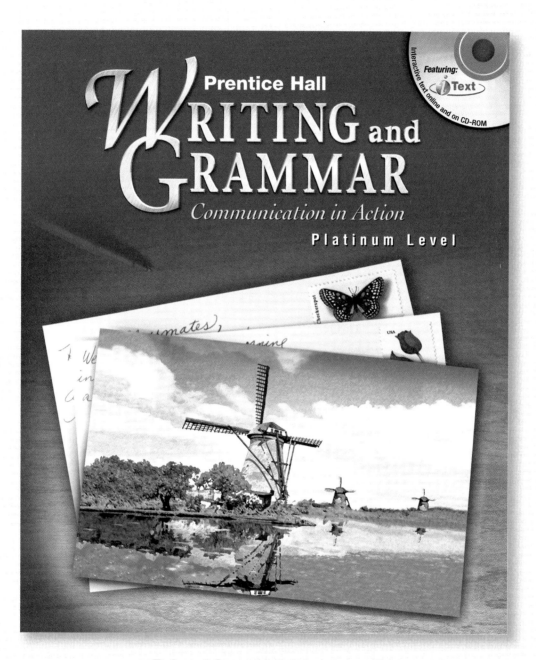

Prentice Hall

Writing and Grammar
Communication in Action

Platinum Level

Featuring: iText
Interactive text online and on CD-ROM

Platinum Level

PEARSON
Prentice Hall

Upper Saddle River, New Jersey
Needham, Massachusetts

WRITING and GRAMMAR
Communication in Action

Copper
Bronze
Silver
Gold
Platinum
Ruby
Diamond

PEARSON
Prentice Hall

ISBN 0-13-116634-4

7 8 9 10   09 08 07 06 05

Go Online
PHSchool.com

Use *i Text* ***Writing and Grammar,*** **the interactive textbook!**

(Includes every grammar exercise in this book!)

- instant feedback on interactive grammar exercises
- interactive writing tools and writing tutorials
- access to the *Prentice Hall Online Essay Scorer*

iText is also available on CD-ROM.

Go on-line to get instant help on the Writing and Grammar Web site!

- additional grammar practice opportunities
- scoring rubrics with scored student models for different modes of writing

Here's how to use the Writing and Grammar Web site:

Look for these Web Codes in your book:

> eek-1001
> eek-1002

Here's how to use Web Codes:

1. Go on-line. Enter URL: PHSchool.com

2. If you want instant feedback on interactive grammar exercises, enter Web Code: eek-1002

   Choose the appropriate chapter from the menu that appears.

3. If you want to review writing rubrics and scored student models, enter Web Code: eek-1001

   Choose the appropriate chapter from the menu that appears.

Program Authors

The program authors guided the direction and philosophy of *Prentice Hall Writing and Grammar: Communication in Action*. Working with the development team, they contributed to the pedagogical integrity of the program and to its relevance to today's teachers and students.

Joyce Armstrong Carroll

In her forty-year career, Joyce Armstrong Carroll, Ed.D., has taught on every grade level from primary to graduate school. In the past twenty years, she has trained teachers in the teaching of writing. A nationally known consultant, she has served as president of TCTE and on NCTE's Commission on Composition. More than fifty of her articles have appeared in journals such as *Curriculum Review, English Journal, Media & Methods, Southwest Philosophical Studies, Ohio English Journal, English in Texas,* and the *Florida English Journal.* With Edward E. Wilson, Dr. Carroll co-authored *Acts of Teaching: How to Teach Writing* and co-edited *Poetry After Lunch: Poems to Read Aloud.* Beyond her direct involvement with the writing pedagogy presented in this series, Dr. Carroll guided the development of the Hands-on Grammar feature. She co-directs the New Jersey Writing Project in Texas.

Edward E. Wilson

A former editor of *English in Texas*, Edward E. Wilson has served as a high-school English teacher and a writing consultant in school districts nationwide. Wilson has served on the Texas Teacher Professional Practices Commission and on NCTE's Commission on Composition. With Dr. Carroll, he co-wrote *Acts of Teaching: How to Teach Writing* and co-edited the award-winning *Poetry After Lunch: Poems to Read Aloud.* In addition to his direct involvement with the writing pedagogy presented in this series, Wilson provided inspiration for the Spotlight on Humanities feature. Wilson's poetry appears in Paul Janeczko's anthology *The Music of What Happens.* Wilson co-directs the New Jersey Writing Project in Texas.

Gary Forlini

Gary Forlini, a nationally known education consultant, developed the grammar, usage, and mechanics instruction and exercises in this series. After teaching in the Pelham, New York, schools for many years, he established Research in Media, an educational research agency that provides information for product developers, school staff developers, media companies, and arts organizations, as well as private-sector corporations and foundations. Mr. Forlini was co-author of the *S.A.T. Home Study* program and has written numerous industry reports on elementary, secondary, and post-secondary education markets.

National Advisory Panel

The teachers and administrators serving on the National Advisory Panel provided ongoing input into the development of *Prentice Hall Writing and Grammar: Communication in Action*. Their valuable insights ensure that the perspectives of teachers and students throughout the country are represented within the instruction in this series.

Dr. Pauline Bigby-Jenkins
Coordinator for Secondary English
  Language Arts
Ann Arbor Public Schools
Ann Arbor, Michigan

Lee Bromberger
English Department Chairperson
Mukwonago High School
Mukwonago, Wisconsin

Mary Chapman
Teacher of English
Free State High School
Lawrence, Kansas

Jim Deatherage
Language Arts Department
  Chairperson
Richland High School
Richland, Washington

Luis Dovalina
Teacher of English
La Joya High School
La Joya, Texas

JoAnn Giardino
Teacher of English
Centennial High School
Columbus, Ohio

Susan Goldberg
Teacher of English
Westlake Middle School
Thornwood, New York

Jean Hicks
Director, Louisville Writing Project
University of Louisville
Louisville, Kentucky

Karen Hurley
Teacher of Language Arts
Perry Meridian Middle School
Indianapolis, Indiana

Karen Lopez
Teacher of English
Hart High School
Newhall, California

Marianne Minshall
Teacher of Reading and Language Arts
Westmore Middle School
Columbus, Ohio

Nancy Monroe
English Department Chairperson
Bolton High School
Alexandria, Louisiana

Ken Spurlock
Assistant Principal
Boone County High School
Florence, Kentucky

Cynthia Katz Tyroff
Staff Development Specialist
  and Teacher of English
Northside Independent School District
San Antonio, Texas

Holly Ward
Teacher of Language Arts
Campbell Middle School
Daytona Beach, Florida

Grammar Review Team

The following teachers reviewed the grammar instruction in this series to ensure accuracy, clarity, and pedagogy.

Kathy Hamilton
Paul Hertzog
Daren Hoisington
Beverly Ladd

Karen Lopez
Dianna Louise Lund
Sean O'Brien

CONTENTS IN BRIEF

CONTENTS
PART 1: WRITING

INTEGRATED SKILLS

INTEGRATED SKILLS

INTEGRATED SKILLS

Chapter 5

Narration

Short Story 76

Student Work
IN PROGRESS

Featured Work:
"Horror Movie"
by Ian Venokur
Columbia High School
Maplewood, New Jersey

INTEGRATED SKILLS

Student Work
IN PROGRESS

Featured Work:
   "Phantom Finish"
   by Leslie Harris
   Sunnyslope High School
   Phoenix, Arizona

INTEGRATED SKILLS

Chapter 7 Persuasion

Persuasive Essay 124

Student Work
IN PROGRESS

Featured Work:
   "Volunteering Is Vital"
by Sharon Goldberg
Miami-Palmetto High School
Pinecrest, Florida

INTEGRATED SKILLS

Chapter 8 Persuasion

Advertisement 152

Student Work IN PROGRESS

Featured Work:
   "Bash at the Lake"
   by Ever Chapa
   La Joya High School
   La Joya, Texas

INTEGRATED SKILLS

Chapter 10 Exposition
Cause-and-Effect Essay 196

Student Work
IN PROGRESS

Featured Work:
"El Niño"
by Jennifer Hoss
Bel Air High School
El Paso, Texas

INTEGRATED SKILLS

Exposition
Problem-and-Solution Essay . . 220

INTEGRATED SKILLS

Research Writing... 244

Student Work
IN PROGRESS

Featured Work:
    "Robert Capa"
  by Michael S. Dougherty
    Central Bucks West
      High School
  Doylestown, Pennsylvania

INTEGRATED SKILLS

Chapter 13 Response to Literature 276

Writing for Assessment 304

Student Work
IN PROGRESS

Featured Work:
   "Why the United States
   Entered World War I"
   by Tricia Bushnell
   Buena High School
   Ventura, California

INTEGRATED SKILLS

Chapter 15 Workplace Writing 322

INTEGRATED SKILLS

PART 2: GRAMMAR, USAGE, AND MECHANICS

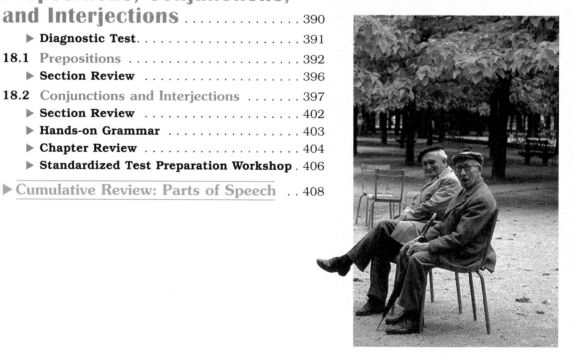

PART 3: ACADEMIC AND WORKPLACE SKILLS

Writing

Femme Cousant, Henri Lebasque, Christie's Images

The Writer in You

▲ **Critical Viewing**
Suppose you wanted
to interview this stu-
dent about her writ-
ing habits. Name
three questions you
might ask. **[Classify]**

You weren't born knowing how to speak. You learned to
speak by listening to others and, eventually, by using words
yourself. The more you spoke, the better you became at it. The
same is true of writing. The best way to discover the writer in
you is, naturally, to write!

Writing in Everyday Life

Writing is already and will continue to be an important part
of your everyday life. The writing you do can be as simple as
jotting down a phone message or writing yourself a quick
reminder or as complex as developing a research paper on a
historical event or preparing a science lab report. You probably do some form of writing—either simple or complex—just
about every day. In this chapter, you will learn strategies to
help you fully take advantage of each writing opportunity so
that you can continue to develop your skills as a writer.

Why Write?

Being a writer helps you respond to the world. Writing is often the most effective way to communicate. Suppose you read an article in a newspaper that makes you feel angry or frustrated. Writing a thoughtful letter to the editor can help you express and share your feelings. Writing can also bring you surprising insights into yourself. For example, when you gather facts for an essay, you might discover interests you never knew you had.

Developing Your Writing Life

One of the keys to improving as a writer is to develop an approach to writing that works for you. Your approach includes where, when, and how you write.

Keep Track of Your Ideas

Experiment with different ways of generating and keeping track of writing ideas. Following are a few techniques you might consider:

Notebook Carry a small notebook with you and record in it anything that captures your interest—places that you visit, events that you witness, interesting news stories. Whenever you need a writing idea, look through your notebook for possibilities.

Clipping File Look through books, magazines, Web pages—even calendars and travel brochures. Capture the interesting pieces of information you come across by keeping a clipping file—a folder containing clippings from the sources you've consulted.

Style Journal Use a style journal to experiment with different writing styles or goals. You might try writing the opening sentence for three different kinds of novels. Or you might take a line of dialogue and write it in four or five different styles. Look at the examples on this page.

Writers in ACTION

Doris Lessing, who has written dozens of widely admired books, stories, and nonfiction works, offers this advice:

"In the writing process, the more the story cooks, the better. The brain works for you even when you are at rest. I find dreams particularly useful. . . . You can only learn to be a better writer by actually writing."

Style Journal

Sample:
Our dog barked when the van drove past our house.

Mystery:
The dog barked suspiciously when the shadowy van slowed down as it passed our house.

Poetic:
Our dog howled mournfully when she heard the van's wheels slur against the rain-slicked pavement.

Children's Rhyme:
Our dog began to bark
As the van drove past the park.
She barked a little more
When the van drove past our door.

Keep Track of Your Writing and Reading

Writing Portfolio Writing is a permanent form of communication. Unlike speech, the writing projects you complete are lasting. You can return to them at any time. Maintaining a writing portfolio of your past works is the best way to monitor your progress as a writer. You can include your favorite writing—whether it is a particularly effective poster or a complete autobiographical narrative. For a longer work, consider including several preliminary drafts to give a snapshot of your writing process in action.

No matter what you include in your portfolio, it will be useful only if you actually reread and review the materials inside. Schedule time at least once a month to review the contents of your portfolio. At that time, you can add new materials or remove those you no longer feel represent your best work.

Reader's Journal When you come across quotations from other writers that strike you as memorable, write them down. Someday, they might be useful for a piece of your own writing.

Try Different Approaches

Selecting Writing Materials The materials you use to write can affect your writing. You might use a pen or pencil and paper or a computer. For some writers, a word processor is an ideal tool for drafting a lengthy report, but a simple pen and pad works best for generating ideas for a poem.

Evaluating Your Writing Time Some writers are more productive in the morning; others work best at night. Learn your time preference by writing the time and date at the beginning of each writing session. When you review your work, look for trends. You might find that your drafting improves in the afternoon, but you get your best prewriting ideas before breakfast.

Improving Your Work Writers' revision strategies vary greatly. You might rewrite obsessively, as Gore Vidal says he does. On the other hand, you might agree with Elie Wiesel, who feels that writing "is more like sculpture where you remove, you eliminate in order to make the work visible." When you revise, you could combine both theories, adding some ideas and taking others away.

Experiment

Discover your own most effective strategies by experimenting. Try new approaches, and then reflect on their success. When you find a technique that works, add it to your set of writing tools.

Planning to Write

Some writing occurs almost automatically. You can fill out a form or leave a phone message without much thought. Other writing requires careful planning. Suppose you are working on an investigative report or a personal essay. If you skip the planning, you might end up frustrated, anxious, or short of time. Structuring your writing life can help you avoid these setbacks.

Organize Your Environment

You need to find and create an environment that supports your writing process.

Choose a Conducive Location Select a place to work where you know you can write productively. Consider each element of your writing environment: the materials available, the mood or feeling of the place, and the presence of distractions or potential inspirations. Of course, you may not always be able to set up the perfect writing environment, so learning to adapt is another important writer's skill. For example, if you have to work in a noisy cafeteria, listening to quiet music on headphones might help you block out the distractions.

▲ Critical Viewing How might an audiocassette recorder help you collect and develop ideas? **[Analyze]**

Budget Your Time A deadline may be inspiring or intimidating. To make a long-term deadline work for you instead of against you, it is important to break it down into short-term goals. Estimate the amount of time you will need for each step of the writing process. Allow enough time in your schedule for stages that take more time than expected. You may want to include group conferences or peer-review meetings in your deadline schedule, but remember to notify others of any changes.

Stop When You Still Have Something to Say When working on a long project, stop working when you still have some ideas left. If you do, you will know exactly where to begin when you start again. Ernest Hemingway described this strategy by saying that he "learned never to empty the well of [his] writing, but always to stop when there was still something there in the deep part of the well, and let it refill at night from the springs that fed it." Jot down a few notes on your plans; then, return to them when you are fresh and ready to write more.

Deadlines for Investigative Report

Sept. 18: Brainstorming session with team.

Sept. 20: Choose topic and begin research.

Sept. 27: Complete research. Assemble notes.

Sept. 29: Develop outline.

Oct. 1: Finish first draft.

Oct. 3: Review draft with peer-review team.

Oct. 4: Finish revising report. Proofread draft.

Oct. 8: Report due.

Sharing Your Work

Work With Others

You will often want to include other people in your writing process. From equal collaborators to helpful peer reviewers, other people can invigorate and improve your writing skills.

Group Brainstorming Writer's block can be frustrating and numbing. If you're stuck for an idea, it can be difficult to find one on your own. Try brainstorming with a group to generate potential ideas. The key to successful brainstorming is not to be critical. Let ideas flow, good and bad. You can always evaluate them later.

Collaborative Writing Writing collaboratively means sharing the steps of the writing process. You might divide jobs for a long project, such as researching and organizing. You can also work more closely, cooperating on each necessary step. Discuss your choices carefully, and make sure each team member has equal input.

Peer Reviewing An "outsider" can often catch mistakes and confusing statements that you, as the writer, may be too close to the project to see. Ask a peer reviewer—a fellow student—to help you catch mistakes and point out parts of your writing that need further elaboration, as well as passages that are particularly strong.

Publish

Sharing your work with an audience can be a satisfying conclusion to any writing project. Your work in print might even inspire other young writers to reach new writing goals. A number of organizations and groups publish the works of students. Look for opportunities to publish your writing, whether through a student Web site or a magazine contest. Ask your librarian or teacher for suggestions, or consult the list of publications on page 869.

Writers in **ACTION**

Editors can help a writer identify passages that aren't working. Author Toni Morrison thinks of a good editor as a "third eye." She praises an editor's ability to be "cool" and "dispassionate" because he or she is not as involved as the writer. "Sometimes it's uncanny: the editor puts his or her finger on exactly the place the writer thought it might fly, but wasn't sure. Good editors identify that place, and sometimes make suggestions."

▼ **Critical Viewing** Suppose that this group of students is collaborating on a literary analysis. How might they divide their writing tasks? **[Analyze]**

What Are the Qualities of Good Writing?

Ideas Strong ideas are the starting point for good writing. Try to begin each piece of writing by focusing on a topic that interests you. In addition, consider whether an idea you are writing about will interest your audience. If not, you may want to consider writing about something else.

Organization Present your ideas and details in a consistent, organized manner that will be easy for readers to follow. Often, your topic and the type of writing that you are doing will dictate a particular method of organization. For example, if you are telling a story, you'll probably want to present events in the order in which they occur.

Voice Voice refers to all of the qualities that make your writing different from that of others. It includes the way you use words and sentences, the types of topics you write about, and the perspective that you bring to those topics. Whenever you write, let your personal voice come through in your writing.

Word Choice Words are the building blocks of a piece of writing. The stronger each block is, the stronger the finished piece will be. Carefully choose each word you use. Make sure that it conveys your intended meaning as precisely as possible. In addition to conveying your meaning, your words should also capture your attitude toward your subject.

Sentence Fluency Read your work aloud to see that each sentence flows smoothly from one to the next. Use transitions to connect your sentences, and vary the length and structure of your sentences to help build a rhythm.

Conventions Don't let errors spoil the impact of your work. Take care to ensure that you have followed the conventions of English grammar, usage, mechanics, and spelling.

Reflecting on Your Writing

Self-questioning is useful for honing your writing skills. Here are some questions that can lead you to discover more about the writer in you:

- Which of your recent writing projects was most successful? Why did you connect so well with this project?

- What specific obstacles have you faced when writing? What strategies might you use to overcome these obstacles?

- What writers do you admire? How does reading their work suggest ideas you can apply to your own writing?

Spotlight on the Humanities

Analyzing How Meaning Is Communicated Through the Arts

Overview

In the chapters that follow, you'll learn a wide variety of ways to express yourself through writing. You can also express yourself through other art forms. Below are some of these art forms.

- **Fine Art** creates meaning through color, line, texture, and subject. Paintings, sketches, sculpture, and collage can convey literal or abstract ideas.

- **Photography** uses still images to create meaning. While a photograph captures still images on film, photographers express ideas through subject, composition, and lighting.

- **Theater** is designed to be performed by actors on a stage. Using props, scenery, sound effects, and lighting, drama brings a story to life. In some cases, music, songs, and dance are incorporated into the story line. For example, in an opera, the story is told completely through song.

- **Film** captures sound and motion to convey an idea. Like dramatic theater, most film tells a story and uses setting, costumes, and characterization to develop a story. A filmmaker can portray a unique point of view using camera angles, lighting, and sound techniques.

- **Music** uses sound to impart meaning. Whether presented as a clarinet solo, an operatic performance, or a symphony, music can create moods or present variations on a theme.

- **Dance** displays meaning through organized movement. It can be performed by a single person, a pair, or large groups.

Introducing Spotlight on the Humanities In the Spotlight on the Humanities features, you will discover how all art is connected—layer upon layer—and how the inspiration that moved the hearts and minds of artists in the past continues to touch artists today.

Writing Activity

Think of a time when you felt inspired to create. Whether it was something artistic or practical, write a journal entry describing your experience as you remember it.

▲ **Critical Viewing**
What ideas can be expressed through a dance like the one shown here?
[Analyze]

Media and Technology Skills

Making Technology Work for You

Activity: Experiment With a Variety of Tools

Technology can help you develop effective writing strategies. Familiarize yourself with the tools available in your classroom, computer lab, library, and home. Here are a few types of technology that many writers employ.

Word-Processing Software Using a word processor simplifies many basic writing tasks. For example, moving a sentence from the beginning to the end of a paragraph is a simple cut-and-paste operation. This chart shows some common word-processing features.

Search and Replace	Also known as a "global replace," this tool can help you quickly change a recurring word.
Spelling and Grammar Check	Many word processors include tools to check your spelling and grammar. These can find many errors, but they do not replace proofreading.
Undo/Redo	These functions allow you to change your mind when you are writing or revising.

Desktop-Publishing Software You might decide to design a newsletter, flyer, brochure, or other work that combines graphics and text. Desktop-publishing software helps you design your project from beginning to end. You can enter text and style fonts. You can also add original art, clip art from professional sources, or photographs.

The Internet The Internet is a worldwide network of computers. When you sign on, you connect your computer to this network and can collect information from sources throughout the world. The Internet is a valuable research tool that contains millions of pages of information on every subject from Abigail Adams to Zoology.

E-mail You might use e-mail (electronic mail) to keep in touch with friends or students at other schools. You can also share samples of your writing through e-mail attachments, allowing a student hundreds of miles away to help you revise a draft. E-mail is also a useful way to request information from businesses or government organizations.

A Few Good Tools

Using tools can help you expand your idea of what a writer does. Consider these possibilities:

- Audiocassette recorders can capture brainstorming sessions or group improvisations.
- Videocassette recorders can collect images for multimedia presentations.
- Scanners allow you to convert photos and artwork into electronic files for use in word-processing or desktop-publishing files.
- Digital cameras take photographs that can be included in computer documents.
- Film cameras take pictures that can be included in brochures or newspapers. You can also have film developed as electronic files. Ask your photo developer for more information.

Standardized Test Preparation Workshop

The Writer in You

Writing is an important part of many standardized tests. On such tests, you will be given a prompt or topic about which to write. When responding to this prompt, you will often have to work within a set time period.

When your work is evaluated, the scorers will look to see that

- you have responded directly to the prompt and performed all of the activities it includes.

- your writing is well-organized and easy-to-follow.

- you have presented and developed a main point and thoroughly supported your main point with facts, examples, and other types of details.

- you have used lively, engaging language.

- you have avoided errors in grammar, usage, mechanics, and spelling.

The process of writing for a test, or any kind of writing, can be divided into stages. Plan to use a specific amount of time for prewriting, drafting, revising, and proofreading.

Following is an example of one type of writing prompt you might find on a standardized test. Use the suggestions on the following page to help you respond. The clocks next to each stage suggest a plan for organizing your time.

Test Tip

Read the test prompt carefully and focus your preparation on the answer. Then, analyze the prompt to provide the types of detail and explanation required.

Sample Prompt

Respond to the following questions in a brief essay. Back up each of your points with examples drawn from your own experience.

In your experience as a writer up to this point, which techniques have you found to be most effective? Why? Which techniques have you found to be less effective? Why?

Prewriting

Allow about a quarter of your time for prewriting.

Prepare a List Quickly list various techniques you have used as a writer, and note why these have or have not been effective.

Review Your List and Narrow Your Focus Review your list, and circle the techniques that you consider most and least effective. Then, arrange the techniques in order from least to most effective. Begin with techniques that you did not find effective.

Drafting

Allow about half of your time for drafting.

Write More Slowly Than Usual You may be working within a set time frame. However, it is important to draft slowly and carefully when you are writing an essay for a standardized test because you will have less time to revise than you will in other writing situations. Review your notes and think through each sentence as you write it so that you can minimize the number of changes you will have to make.

Establish Your Main Points In your introduction, briefly touch on each of the techniques that you will be discussing. Also, try to begin with an attention-grabbing opening sentence.

Elaborate Devote one paragraph to each technique. Elaborate on the technique by providing detailed examples from your own experience. Describe each example as thoroughly as possible, and explain the outcome of using each technique.

Leave a Lasting Impression End with a conclusion that sums up your writing experiences. Consider offering predictions about what you expect to learn as you continue to develop as a writer. Try to end with a concluding sentence that will leave a lasting impression on those who will evaluate your work.

Revising, Editing, and Proofreading

Allow about a quarter of your time to revise, edit, and proofread your work.

Check for Missing Details Review your essay to see whether you have left out any important details. If you find that you have, add the details. Do so neatly, using a caret [^] to indicate where the added material is to be inserted.

Eliminate Errors Check your work carefully for errors in grammar, usage, mechanics, and spelling. These types of errors can hurt your test score.

A Walk Through the Writing Process

Writing, in one form or another, is an essential component of your daily life. Whatever your final product, the writing process—a systematic approach to writing—can help you achieve it. From prewriting to publishing and presenting, being familiar with and using the stages of the writing process will help you write better.

▲ **Critical Viewing**
Identify one way in which computers in the library can improve your writing process. **[Analyze]**

Types of Writing

There are many types of writing. The various types can be grouped into **modes**, a word that refers to the central purpose of a piece of writing. The chart at right shows the modes you'll encounter in this book.

Writing can also be divided into two broader categories: reflexive and extensive, based on the source of inspiration and audience for a piece of writing. When you write reflexively, you choose what to write, what format to use, and whether to share your writing with others. **Reflexive writing**—such as a journal entry, a personal essay, or a list—is writing you do for yourself. **Extensive writing,** which focuses on topics outside of your imagination and experience, is writing that you do for others. Examples of extensive writing include research papers, persuasive essays, and book and theater reviews.

The Modes of Writing
- Narration
- Description
- Persuasion
- Exposition
- Research
- Response to Literature
- Assessment
- Workplace

The Process of Writing

The process of writing occurs in several stages:

- **Prewriting** includes exploring topics, choosing a topic, and beginning to gather and organize details before you write.
- **Drafting** involves getting your ideas down on paper in roughly the format you intend for the finished work.
- **Revising** is the stage in which you rework your first draft to improve its content and structure.
- **Editing and proofreading** involve correcting errors in grammar, spelling, and mechanics.
- **Publishing and presenting** are the sharing of your work with others.

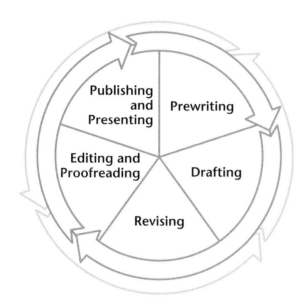

These stages may appear to follow a set sequence, but as writers work, they often skip stages or shift back to earlier stages. For example, as you draft, you may begin making revisions in your work; or as you revise, you may discover that you need to go back and gather more ideas.

A Guided Tour

Use this chapter as a guided tour of the stages of the writing process. Familiarize yourself with the activities of writing. Learn new strategies, look at the way other effective writers employ them, and try them out yourself. In the chapters that follow, you'll see how to apply these and other strategies to specific types of writing.

2.1 *What Is Prewriting?*

Most writers feel challenged when faced with a blank sheet of paper. Writers may grapple with what topic to write about, or they may wonder just how much they have to say about a subject. The prewriting stage helps to get a writer's creative juices flowing. Just as musicians prepare for a performance by practicing, you can warm up to write with your own set of prewriting strategies and techniques.

Choosing Your Topic

To begin writing, you must have a topic. Usually, it is best to write about what you know or about what you find interesting. Take time to explore subjects, issues, and experiences that are meaningful to you. You can use a wide variety of strategies to generate topics. Try this sample strategy:

Learn More

For additional prewriting strategies suited to specific writing tasks, see Chapters 4–15.

SAMPLE STRATEGY

Blueprinting When you blueprint, you draw a map of a place you know well. To try this strategy, draw a floor plan of a classroom in your school. Fill in the room plan with symbols for desks, chairs, computers, chalkboards, bookshelves, windows, doorways, pictures, and whatever else is appropriate. Think about significant events that this room calls to mind, and list the ideas on your blueprint. From that list, select a topic to develop.

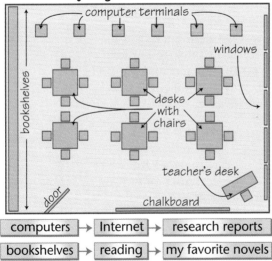

My English Classroom

Narrowing Your Topic

Once you have selected a writing topic, make sure it is not so general that you can't cover it thoroughly in a short piece of writing. Consider whether you can narrow your topic by focusing on a single subtopic or aspect of it. One strategy you might use is shown below.

SAMPLE STRATEGY

Looping to Narrow a Topic Looping is a way of discovering and focusing on the features of a topic that are most important or interesting to you. Begin by freewriting on a general topic, such as sports, friends, or favorite books. Write for five minutes. Then, review what you have written. Circle the most important or significant word. Next, freewrite based on that word for five more minutes. Once again, circle the most important or significant word, and freewrite about it. Continue looping until you are satisfied that your topic is narrow enough. Look at this example:

Looping

Broad topic: Reading

I think I enjoy the time I spend reading because it is private time.

Reading is something I can really get lost in. When I'm reading a

(great book,) not much can distract me.

Reading gives me an alternative to the everyday realities of my own

life and is a great way to disregard anything that annoys me.

Great book:

Novels especially appeal to me for lots of reasons. Sometimes

characters seem really strange and foreign to me, and other times

I can really relate to them. I like to be pulled into the life of another

(character), to feel like I'm experiencing the world being presented in

that novel, and to learn new things.

Narrowed topic:

The characters in novels make reading appealing to me.

Considering Your Audience and Purpose

After you've narrowed your topic, identify your audience—the person or people who will read your work—and your purpose—what you want your writing to accomplish. Your audience and purpose will affect the type of language you use and the types of information you present.

Considering Your Audience It is best not to develop a piece of writing without thinking about who is going to read it. Consider your audience's age, interests, and knowledge of your subject. If you are writing for young children who know little about your topic, use simple language and include the most basic details. If, on the other hand, you are writing for experts or enthusiasts in the field, use sophisticated language and leave out extended explanations of basic details.

Develop an audience profile by asking and answering questions about your audience, such as those on the notepad below. Refer back to your audience profile as you develop your writing.

Considering Your Purpose Identify what you hope to accomplish with your writing. You may be writing to persuade, to entertain, to inform, or to achieve a variety of other specific purposes. Keep your purpose in mind as you decide which details to include, which to leave out, and what type of language to use.

Audience Profile

1. What does my audience already know?

2. What do they need to know?

3. What details will interest or influence my audience?

Gathering Details

Regardless of your subject, it is essential that you back up the points you make with examples, facts, and details. Generally, it is most effective to take some time to gather details before you begin writing. This may involve research in the library or on the Internet or interviews with experts. Consider these strategies for gathering details:

SAMPLE STRATEGY

Using Hexagonal Writing

Hexagonal writing helps you gather details about a literary work in order to write a well-balanced, complete analysis. Create a chart like the one at right. Then, follow the directions shown here to fill it out.

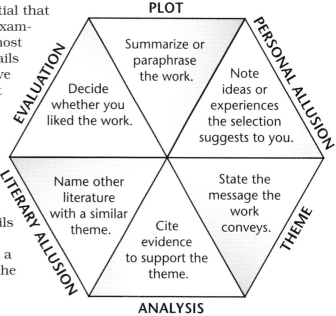

PLOT — Summarize or paraphrase the work.

EVALUATION — Decide whether you liked the work.

PERSONAL ALLUSION — Note ideas or experiences the selection suggests to you.

LITERARY ALLUSION — Name other literature with a similar theme.

THEME — State the message the work conveys.

ANALYSIS — Cite evidence to support the theme.

SAMPLE STRATEGY

Generating Sensory Word Bins When you are writing description, the words you use create an image for your reader. Identify your topic, and then list words that appeal to each of the senses. Look at this example:

Sensory Word Bin: A Summer Storm				
SIGHTS	**SOUNDS**	**SMELLS**	**TASTES**	**PHYSICAL SENSATIONS**
glistening foggy murky	thunder splashes muffled	freshness springlike		heat breeze

▶ **APPLYING THE PREWRITING STRATEGIES**

1. Construct a blueprint of a special place. Then, use your blueprint to identify potential writing topics.
2. Use looping to narrow a topic generated by your blueprint.
3. Identify two different audiences, and devise corresponding audience profiles for an account of a memorable vacation.
4. Use hexagonal writing to gather details about a short story or novel you have recently read.

💻 **Internet Tip**

Using an Internet browser, you can conduct a keyword search on your topic. Be as specific as possible when entering key words, so that you don't come up with more information than you can manage.

2.2 What Is Drafting?

Shaping Your Writing

Match Purpose and Form Each form of writing is linked to a specific purpose. Make sure that your purpose in writing matches that of your chosen form. For instance, if you are writing an editorial, your purpose should be to influence the way others think or act. If you are writing a report or how-to essay, your purpose should be to inform or explain. The purpose of your chosen form will shape your writing, from the details you include to the organization you use. Keep your form and purpose in mind as you draft.

Pull Readers In With an Enticing Lead Begin with an interest-grabbing first paragraph to attract your audience's attention and to stoke their desire to keep reading. To hook with a powerful "lead," employ a controversial quotation, a little-known fact, a bizarre bit of dialogue, or a striking description.

Providing Elaboration

As you draft, elaborate on your main ideas, providing supporting facts, examples, statistics, and other details to help readers understand and accept your points. The SEE method is one strategy that you can use for elaboration.

SAMPLE STRATEGY

Using the SEE Method To use the SEE method (Statement, Extension, and Elaboration), begin each paragraph with a statement that conveys a main idea. Extend that idea by restating or explaining the first sentence. Elaborate on your explanation or restatement by providing supporting details.

STATEMENT: Family reunions can be fun.
EXTENSION: When you get together with relatives, you can enjoy the funny stories they tell.
ELABORATION: No matter how many times you hear about your brother's first report card, you'll still find the exaggerations of the story amusing.

▶ **APPLYING THE DRAFTING STRATEGIES**

1. Write a humorous or startling lead sentence for a description of a basketball game.
2. Complete the following statements. Then, use the SEE technique to elaborate your ideas.
    My favorite actor is ___?___.
    I'd like to travel to ___?___.

Learn More

You can learn about all of the various forms of writing in the writing chapters that follow.

2.3 *What Is Revising?*

Using a Systematic Approach to Revision

Revision is probably the most important stage of the writing process. However, many writers also find it to be the most difficult. In this textbook, you will learn a systematic approach to revision called **ratiocination** (rash´ ē äs ə nā´shen). In everyday use, *ratiocination* refers to the process of reasoning using formal logic. In writing, it refers to the use of a logical step-by-step process to color-code, analyze, evaluate, and rework your writing.

Start by evaluating the overall structure of your work. Then, look at paragraphs, sentences, and words. Throughout the process, use a simple system of highlighting and color-coding to draw your attention to areas that need improvement.

Writers in
ACTION

In The Elements of Style, *William Strunk, Jr., and E. B. White say:*

"Revising is a part of writing. Few writers are so expert that they can produce what they are after on the first try."

Revising Your Overall Structure

There are a variety of things to look for when revising the overall structure of your work, including the following:

- Check to see that your organization makes sense and that it is consistent. You may find it necessary to reorganize parts of your paper.

- Make sure that your introduction will grab your readers' interest and that your conclusion will leave a lasting impression.

- Determine whether you have provided enough support for your main idea. One strategy you can use for this purpose is shown next.

SAMPLE STRATEGY

▶ **REVISION STRATEGY**
Color-Coding Support for Your Main Point

With a red pencil, underline the sentence or sentences that convey the main point of your paper. Then, use a blue pencil to underline the support you've provided for your main point. Once you've finished, you should find that much of your paper is underlined in blue. If not, you probably don't have enough support for your main point. Add more facts, details, or examples to strengthen your writing. In addition, you may want to consider whether all of the passages you have not underlined are necessary.

Revising Your Paragraphs

Once you've reviewed the structure of your draft, check to see that each paragraph focuses on a single aspect of your topic and that all of the sentences within a paragraph relate to one another. Eliminate any sentences that are not clearly related to the others, and look for places where transitions can link the ideas within a paragraph.

Learn More

You will learn more about how to achieve greater sentence variety in Chapter 21.

SAMPLE STRATEGY

▶ **REVISION STRATEGY**
Using Steps, Stacks, Chains, and Balances

- **Steps** When a paragraph presents a series of events or explains a series of steps, check to see that you have used transitions to make the sequence clear to readers. If not, add words such as *first, then,* and *finally.*

- **Stacks** When a paragraph presents a series of related ideas, add transitions such as *in addition* and *as well as.* If certain ideas are more important than others, make sure that you have indicated this with transitions such as *most important.*

- **Chains** When a paragraph explains a cause-and-effect relationship, add transitions such as *consequently* and *as a result* to clarify the relationships among your details.

- **Balances** When the paragraph shows contrast or choice, add words such as *similarly, however, although,* and *rather.*

Revising Your Sentences

Next, study your sentences. Check to see that you have varied their length and structure. Using too many sentences of the same types can make your writing sound choppy.

SAMPLE STRATEGY

▶ **REVISION STRATEGY**
Bracketing Sentence Openers

Use a colored pen to bracket the first three words of each sentence. Review your paper, focusing only on the bracketed words. If you have begun most of your sentences in the same way, rework some of them to produce greater variety.

Revising Your Word Choice

Complete the process of revision by analyzing words you have used. Look for places where you can replace vague or general words with ones that more precisely convey your meaning. Also, check to see whether you have overused certain words. The following strategy will help:

SAMPLE STRATEGY

▶ **REVISION STRATEGY**
Highlighting Repeated Words

Use a highlighter to mark any words you have used more than once. Review the words that you have marked, and consider replacing some to make your writing more lively. Look at this example:

Peer Review

Once you've finished revising on your own, you may want to enlist the help of classmates. Often, others can see problems that are hard for the writer to identify. Use these tips to get the specific feedback you want:

EVALUATING REPEATED WORDS

first flakes of snow began drifting down from the sky
The ~~snow began falling~~ early in the morning. By early afternoon, the ground was covered with several inches of ~~snow.~~ *fluffy white crystals* When evening came, *it was still snowing heavily* ~~the snow was still falling,~~ and by that time, ~~there~~ *the landscape* *was layered with at least a foot of soft white powder* ~~was at least a foot of snow on the ground.~~

Focusing Peer Review	
Purpose	**Ask**
Evaluate introduction	What part of the introduction was most interesting?
Test argument	Which reason was most convincing?
	Which point was least compelling?

▶ **APPLYING THE REVISION STRATEGIES**

Select a piece of writing you did last year. Use the revision strategies presented here to make improvements in this piece. Identify four changes the strategies helped you make.

What Are Editing and Proofreading?

Once you have finished revising for content, proofread your work carefully to find and eliminate errors in grammar, usage, mechanics, and spelling. These types of errors will distract readers and may cause them to respond negatively to your work—even if the content is excellent.

Focusing on Proofreading

To check your writing for errors, get in the habit of reviewing your draft several times. Each time, focus on a specific proofreading topic. Consider these key areas:

Scrutinize Your Spelling The spell-check function of a word-processing program is never fully dependable. Refer to a dictionary to check the spelling of questionable words.

Follow the Conventions of Grammar, Usage, and Mechanics Apply these conventions to everything you write. Examine each sentence, and correct capitalization and punctuation. Check your grammar and usage, and eliminate problematic language or grammatical structures.

Eliminate Run-on Sentences One specific type of error that you may uncover while proofreading is a run-on sentence—two main clauses that are not adequately separated by punctuation. Look at this example:

CORRECTING RUN-ON SENTENCES

> Some whales weigh as much as twenty elephants, they have blood vessels wide enough for a trout to swim through!

Below are two ways to correct a run-on sentence:

- Break it into two simple sentences.

> Some whales weigh as much as twenty elephants. They have blood vessels wide enough for a trout to swim through!

- Rewrite it as a compound sentence.

> Some whales weigh as much as twenty elephants, and they have blood vessels wide enough for a trout to swim through!

▶ **APPLYING THE EDITING AND PROOFREADING STRATEGIES**

With a partner, identify two grammar, usage, or mechanics errors in a recent piece of your writing. Then, discuss ways to locate and correct such problems during the proofreading stage.

Technology Tip

If your word processor has a spell-check feature, use it, but don't expect it to do the job of a good proofreader. Both *where* and *wear* will pass a spell check, but you may not have used the word you wanted.

2.5 What Are Publishing and Presenting?

Moving Forward

This preview of the writing process provides just a glimpse of the strategies and techniques you can employ in your writing process. Each lesson in this section provides specific strategies that will aid you as you write.

Building Your Portfolio Your finished writing products are valuable, so be sure to organize and save them in a folder, a box, or some other secure place. View your portfolio as a record of your development as a writer. Occasionally, you may return to it to compare your latest writing with something you wrote a while ago.

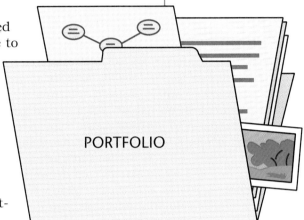

You can also use your portfolio as a repository for future writing ideas, including unfinished writing and thought-provoking photographs or clippings.

Reflecting on Your Writing Each piece of completed writing affects your perceptions about yourself, your topic, and your writing process. Questions posed at the end of each chapter will help you reflect on what you have learned in each of these areas.

Assessing Your Writing A rubric, or set of criteria, on which your work can be evaluated is offered at the end of each chapter. To ensure that you are addressing the main points of the particular mode, refer to the rubric throughout the writing process.

▶ ## APPLYING THE PUBLISHING AND PRESENTING STRATEGIES

1. Reexamine the prewriting activities you used in this introduction to the writing process. Choose one you want to work into a fully developed piece of writing at a later time. Place it in your portfolio. Speak with a writing partner about what made you choose that particular activity.

2. In your writing journal, reflect on your writing process by responding to the following questions:

   • Which techniques helped you the most? Explain.

   • What are your strengths as a writer?

Spotlight on the Humanities

Comparing Themes in Different Media

Focus on Film: Eleonora Duse

When you approach the writing process, you choose your topic, develop your idea, and decide how you want to present the topic to your audience, much like an actor would go about choosing and crafting a role. Considered one of the foremost actors of her time, Italian Eleonora Duse (1858–1924) first attracted attention in 1873 when she played Juliet in Shakespeare's *Romeo and Juliet*. Widely known for her sense of realism, immense emotion, and the poetic spirit in her acting, Duse went on to earn international acclaim as one of the finest dramatic actors of her day. Her work has had great influence.

Dance Named after Eleonora Duse, American ballerina Nora Kaye (1920–1987) was known as the "Duse of Dance." After dancing with the Metropolitan Opera Ballet as a child, Kaye studied with the renowned Russian choreographers Michel Fokine and George Balanchine. In 1939, she joined the American Ballet Theatre. Her performance in the ballet *Pillar of Fire* in 1942 brought her international fame.

Literature Connection Eleonora Duse's premiere performance in New York City was in the play *La dame aux camélias* by the French novelist and playwright Alexandre Dumas (1824–1895). The drama came from his first novel, *Camille*, which appeared in 1848. Born in Paris, Dumas wrote his first volume of poetry in 1847. His feeling for drama and dialogue also made him a first-rate dramatist; his popular plays centered on social and moral problems of the middle class. His father, Alexandre Dumas (1802–1870) was the author of such novels as *The Count of Monte Cristo* and *The Three Musketeers*.

Writing Process Activity: Brainstorming for Ideas

Choose a film, television show, or a song you enjoy. Using it as an inspiration, list several ideas for writing projects. Keep this list in your portfolio for later development.

▲ **Critical Viewing** What emotion does this photograph of Eleonora Duse convey? Explain. **[Interpret]**

Media and Technology Skills

Building an Electronic Portfolio
Activity: Setting Up Your Portfolio

Writing on a computer can help you maintain an organized writing portfolio. Your portfolio can include copies of your writing in several subject areas, as well as your writing and notes for future projects. Keeping an organized electronic portfolio can help you find your past and current projects; it can also help you evaluate your progress as a writer. In some cases, you might decide to revise files that you once thought were in final form.

Learn About It Your computer system, or platform, uses a specific method of organizing files. Although systems vary, many use the terms *file* and *folder* as organizational tools. Each separate work is a file; you can group one or more files into a folder. For example, a folder labeled *Social Studies* might contain all of the files you prepared for that subject.

Structure It Choose a structure that matches the writing you plan to do. Devising a directory structure will help you find your work quickly. Your folder headings should reflect the kinds of writing you do.

<table>
<tr><td>📁 Writing Notes</td><td>📁 English Class</td></tr>
<tr><td>📁 Fiction</td><td>📁 Civics</td></tr>
<tr><td>📁 Poetry</td><td>📁 Algebra I</td></tr>
<tr><td>📁 Nonfiction</td><td>📁 Physics</td></tr>
<tr><td>——Literature</td><td>📁 Journal</td></tr>
<tr><td>——History</td><td></td></tr>
<tr><td>——Spanish</td><td></td></tr>
<tr><td>——Geometry</td><td></td></tr>
</table>

Use It When you start a new file or document, save it in the appropriate folder in your portfolio. When you decide to revise the document, save your first draft by pasting the writing into a new file. Amend the file name to show that it is a revision. Here is one system you might use:

Essay 1	(first draft)	Essay 3	(third draft)
Essay 2	(second draft)	Essay x	(final draft)

Maintain It Adjust your portfolio structure as you use it. You might decide to place early drafts in a separate folder or split one overloaded folder into three smaller categories.

> ### Computer Tips
> - If you store your portfolio on a hard drive, regularly back it up on a disk or CD-R.
> - Store disks and CDs away from heat or magnetic sources.
> - Label disks clearly.
> - If possible, protect your files with a password that will prevent others from reading them.
> - Use your computer system's Search or Find to locate a file that isn't where you thought it was.

Standardized Test Preparation Workshop

Using the Writing Process to Respond to Test Prompts

Using the writing process helps writers produce well-organized, interesting, and coherent works. When responding to a test prompt for a standardized test, use the writing process to construct an effective response. You will be evaluated on your ability to do the following:

- Choose a logical, consistent organization.
- Elaborate with the appropriate amount of detail for your specific audience and purpose.
- Use appropriate transitions so ideas flow together coherently.
- Use complete sentences and follow the rules of grammar.
- Use correct spelling and grammar.

As you learned in this chapter, the process of writing for a test or any kind of writing can be divided into stages. Plan to use a specific amount of time for each task—prewriting, drafting, revising, and proofreading.

Following is an example of one type of writing prompt that you might find on a standardized test. Use the suggestions on the following page to help you respond. The clocks next to each stage show a suggested plan for organizing your time.

Sample Writing Situation

One of the educational topics under discussion addresses whether or not students should attend school year round with only a month off during the summer. Supporters argue that increasing the number of days students attend school will increase student performance. Those who disagree with the idea of year-round schooling argue that the current system is working and that it is unfair to expect teachers to work more days without additional compensation. Which side do you support? Write an essay in which you present your position and provide evidence to support it.

Prewriting

Allow about one quarter of your time for prewriting.

Make a Chart of Pros and Cons Create a simple chart with two columns. On one side, list the arguments for a longer school year; on the other side, list arguments against a longer school year. Review your chart, and choose a side.

Develop a Thesis Statement Your thesis statement is a one- or two-sentence explanation of the main idea that you will present in your essay. Before you begin writing, draft a thesis statement in which you sum up your position on an extended school year.

Gather Support Jot down specific facts and examples that you can use to back up your thesis. For example, you may have a friend whose grades improved greatly after attending summer school.

Drafting

Allow approximately half of your time for drafting.

Organize Your Ideas Present your arguments in the order of their importance. Begin with your least important argument and move toward your most important one.

Develop a Strong Introduction and Conclusion Start with an introduction in which you grab readers' interest with a thought-provoking statement, a quotation, or a surprising observation. Your introduction should also include your thesis statement. End with a conclusion in which you restate your thesis and offer final thoughts that will leave a lasting impression.

Write Thoughtfully Because you have less time to revise than you might in other writing situations, write slowly and carefully. Focus on choosing words that convey your exact meaning and on using transitions to connect your ideas.

Revising, Editing, and Proofreading

Allow about one quarter of your time to revise, edit, and proofread your paper.

Clean It Up Review your essay. Neatly cross out any details that will not influence your audience, and add support for your argument wherever possible. Also, check for errors in spelling. If you are unsure of the spelling of a word, consider replacing it with one you know better. If you are crossing out or erasing, do so neatly.

Sentences, Paragraphs, and Compositions
Structure and Style

What Are Sentences, Paragraphs, and Compositions?

A *sentence* is a group of words with a subject and a predicate that expresses a complete thought. Sentences are the building blocks of your writing.

A *paragraph* is a group of related sentences that presents a unit of thought. Paragraphs provide organization and focus to your writing. When you read, a new paragraph is indicated by visual clues, such as the indentation of the first word of the first sentence or an extra line of space between lines of text.

A *composition* is a connected series of paragraphs on a single topic. There are many types of compositions, including essays, research papers, and workplace writing. The specific types of compositions will be covered in later chapters.

3.1 *Sentence Combining*

Writing Effective Sentences

Effective sentences are the key to appealing and interesting writing. A sentence that is effective by itself, however, may seem uninteresting if it is one in a series of short sentences. Such a series can produce a choppy, repetitive effect.

To keep your sentences interesting, you need to consider sentence variety. By combining two or more short sentences, you can vary your sentences. At the same time, you can show connections between events, stress important information, and create a smooth flow of ideas.

Inserting Words and Phrases

You may combine two related sentences by taking key information from one and inserting it into the other. The information to be inserted may be a word or it may be a phrase. To combine sentences successfully, you may have to change the form of the words and use additional punctuation.

EXAMPLE:	The Spanish artist Joan Miró worked in many different media. <u>Miró is a world-famous artist.</u>
INSERTING A WORD:	The **world-famous** Spanish artist Joan Miró worked in many different media.
EXAMPLE:	Miguel de Cervantes was born outside Madrid. <u>He is the author of *Don Quixote*.</u>
INSERTING A PHRASE:	Miguel de Cervantes, **the author of *Don Quixote*,** was born outside Madrid.

▼ Critical Viewing
How is constructing a building, such as this building by Antoni Gaudí, like combining sentences in a paragraph? **[Connect]**

▶ **Exercise 1** Combining With Words and Phrases

Combine each pair of sentences by inserting key information from one sentence into the other. Add commas as necessary.

1. Antoni Gaudí was a famous architect. He was from Spain.
2. Gaudí is probably best known for the Church of the Sagrada Familia in Barcelona. It is unfinished.
3. The Prado contains collections of paintings by artists such as El Greco, Velázquez, and Goya. The Prado is located in Madrid, Spain.
4. The Canary Islands are located in the Atlantic Ocean off the coast of Africa. They are part of Spain.
5. The wild canary bird is generally green, unlike the canaries bred as pets. It takes its name from the islands on which it lives.

Using Compound Elements

Related sentences may be combined by joining elements from each to form compound subjects, verbs, or objects.

Learn More

For additional information about objects, see Section 19.3; for additional information about prepositional phrases, see Section 20.1.

EXAMPLE: Spain is on my list of places to go on vacation. Gibraltar is also on my list.

COMPOUND SUBJECT: **Spain and Gibraltar** are on my list of places to go on vacation.

EXAMPLE: We visited the Alhambra in Granada, Spain. Then, we toured the gardens and parks.

COMPOUND VERB: We **visited the Alhambra** and **toured the gardens and parks** in Granada, Spain.

EXAMPLE: In the Straits of Gibraltar, tourists can see dolphins. They can also see whales.

COMPOUND OBJECT :   In the Straits of Gibraltar, tourists can see **dolphins and whales.**

EXAMPLE: Gibraltar is famous for its caves. It is also known for the wild Barbary apes.

COMPOUND PREPOSITIONAL PHRASE: Gibraltar is famous **for its caves and the wild Barbary apes.**

▶ **Exercise 2** Using Compound Sentence Elements Combine each pair of sentences using compound elements.

1. Seville is a city in southern Spain. Córdoba is another city in southern Spain.
2. Catalan, a Romance language, is spoken in Catalonia. It is also spoken in Roussillon.
3. Spain is known for its sunny climate. It is also known for its beautiful castles and cathedrals.
4. Spanish fishers catch squid and sardines. They also catch tuna and octopuses.
5. The entertainers in the café danced the flamenco. They played the guitar, too.
6. The Prado, Madrid's great museum, is a main attraction for visitors. El Escorial, a palace outside Madrid, is another.
7. The Spanish are the inventors of *paella*, a rice-based dish. They also invented *gazpacho*, a cold tomato soup.
8. The Spanish parliament, known as the Cortes, is divided into two houses. It has more than 500 members.
9. The Spanish people elect members of the Chamber of Deputies, the lower house of the Cortes. They also vote for the Senate, the upper house of the Cortes.
10. You can see traces of Spain's history in the ruins left by the ancient Romans. You can also see them in the alcazars (palaces) built by the Moors of North Africa.

Forming Compound Sentences

A **compound sentence** consists of two or more independent clauses joined by a comma and a **coordinating conjunction** (*and, but, for, nor, or, so,* or *yet*) or by a semicolon.

EXAMPLE: Soccer is the most popular sport in Spain. Many cities have soccer stadiums that seat tens of thousands of spectators.

COMBINED: Soccer is the most popular sport in Spain, **and** many cities have soccer stadiums that seat tens of thousands of spectators. (comma and coordinating conjunction)

You may also use a semicolon or a semicolon and a transition word called a **conjunctive adverb,** such as *however, nevertheless,* and *consequently.* Notice that you are not simply linking two ideas: You are expressing a relationship between them.

EXAMPLE: We were exhausted after six days of touring. We went on to Madrid anyway.

COMBINED: We were exhausted after six days of touring**; nevertheless,** we went on to Madrid. (semicolon and conjunctive adverb)

⊘ Learn More

For additional information about compound sentences, see Section 21.2; for additional information about using semicolons, see Section 28.3.

To Combine Independent Clauses
Use a coordinating conjunction and a comma.
Coordinating Conjunctions: and, but, for, nor, or, so, yet
Use a semicolon and a conjunctive adverb.
Conjunctive Adverbs: consequently, furthermore, however, otherwise, therefore

▶ Exercise 3 **Forming Compound Sentences** Using the strategy in parentheses, combine each pair of sentences to form a compound sentence.

1. The Strait of Gibraltar connects the Mediterranean Sea with the Atlantic Ocean. The Suez Canal links the Mediterranean Sea with the Red Sea. (comma and coordinating conjunction)
2. Spain is only eight miles from Morocco across the Strait of Gibraltar. The two countries lie on different continents. (semicolon and conjunctive adverb)
3. Rabat is the capital of Morocco. Casablanca is the largest city in Morocco. (comma and coordinating conjunction)
4. Arabic-speakers make up nearly 65 percent of Morocco's population. Berber-speakers constitute the rest of the population. (semicolon)
5. Morocco exports leatherwork and rugs. It imports oil. (comma and coordinating conjunction)

Using Subordination

When one sentence explains more about an idea in another sentence, you can combine the two sentences by rewriting the first sentence as a subordinate clause. Although a **subordinate clause** has a subject and a verb, it cannot stand by itself as a sentence. An **adjective clause** is a subordinate clause that modifies a noun or pronoun by telling *what kind* or *which one*, using a relative pronoun such as *who, whom, whose, which,* or *that*.

EXAMPLE: The Sahara is the world's largest desert. <u>The Sahara includes portions of eleven countries.</u>

COMBINED: The Sahara, **which includes portions of eleven countries,** is the world's largest desert.

An **adverb clause** is a subordinate clause that answers the question *where, when, in what way,* or *why*. All adverb clauses begin with subordinating conjunctions such as *after, although, as, because, before, if, in order that, unless, until, where,* or *wherever*.

EXAMPLE: Most of Libya is covered by the Sahara. <u>For this reason, most of Libya is uninhabitable.</u>

COMBINED: Most of Libya is uninhabitable **because it is covered by the Sahara.**

Subordinating Conjunctions			
after	because	in order that	unless
although	before	since	until
as	even though	so that	when
as if	if	than	while

 **Learn More**

For additional information about clauses, see Section 20.2; for additional information about pronouns, see Section 16.2.

▶ **Exercise 4**   Using Subordination   Combine each pair of sentences using subordinate clauses.

1. The northernmost point in continental Africa is in Tunisia. Tunisia is bordered on the north and east by the Mediterranean Sea. (adjective clause)
2. Most people who live in the Sahara use camels for transportation. Camels can travel far without food or water. (adverb clause)
3. Sometimes, camels use the fatty tissue in the hump for energy. Then, the hump gets smaller and softer. (adverb clause)
4. Scientists believe that camels originated in North America. There are no native camels in North America today. (adverb clause)
5. Our trip to Algeria ended with a visit to the city of Algiers. Algiers is my parents' city of origin. (adjective clause)

3.2 *Writing Effective Paragraphs*

Main Idea and Topic Sentence

In a good paragraph, all of the sentences work together to present and develop one main idea. Often, the main idea is directly stated in a single sentence called the *topic sentence.* All of the other sentences in the paragraph support the topic sentence with examples, details, facts, or reasons.

Sometimes, a paragraph's main idea is *implied,* not directly stated. In such cases, all of the sentences work together to develop the main idea and communicate it to readers.

WRITING MODELS

from The Cabuliwallah
by Rabindranath Tagore
Translated From the Bengali Language

Mini, my five-year-old daughter, cannot live without chattering. I really believe that in all her life she has not wasted one minute in silence. Her mother is often vexed at this and would stop her prattle, but I do not. To see Mini quiet is unnatural, and I cannot bear it for long. Because of this, our conversations are always lively.

> In this paragraph, the stated topic sentence is shown in blue italics. The other sentences support, develop, and illustrate the topic sentence.

from Imitating Nature's Mineral Artistry
Paul O'Neil

The chemical ingredients for a man-made gem are easy to obtain, since most gems consist of relatively common chemical compounds. The art of gem synthesis lies in the technique by which the gem material is liquefied, in a melt or a solution, and then allowed to crystallize slowly and evenly.

> Notice that this paragraph does not contain a topic sentence. Instead, all of the sentences work together to communicate an implied main idea: Creating synthetic gems is an art that requires expertise.

> **Exercise 5** Identifying a Stated Topic Sentence Identify the stated topic sentence of the following paragraph:

A medieval feast was designed to appeal to the senses. The dishes were colorful, such as green eel stew, and highly spiced, such as rabbit seasoned with ginger, cinnamon, saffron, sugar, cloves, and nutmeg. Regarding flavor, two words that appeared often in medieval cooking were *aigre*, a popular sour flavor, and *doux*, meaning "not salty."

> **Exercise 6** Identifying an Implied Main Idea Identify the implied main idea of the following paragraph:

We arrived at the gym an hour before the pep rally started. Helen and I hung red and white streamers from the bleachers, while Alex hung posters from the chalkboards. After twenty minutes, the band filed in, pumping marching music with a rhythmic beat. Next, the bell rang, and suddenly the entire class was piling in, stepping clunkily onto the bleachers. Once everyone was seated, the state champion soccer team stormed the floor, and the crowd went wild.

Writing Topic Sentences

In most of the writing you'll do in school—with the exception of stories and other types of creative writing—you will want to focus on writing paragraphs that contain topic sentences. Following are some tips for writing strong topic sentences:

TIPS FOR WRITING TOPIC SENTENCES

1. Review the details you've gathered for a piece of writing.
2. Identify groups of details to focus on specific topics or subtopics.
3. Jot down a few words to capture the main idea that connects each group of details.
4. Develop a sentence that thoroughly and concisely captures the main idea of a group of details.
5. Once you've completed a paragraph, review your topic sentence, and make sure it still sums up the main idea expressed in the other sentences. Revise it if necessary.

> **Exercise 7** Writing Topic Sentences Write a topic sentence for a paragraph on each of the following topics:
> 1. How computers have changed the quality of life
> 2. The value of holding a position in student government
> 3. Building-accessibility for the physically challenged
> 4. Funding for boys' and girls' sports
> 5. The high cost of concert tickets

Collaborative Writing Tip

Working with a classmate can help you to ensure that your paragraphs have clear and effective topic sentences. Have the classmate read your paragraphs and underline the topic sentence. Check to see that his or her interpretation matches your intentions.

Writing Supporting Sentences

A paragraph's topic sentence should be accompanied by a series of sentences that develop, explain, or illustrate. These other sentences are called *supporting sentences*. Following are some of the types of information that you can include in your supporting sentences:

Use Facts Facts are statements that are provable. They support your key idea by offering backup or proof.

TOPIC SENTENCE: Our car is almost ready for "retirement."
SUPPORTING FACT: Our state has just instituted a strict, new automobile inspection policy.

Use Statistics A statistic is a fact stated with numbers.

TOPIC SENTENCE: Our car is almost ready for "retirement."
SUPPORTING STATISTIC: It has 235,000 miles on it, and we've owned it for 12 years.

Use Examples, Illustrations, or Instances An example, illustration, or instance is a specific person, thing, or event that demonstrates a point.

TOPIC SENTENCE: Our car is almost ready for "retirement."
ILLUSTRATION: Last week, the car broke down, and we had to have it towed.

Use Details Details are the specifics—the parts of the whole. They make your main idea or key point clear by showing how all the pieces fit together.

TOPIC SENTENCE: Our car is almost ready for "retirement."
DETAIL: When our car broke down on the highway last week, it sputtered, slowed down, and finally came to a complete standstill. While we waited for the tow truck, we felt isolated on the highway and annoyed with ourselves for not listening to our trusted mechanic's advice.

▲ **Critical Viewing**
What topic sentence and supporting sentences would you use to describe this car?
[Describe]

▶ **Exercise 8** **Writing Supporting Sentences** Write two supporting sentences for each of the following topic sentences. Use a variety of types of support.
1. The library is a place in which people should gather.
2. Many college students choose a vegetarian diet.
3. It's important to drink plenty of water when you exercise.
4. Music can be beneficial for both the mind and the body.
5. Being on a team builds self-esteem.

Placing Topic Sentences

Most often, topic sentences appear at the start of a paragraph. They can also be placed in the middle or at the end of a paragraph to create different effects. Place a topic sentence

- **at the beginning of a paragraph** so that readers will immediately see the focus of the paragraph and know what to expect in the sentences that follow.

- **in the middle of a paragraph** when you need to provide sentences that lead into or introduce your topic sentence.

- **at the end of a paragraph** when you want to drive home your main point, leaving the point fresh in readers' minds.

Paragraph Patterns Paragraphs can follow a variety of different patterns, depending on the placement of the topic sentence. One common pattern is called TRI (Topic, Restatement, Illustration). A TRI paragraph begins with a topic sentence, which is followed by a restatement of the main idea and one or more sentences illustrating the main idea through facts and examples. The elements of a TRI paragraph can be reorganized to follow other patterns, such as ITR and TIR.

T **R** **I**	Planting perennial beds, borders, or gardens is an investment in years of floral beauty. Most perennial varieties multiply annually, so the initial costs and efforts of planting reap incremental returns in years to come. Under favorable conditions, daffodils, for instance, can cover almost twice as much space in the garden in their second year.

I **T** **R**	Daisies standing guard along the garden border, snapdragons peeking out between holly bushes, and cosmos waving near the side of the house are arranged in colorful groupings. Masses of lavender, lilacs, and forsythia add a brilliant backdrop. The garden is a bright spot in the yard. It presents a splash of color against the expanse of green.

Exercise 9 Placing a Topic Sentence Arrange the sentences below into a TRI pattern. Add transitions as necessary. Then, add two new sentences. Next, reorganize the sentences into a new pattern. Explain the effect created by each pattern.

- Some students do spend hours alone with their computers.
- The fear is that these students will become so used to predictable machines that they will be unable to function with real, fallible human beings.
- Many people think that computers isolate students.

Unity and Coherence

Maintain Unity

A paragraph has unity when all of the sentences support, illustrate, explain, or develop the topic sentence or main idea. To ensure unity as you draft, think about whether each sentence you write connects clearly and logically to the paragraph's topic sentence. When you revise, strengthen the unity of each paragraph by deleting those details or sentences that do not contribute to the support, development, or explanation of the main idea. Look at this example:

The Russian Revolution resulted in the destruction of the monarchy. During the February Revolution of 1917, Czar Nicholas II was forced to leave the throne of Russia. ~~The term Soviet Union was not used until 1917.~~ With the removal of Nicholas's family, the Romanov dynasty was erased. The Russian Empire had been ruled by czars for hundreds of years; it ended when the reign of Nicholas II ceased. ~~Nikolai Lenin died seven years after the revolution, in 1924.~~

▶ **Exercise 10**   **Revising for Unity** On a separate sheet of paper, copy the following paragraph. Mark for deletion the two sentences that interfere with the unity of the paragraph.

The communist government recognized the need for a strong military. Russia signed a treaty with Germany in 1918. There were factions across Russia that did not readily support the new regime. Officials foresaw rebellion and resistance among these groups and needed a well-trained, powerful military force to oppose and put down resisters. To this end, the Red army was established; participation in it became compulsory for city workers and peasants. More than 20 million Russians died during the civil war, which lasted from 1918 to 1921.

▼ Critical Viewing
What can you infer, or conclude, about Russian Czar Nicholas II based on this picture? **[Infer]**

Create Coherence

For a paragraph to have coherence, the supporting ideas must be arranged in a logical order and the sentences must be clearly connected. Following are common organizations:

- **Chronological order** places details in time order.
- **Spatial order** arranges details according to the position in which they appear.
- **Order of importance** presents details from most to least important, or vice versa.
- **Comparison-and-contrast order** discusses all of the details related to one subject, followed by a discussion of all the details related to the other subject; or two or more items are compared point by point.

In addition to using a consistent organization, use transitions to show connections among details.

COMMON TRANSITIONS

To Show Chronological or Sequential Relationships	To Show Spatial Relationships	To Show Comparison-and-Contrast Relationships	To Show Logical Relationships
first	through	along with	if
second	next to	together with	whether
then	above	as well as	unless
next	below	also	therefore
finally	in front of	by the same token	thus
before	behind	similiarly	hence
after	connected to	although	henceforth
at the same time	north	though	in fact
later	south	however	albeit
immediately	inside	despite	
soon	outside	yet	
daily	centered	but	
frequently	middle	on the other hand	
recently	on	in contrast	
when	at the top of	except for	
	at the bottom of		

Learn More

To learn more about creating coherence in various types of writing, see Sections 4.4, 6.4, and 10.4.

> **Exercise 11** **Revising for Coherence** Revise this paragraph to create coherence. Reorganize sentences and add transitions.
> The view was the most beautiful thing Rebecca had ever seen. He was never going to let her talk him into a "little hike" again. She remembered her hiking companion. Hot and tired, he trudged toward her. She looked back down the trail to see Jim.

3.3 *Paragraphs in Essays and Other Compositions*

Writers rarely use paragraphs in isolation. Most writing consists of a series of connected paragraphs that work together to form a composition, such as an essay or a research paper, or another type of writing, such as a short story or an anecdote.

The Parts of a Composition

As you'll learn in the chapters that follow, there are many types of compositions. Compositions include just about any type of writing you do in school, aside from creative writing. While compositions can vary widely in form and purpose, they generally consist of the following elements:

The Introduction

Usually the first paragraph of a composition, the *introduction* introduces the topic, hooks the reader's interest, and presents the thesis statement. The *thesis statement* is a one- or two-sentence summary of the key point of the essay. The thesis statement may be accompanied by a few sentences outlining the subtopics to be covered in the body of the essay.

SAMPLE THESIS STATEMENTS

- Mikhail Gorbachev's policies of openness during the 1980's paved the way for the dismantling of the Soviet Union.

- Hitting a golf ball effectively involves choosing the correct club, assuming the proper position, and swinging smoothly and evenly.

The Body

The *body* of an essay consists of two or more paragraphs that develop and support the thesis. Each body paragraph should focus on a single subtopic and should provide examples, details, facts, reasons, and other types of support. Most often, each body paragraph should include a topic sentence that clearly indicates the subtopic being developed.

The Conclusion

The *conclusion* is the essay's final paragraph. It should reinforce or restate the thesis and offer readers final thoughts on the topic. Ideally, the final sentence should be a forceful, witty, or memorable statement called a *clincher*.

> **Exercise 12** **Analyzing a Composition** Find an article in a newsmagazine that follows the preceding format. Explain each element.

Ⓠ Learn More

To learn more about writing introductions, body paragraphs, and conclusions for various types of compositions, see Sections 10.4 and 13.4.

Types of Paragraphs

There are a number of types of paragraphs you can use in compositions and pieces of creative writing.

Topical Paragraphs

A topical paragraph consists of a topic sentence and several sentences that support or illustrate it. All of the paragraphs on the preceding pages are examples of topical paragraphs.

Functional Paragraphs

Functional paragraphs are used to achieve a specific purpose in an extended piece of writing. Unlike topical paragraphs, they often do not contain a topic sentence. In addition, they are often shorter than topical paragraphs—in some cases, they are only a single sentence. Functional paragraphs may do the following:

- **Indicate dialogue.** One of the conventions of written dialogue is that a new paragraph begins with each change of speaker.

- **Make a transition.** A short paragraph can help a reader move between the ideas of two topical paragraphs.

- **Create emphasis.** A paragraph of a sentence or two that reinforces a main point in a piece of writing will leave a lasting impression with readers. (See the example below.)

WRITING MODEL

from **The Laugher**
Heinrich Böll

I go through life with an impassive expression, from time to time permitting myself a gentle smile, and I often wonder whether I have ever laughed. I think not. My brothers and sisters have always known me for a serious boy.

So I laugh in many different ways, but my own laughter I have never heard.

Because the second paragraph is so brief and direct, it emphasizes the contradiction at the heart of the excerpt: This man goes through life wearing a serious expression, but he laughs inwardly in many different ways.

Paragraph Blocks

Occasionally, you may have so much information that you will need to develop a single idea over several paragraphs. Such "blocks" of paragraphs all support the same main idea or topic sentence. By separating the development of the contributing ideas into paragraph blocks, your ideas become clearer and more accessible.

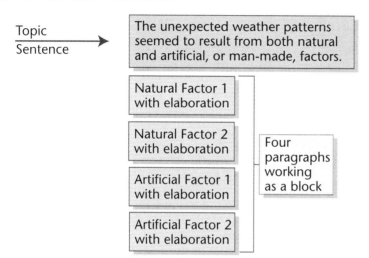

Topic
Sentence → The unexpected weather patterns seemed to result from both natural and artificial, or man-made, factors.

Natural Factor 1 with elaboration

Natural Factor 2 with elaboration

Artificial Factor 1 with elaboration

Artificial Factor 2 with elaboration

Four paragraphs working as a block

▼ Critical Viewing
What topic sentence might you come up with if you were writing a description of this storm? **[Describe]**

Exercise 13 Analyzing Functional Paragraphs and Paragraph Blocks Choose a descriptive essay or factual report. Then, choose a story containing dialogue. In both, locate examples of functional paragraphs that create emphasis, indicate dialogue, and make transitions. Also, locate an example of a paragraph block. Explain to a partner how the functional paragraphs and the paragraph block work within the context of the longer pieces of writing.

Writing Style

Developing Style

You express yourself through your "personal style." It includes your music preferences, the way you dress, how you speak. Style also refers to how you express yourself in writing. These elements work together to determine your writing style:

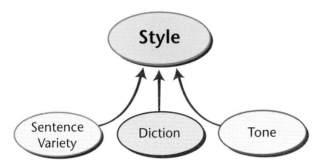

Sentence Variety One of the keys to developing a strong writing style is learning to vary the length and structure of your sentences. Sentences that are all short will sound choppy to readers; sentences that are all very long or all begin in the same way will become boring or hard to follow. Use a mixture of short and long sentences to create a rhythm and emphasize key points. For instance, you can follow a series of long sentences with a short one to drive home an important idea.

Diction Diction refers to a writer's choice of words. When you write, choose your words carefully to have the effect you desire. For example, if you are writing an essay about a serious topic, you will want to use formal language that will command your reader's respect. If, on the other hand, you are writing an amusing story for your friends, you will want to use informal language that matches the way you speak.

Tone The tone of your writing is your attitude toward your subject. Your tone may be formal or informal, friendly or distant, personal or impersonal. A writer offering advice on a serious topic may still choose a lighthearted, amusing tone. When expressing intense personal thoughts about an important topic, however, a writer's tone might reflect awe or respect.

 **Learn More**

When you revise, you can often achieve better sentence variety by combining your short sentences into longer ones. For instruction on combining sentences, see Sections 21.2 and 21.3.

> **Exercise 14** **Analyzing Sentence Variety** Read the Writing Models on pages 33 and 40. Compare and contrast the sentence lengths and structures, the word choice, and the tone of each. Then, write paragraphs of your own, modeled on the style of each piece.

Formal and Informal English

Standard English can be either formal or informal. It is best to use formal English for serious or academic purposes. Informal English is appropriate for stories and casual writing.

Formal English

Formal English should be used for essays, newspaper articles, formal reports, speeches, letters of application, and most school assignments. When using formal English,

- Avoid contractions.
- Do not use slang.
- Use standard English and grammar.
- Use a serious tone and sophisticated vocabulary.

Informal English

The "everyday" English we speak is informal English. You can use informal English when you write dialogue, stories, personal essays, poems, letters to friends, and journal entries. Writing informally allows you to

- Use contractions.
- Use slang and popular expressions, especially to capture the natural sound of speech.

▲ **Critical Viewing** How would you describe this platter of sushi using informal English? How would you describe it using formal English? **[Describe, Compare and Contrast]**

FORMAL ENGLISH:	Sumo wrestling, a special Japanese form of wrestling, may be the most Japanese sport of all. Wrestlers perform ceremonial actions that have traditional significance, like squatting deeply to show respect.
INFORMAL ENGLISH:	I don't think I've ever seen people so crazy about baseball. There's a game every night of the week! It's excellent watching games with a crowd that's totally psyched!

▶ **Exercise 15** **Using Formal and Informal English** Rewrite the following sentences. Use formal English for those written in informal English. Use informal English for those written in formal English.

1. In Japan, the contrast of old and new is very striking.
2. This week, I checked out Tokyo.
3. Sushi and sashimi, two types of raw fish dishes, are eaten with soy sauce.
4. Some people are grossed out by the idea of eating raw fish.
5. If you've never tried sushi or sashimi, you may be floored to discover that they don't have a fishy taste.

Spotlight on the Humanities

Analyzing Culture as Presented in Media

Focus on Dance: Native American Dancing

Just as pieces of writing follow a structure consisting of an organized series of paragraphs, dances follow a structure consisting of an organized pattern of steps. In addition, certain dances involve special costumes.

For Native Americans, dance is highly symbolic and can represent actions by people or events in nature. The costume for the men's traditional dance may include a single bustle with eagle feathers or a breastplate of animal bones. Eagle feathers are sacred to Native Americans and are awarded for bravery. In the women's traditional dance, the costume may include a fringed shawl and a feather fan.

The movements in women's traditional dance are focused; the women move their feet close to the ground, keeping the rhythm of the drum. More complex dances by the men require stamina and athletic ability. Advanced dancing requires the dancer to keep the feathers moving at all times throughout a song. Native American dance has served as a source of inspiration for films and literary works.

▲ Critical Viewing What does this photograph reveal about Native American dance? [Interpret]

Film Connection The 1990 film *Dances With Wolves* uses the image of Native American dance to tell the story of a Civil War soldier and his relationship with a Sioux Indian tribe. Directed by Kevin Costner, the film won seven Academy Awards, including Best Picture, Best Director, and Best Cinematography.

Literature Connection In his book *Desert Dwellers: Native People of the Southwest*, Scott S. Warren captures the costumes and customs of Native American dance in colorful photographs and elaborates on the meaning of movements in dance among the Pueblo, Navajo, and Hopi.

Writing Activity: Composition About a Film

Watch the film *Dances With Wolves*. Write a composition explaining how the image of dance is used in the film to convey a message to the audience. Share your exposition with other class members.

Media and Technology Skills

Recognizing the Varieties of Media Sources of Information

Activity: Keep a Media Log

We receive information from an astonishing variety of media sources. Once, the printed book was the primary source of recorded information. Today, news and other data are stored in newspapers, magazines, network and cable television broadcasts, radio transmissions, and computers connected via the Internet.

You may not be aware of the many sources you use to collect information every day. Keeping a media log will help you assess the channels you use. It might even encourage you to broaden the sources you frequently use.

Think About It Your media log will list the information sources you use every day for one week. Begin by making some predictions about your day-to-day reference sources. Which source do you think you use most often? Write your predictions at the beginning of your media log.

Collect It Keep track of the media sources you use each day. Include everything—from watching television news to getting information from a telephone call. You can organize your list chronologically or by type of media.

Annotate It After you collect your information, use a rating scale to tell how useful each source was. Devise your own rating scale, such as one to five, with five being the highest. Create a code that indicates what each rating means.

Reflect on It When you have completed entries for one week, take time to review your original predictions. Evaluate your use of media sources, and consider making goals for your future research. For example, you might decide to get more information from the Internet.

Varieties of Print Media

When looking for information, be sure to consult a wide variety of print resources. In addition to books, magazines, and newspapers, the following sources of information may contain the facts you need:

- pamphlets and brochures
- government bulletins and documents
- local newsletters
- catalogs and product information sheets
- instruction manuals
- product labels
- direct mail and advertisements

Tuesday

TV: evening news
Newspaper: The Washington Post (news)
Radio: morning weather
record release dates and musician interviews
Telephone: information from poison hotline
Internet: more information about household poisons
record reviews
CD-ROM: looked up poisons in encyclopedia
Magazines: Time magazine (news and reviews)
Scientific American

Standardized Test Preparation Workshop

Strategy, Organization, and Style

Your knowledge of how to write and revise effective paragraphs is often measured on standardized tests. These types of test items consist of a paragraph in which each sentence is numbered and specific questions based on the passage. These test questions often ask about the writer's strategy, organization, sequence of sentences, choice of words, and overall style. The following are three types of questions that you will need to answer:

- **Strategy questions** ask whether a given revision is appropriate in the context of the essay.

- **Organization questions** ask you to choose the most logical sequence of ideas or to decide whether a sentence should be added, deleted, or moved.

- **Style questions** focus on assessing the writer's point of view and the use of appropriate and effective language for the intended audience.

The sample test item that follows will give you practice in answering questions on writing strategy, organization, and style.

Test Tip

Before reading the questions, read the paragraph, noting any places where the text does not flow or seems incorrect. Refer back to this as you answer the questions.

Sample Test Item

Directions: This passage is part of a report that Brooke has written for her geography class. As part of a peer conference, you are asked to read the report and think about suggestions you might make. When you finish reading the report, answer the multiple-choice question that follows.

1 Vietnam is a tropical country in

2 Southeast Asia. Vietnam extends

3 south from China in a long, narrow

4 S-curve.

1 What is the BEST way to combine the sentences in lines 1–4? ("Vietnam . . . S-curve.")

A Vietnam is a tropical country in Southeast Asia, and Vietnam extends south from China in a long, narrow S-curve.

B A tropical country in Southeast Asia, Vietnam extends south from China in a long, narrow S-curve.

C Vietnam is located in Southeast Asia and has an unusual shape.

D Make no change

Answer and Explanation

The correct answer is *B.* Combining the sentences in this way eliminates the unnecessary repetition of the word *Vietnam.*

Practice 1 **Directions:** This paragraph is part of a report that Lauren has written for her art class. As part of a peer conference, you are asked to read the report and think about suggestions you might make. When you finish reading the report, answer the multiple-choice questions that follow.

1 Although Degas is considered one of
2 the Impressionist painters, he did not
3 share their thing about light and color.
4 Instead of concentrating on color and
5 light, he focused on composition, drawing,
6 and form. He created many sculptures.
7 Some of them are quite nice. These were
8 "practice works." They made Degas one
9 of the most important modern sculptors.

1 What is the BEST change, if any, to make the language more appropriate for a formal piece of writing in the sentence in lines 1–3? ("Although . . . color.")

   A Change *thing* to *enthusiasm.*

   B Remove the comma after *painters.*

   C Remove *Impressionist.*

   D Make no change.

2 What is the BEST way, if any, to rewrite the sentence in lines 4–6? ("Instead . . . form.")

   A He didn't want to focus on color and light because he focused on composition, drawing, and form.

   B Instead, he focused on composition, drawing, and form.

   C To focus on color and light was not his primary interest.

   D Make no change.

3 Which sentence would BEST add information about Degas to the passage?

   A Painting and sculpture are powerful art forms.

   B Degas is a well-known painter.

   C Impressionist painting was an important art form.

   D Degas created sculpture to study form and body movements.

4 What is the BEST way to combine the last two sentences? ("These . . . sculptors.")

   A These were "practice works," and they made Degas one of the most important modern sculptors.

   B These practice works made Degas one of the most important modern sculptors.

   C Degas was made one of the most important modern sculptors by these practice works.

   D One of the most important sculptors of our time was Degas.

5 Which of the following sentences, if any, would be the BEST choice to be removed from the passage?

   A Although Edgar Degas is considered one of the Impressionist painters, he did not share their thing about light and color.

   B They made Degas one of the most important sculptors in modern times.

   C Some of them are quite nice.

   D Make no change.

Narration
Autobiographical Writing

A Tough Story, John G. Brown, North Carolina Museum of Art

Autobiographical Narration in Everyday Life

Think for a moment about a typical school day. To whom do you talk? What do you say? Chances are, you probably talk with friends about your experiences since you last met. When you tell a friend about what you did during the weekend or describe a funny thing that happened to you, you are engaging in **autobiographical narration**—telling a story from your own life. These stories may be funny or sad, short or long.

Autobiographical narration sometimes takes written form. You may, for example, write a letter to a cousin about a concert you heard, or you may relate a story about yourself on a job or college application.

▲ **Critical Viewing**
Judging from the details in this piece of fine art, what sort of life story might these boys have to tell? **[Analyze]**

What Is Autobiographical Writing?

Autobiographical writing tells a story about an event or experience in the writer's own life. An autobiographical narrative can be as simple as a description of a recent car trip or as complex as the entire story of a person's life.

Autobiographical writing usually includes

- the writer as the main character.

- a sequence of events.

- conflict or tension between characters or between a character and an outside force.

- an insight gained by the writer.

To preview the criteria on which your autobiographical narrative may be evaluated, see the Rubric for Self-Assessment on page 67.

Writers in
ACTION

American writer and poet Muriel Rukeyser understood the importance of storytelling. In "The Speed of Darkness," she observed the following:

"The universe is made of stories, not of atoms."

Types of Autobiographical Writing

Following are some types of autobiographical writing:

- **Eyewitness accounts** are retellings of events personally witnessed by a writer.

- **Personal narratives** are stories that reveal a writer's opinions, feelings, and insights about an experience.

- **Autobiographical incidents** tell of a memorable or pivotal event in a writer's life.

- **Memoirs** contain a writer's reflections on an important person or event from his or her own life.

- **Anecdotes** are brief, true, and usually humorous stories that contain a definite conclusion.

PREVIEW
Student Work
IN PROGRESS

Erica Jackson, a student at Boone County High School in Florence, Kentucky, wrote a personal narrative called "The Ultimate Challenge." Follow along as she prewrites, drafts, and revises her work. You can read her completed narrative at the end of the lesson.

Linda Greenhouse is a journalist who covers the Supreme Court for The New York Times. *The following article was published in* The New York Times Magazine.

Reading Writing Connection

Reading Strategy: Recognize the Author's Purpose As you read, think about why the author is writing and how he or she wants you to respond. For example, an author may want to warn you about something or to persuade you to think in a specific way. As you read this narrative, examine Greenhouse's word choice and selection of details to identify her purpose for writing.

The Long Tale of Madonna the Iguana

Linda Greenhouse

Madonna the Iguana came into our life when my daughter, Hannah, was 9 years old, desperately wanting a house pet but allergic to almost anything with fur or hair. The little lizard was like a tiny green jewel, small enough to fit in my hand and so fragile I worried each breath might be its last. Five years later, she (we deemed it a female, but we were never really sure) was a muscular, fully grown adult. Five feet long, she had outgrown three enclosures, the last the size of a stall shower, a two-level contraption with sliding glass doors.

She had also outgrown the affections of a teenage girl whose friends now shuddered at the sight of her huge reptilian room-mate. I understood Hannah's embarrassment, but I was proud that while the great majority of iguanas die in their first year as house pets, Madonna was thriving. Without my wanting it to happen, this iguana had found a place in my heart.

So that became our story. A pet outgrew a girl. A girl outgrew her pet. And a mother tried, probably for longer than she should have, to hold on to both.

Notice the play on words in the title. "Tale" could be changed to "tail".

Greenhouse provides a vivid description of the iguana.

Greenhouse herself is the "I" in the story.

"But Madonna doesn't do anything!" Hannah would sometimes say. That was true; these big lizards just bask in the sun munching on leaves and flowers. Visitors often asked if iguanas were smart. Smart enough, was all I could say of a species that had flourished through many millenniums. "Does Madonna love me?" my daughter asked early on. I don't really think so, I replied. "Well, at least does she like me?"

Yet my relationship with Madonna was not just a one-way street. She perked up when I came into the room. She let me peel off her shedding skin like a giant green sunburn, stripes and all. The skin of her feet sometimes came off like a delicate glove, a mysterious artifact from a distant time and place.

At first she wouldn't eat while I watched, and I would peer from the hallway as she delicately picked through her dish to find her favorites—broccoli, green beans and carrots always disappeared before collard greens or kale. Eventually, she ate in front of me. She liked pansies, which I grew as a special treat.

When the window was open, she would climb up the screen and hold herself upright, listening to the birds and watching the breeze intently. I half hoped that the sight of this enormous reptile would terrify someone, but no one noticed.

She did give us a scare when an ice storm knocked out our electricity, forcing us to vacate the house. Not knowing what else to do, we covered Madonna in a towel and left her lying still. Each day for three days, I came back to the cold, dark house to check on her. A mammal might well have died. But her cold blooded reptilian body simply slowed down to the minimum. When the heat came back on, Madonna warmed up and within hours was back to normal, with no damage done.

Dialogue such as this helps bring characters and situations to life for readers.

The autobiographical narrative is told in chronological order, progressing forward in time.

▶ **Critical Viewing** What might account for the popularity of iguanas as house pets? **[Generalize]**

▲ **Critical Viewing** What descriptive words would you choose to paint a verbal portrait of this iguana? **[Analyze]**

When the end came, it was without warning. Just as our Thanksgiving guests were due to arrive, we heard a huge crash from Hannah's room. We raced up the stairs to find the plate glass of Madonna's enclosure shattered. Madonna, uninjured, seemed just as surprised as we were. A random flick of that powerful tail probably hit the glass at a vulnerable point.

The glass could have been replaced. But to me, the message was clear. It was time. Hannah barely blinked. "I'll get a sofa for that corner, where I can stretch out," she said.

An hour on the telephone the next morning confirmed that zoos have no interest in the outgrown pets of families who should have known better in the first place. But we did find a local pet shop that had an empty iguana habitat. Madonna would live there or be placed for adoption in a qualified home.

This event triggers the resolution of the story.

We were at the shop within half an hour, Madonna struggling in the unfamiliar surroundings of a plastic recycling bin. But she didn't fight as the clerk lifted her into her new home, taller and deeper than the one she left behind. She scampered up the climbing log and stared at us, breathing heavily.

I cried on the way home, embarrassed at my inability to stop my tears. "I can't believe I'm crying over an iguana!" I managed to say. "She wasn't just an iguana to you," my husband said. "You took responsibility for her."

I suddenly remembered a scene from "The Little Prince," in which a fox asks a boy to tame him. But why should you want me to tame you? the boy asks. Because, the fox replies, "you become responsible, forever, for what you have tamed."

I never really tamed Madonna, of course, as the fading scars on my arms demonstrate—any more than I can hope to tame my lovely, headstrong 14-year-old daughter, who picked out a new couch before I had even dismantled Madonna's enclosure. A tamed teenager would be as unnatural a creature as a tamed iguana. Both in their natural states are prickly, wary, and inexorably growing into a strength under which things can shatter unexpectedly. In our iguana-less family, as Hannah reclaims her bedroom and looks beyond its walls to the world outside, I will try to remember what Madonna taught: that with responsibility, and love, comes the moment for letting go.

LITERATURE

Desert Exile by Yoshiko Uchida is another example of autobiographical writing. You can find a selection from the work in *Prentice Hall Literature: Timeless Voices, Timeless Themes*, Platinum.

This allusion or reference is both literary and personal.

In the story's last sentence, Greenhouse reveals the insight she gained from her experience.

Reading Writing Connection

Writing Application: Choose Details to Achieve Purpose As you prepare to write your autobiographical narrative, identify your purpose for writing and think about the types of details that will help you achieve that purpose.

Prewriting

Choosing Your Topic

Choose a topic for your autobiographical narrative that you find important or interesting. Following are some ideas for generating topics:

Strategies for Generating Topics

1. **You Were There!** Choose as a topic an exciting event that you witnessed. For example, you could tell about a championship playoff game you attended or about a fantastic concert you heard.

2. **Consider the Moment** Write the following words on a sheet of paper: *Funny, Exciting, Interesting, Puzzling.* Then, try to recall moments in your life that fit each of these categories. Finally, choose one of these moments as the basis of your narrative.

3. **Make a Blueprint** Draw a floor plan of a significant place in your life. Label the rooms or areas, and, if you like, draw in details like furniture or trees. Then, make a list of words, phrases, sentences, names, or activities that come to mind as you "walk through" this special place. Review your ideas, and choose one as the basis of your narrative.

Try it out! Use the interactive Blueprinting activity in **Section 4.2**, on-line or on CD-ROM.

IN PROGRESS

Name: Erica Jackson
Boone County High School
Florence, KY

Using Blueprinting to Find a Topic

Erica Jackson drew a blueprint to come up with a topic for her narrative.

bird's nest

carving initials on tree

water-skiing

painting the fence

TOPIC BANK

Consider these suggestions if you are having difficulty coming up with your own topic:

1. **Anecdote About a Surprise** Recall a time when you were truly surprised. In a brief anecdote, tell the story of the situation and your actions.

2. **Memoir** Think of a person who has influenced your life in a positive way. In a memoir, recount one incident that shows why that person is a worthy role model.

3. **Personal Narrative About a Time of Change** Write about a period of transition in your own life. Describe fully the people and events that prompted such a change.

Backgammon, 1976, Jane Freilicher, Utah Museum of Fine Arts

Responding to Fine Art

4. Look closely at *Backgammon* by Jane Freilicher. Why might the scene pictured inspire a piece of autobiographical writing? Study the setting and characters in the painting, and write an autobiographical narrative that comes to mind.

Responding to Literature

5. "A Child's Christmas in Wales" is a real-life story taken from the life of its writer, Dylan Thomas. Read the story, and search your memory for your own interesting childhood experiences. Choose your own childhood story to tell. "A Child's Christmas in Wales" appears in *Prentice Hall Literature: Timeless Voices, Timeless Themes,* Platinum.

☑ Cooperative Writing Opportunity

6. **School Stories** With a group of classmates, create an anthology of autobiographical narratives about a school-time experience. Have each group member write an autobiographical narrative and submit it to the group. Decide on the order in which to present them, and bind them together in a folder. Take turns reading aloud your finished stories to the group.

Narrowing Your Topic

Once you have chosen your topic, narrow it so that the scope of your narrative is manageable. Use the following technique for narrowing the scope of your topic.

Use Carbon Paper to Narrow a Topic

1. Insert carbon paper between two sheets of notepaper.
2. Using an empty pen or a pen that is "unclicked," write on the top sheet anything that comes to mind about your topic. Write for at least five minutes.
3. Remove the top sheet and the carbon paper, and review what you wrote. Choose the aspect of your topic that interests you most.

Considering Your Audience and Purpose

Your audience and purpose for writing will have an impact on the details that you choose to include and the type of language that you use. The following chart highlights strategies for achieving your purpose, depending on your audience.

Type of Narrative	Audience	Purpose	Strategy
Anecdote about a humorous event	Classmates	To entertain	• Use lighthearted, informal language • Emphasize or exaggerate absurd or comical situations
Memoir about an influential friend	General audience	To inform	• Include ample background information since the audience may not be familiar with the subject • Develop details about the subject that explain his or her actions

⊛ Technology Tip

If you are working on a computer, use the following strategy to narrow your topic:

1. Open up a word-processing document on your computer.
2. Turn off the monitor so that you can't see the document.
3. Freewrite about your general topic for five minutes. Type anything that comes to mind.
4. Turn the monitor back on, and review what you wrote. Choose the aspect of your topic that interests you most.

Gathering Details

Begin gathering details that are necessary to the narrative and interesting to the reader.

Gather Details About the Characters

Before you write your autobiographical narrative, gather details about your characters that will help bring them to life for your readers. Use a character profile like the one that follows to help you gather details about characters—the people in your narrative.

CHARACTER PROFILE

- What is the character's name, age, profession, and background?

- How would you describe the character's personality, habits, and likes or dislikes?

- What dreams or goals does this character have?

- What has this character achieved in life?

- What do other characters in your narrative think about this character?

- Why is the character important to the narrative you are going to relate?

Gather Details About the Setting

The setting is the time and place in which the events of the narrative unfold. The setting locates your reader in your narrative, explaining when and where the action of the story takes place. Fill out a setting chart like the one that follows to help you get started.

Time/Year	Place	Physical Details
nineteenth century	A school in Springfield, MA	A room inside the schoolhouse, hardwood floors

Try it out! Use the interactive Setting Chart in **Section 4.2**, on-line or on CD-ROM.

4.3 **Drafting**

Shaping Your Writing

During the drafting stage, give your narrative its shape. Decide where and how to begin and end it, which characters to develop fully, and which events to highlight.

Create a Plot

Just like fictional stories, autobiographical stories should capture and hold the readers' interest. Think about your real-life story as if it were fiction. To do so, identify the timeline of events and decide on where to begin and end your story.

- List the events, and identify the climax, or high point of interest, in the story.
- Then, arrange the rest of the events so that they follow the structure of a plot diagram.

⊙ **Technology Tip**

In your word-processing program, write several ending paragraphs for your narrative, and then cut and paste each one in your narrative. Which one ties up the loose ends most effectively? Choose one that leaves readers with the strongest image.

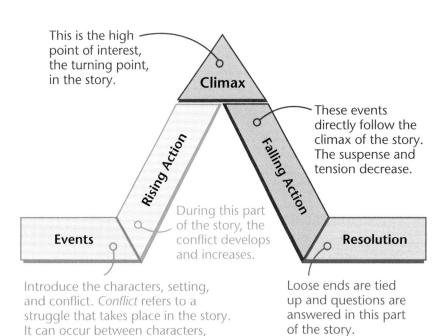

This is the high point of interest, the turning point, in the story.

Climax

Rising Action

Falling Action

These events directly follow the climax of the story. The suspense and tension decrease.

During this part of the story, the conflict develops and increases.

Events

Resolution

Introduce the characters, setting, and conflict. *Conflict* refers to a struggle that takes place in the story. It can occur between characters, between a character and a force of nature (such as a tornado), or within a character's mind.

Loose ends are tied up and questions are answered in this part of the story.

Providing Elaboration

To *elaborate* means "to develop in detail." Make your narrative compelling to readers by using elaboration.

Add Dialogue

One way to add interest to your narrative is to provide dialogue that re-creates conversations or that reveals the thoughts that went through your head while you were in a particular situation. As you draft, develop your character and the characters of others through dialogue.

Explode the Moment

In everyday life, a moment of time passes quickly; there's little opportunity to observe it in detail. In a narrative, a moment can be "exploded." As a writer, you have the luxury of putting it under a magnifying glass, turning it upside down and inside out, and examining it from a variety of angles. Asking questions about an action or event is one way to get started.

Collaborative Writing Tip

Work with a partner to help you explode a moment in your writing. Describe a moment to your partner. Then, have your partner ask you questions about the moment. Use the details that answer the questions to help you explode the moment.

Student Work
IN PROGRESS

Name: Erica Jackson
Boone County High School
Florence, KY

Elaborating by Exploding the Moment

To give depth to her autobiographical narrative, Erica used the technique of exploding the moment.

"Ready!" I called out with clenched fists. The motor raced for the third time, and I felt a gush of wind hit my face. The hair blew off my neck, and I could see the white foam on the peaks of the wake from the boat.

I held on for dear life as the boat pulled me behind it. Wow! What a feeling I had. I was actually skiing!

The highlighted passages "explode the moment," giving readers a vivid sense of Erica's experience.

4.4 *Revising*

Revising Your Overall Structure

A first draft is not a final product. To make it into something wonderful, you need to trim, shape, and polish it. Following are some aspects you should look at as you begin to revise your narrative:

Create Unity

Review the individual elements of your autobiographical narrative to make sure they are unified and that they work together. Each paragraph should help develop the overall impression you want to leave with your readers. Sentences within each paragraph should work to develop the paragraph's main idea.

▶ **REVISION STRATEGY**
Deleting Unrelated Details

Each sentence in the narrative should have a clear relationship to the sentences around it. Delete those sentences or details that do not move events forward or create an image for the readers.

Get instant help! For assistance in creating unity, use the Unity and Coherence Revision Checker, accessible from the menu bar, on-line or on CD-ROM.

Student Work
IN PROGRESS

Name: *Erica Jackson*
Boone County High School
Florence, KY

Deleting Unrelated Details

When Erica reviewed her draft for unity, she discovered that she had included some unrelated details. When she deleted them, her narrative became more focused.

Because these details stray from the main idea of the paragraph, Erica deleted them.

"Are you ready?" my sister shouted from the boat. ~~My sister is an expert water-skier. She's won several local competitions over the years for swimming, diving, and water skiing~~. I paused for a moment, swallowed hard, and nodded.

Revising Your Paragraphs

Form Functional Paragraphs

As you revise, make sure that your paragraphs perform specific narrative functions. Following are major functions your paragraphs might serve:

▶ **REVISION STRATEGY**
Analyzing Paragraphs

To sustain interest: Reread the longer paragraphs in your work to evaluate their ability to hold the readers' interest. If necessary, revise these paragraphs by breaking them into shorter ones that keep the readers involved in the story.

To achieve desired effects: Intersperse short one- or two-sentence paragraphs with longer ones to achieve desired effects, such as indicating a shift in time, a change in mood, or the occurrence of a major event.

To signify a change in speaker: Indicate which character is speaking by beginning a new paragraph each time a different character begins to speak. Because these paragraphs show that another character is speaking, they allow you, the writer, to avoid repeating "he said" or "she said." In the following example, a long paragraph was made into shorter, functional paragraphs.

Draft: In this version, an exchange of dialogue appears in a single paragraph. It is dense to read and doesn't have much of an impact.

> As Bryan and I rode up the mountain in the chair lift, I peppered him with questions about skiing. "What trail should we take?" I asked. "Can I handle an intermediate trail?" "Well," Bryan replied, "we'll just see what's there when we jump off the lift." "Jump off the lift?" I said. "You mean the lift doesn't stop for us?" "No," Bryan said, "the lift keeps moving and you jump off." "Oh," I said, in a small voice.

Revision: By breaking the large paragraph into smaller paragraphs, it's easier to follow the exchange of dialogue. The final line spoken by the narrator has more impact because it stands alone.

> As Bryan and I rode up the mountain in the chair lift, I peppered him with questions about skiing. "What trail should we take?" I asked. "Can I handle an intermediate trail?"
>
> "Well," Bryan replied, "we'll just see what's there when we jump off the lift."
>
> "Jump off the lift? You mean the lift doesn't stop for us?"
>
> "No," Bryan said, "the lift keeps moving and you jump off."
>
> "Oh," I said, in a small voice.

⚙ Grammar and Style Tip

Avoid stringing together too many short sentences with the words *and* or *but*. Varying connecting words is just as important as varying sentence length and structure.

▼ **Critical Viewing**
If this were a movie scene, what lines of dialogue might these skiers be speaking? **[Speculate]**

Revising Your Sentences

Vary Your Sentence Lengths

In narrative writing, variety in sentence length can "spice up" your narrative. Make your writing more expressive by breaking up passages that have consecutive short sentences or consecutive long sentences. Use different sentence types to help make your writing more interesting and mature.

▶ **REVISION STRATEGY**
Color-Coding to Achieve Sentence Variety

Review your draft, and use a blue pencil to highlight sentences of six words or less. Highlight longer sentences in green. Then, examine the balance of sentence lengths and make the following revisions, if necessary.

- Short, simple sentences, which contain only one complete idea, can be combined into compound and complex sentences.

- Long compound and complex sentences can be split into two or three simple sentences.

Simple Sentences: Express only one main idea.		The students wanted to play football. The hailstorm made it impossible to play.
Compound Sentences: Contain two or more complete ideas.	Ideas are joined with the words *and, but, or,* or a semicolon.	The students wanted to play football, **but** the hailstorm made it impossible to play. The students wanted to play football; the hailstorm made it impossible to play.
Complex Sentences: Contain an independent clause with one main idea and one or more subordinate clauses with less important ideas.	Subordinate clauses are introduced by conjunctions, such as *although, because, before, since,* and *while.*	**Although** the students wanted to play football, the hailstorm made it impossible to play.

Get instant help! For assistance in revising sentences, use the Sentence Length Revision Checker, accessible from the menu bar, on-line or on CD-ROM.

Revising Your Word Choice

Evaluate Your Use of *Me, Myself,* and *I*

When you are writing a narrative from the first-person point of view—such as a *memoir, personal narrative,* or *eyewitness account*—you will probably use the personal pronouns *me* and *I*. It's particularly important, therefore, to make sure that you use these pronouns correctly. *I* and *we* are **subject pronouns;** they act as the subjects of a sentence. *Me* and *us* are **object pronouns;** these pronouns receive the action of the verb.

▶ **REVISION STRATEGY**
Color-Coding Personal Pronouns

Read through your draft, and circle each use of the personal pronouns *I, myself,* and *me.* Then, examine each usage, and make sure that you've chosen the correct pronoun based on its function in the sentence. A chart explaining the nominative case and objective case of pronouns appears on the following page.

Student Work
IN PROGRESS

Name: *Erica Jackson*
Boone County High School
Florence, KY

Color-Coding Personal Pronouns

*Erica checked her use of personal pronouns and corrected an error she had made.
She also deleted an unnecessary use of the word* myself.

He had been wanting me to try the whole summer, but (I) hadn't gotten up the nerve to do it. (My) sister and (me) had always been competitive, and she was an expert water-skiier. Also, the thought of making a fool of (myself) in front of everyone didn't sound appealing. At first, (I) was unsure (myself) whether (I) really wanted to undertake skiing, but what did (I) have to lose? . . .

Grammar in Your Writing
Pronoun Case

Case is the form of a noun or pronoun that indicates its use in a sentence. Use the **nominative case** for the subject of a verb and for a predicate nominative. Use the **objective case** for the object of any verb, preposition, or verbal.

Nominative Pronouns	Examples
Subject	*She* is the president of the class. *I* gave my coat to the clerk.
Predicate Nominative	The president is *she*.
(Formal Usage)	It is *I*.
(Informal Usage)	It is *me*.

Objective Pronouns	Examples
Direct Object	Our family praised *her*.
Indirect Object	The organization gave *us* a check.
Object of Preposition	Between *us*, there are no secrets.
Object of Participle	The noise scaring *them* was outside.
Object of Gerund	Helping *them* was my foremost thought.
Object of Infinitive	They want to ask *me* to lead the team.

Find It in Your Reading Read through "The Long Tale of Madonna the Iguana" on pages 50–53. Write down three sentences in which the author uses the personal pronouns *I*, and *me*. Then, explain why each is *nominative case* or *objective case*.

Put It in Your Writing Review your draft to see whether you've used the objective case of a pronoun following a linking verb. If so, replace the objective case pronoun with a subject pronoun and examine the effect on your writing. Decide which better suits your audience and purpose.

For more on pronoun usage, see Chapter 23.

Peer Review

Use a Peer Review Work Sheet

A peer reviewer can help you assess the clarity and effectiveness of your narrative and spot any errors that you have missed.

- Make a Peer Review work sheet like the one below.
- Photocopy the work sheet and distribute it to peer reviewers, along with a copy of your narrative.
- Have reviewers respond by filling in the work sheet.
- Consider the comments of your peer reviewers as you prepare your final draft.

Try it out! Use the interactive Peer Review Work Sheet in **Section 4.4,** on-line or on CD-ROM.

Title_____

Intended Audience_____ **Intended Purpose**_____

Question:	Response/Suggestions for Improvement
Does the opening of the story grab your interest? Would you read on if you came across this story in a magazine?	
Are the characters and settings described well? Why or why not?	
Are the language and details in the story appropriate for the intended audience?	
Are there any story passages that get bogged down in unnecessary detail?	
Are there any other areas that need improvement or other suggestions that you would make?	

Editing and *Proofreading*

Before sharing your narrative, check it for errors in grammar, spelling, punctuation, and capitalization. Since most narratives contain a lot of details involving characters, make sure that you have used pronouns consistently and correctly. Then, use the following strategy to give your narrative a final polish.

Focusing on Punctuating Dialogue

Review the use of dialogue in your draft to be sure you've punctuated dialogue correctly. Use the tips below for further help:

Grammar in Your Life
Paragraphing and Punctuating Dialogue

Quotation Marks Dialogue should be set off with quotation marks. Begin a new paragraph with each new speaker. Look at this example:

"These students are very bored," I said. "They need interesting games that they can play inside in the winter."

"Well, then, perhaps you could invent a new game," the doctor replied.

Punctuation Marks Place punctuation marks that indicate the way in which the dialogue is spoken inside the final quotation mark:

"How about that**!**" exclaimed Judy.

"Who's there**?**" asked the leader.

Find It in Your Reading Find two examples of dialogue within "The Long Tale of Madonna the Iguana" on pages 50–53. Think about why the dialogue is punctuated as it is.

Find It in Your Writing Review the use of dialogue in your narrative. Be sure that you've correctly punctuated each instance of dialogue. Also, check to be sure that you've begun a new paragraph with each new speaker.

For more on the use of quotation marks, see Chapter 28.

4.6 Publishing and Presenting

When you've completed your narrative, share it with others and save a copy for yourself. Following are additional ideas for publishing and presenting your writing:

Building Your Portfolio

1. **Publish in a Print Medium** Submit your narrative to a school newspaper or to a national magazine that publishes student writing. Consult your teacher or librarian to find out about publications that might publish your narrative.

2. **Tell Your Story** Rehearse reading your story aloud. Mark up a copy of the story, and underline words that you plan to emphasize. Also, mark passages you'd like to read more slowly or more quickly. Finally, assemble a group of peers or family, and tell your story to them.

Reflecting on Your Writing

Think for a moment about what it was like to create a piece of autobiographical writing. Then, respond to the following questions, and save your responses in your portfolio.

- As you wrote, what insights did you gain about yourself?
- What "tricks of the trade" did you learn about telling a good story?

Internet Tip

To see model narratives scored with this rubric, go on-line:
PHSchool.com
Enter Web Code:
eek-1001

Rubric for Self-Assessment

Evaluate your autobiographical narrative using the following criteria.

	Score 4	Score 3	Score 2	Score 1
Audience and Purpose	Contains details that engage the audience	Contains details appropriate for an audience	Contains few details that appeal to an audience	Is not written for a specific audience
Organization	Presents events that create an interesting narrative; told from a consistent point of view	Presents a clear sequence of events; told from a specific point of view	Presents a confusing sequence of events; contains a point of view that is inconsistent	Presents no logical order; is told from no consistent point of view
Elaboration	Contains details that create vivid characters; contains dialogue that develops characters and plot	Contains details that develop character and describe setting; contains dialogue	Contains characters and setting; contains some dialogue	Contains few or no details to develop characters or setting; no dialogue provided
Use of Language	Use of language creates a tone; contains no errors in grammar, punctuation, or spelling	Uses vivid words; contains few errors in grammar, punctuation, and spelling	Uses clichés and trite expressions; contains some errors in grammar, punctuation, and spelling	Uses uninspired words; has many errors in grammar, punctuation, and spelling

FINAL DRAFT

◀ **Critical Viewing**
What words would you use to describe the moment captured in this photograph? [**Interpret**]

The Ultimate Challenge

Erica Jackson
Boone County High School
Florence, Kentucky

Splash!

The water smacked the sides of the boat as it slowed to a stop while the sun beat down on the vinyl seats. The humidity made the atmosphere stifling, and the water was as smooth as silk. The lake was so transparent you could see your whole body while taking a refreshing swim. The beaches on either side of me were long and sandy, and towering above them the trees rustled with the slightest breeze. I was relaxing in the front of the boat, sunbathing, when I heard footsteps growing near.

This narrative opens in an attention-getting way.

"Erica, are you ready to try water-skiing?" my dad asked.

He had been wanting me to try the whole summer, but I hadn't gotten up the nerve to do it. My sister and I had always been competitive, and she was an expert water-skiier. Also, the thought of making a fool of myself in front of everyone didn't sound appealing. At first, I was unsure whether I really wanted to undertake skiing, but what did I have to lose? I grabbed my life jacket and put it on.

By this time, my knees were trembling and my heart was pounding. Thoughts raced through my mind. Balancing on the side of the boat as it rocked back and forth, I jumped into the lake. The water engulfed my body, but in the blink of an eye I was back up again.

My dad threw the skis to the left of me, and the rope was thrown in next. I realized it was drifting away quickly. This was the big moment. The temperature of my body seemed to drop suddenly, but I guess that was because I was so nervous.

I maneuvered myself into the skiing position, but my legs wouldn't cooperate. My body went one way, my skis the other. It was such an awkward position that I started laughing at how contorted my body was. Gallons of water went down my throat, and I began gasping for air. I struggled to keep my head above water. When I had finally composed myself, I positioned myself once again for skiing.

I clasped the rope with my left hand and placed it between my skis, which were unmanageable and bobbing up and down with the incoming waves. The rope straightened out and dragged me forward. No turning back now!

"Are you ready?" my sister shouted from the boat. I paused a moment, swallowed hard, and nodded. The knot in my throat was growing as the time drew nearer.

"Ready," I replied, questioning my own decision. I heard the engine roar, and a wall of water blocked my view of the boat. I rocked and then dove forward, still grasping the rope. As my skis flew off my feet, I fell face first into the water.

Smack! My stomach was the first to hit and a throbbing pain ran down my body. Everyone's eyes were on me, staring. I let go of the rope.

"Let the rope pull you up," everyone kept telling me. That was easier said than done.

The rope came around again, and I clenched hard. It straightened out again and I yelled, "Ready!" This time I was positive I would get up. Once again the engine roared, and I was pulled up,

Erica used chronological organization in her personal narrative.

Throughout the narrative, Erica maintains the first-person point of view. Erica is "I," the main character in the narrative.

Use of dialogue helps bring Erica's story to life.

along with the rope. The wall of water hit my body and my legs flew out into a straddle position. My body was screaming out in pain. I let go of the rope and and plunged into the water head first. By this point, I was frustrated. If this is as easy as everyone says it is, then why can't I do it?

My determination took over. Once again, the boat circled around me, and I grabbed the rope. My muscles were tight, but I maneuvered my body into skiing position. It was now or never.

"Ready," I called out with clenched fists. The motor raced for the third time, and I felt a gush of wind hit my face. The hair blew off my neck, and I could see the white foam on the peaks of the wake from the boat. I held on for dear life as the boat pulled me behind it. Wow! What a feeling I had. I was actually skiing!

Learning to ski was not just for my own self-fulfillment. I discovered that nobody is perfect at everything they do. If you learn to accept imperfection, you will still succeed at what you do. This was a lesson that was hard for me to learn, but eventually I learned it was the truth.

Here, Erica directly states the insight she gained as a result of her experience.

◀ **Critical Viewing** Judging from the clues in this photograph, what risks might a water-skiier face? **[Speculate]**

Connected Assignment
Firsthand Biography

One step away from telling your own life story—an autobiography—is telling the life story of someone you know well. In a **firsthand biography,** you use your special view to recount important moments from this person's life. You include your own experiences and interactions with the person to give the biography an intimate and accessible tone. As with any other biography, include facts and descriptive background gained from research.

Use the writing process steps outlined below to write a firsthand biography about someone you know.

▲ Critical Viewing
What interviewing skills does this student seem to be using as she collects details for her firsthand biography? **[Analyze]**

Prewriting Choose someone you know well as the subject of your firsthand biography. You may choose as a subject a person in your family or someone from your school and community who has strongly influenced your life.

Drafting As you draft, focus on bringing your subject to life for your audience. Include examples, dialogue, and vivid descriptions that reveal your subject's personality and life story. Write in the first person to give your biography an "I was there" feeling.

Revising and Editing If possible, have the subject of your firsthand biography read your draft and comment on the truthfulness of the story as it is written. Then, revise your draft, reorganizing events or adding new transitions as necessary. Make sure you've kept consistently to the first-person point of view.

Publishing and Presenting Add photographs or artwork to enhance the text of your firsthand biography. Then, print out a neat copy, and bind it with a cover. You may present your firsthand biography as a gift to its subject, or you may prefer to share it with others who know and appreciate him or her.

Spotlight on the Humanities

Appreciating the Arts
Focus on Film: *Julia*

Narrative writing is writing that tells a story, and one of the most popular forms of twentieth-century storytelling is filmmaking. Nominated for eight Academy Awards, the 1977 film *Julia* is the true story of the friendship between playwright Lillian Hellman and her lifelong friend Julia. Involved with the anti-Nazi movement in Europe in the 1930's, Julia needs Hellman's help to assist in her work. Hellman comes to the aid of her friend and risks her own life in the process. Winner of three Oscars, the film version of *Julia* not only is a study of true friendship and courage, but it is also a dramatic look at the triumph of the human spirit.

▲ **Critical Viewing**
What details in this film still from the movie *Julia* reveal the time and place in which the story is told? **[Distinguish]**

Theater Connection American playwright Lillian Hellman (1905–1984) started her writing career composing book reviews for the *New York Herald Tribune* in the mid-1920's. Her powerful plays embodied strong messages of human courage and determination. The dramas became landmarks in the American theater and are still popular today. Among Hellman's best works are the dramas *The Children's Hour* (produced when she was twenty-eight), *The Little Foxes*, and *Watch on the Rhine*. All were made into films.

Literature Connection Author Dorothy Parker (1893–1967) was with Lillian Hellman in Europe as she traveled toward Nazi Germany for her friend Julia. Born in West End, New Jersey, Parker became known for being the only female founding member of the famous Algonquin Round Table in New York. Located in the Algonquin Hotel, such noted authors as Robert Sherwood, James Thurber, and George Kaufman would gather, creating a literary circle. Dorothy Parker was a drama critic, screenwriter, and book reviewer. She won an Academy Award for her screenplay of the film *A Star Is Born*.

Narrative Writing Activity: Autobiographical Incident

Risking one's life for a friend is an extreme example of helping a friend in need, but at one time or another, we all lend a helping hand to a troubled friend. Write an autobiographical incident about a time that you either helped a friend in need or were helped by a friend.

Media and Technology Skills

Creating a Video Journal
Activity: Record a Trip

A video camera can help you capture the most exciting sights and sounds from any trip—whether you are traveling to a local amusement park, a state fair, or a relative's office. Your video journal will help you remember your trip and share your experience with an audience.

Think About It Choose a specific trip you would like to record with a video camera. Focus on one event from a longer journey. For example, rather than trying to capture an entire trip to New York City, you might create a video journal of your visit to the Statue of Liberty.

Set It Up One key to an effective video journal is to set up imaginative and revealing shots. Don't rely on point-and-shoot views to create an interesting video. Take a few moments to find an unusual angle or an especially powerful view.

Set up and shoot a variety of different shots. You might use:
- long shots to show scenery
- close-ups to show details
- panning shots to show motion or a vast scene
- interviews to share people's reactions

Also, remember that a video camera captures sounds, so background noise—such as birds, traffic, or even wind—can add to the atmosphere of your video.

Close Up

Long Shot

Panned Shot

People's Reactions

Enrich It Your video camera may offer a variety of special effects, such as titles, unusual fades, color tints, or black-and-white options. Read the manual, and experiment to find new ways to enrich your journal.

Edit It After shooting your video, edit it to create a concise and engaging video journal. Use your camera's editing function, or use a double-deck videocassette recorder. Keep your audience in mind as you edit. Try to create a tape that will make your viewers feel as if they were actually along for the ride.

Standardized Test Preparation Workshop

Responding to Narrative Writing Prompts

Test Tip

When sharing your experiences, include only details that relate to the purpose of your response.

The writing prompts on standardized tests often measure your ability to write using the elements of narrative writing. The following criteria upon which your writing will be evaluated include:

- details suitable for the audience and purpose named in the prompt
- a method of organization that allows you to organize details in a meaningful and coherent sequence
- appropriate transitions that help your narrative achieve unity and coherence
- effective use of description, characterization, and other details
- correct grammar, spelling, and punctuation

When writing for a timed test, plan to devote a specified amount of time to prewriting, drafting, revising, and proofreading. Following is an example of a narrative writing prompt. Use the suggestions on the following page to help you respond. The clocks next to each stage show a suggested percentage of time to devote to each stage.

Sample Writing Situation

The Internet is rapidly becoming a primary source of research and communication. It is also becoming an easy and time-saving way to make purchases. Because the Internet is still relatively new, many people are wary of using it for this purpose. Using your own experiences working on the Internet, respond to one of the following prompts:

- Write a letter to a family member who is not familiar with shopping on the Internet. Draw on your own experiences to convince him or her to use the Internet to do some shopping.

- Write an editorial for your town paper directed at working parents on the ease of using the Internet for shopping. Draw on your own experiences to convince them of its many benefits.

Prewriting

Allow close to one quarter of your time for prewriting.

Consider Your Audience Although each prompt is directed at an audience that does not use the Internet to shop, avoid getting caught up in defining technical terms or providing directions on navigation. Use language that is appropriate for your audience. For example, if you are writing to a family member, you may use less formal language and shorter sentences. If you are writing an editorial, you should use more formal language and longer, complex sentences.

Consider Your Purpose Your purpose is to persuade your audience to shop using the Internet. Make a T-chart listing any negative aspects on the left side and positive aspects on the right side. Then, as you make your argument, show how the negative aspects can be overcome.

Gather Details Begin to gather information from your personal experiences of using the Internet for browsing or shopping. List details about your own experiences and the many different types of shopping offered.

Drafting

Allow almost half of your time for drafting.

Elaborate As you draft, give specific details that support your ideas. For example, you may include details from your personal experience, an anecdote about a friend's experience, and factual data about how long it took you to place an order on-line.

Make Clear Connections In order for your audience to follow your ideas, use transitions that indicate the logical connections between ideas. For example, *first*, *second*, *after*, and *then* indicate the time that events occurred, while *most importantly* and *less importantly* indicate order of importance.

Revising, Editing, and Proofreading

Allow almost one quarter of your time to revise and edit. Use the last few minutes to proofread your work.

Make Corrections Review your response for errors. Neatly cross out any details that do not support your purpose. Change language that is inappropriate for your audience, and make sure that transitions keep ideas flowing smoothly. Check for errors in spelling, grammar, and punctuation. When making changes, place one line through text that you want eliminated and place it in brackets. Use a caret [^] to indicate the places you wish to add words.

▲ **Critical Viewing**
What sort of story
might this storyteller
be relating? Explain.
[Speculate]

Short Stories
in Everyday Life

Storytelling is a part of everyday life. Some stories are true:
They relate what happens in the lives of our friends and family.
Other stories are fictional: They may teach or caution or amaze
the listener. These are the stories you read at bedtime and tell
around the campfire. These stories, although fictional, say
something about the teller's beliefs, hopes, and ideas of truth
and beauty.

What Is a Short Story?

Narration is writing that tells a story. A **short story** is a particular kind of narration. It is always fictional and always brief. These stories are meant to be read in a single sitting. Using relatively few words, the writer of a short story aims to create a powerful impression on the reader. Most short stories contain

- a main character, who undergoes a change or learns something during the course of the story.
- a setting, the time and location in which the story takes place.
- a single plot, or series of events, which leads to a climax, or high point of interest.
- a theme, or main message, that is revealed by the story's end.

To preview the criteria on which your short story may be evaluated, see the Rubric for Self-Assessment on page 91.

Writers in
ACTION

Writer Maxine Hong Kingston finds that the process is similar for creating both fiction and nonfiction narratives:

"Narration has to do with movements and story and events and the adventures that we all have in our lives. There's an ongoing movement through time. And when I am writing a story, I am very aware of action that happens now—and then what? Then what happens next? And this way we keep moving."

Types of Short Stories

Although a short story is a specific type of literature, the stories themselves, like longer fictional works, vary widely. Following are a few examples:

- **Adventure stories** keep readers in suspense as they follow the plot twists and turns to the final outcome.
- **Fantasies** depart from reality to explore worlds and characters that stem from the writers' imaginations.
- **Fables** often contain animals as characters, and they convey a specific lesson or observation about life.
- **Science-fiction stories** combine elements of fiction and fantasy with scientific fact.

PREVIEW
Student Work
IN PROGRESS

In this chapter, you'll follow the progress of Ian Venokur, a student at Columbia High School in Maplewood, New Jersey, as he drafts his suspenseful short story "Horror Movie." The final draft of "Horror Movie" appears at the end of the chapter.

Gwendolyn Brooks is a prolific poet and writer of short stories. Her work often focuses on family and the city of Chicago, where she grew up. Her first collection of poetry, A Street in Bronzeville, *describes her childhood in that city. Brooks was the first African American woman to receive the Pulitzer Prize for Poetry.*

Reading | Writing Connection

Reading Strategy: **Predict** In the following short story, the main character catches a mouse and muses about its life. As you read, use clues in the text to **predict** what will happen to the mouse.

Maud Martha Spares the Mouse

from Maud Martha

Gwendolyn Brooks

There. She had it at last. The weeks it had devoted to eluding her, the tricks, the clever hide-and-go-seeks, the routes it had in all sobriety devised, together with the delicious moments it had, undoubtedly, laughed up its sleeve—all to no ultimate avail. She had that mouse.

It shook its little self, as best it could, in the trap. Its bright black eyes contained no appeal—the little creature seemed to understand that there was no hope of mercy from the eternal enemy, no hope of reprieve or postponement—but a fine small dignity. It waited. It looked at Maud Martha.

She wondered what else it was thinking. Perhaps that there was not enough food in its larder. Perhaps that little Betty, a puny child from the start, would not, now, be getting fed. Perhaps that, now, the family's seasonal house-cleaning, for lack of expert direction, would be left undone. It might be regretting that

The story's two characters, Maud Martha and the mouse, are introduced in the opening paragraph.

By describing Maud Martha's speculations about the mouse's thoughts, Brooks helps reveal Maud Martha's personality to readers.

◀ **Critical Viewing**
Why might a person
want to spare the life
of a mouse such as
the one pictured?
[Relate]

LITERATURE

"The Contents of the
Dead Man's Pockets,"
by Jack Finney, is
another short story
that revolves around
a character's decision.
You can find this story
in *Prentice Hall
Literature: Timeless
Voices, Timeless
Themes,* Platinum.

young Bobby's education was now at an end. It might be nursing
personal regrets. No more the mysterious shadows of the kitch-
enette, the uncharted twists, the unguessed halls. No more the
sweet delights of the chase, the charms of being unsuccessfully
hounded, thrown at.

Maud Martha could not bear the little look.

"Go home to your children," she urged. "To your wife or husband." She opened the trap. The mouse vanished.

Suddenly, she was conscious of a new cleanness in her. A wide
air walked in her. A life had blundered its way into her power and
it had been hers to preserve or destroy. She had not destroyed. In
the center of that simple restraint was—creation. She had created
a piece of life. It was wonderful.

"Why," she thought, as her height doubled, "why, I'm good! I
am *good*."

She ironed her aprons. Her back was straight. Her eyes were
mild, and soft with a godlike loving-kindness.

*The plot, which
revolves entirely
around Maud
Martha's decision,
reaches its climax
when she decides to
free the mouse.*

*The story's theme is
revealed as the
readers discover the
impact that Maud
Martha's decision
has on her life.*

Reading Writing Connection

**Writing Application: Help Your Readers Make
Predictions** What clues in the story's text
helped you **predict** the mouse's fate? If you
were to write a story about a fateful decision, what details might
you include to help your readers predict the story's outcome?

5.2 *Prewriting*

Choosing Your Topic

Sometimes, ideas for stories come easily and quickly to writers; other times, writers use various strategies to come up with ideas. Below are several strategies you can use to generate ideas for your short story:

Strategies for Generating Topics

1. **Sketch a Character or Setting** Use your imagination to sketch a character or setting. Then, review your sketch, and jot down story ideas that stem from it. Choose one idea to develop into your short story.

2. **Browse Through Quotations** "There is nothing to fear but fear itself!" "One is the loneliest number." Sometimes, looking through a book of quotations can provide you with a theme for a story. Find a quotation or theme that intrigues you, and then build a story around it.

3. **Freewrite** Freewrite for ten minutes about whatever pops into your mind. Review what you have written, looking for an interesting theme or idea. Then, develop your short story around that idea.

Try it out! Use the interactive Freewriting activity in **Section 5.2**, on-line or on CD-ROM.

Student Work
IN PROGRESS

Name: Ian Venokur
Columbia High School
Maplewood, NJ

Freewriting to Discover a Topic

Ian Venokur decided to freewrite about events in his own life to find inspiration for his short story. He began by writing about the events of the previous weekend. When he reviewed his prewriting, he found that a number of details in his freewriting were like elements of a scary movie. Because he was working to catch ideas quickly, Ian's freewriting included sentence fragments. These sentence errors can be corrected in a final draft.

The weekend. After school Friday went skateboarding, dull. Was (home alone) at night. Mom and dad went out. Gave me the usual business about (locking up) etc., etc., etc., Rented a couple (horror) movies.

A horror story about watching horror movies!

TOPIC BANK

For more specific story ideas, consider the possibilities below:

1. **Story With a Theme** Write a short story around the theme "All's well that ends well." The theme may be implied or directly stated.

2. **Story About a Struggle With Nature** Conflict is the heart of a short story. Develop a conflict between a character and a dangerous foe—nature. Hurricanes, anacondas, a sudden flash flood along a remote hiking trail—you choose the specific force with which the character clashes.

Responding to Fine Art

3. Study the images presented in *Students of Modeling and Painting*, shown at right. Use the characters or setting within the painting to spark story ideas.

Responding to Literature

Students of Modeling and Painting Anonymous, Private Collection

4. "The Monkey's Paw" by W. W. Jacobs is a chilling short story. First, read the story. Then, write your own short story in response. Your story may update the original version or continue Jacobs's story. "The Monkey's Paw" appears in *Prentice Hall Literature: Timeless Voices, Timeless Themes*, Platinum.

☑ Cooperative Writing Opportunity

5. **Story Anthology** Working in a group, divide into subgroups of three. One group will fill out note cards with descriptions of characters; another group will fill out cards describing various settings; and the last group will describe possible conflicts. Each group should place their cards into a box. Then, have the group select one card from each box to provide the framework for a short story. Have each group member write a short story using the selected cards as a basis. When stories are finished, have each writer read his or her story aloud while the group notes similarities and differences among them. Bind finished stories together in an anthology.

Narrowing Your Topic

A short story has to be short, containing a single main character, a limited setting, and a focused plot. To ensure that your story will be narrow and focused, answer the following questions as you plan your story. Refer to your answers to help you draft and revise.

- Who is the main character?
- What is the main character's problem?
- Will the main character solve the problem?
- What does he or she learn during the course of the story?

Considering Your Audience and Purpose

Though your general purpose for writing a short story is probably to entertain, you should focus on a more specific purpose as well. This purpose will affect the language and details you choose.

Create a Purpose Planner

Because short stories are meant to convey a single strong impression, think about the impression you want your story to leave on the reader. This will become your purpose for writing. Once you identify your purpose, develop a plan for achieving that purpose.

Create a purpose planner like the one below. Use the purpose planner as you gather details for your short story.

Purpose	Details to Achieve This Purpose
To amuse	Create eccentric characters; use exaggeration
To teach	State your theme; use main character as example
To horrify	Create a mood of horror through word choice; leave things unsaid and mysterious; create suspense by foreshadowing, or by dropping hints about the story's outcome

Gathering Details

While the plot is the "engine" of your story, details help to develop the characters, and setting helps to bring your short story to life for your readers. Before you begin drafting your story, gather details about your characters and setting.

Gathering Details About Characters Characters are people, animals, alien life forms, or other creatures that take part in the action of a narrative. Effective characters are memorable, believable, and understandable. Before you begin drafting, jot down details about each character.

Gathering Details About Setting The setting is the time and place in which story events unfold. It includes the historical period, year, season, and time of day; it also includes the planet, country, city, block, or building, as well as specific physical features—such as furniture, plants, and weather conditions. To gather details about the setting, make a setting chart like the one shown below.

Try it out! Use the interactive Setting Chart in **Section 5.2**, on-line or on CD-ROM.

Student Work
IN PROGRESS

Name: Ian Venokur
Columbia High School
Maplewood, NJ

Gathering Details About Setting

Ian used a chart to gather details about the setting of his story.

Time	Place	Weather/Other
weekend early evening to very late at night	house, 163 Willowbend Lane family room: brown sofa; the basement: dark (burnt-out light bulb), cold concrete floor, spooky banister leading down	howling winds, thunderstorm, lightning

Drafting

Shaping Your Writing

As you draft your narrative, keep your central conflict in mind and shape the story around it. You may want to use a plot diagram to plan the events leading up to and following the climax of your plot.

Make a Plot Diagram

A plot usually contains the following elements:

- In the **exposition,** the characters and setting are introduced, as is the **conflict**—the struggle between characters or between a character and some other force.

- During the **rising action,** the tension builds as the conflict becomes more evident.

- The **climax** is the high point of interest in the story, during which one of the battling forces wins and the conflict is resolved.

- The **falling action** refers to the events that immediately follow the climax.

- The section of the story in which loose ends are tied up is called the **resolution.**

Doug's parents arrive home just as Doug panics.

CLIMAX

RISING ACTION

FALLING ACTION

EXPOSITION

RESOLUTION

Doug's parents go away, leaving Doug alone for the first time.

Doug watches horror movies. He wakes up, alarmed at a noise. He decides to check the basement door. He gets locked in the basement.

Doug explains to his parents why he was in the basement.

Doug realizes that he learned an important lesson about himself.

Providing Elaboration

Use Dialogue to Develop and Reveal Character

Often, the most effective way to convey the traits and attributes of your characters is through dialogue. Dialogue is the exact words that your characters say aloud or think to themselves. Through dialogue, you show rather than tell readers about the characters in your story. As you draft, look for opportunities to use dialogue rather than description.

Telling Through Description

Terence caught sight of Pat and enthusiastically greeted him in the hallway. Pat, feeling acutely embarrassed, tried to avoid his friend but had no choice. At first, Terence noticed nothing unusual about his friend's behavior, but puzzled by Pat's reluctance to talk, Terence eventually left.

Showing Through Dialogue

"Hey, pal! Great to see you!" boomed Terence, catching sight of Pat.

"Yeah," Pat said weakly, "great to see you too."

"What luck, running into you here and all."

"Yeah, luck, . . . huh?"

"Anything wrong, Pat? You seem kinda quiet."

"No, no, . . . everything's okay."

"Right," said Terence uneasily, "I guess I'll catch you later."

▲ Critical Viewing
If you were to write dialogue to accompany the scene pictured, what would it say? [Analyze]

Use Dialogue to Further the Plot Events

When drafting your story, avoid always having your narrator explain what events happened next. Instead, let the dialogue sometimes reveal what happened to whom.

Description of Plot Events

Jenny was very angry with her friend Bob for forgetting to drive her to the cast party after the show. After all, Jenny was in the play and had worked hard all month during rehearsal. Now, she just wanted to cry.

Plot Events Revealed Through Dialogue

"Bob! How *could* you leave me behind? I've worked so hard all month, rehearsing and rehearsing this play so I'd be good in it. And you leave for the cast party without me! I could just cry."

5.4 *Revising*

Revising Your Overall Structure

Critically examine your short story to ensure that it's fast-moving and interesting. The following strategies will help you evaluate the plot of your story.

▶ **REVISION STRATEGY**
Identifying the Purpose of Plot Events

Short stories that contain too many plot events may be slow-moving and boring. Stories containing plot events that are not clearly connected to the rest of the story may be confusing and hard to follow. Review your draft critically, examining your story's plot events. Then, fill in a chart like the one at right, in which you identify plot events and evaluate their usefulness to the plot. Cut plot events that do not further the plot, and make clear connections between the other plot events to show readers how they relate to each other.

PLOT ANALYZER

	How Does It Further Plot?	What Is Its Purpose?
Event A:		

Revising Your Paragraphs

Revise the Dialogue to Make It Realistic

The challenge in writing dialogue is to make it sound as if your characters are real people, speaking as they would in the real world. For example, in the real world, people often use sentence fragments and slang in conversation. Use the following strategy to help make your dialogue more realistic:

▶ **REVISION STRATEGY**
Using Contractions in Dialogue

Only in rare situations would you encounter someone who avoids contractions in everyday speech. When revising your dialogue, combine word pairs, such as *I will* and *have not*, to make contractions.

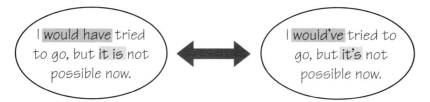

I would have tried to go, but it is not possible now. ⬌ I would've tried to go, but it's not possible now.

Revising Your Sentences
Change the Passive Voice to Active Voice

Your short story should engage and hold the interest of your readers. One way to do this is to write it in the active voice. The active voice, in which the subject performs the action, is livelier and more direct than the passive voice, in which the action is performed on the subject. The use of too many passive sentences may result in clunky and lifeless writing.

▶**REVISION STRATEGY**
Color-Coding Passive Sentences

Use a colored highlighter to mark instances of passive voice in your narrative. Passive verbs always have two parts: a form of *be* plus the past participle of a transitive verb. Once you've color-coded passive voice passages, review them carefully. If your use of the passive voice is unintentional, revise the passage to be in the active voice.

ⓘ Learn More

For more instruction on passive and active voice, see the Grammar in Your Writing feature on page 88.

Student Work
IN PROGRESS

Name: *Ian Venokur*
Columbia High School
Maplewood, NJ

Color-Coding Passive Sentences
Ian color-coded the passages containing the passive voice. To give his story energy and interest, he changed the passive voice to active voice.

                              his parents left him alone
It was the first time ~~he had been left alone by his parents~~
                         ∧
for a night. Doug couldn't be happier. He had prepared
for it all week by picking out the movies he wanted to see
                                                      keep
and the junk food he wanted to eat. "Now, the doors
                                         ∧
~~should be kept~~ locked,........."

Grammar in Your Writing
Verbs: Active and Passive Voice

Differences Between Active and Passive Voice

There are two voices in English: **active** and **passive.** Only action verbs show voice; linking verbs do not. The voice is determined by the relationship between the subject and the verb. In a sentence in the active voice, the subject performs the action expressed by the verb. In the sentence below, the subject is *balloonists.*

> s
> **Active Voice:** Two balloonists sought the trophy.

In a sentence in the passive voice, the subject receives the action expressed by the verb. In the sentence below, the subject is *trophy.* Note that a passive voice verb contains a form of the helping verb *be* and the past participle of the main verb.

> s
> **Passive Voice:** The trophy was sought by two balloonists.

Use Voice Correctly

Because the active voice is more direct and lively, you should generally use it in your writing. However, if you want to emphasize the receiver of the action rather than the performer of an action, use the passive voice.

Use the passive voice to emphasize the receiver of the action: George Ramirez was awarded Student of the Year by school officials.

The passive voice is also effective when the performer of the action is not important or is not known.

Use the passive voice when the performer of the action is unknown: The mysterious package was left in the cafeteria.

Find It in Your Reading Find two examples of active voice in "Maud Martha Spares the Mouse" on pp. 78–79. Explain how the passages would differ if they had been written in the passive voice.

Find It in Your Writing Find an instance of passive voice in your short story. Then, decide whether its meaning would be better served in the passive voice or if the passage would have more impact if written in the active voice.

For more on passive and active voice, see Chapter 22.

Revising Your Word Choice

▶ **REVISION STRATEGY**
Evaluating the Use of Tag Words

Tag words describe the way a character in a narrative speaks. For example, "he *said*" and "they *whispered*" are examples of tag words. When the same tag words are used repeatedly, writing may get repetitive and dull. On the other hand, the overuse of tag words or too large a variety of tag words may be annoying to readers. Keep the following tips in mind as you revise your draft:

- Rely mainly on *said* as a tag word, and let the actual dialogue convey the *emotion*—the way the line would be stated:

EXAMPLE: "Are you coming?" Stephen asked. "It's getting late, and I'm rather tired."

"Yes, I'm coming" Miranda said.

- Try to limit the use of tag words in extended passages of dialogue. It has to be clear to readers, however, who is addressing whom.

EXAMPLE: Stephen and Miranda discussed leaving the party.

"Are you coming? It's getting late, and my dad needs the car back."

"Yes, I'm coming."

- Vary the use of tag words to avoid repetition:

EXAMPLE: "Are you coming?" Stephen demanded. "It's getting late, and my dad needs the car back."

"Yes, I'm coming," sulked Miranda.

Peer Review

Consult with peer reviewers as you revise your short story. Use the "Say Back" Sheet for getting useful feedback from peer reviewers.

"Say Back"

Assemble a group of four or five peer reviewers. Read your story aloud to them once. Then, distribute a work sheet to them like the one shown at right. Read your story again to the group, and instruct them to fill out the work sheet. Consider the comments of your peer reviewers as you revise your short story a final time.

Try it out! Use the interactive "Say Back" Sheet in **Section 5.4**, on-line or on CD-ROM.

> **"SAY BACK" SHEET**
>
> What I liked about the story: _____
>
> _____
>
> What I'd like to know more about: _____
>
> _____

Editing and Proofreading

An error-free, clearly written story will be easier for readers to follow and enjoy. When you have finished revising your narrative, check for errors in grammar, spelling, and punctuation.

Focusing on Punctuation

Check your short story to be sure that you have correctly punctuated passages of dialogue. First, read through your draft and locate all opening quotation marks. Then, make sure that for each opening quotation mark, there is a closing quotation mark. Also, check to see that you have correctly placed end marks in passages of dialogue.

⊙ Technology Tip

Use the Find feature of your computer's word-processing program to quickly locate all opening quotation marks. Then, check to see that each has a corresponding closing quotation mark.

Grammar in Your Writing
Formatting and Punctuating Dialogue

Because short stories often make extensive use of dialogue, it's particularly important to understand how to format and punctuate it correctly.

- A character's exact words are enclosed in quotation marks.
- Commas separate quotations from words that identify the speaker. The comma always appears inside the closing quotation mark.
- A new paragraph begins each time the speaker changes.
- When a paragraph ends while a character is still speaking, quotation marks do not appear at the end of that paragraph. However, quotation marks do appear at the beginning of the next paragraph.

Find It in Your Reading Find an example of dialogue in "Maud Martha Spares the Mouse" on pages 78–79. Explain the conventions used for punctuating and formatting the character's dialogue.

Find It in Your Writing Find the first passage of dialogue in your short story. Look at the end punctuation to be sure that it matches the way in which a character is speaking. For example, if the character is surprised, use an exclamation mark. Then, check to be sure that the dialogue is punctuated and formatted correctly.

For more on punctuating and formatting dialogue, see Chapter 28.

5.6 *Publishing and Presenting*

Following are a few ideas for publishing and presenting your short story:

Building Your Portfolio

1. **Verbal Sharing** With a partner, take turns reading your narratives aloud or organize a reading in which several people read their short stories. Place a copy of the story or a tape of the reading into your portfolio.

2. **Anthology** Present your short story as part of a larger collection of short stories. In your anthology, include works written by your classmates. Organize the stories by theme.

Reflecting on Your Writing

Think back for a moment about your experience writing a short story. Then, answer the following questions, and save your responses in your portfolio.

• Which part of writing a story appealed to you most? Why?

• If you were to write another short story, on which stage of the writing process would you spend more time?

 **Internet Tip**

To see model stories scored with this rubric, go on-line:
PHSchool.com
Enter Web Code:
eek-1001

Rubric for Self-Assessment

Use the following criteria to evaluate your short story.

	Score 4	Score 3	Score 2	Score 1
Audience and Purpose	Contains details that engage and impact the audience	Contains details that appeal to an audience	Contains few details that contribute to its purpose or that appeal to an audience	Contains no purpose; is not written for a specific audience
Organization	Presents events that create an interesting, clear narrative; told from a consistent point of view	Presents sequence of events; told from a specific point of view	Presents a confusing sequence of events; contains inconsistent points of view	Presents no logical order; is told from no consistent point of view
Elaboration	Contains details that provide insight into characters; contains dialogue that reveals characters and furthers the plot	Contains details and dialogue that develop characters	Contains characters and setting; contains some dialogue	Contains few or no details to develop characters or setting; no dialogue provided
Use of Language	Uses word choice and tone to reveal story's theme; contains no errors in grammar, punctuation, or spelling	Uses interesting and fresh word choices; contains few errors in grammar, punctuation, and spelling	Uses clichés and trite expressions; contains some errors in grammar, punctuation, and spelling	Uses uninspired word choices; has many errors in grammar, punctuation, and spelling

FINAL DRAFT

Horror Movie

**Ian Venokur
Columbia High School
Maplewood, New Jersey**

It was the first time his parents had left him home alone for a night, and Doug couldn't have been happier. He had prepared for it all week by picking out the movies he wanted to see and the snack food he wanted to eat. "Now keep the doors locked, go to bed before midnight, and be *safe*," Doug's parents reminded him at least five hundred times while they walked toward the car.

"I can handle it, Mom." Doug responded. It frustrated him that his mother refused to accept the fact that he was grown up. "Have fun! I'll be fine!" Doug yelled to his parents as they pulled out of their driveway.

"Finally," Doug said to himself. What to do first? The possibilities seemed endless to the new king of 163 Willowbend Lane. The microwave clock read 7:00 P.M. "Perfect! Movie time." Doug dashed to the kitchen table where the Movie-Town bag lay on its side. Doug popped in *Hangman Twelve* and sat down on the family couch in the television room.

Two bags of corn chips, a bowl of popcorn, and three movies later, Doug lay with a stomachache and heavy eyelids. He decided to go to his royal bathroom to brush his teeth and flop in bed.

In the exposition, Ian has introduced everything his readers need in order to get involved in the story—the characters, the setting, and a situation to which they can relate.

Ian included variety in his tag words, such as "responded" and "yelled."

By using dialogue here, Ian reveals Doug's inner thoughts and personality.

Around 2:00 A.M., Doug woke up. Still groggy, he wondered what disturbed him, and he strained his ears to listen. The basement door was locked . . . right? I remembered to do that. But he crept downstairs to check it anyway.

The whole house was dark, but Doug's eyes were focused on the door to the basement, which was open a crack. Everything inside of him told him to turn back, but for some reason Doug continued until he stood directly in front of the door. By this time, he was sweating and his heart was racing. As fate would have it, the light bulb was burnt out. "It'll only take a minute . . . ," Doug reassured himself as he took the first step into the darkness.

He reached out and grabbed the banister. It would be his only guide, because it was pitch black and he was alone. Doug's foot touched the cold concrete floor. He knew that the outside basement door was only about ten feet from where he stood, but he could not see it. "I have nothing to worry about, I'll be back upstairs in a minute," Doug proclaimed to his audience of none.

Doug's forehead was the first thing to reach the door; the rest of his body followed. He fumbled for the handle and then the lock.

The familiar click of the key turning put his fears to rest. Smiling to himself, Doug began backtracking toward the stairs. Step by step, Doug's triumph grew larger and larger, and greater and greater, until he reached the doorway back to the kitchen.

The door was stuck. Suddenly, Doug was shocked back to reality as he pulled the metal handle with all his might. He fought back his rising horror as best he could. But it was no good. Doug sank weakly on the top stair. To keep his fears aways, he loudly began reciting nursery rhymes. "Hey diddle, diddle, . . ."

Without warning, the door gave way behind his back. His mother gasped and shouted, "Douglas! What are you *doing*?"

"I knew he wasn't ready to stay home alone," Doug's dad chipped in.

"I couldn't sleep," Doug said.

"But why are you in the basement?"

"It's all right, Mom. I came down to lock the basement door, and I just felt like staying down here." Doug did not allow himself to tell the whole story.

"As long as you're OK."

"I'm fine, Mom." And Doug knew that next time, he would be.

Details about the setting ("pitch black," "cold concrete floor") contribute to the atmosphere of suspense.

The climax of the story occurs as Doug realizes he is locked in the basement.

The final statement of the story reveals what Doug, the main character, learns from his experience.

Connected Assignment
Drama

Like a short story, **drama** contains characters who face a problem or conflict. The major difference is that drama is written to be performed by actors on a stage. Costumes, lighting, music, and sound effects add to the total effect of drama.

Most dramas

- are generated in a script format.

- contain stage directions to indicate props, movements, and information about characters' motives.

- contain dialogue that develops characters and furthers the plot.

The following excerpt is from a radio play—a type of drama. It contains a typical script format and basic elements of a drama.

▲ **Critical Viewing** Judging from the details in this photograph, would you think this was an audition or a rehearsal? Explain. **[Interpret]**

MODEL

from *Invasion From Mars*
Howard Koch

OPERATOR FIVE. This is 8X3R . . . coming back at 2X2L.

OPERATOR FOUR. How's reception? How's reception? K, please. Where are you, 8X3R?

What's the matter? Where are you?

[*Bells ringing over city gradually diminishing*]

ANNOUNCER. I'm speaking from the roof of Broadcasting Building, New York City. The bells you hear are ringing to warn the people to evacuate the city as the Martians approach.

Prewriting Choose an idea to center your drama around. Following are some suggestions to help you come up with an idea for a drama:

- **Start with a character.** Jot down a description of your main character: his or her appearance, goals, problem, family life, and dreams.

- **Start with a conflict.** Choose an exciting or a thought-provoking problem that your characters will grapple with during the course of your drama.

- **Start with a theme.** Decide on a main message that you would like to convey through your drama.

- **Start with a setting.** Create a wild, unique, beautiful, or realistic setting to act as a backdrop for your characters. Your setting might also play a role in your drama if you pit your characters against some force of nature, like a typhoon.

Gather Details Once you have a basic story idea, gather details about the setting, characters, and plot. Then, bring your characters to life by listing details about them, such as name, age, job, education, physical appearance, mannerisms, views, and especially speech style.

Drafting As you draft, tell the story of your drama. Elaborate by writing dialogue that develops characters and furthers the action of the drama. Also, insert stage directions that give information about the set, actors' movements, and characters' motivations. The diagram shown here indicates the correct terms to describe stage locations, as seen from the stage.

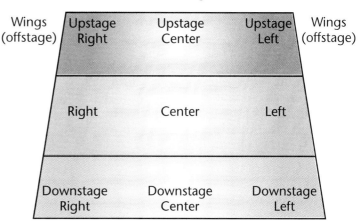

The Stage

Wings (offstage)	Upstage Right	Upstage Center	Upstage Left	Wings (offstage)
	Right	Center	Left	
	Downstage Right	Downstage Center	Downstage Left	

The Audience

Revising and Editing Read your drama aloud to friends. Ask them to note and correct any dialogue that seems stilted, inconsistent, or unrealistic. If appropriate, use phrases or informal slang to add realism to the dialogue. If needed, add stage directions to more specifically describe the characters' actions or moods, along with the use of props or sound effects.

Publishing and Presenting Cast the parts in your play, and read it for the class. Decide whether you will include lighting and sound effects or whether you would rather assign an actor to read stage directions aloud.

Spotlight on the Humanities

Recognizing the Oral Tradition

Focus on Music: "The Ballad of John Henry"

Some stories are told through music. Embedded in the roots of American folklore, "John Henry, the Steel Driving Man" is a ballad—a narrative set to music—about an African American railroad worker who was seven feet tall and as strong as thirty men. Renowned for his superhuman strength, Henry, using only his hammer, raced a mechanical steam drill to cut a railroad tunnel through a mountain. John Henry won the race, but after the tremendous exertion, his heart gave out, and he lost his life. Many different forms of this ballad exist, with the oldest printed copy dated around 1900. This ballad has been sung by such notables as Woody Guthrie, Pete Seeger, and Burl Ives.

He Laid Down His Hammer and Cried, 1944-47, Palmer C. Hayden, Museum of African American Art, Los Angeles, CA

▲ **Critical Viewing** What details in this painting help convey John Henry's legendary strength? **[Connect]**

Art Connection Various artists have captured through clay, paint, and watercolor the hero John Henry. Jerry Pinkney (born 1939) created a watercolor of John Henry for the jacket illustration of the book by Julius Lester. The 1994 watercolor captures the herculean features of John Henry as well as the rough landscape of the railroad man's life.

Film Connection The legendary John Henry pitted his strength against that of a machine. This conflict—"man against the machine"—has been explored a number of times throughout the years. A notable and memorable example of this theme is presented in *2001: A Space Odyssey,* in which an astronaut matches wits with a computer named Hal.

Narrative Writing Activity: Short Story Based on a Favorite Song

Select a favorite song from an artist or a band you enjoy. Then, write a short story based on the lyrics of the song. Add details and additional information that will make your song a compelling short story.

Media and Technology Skills

Using Media to Convey Ideas

Activity: Video Adaptation of a Short Story

A short video can bring to life the action, mood, theme, and style of a story. A viewer audience receives more sensory information than a reader does: The film uses motion and imagery to provide a narrative.

Many effective film adaptations change the time or place of a story. Your adaptation might reset a historical tale in modern times or change characters from adults to high-school students.

Think About It Select a short story to adapt that has a concise plot and interesting characters. Look especially for a story that has a strong visual element—for instance, a vivid setting.

Storyboard It Sketch a storyboard to plan your film. A storyboard is an illustrated sequence of sketches that shows the scenes in order. You can include ideas for camera angles, close-ups, distance shots, and fades.

Filming Tips
- Place the camera on a tripod to achieve a steady, professional image.
- Film test-footage to check lighting levels.
- Vary the distance of the camera. Use close-ups to draw the viewer into emotional moments. Use distant shots to establish new settings.

Susan sends an e-mail.   Fade out.   Zoom in on Hillary's desk.   Hillary runs in and signs onto the Net.

Script It Developing a storyboard will help you decide what scenes and dialogue you need for your film. Write a shooting script by indicating the location of each scene and the characters' dialogue. Try improvising scenes to help give each character a distinctive voice.

Design It Create the sets and costumes you will need. Remember that costumes provide important information about the characters' personalities and preferences. You may need to find or build specific props that are key to your story's development.

Shoot It Use your storyboard to guide the filming. Shoot several versions, or takes, of each scene. Then, use your camera's or video-cassette recorder's editing functions to select the best takes, and copy them onto a new tape. During editing, you can also add titles and music to polish your video.

Standardized Test Preparation Workshop

Responding to Questions About Short Stories

Knowing how the elements of a short story work helps you write about short stories. Some standardized tests require you to write a short response about a story you have read. Before responding to a test prompt on a short story, think about how its narrative elements contribute to the story's effectiveness. Take the following elements into consideration: **plot**—the story's sequence of events; **characters**—people, animals, or other beings who perform the action; **setting**—time and place in which the story takes place; and **theme**—the story's central message. The following are some of the criteria upon which your response will be evaluated:

- a clear and logical organization of ideas

- details and precise language that fully develop your ideas

- a focused purpose for writing

- correct spelling, capitalization, punctuation, grammar, usage, and sentence structure

Choose one of the following sample prompts for the short story "Maud Martha Spares the Mouse," and write a short response.

Test Tips

- When writing about a short story, be careful not to simply retell the story. Instead, focus on responding to the prompt.
- When writing for a timed test, plan to devote a certain amount of time to prewriting, drafting, revising, and proofreading.

Sample Writing Situations

Read this quote:

"A life had blundered its way into her power and it had been hers to preserve or destroy. She had not destroyed. . . . She had created a piece of life. It was wonderful."

What does the quotation above reveal about how Maud views her decision? Describe a time when you made a decision that made you feel good about yourself, and compare it to Maud Martha's decision and her feelings. Use details and information from the story to support your answer.

The quotation from "Maud Martha Spares the Mouse" reveals a message or theme to readers. Explain how the story's narrative elements—character, plot, and setting—help to convey its theme. Use details and information from the story to support your answer.

Prewriting

Allow close to one fourth of your time for prewriting.

Gather Details Respond to the prompt by listing several details that support your response. For example, you may jot down lines from the story, references to other stories, and personal observations. If you are comparing and contrasting two or more ideas, you may use a Venn diagram as you gather similarities and differences between ideas.

Organize Details Organize your details in a logical and effective order. If you are discussing plot events, you may want to organize them chronologically, or in time order. If you are comparing and contrasting, you may use point-by-point or subject-by-subject organization. If you are discussing a single element of literature, you may want to use order of importance to organize your paragraphs.

Drafting

Allow almost half of your time for drafting.

Write a Topic Sentence Write a topic sentence that tells specifically what the main idea and purpose of your response will be.

Use the Story as Support Develop your short response using details from the story and your own experience to elaborate upon your topic sentence.

Conclude Effectively Write a concluding sentence in which you sum up the main idea of your response.

Revising, Editing, and Proofreading

Allow almost one fourth of your time to revise and edit. Use the last few minutes to proofread your work.

Check Language and Details After you have drafted your response, read through it again to make sure that you have included only those details that directly support the main point of your response. Eliminate those details that do not.

Make Corrections Review your response for errors. Neatly cross out details that do not support your purpose. Eliminate language that is vague, and replace it with precise, strong words. Check for errors in spelling, grammar, and punctuation. When making changes, draw a line through text that you want eliminated. Use a caret [^] to indicate the places that you are adding or revising words.

Description in Everyday Life

Before you leave your home each day, you probably use description. For example, you might describe how well you slept or how a new cereal tasted. Through description, patients tell doctors about their illnesses, travel agencies tempt homebodies to new horizons, victims lead detectives to criminals, and screenwriters portray environments for movie producers to build or find.

Description also takes written form. For example, you might write a description about last night's championship game in an e-mail to a friend, or you might describe a chemical reaction in a report for your chemistry class. In the workplace, too, description plays a vital role. Precise descriptions may convey company procedures, explain benefits packages, or provide detailed instructions for accessing a phone-mail system.

▲ Critical Viewing
If you were to describe the scene pictured above, what words would you select? Why?
[Interpret]

What Is Description?

You experience your world through your senses: sight, hearing, taste, smell, and touch. **Description** is writing that enables you to re-create your experiences vividly and share them with others. Most descriptive writing contains

- sensory language that shares what the writer sees, hears, tastes, smells, and touches.
- precise language, including vivid verbs and precise nouns.
- figurative language, such as personification, exaggeration, simile, and metaphor.
- a logical organization, such as chronological or spatial order.

To see the criteria on which your final essay may be evaluated, preview the Rubric for Self-Assessment on page 115.

Types of Description

Most writing contains description. Following are a few types of writing that depend heavily on descriptive language:

- **Descriptions of a person, place, or thing** contain sensory details that bring to life actual people, places, and things.
- **Observations** describe an event the writer has witnessed. Often, the event takes place over an extended period of time.
- **Travel brochures** contain factual information as well as persuasive language to encourage tourism.
- **Character sketches** describe fictional characters—their appearances, personalities, hopes, and dreams.

Writers in ACTION

Colleen J. McElroy, poet and author, often uses descriptive details in her writing. Like most writers, she understands the power of description. She has the following to say about finding inspiration for writing a description:

"What makes a description good for me is not so much reporting it, but finding the impression. You're looking for that thing that's in the corner of the eye— or that smell that sort of drifts by— and it reminds you of some place."

PREVIEW
Student Work
IN PROGRESS

Leslie Harris, a student at Sunnyslope High School in Phoenix, Arizona, wrote a description of her impressions during the seconds before the start of a footrace. Follow along as Leslie plans, drafts, and revises her writing. A final draft of her description appears at the end of the chapter.

6.1 Model From Literature

Dear America: Letters Home From Vietnam is a collection of actual letters written by various American solders while they were posted in Vietnam during the war. The following letters were written in the spring of 1967 by Richard Loffler, Sp/4, 36th Sig. Bn., 2nd Sig Gp., Long Binh, Bear Cat, 1966–1967.

Reading ⟷ **Writing**
Connection

Reading Strategy: Envision When you envision a writer's words, you mentally picture what is being described. As you read these letters, pay attention to the descriptive details to help you envision the scenery and the experiences of the author.

from *Letters Home From Vietnam*

March 26, 1967
Dear Folks,

New place, new faces, a few old. I've been transferred to a region near Bien Hoa, almost 20 miles southeast of Saigon. Our base is about one mile square. Scraped out of the jungle, with the name of Bear Cat; it's the code name for the home base of the Big Red "One" (First Infantry Division).

We came by chopper. Ride was all vibration—hot, noisy, kerosene smell, door open wide, man at machine-gun–ready. This camp has dust over everything. A beige landscape. It's a fine powder that blows at the slightest breeze. Clouds of it blow into the mess hall while you're eating and get in your food, mouth—gritty, gritty.

I'm with a signal company again and still have my draftsman's job—doing charts, etc.

I've heard the camp has been shelled in the past. This means a red alert is in progress. You have to grab your flak jacket, rifle and ammo, and go stand at a post for a half hour or so until the "danger" is over. 105-millimeter cannons surround the perimeter of the camp and go off any time and rumble the tents, and the middle of your stomach. It's not bad, though. 242 days to go.

▲ **Critical Viewing**
What situation might the soldier pictured be facing? Explain why you think as you do. **[Analyze]**

The opening of the letter contains both factual details and figurative language.

This paragraph is full of descriptive details such as "hot," "noisy," "beige," and "gritty."

April 15, 1967

Dear Folks,

This is your "on the spot" correspondent in the BIG NAM reporting. . . .

Answers to pertinent questions first. Yes, we sleep on cots. One can buy mattresses and pillows at a Vietnamese store outside our base. I have a towel for a pillow and roll myself in the blanket. Just not energetic enough to get sheets and pillow.

On a trip to Vung Tau, I noticed red flowers abundant. Small, white, bell-shaped type are shaped by kids into garlands for the neck. They sell for five piasters. Trees are scrubby junk or a banana type. Soil is really hard as rock for about three feet down, then becomes sandy.

Well, guard duty is a drag. We go to a commercial post (a solitary telephone sitting on a bench) at 2:30 P.M. for instructions, then are driven out to the bunkers—sandbag shelters with broken cots inside. There are peepholes for observation. Chow is brought out to us at dusk. Three guys to a bunker. Two stay awake at all times. We eat, and sit, and sit, and sit. Then the cannons start.

Here are the noises of the ritual of firing one round: Whhiirrrrrrr-klick. Sskkllaannkkk. WWhhiiirrr-kkllaannk. That was the charge and shell being loaded into the breech. More whirring follows; asimuth and elevation controls are set. Then a guy gives a short "yell" and then an instant's silence. Then a BAM-BOOM-TTHHAATT sound combination that bounces the ground, the cot, and you. Maybe a half hour of this is followed by an hour and a half of silence. Then BBAAMM, BAAAMM for another half hour. This goes on all night. Flares can be seen nearby, fired off when somebody sees "sumthin out dare." There [are] the whining choppers slipping by, landing lights glowing red. Mice and rats squeak, and the night goes on.

Well, the routine goes on. We're just "paper soldiers," that is, the people doing administration, although somebody has got to do it. The "roughness" we endure is only the water rationing, being hot, and the somewhat dreary atmosphere of it all. Dirty Boy Scouts moved up a notch.

Hope all are in good health.

Sp/4 Richard Loffler, 36th Sig. Bn., 2nd Sig. Gp., Long Binh, Bear Cat, 1966–1967.

Because the audience for this letter is the soldier's family, the soldier uses slang and informal language.

Onomatopoeia—the use of words that imitate sounds—makes this descriptive paragraph a vivid re-creation of the sounds of battle.

Reading Writing Connection

Writing Application: Envision Before you begin writing your description, envision your subject and think of words and phrases that will help you to convey that vision to readers.

Prewriting

Choosing Your Topic

Memorable people, remarkable places, unusual events, and intriguing ideas all make great topics for description. Following are more ideas for coming up with a topic for description.

Strategies for Generating Topics

1. **Draw or Sketch** Use a drawing pencil and paper to sketch a person, place, thing, or event you find interesting. Your sketch may be as abstract or realistic as you like. When you are finished sketching, choose an aspect of the drawing to develop into a description.

2. **Browse in a Calendar** Look through this year's or last year's calendar or date book to spark memories of people and events of the past year. For example, a certain date might remind you of someone you met, a game you played, or your grandfather's birthday party. Choose one of those memories to form the heart of your description.

OCTOBER						
Sunday	Monday	Tuesday	Wednesday	Thursday	Friday	Saturday
					1 Mom's Surprise Party	2
3	4	5	6	7	8	9
10 Pumpkin Picking	11	12	13	14	15 Choir Concert in Gym	16
17	18	19	20	21	22	23
24	25					

3. **Make a Blueprint** Draw the floor plan of a place you know well. Next, label each room or area with a name that makes it personal for you, such as *My Studio, Kai's Hideout,* or *Mom's Den.* Also, jot down memories or ideas you associate with each room. Then, select the most interesting idea, and make it the topic of your description.

TOPIC BANK

To get more specific writing ideas for a description, read the following suggestions:

1. **Describe an Idea: Democracy** Think about the concept of democracy and the images it conjures up for you. For example, you may think of a person voting, a town meeting, or a king losing his crown. Then, develop this idea, and write a description of "democracy."

2. **Recall a Challenging Moment** What was the last big challenge you faced? Write some adjectives or sensory images that arise from your memory of facing that challenge. Then, work your ideas into a description.

Responding to Fine Art

3. *Studio Interior* by Jane Freilicher depicts a picture within a picture. Imagine yourself in the artist's studio, and write a description of what you see, as though speaking to a friend far away. You may describe what is actually in the picture or what you imagine lies beyond the window.

Studio Interior, 1982, Jane Freilicher, Tibor De Nagy

Responding to Literature

4. In "Jazz Fantasia," the poet Carl Sandburg uses vivid descriptive language to bring to life jazz music. Write a description in response to this poem by bringing to life your ideas about jazz or any other type of music you like. "Jazz Fantasia" appears in *Prentice Hall Literature: Timeless Voices, Timeless Themes*, Platinum.

☑ Cooperative Writing Opportunity

5. **Descriptions of a Place** With a classmate, choose a place with which you're both familiar. Once you agree on a place, each of you should use it as the topic for a description. When you are finished writing, trade papers and note the similarities and differences between your descriptions.

Narrowing Your Topic

Use a topic web to explore several aspects of a topic. Then, choose the aspect that most interests you to write about.

Make a Web

Write your broad topic at the top of a piece of paper, and then write subtopics in circles connected to your broad topic by lines. Following is an example:

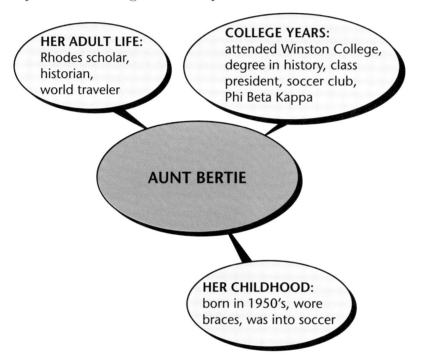

HER ADULT LIFE:
Rhodes scholar,
historian,
world traveler

COLLEGE YEARS:
attended Winston College,
degree in history, class
president, soccer club,
Phi Beta Kappa

AUNT BERTIE

HER CHILDHOOD:
born in 1950's, wore
braces, was into soccer

Considering Your Audience and Purpose

Choose details for your description that your audience will understand and appreciate. Your choice of details and your tone, or attitude toward your subject, will also help you to achieve your purpose, your overall reason for writing. In the following example, the details and writer's tone vary because the audiences and purposes differ.

Audience: Friends
Purpose: To impress

I lunge through the pressing cluster of runners near the finish line. I push so hard I twist my right ankle. Despite the shooting pain, I manage to limp over the finish line first.

Audience: Doctor
Purpose: To diagnose

The right Achilles tendon is so tight and numb that my foot will flex no more than an inch. Inward and outward motion of the foot is difficult, and I feel a shooting pain with each slow step.

Gathering Details

Gather a wide range of descriptive details using the cubing technique, which is explained below.

Use the Cubing Technique

Just as a cube has six sides or aspects, so may your description topic have different aspects. Following are six ways to look at your topic. Jot down your responses to the directions. Then, use your responses as you draft your description.

1. **Describe It** Provide details about your subject's appearance, importance, or personality.
2. **Associate It** Tell what related thoughts come to mind when you think of your subject.
3. **Apply It** Provide examples of what you can do with or learn from your subject.
4. **Analyze It by Breaking It Into Parts** Describe your subject aspect by aspect, using factual terms.
5. **Compare or Contrast It** Tell what your subject is similar to or different from.
6. **Argue for or Against It** Give details that explain your subject's value or problems.

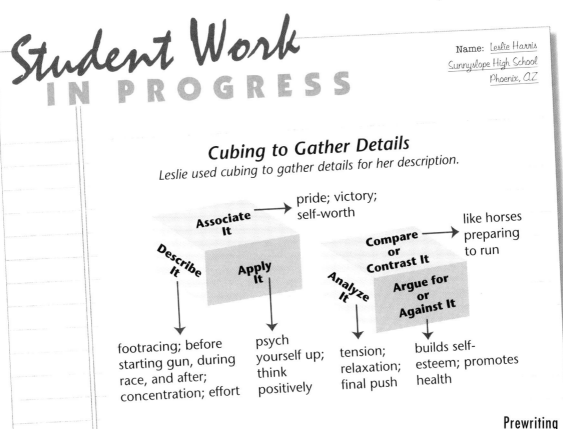

Student Work
IN PROGRESS

Name: Leslie Harris
Sunnyslope High School
Phoenix, AZ

Cubing to Gather Details

Leslie used cubing to gather details for her description.

Associate It → pride; victory; self-worth

Describe It

Apply It

Compare or Contrast It → like horses preparing to run

Analyze It

Argue for or Against It

footracing; before starting gun, during race, and after; concentration; effort

psych yourself up; think positively

tension; relaxation; final push

builds self-esteem; promotes health

Drafting

Shaping Your Writing
Create a Mood

Once you have gathered a wide range of details that appeal to the senses, choose the ones that create an overall mood, or atmosphere. The mood your description provides will add to your readers' understanding and to their enjoyment of your writing.

In the following models, the choice of descriptive details gives each description a definite mood:

Joyous Mood The morning sunlight hit the window above my bed and sent dizzying rays of light dancing over the wall. I sprang up and looked outside. The whiteness was almost blinding in its brilliance. It had snowed!

Awed Mood The morning sun was different that morning. It was shining, clear and true, throwing intricate, mysterious patterns onto the wall. With bemused anticipation, I sat up and peered out the window. Snow had fallen overnight, transforming the town into a heartbreakingly beautiful wonderland.

▲ Critical Viewing
What mood does the image in this photograph convey? Explain. **[Analyze]**

Providing Elaboration
Create Figurative Language

As you draft, use figurative language to make your description memorable and unique. Following are some commonly used types of figurative language:

Simile	A simile compares two unlike things using the words *like* or *as*.	The dog was *as fast as* a rocket.
Metaphor	A metaphor compares two unlike things by stating that one thing *is* the other.	The *ball of fire* rises each morning over the horizon.
Hyperbole	Hyperbole is exaggeration that is usually used to create a comic effect.	The guard was *twelve feet tall, with muscles of steel.*
Personification	Personification applies human qualities or behavior to something nonhuman.	The washing machine *danced* across the basement floor!

6.4 *Revising*

Revising Your Overall Structure

Review your description to be sure that you've used a consistent, logical, and effective structural organization.

▶ **REVISION STRATEGY**
Outlining Details to Check Your Organization

Create an outline to show the content and order of each paragraph in your description. Then, review your outline and rearrange paragraphs, if necessary, to make your description more effective. Following are some organizational strategies you might want to use as you reorganize your description:

- **General to Specific** Use this structure when describing a person, thing, or an idea.

- **Chronological Organization** Use chronological, or time, order to bring events to life for readers.

- **Spatial Organization** Use spatial organization to describe where things are located in relation to each other; for example, a place, a building, or an object.

Revising Your Paragraphs

Check Unity

Review the paragraphs in your description to be sure that the main idea of each describes an aspect of your overall topic. Also, make sure that individual sentences within a paragraph support the topic sentence.

▶ **REVISION STRATEGY**
Color-Coding to Check Unity

With a highlighter, color-code the main idea of each paragraph. If any main ideas do not support the topic of your description, rewrite or delete them. Then, use a different-colored highlighter to call out the sentences within each paragraph that support the main idea. Rewrite or delete sentences that stray from the paragraph's main idea.

Jasmine's singing voice had the power to enthrall an audience. Her voice range was impressive, spanning three octaves. An octave is a set of eight notes on a diatonic scale. An easy way to remember what an octave is is the song "Do, a deer." But it was the bell-like quality of her voice that truly set Jasmine apart as a singer.

Get instant help! To create your outline, use the Essay Builder, accessible from the menu bar, on-line or on CD-ROM.

Revising Your Sentences
Add Modifiers to Enhance Your Description

Enliven your description by adding modifiers to dull sentences. Through the use of modifiers, you give more information about the subject or verb of a sentence. Modifiers may be single words (adjectives and adverbs) or they may be in the form of a phrase (adjectival and adverbial phrases and clauses).

▶ **REVISION STRATEGY**
Adding Modifiers

First, read through your draft and circle any passages that seem terse, dull, or incomplete. Then, add descriptive details, answering the questions *Who? What? Where? When? Why?* and *How?* through the use of modifiers. Your modifiers may be single words, phrases, or clauses.

Student Work
IN PROGRESS

Name: *Leslie Harris*
Sunnyslope High School
Phoenix, AZ

Adding Modifiers
Leslie added some modifiers to her description to add depth and to enhance her readers' understanding of her subject.

Leslie's thoughts are more fully explained with this detail.

The gun explodes, sentencing me to a half mile, while at the same time setting me free, and a rush of adrenaline shoots through my body. I start out hard, sprinting in front of the others, and cutting to the inside lane. Extend, extend, I remind myself. Relax, stretch it out. More arms. Faster. As I run by the bleachers, Spectators are screaming encouragement, but the only sound I hear is that shot signaling my final lap.

This detail was added to help define "start out hard."

By telling "when," this helps clarify the sentence for readers.

Grammar in Your Writing
Dangling and Misplaced Modifiers

A **modifier** is a word or phrase that helps describe nouns or verbs in a sentence. An essential ingredient of clear writing is effectively placed modifiers. A modifier should be placed as close as possible to the word it modifies.

Misplaced Modifiers

A **misplaced modifier** appears to modify the wrong word in a sentence. In the sentence below that contains the misplaced modifier, the reader may at first think that "we" were covered with cobwebs and mold, not the cabinet.

Sentence with misplaced modifier: Covered with cobwebs and mold, we cleaned the old cabinet.

Corrected sentence: We cleaned the old cabinet that was covered with cobwebs and mold.

Dangling Modifiers

A **dangling modifier** appears to modify either the wrong word or no word at all because the word it should logically modify is missing. In the sentence below that contains the dangling modifier, the reader may wonder what, exactly, is "pistoning like spark plugs"?

Sentence with dangling modifier: Pistoning like spark plugs in a human engine, the track was pounded.

Corrected sentence: Pistoning like spark plugs in a human engine, the runner's feet pounded the track.

Find It in Your Reading Read the excerpt from *Letters Home From Vietnam* on pages 102–103. Locate three sentences that contain modifiers. On a separate sheet of paper, circle each modifier and the word it modifies. Observe where the modifier appears in relation to the word it modifies. Then, answer the following question for each word-modifier combination you identified. Could the modifier be closer to the word it modifies, or does the sentence work fine as is?

Find It in Your Writing Review your draft to identify and correct any dangling or misplaced modifiers. Be sure you have placed your modifiers near their subjects. Be particularly careful about sentences that contain passive voice; they are more likely to contain dangling modifiers.

For more on misplaced and dangling modifiers, see Chapter 21.

Revising Your Word Choice

Replace Vague Words

A vague word—whether it is a noun, a verb, or a modifier—cannot communicate your unique experience. Reread your draft, and replace words that are vague with more precise words.

Vague Words	Precise Words
good	delicious, excellent, well-mannered
looked	stared, glanced, peered, squinted
store	grocery, delicatessen, boutique
cold	freezing, chilly, brisk, frigid

▶ **REVISION STRATEGY**
Circling and Replacing

Read through your description, and circle words that are vague, dull, or inaccurate. Then replace those circled words or phrases with choices that better reflect what it is you are describing.

Student Work
IN PROGRESS

Name: Leslie Harris
Sunnyslope High School
Phoenix, AZ

Replacing Vague Words
Leslie replaced vague words with more precise words
to make her narrative more engaging.

I am ⟨sure⟩ [determined] that I am going to win. All the way
through, I ⟨think⟩ [mentally chant] run all the way through the
finish line. And then, as ⟨soon⟩ [abruptly] as I started, I am
⟨done⟩ [finished], drained of nervousness and the ability to
remain standing. I open my eyes, knowing that I
am now ⟨ready⟩ [prepared] and confident enough to run.

Peer Review

One way to get feedback on your description is to work with a group of peers and have them comment on the effectiveness of your writing. Use the following activity as you edit your description.

Create a Plus-and-Minus Chart

Use the following guidelines as you work with your peers to revise your description:

1. Work in a group of three to five students.
2. Prepare a chart like the one shown, and give copies to peers.
3. Read your description aloud to your peers.
4. Then, read the first entry on the chart, and ask your peers to make a thumbs-up sign if their response is positive and a thumbs-down sign if their response is negative. Enter your peers' responses on your chart.
5. Review the responses, and make revisions to your draft as necessary.

▲ Critical Viewing
Why is it useful to compare and contrast reviewers' reactions to your writing? [Apply]

Plus-and-Minus Chart

	Reviewer #1	Reviewer #2	Reviewer #3
1. The title is appropriate and interesting.	+	+	-
2. The description contains details like vivid verbs and precise nouns.	-	-	+
3. The description creates a definite mood, or atmosphere.	-	-	-
4. The writing is unified.	+	+	+
5. Each sentence is clear, with no misplaced or dangling modifiers.	+	+	-

Editing and *Proofreading*

Before you share your description with others, take time to polish it. Correct errors in grammar and punctuation, and make sure that you have spelled everything correctly.

Focusing on Commas

Review your description carefully, and check to be sure that you have correctly used commas to separate adjectives of equal rank and to separate a series of adjectives.

Grammar in Your Writing
Using Commas Correctly

Commas are used to separate items in a series and to separate certain kinds of adjectives.

Serial commas: Use commas to separate three or more words, phrases, or clauses in a series. In the example below, the first two adjectives are followed by a comma. The third adjective does not need a comma.

Example: The restless, tired, and hungry crowd gathered near the mountaintop.

Adjectives of equal rank: Use commas to separate adjectives of equal rank, called coordinate adjectives. In the sentence below, the adjectives *moist* and *delicious* could be switched without changing the meaning.

Example: The moist, delicious pie was a hit after dinner.

Adjectives of unequal rank: If one adjective has a closer relationship to the noun than the other, no comma appears between them. Below, the adjective *talented* has a closer relationship to *acrobats* than does *twenty*.

Example: Twenty talented acrobats appeared in the circus ring.

Find It in Your Reading Read through the excerpt from *Letters Home From Vietnam* on pages 102–103, and find adjectives that the writer does not separate with commas. Explain why commas are not needed.

Find It in Your Writing Check your description to make sure that you have used commas with adjectives correctly. Find items in a series of adjectives. If there are none, challenge yourself to add a series of adjectives.

To learn more about the correct use of commas, see Chapter 28.

6.6 Publishing and Presenting

Use the following ideas for sharing your description with others:

Building Your Portfolio

1. **Display** Request a bulletin board at school where you can post your description. Place photos or illustrations around your paper to further enhance its effectiveness.

2. **Audiotape** Capture your description on audiotape. First, rehearse yourself reading your paper. Mark on your copy where you will pause and what words require special emphasis. Then, record your reading. Play the tape back for family and friends.

Reflecting on Your Writing

After you have finished your description, think about the experience of writing it. Use these questions to direct your reflection, and record your responses in your portfolio.

- What did you learn about the subject you chose?
- Which strategy for choosing a topic would you use for a future descriptive essay?

Internet Tip

To see descriptions scored with this rubric, go on-line:
PHSchool.com
Enter Web Code:
eek-1001

Rubric for Self-Assessment

Use the following criteria to evaluate your description.

	Score 4	Score 3	Score 2	Score 1
Audience and Purpose	Contains details that work together to create a tone	Creates a tone through use of details	Contains extraneous details that detract from the tone	Contains details that are unfocused and create no tone
Organization	Is organized consistently, logically, and effectively	Is organized consistently	Is organized, but not consistently	Is disorganized and confusing
Elaboration	Contains creative use of figurative language, creating interesting comparisons	Contains figurative language that creates comparisons	Contains figurative language, but the comparisons are not fresh	Contains no figurative language
Use of Language	Contains sensory language that appeals to the five senses; contains no errors in grammar, punctuation, or spelling	Contains some sensory language; contains few errors in grammar, punctuation, and spelling	Contains some sensory language, but it appeals to only one or two of the senses; contains some errors in grammar, punctuation, and spelling	Contains no sensory language; contains many errors in grammar, punctuation, and spelling

Student Work
IN PROGRESS

FINAL DRAFT

◀ **Critical Viewing**
What sports require the kind of concentration you see on the face of this athlete? Explain. **[Relate]**

Phantom Finish

Leslie Harris
Sunnyslope High School
Phoenix, Arizona

Fears sprout wings, taking flight in the depths of my stomach, and my mutinous mouth refuses to swallow. Breathe, I tell myself. Settle down. Every logical part of me assures myself that it's no big deal; I have nothing to be afraid of. But my stomach will not stop its incessant churning, and my chest is tight with anticipation. Realizing that no one else can calm my fears, I slowly exhale, forcing myself to relax and focus on the event ahead. Closing my eyes, I envision myself at the starting line, feeling vul-

Sensory details like "taking flight" and "churning" help readers understand Leslie's experience.

nerable and uncertain of my abilities. Faceless competitors sur-round me, jumping, stretching, and talking amongst themselves. Each of us presents a recognized threat to the other, and good luck wishes fill the air like cheap perfume. I am quiet and withdrawn, mentally preparing and hoping that hours of painful training will pay off. Too soon come those haunting words: "On your mark." My heart beats wildly in opposition with my stiffened and tense body. The gun explodes, sentencing me to a half mile, while at the same time setting me free, and a rush of adrenaline shoots through my body. I start out hard, sprinting in front of the others, and cutting to the inside lane. Extend, extend, I remind myself. Relax, stretch it out. More arms. Faster. As I run by the bleachers, spectators are screaming encouragement, but the only sound I hear is that shot signaling my final lap. "Faster" it screams, and I obey its command. Pounding footsteps on my heels torture me, and the visible shad-ows of opponents barely behind, force my straining body to test its limits. Final 200, final 200. I sprint harder than ever before; I am determined that I am going to win. All the way through, I mentally chant: "Run all the way through the finish line." And then, as abruptly as I started, I am finished, drained of nervousness and the ability to remain standing. I open my eyes, knowing that I am now prepared and confident enough to run. Just then, a competitor compliments me: "You're always so calm before you run." At this I simply smile; little does she know.

This metaphor compares insincere good luck wishes to cheap perfume filling the air.

Chronological organi-zation carries the readers along with Leslie through the race.

Here, Leslie uses vivid, precise words like "pounding" and "force" to create a specific mood.

◀ **Critical Viewing**
What qualities are needed to be a suc-cessful runner like the ones pictured? **[Analyze]**

Connected Assignment
Poem

Like writers of description, poets carefully choose words. In their **poems**, they use words to create images, moods, sounds, and to communicate ideas. Some poems tell a story; others describe something or express a feeling or an idea. Poems come in many forms: some are epic in length, and others are a few lines long. Some poems have rigid structures and rhyming rules, and others do not. Below are examples of two types of poems: haiku and free verse.

Write your own poem, following the writing process suggestions outlined on the page at right.

▲ **Critical Viewing** If you were to write a poem inspired by this photograph, what would be its title? **[Analyze]**

MODEL

Bashō
Translated by Harold G. Henderson

The sun's way:
Hollyhocks turn toward it
Through all the rain of May.

Poverty's child—
He starts to grind the rice,
And gazes at the moon.

Night Clouds
Amy Lowell

The white mares of the moon rush along the sky
Beating their golden hoofs upon the glass Heavens;
The white mares of the moon are all standing on their hind
        legs
Pawing at the green porcelain doors of the remote Heavens.
Fly, Mares!
Strain your utmost.
Scatter the milky dust of stars,
Or the tiger sun will leap upon you and destroy you
With one lick of his vermilion tongue.

Prewriting Before you begin writing your poem, take some time to decide on its format, subject matter, and the impact you want to have on your readers.

Choose a Format Sometimes, it helps to choose a format for a poem before you choose its subject. Select a format that you like, such as a haiku or limerick. Read a few examples to remind yourself of the format's line structure and rhythm. Then, sort through recent experiences for moments that captivated your senses.

Select Subject Matter Think about what you want the subject of your poem to be. For example, you may want to explore what it feels like to be a turnip, or you may want to tell the story of your ninth birthday party.

Gather Details With a format and topic in hand, brainstorm for images that will convey ideas about your poem's subject. Record sensory images in a chart like the one below, that lists sights, sounds, tastes, smells, and touch.

SENSORY CHART				
Sight	**Sound**	**Taste**	**Smell**	**Touch**
bright	musical	salty	foul	rough
beautiful	noisy	sour	fragrant	bumpy
hazy	echoing	spicy	fresh-baked	furry

Drafting Let your chosen format help you draft and guide the number of syllables, lines, or stanzas that you write. Then, give your imagination license to run free. Experiment with unexpected word order, and create unusual metaphors. Include sound devices such as alliteration (repeated beginning consonants) and onomatopoeia (words that sound like their meaning) to support the desired mood.

Revising and Editing Read your poem aloud to a friend or to yourself. Listen for the sound, of the words, and picture the images. Add or change wording to make your images more vivid and powerful. Rearrange words to catch the desired rhythm.

Publishing and Presenting Hold a poetry reading with a group of peers. Take turns reading your poems aloud. Then, following the reading, discuss your experiences as poets and your ideas for upcoming poems.

Spotlight on the Humanities

Making Cultural Connections

Focus on Dance: Flamenco

If you were going to describe a dance performance to a friend, you would use vivid verbs and adverbs to paint a picture of the performance. In the fifteenth century, flamenco arose as a popular art form among the people of southern Spain. A type of folk-loric dance, flamenco is a combination of singing, dancing, and guitar music. The complicated footwork mirrors its complex rhythms, making it challenging for the dancer and exciting for an audience to watch.

Art Connection Born in Mexico, Diego Rivera (1886–1957) is considered one of the great artists of the twentieth century. As in the painting at right, Rivera often used Hispanic dancers as the subject of his paintings, capturing the costumes and flavor of Mexican culture in his work. Rivera will forever be remembered for his great mural paintings, which captured the essence of Mexican society.

Portrait of Dolores Olmedo, Diego Rivera

▲ **Critical Viewing** Why might female folkloric dancers, like the one pictured, wear flowing skirts? **[Speculate]**

Literature Connection In her poem "Mexican Magician," twentieth-century American poet Pat Mora compares the daily activities of a baker with the movements of a Mexican dance.

> All day the panadero
> in white apron and call cap,
> stirs flour, eggs and sugar
> then salsas with his broom. . . .
> His hips sway while he sprinkles
> cookies with sweet confetti,
> dance-dancing panadero,
> magician with a flair.

Pat Mora, a native Texan, continues to write books for children and adults. Recipient of a Poetry Fellowship from the National Endowment for the Arts in 1994, she currently lives in New Mexico.

Description Writing Activity: Dance Description

Describe a dance performance that you've seen recently. Use descriptive details and vivid verbs to bring the dance to life for your readers—but do so without naming the type of dance you are describing. Share your dance description with your class, and see whether they can guess the type of dance you described.

Media and Technology Skills

Evaluating Images

Activity: Rating a News Set

The production values of any television program send carefully planned messages to viewers. Designers work with producers to create sets, lights, costumes, and logos that project the desired "look." A passive television audience can be unconsciously manipulated by these carefully constructed images. You can easily see through these images by becoming an active, analytical viewer.

Think About It Consider the messages sent by your preferred television news program. Write down four or five words that describe the overall feeling or tone of the program. These words may help you understand your unconscious impression. Next, you will become an active viewer and take a close look at the production elements that might contribute to your perception.

Describe It Watch the program you have selected, and create a chart describing each of these production elements.

LOGO	SETS	PROPS	COSTUMES	LIGHTING
First-Witness News	Small set, very sparsely furnished	Only a long desk	Anchors are wearing serious business suits	Very bright lighting

Use specific descriptive language to help you analyze each element. You might find it useful to turn the sound down or off so that you are focusing primarily on the images.

Rate It Review your descriptions to make specific generalizations about the way the news program uses images to create a look or identity. Refer to your initial impressions to see whether your previous perceptions match the results of your analysis.

After analyzing the production elements, you can share your evaluation by giving the news program a rating. You might use a letter grade (A, B, C, etc.) or a five-star scale. You may wish to give ratings for a variety of aspects, such as overall appearance, professional feeling, or attitude.

Identifying Image Trends

Being an active viewer includes recognizing various uses of images in film and video. Think about which of these trends you have noticed and whether or not you find them effective:

- Fast-cutting techniques appear often in music videos.
- Some stations place their logo in a corner of the screen at all times.
- Some commercials or promotional spots use quirky camera angles and speeded-up or unfocused footage.

Standardized Test Preparation Workshop

Strategy, Organization, and Style

On a standardized test, you may be asked to read a descriptive passage in which each sentence is numbered. Following the passage will be several multiple-choice questions based on the reading.

The following are three types of questions that you will need to answer:

- **Strategy questions** ask whether a given revision is appropriate in the context of the essay.

- **Organization questions** ask you to choose the most logical sequence of ideas.

- **Style questions** focus on conveying the writer's point of view and the use of appropriate and effective language.

Sample Test Item

Directions: Read the passage, and then answer the questions that follow.

1 The <u>original</u> garden plan had no fence.
2 Several <u>rabbit</u> families resided in our back-
3 yard. Mark was able to <u>build</u> a picket fence
4 to enclose the raised beds. Even so, the
5 baby rabbits were able to <u>get</u> into the garden.

1 Which of the following is the **BEST** revision of lines 1 to 3?

  A The original garden plan had no fence; then, we learned that several rabbit families resided in our backyard.

  B The original garden plan had no fence and several rabbit families resided in our backyard.

  C The original garden plan had no fence, and lots of rabbits lived there.

  D Correct as is.

Answer and Explanation

The correct answer is *A*. The transition word *then* links the two clauses and alerts the reader to the chronological order of the passage.

▶ **Practice 1** **Directions:** Read the passage, and then answer the questions that follow. Choose the letter of the **BEST** answer.

1 There are woods surrounding poet Carl
2 Sandburg's home, in Flat Rock, North
3 Carolina. They are thick with young
4 pines, and old rhododendrons. The
5 beautiful mountainside property is now
6 a national park. A small parking lot
7 limits the number of guests in the park.
8 A long trail climbs up the hill parallel
9 to an enormous grassy expanse of lawn.
10 The park offers several benches along the
11 many hiking trails, as well as many direc-
12 tional signs to help trail-weary hikers
13 find their way around the property.

14 For small children and animal lovers,
15 perhaps the main attractions are the
16 barns and fields. Park patrons are
17 invited to enter the fenced meadows
18 where the nanny goats and kids wan-
19 der. The more aggressive billy goats are
20 penned separately. Mrs. Sandburg ded-
21 icated much of her time to raising
22 several kinds of goats.

23 The house itself sits about two thirds of
24 the way up the mountain. Across the
25 lawn from the trail is an outdoor
26 amphitheater with wooden benches
27 and a small wooden stage. Behind the
28 large white house are several out-
29 buildings, including the park ranger's
30 residence, and several barns that used
31 to house the Sandburg vehicles.

1 Which of the following is the **BEST** order for the paragraphs?
A 3,2,1
B 2,3,1
C 1,3,2
D Correct as is.

2 Which of the following would be the best way to write lines 1–3?
F There are woods surrounding poet Carl Sandburg's home, in Flat Rock, North Carolina, they are thick with young pines and old rhododendrons.
G The woods surrounding poet Carl Sandburg's home, in Flat Rock, North Carolina, are thick with young pines and old rhododendrons.
H There are woods surrounding poet Carl Sandburg's home, in Flat Rock, North Carolina; they are thick with young pines and old rhododendrons.
J The thick woods surrounding poet Carl Sandburg's home, in Flat Rock, North Carolina, have many young pines and old rhododendrons.

3 If the author wanted to include more information about what adults might enjoy at the park, which of the following would be an appropriate addition?
A Mr. and Mrs. Sandburg loved their home in Flat Rock.
B There are currently many goats living at the Sandburg Park.
C Sandburg wrote the poem *Skyscraper*.
D The samples of Sandburg's poetry are displayed in his own unique handwriting.

4 Which of the following words, if any, would be more descriptive than the word *small* in line 27?
F little
G tiny
H miniature
J Correct as is.

5 Which sentence should be deleted to eliminate irrelevant information?
A the sentence in lines 1–2
B the sentence in lines 6–7
C the sentence in lines 14–16
D the sentence in lines 20–22

Persuasion

Persuasive Essay

Persuasion in Everyday Life

The art of persuasion—getting others to do something or to think as you do—is a part of daily life. Persuasion may involve convincing a friend to see a movie with you or bargaining over the cost of a comic book at a flea market. Persuasion sometimes is verbal, sometimes visual, sometimes written, and often a combination of all these elements.

Persuasion is often a part of various types of writing, as well as a type of writing itself. For example, a character in a short story may speak persuasively to a group of friends, or a poem may contain a plea to readers about an important issue. Persuasive writing gives you an opportunity to make your voice heard and to express your opinion on an issue about which you feel strongly. In this chapter, you'll learn how to create a persuasive essay that is clear, organized, and forceful.

▲ Critical Viewing
Kofi Annan, pictured above, is giving a speech in his role as Secretary General of the United Nations. Why might a member of the United Nations find persuasive skills useful? [Connect]

What Is a Persuasive Essay?

A **persuasive essay** is a piece of writing that tries to convince readers to accept a particular viewpoint or to take a certain action. Most effective persuasive essays contain

- a clearly stated opinion or argument on an issue that has more than one side.
- evidence to support the opinion or argument.
- memorable and convincing details and vivid, persuasive language.
- an effective, logical organization.

To preview the criteria on which your persuasive essay may be evaluated, see the Rubric for Self-Assessment on page 143.

Writers in ACTION

Dean Rusk, former secretary of state, shares the following insight about the art of persuasion:

"One of the best ways to persuade others is with your ears—by listening to them."

Types of Persuasive Essays

In addition to persuasive essays, there are many other forms of persuasion:

- **Editorials and letters to the editor** appear in newspapers. Editorials express the newspaper's stand on a current issue; letters to the editor present readers' viewpoints.
- **Persuasive speeches** are an oral form of a persuasive essay. They often contain allusions and sound devices to make them stirring and memorable.
- **Position papers** address one side of a controversial issue. They are often directed at a person or group with some power to shape policy on a particular issue.
- **Grant proposals** make a request for financing a program or a project of the writer's. They are usually addressed to members of a government agency or private corporation.

PREVIEW
Student Work IN PROGRESS

In this chapter, you'll follow the work of Sharon Goldberg, a student at Miami-Palmetto High School in Pinecrest, Florida, as she drafts a persuasive essay that expresses her opinion on the importance of volunteerism. Sharon's completed essay appears at the end of the chapter.

Model From Literature

Ellen Goodman is a newspaper columnist based at the Boston Globe. *She won the Pulitzer Prize for Distinguished Commentary in 1980.*

George F. Will won the Pulitzer Prize for Commentary in 1977. In addition to authoring a syndicated newspaper column, he is a commentator for a network news program.

Reading Strategy:
Identify the Author's Main Points As you read a persuasive essay, look for the **main points** the author provides to support his or her argument. If those main points are few or weak, you should consider seriously whether to agree with his or her viewpoint.

▲ **Critical Viewing**
This photograph shows Walter Polovchak walking to a press conference. Would you consider a boy this age able to make life decisions? Why or why not? **[Make a Judgment]**

Two Views

The following persuasive articles were written in response to a controversial issue: A twelve-year-old boy, Walter Polovchak, wanted to stay behind in the United States when his parents decided to move back home—to the Soviet Union. Americans were sharply divided on the issue. Some felt that keeping the Polovchak family together was most important; others thought that Walter should have the right to live in a free country.

The State's Nose in Family Life
Ellen Goodman

Imagine that you, a parent of sound mind and body, are moving cross-country. You've had enough of California and want to try New England.

The children, however, don't want to move. They like the weather, their friends, the school, the usual.

You argue about it, of course; that's what families do. Eventually, you decide that the 17-year-old has a right to stay with her aunt and uncle because she is, after all, one year away from being on her own. But the 12-year-old must come along.

Goodman opens her persuasive essay by comparing the Polovchaks' situation with a situation to which her readers can relate.

Rebelling, the boy runs away. But when the state finds him, they do not return him. Instead, they grant your son asylum in California.

Asylum from you.

Or maybe it wasn't California. Perhaps you have emigrated to a socialist country and seven months later, disillusioned, want to come home. But this time the state grants your 12-year-old political asylum to save him from a lifetime of materialism, capitalism—who knows what?—in the United States.

If you can imagine these situations, you can feel what has happened to the Polovchak family of Chicago and the Ukraine. The Polovchaks, five of them, emigrated to this country, apparently encouraged by a family member who promised them a leg up into American life. Now, disappointed, the parents want to go back, taking Walter and his younger brother with them.

But the U.S. government has offered Walter asylum and a lawyer and the temporary custody of the state. Two parents, who have neither abused nor neglected their son, have temporarily lost their right to make decisions for their boy, for reasons that are blatantly political.

If it happened to an American family, it would be an outrage. If it happened to an American family in the Soviet Union, it would make furious headlines. It goes against the basic American principle of keeping the state—whenever possible—out of family life.

"There is nothing that any of us would find in the current situation to justify the state entertaining this case," says Yale Law School's Joseph Goldstein, who has written extensively about parents' and children's rights. "We don't put someone else in the place of the parents unless they are disqualified. These parents did not abuse or neglect their children."

Psychiatrist Allen Stone, who teaches family law at Harvard, had very much the same reaction: "This is totally outside the range of what family law and family courts ought to be doing. The notion that they would interfere in an ongoing, intact family boggles the mind. It just boggles the mind."

The fact is that we have given much more weight to this Ukrainian boy's testimony than to any American boy of the same age. We have given his parents' views much less weight, because they want him to return with them to the Soviet Union.

But it is almost impossible to assess the boy's own frame of mind and values. Is he a 12-year-old who merely likes the ice cream and bicycles of America? "There is lots of food here," he said. "You can buy many things and I liked school."

For another example of persuasive writing, read "Keep Memory Alive" by Eli Wiesel. The essay appears in *Prentice Hall Literature: Timeless Voices, Timeless Themes,* Platinum.

This expert testimony, in the form of a quotation, helps support Goodman's argument.

Goodman includes quotations from Walter to emphasize how immature he really is.

Is he, like so many his age, testing the limits, tasting his first tidbits of rebellion? Or can he be mature enough to choose political freedom above family?

It is equally difficult to determine what is best for the boy. There are psychological terrors as well as exhilarations for a child who "wins" such an early and terminal battle with his parents. There are also troubles ahead for a child who returns unwillingly, an embarrassment, to the Ukraine.

But our laws assume (except in rare instances) that the parent is best judge of the state of mind, the needs and the future of the child. Whether we approve or not, we do not interfere unless they have been proven unfit.

No matter what fantasies we have about rescuing Walter Polovchak, no matter how certain we are that his parents are wrong, we can't have two standards of law—one for Americans and one for Soviet immigrants.

Parallel structure helps makes Goodman's point memorable and effective.

In a Chicago courtroom on Aug. 4, Judge Joseph Mooney ruled that the boy should remain in the custody of the state, and the care of his aunt and uncle, for five more weeks. But his intention is clearly to reunite this family, "whatever the political consequences." And he is right.

The irony is that we criticize, even denounce, the power of the state in the Soviet Union, the way it interferes in private lives. We pride ourselves on being different, pride ourselves on protecting the integrity of the family from the state. But in the case of Walter Polovchak we very nearly lost that difference.

"The Littlest Defector" Deserves Asylum
George Will

Washington—The case of Walter Polovchak, "the littlest defector," dramatized the difficulties, logical and political, that occur when people do not take seriously the radical evil of totalitarian states. Americans who oppose Walter's plea for political asylum are disregarding the premise of the United States, or the manifest nature of the USSR, or both.

In his opening paragraph, George Will uses powerful words and phrases such as "radical evil" and "totalitarian states" to make his opinion clear.

Eight months ago Walter, 12, and his family emigrated from the Soviet Union to Chicago. The father is unhappy and wants to return with his wife, Walter, and another son, 6. His daughter, 17, has her own visa and has no intention of leaving the United States. She and Walter are staying with relatives in Chicago, pending disposition of Walter's case.

People opposed to the Illinois court's intervention say the case is "political." Usually that adjective is used to imply that there are

◀ **Critical Viewing** What message do you think this photograph of Walter conveys? Explain. **[Interpret]**

no legal standards to control judgment, or that the Constitution commits disposition of such matters to another branch of government. Whatever constitutional problem, if any, lurks here, most of those who complain that Walter's case is "political" seem to mean something else.

They seem to mean only that if Walter were resisting return to, say, Denmark rather than to a closed, totalitarian society, the court probably would not have given Walter a hearing. To which, the answer is: Of course. Justice cannot be done here without taking cognizance of the two regimes, under one of which Walter will live.

Many who oppose granting asylum say Walter is not "mature enough" to choose freedom above family. And they stress American respect for parental authority.

But the fundamental question pertains to claims that are being made to rights that are not contingent upon maturity: Should Walter's parents have the right to choose for him a future in which the possibility of freedom is foreclosed? A nation that asserts that fundamental rights are "inalienable" should not spurn the pleas of a boy whose parents are asserting a right to alienate his fundamental rights, permanently.

In his final paragraph, Will makes his strongest argument: Should Walter's future freedom be decided for him by his parents?

Writing Application: Include Main Points
As you prepare to write your persuasive piece, think about the main points you will make to support your opinion or viewpoint.

Model from Literature • **129**

Prewriting

Choosing Your Topic

To write a powerful persuasive essay, start with a topic that is important to you. For help in generating topics, use the strategies below:

Strategies for Generating Topics

1. **Scan Newspapers** Scan a newspaper, looking for stories that matter to you on a personal level. What do you see that makes you angry, strikes you as unfair, or cries out "this needs to be changed"? Use one of the news stories to provide you with a topic for your persuasive essay.

2. **Make a Quicklist** Come up with a topic for your persuasive writing by listing types of issues. For example, write headings like Community Issues, Political Issues, and Social Issues at the top of a sheet of paper, and quickly list ideas inspired by each. Review your lists, and choose the issue that interests you most as the topic of your persuasive essay.

3. **Use Sentence Starters** To come up with a topic, copy the following sentence starters and fill in the blanks. Then, review your completed sentences. Choose one issue as the topic of your persuasive essay.

   - If I became (mayor/president/school principal), the first thing I would do is ___?___ .

   - Something that needs to be changed at this school is ___?___ .

   - Teenagers today should ___?___ .

Get instant help! To make your Quicklist, use the Essay Builder, accessible from the menu bar, on-line or on CD-ROM.

Student Work
IN PROGRESS

Name: *Sharon Goldberg*
Miami-Palmetto High School
Pinecrest, FL

Using Sentence Starters to Choose a Topic
Using sentence starters helped Sharon Goldberg focus on an issue that was important to her.

- Something that needs to be changed at this school is *cafeteria food*

- Teenagers today should *help others*

TOPIC BANK

If you are having difficulty finding a suitable topic for your persuasive piece, use one of the following:

1. **Persuasive Speech** Choose a global issue—child labor laws or deforestation, for example—about which you would like to take a stand. Write and deliver a persuasive speech in which you support your opinion.

2. **Persuasive Essay** Write an essay in which you support one candidate over another. Candidates may be actual, perhaps someone running for student council president, or imaginary, as in Hero of the Year.

Responding to Fine Art

3. Study *Arrivals and Departures* by Chester Arnold. Determine what you think the artist's message is. Then, write a persuasive essay in which you agree or disagree with that message.

Responding to Literature

4. "There Will Come Soft Rains" by Ray Bradbury is set in a technologically advanced world. Read the story and draw on its images to write a persuasive essay on the effects of technology on our lives. You can find the story in *Prentice Hall Literature: Timeless Voices, Timeless Themes*, Platinum.

Arrivals and Departures, 1999, Chester Arnold, The Seven Bridges Foundation, Greenwich, CT

☑ Cooperative Writing Opportunity

5. **Editorial Page** Most newspapers contain an editorial page on which appear editorials, cartoons, and letters to the editor. Work with a small group to prepare an editorial page about a particular issue. First, discuss and decide on your school's most pressing issue. Then, assign one student to conduct a survey about the issue, another to write a letter to the editor about the issue, and another to draw a cartoon about the issue. When finished, work together to lay out the editorial page. Photocopy your completed project, and distribute it to classmates.

Narrowing Your Topic

Once you've chosen a general topic, narrow it into one you can argue effectively. Looping is one strategy you can use to ensure that your topic isn't too broad.

Narrow a Topic by Looping

1. Write freely on your general topic for about five minutes.
2. Read what you have written. Circle the most important idea.
3. Write freely on that idea for about five minutes.
4. Repeat the process until you have found a topic that is narrow enough to address in your persuasive essay.
5. If you keep writing, you may even be able to identify a thesis statement, or main idea, that you want your persuasive essay to communicate.

Student Work
IN PROGRESS

Name: *Sharon Goldberg*
Miami-Palmetto High School
Pinecrest, FL

Looping to Narrow a Topic

Sharon used looping to narrow her broad persuasive topic.

Broad Topic: Helping Others

It's important to help others. Those in service industries—like nursing and the fire and police departments—devote their lives to the public. Some people prefer to help in other ways. From retirees who help care for children in need to families who donate food to the hungry to teenagers who work in their communities, everyone can make a difference.

More Narrowed Topic: Everyone Can Make a Difference

Working with others gives volunteers a sense of perspective. Volunteering their extra time keeps teens focused and gives them a sense of responsibility and accomplishment. Schools should offer course credit to teens who take on a volunteering role in the community. Everyone in the community—from elementary-school children to people who have retired—should take time to help others.

Thesis Statement: Volunteerism is vital.

Considering Your Audience and Purpose

As you draft, identify your audience and their opinions. This will help you achieve your purpose—to persuade them.

Write for Various Audiences

A hostile audience is one that will not be immediately receptive to your argument. A friendly audience is one that is likely to be more sympathetic. Depending on whether you expect your audience to be hostile, friendly, or a mix, vary your argument accordingly.

EXAMPLE: Imagine that you are writing an editorial calling for a ban on bicycle traffic from a park pathway.

Hostile Audience: Bicycle Riders

Emphasize alternative paths that would remain available for people who ride bicycles.

Friendly Audience: Families With Small Children

Emphasize the dangers that are posed when bikes and pedestrians mix.

Create a Purpose Planner

Ultimately, you hope your persuasive writing will change the thinking or behavior of your audience. To do so, choose details that will lead your audience to think or behave in a certain way. A purpose planner can help you achieve your particular goals. Use the following purpose planner as a guide for making your own.

Purpose >	Plan
To warn >	• Provide details about children who have been injured by careless bikers. • Use emotionally charged language.
To inform >	• Demonstrate that bicyclists have several alternative routes available. • Provide statistics about bike-pedestrian accidents.

Gathering Evidence

You'll need facts and details from a variety of sources to support your position. Follow these strategies as you gather the evidence you need:

1. **Find Unbiased Research** The foundation of an effective persuasive essay should contain reliable evidence in support of its position. Evidence from biased or unreliable sources will weaken your argument. As you perform research for your editorial, find sources of information that are objective and bias-free.

2. **Conduct Interviews** For some issues, the most powerful evidence you can use to support your argument is evidence that you collect yourself. Interview an expert in that field. His or her words will prove more persuasive than a quotation from an unqualified person.

3. **Make a Pro-and-Con Chart** Make a chart to help you see both sides of an issue. In the left column, list your arguments, or "pros"; in the right column, list opposing arguments, or "cons." When it's complete, note the evidence in the "Opposing" column. Brainstorm for ways to counter-argue the evidence listed there.

Student Work
IN PROGRESS

Name: Sharon Goldberg
Miami-Palmetto High School
Pinecrest, FL

Gathering Evidence With a T-Chart
Sharon made a T-chart to examine both sides of the issue about volunteering.

Supporting	Opposing
✓ Volunteering helps the community.	Paying taxes is enough help.
✓ Volunteers learn life skills.	Volunteering takes away from study and homework time.
✓ Volunteering can build self-esteem.	Sports and clubs build self-esteem.

7.3 **Drafting**

Shaping Your Writing

Structure your persuasive writing in the way that best suits your argument and your evidence.

Use TRI/PS/QA to Structure Paragraphs

As you draft paragraphs, think first about what you want to say and then choose a logical organization for each. Following are some ideas for organizing your paragraphs:

TRI stands for **T**opic, **R**estatement, **I**llustration. This type of organization helps readers follow along as you explain your ideas. The elements TRI can occur in any order within a paragraph (TIR). You could also include two illustrations, or even three, within the same paragraph (TRII).

T
R — **Example:** Ursuline Avenue should and must be converted to a one-way street. It cannot support two-way traffic because it is too narrow and it has too much traffic.
I — For example, in a three-month period last year, there were eleven accidents on Ursuline Avenue and at least thirty traffic tie-ups caused by traffic-flow problems.

PS stands for **P**roblem and **S**olution. This type of organization emphasizes the problem-and-solution relationship between the facts you are presenting. To use this type of structure, begin by stating a problem. Follow it with one or more solutions to that problem.

P — **Example:** Our town has been severely damaged by floods over the past ten years. Local officials must look
S — into the solutions of people in areas that have experienced similar problems. Starting from scratch won't gain us anything. We must use the knowledge and experience of others as a starting point so that we can solve our flooding problems soon.

QA stands for **Q**uestion and **A**nswer. Use this method of organization when you anticipate that your audience will have specific questions about your topic. Begin by posing a question or problem. Then, present your answer or answers in response to the question.

Q — **Example:** Why is it necessary to build a new computer laboratory? The future is now. Students must become
A — familiar with current technology in order to better their chances of developing viable work skills. Current software applications will not run on our old computers, so many students miss out on becoming familiar with those all-important workplace tools.

Providing Elaboration

Elaborate on your ideas by providing details that explain, restate, illustrate, or expand on them.

Build Your Argument With Evidence

As you draft, build and support your argument by providing evidence or support. Choose details of various types from various sources. Following are types of evidence you should consider including in your persuasive essay:

- **Historical details** may be provided through excerpts from government records, war records, and almanacs.

EXAMPLE: The Central School Stage Band has been in existence since 1922.

- **Statistical information** may be researched or gathered firsthand. This type of information may come from results of surveys, polls, scientific data, and weather records.

EXAMPLE: Four out of five high-school musicians go on to higher education.

- **Expert testimony** is provided by someone who is considered extremely knowledgeable about or familiar with your topic.

EXAMPLE: Dr, Rita Sohns, head of the American Student Agenda, strongly advocates music programs in schools. She said, "There is no better way to learn discipline, art, and camaraderie, than through participation in music programs."

- **Textual evidence** may come from literature, letters, and personal documents.

EXAMPLE: In an open letter to Principal Ordonez, the band requested "funding for new sheet music and new instruments."

▼ Critical Viewing
If you were to persuade someone to take up a musical instrument, what reasons would you give? [Relate]

7.4 **Revising**

Revising Your Overall Structure

Once you've completed your first draft, make sure that it contains the details needed to be effective. Also, check to be sure that you develop and support your argument in the body of your paper.

▶ **REVISION STRATEGY**
Color-Coding to Identify Support

Reread your essay to see whether you have included enough supporting details to make your argument successful. As you read, use a colored pencil to circle each topic sentence. Then, use a different-colored pencil to circle supporting details.

Next, review your markings. If a topic sentence has fewer than two supporting details, add more evidence to support it or reconsider whether the point is worth including.

▲ **Critical Viewing**
In what ways can hospital volunteers improve the quality of patient care? **[Speculate]**

Student Work
IN PROGRESS

Name: *Sharon Goldberg*
Miami-Palmetto High School
Pinecrest, FL

Color-Coding to Identify Support
Sharon used color-coding to identify the types of support she used in her essay. She revised accordingly and added a different type of support—a quotation—to give this paragraph more depth.

Not only is it necessary to perform community-service hours to graduate from high schools, but it is also essential to provide time and commitment voluntarily to the surrounding community. Young students, for example, should assist at a hospital or a nursing facility as much as possible without interfering with their schoolwork. These services should provide the satisfaction of knowing that the volunteers have made a difference in someone's life.

"Don't give until it hurts, but give until it feels good" is a statement that accurately describes how an individual should volunteer.

Revising Your Paragraphs

Make the main points in your essay memorable by using *parallelism*—the use of patterns or repetitions of grammatical structures. Parallclism adds rhythm and balance to your writing. Use it to emphasize important points and to forge links between related ideas.

▶ REVISION STRATEGY
Forming Parallel Structures

To form parallel structures in your draft, locate an important word, phrase, clause, or question. Then, experiment with building upon that word, phrase, clause, or question to make it into a passage containing parallelism.

PARALLEL QUESTIONS: Who will step up first? Who will lead the way? Who will win the day?

PARALLEL PHRASES: If you care, if you can, and if you would, lend a hand now.

PARALLEL CLAUSES: Although we strive for greatness, although we work hard, although we deserve the best, sometimes, it's just not enough.

Student Work
IN PROGRESS

Name: Sharon Goldberg
Miami-Palmetto High School
Pinecrest, FL

Making Use of Parallelism

As she revised, Sharon made use of parallelism to make her introduction more memorable and stirring.

Reading a book to a blind person. ~~At a nursing home,~~

(cap) Feeding a debilitated patient ∧ (at a nursing home.) Tutoring a younger child.

These are examples of community service projects that provide the performer of such deeds with feelings of self-worth and gratification. By serving others in the community, the individual is helping himself or herself to grow and to acquire knowledge and wisdom.

Grammar in Your Writing
Adding Parallel Clauses

A **clause** is a group of words with its own subject and verb. One way to make your persuasive essay memorable is by adding **parallel clauses.** These are clauses within a sentence that have matching grammatical forms or patterns.

Following are some tips for revising your sentences to form parallel clauses.

1. Make sure that the verbs in each clause are in the same tense.

NOT PARALLEL:	The Garden Group planted, the Garden Group hoed, the Garden Group was persevering, and the Garden Group triumphed.
PARALLEL:	The Garden Group planted, the Garden Group hoed, the Garden Group persevered, and the Garden Group triumphed.

2. Don't change the subject in subsequent clauses.

NOT PARALLEL:	After his efforts on our behalf, after Matt's sacrifices on our behalf, and after his achievements on our behalf, isn't it time to elect him president of the class?
PARALLEL:	After Matt's efforts on our behalf, after his sacrifices on our behalf, and after his achievements on our behalf, isn't it time to elect him president of the class?

3. Always use the same type of subordinate clause:

NOT PARALLEL:	The corporation will sponsor only those projects that are worthy and it thinks have a chance at winning awards.
PARALLEL:	The corporation will sponsor only those projects that are worthy and that might win awards.

Find It in Your Reading Find an example of parallelism in the essay by Ellen Goodman on pages 126–128. Explain the impact that parallelism has on the passage.

Find It in Your Writing As you revise your essay, look for two examples of parallel clauses. If you cannot identify any, revise to insert them.

For more on parallel clauses, see Chapter 20.

Revising Your Sentences

Add Variety to Your Sentences

Writing is much more persuasive if it is interesting. One way to add interest to your writing is to use a variety of sentence types and lengths. Review your draft, and analyze the sentences you have used. If you tend to use too many sentences of one type and of one average length, revise to make your writing more interesting to read and hear.

▶ **REVISION STRATEGY**
Color-Coding Clues to Sentence Types

Use this strategy to analyze the sentence variety in your writing:

1. Read through your essay. Underline declarative sentences in red, interrogative sentences in green, exclamatory sentences in blue, and imperative sentences in black.

2. Review the underlined material. If you have little or no variety in sentence types, revise to make your writing more interesting.

Learn More

To learn more about revising to create effective sentences, see Chapter 21.

Student Work
IN PROGRESS

Name: *Sharon Goldberg*
Miami-Palmetto High School
Pinecrest, FL

Color-Coding Sentence Types

When Sharon discovered that she used only declarative sentences in this paragraph, she revised a sentence to provide sentence variety. Her revised sentence is circled.

"Don't give until it hurts, but give until it feels good" is a statement that accurately describes how an individual should volunteer. These services should provide the satisfaction of knowing that the volunteer has made a difference in someone's life. Similarly, community service activities serve as a learning tool for those involved. Why Although traditional teaching techniques require students to sit in a classroom and study from books or that which is written on a traditional chalkboard when community service projects give individuals hands-on experiences ?

Revising Your Word Choice

Revise Informal Language

The words you choose can influence the power of your essay. Using slang and informal language can mean that your writing may not be taken seriously. Instead, use formal language that reflects the seriousness of your topic.

Informal Language

The town dump has to be cleaned up before it makes everyone really sick.

Formal Language

Conditions at the town's garbage collection center must be made more sanitary before it poses a health risk for residents.

⚙ Grammar and Style Tip

Use a thesaurus to come up with alternative, more formal word choices for your persuasive writing.

Peer Review

Use Point/Counterpoint

Anticipating counterarguments can strengthen your editorial. Share your revised draft with a partner who takes on the role of the opposition. Together, make a list of the main points in your writing. Then, ask your partner to come up with counter-points, or opposing arguments for these points.

When your partner has finished, find evidence to weaken the opposition's argument. Incorporate that evidence into your draft to strengthen your own argument.

▶ Critical Viewing
Why is it useful to work with a peer while revising? **[Reflect]**

Editing and Proofreading

Before you revise your final draft, proofread your writing, and correct errors in grammar, spelling, and punctuation.

Focusing on Spelling

Your readers will equate careless writing with a careless argument. Make sure that your persuasive essay is free of spelling errors. As you proofread, look for words you frequently misspell, as well as words with tricky endings, such as -*ance* and -*ence*.

Grammar in Your Writing
Words That End in -*ance* and -*ence*

Word endings that sound similar are sometimes difficult to spell. Among the most misspelled word endings are -*ance* and -*ence*.

If a noun ends in -*ance*, the corresponding adjective will end in -*ant*. If the noun ends in -*ence*, the corresponding adjective will end in -*ent*.

abundance/abundant   independence/independent

> **Common Words Ending in -*ance*:** abundance; acquaintance; appearance; brilliance; defiance; importance; radiance; resonance; romance; tolerance

> **Common Words Ending in -*ence*:** absence; convenience; correspondence; difference; excellence; independence; patience; presence; reference; violence

Find It in Your Reading Read the persuasive essays by Ellen Goodman and George Will on pages 126–129. Within them, find two words that end in -*ance* and two that end in -*ence*. Practice writing and spelling those words.

Find It in Your Writing As you proofread your essay, check to be sure that you have spelled words ending in -*ance* and -*ence* correctly.

For more on spelling word endings, see Chapter 30.

7.6 Publishing and Presenting

Building Your Portfolio

The purpose of persuasive writing is to influence your audience. To achieve this goal, find a way to share your work with others. Below are a few possibilities for presenting your finished work:

1. **School Paper** If the topic of your persuasive writing is school- or community-related, publish it in your school newspaper.
2. **Local Newspaper** The editorial page of your local newspaper is a place to make your voice heard. Contact the paper for the proper procedures for submitting a letter to the editor, and revise your writing to conform to the newspaper's guidelines.

Reflecting on Your Writing

Once you have completed your persuasive essay, reflect on the experience of writing it. Answer the following questions, and record your responses in your portfolio:

- What did you discover about your topic as you wrote about it?
- What did you learn about the process of writing persuasively? Can you apply what you learned to other types of writing?

 **Internet Tip**

To see persuasive essays scored with this rubric, go on-line:
PHSchool.com
Enter Web Code:
eek-1001

Rubric for Self-Assessment

Use the following criteria to evaluate your persuasive writing:

	Score 4	Score 3	Score 2	Score 1
Audience and Purpose	Demonstrates effective word choice; clearly states focus on persuasive task	Demonstrates good word choice; states focus on persuasive task	Shows some good word choices; minimally states focus on persuasive task	Shows lack of attention to persuasive task
Organization	Uses clear, consistent organizational strategy	Uses clear organizational strategy with occasional inconsistencies	Uses inconsistent organizational strategy; illogically presented	Lacks organizational strategy
Elaboration	Provides specific, well-elaborated reasons that support the writer's position	Provides two or more moderately elaborated reasons to support the writer's position	Provides several reasons, but only one is elaborated	Provides no specific reasons or elaboration
Use of Language	Incorporates many transitions to provide clarity of expression; has very few mechanical errors	Incorporates some transitions to help flow of ideas; has few mechanical errors	Incorporates few transitions; does not connect ideas well; has many mechanical errors	Fails to connect ideas; has many mechanical errors

Student Work
IN PROGRESS

FINAL DRAFT

Volunteering Is Vital

Sharon Goldberg
Miami-Palmetto High School
Pinecrest, Florida

▲ **Critical Viewing**
How well do the volunteers in this photograph seem to be working as a team? Explain. **[Evaluate]**

Reading a book to a blind person, feeding a debilitated patient in a nursing home, and tutoring a young child are all examples of community service projects. Such projects not only help others, they also help build feelings of self-worth and gratification in the volunteer. By serving others, volunteers acquire knowledge and wisdom. In fact, volunteering is an important part of life and growing up.

Using parallel structure in the essay's opening sentence helps Sharon grab the attention of her audience. Her main point is revealed at the end of the intro-duction.

The importance of volunteerism is starting to catch on. Many local high schools, for example, are making volunteer service in a community project a requirement for graduation. In one scenario, students may assist at a hospital or nursing facility. In another, students may help refurbish a local playground. Students are encouraged to work as much as possible, as long as it does not interfere with their schoolwork. As the saying goes, "Don't give until it hurts; give until it feels good!"

Sharon gives examples to illustrate the types of community service projects that exist.

Similarly, community service projects serve as learning tools for those involved. Although classroom study is important, community service projects give individuals hands-on experience. Through such experiences, volunteers learn about real-life situations. How so? For example, helping to build a house for an impoverished family gives the volunteer a greater sense of what it is like to give (the volunteering experience) and to receive (the thanks of the new homeowner). At the same time, volunteers are acquiring life skills, such as learning how to put up drywall and how to operate a power saw. Learning to work as part of the home-building team provides the volunteer with an experience that will most likely be cherished forever.

Specific examples of the benefits of volunteering help Sharon support her argument.

In addition, the performance of community service provides students with the opportunity to become familiar with potential careers. If a student wanted to pursue an acting career, what could be more appropriate than volunteering at a local theater? If a teenager is interested in becoming a veterinarian, why not spend time working in an animal shelter? Volunteering is like a blank canvas; how one fills the space for the enrichment of others can be determined only by the interests of the giver and the needs of the community.

This essay is organized aspect by aspect: Sharon examines different aspects of the benefits of volunteering in successive paragraphs.

Although many people associate volunteering with working at a hospital, anyone can use a helping hand. People do not need to be poor or infirm to welcome assistance. A beautification project in which community members assist the police department in painting over graffiti is an example, as is helping out at a soup kitchen or tutoring younger children.

Using sentences of various lengths helps keep Sharon's writing interesting.

Some people avoid community service; they would rather give money and not get personally involved. Community service, however, can furnish volunteers with self-fulfillment, gratification, and peace, knowing that they have helped to make a difference. This is one reason that so many people take part in volunteering activities in later life. Volunteerism provides senior citizens with a purpose, which, in turn, promotes their happiness and satisfaction with life even after retirement.

Just think how wonderful your community could be if you and your peers take the time to volunteer. Serve meals to the hungry. Plant a tree in the park. Pick up garbage by the lake. Aside from feeling great about yourself, you will have helped someone in need, helped your community look better, and helped yourself become a mature, contributing member of society.

In the essay's final paragraph, Sharon sums up her argument and restates her main idea—that volunteerism is an important part of life.

Connected Assignment
Editorial

Like persuasive essays and speeches, **editorials** are a form of persuasion that allows people to share their opinions. In editorials, writers express their ideas about current events or political issues. In some instances, editorials are written to reveal an organization's official position on an issue. Editorials may appear in newspapers, in journals, on radio, or on television.

An effective editorial
- clearly states the writer's position on an issue.
- contains details that support the writer's opinion.
- uses a respectful yet persuasive tone.
- is brief and to the point.
- is logically and effectively organized.

Write your own editorial on a current issue that interests you. Use the following strategies to help you:

Prewriting

Choosing Your Topic To find a topic for your editorial, scan the editorial page of the newspaper or listen to an editorial on the television news. You can also talk to family members or friends about issues currently in the news. Think about the opinions people present, and note your reactions. Then, review the issues, and choose one to form the heart of your editorial.

Narrowing Your Topic Your topic should be narrow enough to address fully in your editorial. For example, you should be able to reveal your opinion in a single thesis statement. For help narrowing your topic, make a list of the various aspects of your broad topic. Then, choose one of those aspects as your focus.

Gathering Details Once your topic is narrow enough, gather details to support your opinion or main idea. If you quote outside sources, make sure that they are reputable and unbiased. To add variety to the details you use as support, find examples of the following: quotations, historical events, statistical data, expert testimonies, and personal observations.

Drafting Adopt a firm and persuasive tone as you draft. Keep your audience in mind by defining any terms readers may not know and providing necessary background information. Refer to your prewriting plan as you present your position, and support it with details. Show that you care about your topic by bringing it to life with vivid verbs and precise nouns.

Revising and Editing Check your editorial to be sure that it is free of faulty logic such as bandwagon appeals (Everyone's doing it, so you should too!); circular reasoning (Rain forests should be preserved because it's important to preserve them.); and loaded language (Don't be a loser; buy Chooser!).

Read your editorial critically, and add details where needed. Delete details if they are unnecessary or beside the point. To get a fresh perspective on the effectiveness of your writing, consult a peer editor, and take his or her comments into consideration as you revise.

Carefully proofread your editorial, and correct any errors you find in grammar, spelling, and punctuation. Also, check to be sure that you have cited the quotation correctly and consistently and correctly spelled the names of experts or sources. Use the chart at right to help guide your editing.

Publishing and Presenting
Neatly print out a copy of your editorial. Share it with friends, or send it to the editors of your school newspaper and ask them to publish it on their Op Ed page.

> ## Editing Tips
>
> ☑ **Experts:** *If you quoted experts in your editorial, be sure their names, positions, and organizational affiliations are properly spelled and capitalized.*
>
> ☑ **Titles:** *Whether it's a newspaper, book, or periodical, make sure that any titles you mentioned are formatted correctly.*
>
> ☑ **Names: Edwin or Edward?** *Don't take a guess at people's names. Be sure instead. If necessary, call back interview subjects to double-check spellings and personal information.*
>
> ☑ **Addresses:** *Confirm that all addresses are correct and properly punctuated.*

Spotlight on the Humanities

Recognizing Messages in Art

Focus on Art: *Snap the Whip*

Persuasion comes in many forms—speeches, essays, television ads, and even works of art. One such persuasive painting is *Snap the Whip* by Winslow Homer. It was painted in 1872, after the Civil War. During this time, reformers in education promoted free, unbridled development of children, as opposed to strict discipline and demands for obedience. Homer's message in *Snap the Whip* reflects this new ideology of the educational reformers. In the painting, the boys are running free, and the little red schoolhouse in the background symbolizes a more innocent era.

Snap the Whip, 1872, Winslow Homer

▲ **Critical Viewing**
What overall message is conveyed in this painting? **[Interpret]**

Literature Connection Authors throughout the years have used the pen to address injustices and to advocate reform. Charles Dickens was among the most influential novelists to use his novels and characters to make persuasive points. In *Hard Times*, for example, Dickens lampoons the educational practices of the day through the characters of Gradgrind and M'Choakumchild.

Music Connection Persuasive messages are often transmitted through song. From "Yankee Doodle," which dates back to the Revolutionary War, to the sixties anthem "The Times They Are A-Changin'," songs combine the power of music with the power of words, giving listeners something to think about.

Persuasive Writing Application: Multigenre Persuasive Message

Persuasion can appear in art, music, song, and poetry. Think of a persuasive message you would like to convey about an issue that matters to you. Do research on the issue. Then, produce a multigenre project in which you convey your message in three or more forms. For example, you may create a piece of art that conveys your persuasive theme, design a public-service announcement that has the same message, and follow up with a poem exploring that same idea. Share your multigenre persuasive project with others in your class.

Media and Technology Skills

Recognizing Persuasion in the Media

Activity: Identify Persuasive Strategies in Commercials

Media researchers estimate that the average American views close to 20,000 television commercials every year. Even if you watch less television than most people, chances are good that you sit through thousands of carefully produced advertisements. Identifying the persuasive techniques in commercials can help you become an active viewer and resist the powerful pull of these advertisements.

Think About It Think about the last five items you purchased. Consider how your buying decisions were affected by advertising. Then, evaluate your satisfaction with each product. Compare your expectations with the actual performance of each item.

Describe It Conduct a viewing survey of at least five television commercials. Begin by describing the basic elements of each commercial. Use a chart like the one below to help you.

Product	Setting	Actors	Events/Plot	Special Features
Stone-washed jeans	A high-school parking lot after school	Five teenagers, all wearing the product	Kids are carrying backpacks and kidding around.	Camera keeps shifting back to the jeans; emphasizes that the jeans make the kids popular

Analyze It After describing each commercial, study how the elements work together to persuade an audience. Draw a conclusion about why the advertisers chose this strategy to appeal to an audience. You may analyze commercials that use some of these strategies:

- **Testimonials** add glamour to a product's image. Recommendations from "real-life" people make an ad's claims seem more believable.

- **Bandwagon appeals** rely on peer pressure to encourage buyers to join a trend.

- **Identity advertising** promotes specific appeals that have more to do with lifestyles than with product qualities.

Publish It Start a Media Watch column for your class or school newspaper. Each column can analyze current commercials and expose the persuasive techniques at work.

Check Your TV Pulse

Find out how your viewing habits compare with those of the average American teenager. Keep an exact record of your television viewing for one week. Then, compare your results with the information in the chart below.

TV Viewing Habits/Ages 12–17
- M–F, 10 A.M. to 4:30 P.M.: 1 hr., 46 min.
- M–F, 4:30 P.M. to 7:30 P.M.: 2 hr., 51 min.
- M–Sun, 8 P.M. to 11 P.M.: 6 hr., 2 min.
- Sat. 7 A.M. to 1 P.M.: 38 min.
- M–F, 11:30 P.M. to 1 A.M.: 46 min.
- * Source: World Almanac Book of Facts, 1999

Standardized Test Preparation Workshop

Responding to Persuasive Writing Prompts

Some persuasive writing prompts on standardized tests examine your ability to present, argue, and defend a position. You must clearly state your position and support it with specific examples, reasons, or details. You will be evaluated on your ability to do the following:

- Develop a clearly stated position in response to the essay prompt.
- Identify and include compelling details suited to the essay's audience and purpose.
- Organize ideas in a logical way, and express them with effective language.
- Use correct grammar, spelling, and punctuation.

As you generate standardized test responses, rely on the basic writing process stages—prewriting, drafting, revising, editing, and proofreading—to lead you through the task. Be aware, however, of how much time you are allotted for completing your response.

Below is an example of a typical standardized test persuasive writing prompt. Before developing your response, read the tips on the next page. Also, note the time-planning suggestions on the clocks next to each stage.

Test Tip

When writing a persuasive test response, make sure to state your position clearly. Choose reasons and language that are appropriate to the specified audience.

Sample Writing Situation

> Many schools have budget issues that require a choice to be made between one service or program and another. Your school board is planning to cut one school program in order to stay within next year's budget. In a letter to the board, explain which program you think is least valuable and might be cut in order to maintain other programs. Support your position with convincing reasons, facts, and examples.

Prewriting

Allow about one quarter of your time for shaping your argument and identifying supporting details.

Look at Both Sides Quickly jot down your ideas in a pro-and-con chart to help you see both sides of the issue. This will help you solidify your own argument and develop reasons that address those who would argue in favor of keeping the program you suggest eliminating.

Support Your Ideas Look at your notes to identify details that will influence your audience of board members. Your goal is to persuade your audience to agree with your ideas, not to attack people who hold opposing views. Come up with supporting details or reasons that are specific and effective but not inflammatory.

Drafting

Allow about half of your time for drafting. Leave space for text you may want to insert when revising.

Begin, Develop, and Conclude As you draft, write an introduction that reveals your purpose and main idea. Also, in your introduction, establish your tone and get the audience "on your side." Then, in the body of the essay, develop your argument. Give reasons that your audience should agree with you. Summarize your most important points, and restate your main idea in your conclusion.

Craft Your Language Effective persuasion contains not only credible ideas but high-impact language. Choose vivid verbs, nouns, and adjectives that engage readers in your essay. Mix punchy, short sentences with longer, more elaborate language for variety.

Revising, Editing, and Proofreading

Allow almost one quarter of your time for revising and editing. In the last few minutes, proofread carefully.

Verify Your Response Reread the test prompt to be sure that you have fully and completely responded to it. If you have not, revise your letter to make sure that it addresses the prompt.

Review Your Tone Read over your work, and listen to its tone. Replace words that have negative connotations, and delete critical language that may alienate undecided readers. If time allows, recopy your work neatly. Otherwise, carefully insert changes to your draft.

Correct the Errors Work steadily and carefully to review your essay for spelling and punctuation errors. Sometimes, reading backward makes these errors easier to spot. Make all changes with proofreader's marks and neatly drawn deletion lines.

Persuasion
Advertisement

Advertisements in Everyday Life

Advertisements are all around you. For example, when you watch television, you probably spend at least fifteen minutes every hour watching commercials—advertisements of various companies pitching their products. Advertisements also appear on magazines and billboards and even on T-shirts and hats. In recent years, ads have become common sights on the Internet as well, blinking and winking to grab the attention of those surfing the Web.

▲ Critical Viewing
Judging from this photograph, why might it be important for an advertisement to be eye-catching?
[Connect]

What Is an Advertisement?

An **advertisement** is a persuasive message paid for by an individual or company. Ads attempt to persuade people to buy something, accept an idea, vote for a candidate, or support a cause.

Advertisements take many forms—from media ads on television and radio to print ads in newspapers, magazines, and flyers to creative visual ads, such as skywriting or walking billboards.

Most effective advertisements contain

- a slogan or catchy phrase that grabs the audience's attention.
- reasons the customer should purchase the product or service.
- details that tell who to call or where to purchase the product or service.

To preview the criteria upon which your advertisement may be evaluated, see the Rubric for Self-Assessment on page 164.

Writers in **ACTION**

As a person who did fund-raising for and advanced the ideas of the Asia Society in New York City, Sayu Bhojwani has firsthand experience writing persuasively:

"The most important aspect of persuasive writing is to be able to convey to your reader a certain emotion or concept. In the type of work that I do, it's usually a concept.... We want to convey a sense of innovation and newness, to get a reader in."

Types of Advertisements

Although most people think of advertising as only commercial ads used to sell consumer products, advertisements can take many forms:

- **Public-service announcements,** sent out by nonprofit organizations, discuss topics such as public safety or health.
- **Merchandise ads** are print, broadcast, or visual messages about products that consumers can purchase.
- **Service ads** are print, broadcast, or visual messages about services—cleaning, entertaining, or self-improvement.

PREVIEW *Student Work* **IN PROGRESS**

In this chapter, you'll follow the progress of Ever Chapa, a student at La Joya High School in La Joya, Texas, as he drafts an advertisement for a college fair. Follow along as Ever uses prewriting, drafting, and revising strategies to develop his ad. Ever's completed advertisement appears at the end of the chapter.

Model From Literature

The following advertisement appeared in a magazine about nature and travel.

This advertisement contains an interesting use of language. The text is like a recipe that creates something wonderful—Costa Rica.

This statistic is presented in an appealing way.

Parallel structure runs through this advertisement: Each sentence is an imperative.

The ad's tag line—no artifical ingredients—continues the recipe metaphor.

Reading Writing Connection

Writing Application: Use Creative Language
You'll notice that the ad above contains creative use of language. As you prepare to write your own ad, think about creative ways you can use language.

8.2 *Prewriting*

Choosing Your Topic

You can write an advertisement for a product, a political candidate, or a service. Use the following strategies to help you come up with a topic for your advertisement:

Strategies for Generating Topics

1. **Conduct a Survey** Ask the following survey question: What gift would you most like to receive for your birthday? Review the responses, and choose one to form the topic of your advertisement.

2. **Blueprint** Draw the floor plan of a room in your everyday environment. Fill the room of your drawing with appropriate gadgets, clothes, or art objects. As you draw the items, decide which object appeals to you most. Make that one the subject of your advertisement.

Try it out! Use the interactive Blueprint activity in **Section 8.2**, on-line or on CD-ROM.

TOPIC BANK

If you need a specific topic for your advertisement, follow these suggestions:

1. **Advertisement for a School Function** Write and design a poster publicizing a school music festival.

Responding to Literature

2. In the ancient Greek tragedy *Antigone*, a woman defies the order of a stern king and gives her dead brother an appropriate burial. Think of images from this or another play that would make an exciting poster for a theatrical production. Then, create such a poster. You can read *Antigone* in *Prentice Hall Literature: Timeless Voices, Timeless Themes*, Platinum.

☑ Cooperative Writing Opportunity

3. With a partner, create a short list of favorite television or radio ads. Choose one that you both like, and write another ad for that product. Display your ad in your classroom.

Narrowing Your Topic

An advertisement should almost always have a narrow focus: Most effective ads are short and memorable. To narrow your topic for your advertisement, answer the following questions:

- What product/person/service am I selling or promoting?
- What is the one thing I'd like to communicate to my audience about this product/person/service?

As you draft your ad, refer to your responses to ensure that your focus has remained narrow.

Considering Your Audience and Purpose

As you think about the advertisement you are going to write, consider whom it is you are trying to persuade. Then, decide on the language and details that will impress them most.

Choose Your Words Carefully

One way to achieve your purpose is to choose words that will most appeal to your audience. Select your words carefully, taking into consideration their denotation and connotation. A word's *denotation* is its dictionary meaning. Its *connotation* is the positive or negative association the word conjures up. In your ad, take advantage of a word's connotation as well as its denotation.

Audience: Sporty Women

Audience: Romantic Women

Gathering Details

Put yourself in the place of your audience. Then, answer the questions you, as the audience, have about the product, service, or person you are promoting. Be sure to answer those questions somewhere in the advertisement you write.

Gather Details for a Product
- What is it?
- What makes it special or different?
- How much does it cost?
- Where can I buy it?

Gather Details for a Campaign
- What are his or her qualifications?
- What is his or her stand on ___?___?
- Who else supports this candidate?

Gather Details for an Event
- Who is sponsoring the event?
- Where is the event to be held? At what time?
- How much is the cost of admission?

Student Work
IN PROGRESS

Name: *Ever Chapa*
La Joya High School
La Joya, TX

Gathering Details for an Event
Because Ever was writing an ad for an event, he made a list of questions his audience would want answered.

Who? **Representatives from colleges**

What? **College fair**

When? **Saturday, August 9, 2000**
12:00 P.M. to 8:00 P.M.

Where? **Westside Lake Park**

Why? **To provide information about colleges, tuition, courses, requirements, etc.**

How much? **Free**

Drafting

Shaping Your Writing

When drafting your ad, be sure to grab the audience's attention right away. To do this, start with the most appealing characteristic of the product.

Order Details From Most Important to Least Important

Know what is most important to your audience, and tell them about that up front. Then, follow with details that your audience will also want to know.

In the advertisement at right, details are arranged in descending order of importance: The most important detail is that the lawn service is half price. The least important detail is that referrals are available.

Providing Elaboration

Include Testimonials, Statistics, and Graphics

Elaborate your advertisement, using pictures, quotations, and facts that will convince your audience of your product's superiority:

Testimonials are quotes from satisfied users:

Mary Kay Louis of Denver, Colorado, says "I'll never leave home without my Timetip wristwatch!"

Statistics are numerical facts that favor the use of the product or service being advertised:

More than 70 percent of the people polled by Dennton University say that they'd like to try a Timetip wristwatch.

Attractive graphics could include photographs of people using your product or service, diagrams that show the benefits of your product, or illustrations of the product or service.

8.4 *Revising*

Revising Your Overall Structure

Prominently Place the Main Idea

In most advertisements, the most important idea occupies the most prominent place. (If your advertisement is written for radio, you will probably want to lead off with your most important idea.)

▶ **REVISION STRATEGY**
Experimenting With Placement of Your Main Idea

Critically examine the layout of your advertisement, and juggle the placement of your most important idea until it achieves the maximum impact.

Revising Your Paragraphs

▶ **REVISION STRATEGY**
Circling the Important Details

Trim unnecessary information from your paragraphs so that every detail and concept is essential to the message and its delivery. To do this, circle the most important details and delete uncircled material.

Student Work IN PROGRESS

Name: *Ever Chapa*
La Joya High School
La Joya, TX

Circling Important Details

Ever Chapa circled the most important details in his advertisement. Then, he deleted or rewrote the uncircled details.

(Attention all SENIORS!) ~~You know who you are.~~ (Come join the fun) at the first annual Bash at the Lake. ~~Who said getting the scoop on what colleges have to offer you has to be boring?~~ (Come out and learn more about local scholarships and grants.)

Revising Your Sentences

Vary Sentence Types

Any writing is more enjoyable and engaging when its rhythms vary. By varying sentence type, you vary the rhythm of your prose. There are four basic sentence types: declarative, interrogative, exclamatory, and imperative.

▶ **REVISION STRATEGY**
Color-Coding End Marks

Read through your draft, and use a colored pen or pencil to call out various end marks. By doing this, you'll be able to see whether, for example, you have mostly declarative or imperative sentences, interrogative sentences, or exclamatory sentences.

First, draw a circle around periods, a square around question marks, and triangles around exclamation marks. Then, review your draft. If you have too many end marks of one shape, you may want to vary your sentence types to make your advertisement more interesting to read.

Student Work
IN PROGRESS

Name: _Ever Chapa_
La Joya High School
La Joya, TX

Coding to Identify Sentence Types

When Ever reviewed his draft, he found that too many of his sentences were declarative. He made the following changes to enliven his writing and keep the interest of his audience.

BASH AT THE LAKE

Attention all seniors !

What's happening with your future?

Come to the first annual Bash at the Lake to find out!
Learn about various colleges and what they have to offer

YOU

Why not Get the *real scoop* on local

scholarships and grants?

Create Parallel Structure

Although it can be effective to vary your sentence types in an advertisement, you can make your advertisement memorable if you create parallel structure by repeating sentence types for effect. In the following example, three interrogative sentences are followed by an exclamatory sentence to create an impact.

EXAMPLE: Is your breakfast cereal boring? Is it bland? Is it full of sugar? Then, try Crackle, a new type of cereal that is sure to enliven your mornings!

▶**REVISION STRATEGY**
Extending an Idea
Read through your draft, and locate an idea that you'd like to emphasize. Then, build on that idea by creating short sentences of the same type to make the idea memorable to readers.

Grammar in Your Writing
The Four Functions of Sentences

Just as sentences can have varied structures, they can have varied functions as well. Try to include declarative, interrogative, exclamatory, and imperative sentences in your writing.

The Four Functions of Sentences Every sentence fulfills one of the following four functions:

Declarative—a sentence that makes a statement
Example: This product whitens and brightens your teeth.

Interrogative—a sentence that asks a question
Example: Do you need a new bicycle?

Exclamatory—a sentence that expresses strong emotion
Example: Try our great-tasting soup!

Imperative—a sentence that gives a command
Example: Be the first to buy this product.

Find It in Your Writing Review your draft to identify sentences that fulfill each of the four functions. Be sure that you have used the appropriate end marks. If you cannot identify all four functions, challenge yourself to add at least one more to your writing.

To learn more about types of sentences, see Chapter 21.

Revising Your Word Choice

In advertising, you want to keep your sentences short and powerful. You don't want to use too many words, so choose carefully. Verbs, especially, can help you stimulate the readers' imagination or motivate them to do something.

▶ REVISION STRATEGY
Replace Dull Words

When you want to attract attention, use verbs that vividly describe the action you want readers to take.

	DULL VERBS	VIVID VERBS
Example:	*Get* into our car.	*Jump* into our car.
Example:	*See* Williamsburg, Virginia, and *see* the eighteenth century.	*Come* to Williamsburg, Virginia, and *relive* the eighteenth century.

Peer Review

Question a Peer

With a partner, exchange advertisement drafts. Then, have your partner answer the following questions, or create questions of your own that you'd like to have answered.

- What is the main idea conveyed by my advertisement?
- Do any images within the ad seem distasteful? If so, which?
- Which words seem weak or inappropriate? What replacements do you suggest?
- Is any information left out of the ad that you would like to know? If so, what?
- Does my ad need to be enlivened with graphics, charts, or photographs? What type would be effective?
- If you could change one thing about my advertisement, what would it be?

Review the responses of your partner. Then, incorporate changes into your ad, and review it again.

Get instant help! For assistance in replacing dull words, use the Word Bins, accessible from the menu bar, on-line or on CD-ROM.

8.5 *Editing and Proofreading*

Correct Use of *Your* and *You're*

Homophones—words that sound the same—are sometimes used incorrectly. For example, you might write the contraction *you're* instead of the possessive *your*. Read through your advertisement carefully to make sure that you have chosen the correct homophones.

EXAMPLE: These walking shoes are made for you're comfort.
CORRECT: These walking shoes are made for your comfort.

EXAMPLE: Your going to notice the cushioned insole.
CORRECT: You're going to notice the cushioned insole.

Grammar in Your Writing
Homophones

Homophones are words that sound the same but have different spellings and meanings. Some homophones that are commonly confused include the following:

It's	Its	
By	Buy	
Who's	Whose	
To	Too	Two

Find It in Your Reading Find a homophone in the advertisement on page 154. Then, write down the related homophones and their meanings.

Find It in Your Writing As you proofread your advertisement, check that you have written all homophones correctly.

For more on spelling homophones, see Chapter 30.

Publishing and Presenting

Building Your Portfolio

Use the following suggestions for sharing your advertisement:

1. **Post It** If your advertisement is for a real product or service, get permission to post it throughout your school or in your community.
2. **Record It** Rework your advertisement for radio presentation. Add sound effects and tape-record your efforts. Play the ad for your peers.

Reflecting on Your Writing

Consider the experience of writing your advertisement. Then, answer the following questions, and record your responses in your portfolio.

- In the process of writing, what did you learn about how you relate to your audience?
- Which strategies for prewriting, drafting, revising, or editing might you recommend to a friend?

 **Internet Tip**

To see an advertisement scored with this rubric, go on-line:
PHSchool.com
Enter Web Code:
eek-1001

Rubric for Self-Assessment

Use the following criteria to evaluate your advertisement.

	Score 4	Score 3	Score 2	Score 1
Audience and Purpose	Presents effective slogan; clearly addresses persuasive task	Presents good slogan; addresses persuasive task	Presents slogan; minimally addresses persuasive task	Does not present slogan; shows lack of attention to persuasive task
Organization	Uses clear, consistent organizational strategy	Uses clear organizational strategy with few inconsistencies	Uses inconsistent organizational strategy; creates illogical presentation	Demonstrates lack of organizational strategy; creates confusing presentation
Elaboration	Successfully combines words and images to provide convincing, unified support for a position	Combines words and images to provide unified support for a position	Includes some words or images that detract from a position	Uses words and images that do not support a position
Use of Language	Successfully communicates an idea through clever use of language; includes very few mechanical errors	Conveys an idea through adequate use of language; includes few mechanical errors	Misuses language and lessens impact of ideas; includes many mechanical errors	Demonstrates poor use of language and confuses meaning; includes many mechanical errors

FINAL DRAFT

Ever Chapa
La Joya High School
La Joya, Texas

BASH AT THE LAKE

Attention all seniors!

Representatives from more than
ninety colleges!
Five hot bands!
Food!

Westside Lake Park
Saturday, August 9, 2000
12:00 P.M. to 8:00 P.M.

Free of charge for everyone

High-school seniors are encouraged to attend.
(10 Senior Points for those who come!!!)
Parents are also encouraged to attend.

Come join the fun at the first annual **BASH AT THE LAKE.**

Learn about various colleges and what they have to offer YOU.

Get the *real scoop* on local scholarships and grants.

Capital letters emphasize the main idea.

Details that make the event more attractive are featured to the side of the main ad.

Colorful text emphasizes the time and place of the event.

Ever used boldface text to highlight the fact that the event is free.

Colloquial terms like "real scoop" appeal to the audience of high-school students.

Connected Assignment
Flyer

A flyer is an advertisement that is printed on a sheet of paper. Flyers vary in complexity from a simple photocopied piece of paper to a high-gloss, printed color piece, but the basic features are the same. Flyers are delivered by hand or through the mail. They convey current information about a product or service and seek to grab readers' attention on the spot.

An example of a flyer appears below. Use the writing process tips suggested on the next page to create your own flyer.

▲ Critical Viewing
What use would a flyer, such as the one shown here, serve at a job fair? [Connect]

GET YOUR CAR WASHED!

On Saturday, May 15th, come over to Yallum High School to get your car washed.

From 10:00 A.M. to 4:00 P.M.
South Parking Lot
(behind the stadium)
Each car wash costs $5.00

Proceeds benefit the High-School Marching Band.
We need: New uniforms, Sheet music, Money for our band trip...

Sponsored by the Music Boosters Assoc.

Prewriting Skim through the handouts you've received at school this week, or ask the office to show you some examples. Then, think about activities or events that you might need to advertise to others. Also, think about products or services available that classmates might find useful.

Having no more space available than a page printed on both sides, you must give your message a focus. Use an inverted pyramid chart to narrow your topic until you can state the main message in one sentence. Then, brainstorm for adjectives and vivid verbs that capture the excitement of your product or service.

Mindy's is a great new restaurant serving our town. It offers wonderful burgers and shakes. Its prices are reasonable, and the service is terrific.

Mindy's has great food and service.

Eat at Mindy's.

Drafting People will look at your flyer for just a second before deciding to read it or toss it. Grab them in that instant with powerful language and engaging visuals. Reshape your prewriting sentence into a slogan or headline. Then, use sound devices such as alliteration (repeated initial consonants) to help your message stick with your readers.

Revising and Editing Study your flyer from a distance to make sure that its visual appeal works. Make sure that your text is large enough to read quickly and that all the key information is easily accessible. Add vivid verbs that lend zest to your language and present your product or service in the most positive light.

Publishing and Presenting Photocopy your flyer. Then, hand out copies to friends, and get their reactions to the information printed on it.

Technology Tip

Become familiar with the features of your word-processing software. Then, use features like centering text, boldfacing, and adding bullets to enhance the appearance of your flyer.

Spotlight on the Humanities

Recognizing Theater Connections

Focus on Theater: *A Funny Thing Happened on the Way to the Forum*

Before a play or film opens, it is usually backed by an ad campaign promoting it to guarantee that an audience will support it. In fact, one of the most successful forms of persuasion is advertising—convincing an audience that a performance or product is something they must see or purchase. Winner of five Tony Awards, the musical *A Funny Thing Happened on the Way to the Forum* opened on Broadway on May 8, 1962. Based on the writings of the ancient Roman playwright Plautus, the music and lyrics were written by Stephen Sondheim, and the book was created by Burt Shevelove and Larry Gelbart. The writers, hoping to give Broadway a taste of what once delighted ancient Roman audiences, carefully studied all twenty-one of Plautus' surviving comedies and then created their own original story, drawing characters and situations freely from many of the old scripts.

▲ **Critical Viewing**
Judging from this photograph, what sort of play is *A Funny Thing Happened on the Way to the Forum?* Explain. [**Speculate**]

Literature Connection Born Titus Maccius Plautus (ca. 254–184 B.C.), this Roman playwright first worked as a stagehand. He may have acted, also. At least 130 plays were attributed to Plautus, and 21 of these were authentically his own.

Art Connection The Forum Romanum in the city of Rome lies between the Palatine and Capitoline hills. Used as a location for public meetings and courts of law, the Forum was also a center for shopping and open-air markets. It was also the site of several monuments. Among the monuments lies the tomb of Romulus, the founder of Rome.

Persuasive Writing Activity: Advertisement for Current Play or Film

A Funny Thing Happened on the Way to the Forum enjoyed another successful run on Broadway in 1997 and 1998, thanks to its reputation and an aggressive advertising campaign that boasted top-name celebrities in the title roles. Choose a film or play that is currently being performed, and write an advertisement for it that will be sure to bring audiences flocking to the theaters.

Media and Technology Skills

Using Technology to Extend Meaning

Activity: Enhance a Print Piece

In bookstores, thousands of books compete for your attention. An effective cover can make one book stand out from the crowd. You can apply visual strategies to enhance any writing project. A word processor or page-layout program can help you to increase visual impact and appeal. To enhance an advertisement, brochure, or other writing, become familiar with the features offered by the programs you use most frequently.

Think About It Choose a writing project that you would like to publish in a more elaborate format. Think about how visual imagery can help you reach a wider audience, and choose a relevant format. For example, you might turn a personal advertisement into a brochure or a short story into a small booklet.

Lay It Out Choose a layout that is appropriate for the format you have chosen. You might consider these layouts:

- newspaper style, with headlines and several articles per page
- magazine style, with headlines and one article per page
- brochures, created by folding two-sided printouts
- newsletter style, with headlines and two or three columns of text

Display It After choosing your layout, decide what type styles, or fonts, you will use. Some fonts are designed to be used for headlines; others are best used for running text. Headline fonts are often more detailed or ornate; text fonts should be clear and easy to read even in small sizes.

> **Printing Formats**
>
> You can turn an 8-1/2" x 11" sheet of paper into a professional-looking brochure by printing on both sides and then folding it. If you are planning to fold your work, lay out the columns so that they will follow the correct order when folded.

Example Font

Example Font

Illustrate It You can import a variety of images to add visual appeal. Consider importing digital photographs or artwork. You can create your own artwork using a graphics program, or you can find ready-made art in a clip art source.

Standardized Test Preparation Workshop

Analyzing Persuasive Texts

Standardized test questions often measure your ability to evaluate an advertisement. All advertisements, whether for political campaigns or consumer products, have the same goal—to get you to act. As an educated reader, you must look past the attempts to persuade to find the factual, relevant information. The following methods will help you evaluate an advertisement:

- Search for facts.
- See whether the argument or claim is supported.
- Check for missing information, vague statements, or partial truths.
- Recognize false conclusions and oversimplifications, such as overgeneralizations, loaded language, circular reasoning, questionable cause-and-effect statements, either/or arguments, or bandwagon appeals.

The following sample test items will give you practice with these types of questions.

Test Tip

When evaluating an advertisement, it is just as important to consider whether information has been left out as it is to weigh information that has been included.

Sample Test Items

Directions: Read the passage, and then choose the best answer to each question.

This week, only at Athletes' World locations in Dallas: *Striker* Athletic Shoes on sale! With *Striker* on your feet, you'll be a starter on your team!

1 What important information has been left out of this advertisement?
  A name brand of the shoes
  B time frame of the sale
  C name of the store where the sale is
  D price of shoes on sale

2 What type of unreasonable appeal does "With *Striker* on your feet, you'll be a starter on your team!" exemplify?
  A circular reasoning
  B bandwagon appeal
  C questionable cause and effect
  D overgeneralization

Answers and Explanations

The correct answer is *D*. The price of the shoes is not given in the ad.

The correct answer is *C*. The ad implies that the reader need only wear *Striker* shoes to be one of the best players on a sports team.

▶ **Practice 1** **Directions:** Read the passage, and then choose the letter of the best answer to each question.

There is a new craze hitting Harleville: RECYCLE TODAY!!! Before you throw away that soup can, before you trash that newspaper—think about our children. Money earned from recycling could be put toward a new city park. The Mayor, the City Council, and the Police Chief have all endorsed our new recycling program. Remember, neglecting our environment is neglecting our children! Let's all RECYCLE TODAY to give our children a new park tomorrow.

1 You can tell the writer is
  A indifferent to recycling
  B in favor of recycling
  C opposed to recycling
  D trying to endorse town officials

2 Which of the following is an example of loaded language—appealing to readers' fears or prejudices?
  F ". . . and the Police Chief have all endorsed . . . "
  G "Money earned from recycling could be put toward a new city park."
  H ". . . neglecting our environment is neglecting our children!"
  J none of the above

3 The author implies that the town of Harleville is
  A refusing to recycle
  B building a recycling plant
  C earning money from recycling
  D none of the above

4 Which of the following statements is an example of a partial truth?
  F "Let's all RECYCLE TODAY to give our children a new park tomorrow."
  G "before you trash that newspaper— think about our children"
  H "The City Council, . . . all endorsed our new recycling program."
  J none of the above

5 The statement, "There is a new craze hitting Harleville: RECYCLE TODAY!!!" is an example of which of the following types of persuasive reasoning?
  A circular reasoning
  B either/or argument
  C questionable cause and effect
  D bandwagon appeal

6 What fact does the author state in the article?
  F Money from recycling will be spent a new park.
  G Everyone in Harleville recycles.
  H The Police Chief has endorsed Harleville's recycling program.
  J A large amount of money will be earned from the recycling program.

7 What conclusion is NOT supported by information given in the article?
  A Some citizens of Harleville are recycling.
  B The recycling program includes tin cans and newspapers.
  C The author would like to raise money to build new parks.
  D The mayor of Harleville wants to use recycling revenue to build new parks.

Comparing and Contrasting in Everyday Life

Comparing and contrasting are processes that you perform every day. Whether you're deciding which movie to see or which jacket to buy, you analyze the similarities and differences between the choices and make judgments about the positive qualities or shortcomings of each one.

Developing your ability to compare and contrast is useful any time you have to make a major decision. When the time comes to decide which college to attend or which job offer to accept, being able to clearly assess your options will help you take the best possible course of action.

▲ Critical Viewing
What sort of features or qualities might these shoppers be comparing and contrasting? [Analyze]

What Is a Comparison-and-Contrast Essay?

To *compare* is to show how two or more things are similar. To *contrast* is to show how two or more things are different. An essay exploring the similarities and differences between two or more subjects is a **comparison-and-contrast essay.**

Most effective comparison-and-contrast essays contain

- two or more subjects that are being compared and contrasted.
- details that reveal the similarities and differences between the subjects.
- transitions that make relationships between the subjects clear.
- an effective structure, such as point-by-point or subject-by-subject organization.

To preview the criteria on which your comparison-and-contrast essay may be evaluated, see the Self-Assessment Rubric on page 188.

Types of Comparison-and-Contrast Essays

Topics for a comparison-and-contrast essay range widely. Following are some examples:

- significant events from history
- works of art, literature, or music
- lives and achievements of historical figures
- effects of different laws or policies

Writers in ACTION

Journalist and author Joseph Epstein considers himself lucky to have discovered at an early age that essay-writing was his preferred form of expression. He reveals the following insight about what makes essay-writing so appealing:

"Writing an essay has for me tended to be an act of self-discovery. By this I mean that I come to the writing of an essay not knowing what I think of the subject, except in an [unformed] way; or if I believe I know what I think, the writing itself leads me into aspects of the subject whose importance or even existence I hadn't earlier recognized."

PREVIEW *Student Work* **IN PROGRESS**

Follow the progress of Emily Agy, a student at Pleasant Valley High School, in Pleasant Valley, Iowa, as she drafts a newspaper article that explores the similarities and differences between life in the United States and life in England. The completed article appears at the end of the chapter.

Model From Literature

William Zinsser was for thirteen years an editor, critic, and editorial writer with the New York Herald Tribune. *He now teaches writing at the New School in New York City.*

Reading Strategy: Recognize Patterns
Recognizing how material is organized can help you to understand and evaluate it. As you read this essay, look at each paragraph's first line to see if the essay is ordered chronologically or in order of importance.

Two Writing Processes

William Zinsser

A school in Connecticut once held "a day devoted to the arts," and I was asked if I would come and talk about writing as a vocation. When I arrived I found that a second speaker had been invited—Dr. Brock (as I'll call him), a surgeon who had recently begun to write and had sold some stories to magazines. He was going to talk about writing as an avocation. That made us a panel, and we sat down to face a crowd of students and teachers and parents, all eager to learn the secrets of our glamorous work.

Dr. Brock was dressed in a bright red jacket, looking vaguely bohemian, as authors are supposed to look, and the first question went to him. What was it like to be a writer?

He said it was tremendous fun. Coming home from an arduous day at the hospital, he would go straight to his yellow pad and write his tensions away. The words just flowed. It was easy. I then said that writing wasn't easy and wasn't fun. It was hard and lonely, and the words seldom just flowed.

Next Dr. Brock was asked if it was important to rewrite. Absolutely not, he said. "Let it all hang out," he told us, and whatever form the sentences take will reflect the writer at his most natural. I then said that rewriting is the essence of writing. I pointed out that professional writers rewrite their sentences over and over and then rewrite what they have rewritten.

▲ **Critical Viewing**
For what type of writing might you use the type of pen pictured? Why? **[Assess]**

Early in the essay, it becomes apparent that Zinsser and Brock have different ideas about what it means to be a writer.

"What do you do on days when it isn't going well?" Dr. Brock was asked. He said he just stopped writing and put the work aside for a day when it would go better. I then said that the professional writer must establish a daily schedule and stick to it. I said that writing is a craft, not an art, and that the man who runs away from his craft because he lacks inspiration is fooling himself. He is also going broke.

"What if you're feeling depressed or unhappy?" a student asked. "Won't that affect your writing?"

Probably it will, Dr. Brock replied. Go fishing. Take a walk. Probably it won't, I said. If your job is to write every day, you learn to do it like any other job.

A student asked if we found it useful to circulate in the literary world. Dr. Brock said he was greatly enjoying his new life as a man of letters, and he told several stories of being taken to lunch by his publisher and his agent at Manhattan restaurants where writers and editors gather. I said that professional writers are solitary drudges who seldom see other writers.

"Do you put symbolism in your writing?" a student asked me.

"Not if I can help it," I replied. I have an unbroken record of missing the deeper meaning in any story, play or movie, and as for dance and mime, I have never had any idea of what is being conveyed.

"I *love* symbols!" Dr. Brock exclaimed, and he described with gusto the joys of weaving them through his work.

So the morning went, and it was a revelation to all of us. At the end Dr. Brock told me he was enormously interested in my answers—it had never occurred to him that writing could be hard. I told him I was just as interested in *his* answers—it had never occurred to me that writing could be easy. Maybe I should take up surgery on the side.

As for the students, anyone might think we left them bewildered. But in fact we probably gave them a broader glimpse of the writing process than if only one of us had talked. For there isn't any "right" way to do such personal work. There are all kinds of writers and all kinds of methods, and any method that helps you to say what you want to say is the right method for you. . . .

Here, it becomes clear that Zinsser is comparing and contrasting the writing methods of two writers: himself and Dr. Brock.

LITERATURE

Two critical essays written by Vincent Canby and Roger Ebert provide two opinions on the same topic. The essays appear in *Prentice Hall Literature: Timeless Voices, Timeless Themes,* Platinum.

Transitions such as "At the end" help readers follow Zinsser's thoughts.

The essay contains a clear and logical organization—point-by-point organization—that is consistent throughout.

Reading Writing Connection

Writing Application: Use Patterns Before you draft your essay, decide on a method of organization to help your readers follow along.

^{9.2} *Prewriting*

Choosing Your Topic

Choose two or more subjects to explore in a comparison-and-contrast essay. For help getting started, consider the strategies below:

Strategies for Generating Topics

1. **Freewrite** Freewrite for five minutes about recent decisions you have made. For example, have you recently purchased one brand of clothing over another brand? If so, why? Review your freewriting, and use an idea from it to form the basis of your comparison-and-contrast essay.

2. **List** First, choose a broad subject area, such as music, art, history, sports, or characters in a novel. Then, list items that come to mind within that subject area—your favorite examples or ones that you find particularly interesting. Finally, examine your list to find connections between the two or more items you recorded. Strong connections between items indicate that they might be effective subjects for a comparison-and-contrast essay. If so, choose those items and build your comparison-and-contrast essay around them. Here's an example:

Get instant help! Freewrite or list your items using the Essay Builder, accessible from the menu bar, on-line or on CD-ROM.

SPACE	*Broad Subject Area*
Moon	
Sun	
Saturn	
Andromeda	*Topic: Comparison and Contrast of Galaxies*
Jupiter	
Black holes	
Asteroids	
Milky Way Galaxy	

TOPIC BANK

For more specific suggestions for your comparison-and-contrast essay, consider the following ideas:

1. **Historical and Current Situations** Write an essay in which you compare and contrast an event or situation from history with one that is occurring today. For example, you could compare and contrast the Information Age with the Industrial Revolution.

2. **Two Products** Select two competing products that you would consider buying. In your essay, focus on the merits or shortcomings of each one. Finally, provide the reader with a recommendation about which one is the better product or the better value.

Responding to Fine Art

3. Study *Minor League*, by Clyde Singer. Then, write a comparison-and-contrast essay about two favorite athletes or baseball today compared with baseball of the 1920's.

Minor League, Clyde Singer, Butler Institute of American Art

Responding to Literature

4. Compare and contrast "I Am Not One of Those Who Left the Land" by Anna Akhmatova and "Speech During the Invasion of Constantinople" by Empress Theodora. You can find both selections in *Prentice Hall Literature: Timeless Voices, Timeless Themes*, Platinum. Focus on the similarities and differences in the speakers, the situations they face, and the character traits they exhibit.

☑ Cooperative Writing Opportunity

5. **Display** Work in a group to discover the similarities and differences between a typhoon and a hurricane. Split your group into two: one group will research similarities and the other, differences. Then, collaborate to prepare a comparison-and-contrast display. Assign some group members to create visuals such as maps and diagrams. Let other group members write captions and explanations of the visuals. Display your completed work in the classroom.

Evaluating Your Topic

Evaluate your topic to make sure the subjects you have chosen share a valid basis for comparison. Don't compare dissimilar subjects, such as the work of an artist with that of a musician, unless you have a compelling reason for doing so.

Also, make sure that the focus of your comparison isn't too broad. For example, the complete body of work of two writers is too much to handle in a single essay; two of their works or characters is a much more manageable challenge.

Use a Venn Diagram

To evaluate whether or not your subjects have enough points of comparison and contrast, use a Venn diagram.

Try it out! Use the interactive Venn Diagram in **Section 9.2**, on-line or on CD-ROM.

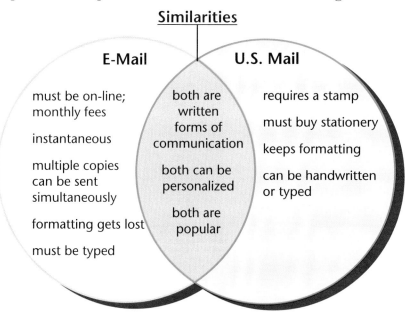

Similarities

E-Mail

U.S. Mail

must be on-line; monthly fees

instantaneous

multiple copies can be sent simultaneously

formatting gets lost

must be typed

both are written forms of communication

both can be personalized

both are popular

requires a stamp

must buy stationery

keeps formatting

can be handwritten or typed

Considering Your Audience and Purpose

The audience and purpose for your essay will affect the type of information you include in it. Use these questions to help you consider your audience:

- Who will read your essay? Peers? A review panel?
- How familiar will they be with the topic? What aspects of the topic will be most interesting to them?

Use these questions to help you consider your purpose:

- What aspects of the topic are most important to emphasize?
- How will your audience use the information you are providing?

Gathering Details

Gather enough details, descriptions, facts, examples, and reasons to provide your audience with a clear understanding of each subject being compared and to support your statements about the similarities and differences between them. Below are three ways to gather details:

Use Personal Experience

Experience counts. Use yours if you are comparing products, places, or things with which you have direct experience or if you are comparing works of art, literature, or music. For example, if you are comparing two products, use your own experience with each of them as evidence.

Use Primary Sources

Primary sources include original documents, such as scientific reports, company brochures, speeches, diary entries, journals, letters, or interview responses. Primary source material provides the words or works of people who were participants in or eyewitnesses to an event.

Use Secondary Sources

Secondary sources come from a published work in which the writer presents ideas about a subject based on evidence from several primary sources. For example, a biography of a president of the United States would be a secondary source. To write one, its author would draw upon primary sources, including letters from the president and interviews with people who worked with the president.

The following chart gives examples of different types of details gathered in various ways:

Subjects	Personal Experience	Primary Source	Secondary Source
two mountain-bike models	your experience riding each model	specification sheets from the manufacturers	newspaper article on this year's mountain-bike models
tornadoes and hurricanes	your experience with those types of weather phenomena	interviews with people who survived a category 5 hurricane	encyclopedia entry on hurricanes

 Internet Tip

If you are comparing and contrasting two or more products in your essay, take advantage of official company Web sites. Many companies maintain Web sites with detailed information (including technical specifications) about their products. Use a search engine to find the company's URL, or web address.

9.3 *Drafting*

Shaping Your Writing

An effective comparison-and-contrast essay is usually organized in one of two ways:

Use Subject-by-Subject Organization

In a subject-by-subject organization, first discuss all the aspects of one subject and then discuss all the aspects of the second subject. For example, you could discuss figure skating first and then discuss hockey skating.

Use Point-by-Point Organization

In a point-by-point organization, each aspect or point of comparison and contrast is discussed in turn. You might, for instance, discuss the cost of product A and the cost of product B, and then discuss the appearance of product A and that of product B, and so on.

Try it out! Use the interactive Point-by-Point activity in **Section 9.3**, on-line or on CD-ROM.

Student Work
IN PROGRESS

Name: Emily Agy
Pleasant Valley High School
Pleasant Valley, IA

Using Point-by-Point Organization
Emily decided to structure her article using point-by-point organization. She wrote each point of comparison on a self-sticking note so she could rearrange the order in which she planned to present each point of comparison.

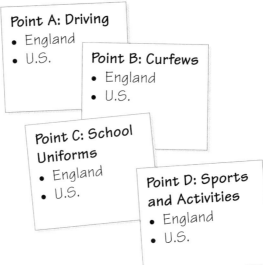

Point A: Driving
- England
- U.S.

Point B: Curfews
- England
- U.S.

Point C: School Uniforms
- England
- U.S.

Point D: Sports and Activities
- England
- U.S.

Providing Elaboration
Give Examples

During the drafting process, make sure you provide support for each of the statements you make about your subjects. Elaborate on your points by providing specific details and examples that clarify the similarities and differences between the subjects.

Provide Facts

Provide facts to give your readers a clear understanding of each subject under discussion.

EXAMPLE: Bike 3000 is suitable for the toughest terrain. It is tough enough to handle boulder-strewn trails and has special gearing for handling steep inclines. Advanced brakes help riders make quick stops on wet surfaces.

Cite Quotations and Figures

Use quotations and statistical or numerical figures to lend authority to the points you make in your comparison-and-contrast essay.

▲ Critical Viewing
If you were thinking of purchasing a bike like the one shown, about what features would you want to know? **[Relate]**

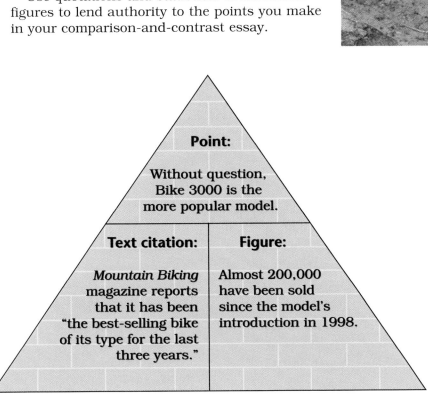

Point:

Without question, Bike 3000 is the more popular model.

Text citation:	**Figure:**
Mountain Biking magazine reports that it has been "the best-selling bike of its type for the last three years."	Almost 200,000 have been sold since the model's introduction in 1998.

Revising

Revising Your Overall Structure

Because your essay has two or more subjects, it's particularly important to make sure that its structure is sound. If the structure of the essay is disorganized, a reader may become confused about which subject you are discussing. You also need to ensure that your essay is balanced—that equal space is devoted to each subject.

▶ **REVISION STRATEGY**
Color-Coding by Subject

Using a highlighter of one color, go through your essay and mark each detail you have included about subject A. Then, use a highlighter of a second color to mark each detail you have included about subject B. Examine the essay. Is there a lot of one color and just a little of the other? If so, add more information about the other subject.

Also, check to be sure that your essay consistently follows either point-by-point or subject-by-subject organization. If the essay is well structured, your highlighted body paragraphs will form a pattern of color.

Student Work
IN PROGRESS

Name: Emily Agy
Pleasant Valley High School
Pleasant Valley, IA

Color-Coding to Check Structure
Emily highlighted information about England and the U.S. in different colors to make sure she had included sufficient details about both countries.

There are many differences when it comes to extracurricular school-sponsored activities. "Here there are all kinds of activities: football teams, field hockey teams, language clubs, etc. In England, we don't have extracurricular activities at school. If you want to play sports, you have to find the time to do it yourself...."

Revising Your Paragraphs

Once you've evaluated the balance and structure of your essay, analyze your writing at the paragraph level. You may want to reorganize some of your paragraphs to give your essay variety and to make it more interesting to read. Read the following examples to come up with ways to structure your paragraphs.

▶ REVISION STRATEGY
Using TRI/PS/QA

TRI: *TRI* stands for Topic, Restatement, and Illustration.

Michael Jordan has had a serious impact on the American economy. Some estimate that the "Jordan Effect" reached as high as $10 billion dollars over the course of his career. If that seems high, consider $165 million in basketball tickets, the $230 million worldwide gross of the movie he starred in, and almost $3 billion in Jordan-related merchandise.

Topic

Restatement

Illustration

PS: *PS* stands for Problem and Solution. In this kind of structure, both a problem and a solution are presented.

PROBLEM

A mountain bike must be able to withstand repeated bumps and jolts as it navigates the trails. Bike 3000 handles this requirement by incorporating a special frame geometry that disperses shocks more efficiently than conventional bikes.

SOLUTION

QA: *QA* stands for Question and Answer. Using this organization, a paragraph poses and answers a question.

QUESTION

How did Tiger Woods gain so much acclaim, so quickly? The answer is a stunning string of victories in both his amateur and professional careers.

ANSWER

Revising Your Sentences

Read your comparison-and-contrast essay carefully, examining the sentences you have written. Correct run-ons and fragments by joining or breaking up groups of words as needed. Also revise complete sentences to create variety within your essay. Make sure that your sentences flow smoothly and connect ideas.

Improve Connections Between Ideas

Review your draft, paying special attention to how well your ideas connect and flow together. If your sentences are choppy and unconnected, consider combining them. When combining sentences, use appropriate conjunctions to clearly indicate how the ideas within them are related.

▶ **REVISION STRATEGY**
Using Conjunctions to Combine Sentences

Read your draft critically to make sure that your ideas flow smoothly and logically. Whenever you find a passage that contains short, choppy sentences, combine the sentences and use a conjunction within the sentence to indicate relationships. Use a coordinating conjunction to link ideas of equal importance. Use a subordinating conjunction to indicate that one idea within a sentence is dependent upon another.

Student Work
IN PROGRESS

Name: Emily Agy
Pleasant Valley High School
Pleasant Valley, IA

Adding Conjunctions to Connect

After reviewing her opening paragraph, Emily decided that her sentences were too short and choppy. She decided to add conjunctions to connect her ideas more smoothly.

It's one thing to move from one state to another. ~~To~~ but move from a different country to the United States must certainly be a challenge. Michael Johnson, a fifteen-year-old sophomore recently moved from Southend-on-Sea, England. Johnson was recently interviewed at a journalism club meeting where students. ~~During the interview,~~ he explained the differences between life in the United States and life in England.

Grammar in Your Writing
Conjunctions

A conjunction is a word used to connect other words or groups of words. In English, there are three main kinds of conjunctions: *coordinating conjunctions, correlative conjunctions,* and *subordinating conjunctions.*

Coordinating conjunctions connect similar kinds or groups of words. There are seven coordinating conjunctions: *and, but, or, nor, for, yet,* and *so.*

Examples:

The golfers and basketball players arrived at the tournament.

The carryall bag given out to students was sturdy yet lightweight.

Carry the picnic basket or the blanket outside.

Correlative conjunctions are used in pairs to connect similar words or groups of words. Examples of correlative conjunction pairs include *neither/nor, just as/so, both/and,* and *whether/or.*

Examples:

Neither thunder nor lightning had much of an effect on our sleepy cat.

Both Charles and Ed promised to help us get ready for the dance.

Just as bees fly to honey, so my car gravitates to potholes.

Subordinating conjunctions connect two complete ideas by placing one idea below the other in rank or importance. Commonly used subordinating conjunctions include *after, before, because, even if, since, so that, unless, until, when,* and *while.*

Examples:

He achieved a great deal of success because he practiced regularly.

We can go to the park today, even if it rains.

Now that the show is over, you can go home.

Find It in Your Reading Find an example of a coordinating conjunction and of a subordinating conjunction in "Two Writing Processes" on pages 174–175. Then, explain how the conjunctions help to show the relationships between the ideas being connected.

Find It in Your Writing As you revise your comparison-and-contrast essay, look for one example of each type of conjunction. Examine each conjunction to make sure it shows the relationship you intend. If you can't find any, challenge yourself to combine ideas with conjunctions.

For more on conjunctions, see Chapter 18.

Revising Your Word Choice
Add Transitions to Clarify Relationships

Transitions indicate relationships. You can improve the clarity of your writing by adding transitions that express the relationships between the ideas in your essay.

Common Transitions			
Time Relationships	Spatial Relationships	Comparison-and-Contrast Relationships	Logical Relationships
before; during after; first; second; last; next; then; when; at the same time; now; later; immediately; soon; recently	above; below; behind; in front of; alongside; next to; north; south; east; west; inside; outside; beneath; at the top of; at the bottom of	along with; together with; as well as; also; similarly; although; though; however; nevertheless; yet; but; on the other hand; in contrast	if; whether; unless; therefore; thus; hence; in fact; in essence; for example; for instance

▶ **REVISION STRATEGY**
Reading Aloud

Read aloud pairs of sentences in your draft. For example, read the first and second sentence, then the second and third sentence, and so on. Pause after each pair and ask: Would adding transitions clarify the relationship between the two sentences? If so, add a transition from the chart above. Reread the sentence to be sure that the transition works well.

Peer Review
Ask Questions

Work with a peer to revise your essay. Write down five questions about your essay that you would like your peer reviewer to answer. Then, exchange drafts and questions with your peer reviewer. Take your peer's comments into consideration as you prepare a final draft.

Sample Questions:

• What types of details would enhance my essay?

• Have I provided a balanced treatment of the two subjects?

• What aspects of the essay need improvement? Why?

9.5 Editing and Proofreading

Before sharing your comparison-and-contrast essay with others, proofread it carefully to correct errors in spelling, punctuation, and grammar.

Focusing on Punctuation

Because comparison-and-contrast essays discuss two or more subjects, they often contain compound sentences. Pay close attention to your punctuation of compound sentences to ensure that you have correctly used commas within them.

⊛ **Technology Tip**

Use the Find feature of your word-processing software to locate conjunctions like *and, but,* and *yet*. When each is found, examine the sentence to see if it is compound. If so, make sure that it has a comma before the conjunction.

Grammar in Your Writing
Punctuating Compound Sentences

A **compound sentence** consists of two or more independent clauses joined by a comma and a coordinating conjunction or by a semicolon. Use the following rules for properly punctuating compound sentences:

- Use a comma before the conjunction that joins the clauses of a compound sentence.

  Eighteen tourists remained on the island, **but** most were safely evacuated before the hurricane struck.

- Use a semicolon when no conjunction is used to join closely related independent clauses.

  The tour bus was forced to take a detour; mudslides had made the main road impassable.

Find It in Your Reading Find three examples of compound sentences in "Two Writing Processes," on pages 174–175. Explain the rules for punctuating them.

Find It in Your Writing As you proofread your comparison-and-contrast essay, check to be sure that you have punctuated all compound sentences correctly.

For more on compound sentences, see Chapter 20.

9.6 Publishing and Presenting

Consider the following possibilities for publishing and presenting your comparison-and-contrast essay:

Building Your Portfolio

1. **Presentation** Present your comparison-and-contrast essay to the class. Gather or create visual aids such as photographs and charts, and decide on the order in which you'll present them. Rehearse your presentation to give it polish.

2. **Electronic Essay** Add to the details in your essay with digitized photographs, sound or video clips, or other multimedia elements. Share your essay with others by posting it on a Web site or uploading it onto a classroom computer.

Reflecting on Your Writing

Think back on your writing experience. Then, answer the following questions and save your responses in your portfolio.

- What surprises did you encounter while gathering details for your essay?
- If you could start over, would you choose the same subjects to compare and contrast? Why or why not?

 **Internet Tip**

To see model essays scored with this rubric, go on-line: PHSchool.com
Enter Web Code: eek-1001

Rubric for Self-Assessment

Use the following criteria to evaluate your comparison-and-contrast essay:

	Score 4	Score 3	Score 2	Score 1
Audience and Purpose	Chooses details and language that engage audience and achieve purpose	Chooses details and language appropriate for audience and purpose	Chooses details that mostly suit audience and purpose	Chooses details inappropriate for audience and that do not fulfill any purpose
Organization	Clearly presents information in a consistent organization best suited to the topic	Presents information using an organization suited to the topic	Chooses an organization not suited to comparison and contrast	Shows a lack of organizational strategy
Elaboration	Elaborates several ideas, with facts, details, or examples; links all information to comparison and contrast	Elaborates most ideas with facts, details, or examples; links most information to comparison and contrast	Does not elaborate all ideas; does not link some details to comparison and contrast	Does not provide facts or examples to support a comparison and contrast
Use of Language	Demonstrates excellent sentence and vocabulary variety; includes very few mechanical errors	Demonstrates adequate sentence and vocabulary variety; includes few mechanical errors	Demonstrates repetitive use of sentence structure and vocabulary; includes many mechanical errors	Demonstrates poor use of language; generates confusion; includes many mechanical errors

9.7 *Student Work* IN PROGRESS

FINAL DRAFT

▲ **Critical Viewing**
In what ways are these groups of students similar and different? **[Compare and Contrast]**

Life in Britain Versus Life in the U.S.

Emily Agy
Pleasant Valley High School
Pleasant Valley, Iowa

It's one thing to move from one state to another, but to move from a different country to the United States must certainly be a challenge. Michael Johnson, a fifteen-year-old sophomore, recently moved here from Southend-on-Sea, England. Johnson was interviewed by students taking a journalism course, to whom he explained the differences between the United States and England.

Emily clearly identifies the subjects of the comparison—life in the United States and in England.

When asked to name a few differences, Johnson replied, "Petrol (gasoline) is a lot more expensive at home and brand names of clothing are more expensive." He was eager to point out that living in England certainly isn't without its major benefits, though. "I think I've a lot less freedom here than in England. For example, in England, teenagers are treated more like adults. They are less supervised by parents and teachers."

Is driving on the right side of the street hard to get used to? This question was of great interest to the students. "Surprisingly, no," answered Michael. The steering wheel and driving controls are the same in both countries. But they are located on the left side in American cars and on the right side in British cars. If you simply remember that the driver always should be closer to the road's center than the passenger, you're all right."

Another main question was whether the school system was the same as in the United States. There are some similarities. For example, students attend school for the same number of years, and the school year is about the same length. They also study the same basic disciplines such as math, science, and literature. The major difference was that the classes are not structured the same in England. "Teenagers in England have more of a choice of what classes we take, and the schedule varies daily," Johnson said. In the United States, students may choose only one or two classes, and the schedule for classes is set.

Another difference is the school uniform. While it isn't uncommon to have a school uniform in the United States, we do not wear uniforms in Pleasant Valley High School. A typical school

uniform for boys in England consists of, "Shoes, blue pants, shirt, tie, and blazer," Johnson said.

Although both American and English students love team sports, there are many differences when it comes to extracurricular school-sponsored activities. "Here, there are all kinds of activities: football teams, field hockey teams, language clubs, and so on. In England, we don't have extracurricular activities at school. If you want to play sports, you have to find the time to do it yourself. There *are* sports, but they aren't this big; for instance, we haven't got a stadium like you have."

All in all, we, the journalism students, learned that despite the differences, teenagers in England and teenagers in the United States have more in common than we originally believed. Long live the Queen!

Point-by-point organization makes this essay easy to follow.

Emily chooses details that will interest her audience, such as school clothing and class structure.

Supporting details such as these help explain the similarities and differences.

Connected Assignment *Consumer Report*

When you want to compare and contrast several products or services, you can read a **consumer report.** In these reports, writers analyze different features of the products or services being discussed and come up with a recommendation. Consumer reports often take readers step by step through data such as user polls, expert opinions, and test results. They may use tables, graphs, or charts to show at a glance how the products or services compare and contrast.

Write your own consumer report about a product or service you know well. Use the writing process tips outlined below to help you.

Prewriting Decide on two or more products or services to compare and contrast. To come up with an idea, think about products you are interested in buying or a service, such as car washes, that you have used.

Before you draft, collect details that describe the features of the products or services about which you are writing. Use a chart like this one to help you organize the information as you find it.

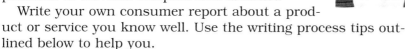

PACKAGING	
Product A	Product B

Drafting Open your draft with a general statement about the product type and a quick explanation of the features you will be examining. Refer to the chart often as you address each feature and evaluate the pros and cons of each product example. Close with a recommendation about which product or service you find superior.

Revising and Editing Check for consistency in your organization. For example, if have used point-by-point organization, don't switch to subject-by-subject organization later in the report. Confirm that all product names are accurate and correctly spelled. Strengthen your conclusion by correcting wordiness and adding persuasive modifiers.

Publishing and Presenting Make a neat copy of your consumer report, and post it for others to read. If time allows, collect consumer reports from your peers and assemble them into a binder for classmates to use as a reference.

Spotlight on the Humanities

Examining Cultures Through Film

Focus on Film: *The Good Earth*

Through the magic of cinema, you may experience a world other than your own and compare and contrast the characters' experiences with your own. Released in 1937, *The Good Earth* is considered by many movie fans to be one of the best films ever made. Based upon the novel by Pearl Buck, the motion picture stars legendary actor Paul Muni and actress Luise Rainer. The film follows an Asian rice-farming family through their reverence for the land and the fortunes and misfortunes that overtake their lives. Luise Rainer won an Academy Award for Best Actress, and the film also won an Oscar for Best Cinematography.

Literature Connection American author Pearl S. Buck (1892–1973) is one of only nine women to win the Nobel Prize for Literature. She was not only an author, but also a philanthropist, editor, and crusader for women's rights. After growing up in China with her missionary parents, Buck returned to the United States to attend college. She later returned to China and traveled the countryside acting as an interpreter for her husband, Dr. John Lossing Buck. Her novel *The Good Earth* sold over 1,800,000 copies in 1931 and was awarded the Pulitzer Prize in 1932. *The Good Earth* has been translated into thirty languages.

Art Connection Nature and the importance of the land appear consistently in traditional Chinese art. The land is represented distinctively in hanging scrolls, usually done with ink on paper, showing images of rocks, trees, and the outline of distant mountains. These hanging scrolls were common in the eleventh, twelfth, thirteenth, and fourteenth centuries in China.

▲ Critical Viewing
In what ways is this movie poster similar to or different from movie posters of today? [**Compare and Contrast**]

Writing Application: Response to a Favorite Film

You've probably seen many wonderful films based on novels that moved you to tears or made you laugh out loud until your stomach ached. Choose one of your favorite movies that was based on a short story or novel, and write a response to it. In your response, tell what you liked about the film and, if you read the story as well, whether you preferred the film or the book and why.

Media and Technology Skills

Analyze Relationships Between Media

Activity: Compare Versions of a News Story

Different media have different strengths and weaknesses. Imagine that a flood takes place in a nearby town. A newspaper could present in-depth coverage of the event, including several first-person accounts, photographs, and a comparison with earlier floods in your region. A television report would be shorter, but its video footage helps viewers understand the tragedy of the event.

Think About It You can discover a lot about a medium's strengths and the producer's perspectives by comparing two different versions of the same news story. Choose a local, state, or national story and compare the way it is presented in your local newspaper and on a local television broadcast.

Summarize It Begin by summarizing the coverage presented in each source. You may want to use a chart like this one to collect details about each story.

	Newspaper Report	Television Report
Facts		
Images		
Sources Cited		
Length (estimated word count; length of time)		
Position (front page/ back page; first in program, and so on)		

Comparing Other Media Sources

Comparing Other Media Sources
Extend your comparison to include one or more of the following sources of information. Review the medium's coverage of the same story:
• radio newscast
• weekly newsmagazine
• Internet news resource or on-line newspaper

From Page to Screen
Reading television transcripts can help you evaluate the difference between the written material spoken during a news report and the completed report with video and audio. Write to a network program to request a transcript from a specific program. After reading the transcript, share your reactions with your class.

Compare It After reviewing both sources, consider their similarities and differences. Ask questions such as the following:

• Which source assigned greater importance to the story?

• How did each source adapt the story to suit the needs of its medium?

• Which source gave its audience more information?

Write a review in which you compare and contrast the two stories. You may wish to provide a rating for each source, indicating which source you find more reliable.

Standardized Test Preparation Workshop

Responding to Comparison-and-Contrast Prompts

On a standardized test, you may be asked to analyze literature, evaluate ideas, or make a judgment and explain your reasons. In responding to these types of prompts, you will often compare and contrast characters, concepts, or choices. You will be asked to identify similarities and differences. You may also be asked to develop a position or draw a conclusion based on the similarities and differences you identify. You will be evaluated on your ability to do the following:

- recognize similarities and differences among the two or more choices
- structure your ideas in a format appropriate for comparing and contrasting
- choose supporting details that develop your ideas
- use correct spelling, language, and grammar

Use the basic writing process stages—prewriting, drafting, revising, editing, and proofreading—as you prepare your test responses. As part of your strategy, plan to devote a set amount of time for each stage of the writing process.

Below is an example of a standardized test writing prompt that involves comparing and contrasting. Develop a response, using the suggestions on the next page for guidance. The clock next to each stage shows a suggested portion of your time to devote to that stage.

Test Tip

When writing a comparison-and-contrast essay about a creative work, make sure to provide sufficient context for readers who may be unfamiliar with the work. Also, choose items for comparison and supporting details that are appropriate to the specified audience.

Sample Writing Situation

Read "The Masque of the Red Death" by Edgar Allan Poe. Then, respond to the following prompt.

In "The Masque of the Red Death," the people inside the abbey have a very different life from the people outside the abbey. In an essay, explain how this contrast and the common fate that the characters share reveal the theme of the story.

Prewriting

Allow about one quarter of your time for finding a specific topic and identifying comparison-and-contrast details.

Gather Details Use a Venn diagram to jot down the similarities and differences between the Prince's party and the situation of the common people (as described in the opening of the story and as you infer from details in the story.) For example, Poe describes the music and dancing within the abbey. The contrasting detail might be the crying and suffering outside the abbey.

Organize Details Study the details you collected, and decide on a method of organization that will help you achieve your purpose of showing the theme. You might find subject-by-subject organization the most effective method for showing an overall contrast between the rich and the poor. In this case, write about all the details on one side of your Venn diagram before moving on to the other side.

Drafting

Allow about half of your time for drafting. Write neatly, and leave space for text you may want to insert when revising.

Write an Introduction, Body, and Conclusion Use a traditional format for your comparison-and-contrast essay. In your introduction, you should state your thesis, or main point, so a sentence that states how the contrast in the story illustrates its theme. (Whenever you respond to a prompt, reread the prompt to be sure that your thesis statement addresses the prompt.) Then, develop your ideas in the body of your essay. Conclude by restating your thesis, and leave your readers with a powerful image from the story, such as the clock or the strange visitor.

Revising, Editing, and Proofreading

Allow about one quarter of your time for revising. Allow about five minutes to check your work for spelling, punctuation, or grammar errors.

Close the Gaps Read through your essay, and look for places where you can elaborate further. If you have written that the party was extravagant, make sure you have included several details that show how extravagant the party was. If you have not included several such details, add them at this time. Also, add transitions, if necessary, to indicate places that you change from describing life inside the abbey to life outside the abbey.

Reread After making your revisions, spend a few minutes checking that you have used capitals for characters' names and the beginnings of sentences. Double-check your use of end marks and commas as well. Correct as necessary.

Exposition
Cause-and-Effect Essay

Cause-and-Effect Relationships in Everyday Life

Identifying causes and effects is a part of daily life. Giving advice to a friend based on the effects you predict, fireproofing a potential fire hazard, and arguing about the best way to solve a problem—all these activities show an awareness of cause-and-effect relationships.

Cause-and-effect relationships are also explored in writing. Feature articles in your daily newspaper often describe causes and effects related to politics, crime, or the environment. History textbooks are primarily focused on causes and effects, as well. Even something as common as a recipe may describe a cause-and-effect process.

▲ Critical Viewing
When you look at this picture, what causes and effects come to mind?
[Relate]

What Is a Cause-and-Effect Essay?

Exposition is writing that informs or explains. A **cause-and-effect essay** is a piece of exposition that describes the relationship between an event or circumstance and its causes. Good cause-and-effect essays contain

- a clearly stated topic that explains what cause-and-effect relationships will be explored.

- an effective and logical method of organization.

- details and examples that elaborate upon the writer's statements.

- transitions that smoothly and clearly connect the writer's ideas.

To preview the criteria on which your cause-and-effect essay may be evaluated, see the Rubric for Self-Assessment on page 212.

Types of Cause-and-Effect Essays

Cause-and-effect relationships are explored in many types of writing, including the ones listed below:

- **Historical articles** explain how events in history contributed to or resulted in other events.

- **Process explanations** take readers step by step through a process, such as a math formula or a scientific technique.

- **Predictions** make educated guesses about future events based on knowledge of cause-and-effect relationships.

Writers in
ACTION

Writer Rudolfo Anaya discusses the process of writing an expository essay:

"In expository writing you're guided by an idea that you want to develop. It may be a paragraph, it may be ten pages, but what you really have is a subject, and you want to convey it...."

PREVIEW
Student Work
IN PROGRESS

In this chapter, you'll follow the progress of Jennifer Hoss, a student at Bel Air High School in El Paso, Texas, as she writes a cause-and-effect essay entitled "El Niño." At the end of the chapter, you can read Jennifer's completed work.

Model From Literature

California native Cindy Lin attended Columbia University's Graduate School of Journalism. Following a two-year period teaching high school in Japan, Lin now reports for an educational news station in New York City.

Reading **Writing** **Connection**

Reading Strategy: Question As you read works of nonfiction such as the following, question the author's statements, and check to be sure they are supported with evidence.

▲ **Critical Viewing** What might be the causes of urban development such as you see in the background of this photograph? **[Speculate]**

Growing Pains in China

Cindy Lin

If you go to the big cities in China today, you'll see skylines teeming with new skyscrapers and stores filled with consumer goods like refrigerators and designer handbags. You'll see a lot of billboards and ads for American products, and people dressed in Western clothes. In fact, they look like many big cities in the United States.

But as recently as the 1980's, things in China were very different. Few people owned televisions, and even fewer people had cars. There wasn't much choice in what you could buy, because food and clothing were rationed and foreign imports were restricted. The government owned and controlled everything, including deciding which products got made and in what quantities. The result was massive state-run companies that, while usually not profitable or efficient, employed thousands of people for life.

That all began to change in the early 1980's, after diplomatic relations with the U.S. and China resumed in 1979. China's leaders instituted reforms, such as allowing farmers to keep a small portion

In the opening paragraph, Lin describes the effect—China's newfound prosperity —that she plans to explore.

Transitions such as "because" help readers make connections between causes and effects.

of what they grew to sell on their own, inviting foreign investment and encouraging the privatization of state-owned companies. Money from foreign investors flowed into China—$67 billion in the last two years alone—as companies hurried to establish their products in a market with 1.25 billion people.

Now, 93 percent of Chinese households have a television set, and other goods such as washing machines and refrigerators are becoming common as well. But not everyone is benefiting from the changes in China—an estimated 100 million people are unemployed in China's cities and more than 80 million peasants in the country live in poverty, earning less than $100 a year.

SO WHO WINS AND WHO LOSES?

China's emerging middle class is reaping the benefits of change in China. They are the educated ones—usually in the cities—who can adjust to change and take the opportunity to start their own business or move into a management position at the growing numbers of new, privately owned businesses.

Those with little skills or education, who expected to work for a lifetime doing the same job, are now the ones who struggle. As state-owned companies have shut down or laid them off, the unskilled laborers become part of the staggering numbers of unemployed. Elderly retirees who exist on tiny government pensions also can't keep up with the changes, and people in the country who are too far from the big job markets of the cities continue to be mired in poverty.

For much of this century, Americans also expected to work at the same job or company for their entire careers. While American companies may be privately run, competition from other companies both domestically and abroad (such as in the auto industry) led to a spate of layoffs and factory closings in the late 1980's and early 1990's. People have since discovered that the more varied skills and education they have, the easier it will be for them to find work—especially in the event of change.

A chronological organization helps Lin trace the various causes leading to China's present-day conditions.

Statistical details such as the ones in this paragraph support Lin's ideas.

LITERATURE

R.K. Narayan's "Like the Sun" traces the effects of one man's attempts to tell the truth. The short story appears in *Prentice Hall Literature: Timeless Voices, Timeless Themes,* Platinum.

In her concluding paragraph, Lin notes that the cause-and-effect relationships that existed in China also hold true in the United States.

▲ Critical Viewing Would you say that the photograph shows a town with a healthy economy or a poor one? Explain. **[Make a Judgment]**

Reading Writing Connection

Writing Application: Answer Readers' Questions As you prepare to write your cause-and-effect essay, think about the questions your readers may ask. Be sure you answer those questions as you draft your essay.

Prewriting

Choosing Your Topic

Choose a topic for your cause-and-effect essay that you find interesting and that centers around a cause-and-effect relationship.

Strategies for Choosing a Topic

1. **Sketch a Scene** Draw a scene from the world of nature. Review your sketch to find interesting details that make a good writing topic. For example, you might draw a field of dandelions and clover that has a pond in the middle of it. You might then decide to write about the effects of last year's drought on local flowers and crops.

2. **Make a List** List interesting events or scientific phenomena. After five minutes, circle the one you find most interesting. Then, write for another five minutes, listing any causes and effects that spring to mind when you think of that topic. Review what you wrote, and develop your topic into a cause-and-effect essay. If you find that your topic doesn't have a strong enough cause-and-effect relationship, continue the listing process until you find one that does.

3. **Scan a Newspaper** Scan a newspaper, looking for topics that you can link to causes or effects. Keep a list of the possible topics as you come across them. Then, review your list, and choose as a topic the item you find most interesting.

Get instant help! Make your list using the Essay Builder, accessible from the menu bar, on-line or on CD-ROM.

Student Work
IN PROGRESS

Name: *Jennifer Hoss*
Bel Air High School
El Paso, TX

Doing a Newspaper Scan to Find a Topic
Jennifer Hoss found her topic by flipping through a newspaper. She jotted down articles that explained causes and effects and chose the one she liked the best as her topic.

1. Academic scores rise dramatically
2. Indonesia elects a new president
3. Scientists analyze tissue from a twenty-five-thousand-year-old frozen woolly mammoth
4. El Niño crop failure blamed for high cost of chilies

TOPIC BANK

If you are having difficulty finding a specific topic for your cause-and-effect essay, use the following ideas:

1. **Influences of the Blues on Popular Music** Write an essay that reveals how blues instruments, blues singers, and recurring themes in blues songs affect music today.

2. **Causes of Changes in Rain Forests** In a cause-and-effect essay, explore the various factors that have led to the rain forest's acreage being decreased. You can find information about deforestation in current periodicals available at the library.

Responding to Fine Art

3. *Rolling Power* depicts a close-up view of the workings of a locomotive. Write a cause-and-effect essay, explaining how steam engines propel locomotives. As an alternative, explore the cause-and-effect relationship between the development of the railroad and patterns of settlement westward across the United States.

Rolling Power, Smith College Museum of Art

Responding to Literature

4. Read the short story "The Dog That Bit People" by James Thurber. In an essay, explain how Thurber exaggerates cause-and-effect relationships to create humor. You can find the story in *Prentice Hall Literature: Timeless Voices, Timeless Themes,* Platinum.

☑ Cooperative Writing Opportunity

5. **History or Science Display** Work with a group to plan a cause-and-effect display for the classroom. Choose a significant moment in history or science. Then, divide into two subgroups, with one group making a timeline that traces the causes leading up to that significant moment and the other group making a timeline showing effects. Share your work with the class.

Narrowing Your Topic

Once you have a general idea for a topic, work with the material until it is narrow enough to cover effectively within the scope of your essay. Cubing is one narrowing technique that you can use.

Use the Cubing Technique

Cubing lets you focus on details by helping you identify six perspectives or aspects of your topic. Answer the six questions, and decide to focus your essay on one or two of the perspectives or aspects you explored.

1. **Describe It** How would you describe your topic to someone who is unfamiliar with it?
2. **Associate It** What other situations or events does your topic bring to mind?
3. **Apply It** Why is your topic important? Why is it useful to explore?
4. **Analyze It** Where is it? When did it happen? Why might it happen again? Can anything stop it from happening?
5. **Compare or Contrast It** How does your topic compare and contrast with similar topics?
6. **Argue for or Against It** What are the positive and negative effects of your topic?

Considering Your Audience and Purpose

Before you gather details, identify your audience and your purpose. Your audience and purpose will affect your word choice, the details you include, and the way in which you present those details. For help identifying the types of details and style of language that will be most effective, devise a plan like the one that appears below.

Audience:	School Board
Purpose:	To explain effects of decreased music funding
Details:	Facts and statistics; cause-and-effect chart; examples
Style of Language:	Formal word choice; vivid persuasive language; tone of respect

Gathering Details

Before you draft, collect and organize details for your cause-and-effect essay. Following are two methods for collecting and organizing details:

Collect Note Cards

When you research a topic, it's important to keep note cards for each cause-and-effect idea and its source. Before you begin to draft your essay, collect note cards from at least three or four sources either at home or at the library. On each note card, record the quotation or the idea you want to include in your report. Mark the note card with a number that identifies its source and the page number(s) on which the information can be found.

As an alternative, photocopy source pages and highlight the information you use.

Chart Causes and Effects

On a sheet of paper, write the effect, or event, that is your subject. Then, use arrows and boxes to show events or conditions that are caused by or result from your topic. If one event has several different effects, use a separate arrow to point to each.

Technology Tip

If you find information on the Internet, print out the pages containing the information you plan to use. Make sure to print out or write down the Web address, too.

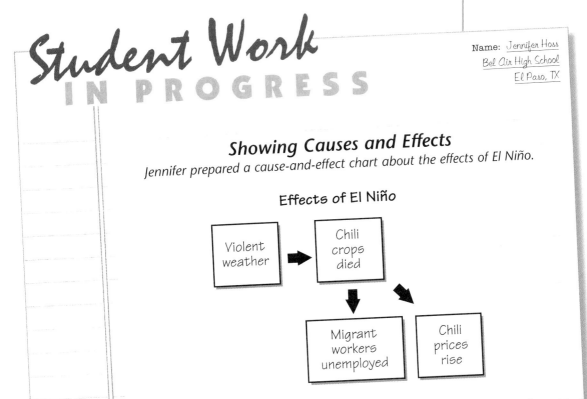

Student Work
IN PROGRESS

Name: *Jennifer Hoss*
Bel Air High School
El Paso, TX

Showing Causes and Effects
Jennifer prepared a cause-and-effect chart about the effects of El Niño.

Effects of El Niño

Violent weather → Chili crops died → Migrant workers unemployed / Chili prices rise

Drafting

Shaping Your Writing

Now that you have gathered details on your topic, shape the structure of your essay. Choose a logical method of organization for your cause-and-effect essay.

Choose a Logical Organization

Chronological Organization Chronological, or time, organization is a logical choice for structuring a cause-and-effect essay. You can start either with the effect and go back through its causes one at a time, in chronological order, or you can start with the cause and proceed to describe its effects in time order.

Effects Organized Chronologically:

After the *Titanic* sank, new marine regulations were put into effect. The tragedy of the *Titanic* caused mariners to firm up regulations about radio contact and lifeboats. Marine regulations instituted after the *Titanic* included these mandates: constant radio contact between vessels and sufficient lifeboats to hold all passengers.

▼ **Critical Viewing** What effect has time had on the *Titanic,* shown in this recent photograph? **[Analyze]**

Order-of-Importance Organization Order-of-importance organization allows you to build an argument or to present various causes or effects in the order of their relative importance. You can either begin with the most important detail and end with the least important detail or reverse it, beginning with the least important detail and ending with the most important detail.

Effects Organized in Order of Importance:

The *Titanic's* voyage proved to be a disaster because of many causes. Chief among them was the failure of the crew to navigate around the iceberg. The resulting damage to the ship's hull made its sinking inevitable. . . .

Another contributing cause was the lack of adequate lifeboats and safety instruction. Because the *Titanic* was "unsinkable," the company that made the ship did not provide enough safety equipment to ensure the safety of passengers and crew.

The weather conditions certainly did not help. . . .

Providing Elaboration

Elaborate as you draft to add depth and detail to your cause-and-effect essay. Types of elaboration include examples, statistics, quotations, and other types of details that support your ideas. Use the following strategy to help you elaborate:

Use the SEE Technique for Elaboration

Use the SEE technique to layer, or give depth, to your writing as you draft. First, write a basic statement about your topic. Next, write a sentence that extends that statement. Finally, write a sentence that elaborates on the extension.

STATEMENT: **State the main idea of the paragraph.**

Exercise is beneficial to your health.

EXTENSION: **Restate the idea.**

People who exercise regularly live longer, fuller lives.

ELABORATION: **Add information that further explains or defines the main idea.**

For example, a person who works out for twenty minutes three times a week is often in far better shape than a person who has no regular routine.

Student Work
IN PROGRESS

Name: *Jennifer Hoss*
Bel Air High School
El Paso, TX

Using SEE to Elaborate

Using the SEE technique, Jennifer gave depth to her essay.

El Niño has since passed, but the world is still suffering from | Statement
its aftermath. Weather conditions, for example, have differed | Extension
from normal. Records from the past have shown that the |
winters following El Niño have been some of the coldest and | Elaboration
fiercest in history.

Revising

Revising Your Overall Structure

As you look at the structure of your essay, make sure that the ideas you've presented appear in logical order and are clearly connected to each other.

Strengthen Your Introduction and Conclusion

In your introduction, clearly present the main idea of your cause-and-effect essay. You may also mention reasons for your choice of topic and give readers an idea about why it is interesting or important.

▶ **REVISION STRATEGY**
Circling to Identify Relationships

To make sure that your introduction and conclusion "match up," circle the main idea you present in your introduction. Then, find and circle in your conclusion a restatement of that main idea. If your conclusion does not contain such a restatement, either rewrite your introduction or rewrite your conclusion so that they work together effectively.

Following is an example of the circling strategy:

INTRODUCTION

The ancient Peruvian society was based upon agriculture. As a result, their need for social cooperation was great. For instance, crops needed to be gathered and stored so that all the people could eat them. Just as important were the division of labor among farming, home-building, child-rearing, and hunting. When the Incas conquered Peru's tribes, the Incas continued to support the existing social structure.

↓

CONCLUSION

With a brilliant government strategy, the Incas maintained the social structures the conquered tribes already had in place and expanded them to include an empire. Because of the Incas' wise and thoughtful governing methods, they went on to rule a peaceful and prosperous society for more than a thousand years.

Revising Your Paragraphs

Review your paragraphs to be sure that each develops a single idea and that the paragraphs themselves flow together smoothly. Check to be sure that topical paragraphs—those that contain a topic sentence—are unified.

Strengthen the Unity of Paragraphs

Revise your topical paragraphs to make them unified—to make sure that each has a topic sentence and that the other sentences within the paragraph support or develop the main idea expressed in the topic sentence.

▶**REVISION STRATEGY**
Color-Coding to Identify Related Details

Circle each topic sentence in every topical paragraph. (Functional paragraphs—those that perform a specific function—do not have topic sentences.) Then, using a pencil of a different color, circle the details that support the topic sentence. Examine sentences you have *not* circled. If they do not support the topic sentence, either rewrite or delete them.

Learn More

To learn more about unified paragraphs, see Chapter 3.

Student Work
IN PROGRESS

Name: Jennifer Hoss
Bel Air High School
El Paso, TX

Color-Coding to Identify Related Details
To make her writing more unified, Jennifer deleted an unrelated detail.

Because of adverse weather conditions brought on by El Niño, the Southwest's world-famous chili crops began to die. ~~The Southwest is in an area comprising New Mexico, Arizona, Texas, and California.~~ This in turn put many migrant workers, who harvest chili peppers, out of work and it raised the price of chili to much higher than it had been before. What was once affordable by the pound became a precious commodity. The Southwestern tradition of having a delicious red or green chili with every meal or as a staple ingredient was now not possible for some people until the prices fell.

Revising Your Sentences

Now that your paragraphs are unified, look even more closely at your writing. Within each sentence, check to see that the relationships are logical.

▶ **REVISION STRATEGY**
Clarifying Relationships

Within each sentence, make sure that the connections among words, phrases, and clauses are clear. Read each sentence carefully. If there is more than one thought within the sentence, you may have to add a transition to show how those thoughts are related. Some transitions indicate meaning or clarify the significance of a detail. For example, the phrase *not only* indicates that a detail is just one of many.

Student Work
IN PROGRESS

Name: *Jennifer Hoss*
Bel Air High School
El Paso, TX

Clarifying Relationships With Transitions
To make the relationships more clear, Jennifer added several transitions to her draft.

The phrase *not only* alerts readers that there is more than one effect being discussed.

Because of adverse weather conditions the Southwest's world-famous chili crops began to die, and harvesting was delayed. This *not only* put many migrant workers out of work *but* and it also raised the price of chili to much higher amounts than it had been before. What was once affordable by the pound *now* became a precious commodity. The Southwestern tradition of having a delicious red or green chili with every meal or as a staple ingredient was put on the shelf for some people until the prices fell.

By changing *and* to *but*, Jennifer clarifies the importance of the second detail in the sentence.

The word *now* was added to make the cause-and-effect relationship more clear.

Grammar in Your Writing
Transitional Phrases

A **phrase** is a group of words without a subject and verb. In your cause-and-effect essay, use transitional phrases to show connections between ideas. A phrase may appear at the beginning of the sentence, between the subject and the verb, or at the end of a sentence:

Beginning:
After lunch, we worked enthusiastically.

Between the Subject and Verb:
We, after eating lunch, worked enthusiastically.

End:
We worked enthusiastically after eating lunch.

There are many types of phrases that you can use as transitions, connecting ideas in your writing.

A **prepositional phrase** is a group of words made up of a preposition and a noun or pronoun, called the object of the preposition:

Inside the studio, the sound engineers began mixing the demo.

A **participial phrase** is a participle modified by an adverb or adverb phrase or accompanied by a complement. The entire phrase acts as an adjective:

Using a high-powered lens, Annette could just make out the letters.

An **infinitive phrase** is an infinitive with modifiers, complements, or a subject, all acting together as a single part of speech:

To avoid the iceberg, the captain had to steer hard to starboard.

Find It in Your Reading Read through "Growing Pains in China" by Cindy Lin, on pages 198–199. Identify three sentences that contain transitional phrases—phrases that connect ideas. Explain the ways in which those phrases help to clarify the relationships within the essay.

Find It in Your Writing Review your draft to identify where you have used phrases to show transitions. If you cannot identify six phrases, challenge yourself to add at least one more to your writing. Notice the improvement.

For more on phrases, see Chapter 20.

Revising Your Word Choice

Review Your Word Choice

If you use the same word or form of it several times within a passage, your writing can sound tedious and awkward. Learn to distinguish between useful repetition and careless repetition. Useful repetition helps to emphasize a point or to make a passage memorable. Careless repetition creates a dull impression on the reader.

USEFUL REPETITION:	In the 1920's, people *flocked* to theaters to see plays; in the 1930's, they *flocked* to theaters to see movies.
CARELESS REPETITION:	Because I have always loved the *theater*, I'm studying *theater* and *theater* arts in school.

▶ **REVISION STRATEGY**
Underlining Repeated Words and Forms of Words

Read through your draft, and underline repeated words or forms of words. Then, review your draft. If passages containing repetition are not intended, replace some of the repeated words with synonyms, words with the same meaning.

OVERUSED WORD:	They *housed* the furniture for the *house* in a shed out back.
VARIED WORDS:	They *stored* the furniture for the *house* in a shed out back.
OVERUSED WORD:	We tried to *locate* a better *location* for our party.
VARIED WORDS:	We tried to *find* a better *location* for our party.

> **⚙ Grammar and Style Tip**
>
> If there is a thesaurus in your word-processing program, use it to locate alternative word choices.

Peer Review

"Say Back"

Work with a small group of peers to get feedback on your writing.

- Read your paper aloud to your peer editors twice.

- Have peers jot down two positive comments and three constructive comments for improvement.

- One by one, have your peers read aloud their comments to you.

- Take their comments into consideration as you prepare your final draft.

10.5 Editing and Proofreading

Reread your cause-and-effect essay carefully, correcting any mistakes you find in spelling, punctuation, and grammar. Double-check statistics or other details you present as fact.

Focusing on Commonly Confused Words

Proofread your essay carefully. Make sure you've correctly used the following commonly confused words: *since, because, then,* and *than.*

⊙ Technology Tip

Use the Find feature of your word-processing program to locate the words *since, because, then,* and *than.* Once you've located those words, check to be sure your usage of them is correct.

Grammar in Your Writing
Using *Since, Because, Then,* and *Than* Correctly

As you proofread, make sure that you have used these words appropriately.

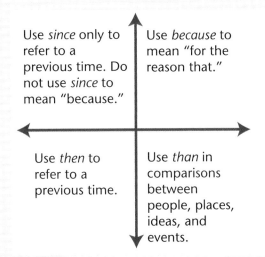

Use *since* only to refer to a previous time. Do not use *since* to mean "because."

Use *because* to mean "for the reason that."

Use *then* to refer to a previous time.

Use *than* in comparisons between people, places, ideas, and events.

Find It in Your Reading In "Growing Pains in China," which appears on pages 198–199, Cindy Lin correctly uses the word *since.* Find the usage, and explain why her choice was correct.

Find It in Your Writing As you proofread your cause-and-effect essay, check to be sure you have used the words *since, because, then,* and *than* correctly. If you have not used any of those words, challenge yourself to add them to make clear connections between your ideas.

For more on word usage, see Chapter 26.

10.6 Publishing and Presenting

When you are finished writing your cause-and-effect essay, share it with others. Following are some ideas for sharing your writing:

Building Your Portfolio

1. **Presentation** Use your essay as the basis of a cause-and-effect presentation. Use photographs, charts, and diagrams as you explain the topic of your essay. Save the essay and visuals in your portfolio.

2. **E-mail** Share your essay electronically. Type the essay using word-processing software. Then, attach the file to an e-mail to a friend or relative.

Reflecting on Your Writing

Think back on your experience of writing a cause-and-effect essay. Then, respond to the following questions, and save your responses in your portfolio.

- During the process of writing, what did you learn about the subject you chose?

- Which strategy for writing a cause-and-effect essay might you recommend to someone as being most useful? Why?

 Internet Tip

To see model essays scored with this rubric, go on-line:
PHSchool.com
Enter Web Code:
eek-1001

Rubric for Self-Assessment

Use the following criteria to evaluate your cause-and-effect essay:

	Score 4	Score 3	Score 2	Score 1
Audience and Purpose	Consistently targets an audience through word choice and details; clearly identifies purpose in thesis statement	Targets an audience through most word choice and details; identifies purpose in thesis statement	Misses target audience by including a wide range of word choice and details; presents no clear purpose	Addresses no specific audience or purpose
Organization	Presents a clear, consistent organizational strategy to show cause and effect	Presents a clear organizational strategy with occasional inconsistencies; shows cause and effect	Presents an inconsistent organizational strategy; creates illogical presentation of causes and effects	Demonstrates a lack of organizational strategy; creates a confusing presentation
Elaboration	Successfully links causes with effects; fully elaborates connections among ideas	Links causes with effects; elaborates connections among most ideas	Links some causes with some effects; elaborates connections among most ideas	Develops and elaborates no links between causes and effects
Use of Language	Chooses clear transitions to convey ideas; presents very few mechanical errors	Chooses transitions to convey ideas; presents few mechanical errors	Misses some opportunities for transitions to convey ideas; presents many mechanical errors	Demonstrates poor use of language; presents many mechanical errors

10.7 Student Work
IN PROGRESS

FINAL DRAFT

El Niño

Jennifer Hoss
Bel Air High School
El Paso, Texas

For the past year or so, El Niño has been a troublemaking culprit, causing mischief and mayhem with the chili pepper crop in the United States Southwest. In addition to causing local trouble, El Niño has been the cause of terrible occurrences around the globe, and it is not the innocent-faced little boy the direct Spanish translation suggests. In fact, the awful effects of El Niño may be yet to come.

El Niño is a weather pattern that brings with it rain, wind, drought, thunderstorms, heat, and other examples of Mother Nature's fury. Past El Niños have occurred in 1953, 1957–58, 1965, 1972–73, 1976–77, and 1982. To put it in simple terms, El Niño is caused by a cooling of the waters in the Peru Current off the coast of South America. The change in temperature occurs because for most of the year, the east Pacific is cooler than the west Pacific. The trade winds drag the warmer water west, and it "piles up" on the ocean's surface, resulting in heavy rainfall. The opposite situation exists on the eastern boundary: The cooler waters experience relatively dry weather. During El Niño, this situation is upset. The water on the west comes back east in big waves and the west becomes dry, whereas the east experiences heavy rainfall.

The El Niño weather pattern produces more than violent weather, however: It also has had a huge effect here in the United States, wreaking havoc on the chili crops of western Texas and southern New Mexico.

▲ **Critical Viewing**
What weather conditions might have caused the situation pictured? **[Connect]**

The first paragraph of Jennifer's essay reveals her topic: the causes and effects of El Niño.

In the second paragraph, Jennifer discusses some causes of the El Niño weather pattern.

Jennifer's essay is logically organized: The first half explains causes of El Niño; the second half explains the effects of El Niño.

Because of adverse weather conditions brought on by El Niño, the Southwest's world-famous chili crops began to die. This not only put many migrant workers out of work, but it also raised the price of chili much higher than it had been before. What was once affordable by the pound became a precious commodity. The southwestern tradition of having a delicious red or green chili with every meal or as a staple ingredient was now not possible for some people until the prices fell.

Transitions like "because" and "in turn" help connect the ideas in this paragraph.

While chili-loving patrons from across the globe may have suffered, chili farmers have suffered even more. Acres of crops were ruined or even killed by extremely high winds and excessive rain storms. If that weren't enough, the winds and rain brought along with them a virus that added to the devastation of the chili crops. Millions of dollars washed away with the rain, leaving farmers, families, and migrant workers without a means of making a living.

Jennifer provides specific examples to support her statement that chili farmers have suffered more than others.

This year's El Niño has passed, but the world is still suffering from its aftermath. Records from the past have shown that the winters following El Niño have been some of the coldest and fiercest in history. In fact, some scientists argue that El Niño and the ice ages may actually be connected. Cold winters often signal the coming of poor summer crops, so perhaps the worst effects of El Niño have yet to be seen.

In the last paragraph, Jennifer concludes with a chilling prediction: El Niño's worst effect may be yet to come.

Connected Assignment Documentary

What Is a Documentary?

Documentaries are films that focus on real-life people and issues. Because they often deal with specific problems or issues, they usually demonstrate or track cause-and-effect relationships. An overarching narrative often ties all the pieces together and emphasizes cause-and-effect links.

The basis for a documentary is a script, written in stage format with stage directions and dialogue. In such a script, stage directions indicate the sequence of elements and camera shots along with any of the actors' movements.

Write your own documentary script. Use the following writing process guidelines:

▲ **Critical Viewing**
Judging from this photograph, does the person who's filming seem experienced? Explain why or why not. **[Make a Judgment]**

Prewriting Find a topic by thinking about your community and its history or problems. Look for trends that you can explain and new developments you can track to their results.

Research your topic at the library and through visits to locations. Conduct tape-recorded interviews, and take notes about your observations. Then, jot down your ideas for ways to present your findings visually. Also, look for existing visuals such as film clips. Generate index cards for each key idea, and note possible ways to express it. Then, focus on structuring the cause-and-effect relationship you want to show.

Drafting As you draft, bring your vision to life. Mix voice-over narration and still images (shots of letters or the outside of a building, for example) with live action scenes. When you're happy with the sequence and blend of visuals, write the narration in the dialogue portion of the script. Within the narrative, provide any necessary background information, identify people and places, and highlight cause-and-effect links.

Revising and Editing Mentally "view" your documentary as you read your script. Improve clarity by adding explanations, and strengthen connections by adding transitional sentences or phrases.

Publishing and Presenting Film your documentary, or a portion of it, and hold a screening for friends, peers, teachers, and relatives. Have a question-and-answer session following the screening.

Spotlight on the Humanities

Examining Images

Focus on Art: *Tristan and Isolde*

Powerful stories can have a ripple effect through the ages. For example, artist Ferdinand Leeke painted his famous rendition of Tristan and Isolde in 1889. His depiction was inspired by composer Richard Wagner's opera *Tristan and Isolde*, which, in turn, was inspired by the centuries-old legend of Tristan and Iseult.

Literature Connection Known as one of the world's greatest love stories, the Celtic tale of Tristan and Iseult was written in the mid-twelfth century by a French poet. The tale centers on a princess and a knight, who accidentally drink a love potion and immediately fall in love. When Tristan is wounded, he calls for Iseult because he believes only she can save him. Another woman, Iseult of the White Hands, tells him deceivingly that the first Iseult refused his request. Tristan dies of a broken heart. When the first Iseult hears what has happened, she also dies of a broken heart. Tristan and Iseult were buried side by side. A vine grew from Tristan's grave, and a rose grew from Iseult's. The vine and rose met, entwined, and never separated.

Music Connection Between 1857–1859 German composer Richard Wagner wrote the words and music for his opera *Tristan and Isolde*. The three-act opera tells of the fatal love of the Irish princess Isolde and the Cornish knight Tristan. Wagner had to wait six years before he found a patron—King Ludwig II of Bavaria—to finance the production of the opera. Its leading roles are considered very difficult to perform.

Tristan and Isolde, 1912, John Duncan, City of Edinburgh Museums and Art Galleries

▲ **Critical Viewing**
Do the figures in this painting seem romanticized or realistic? Explain. **[Assess]**

Cause-and-Effect Writing Activity: Annotated Timeline of a Story's History

Throughout the ages, popular stories have developed and then were told and retold time and again. Choose one such story, and trace its history. Develop an annotated timeline in which you chronicle the story's history, the differences among versions, and the cultural and historical influences that might be the cause of such variations. Include visuals, and post your finished timeline in the classroom.

Media and Technology Skills

Examining the Effects of Media on Perceptions of Reality

Activity: Prepare a Multimedia Evaluation

Television viewers often unconsciously absorb the images and ideas broadcast day and night. You can analyze the effects of specific television genres or programs to understand how people's choices and attitudes are influenced by what they view.

Situation comedies, or sitcoms, are one of television's most successful genres. By carefully analyzing today's most popular sitcoms, you can uncover ways in which these programs shape viewers' perspectives.

Learn About It Begin by finding out which current sitcoms are most popular. An entertainment magazine might report weekly Nielsen ratings, which describe television viewing patterns. If you prefer, conduct your own survey to discover which television programs are most popular.

Record It Record and view several episodes of the program you plan to evaluate. Make an annotated episode log to help you remember the original broadcast date and theme or topic of each episode.

Date Aired	Plot Summary	Theme
3/21/00	George gets fired.	Have a backup plan.

Evaluate It After viewing three or four episodes, evaluate the program's underlying principles. To think about how the program might affect viewers, ask questions such as the following:

- What beliefs or values do most of the characters share?

- Have any of the characters' clothing styles become popular because of this series?

- What recurring motifs or events occur on almost every episode?

- Are there any "catch phrases" or familiar sayings associated with this show?

- Which specific scenes best reflect the program's attitudes?

Present It Recap your analysis for your class in a multimedia presentation. Select brief scenes from the episodes you recorded that illustrate your evaluation. You can use video editing to create a high-lights tape or simply cue up desired scenes. Allow time for your audience to share their insights into each program's effects.

What You'll Need
- Television
- Videocassette Recorder (editing features optional)

Perspective on the Past
- Viewing television programs of the past can help you understand how these sources influence people.

Standardized Test Preparation Workshop

Analyzing Cause-and-Effect Relationships

On some standardized tests, you will be prompted to evaluate and show your understanding of various cause-and-effect relationships. These prompts measure your ability to identify, analyze, and explain in writing the causal relationship between two or more events or circumstances. You will be tested on your ability to

- Clearly answer or respond to the prompt.

- Provide sufficient details that elaborate upon and support your statements.

- Organize details in a clear and coherent format.

- Use correct grammar, spelling, and punctuation.

As you draft your response to a writing prompt, follow the stages of the writing process. Devote sufficient time to prewriting, drafting, revising, and proofreading, bearing in mind the time constraints of a standardized test.

Following is an example of a cause-and-effect writing prompt. Use the suggestions on the following page to help you respond. The clocks next to each stage show the suggested percentage of time to devote to each stage.

Sample Writing Situation

Read the following writing prompt, and draft a response. Use specific details to support your ideas.

Suppose it is discovered that the planet Mars is able to support human life. How might things change on Earth in terms of global politics, science, education, social programs, and so on? Give specific examples of the changes you foresee.

Prewriting

Allow one quarter of your time for prewriting.

Gather Information Quickly jot down ideas that you have in response to the writing prompt. When finished, review your list to decide on a focus for your response. For example, you may want to focus on how world governments will decide on "ownership" of Mars territory.

Organize Your Ideas Once you have focused your ideas, decide on the most effective and logical organizational method. Because you will be discussing cause-and-effect relationships, you may consider chronological organization—showing the flow of causes and effects—or you may choose to examine multiple effects of a single cause.

Drafting

Allow approximately half of your time for drafting.

Elaborate As you draft your response, include various types of supporting details. For example, you could cite historical similarities that give your prediction believability or you could use statistical figures to explain your ideas in depth. Also, give examples of how you think people will behave following the announcement that people will be able to live on Mars.

Create a Tone Choose your words carefully as you draft, to create a tone or to reveal your attitude about your subject. In this response, you are revealing a prediction; therefore, your tone should be convincing and authoritative.

Revising, Editing, and Proofreading

Allow one quarter of your time to revise and proofread your response.

Strengthen Unity Read through your response to make sure that each paragraph addresses the prompt. Revise or delete paragraphs that stray from your main point. Also, check details within paragraphs to make sure they support each paragraph's main idea. If you find a detail that does not, either rewrite it or delete it.

Check Verb Tense Be especially careful to review your use of verb tense throughout your response. Because you are writing a prediction, you probably will make use of the future tense as well as the present and past tenses.

Correct Errors Proofread carefully to locate and correct any and all errors you have made in grammar, spelling, and punctuation. Also, check to be sure that you have indented each paragraph and that you have titled and signed your response.

Chapter 11

Exposition

Problem-and-Solution Essay

Problem-and-Solution Essays in Everyday Life

Tackling difficult problems can help you develop powerful and effective strategies for daily life. As the poet Jean Toomer said, "We learn the rope of life by untying its knots." Writing about problems and solutions can help you find innovative solutions to your problems and allow you to share your discoveries with an audience. You might write a letter to a relative suggesting a way to resolve a family conflict or share your new solution to a school dilemma in a newspaper editorial.

▲ **Critical Viewing**
What problem might the people in this photograph be working together to solve? **[Speculate]**

What Is a Problem-and-Solution Essay?

Exposition is writing that explains or informs. A **problem-and-solution essay** is a specific type of exposition that identifies a problem and presents one or more potential solutions. An effective problem-and-solution essay

- clearly states a specific, real-life problem.
- identifies the most important aspects of the problem.
- presents one or more possible solutions.
- supports each solution with specific details and logical reasons.

To preview the criteria on which your problem-and-solution essay may be evaluated, see the Rubric for Self-Assessment on page 236.

Types of Problem-and-Solution Essays

Problem-and-solution essays may address a wide variety of issues. Following are some of the specific types of issues they can address:

- **Consumer issues** include problems with products or services and how they can be remedied.
- **Local issues** may be problems facing your community, such as issues of school funding and library staffing.
- **Business issues** involve problems facing a company or business, such as budget shortages or schedule delays.

Writers in
ACTION

Without challenges, life would become too predictable and even a bit boring. Author Marsha Sinetar acknowledges the importance of working on hard challenges:

"Rather than denying problems, focus inventively, intentionally on what solutions might look or feel like. . . . Our mind is meant to generate ideas that help us escape circumstantial traps—if we trust it to do so."

PREVIEW
Student Work
IN PROGRESS

Patrick Swan, of Muncie High School in Muncie, Indiana, realized that the parking situation at his school was out of control. Follow along as he uses prewriting, drafting, and revising techniques to develop an essay that analyzes the problem and proposes a solution. A final version of Pat's problem-and-solution editorial appears at the end of the chapter.

Mark Carwardine has a degree in zoology from London University. Since 1986, he has been a writer, consultant, lecturer, and broadcaster.

Reading Strategy: Evaluate the Author's Message When you read a problem-and-solution essay, don't accept a proposed solution unless the author has included thorough support.

from

Caring for Whales, Dolphins, and Porpoises

Mark Carwardine

The final death toll is shocking: about a million sperm whales, at least half a million fin whales, more than 350,000 blue whales, nearly a quarter of a million humpbacks, and literally hundreds of thousands of others. Two million whales were killed in the Southern Ocean alone. Some years were particularly bad: In the 1930–31 season, 28,325 blue whales were killed; more than 30 years later, in 1963–64, no fewer than 29,255 sperm whales met their death—we still had not learned the lessons of the past. Today, we are left with merely the tattered remnants: In most cases, no more than 5–10 percent of the original great whale populations remain.

By the time the animals were given official protection, it was almost too late and, indeed, some species may never recover. . . . But there is some good news, as well. Against all the odds, several species appear to be bouncing back. The gray whale is the ultimate success story. The North Atlantic stock was probably wiped out by early whalers, and only a remnant population survives in the western North Pacific. But in the eastern North Pacific, it has made such a dramatic recovery that it is now believed to be at least as abundant as in the days before whaling. Meanwhile, there

▲ Critical Viewing Why is this photograph an appropriate choice for a problem-and-solution essay about whaling? **[Connect]**

Carwardine begins with a direct statement of the problem. Next, he uses detailed statistics to elaborate on the situation.

Carwardine points out that some progress has been made already in addressing the problem.

has been a dramatic increase in blue whale numbers off the coast of California, where about 2,000 animals gather for the summer and autumn. Humpbacks and southern right whales are also making a comeback in many places.

It is only natural that, from time to time, everyone involved in whale conservation feels a sense of despair and helplessness. But progress is being made, albeit slowly, and the attitudes of governments and other key decision makers are gradually changing. In the past decade, there have been many success stories, from the establishment of the Southern Ocean Whale Sanctuary, surrounding Antarctica, to the passing of a new law to ban dolphin hunting in Peru. . . .

There are no easy solutions to most of the problems facing whales, dolphins, and porpoises. The issues are complex and there are often many vested interests involved. Solutions do exist, but they are often complex themselves and it may be many long years before they are put into effect.

The work undertaken by organizations such as the British-based Whale and Dolphin Conservation Society, the largest charity of its kind dedicated to the conservation, welfare, and appreciation of cetaceans, is necessarily wide ranging. It includes anything from the development of good working relationships with key politicians to working toward a feeling of mutual respect and cooperation with local fishers.

It involves encouraging and assisting schoolchildren to take an interest in conservation, and focusing world attention on key issues, such as commercial whaling and destructive fishing methods. It entails producing action plans for saving endangered species, or populations, and developing realistic economic alternatives to hunting and killing. It involves undercover operations to gather important information on a wide range of illegal activities, improving the enforcement of existing laws and regulations, and much more. Above all, constant vigilance is essential because, even when important progress has been made, it can always be weakened or revoked.

Carwardine does not oversimplify the solutions. Because the problem is a large and complex one, the solutions are detailed and complex.

Here, Carwardine acknowledges that the solutions must work for all involved and be reached through cooperation between conservationists and fishers.

In the final paragraph, Carwardine organizes proposed actions in order of importance. He concludes by pointing out that the solutions must be realistic and sustainable.

LITERATURE

In "Leiningen Versus the Ants," by Carl Stephenson, the story's characters are faced with a problem for which they need to find an immediate solution. This story appears in *Prentice Hall Literature: Timeless Voices, Timeless Themes*, Platinum.

Reading • **Writing** • **Connection**

Writing Application: Provide Support for Your Message When you write your problem-and-solution essay, provide thorough support for the solution you propose.

⬤11.2 *Prewriting*

Choosing Your Topic

Begin by identifying an important problem about which you feel strongly. Your essay will be more effective if you choose a significant and meaningful problem rather than a simple one that can be solved easily. Use these strategies to find a topic you would like to develop:

Strategies for Generating Topics

1. **Talk With a Peer** Talking with a partner can help you identify important problems in your school and community. You can also talk about state or national problems. Begin by working together to brainstorm for a list of problems. As you work, use a chart like the one below to gather ideas. When your chart is completed, choose the item you find most interesting to become the topic for your problem-and-solution essay.

School	City	Nation	World
Overcrowded classes Chaotic parking lot	Dangerous intersection at Elm and Watson Zoo closing	Highway safety Government corruption Campaign financing	International policies Diminishing resources World hunger

2. **Use Sentence Starters** Complete the sentence starters below to help you come up with a topic. Don't stop with one response. Try to come up with three or four endings for each sentence. Then, review your ideas to find a problem that is important to you.

Possible Sentence Starters
- The biggest problem facing students today is . . .
- The world would be a much better place if we could solve the problem of . . .
- I wish that we could eliminate the problem of . . .
- One problem we could solve if we all work together is . . .

Try it out! Use the interactive Sentence Starters activity in **Section 11.2**, on-line or on CD-ROM.

TOPIC BANK

Consider these suggestions if you are having difficulty coming up with your own topic:

1. **Solution to a Math Problem** Write an essay in which you explain a complex math problem and its solution.

2. **Editorial Addressing a Local Issue** Choose a problem that faces your school or neighborhood, and write an editorial presenting a solution.

Responding to Fine Art

3. *Unloading the Cargo*, by Ralston Crawford, depicts the unloading of a ship's cargo. What sorts of problems might such a task involve overcoming? Write a problem-and-solution essay that describes one such problem and details the solution.

Unloading the Cargo, 1942, Ralston Crawford

Responding to Literature

4. In James Thurber's humorous story "The Dog That Bit People," the characters are confronted with a dog's behavior problems. Write a problem-and-solution essay proposing steps that could be taken to change the dog's behavior. You can find "The Dog That Bit People" in *Prentice Hall Literature: Timeless Voices, Timeless Themes*, Platinum.

✔ Cooperative Writing Opportunity

5. **Letter of Petition** Work with a team to identify a problem that affects everyone in your school. Brainstorm together to generate a reasonable solution. Then, have one team member draft the petition, another team member edit and proofread it, and another team member type it and design it. Work as a team to photocopy the petition and get as many students as possible to sign it. Finally, send the signed petition to decision makers who can help you solve the problem.

Narrowing Your Topic

If your topic is broad, narrow it so that you can focus on presenting a solution to a single problem.

Use Looping to Narrow Your Topic

Looping can help you focus on key aspects of your topic. Begin by writing freely on your topic for about five minutes. Read what you have written, and circle the most interesting or important idea. Then, write about that idea for five minutes. Repeat this process until you arrive at a topic narrow enough to address thoroughly in your essay.

Problem: Pollution

I think pollution is a big problem. Soon, we won't be able to enjoy the environment because it will be so polluted. It's not just the land, it's the water and air, too.

Water Pollution: Acid rain is a problem. And oil spills in oceans. Even our local stream has suds in it. Lakes can get polluted, too.

Miller Stream: The stream behind the school is unsafe because of phosphates dumped into it from local businesses.

Considering Your Audience and Purpose

The type of language you use will depend on the audience for your problem-and-solution essay. Some audiences, such as a group of friends, will relate best to informal language. Many other audiences, however, will respond better if you use formal language to communicate your ideas.

FORMAL LANGUAGE	INFORMAL LANGUAGE
The parking situation in the eastern lot is dangerous.	The parking lot is a mess.
The most effective solution to the problem of truancy is to make the issue of attendance important to students.	The best way to stop kids from cutting class is to make them feel that attendance is a big deal.

Gathering Information

To develop a successful essay, you need a strong set of facts, statistics, and other types of support. Most likely, you'll find it necessary to conduct research in the library or on the Internet to gather the material you need.

Gather Various Types of Details

As you gather details, look to find those that fully explain the problem you are proposing to solve and the steps or aspects of the solution.

- **Cite examples:** Give examples from research or real life to explain the problem and its history.

- **Interview:** Talk to people who have a deep knowledge of the problem or who have definite ideas on how to solve it.

- **Survey:** Create and distribute a survey that probes for ideas about the problem and possible solutions. Tabulate the responses, and cite the results in your essay.

Student Work
IN PROGRESS

Name: *Patrick Swan*
Muncie Central High School
Muncie, IN

Collecting Details

Pat gathered details that will help him explain the problem and solution that form the heart of his essay.

<u>Problem:</u> "In our school, people without permits frequently take up parking spots, forcing people with permits to park illegally."—Phone interview with Principal Suding from Yorktown High School

<u>Solution:</u> Penalties for parking without a permit
   1. First offense: a warning
   2. Second offense: a detention
   3. Third offense: loss of parking privileges for duration of school year

11.3 *Drafting*

Shaping Your Writing

Start With the Problem

As inventor Charles Kettering once said, "A problem well stated is a problem half solved." Your problem-and-solution essay should begin with a detailed description of the problem. Make sure your audience understands all of the important aspects of your problem. Once the problem is clear, you can write about the solution or solutions you propose.

Using an Outline An outline can help you organize your ideas before you begin to draft. Look at the examples below. The first example shows how to organize an essay presenting a single solution to a problem. The second example shows how to organize an essay proposing more than one solution. Use the organization that fits your topic.

Get instant help! To create your outline, use the Essay Builder, accessible from the menu bar, on-line or on CD-ROM.

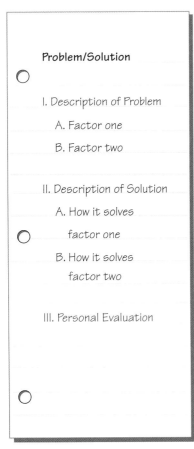

Problem/Solution

I. Description of Problem

   A. Factor one

   B. Factor two

II. Description of Solution

   A. How it solves

      factor one

   B. How it solves

      factor two

III. Personal Evaluation

Problem/Solution/Solution

I. Description of Problem

   A. Factor one

   B. Factor two

II. First Solution

   A. Advantages

   B. Disadvantages

III. Second Solution

   A. Advantages

   B. Disadvantages

IV. Personal Evaluation

Providing Elaboration

Following your outline, begin writing your first draft. Support each major point in your outline by adding facts and other details, expanding on ideas, and discussing important related concepts. This elaboration will help you convince readers of the soundness of your solution.

Expand on Your Outline

Support each major point in your essay by providing clear and relevant details. Doing so will help readers understand and accept the solution you are proposing.

Student Work
IN PROGRESS

Name: *Patrick Swan*
Muncie Central High School
Muncie, IN

Expanding on an Outline

Working from an outline, Pat expanded each point by giving specific examples. Notice how he elaborated one heading in the outline.

I. The parking lot is a mess

   A. Students park carelessly

   B. Unauthorized parking

   C. Damage to cars caused by vandalism and reckless driving

II. Parking Permits

   A. Students are accountable for their driving and parking

   B. Unauthorized parkers are easily identified

   C. Permits have worked at other schools

     1. Yorktown
     2. Delta

   D. Details of the plan

Unauthorized parking is another part of the problem. People who are not connected with the high school take advantage of the lot's central location. Commuters and shoppers take up spaces meant for students, teachers, and other school employees. This is not a new problem. According to former assistant principal James Suding, now principal at Yorktown High School, "Everyone from the community used to meet at Central and carpool. It's always been a mess there."

Revising

As you review your first draft, you will find many ways to improve your writing. You might begin by focusing on the overall structure to make sure the whole essay "hangs together." After that, look at each paragraph, sentence, and word to sharpen your work.

Revising Your Overall Structure

Solve the Problem

The success of a problem-and-solution essay depends on two things: You need to clearly define the problem, and you need to describe a specific and effective solution. The structure of your essay should make it easy to see how your solution answers every aspect of the problem.

▶ **REVISION STRATEGY**
Connecting Ideas

Use a highlighter to connect parts of the problem to related parts of the solution.

- Highlight or underline each problem or part of a problem and label it *P*.

- Highlight or underline each solution. Label it *S*. Connect related problems and solutions.

If you find a problem that has no matching solution, you need to expand your solutions. If you find a solution that doesn't fit part of the problem, it is probably unnecessary. You should consider cutting it.

▼ Critical Viewing
What sort of problems might someone encounter while wading this stream? **[Anayze]**

CONNECTING PROBLEMS TO SOLUTIONS

P   . . . A primary cause of the pollution is restaurants that use phosphates in their dishwashing liquids. Acid rain also contributes to the poor water quality. . . .

S   Requiring all local businesses to use phosphate-free detergents will greatly improve the water quality of Hawkins Stream. These detergents are slightly more expensive but clean equally well. . . .

Revising Your Paragraphs

Focus Each Paragraph on a Single Topic

Every paragraph in your problem-and-solution essay should develop a single idea or topic. You can test each paragraph by asking questions as you revise.

▶ **REVISION STRATEGY**

Questioning Your Paragraph Choices

Review your essay, and evaluate each paragraph as a separate unit. When you come to the end of a paragraph, pause to ask yourself why you grouped these sentences together.

- **Does the paragraph focus on one idea?** State the idea, and describe how each sentence expands on, supports, or clarifies that idea.

- **Does every sentence relate to the main idea?** If you find sentences on different topics, consider cutting them or moving them to other, more appropriate paragraphs.

- **Do two paragraphs discuss the same topic?** Consider combining the paragraphs to improve the flow of ideas.

Student Work
IN PROGRESS

Name: *Patrick Swan*
Muncie Central High School
Muncie, IN

Focusing a Paragraph

Pat made several adjustments after considering the paragraphs in his problem-and-solution essay.

This solution has worked well at two local high schools. Both Yorktown and Delta high schools require students and faculty members to display parking permits. ~~The parking lots at these school are always filled to capacity.~~ The lots are patrolled periodically to identify cars without permits on display.

Administrators at both schools report that the permits have been popular and effective. Consequences have been created for students who fail to purchase a permit.

Revising Your Sentences

Fix Unnecessary Shifts in Tense

Your sentences should use verb tenses to indicate clearly when an event occurred. It is often best to stay with a single tense. For example, if you are writing about a problem in the past, make sure that all your verbs are in the past tense.

Mixed Tenses

The stream <u>has contained</u> high levels of dangerous chemicals. The surrounding ecosystem <u>will be</u> greatly affected. Fish living in the stream <u>suffered</u> because of the poor water quality. Birds that eat these fish <u>have gotten</u> sick, too.

Consistent Tense

The stream <u>contains</u> high levels of dangerous chemicals. The surrounding ecosystem <u>is</u> greatly affected. Fish living in the stream <u>suffer</u> because of the poor water quality. Birds that eat these fish <u>get</u> sick, too.

▶ **REVISION STRATEGY**
Naming Each Tense

Read through your draft. Find each verb, and name the tense. If you find more than one verb tense in a sentence or paragraph, make sure that the tense shift is necessary. If it is not, revise accordingly.

Student Work
IN PROGRESS

Name: Patrick Swan
Muncie Central High School
Muncie, IN

Fixing Verb Tenses

Pat revised this paragraph to put each verb in the future tense.

Unauthorized parking will also be greatly reduced. Administrators can [will be able to] recognize unauthorized cars because those cars don't [won't] have permits. The plan would also have helped [will also help] our school identify potential suspects in cases of damaged and vandalized automobiles.

Grammar in Your Writing
The Six Tenses of Verbs

There are six verb tenses. Each tense has a basic form, as shown in this chart.

Basic Forms

Present	I *look* for a solution.
Past	I *looked* for a solution yesterday.
Future	I *will look* for a solution tomorrow.
Present Perfect	I *have looked* for a solution before.
Past Perfect	I *had looked* for a solution until I almost gave up.
Future Perfect	I *will have looked* for a solution by the end of next week.

Each tense also has a progressive form, ending in *-ing.*

Progressive Forms

Present Progressive	I *am looking* for a solution.
Past Progressive	I *was looking* for a solution yesterday.
Future Progressive	I *will be looking* for a solution tomorrow.
Present Perfect Progressive	I *have been looking* for a solution since last week.
Past Perfect Progressive	I *had been looking* for a solution when I found the answer.
Future Perfect Progressive	I *will have been looking* for a solution for two weeks.

Find It in Your Reading Review "Caring for Whales, Dolphins, and Porpoises" on pages 222–223. Choose one paragraph, and identify the tense of each verb. Explain the reason for any shifts in tense that you find.

Find It in Your Writing Identify the tense of each verb in your draft. Highlight paragraphs that have more than one verb tense. Evaluate whether or not each shift in tense is necessary.

To learn more about verb tenses, see Chapter 22.

Revising Your Word Choice

Revise Your Word Choice to Create a Tone

The words you select help set the tone of your writing—the attitude toward your subject that you convey to your readers. Decide on a tone you would like to convey, and revise your choice of words to help you achieve that tone.

The following chart shows how an alteration in word choice can affect the tone of a piece of writing.

Optimistic Tone	Discovering an effective solution will be most challenging.
Pessimistic Tone	Reaching a workable solution will be extremely difficult.
Informal Tone	Getting at a decent answer will be really hard.

▶ **REVISION STRATEGY**
Highlighting Key Words

Changing just a few words can adjust or heighten the tone you want to develop. Highlight two or three key words in each paragraph, and brainstorm for ideas for words that might replace them. Weigh your choices carefully, and then make any desired changes.

Peer Review

Key Questions

The actor Robert Redford has said that "problems can become opportunities when the right people come together." Revising your problem-and-solution essay with a partner is an excellent way to use teamwork to make effective changes. Have a partner or group read your problem-and-solution essay. Use these questions as a starting point for your discussion:

▼ Critical Viewing
Do the students in the photograph seem to be working well together? Explain. **[Analyze]**

• How complete is the description of the problem?

• How well does the solution match the problem?

• Are there any important parts of the problem that are not discussed?

After listening to your classmates, consider using their suggestions to improve your work.

11.5 Editing and Proofreading

Because spelling and grammar errors can make your writing confusing and distract your readers' attention, make sure that your essay is error-free.

Focusing on *That* and *Which*

The words *that* and *which* are often misused, even by experienced writers. As you check your essay for errors, look to see whether you have used *that* and *which* correctly. Highlight each use of both words, and decide whether or not you have chosen the appropriate word.

Use the following information to help you determine whether your use of *that* and *which* is correct.

Speaking and Listening Tip

It is often helpful to read your writing aloud to check for errors. If you stumble over words while reading, look to see whether you have come across a typographical error or an error in punctuation.

Grammar in Your Writing
Restrictive and Nonrestrictive Clauses

Adjective clauses often begin with *that* or *which.* You can decide which word to use by deciding whether the clause is restrictive or nonrestrictive.

A **restrictive clause** contains information that is essential to the meaning of the noun it modifies. It can expand, limit, or define the noun. Begin a restrictive clause with *that:*

The essay that I wrote was published in the school newspaper.
I found a solution that was simple and effective.

A **nonrestrictive clause** contains information that is not essential to the meaning of the noun it modifies. Begin a nonrestrictive clause with *which.* Set off a nonrestrictive clause with commas:

The mayor's speech, which was about crime, was quite rousing.
"How to Stop Litter," which I wrote last year, won first prize in an essay contest.

Find It in Your Writing As you proofread, locate instances in which you used *that* and *which.* Then, check to be sure you've used those words correctly.

For more on restrictive and nonrestrictive clauses, see Chapter 20.

Publishing and Presenting

Once you have polished and completed your problem-and-solution essay, share your final draft with an audience. Your readers will enjoy learning about your solutions, and you will have the satisfaction of knowing that you have made a helpful proposal.

Building Your Portfolio

1. **Encourage Responses** Sponsor a group read-aloud of several problem-and-solution essays. Take time to discuss the proposed problems and solutions in each essay.
2. **Submit Your Essay** Send your essay to the editors of a magazine or Web site that accepts student writing. Use writers' directories to help you locate addresses.

Reflecting on Your Writing

Reflect on your writing experience by answering these questions. Save your responses in your portfolio.

- Which was more difficult to write about, the problem or the solution? Why?
- What strategies did you use to make sure that your solution was complete and effective?

 **Internet Tip**

To see model essays scored with this rubric, go on-line:
PHSchool.com
Enter Web Code:
eek-1001

Rubric for Self-Assessment

Use the following criteria to evaluate your problem-and-solution essay.

	Score 4	Score 3	Score 2	Score 1
Audience and Purpose	Contains language and details to engage audience and accomplishes purpose	Contains language and details appropriate for audience and that help contribute to purpose	Contains some language and details not suited for audience; contains some details that detract from purpose	Contains language and details that are not geared for a particular audience; has an unclear purpose
Organization	Is organized consistently, logically, and effectively	Has consistent organization	Has some organization, but its organization is not consistent	Is disorganized and confusing
Elaboration	Has a solution that is clearly laid out, along with details that support or explain	Has a solution that is supported with details	Has a stated solution, but it contains few details to support it	Has unclear solution, and no details are given to support it
Use of Language	Contains language that helps the writer achieve an effective tone; contains no errors in grammar, punctuation, or spelling	Contains language that creates a tone; contains few errors in grammar, punctuation, and spelling	Contains few examples of language that create tone; contains some errors in grammar, punctuation, and spelling	Demonstrates no attempt to create tone through word choice; contains many errors in grammar, punctuation, and spelling

11.7 Student Work IN PROGRESS

FINAL DRAFT

▼ **Critical Viewing**
What problems might exist in a parking lot such as the one shown? **[Analyze]**

Parking Permits Needed to Regulate Student Parking

Patrick Swan
Muncie Central High School
Muncie, Indiana

Our parking lot is a mess.

Students drive in from all angles and park anywhere. Because school starts earlier this year, many student drivers are even more rushed, to avoid being tardy. Their haste adds to the parking lot chaos.

Unauthorized parking is another part of the problem. People who are not connected with the high school take advantage of the lot's central location. Commuters and shoppers take up spaces meant for students, teachers, and other school employees. This is not a new problem. According to former assistant principal James Suding, now principal at Yorktown High School, "Everyone from the community used to meet at Central and carpool. It's always been a mess there."

The parking lot has become unsafe for both cars and pedestrians. There has been a noticeable increase in vandalism, damage to cars, and small fender benders. If you park in our lot, you are lucky if your car leaves without being nicked, scratched, painted, or dented.

Although there is assistance from administration members and security guards to control traffic after school, there is no master plan to indicate who is parking where and for what reason.

An informal statement of the problem grabs readers' attention in the essay's first sentence. Pat then describes the problem more fully, using formal language.

Pat quotes a knowledgeable source, a high-school principal, to further explain the problem.

We think we have a solution.

It only makes sense that students, faculty, and staff members ought to be issued parking permits, which will be kept on file in the front office. Using this plan, administrators can easily find the owner of any car that is improperly parked. If students know that they can easily be traced, they will drive and park more carefully.

Unauthorized parking will also be greatly reduced. Administrators will be able to recognize unauthorized cars because those cars won't have permits. The plan will also help our school identify potential suspects in cases of damaged and vandalized automobiles.

This solution has worked well at two local high schools. Both Yorktown and Delta high schools require students and faculty members to display parking permits. The lots are patrolled periodically to identify cars without permits on display. Administrators at both schools report that the permits have been popular and effective.

Consequences have been created for students who fail to purchase a permit. The first offense results in a warning, followed by a detention for the second offense, and the third results in loss of parking privileges for the remainder of the year. However, according to Suding, "We haven't had much trouble with students parking in reserved spots or not getting a pass."

Yorktown High School also uses the permits as an extra source of revenue. Students there have the opportunity to buy reserved spots at the front of the parking lot, near the building. The school uses the money as a fund-raising opportunity for any club or organization. At a cost of five dollars per semester, 64 students have reserved spots for this fall. Other parking passes cost the students one dollar for general parking outside the reserved area.

We can take a tip from our neighboring high schools and organize the parking situation at Central High School. One dollar is a low price to pay for keeping your car and its contents safe.

Pat clearly indicates the structure of the essay by announcing that he will discuss the solution.

Each part of the solution corresponds to part of the problem identified earlier in the essay.

Pat's word choices help him create a formal, direct tone. Doing so helps ensure that Pat's audience will take his ideas seriously.

The closing statement helps convince Pat's audience that his solution is a good one.

◄ **Critical Viewing**
Give two reasons for the importance of having an organized parking lot such as the one pictured. **[Apply]**

Connected Assignment *Advice Column*

One way to solve a problem is to seek expert advice. You can often find expert advice in question-and-answer forums or in advice columns in magazines or newspapers. Topics may range from gardening to computer use to chess strategies to parenting. In such a column, one writer presents a problem and another writer responds with a proposed solution. Sometimes, however, the columnist presents both aspects after receiving an inquiring letter.

Write your own advice column, inventing the problem and coming up with a solution. Use the writing process skills outlined below to guide you.

Prewriting Make a T-chart of problems you've recently encountered. In the left-hand column, write down possible problems that an advice-seeker might have. In the right-hand column, jot down the solutions, or advice, you would give to address each problem.

Review your chart, and choose as a topic the advice you feel most confident about giving.

▲ Critical Viewing
Would you say the person in the photograph is posing a problem or presenting a solution? Why? **[Speculate]**

Problem	Solution
noise	ear plugs
	white-noise machine

Drafting Keep your audience—the advice-seeker and your readers—in mind as you draft your advice column. For example, you may want to adopt a friendly and persuasive tone as you present your solution. As you give advice, support it with examples, quotations, and other types of evidence.

Revising and Editing Review your advice column to ensure that both the problem and the solution are clearly stated. Add to or modify your language to create an upbeat and positive tone, especially in the advice portion.

Publishing and Presenting Share your advice column with others. Ask them whether or not they agree with the advice you have given.

Spotlight on the Humanities

Appreciating the Arts

Focus on Theater:
Man of La Mancha

If only there were a solution to every problem in life, as legendary fictitious hero Don Quixote believed. The musical *Man of La Mancha*, whose main character is Don Quixote, premiered on the Broadway stage in 1965. With music by Mitch Leigh, lyrics by Joe Darion, and book by Dale Wasserman, the musical ran for six years on Broadway. The show won six Tony Awards, including Best Musical of the 1965–1966 season, and the New York Drama Critics Circle choice for Best Musical.

▲ **Critical Viewing** Can you tell from this photograph which figure is Don Quixote and which is Sancho Panza, his servant? Explain. **[Distinguish]**

Literature Connection Written by Miguel de Cervantes Saavedra in 1605, *Don Quixote de la Mancha* is one of the most famous books in literature. The novel tells the story of Don Quixote, who decides to right the wrongs of the world. He is so taken with the concept of romanticized chivalry, however, that he becomes blind to the world around him. He soon believes that windmills are giants and flocks of sheep are armies. Cervantes's novel was first translated into English in 1616.

Music Connection German composer Richard Strauss (1864–1949) wrote a tone poem in 1897 based on Cervantes's *Don Quixote de la Mancha*. The tone poem is considered to be one of Strauss's most important orchestral pieces.

Problem-and-Solution Writing Activity:
Solutions to Problems at School

Perhaps students in your school are constantly complaining about the quality of their school lunches. Maybe your school could use several "late buses" to accommodate students participating in after-school activities. Create a chart that vividly illustrates several problems you perceive and how you would solve each one. Color-code or illustrate your chart to make problems stand out from solutions. Post your completed chart in your classroom.

Media and Technology Skills

Using Technology to Find Answers

Activity: Create a Research Quiz

Research today may involve a wide variety of media sources, from books and magazines to software and the Internet. Using a variety of sources will increase your ability to locate the information you need efficiently. Using several different information sources, create a challenging quiz for your classmates to solve.

Think About It Choose a format and topic for your research quiz. Your quiz format may be multiple choice, true or false, short answer, or a combination of formats.

Research It Plan to use at least three different sources of information to collect facts and details for your challenge. You might use any of these sources:

- **CD-ROMs:** CD-ROMs contain many types of media, such as music, art, photographs, and illustrations.
- **Software tools:** Many software programs come with built-in tools that can provide valuable information. For example, most word processors include a thesaurus and a spell checker.
- **Internet search engines:** The Internet contains millions of pages of information, but finding the facts you need can be difficult. Search engines help you find sites that mention specific topics.

Write It Create your research challenge by writing eight to ten questions. Make sure that the information required is found in a variety of different sources. In addition to the questions, prepare a hint sheet that lists the information sources you used to write the questions. Fold the hint sheet, and place it in an envelope.

> **Hint Sheet**
>
> 1. Internet
> 2. Encyclopedia

Swap It Exchange quizzes and hints with another classmate or team. Keep track of the sources you use to solve each question. Refer to the hint sheet if you have difficulty answering a question. Score one another's tests, and discuss what you learned about conducting research.

Using Internet Search Engines

Use these tips to help you use search engines effectively:

- Always try more than one search engine. Because the indexes and methods differ, you may get very different results at each site.
- If a search generates too many hits, or matches, try a more specific search. Add one or more words to narrow your search.
- To search for a multi-word name or phrase, enclose all the words in quotation marks.
- Many search engines allow you to use the words *AND, OR,* and *NOT* when searching for information. Click on Advanced Search options to learn how to use these features.

Standardized Test Preparation Workshop

Responding to Problem-and-Solution Prompts

Problem-and-solution prompts, in which you are asked to propose a solution to a stated problem, appear on some standardized tests. They measure your ability to analyze a problem, identify and propose an arguable solution, and defend that solution with specific reasons. You will be evaluated on your ability to do the following:

- organize your ideas and information in a clear and coherent manner

- include specific and compelling details tailored to the specific audience and purpose

- generate well-paced and engaging arguments

- apply grammar, spelling, and punctuation conventions

Writing for a test differs from other writing primarily in the time limitation placed upon your writing. You can still, however, apply the writing process stages—prewriting, drafting, revising, editing, and proofreading—to ensure that your writing is as effective as it can be.

Below is an example of one kind of problem-and-solution prompt that might appear on a standardized test. Let the writing process steps on the next page guide you in generating a response. Check the clocks next to each stage for ideas on how much time to allow along the way.

Sample Writing Situation

More and more young people are leaving your community after high school. What can be done to change this? Write a letter to the community government proposing a solution to this troubling problem. Discuss the roots of the problem as you see them, and cite specific reasons why your proposed solution will improve the situation. Make sure that you explain any steps needed to implement the solution you are proposing.

Prewriting

Allow about one fourth of your time for developing your solution and identifying supporting reasons.

Identify a Solution First, identify the solution to the problem posed in the prompt. When proposing a solution, it's critical that it be possible, practical, and realistic. Readers will ignore your proposal if they find it irresponsible. Before you begin drafting, evaluate whether or not your solution is realistic.

Drafting

Allow approximately half of your time for drafting. Write neatly and leave space to insert revisions later.

Organize Ideas Use a T-chart to organize information about both the problem and your proposed solution. Identify specific details concerning the problem, such as financial costs, human impact, and community response.

Stay Upbeat As you propose solutions, stress their benefits to the community. Briefly outline exactly how the solution will function and how it will solve the problem. Make sure you stress why the problem should be solved.

Revising, Editing, and Proofreading

Allow about one fourth of your time for revising and editing, and about five minutes for proofreading. Make changes neatly with a proofreader's insertion mark [^] or, if time permits, rewrite your work.

Rearrange Details Examine your draft to be sure that you have chosen a logical and effective organizational strategy. If not, rearrange details to more clearly show the relationship between the problem you have outlined and the solutions you are proposing.

Add Details Reread your essay. Look for places where an added step will clarify exactly how the solution will solve the problem. Insert transition words or rearrange sentences to reinforce the cause-and-effect link you are making.

Fix the Errors Proofread carefully to fix errors in grammar, spelling, and punctuation. Cross out errors with a single line, and neatly write in your correction above the line.

Research Writing

Researching in Everyday Life

Our era has been called the Age of Information because there are so many different sources of information—from traditional print sources, like books and magazines, to multimedia sources, including film and video, CD-ROMs, and the Internet. You conduct research every time you tap into any information source. For example, you become a researcher when you look up a telephone number, talk to your doctor about nutrition, or read about the life of a favorite celebrity.

Research often serves as a foundation for writing. For an end-of-semester essay, for example, you might incorporate historical research. Later in life, you may find that researching skills help you to produce business reports, write historic plays, or re-create historic homes.

▲ Critical Viewing
What three research ideas does this photograph inspire? Why? [**Analyze**]

What Is Research Writing?

Research writing—writing based on information gathered from outside sources—gives you the power to become an expert on any subject. This focused study of a topic helps you to explore and connect ideas, make discoveries, and share your findings with an audience. Effective research writing

- focuses on a specific, narrow topic, which is usually summarized in a thesis statement.
- presents relevant information from a wide variety of sources.
- structures the information logically and effectively.
- identifies the sources from which the information was drawn.

To preview the criteria on which your research writing may be evaluated, see the Rubric for Self-Assessment on page 266.

Types of Research Writing

Besides the formal research report, there are many other specialized types of writing that depend on accurate and insightful research:

- **Multimedia presentations** support written information with a variety of media, including slide shows, videos, audio recordings, and fine art.
- **Statistical reports** explore a subject through numerical data.
- **Annotated bibliographies** are a compilation and evaluation of resources available about a specific subject.
- **Experiment journals** are a record of the process and results of an experiment.

Writers in ACTION

Authors of all types of writing recognize the usefulness of research. Author N. Scott Momaday, for example, has the following to say about the importance of research:

"Research is absolutely essential to me as a writer. . . . In the case of The Way to Rainy Mountain, *I needed additional information. I needed to know about the history and the pre-history of the Kiowa people. And so I made the migration trip myself. . . . I saw firsthand the landscape that they had passed through, and I imagined —with the help of the stories—what it must have been like to come across this vast sea of plains."*

PREVIEW Student Work IN PROGRESS

While taking a class in photography, Michael S. Dougherty, a student at Central Bucks West High School in Doylestown, Pennsylvania, became interested in war photographers. In this chapter, you will see how he applied his curiosity about this subject to develop a strong piece of research writing. His completed report appears at the end of this chapter.

Model From Literature

Barbara Babcock is a Professor of English at the University of Arizona. She has published and lectured frequently on the subject of Pueblo ceramics. Guy and Doris Monthan, a husband-and-wife photographer-writer team, have for many years collaborated on writing about Native American art.

Reading **Writing**
Connection

Reading Strategy: Reread to Find Context Clues Reports involving research may sometimes contain specialized language with which you are unfamiliar. If you come across unfamiliar terminology, reread confusing passages to clarify their meaning.

▲ **Critical Viewing** If they could speak, what story might these Storyteller figures have to tell? Explain. **[Interpret]**

from

The Figurative Tradition

Barbara A. Babcock and Guy and Doris Monthan

In April 1981, the Third Annual Storyteller Show opened at the Adobe Gallery in Albuquerque, and, in contrast to the gallery's first show in 1979, in which the work of ten Rio Grande Pueblo potters was represented, there were over two hundred figures by sixty-three potters. When I reported this substantial development in the Storyteller revolution to Cochiti potter Helen Cordero, she replied, "See, I just don't know. I guess I really started something" (Cordero). And so, indeed, she did. When Helen Cordero shaped the first Storyteller doll in 1964, she made one of the oldest forms of Native American self-portraiture her own, reinvented a long-standing but moribund Cochiti tradition of figurative pottery, and engendered a revolution in Pueblo ceramics comparable to the revivals begun by Nampeyo, the Hopi-Tewa potter of Hano, and Maria Martinez of the Tewa Pueblo of San Ildefonso. In the last

The introduction begins with a recollection of an actual event in Babcock's life. By sharing this information, Babcock draws the reader into the report.

A quotation from an interview is placed in quotation marks.

two decades, Pueblo figurative pottery has been rediscovered, redefined, and reinvented by both producers and consumers. The "little people" that Helen Cordero has created have become prize-winning and world-famous collectors' items, and by the mid-1980's Storytellers and related figures were being made by more than 175 potters throughout the New Mexico Pueblos. In addition, figurines were being judged in categories other than "Pottery, Miscellaneous" and were regularly winning prizes at the Santa Fe Indian Market, sponsored by the Southwestern Association on Indian Affairs (SWAIA), and other major arts and crafts fairs throughout the Southwest; and galleries throughout the United States were having shows devoted entirely to figurative pottery. In the late 1970's and early 1980's, Sotheby Parke Bernet auctioned off old Cochiti figures for four-digit figures; and, for the first time in several centuries, Pueblo ceramic figurines began to be valued and respected as art.

Like most writings based on research, this piece contains formal language.

Pueblo culture, which has endured in the southwestern United States for almost two thousand years, is distinguished both by its instinct for survival and its capacity to revitalize itself (Dozier; Ortiz). Without pottery to store water and grain, settled Puebloan existence as it developed in the first centuries A.D. and was lived until the last decades of the nineteenth century would have been literally inconceivable. In the twentieth century, pottery has rarely been used for the storage, preparation, and consumption of food-stuffs, but it has become increasingly important symbolically and economically as a form of Pueblo cultural identity and survival (Brody, *The Creative Consumer* 70–84: Brody, *Pueblo Fine Arts* 603–608). The invention of the Storyteller and the attendant revival and expansion of figurative pottery making epitomize this capacity for revitalization, and the pages which follow document and describe these important changes and significant develop-ments in the shape of Pueblo pottery.

Background informa-tion contained in this paragraph helps the audience under-stand Babcock's subject more fully.

Archaeologists conjecture that ceramic technology was intro-duced into what is now the American Southwest from Mesoamerica about 500 B.C. Within centuries, pottery making had become an integral element of the three major prehistoric sedentary cultures: the Hohokam of the southern Arizona desert; the Mogollan of mountainous eastern Arizona and southwestern New Mexico; and the Anasazi in the high plateau country of northern Arizona and New Mexico and southern Utah and Colorado. In addition to utility ware, these Puebloan predecessors shaped and painted ceramic images of themselves, their gods, and the animals around them. The representative impulse in prehis-toric pottery takes several forms: fetish, figurine, and effigy or

LITERATURE

"Imitating Nature's Mineral Artistry" by Paul O'Neil is a research report on the formation of crystals. The selection appears in *Prentice Hall Literature: Timeless Voices, Timeless Themes, Platinum.*

effigy vessel, as well as both three-dimensional appliquéd figures and two-dimensional, painted figures on nonfigurative and figurative shapes. . . .

Both fired and unfired ceramic figurines of animals, birds, and humans have been found throughout the prehistoric Southwest, widely distributed in space and time. Morss has argued that "the earliest known occurrence of figurines . . . in the whole Southwest is in the early pit house village of the Hilltop Phase known as Bluff Ruin, in Forrestdale Valley in eastern Arizona, which is rather closely dated by a good cluster of tree-ring dates falling between A.D. 287 and 312 (Morss 27). Haury, however, dates Hohokam figurines found at Snaketown from the earliest, or Vahki, phase of the Pioneer Period, 300 B.C.–A.D. 100 (233–245). While the baseline for the figurine complex in the Southwest is debatable, there is no question that among the Anasazi true figurines were an integral element of Basketmaker III culture (A.D. 400–A.D. 650) and that the most common forms were human females. Most of these figurines consist of a minimally modeled slab or cylinder of clay no longer than six inches, with frontal orientation and perforated or appliquéd features; rarely are they painted or fired. The most interesting and elaborately modeled of Anasazi Basketmaker figurines are the Pillings figurines from northeast Utah described by Morss. . . .

Like figurines, human and animal effigy vessels have been found in three prehistoric southwestern cultures. The largest numbers of such forms are Anasazi in origin and date from Pueblo II and III (A.D. 900–A.D. 1300). In addition to effigy-handled vessels—such as mugs, pitchers, and jars, as well as ladles with "babe-in-cradle" handles—the most common effigy vessels are bird forms (Morss 27; Hammack 33–34). Inevitably, analyses of representational prehistoric art in general and of effigy vessels in particular lead archaeologists to look south, not only to the figurine complexes of the high cultures of Mesoamerica, but to Casas Grandes, the great trading center in what became northern Chihuahua. The largest community in the Southwest, Casas Grandes developed in the eleventh and twelfth centuries; between A.D. 1060 and A.D. 1340, it produced the finest of painted prehistoric effigy jars. The work of eleventh-century Casas ceramists was widely traded; Casas pottery (and its influence) has been found as far north as the great Anasazi Pueblo of Mesa Verde. Most of these polychrome figurative vessels are human, and in both their modeled form and painted decoration bear a striking resemblance to historic Pueblo figurines and effigies, especially

Babcock gives specific dates and other factual details she found while researching.

Transitions such as "in addition to" help to connect Babcock's ideas.

Source information appearing in parentheses follows details that Babcock found from outside sources.

those produced at Cochiti Pueblo in the last half of the nineteenth century. It does not seem possible that almost a thousand years elapsed between effigies such as the Casas mother and child and the "Madonna" or "Singing-Mother" figures produced at Cochiti in the late 1800's and early 1900's (DiPeso 32–37, 90). . . .

The figure of a woman holding or carrying a child or two, which Cochiti potters called a "Singing Mother" or "Madonna," was the most popular human form made at Cochiti between 1920 and 1960. But only a few women, such as Teresita Romero, Damacia Cordero, and Laurencita Herrara, made them, and, as Helen Cordero has said, "for a long time pottery was silent in the Pueblo" (Cordero). In the mid-1980's, when pottery was anything but silent at Cochiti and over fifty potters were making Storytellers and related figurines, many potters would tell you that their mother or aunt or grandmother "made Storytellers a long time ago." They were referring, I have discovered, not to the Storyteller as later conceived and made popular by Helen Cordero, but to this Cochiti traditional of pottery mothers singing to their children.

▼ **Critical Viewing**
What value would you place on a piece of art like this one? Why? [**Make a Judgment**]

Babcock wraps up her report by returning to the subject of Storyteller pottery as it is today.

A works-cited list provides complete information about the source material Babcock used.

Works Cited

Brody, J. J. "The Creative Consumer: Survival, Revival, and Invention in Southwest Indian Arts." *Ethnic and Tourist Arts*. Ed. Nelson Graburn. Berkeley: University of California Press, 1976. 70–84.

Brody, J. J. "Pueblo Fine Arts." *Handbook of North American Indians*, Vol. 9. (1979): 603–608.

Cordero, Helen. Personal Interview. 1981.

Di Peso, Charles C. "Casas Grandes Effigy Vessels". *American Indian Art* 2:4 (1977): 32–37, 90.

Dozier, Edward P. *The Pueblo Indians of North America*. New York: Holt, Rinehart and Winston, 1970.

Haury, Emil. "Figurines and Miscellaneous Clay Object." *Medallion Papers*. Vol. 25 (1937): 233–245.

Hammack, Laurens C. "Effigy Vessels in the Prehistoric American Southwest." *Arizona Highways* 50:2 (1974): 33–34.

Morss, Noel. "Clay Figurines of the American Southwest." *Papers of the Peabody Museum* 49:1. Cambridge, Mass.: Peabody Museum Press, 1954. 27.

Ortiz, Alfonso, ed. "The Dynamics of Pueblo Cultural Survival." American Anthropological Association Meeting. Washington, D.C. 1976.

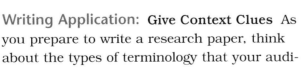

Reading Writing Connection

Writing Application: Give Context Clues As you prepare to write a research paper, think about the types of terminology that your audience may find baffling and the context clues you could use to help them understand those terms.

Prewriting

Choosing Your Topic

Choosing a subject for research writing is a matter of following your instincts and interests. Consider as a topic anything you would like to know more about, from antibiotics to zoology. These strategies can help you find topics to explore:

Strategies for Generating Topics

1. **Refer to a Map, Globe, or Atlas** A map, globe, or atlas can be a useful springboard to a world of research topics in geography, social studies, history, and other areas. Turn to a random page of an atlas or spin a globe of the world, and see where your finger lands; or open to a region you want to visit or know more about, and really inspect the surrounding terrain. Make a list of potential topics, and then evaluate your list. Choose one item as the topic for your research.

2. **Scan Headlines** A newspaper or magazine can provide many inspirations for subjects that connect to contemporary issues. Use a marker or self-sticking notes to indicate intriguing headlines or articles. Review your notes to find a topic you want to investigate in a research report.

3. **Make a Celebrity List** Biographical research can give you remarkable insights into the people you admire and respect. Make a list of celebrities about whom you would like to know more. You might organize your list into categories of accomplishment, such as athletes, actors, politicians, philanthropists, scientists, or philosophers. Review your list, and select the person you find most interesting to research. A sample listing of possible research subjects appears below:

Try it out! Use the interactive Make a Celebrity List activity in **Section 12.2**, on-line or on CD-ROM.

Artists	Authors	Composers and Musicians
Diego Rivera	Michael Crichton	Duke Ellington
Henri Matisse	Mark Twain	Edith Piaf
Georgia O'Keeffe	Edith Wharton	Wolfgang Amadeus Mozart
Charles Schultz	George Eliot	George Gershwin
Mary Cassatt	John Updike	Elvis Presley
Jan van Eyck	Agatha Christie	Suzanne Vega
Camille Pissarro	Carl Sagan	Lyle Lovett
Henry Moore	Jamaica Kincaid	Paul McCartney

TOPIC BANK

Use these topics to help launch your research writing.

1. **Essay on a Historical Personality** Choose an influential historical personality, such as Genghis Khan, Joan of Arc, or Henry VIII. Begin by reading an encyclopedia entry to get a helpful overview, and choose one specific aspect of the person's life to research.

2. **Investigation of a Scientific Phenomenon** Select a unique occurrence on Earth or in space, such as fjords, coral atolls, or the aurora borealis. Browse through a science textbook to find a topic and some initial information. Use several additional sources to help you present a complete explanation for your audience.

Responding to Fine Art

Federal Brigade Commanded by General Winfield Scott, Julian Scott, Smithsonian Institution

3. List the historical conflicts that come to mind as you study the painting *Federal Brigade Commanded by General Winfield Scott* by Julian Scott. Choose one of these conflicts to research.

Responding to Literature

4. Read "A Marginal World" by Rachel Carson, a description of the ecology of the edge of the sea. Identify a topic she discusses that interests you and write a research report on it. The selection appears in *Prentice Hall Literature: Timeless Voices, Timeless Themes,* Platinum.

☑ Cooperative Writing Opportunity

5. **Readers' Guide** With a group, choose a popular author, and prepare a readers' guide to the author's works. Divide the author's writings evenly among group members. Then, have each student compose entries giving publication information, a summary of the work, the critical reaction to the work, and a rating or an evaluation. Share your completed readers' guide with the class.

Narrowing Your Topic

If your topic is not narrow enough to be covered fully within the space limitations of your essay, narrow it before you begin your research.

Use Research Clues to Narrow Your Topic

Use library or Internet sources for ideas on ways to divide subjects for a narrower focus.

- **Look at encyclopedia entries,** which often include sub-headings and highlighted key words. Both of these features can help you identify narrower topics you might consider.

- **Read the table of contents** of books and the title and sub-headings of magazine articles and Web pages to get ideas about different aspects of your topic.

- **Scan book indexes** to find groupings of related ideas.

Considering Your Audience and Purpose

As you gather details for your research report, choose words and details that will appeal to your audience and help you to accomplish your purpose for writing.

Use Formal Language

To reflect a serious tone, most writers of research reports use formal language. The features of formal language include sophisticated vocabulary, sentences with varied structures, and avoidance of slang and contractions. As you gather details about your topic, keep in mind that your details and word choice should be precise and formal.

▼ Critical Viewing
How is the scene in this illustration similar to and different from modern work-day conditions? **[Compare and Contrast]**

Informal Language	Formal Language
Back in the 1850's and later, things changed a great deal for lots of women, especially in New England. Factories began to make the same stuff that women made at home. So the women didn't have any choice. They had to take factory jobs.	During the second half of the nineteenth century, the lives of many New England women changed dramatically. As factories began to compete with home industries, many women who had earned money by sewing and knitting at home were compelled to take factory jobs for the first time.

Gathering Information

Make a research plan to find the information you need from the wide array of sources available.

Perform Library Research

Historian Barbara Tuchman acknowledges, "To a historian, libraries are food, shelter, and even muse." Develop your library skills to help you use your library time effectively.

- Discover how your library is organized. Use the catalog to search for titles. Remember that books are organized by categories, so when you find a useful volume, be sure to explore the nearby titles as well.

- Use indexes like the *Readers' Guide to Periodical Literature* and bibliographies to find information about publications related to specific types of subjects.

- Many libraries today offer Internet access so that you can search for topics on the World Wide Web. Use key words to focus and speed your research.

To organize your library research plan, make a K-W-L Chart, filling in what you **k**now, what you **w**ant to know and what you **l**earned during your research.

Student Work
IN PROGRESS

Name: *Michael S. Dougherty*
Central Bucks West High School
Doylestown, PA

Guiding Research With a K-W-L Chart

After narrowing the subject of war photography to focus on one photographer, Robert Capa, Michael used a K-W-L chart to guide his library research.

Know	Want to Know	What I Learned
Robert Capa was a successful war photographer.	How did he get his start?	At the age of 18, he worked as a darkroom apprentice in Berlin.
Capa was often present during war battles.	How did he feel about being at battle scenes?	"It is not always easy to stand aside and be unable to do anything except record the suffering around one."

Take Organized Notes

One major challenge of conducting research is keeping track of all the information you discover. Use the following tips to organize your material.

Source cards list the publication information for each source you consult. When you find a source that you might use, make a source card for it and assign it a number.

Note cards list specific details for use in your writing, such as direct quotations or summaries of important facts.

Photocopy and highlight pages from sources you plan to use. Also, photocopy copyright information to use in your works-cited list.

Print copies of on-line source information for later reference. Be sure that the Web address can be clearly seen in the printout.

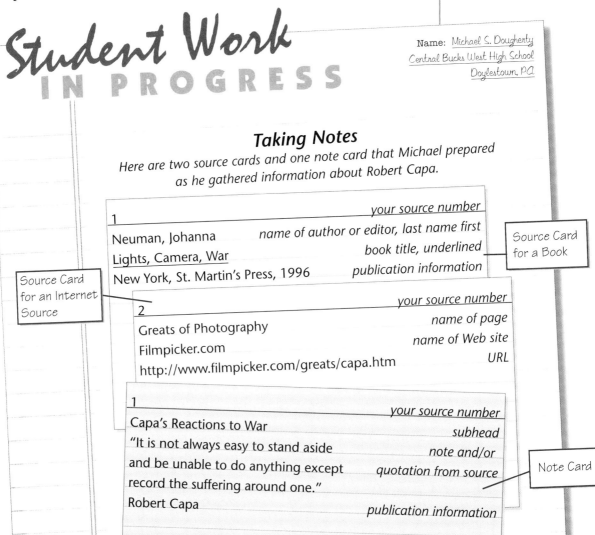

Student Work
IN PROGRESS

Name: Michael S. Dougherty
Central Bucks West High School
Doylestown, PA

Taking Notes

Here are two source cards and one note card that Michael prepared as he gathered information about Robert Capa.

1   your source number
Neuman, Johanna   name of author or editor, last name first
Lights, Camera, War   book title, underlined
New York, St. Martin's Press, 1996   publication information

> Source Card for a Book

> Source Card for an Internet Source

2   your source number
Greats of Photography   name of page
Filmpicker.com   name of Web site
http://www.filmpicker.com/greats/capa.htm   URL

1   your source number
Capa's Reactions to War   subhead
"It is not always easy to stand aside   note and/or
and be unable to do anything except   quotation from source
record the suffering around one."
Robert Capa
    publication information

> Note Card

Doing Investigative Research

Consider supplementing the information that you collect from published sources with your own investigative research. Conducting your own interviews, polls, and surveys can make your writing uniquely powerful: You can present facts and quotations that no one else can.

- **Interviews** Conduct an interview to get information directly from a primary source. Prepare for your interview by finding out about the subject you will interview. Familiarize yourself with the person's background so that you can ask informed questions. Be sure to compile a list of questions beforehand, but feel free to depart from your list when additional questions arise naturally.

Interview Tips

√ Prepare questions in advance.

√ Avoid asking "yes" and "no" questions.

√ Wait for answers. Don't interrupt the interviewee.

√ Ask permission to tape the interview.

- **Polls and Surveys** Use polls and surveys to gather information about public opinion. Write survey questions that are unbiased and easy to tabulate. Choose a random sample for your target group. Be careful when you interpret your poll results. Your group may not be representative of a larger population. For example, if you interview only seniors at your school, their opinions will not reflect those of all students in the school.

- **Experiments** Conduct experiments to test theories in science or social sciences. For example, to test a theory about student alertness, you might give different groups of students the same quick quiz early in the morning and late in the afternoon to see which group does better.

Whenever you conduct your own investigations, take careful notes using source cards and note cards. You may want to include information about your interviews or polls in your bibliography.

🔋 Research Tip

To write an effective survey, provide a limited number of responses. For example, ask people to rate their opinions using a 1–10 scale or to categorize their feelings according to terms like "strongly support," "support," "oppose," and "strongly oppose."

▼ Critical Viewing
What sort of research is the pictured student performing? Explain. **[Analyze]**

Drafting

Shaping Your Writing

Research writing needs an effective organization in order to communicate clearly with an audience.

Arrange Your Findings

Use your note cards or photocopied materials to identify major aspects of your topic. Gather related notes together, and consider their relationships. Arranging your notes on a table or adjusting their arrangement in a stack can help you try out different organizations.

Choose an Organizational Strategy

One of the most important decisions you will make as you draft is how to organize your information. A carefully planned structure can make the difference between powerful writing and confusing disorder. The chart below shows several common ways of organizing research writing. Choose a logical organization that matches the content and purpose of your writing.

Description	Uses
Chronological Order: Events are presented in time order.	Chronological order is useful for research reports on historical topics and for experiment journals. For example, if you were writing about a time in history, you could trace actual events.
Part-to-Whole Order: Aspects or parts of a larger topic are described one by one to build a complete picture.	Use this organization to examine the categories that make up a whole. For example, if you were writing about volcanoes, you could show how the location of volcanoes and volcanic eruptions have helped scientists learn about the Earth's interior.
Order of Importance: Details are presented from most important to least important or from least important to most important.	Order of importance can help you build an argument. To write about safety and skiing, you might begin with the least important or most obvious—wearing warm gloves—and end with the most important safety factor—avoiding restricted zones.

Prepare an Outline

Prepare an outline to organize the details you have gathered. Begin by reviewing the notes or research materials you have photocopied and grouped. Then, use Roman numerals to indicate major sections of your report. Use capital letters to indicate subsections of each major section, and use Arabic numbers to indicate specifics you plan to discuss within each subsection. As you develop an outline, the entries at each level should be nearly equal in importance.

Your outline may be as broad or detailed as you like. Following are two types of outlines you may like to consider:

- A "sentence outline" can be used to help you rough out your ideas.

- A traditional outline will help you determine the major sections of your topic and will guide you as you write.

Name: Michael S. Dougherty
Central Bucks West High School
Doylestown, PA

Preparing an Outline

Michael created an outline to help him organize while drafting. His research report is organized chronologically.

I. Introduction: War Journalists

II. Birth and life in Hungary
  A. born Andrei Friedmann
  B. exiled due to activism

III. Germany
  A. darkroom apprentice
  B. first assignment: photographing Leon Trotsky
  C. left Germany because of Hitler's rise

IV. Paris
  A. Friedman invents Robert Capa to increase his prices
  B. An editor finds out
  C. Assumes the name Robert Capa

Providing Elaboration

Elaborate on Notes

As you draft, refer to your note cards or photocopies of source material to provide facts, statistics, and quotations you have discovered. In addition to citing your findings, also provide your own ideas, examples, and analyses as you weave together the information you found while researching. For example, if you give a statistic, also tell why you find the statistic interesting or significant.

Be sure to paraphrase the words of a source unless you plan to put the person's exact words within quotation marks. All source material, whether taken word for word or paraphrased, must be cited in your report.

Student Work
IN PROGRESS

Name: Michael S. Dougherty
Central Bucks West High School
Doylestown, PA

Elaborating on Notes

Michael referred to his notes as he drafted his report on Robert Capa. In addition to using the facts he found in his notes, Michael added his own insights to elaborate on what he found.

He was the sole photographer of the bloodiest landing, Omaha Beach, and took 106 photographs in what he considered to be an outstanding personal victory. Unfortunately, a darkroom assistant turned on too much heat while developing the pictures and destroyed all but eight. Despite such setbacks, Capa remained dedicated to photographing the war effort, making several other parachute landings as well (Stein 189).

Although his talents as a war journalist were outstanding, photographing the frightening images of war was never an easy task for Capa. As he once said, "It is not always easy to stand aside and be unable to do anything except record the suffering around one." Capa's humanity and compassion shine through his powerful photographs.

> Although Michael paraphrased his source material, he was careful to include an in-text citation to credit the source's information.

> Michael used what he found out about Capa to come up with this analysis.

12.4 Revising

Writer E. B. White once commented, "When you say something, make sure you have said it. The chances of your having said it are only fair." During revision, you have the opportunity to make sure that you have said what you wanted to say. You can make adjustments in your paper's organization, presentation of ideas, and language.

Revising Your Overall Structure

Create Unity

The first step in revising is to consider the "big picture." Your research writing needs to show unity, that is, a sense that the entire work relates to one specific subject. While you were drafting, your primary goal was to get the words down on paper. During revision, you take a close look at those words to make sure that you haven't strayed from your main idea, added empty padding to fill space, or used an illogical organization that is certain to baffle your audience.

▶ **REVISION STRATEGY**
Using Marginal Notes to Identify the Structure

Review the major sections and subsections in your report by writing notes about the main points of each paragraph. To make these notes stand out, work with a red pen or place self-sticking notes in the margins of your draft. After writing marginal comments or descriptions, read them from beginning to end to make sure that the flow makes sense. You might consider rearranging sections that flow awkwardly or cutting sections that stray from the central topic.

In the example at right, one unrelated section of a research paper about the Channel was deleted and another was moved to a more appropriate position.

Technology Tip

If you are working electronically, boldface any passages that are word-for-word quotations from a source. When you revise, you can quickly proofread those passages against the original source to check for accuracy.

THE ENGLISH CHANNEL TUNNEL

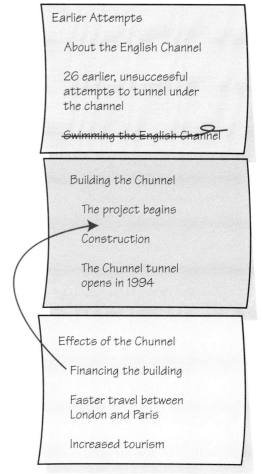

Earlier Attempts

About the English Channel

26 earlier, unsuccessful attempts to tunnel under the channel

~~Swimming the English Channel~~

Building the Chunnel

The project begins

Construction

The Chunnel tunnel opens in 1994

Effects of the Chunnel

Financing the building

Faster travel between London and Paris

Increased tourism

Revising Your Paragraphs

Every paragraph you write should have a clear organization that explains a single idea.

▶ **REVISION STRATEGY**
Coding to Identify the Structure

There are many different patterns you can use to organize your paragraphs. Three of the most common patterns are identified by the initials *TRI*, *PS*, and *QA*. Read through each paragraph in your research writing, and identify its structure. Revise paragraphs so that each is structured effectively.

T R I

When almost 100,000 people flooded to California in search of gold in 1848 and 1849, some cities grew almost instantly. } Topic

These cities were known as "boom towns." } Restatement

One city on the Yuba River had only two houses in September 1848. A year later, those two houses had expanded into a city of 1,000 inhabitants. } Illustration

P S

Scientists are searching for new ways to handle epidemics that are spread by insects like mosquitoes. } Problem

Spraying can often kill the insects, but it affects other animals and the environment as well. Intervention on the genetic level may offer the most promising solution. Soon, researchers might be able to generate mosquitoes that cannot carry specific germs. } Solution

Q A

How did *gerrymandering* get its name? } Question

Elbridge Gerry, an early Massachusetts governor, redivided election districts to strengthen his party. Artist Gilbert Stuart noticed that one of the new districts had the shape of a salamander. He drew a head, wings, and a tail onto the map. A newspaper editor added the caption "Gerrymander." } Answer

🔵 Learn More

To learn more about writing effective paragraphs, see Chapter 3.

Revising Your Sentences

When most of the sentences within a written work are similar in length, type, or structure, it can have a numbing effect on the audience. Read through your draft carefully, and vary the length, type, and structure of your sentences to ensure that your writing is lively.

Invert Some Sentences for Variety

Most sentences contain a subject followed by a verb. To add variety to your sentences, you may want to invert the order of the subject and verb. As you do so, be careful not to introduce an error in subject-verb agreement.

▶ **REVISION STRATEGY**
Color-Coding to Identify Subject-Verb Patterns

First, circle the subjects and verbs in each sentence. Review your draft. If every sentence contains the traditional subject-verb order, invert a sentence to add variety to your writing.

Student Work
IN PROGRESS

Name: Michael S. Dougherty
Central Bucks West High School
Doylestown, PA

Color-Coding to Identify Patterns

While revising, Michael noticed that he always used a subject-verb pattern. He inverted a sentence in this paragraph to add variety to his writing.

Americans (honor and respect) the brave citizens who, over the years, have fought for their country. (They) (have ensured) the tranquillity of our people by bearing arms against the ever-changing threats to our nation's security. *Often overlooked, however, are* Scores of men and women who have gone into battle defenseless against enemy attacks (are often overlooked) however: wartime journalists. With only a camera or a pad and pencil in hand, (they) (live) a soldier's life while working a civilian job. Looking danger in the face, this unarmed (crew) (records) the dramatic details of war to inform people at home, as well as generations to come.

Grammar in Your Writing
Special Problems With Agreement

All sentences contain at least one subject and one verb. The subject and verb pairs should agree in number. In some instances, knowing how to make the subject and verb agree may not be immediately clear.

Inverted Sentences

When a verb precedes its subject in a sentence, the sentence is said to be inverted. A subject that comes after its verb must agree with it in number:

Under the boardwalk was a tiny crab.

There are no more seats left in the auditorium.

Collective Nouns

Collective nouns—such as *audience, class, couple, crowd, faculty, group,* and *team*—can be either singular or plural depending upon how they are used.

If a collective noun refers to a whole group, use a singular verb:

The army approaches the border.
The jury listens to the evidence.

If a collective noun refers to individual group members, use a plural verb:

The faculty discuss the proposal.
The jury are unable to reach a consensus.

Confusing Plurals

Some nouns are plural in form but singular in meaning. Many of these nouns name branches of knowledge: *ethics, mathematics, physics, politics, social studies.* Others name a single unit or idea: *measles, news, series.*

If a noun is plural in form but singular in meaning, use a singular verb:

Physics is an interesting subject.
The news today seems good.

Find It in Your Reading Review the excerpt from *The Figurative Tradition* on pages 246–249 of this chapter. Within it, identify one collective noun and one noun that is plural in form but singular in meaning.

Find It in Your Writing Review the subject-verb agreement in your sentences, paying close attention to your use of collective nouns and plurals. Circle any subject-verb pairs that you want to reconsider. Discuss circled pairs with a peer reviewer.

To learn more about agreement, see Chapter 24.

Revising Your Word Choice

Delete Instances of Wordiness

Direct writing is more effective and interesting than writing that is weighed down with unnecessary words. Review your draft, and eliminate instances of wordiness.

WORDY: As a matter of fact, there are many qualities in Capa's photographs that are beautiful, despite the fact that they depict war.

CONCISE: Many of Capa's photographs are beautiful, even though they depict war.

▶ **REVISION STRATEGY**
Deleting Empty Words

This chart shows some common phrases that are often unnecessary. Read through your draft to locate the following phrases. If the phrase does not help connect ideas, delete it.

EMPTY WORDS AND PHRASES

as a matter of fact	in my opinion	to the extent that
as I said before	it is a fact that	the reason was that
by way of	it is also true that	there is/there are
despite the fact that	needless to say	the thing is
given the fact that	of course	the type of
indeed	on account of the fact that	what I mean is

Peer Review

Review With a K-W-L Chart

Determine how effectively your research writing meets your audience's needs by asking a peer reviewer or review team to complete a K-W-L chart as they review your work. Briefly describe the topic, and have your reviewers write what they **k**now about the topic and what they **w**ant to know. After reading your essay, reviewers complete the chart by adding what they **l**earned.

Use the charts to focus a group discussion. Then, incorporate appropriate suggestions from your peers as you revise your research writing.

12.5 Editing and Proofreading

Before you hand in your final draft, prepare a works-cited list, and proofread your draft to correct errors in spelling, grammar, and punctuation.

Preparing a Reference List

No research paper is complete without a reference list. Before you turn in your paper, compile a works-cited list on which you completely and accurately document the source material for your research paper. Check with your teacher to confirm the type of format your works-cited list should take.

Following is a list of style manuals you may want to consult as you put together your works-cited list:

- *Modern Language Association Handbook* (MLA)
- *American Psychological Association Handbook* (APA)
- *The Chicago Manual of Style* (CMS)

Focusing on Proofreading

Proofread to make sure all quoted passages, book titles, author names, and page references within parenthetical citations and on your works-cited page are correct. Also, check to be sure that your use of colons, commas, and other punctuation symbols conforms to a specific style of citation.

- Underline the titles of long written works and the titles of publications that are printed as a single work.
- Also, underline the titles of movies, TV and radio series, lengthy works of music, paintings, and sculptures.
- Use quotation marks around the titles of short works.
- Use quotation marks to set off titles of photographs.

Research writing often refers to titles of works, from books and articles to artworks and Internet sites. Check that you have capitalized and punctuated each title correctly.

Remember to capitalize the first, last, and key words in a title. Conjunctions and prepositions shorter than four letters are not considered key words.

Grammar in Your Writing
Citing Sources

In your research paper, be sure to credit the sources of information. To do this, include endnotes, footnotes, or internal citations within the text. Also, prepare a bibliography or works-cited list that will appear on the last page of your writing.

Footnotes and Endnotes When using footnotes and endnotes to provide internal documentation, include full details about the source and cite the page number. Indicate a footnote or an endnote by placing a number at the bottom of the page on which the information cited appears; for an endnote, place the documentation in numerical order on a page preceding the reference list.

> **Example footnote:** Bruce Goldfarb, *King of the Desert* (New York: Leland, 1999)

Parenthetical Documentation Using parenthetical references allows readers to learn about sources quickly and easily, without having to refer to a footnote. A parenthetical reference usually includes the author's last name and the page numbers from which the information is taken. The full publication information about each source to which you refer in parentheses will appear on your works-cited list.

> **Example:** Two thirds of employed actors appear only in commercials (Fleming 55).

Works-Cited List A works-cited list appears at the end of a piece of research writing and includes the publication information for any source used or quoted. Titles are usually arranged in alphabetical order by author's last name and are underscored or italicized. Your source cards will have all of the information you need to include on this list.

Bibliography Present your sources in a standardized format based on the type of resource referenced. Include the author's names, source title, place of publication, publisher, and date of publication.

> **Example entry:** Dryson, Edna. *Knowing a Thing or Two*. Chicago: Tower, 2000.

Find It in Your Reading Review the works-cited list in the excerpt from *The Figurative Tradition* on pages 246–249. Explain why each title is underlined or set in quotation marks.

Find It in Your Writing Check the punctuation of the titles in your research writing. Make sure that you have used capitalization, underlining, and quotation marks correctly.

To learn more about punctuating cited sources, see Citing Sources and Preparing Manuscript on pp. 848–854.

Publishing and Presenting

Following are some ways to share your research writing:

Building Your Portfolio

1. **Class Anthology** Assemble an anthology of essays by combining your class's examples of research writing. Discuss the organization and title of the anthology, and work together to write an introduction or foreword explaining the project. Bind the anthology, and make it available to classmates.

2. **Internet Publication** Use the Internet to share your research writing. Send your finished draft to a friend or relative by e-mail, or submit your writing to a Web site that publishes student writing.

Reflecting on Your Writing

Think over your research writing experience. Then, answer the following questions, and record your responses in your portfolio.

- Where did you find the most useful information?
- Which writing strategies worked so well that you would like to try them again?

Internet Tip

To see model research papers scored with this rubric, go on-line:
PHSchool.com
Enter Web Code:
eek-1001

Rubric for Self-Assessment

Evaluate your research writing using the following criteria.

	Score 4	Score 3	Score 2	Score 1
Audience and Purpose	Focuses on a clearly stated thesis, starting from a well-framed question; gives complete citations	Focuses on a clearly stated thesis; gives citations	Focuses mainly on the chosen topic; gives some citations	Presents information without a clear focus; few or no citations
Organization	Presents information in logical order, emphasizing details of central importance	Presents information in logical order	Presents information logically, but organization is poor in places	Presents information in a scattered, disorganized manner
Elaboration	Draws clear conclusions from information gathered from multiple sources	Draws conclusions from information gathered from multiple sources	Explains and interprets some information	Presents information with little or no interpretation or synthesis
Use of Language	Shows overall clarity and fluency; contains few mechanical errors	Shows good sentence variety; contains some errors in spelling, puncutation, or usage	Uses awkward or overly simple sentence structures; contains many mechanical errors	Contains incomplete thoughts and mechanical errors that make the writing confusing

12.7 Student Work
IN PROGRESS

FINAL DRAFT

Robert Capa

Michael S. Dougherty
Central Bucks West High School
Doylestown, Pennsylvania

Americans honor and respect the brave citizens who, over the years, have fought for their country. They have ensured the tranquillity of our people by bearing arms against the ever-changing threats to our nation's security. Often overlooked, however, are scores of men and women who have gone into battle defenseless against enemy attacks: wartime journalists. With only a camera or a pad and pencil in hand, they live a soldier's life while working a civilian job. Looking danger in the face, this unarmed crew records the dramatic details of war to inform people at home, as well as generations to come. The public certainly owes much to these brave and loyal workers. One of the most renowned of these war journalists was a photographer named Robert Capa, who dedicated his life to capturing the essence of war on film.

Capa was born Andrei Friedmann in Budapest, Hungary, in 1913. Little is known about his childhood, except that he did not have formal training in photography. Indeed, he taught himself everything that he learned in this field (Adato 98). While a high-school student in Hungary, he was exiled because of his political beliefs. Leaving his home country would have a strong influence on his life and career as a photographer.

In 1931, Friedmann got a job with a picture agency in Berlin, where he took his first assignment. He traveled to Copenhagen to photograph Russian Communist leader Leon Trotsky. Upon completing this assignment, he returned to Germany but was driven out by Hitler's menacing regime. Cast out from his second home, Friedmann found a new, more welcoming home in Paris, France.

While he was in Paris, Friedmann's career began to flourish, but not without an initial struggle. Even at the start of

Michael builds his opening paragraph to a thesis statement that describes the topic of his essay.

▼ **Critical Viewing**
What type of personality might you guess Capa to have had, based on this photograph? Explain.
[Speculate]

his year in Paris, Friedmann was proud of the powerful images he was creating. However, he was dismayed that they were not selling for very much money, so he devised a plan that would benefit him and his wife financially. In order to sell prints for higher prices, Friedmann posed as the assistant to a completely fictitious American photographer named Robert Capa. For a while, he and his wife, who pretended to be the famous American's secretary, were making a substantial profit with this scheme. Unfortunately, in 1936, an editor recognized their fraud and threatened to expose them. Instead of abandoning the name, as the editor suggested, Friedmann decided to resolve the situation by adopting it. For the rest of his life, Andrei Friedmann was known as Robert Capa.

Michael clearly and effectively organizes his paper using chronological organization of details.

Later the same year, a conflict in Spain began to attract some of the world's attention away from the rising Nazi regime. Attracted by the limitless possibilities that war-field photography offered, Capa got a job with *Life* magazine and left France to cover the war. It was here that he developed a knack for war photography that made him famous. By shooting such remarkable images as "Death of a Loyalist Militiaman Frederico Borrell García, Cerro Muriano (Córdoba Front), 1936," Capa's reputation steadily grew until the European and American Press circles named him the "greatest war photographer in the world" (Emery 538).

Parenthetical documentation is used to name the sources of information. The full citation for the source appears at the end. The numbers indicate the page number.

In the following years, Robert Capa spent time covering China's war with Japan. He documented this war, but he was given his greatest opportunity when the Allied Forces declared war against Hitler's Axis Powers, which signaled the beginning of World War II.

As a Hungarian citizen based in America during this war, Capa suffered greatly. Because the Allies had declared war against the Axis, many Americans felt angry with Middle Europeans. Capa, a citizen of a country united with others against America, was categorized as an enemy alien. He was fired from his job at *Life* and found it difficult to make ends meet (Lande 251).

Michael uses formal language to share the facts and details he discovered during research.

Finally in 1943, Capa was hired to cover the war overseas for *Collier's* magazine. His first assignment was the North African invasion. Dodging bullets as he traveled across the countryside, Capa was always in the center of the action. He made many friends, but he was eventually fired from *Collier's* for pooling, or sharing, his pictures with them. Scrambling for a new assignment, Capa took a job once again for *Life*. He was assigned to fill in for a sick man who was scheduled to jump out of a plane with a squad of paratroopers. Although he was nervous, Capa showed his dedication to his job by hurling himself from the plane into the African canopy (Stein 188).

Michael italicized the titles of magazines. He proofread his writing carefully to make sure that it was free of distracting errors.

Capa's success was capped, however, when he was selected as one of four photographers who would make the D-Day landing in Normandy. He was the sole photographer of the bloodiest landing, Omaha Beach, and took 106 photographs in what he considered to be an outstanding personal victory (Neuman 85). Unfortunately, a darkroom assistant turned on too much heat while developing the pictures and destroyed all but eight. Despite such setbacks, Capa remained dedicated to photographing the war effort, making several other parachute landings as well (Stein 189).

Although his talents as a war journalist were outstanding, photographing the frightening images of war was never an easy task for Capa. As he once said, "It is not always easy to stand aside and be unable to do anything except record the suffering around one." Capa's humanity and compassion shine through his powerful photographs.

World War II eventually ended, but Capa's career moved forcefully ahead. After only three years, a conflict between the Israelis and Arabs broke out. Capa was one of the first men there and one of the first in Indochina to record fighting between the French and the Viet Minh.

Tragically, covering this event in 1954, Robert Capa was killed after stepping on a land mine. He had lived for forty years and covered four major wars. By capturing the horrifying and moving images of war, Robert Capa served America and its journalism well, eventually sacrificing his life for a profession he loved.

▲ **Critical Viewing**
This photograph shows the Normandy invasion in action. If the invasion were to take place today, how would it be similar and different? Explain. **[Modify]**

Michael closes with a strong restatement of his opening thesis.

Works Cited

Adato, Allison. "The Double Life of a Legendary War Photographer."
   Life, March 1997: 98–103.
Emery, Edwin. *The Press and America: An Interpretive History of
   the Mass Media*. 3rd Edition. Englewood Cliffs, NJ: Prentice
   Hall, Inc., 1972.
Lande, Nathaniel. *Dispatches from the Front: News Accounts of
   American Wars*, 1776–1991. New York: Henry Holt and Company, 1995.
Neuman, Johanna. *Lights, Camera, War*. New York: St. Martin's
   Press, 1996.
Stein, M. L. *Under Fire: The Story of American War Correspondents*.
   New York: Julian Messner, 1968.

Connected Assignment
Documented Essay

In a **documented essay,** a thesis or main idea is presented and supported with evidence that comes in part from research. A documented essay is generally less formal than a traditional report. It also may contain fewer research sources and focus on a contemporary topic. Evidence within a documented essay might include more immediate or subjective information, such as interviews rather than just factual data. Also, sources are cited in full in parentheses immediately following appropriate text; no works-cited list is provided. Finally, like a magazine article, a documented essay may reflect a more informal tone than a traditional research paper.

An effective documented essay contains

▲ Critical Viewing What sources might you use to find information about the Hubble Telescope, pictured here? **[Hypothesize]**

- a thesis or main idea.

- evidence or details to support that main idea.

- language appropriate for its audience and purpose.

- an effective and logical organization.

- parenthetical citations that reveal source information.

Develop your own documented essay, using the writing process skills that follow:

Prewriting

Choosing Your Topic Make sure to choose a topic you're genuinely interested in—you'll need to immerse yourself in it to write a successful documented essay. Listen to or watch the day's headline news, read the school's newspaper, or exchange ideas with a friend.

Narrowing Your Topic Once you have chosen a topic, narrow it so that you can discuss it fully within the space limitations of your essay. To narrow your topic, make a web by writing your broad topic in the center. Then, list related subtopics around the broad topic. Choose one of the subtopics as the focus for your documented essay.

Gathering and Organizing Details Gather details from a variety of sources to support the main idea of your documented essay. Some details you may research in books or on-line; some you may discover for yourself by interviewing or conducting surveys. Take careful notes as you gather details. Be sure that you accurately copy down all the source information you will use in parenthetical documentation.

Once you have a body of facts and examples, decide on the most effective way in which to present them. Develop an outline like the one that follows to organize your documented essay.

I. Hubble Telescope

   A. History & Development
      1. Invention team
      2. Sponsor

   B. Current Mission
      1. Successes
      2. Failures

   C. Future Missions
      1. Goals
      2. Next generation

Drafting Open your essay by stating your thesis or main idea. You may also want to grab the interest of your audience by sharing an interesting anecdote or posing an interesting question. In the body of the essay, weave illustrative examples with explanatory text. Refer to your outline to ensure that your essay is logically organized. Insert parenthetical documentation of source material as you draft.

Revising and Editing Ask a peer to read your essay aloud. Listen for and correct any inconsistencies in tone or attitude toward your subject. Add or clarify details by scanning your notes. Double-check all details for accuracy, and proofread carefully. Where appropriate, consider putting large blocks of data into a chart or graph to make your presentation more appealing.

Publishing and Presenting Hand write or print out a neat copy of your documented essay. Add photographs, charts, and other visuals to enhance the information within the text. Then, share your essay with peers or family members.

Grammar and Style Tip

As you draft, use transitions such as *then*, *since*, and *however* to make connections between your ideas.

Spotlight on the Humanities

Recognizing Musical Achievements

Focus on Music: Franz Schubert

Research allows you to study the past as well as the present, finding out about famous people and events of centuries ago. Born in Vienna, Franz Schubert (1797–1828) grew up in a musical family but remained a fairly unknown composer throughout his lifetime. The lyrical quality of Schubert's work made it compatible with the music form known as the *lied*. Later in his life, he composed pieces inspired by the nineteenth-century poet Johann Wolfgang von Goethe. Schubert's expressive music reflected the poetry of writers such as Goethe. Schubert established the German *lied* as a new art form in the nineteenth century.

Film Connection The rivalry between Wolfgang Amadeus Mozart and Schubert's teacher Antonio Salieri is the focus of the film *Amadeus* (1984). Originally a Broadway play by Peter Shaffer, the film won eight Academy Awards, including Best Picture, Best Director, and Best Actor.

Literature Connection Franz Schubert was inspired by the words of poet and writer Johann Wolfgang von Goethe (1749–1832), who was at the center of the literary movements during the "Age of Goethe" in Germany (1770–1832). The poetry, dramas, novels, and essays of Goethe have influenced writers of such esteem as Samuel Taylor Coleridge, Percy Bysshe Shelley, Henry Wadsworth Longfellow, and Harriet Beecher Stowe.

Research Writing Activity:
Research Report on Franz Schubert

It may have surprised you to read that Schubert was a relatively unknown composer throughout his lifetime. For other interesting facts and anecdotes about Schubert's life and works, research him at your local library or on the Internet. Then, write a research report on Schubert's life and inspirational works. Share your research paper with your classmates.

Media and Technology Skills

Using Media to Produce a Documentary

Activity: Produce a Video Report

Documentaries are nonfiction films that share many kinds of information with an audience. You can use a video camera to produce a well-researched and effective documentary that uses images, sounds, and narration to communicate ideas.

Think About It Shoot a 5–6 minute documentary based on research into a topic. As you select a topic, consider the possibilities that video offers. For example, you may want to include interviews with local experts or family members. The people available to you may suggest suitable topics or themes.

Research It Use a variety of sources to collect information for your documentary. Look for opportunities to expand your research to include the Internet, CD-ROMs, and other media.

Storyboard It While you gather facts, you will begin to plan your documentary. A storyboard will help you plan the sequence of shots. It might also help guide your research by suggesting new directions or missing elements.

<aside>

Filming Tips

- Film a variety of locations to add interest.
- Choose interview settings that are not too distracting.
- Vary the distance of the camera from interview subjects.
- Look for ways to incorporate motion as you film. Pan the camera across a photograph or landscape; have your narrator speak while walking.
- To achieve a clear still image, place the camera on a tripod.

</aside>

Introduction:
Our Local Fire Department

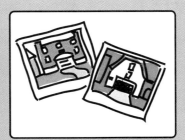

Narrated history, with
photographs

Interview with Captain
Isaiah Acevedo

Script It Once you have determined the flow of elements, write the script for the documentary's narration. Use a direct, explanatory tone. Practice reading your script several times, looking for phrases that sound awkward or confusing.

Produce It Shoot your documentary. Film several versions of each scene to be sure you have one that is clear and effective. During editing, follow the sequence of your storyboard, adding titles to clarify ideas or identify sources or settings.

Standardized Test Preparation Workshop

Applying Revising and Editing Skills to Writing

Your skills at revising and editing a passage will be assessed on some standardized tests. These skills are also useful to have when you are writing a research paper. When you are prompted to revise and edit, these strategies will assist you in formulating your answers:

- Check that the writer has not strayed from the main idea of the passage.
- Analyze the passage for sentences that seem misplaced or that contain details insignificant to the rest of the passage.
- While reading, think of suitable ways to clarify the structure of the paragraphs and sentences.
- Check for correct grammar and punctuation.
- Check for the proper use of verb tenses.
- When deciding how to best reword a sentence, be certain to avoid redundancies, jargon, and padded phrases.

The following is a sample prompt for revising and editing:

Test Tip

Always read the questions carefully, and make sure you comprehend what is being asked.

Sample Test Item	Answer and Explanation
Directions: Read the passage, and choose the best answer to each question: [1]Irony is the literary technique that involve surprising, interesting, or amusing contradictions at work. [2]These differences can result from clashes between what a character believes and what is actually the case. [3]Irony might also result from clashes between what a character expects to happen and what actually happens.	
1 What is the most fitting change to make to the preceding passage? **A** Part 1: change <u>involve</u> to <u>involves</u> **B** Part 2: insert a <u>comma</u> after <u>and</u> **C** Part 3: change <u>expects</u> to <u>expected</u> **D** Make no change	The answer is *A.* This question addresses subject-verb agreement. In this case, the subject of the sentence, *literary technique,* is singular. Therefore, the verb should be in a singular form: *involves.*

Practice 1 **Directions:** Read the passage, and choose the best answers to the following questions.

¹The ancient Greek dramatist Sophocles wrote one hundred plays, but only seven remains in existence. ²The most famous are the three dealing with Oedipus and his children: *Oedipus Rex (Oedipus the King), Oedipus at Colonus,* and *Antigone.* ³Today, there are many stage actors who vie for the role of Oedipus. ⁴This trilogy was written over a span of forty years. ⁵Born in Colonus, near Athens, Sophocles was one of the most respected Greek dramatists of his time. ⁶He was admired not only for his poetic and dramatic skills, but also for his good looks and musical talent. ⁷Sophocles frequently won first place in the competitions of plays performed in the Dionysian festivals. ⁸With his first tragedy, written at age twenty-seven, he defeated the highly respected Aeschylus. ⁹Sophocles made some changes to the traditions of Greek theater. ¹⁰One of the most important changes, was to increase the size of the chorus.

1 What is the best change to make to part 1?

A Change <u>dramatist</u> to <u>Dramatist</u>.

B Change <u>ancient</u> to <u>Ancient</u>.

C Change <u>remains</u> to <u>remain</u>.

D Make no change

2 Which of the following changes, if any, is needed in the passage?

A Delete part 3.

B Delete part 6.

C Delete part 4.

D Make no change.

3 Which of the following should have a comma deleted?

A Part 1

B Part 10

C Part 6

D Make no change

4 Which is the best way to combine the sentences in part 9 and part 10?

A Sophocles made some changes to the traditions of Greek theater, and one of the most important changes was to increase the size of the chorus.

B Such as Sophocles made, one of the most important changes to Greek theater was an increase in the size of the chorus.

C Sophocles, who had made some changes to the traditions of Greek theater, made one of the most important changes, which was to increase the size of the chorus.

D An increase in the size of the chorus is one of the most important changes Sophocles made to Greek theater, among the other changes he made.

5 Which of these sentences would best fit after part 5?

A Sophocles passed through life virtually unnoticed, and not accepted by Greek society.

B Sophocles lived a long, healthy life, and died before Athens fell from glory.

C Of the major Greek tragedy writers of his time, Sophocles is the only one not mocked in the comedies of Greek playwright Aristophanes.

D His works, however, are not worthy enough of being deemed scholarly nor classical.

6 Which of the following changes, if any, is needed in part 2?

A Place the comma inside the parentheses.

B Replace the colon with a comma.

C Change <u>King</u> to <u>king</u>.

D Make no change

Responding to Literature in Everyday Life

You probably respond to literature in everyday life more often than you realize. For example, when you lend a book to a friend with a comment like "It's really funny," or when you summarize the plot of a favorite childhood story, you are responding to literature. Other ways of responding to literature in everyday life include silently identifying with a character in a book you're reading or sharing your views about a story or poem with a teacher or friend.

Responses to literature also appear in written form in every-day life. For example, your morning newspaper may contain a review of a new novel or collection of poetry. On-line, Web sites may be devoted to sharing readers' responses to a particular author's works or to a genre of literature.

▲ Critical Viewing
What clues indicate that this student is enjoying what she is reading? Explain.
[Make a Judgment]

What Is a Response to Literature?

A **response to literature** is a reader's reaction to any aspect of the literature he or she is reading. Some responses are formal and academic in tone; others are informal and more personal. Most responses to literature contain

- a reaction to a poem, story, essay, or other work of literature.

- references to or passages from works that support the writer's main points.

- personal and literary allusions, quotations, and other examples that support the writer's opinions.

- an effective and logical organization.

- a conclusion or evaluation that sums up the writer's response to the work.

To preview the criteria on which your response to literature may be evaluated, see the Rubric for Self-Assessment on page 294.

Types of Responses to Literature

Readers can respond to literature in various ways:

- **Journal entries** contain a reader's unique responses. They are generally informal and not shared with others.

- **Critical reviews** discuss various elements of a literary work—characters, plot, theme—and offer opinions about the work's effectiveness.

- **Literary analyses** examine various aspects of a work of literature. Often, an analysis compares the work with other works and offers an opinion of the work's literary importance.

Writers in
ACTION

Literature is meant to be read, shared, and responded to. For Miguel Algarín, teacher and poet, responding to literature is a way of life:

"A lot of the responding I do is face-to-face. It's people bringing their work and looking for me to respond while they're here. . . . I've made a passionate life out of talking about how other people have written . . . and talking to other people through my writing about how I felt it."

PREVIEW
Student Work
IN PROGRESS

Follow the progress of Sheetal Wadera, a student at Hightower High School in Missouri City, Texas, as she drafts her response to Homer's *Odyssey*. Sheetal's completed response appears at the end of this chapter.

Paul Montazzoli is a graduate of Rutgers University. He works in New York City as a freelance editor and book reviewer.

Reading Strategy: Identify Support for the Author's Points As you read nonfiction essays like this response to literature, look for examples, quotations, and other types of details that support the author's points. If there are few supporting details, you should question the author's ideas.

▲ **Critical Viewing**
What sort of story would you set in Notre-Dame, pictured here? Why? **[Relate]**

from the Introduction to The Hunchback of Notre-Dame

Paul Montazzoli

The Victor Hugo who wrote *The Hunchback of Notre-Dame* was a twenty-nine-year-old firebrand burning at full blaze—sure of his own genius, gripped by an epic vision of Homeric proportions, and in no mood to bow down to church, state, or public taste. . . . Indeed, *The Hunchback of Notre-Dame* must have irked even some of Hugo's fellow Romantics, for it does not show that favorite period of Romantic nostalgia—the Middle Ages—as they liked to show it: a soft-focus tableau of saints, lords, ladies, and knights. Medieval life in this prose epic is as full of squalor as of splendor, and far too dynamic ever to hold still for a tableau. The book gives its specific setting—fifteenth-century Paris—all the variety and danger, the dash and the dreariness, that great cities have always had.

In the introduction, Montazzoli reveals his topic: his response to The Hunchback of Notre-Dame.

One way to respond to literature is to compare it with other works of the same period or literary movement.

Imagine yourself living in this city—it is not difficult. You swing around a drab, dirty corner—and your head is thrown back by the vision of the exalted towers of Notre-Dame. You stand on your toes and peer above the heads of a jeering crowd in a square— and catch sight of an impossibly deformed creature with bristling red hair, writhing and sweating in the sun as he is turned slowly on a pillory. You loll about the plaza in front of the cathedral, watching the gaudily dressed passersby—and are jostled by a priest in somber clothes and with a somber face, who is walking quickly—almost ferociously—through the crowd. Before he disappears into it, you make out in his eyes glimmers of complicated secrets that you want to know and fear to know.

No doubt the central figure of the book is that horrendous one you saw on the turning wheel. Why did Hugo make him *so* horrendous—with his crooked legs, enormous hump, and eye covered by a pronounced wart? To shock us, undoubtedly—though, since we are not dealing with a horror movie but with a tragic novel, the shock is not meant to vibrate in us for a minute and then pass, but to lead us to pity and wonder. The pity is for Quasimodo, the hunchback, and the wonder is for Fate, which made him what he is.

"Oh! Why am I not of stone, like thee?" Quasimodo asks one of the sculpted goblins in the cathedral. His question curiously inverts one that King Lear asks the dead Cordelia in the last scene of Shakespeare's play: "Why should a dog, a horse, a rat, have life,/ And thou no breath at all?" The tragic substance of the two questions is the same: life is given or denied by Fate with no regard for justice or the needs of the human heart.

In Quasimodo's disharmonious features, Hugo embodied the chaos of the world as he perceived it— a world of plague, riot, and passion, of titanic clashing energies both psychic and material. In those same features he also imaged the deformities in the soul of that priest who jostled you in the crowd, and who happened to be Quasimodo's beloved master, the

Here, Montazzoli uses his own imagination as he responds to Hugo's work.

▼ **Critical Viewing**
How well does this actor's makeup and costume convey Hugo's Quasimodo? Explain. **[Criticize]**

Model From Literature • 279

archdeacon Claude Frollo. This soul is an impressive one, however bent and twisted: Claude is no stage villain, but a complex mixture of overardent intellectuality, misguided generosity, and undeterable spite.

Another intention behind the hunchback's singular grotesqueness is less obvious. In Quasimodo's body, chaos meets order and the inhuman confronts the human. The mystical vision also admits a joining of opposites—all the contraries of the world blending into a whole, though the result is not disharmony but harmony. In a skewed, ironic way, the figure of Quasimodo alludes to mysticism. Thus, his close relation to the cathedral of Notre-Dame—a sublime vision in stone—and to its awesome bells seems oddly appropriate at the same time that it arrestingly contrasts the ugly and the beautiful.

Looked at another way, Quasimodo represents a crossing of the human into the bestial, or the bestial into the human. Here is a glimpse at one of the chief underlying patterns of the book: the crossing of boundaries. For example, in Book II, the poet Pierre Gringoire—bumbling innocent that he is—crosses unawares into the Court of Miracles, the center of the Vagabonds' domain of illegality, where the king's writ does not run.

There are many less literal but more dramatic examples. Spurred

This response to literature is well organized: Each paragraph explores a specific aspect of the author's response.

▼ **Critical Viewing**
Explain the ways in which this scene illustrates "chaos meeting order." **[Connect]**

on by passion, the characters in the book again and again take up the dare of a society that confines its members to specialized roles in rigid hierarchies, and grants outsiders no respect at all. . . .

The society these characters struggle against represented, for Hugo, an attempt to create a zone of reason and order within a world tending naturally to blind conflict and chaos. This attempt—and perhaps all such attempts—he regarded as futile. For example, *The Hunchback of Notre-Dame* shows us a Paris made up of a patchwork of many judicial sovereignties, whose boundaries and prerogatives often blur together. Where so many are responsible, none are responsible, and the city seems to live under no law at all. The justice that *is* dispensed tends to be laughable or lamentable. As for the supreme judge, Louis XI, his arbitrary cruelty mimics that of Fate itself. . . .

While the characters are driven by passions ranging from the merely fierce to the berserk, and an already weak social fabric is torn and mangled by violence, the voice that conveys this anguishing picture is surprisingly calm and detached. It is as if the narrator were determined to keep his balance at the edge of the abyss of unreason opened up by his own tale. His favorite approaches include dry reportage, enthusiastic lecturing, suave irony, and poetic whimsy, all of which provide satisfying counterpoint to the stupendous flux of the action. Unlike many narrators in nineteenth-century fiction, only occasionally and moderately does he exhibit astonishment or pity. Generally he leaves these emotions to the characters and the reader. For example, his accounts of the four appalling deaths in Book IX are sharply focused and unflinching, and he does not pause to sympathize, eulogize, or blame. In one case, he dryly provides one exact, hair-raising detail after another until the effect is excruciating.

The author of *The Hunchback of Notre-Dame* desired not to soothe and lull his audience with confections, but to move and disturb it with tragedy. The book shows man as a victim or a victimizer in society, and a victim and an orphan in the cosmos. Significantly, the main characters include three actual orphans, one foundling, and one kidnapped child. There is no hedging of the truth. Into this gorgeous, savage, and wholly unconsoling masterpiece, Victor Hugo put all the candor as well as all the intensity of his youthful genius.

Specific allusions to elements from The Hunchback of Notre-Dame *support Montazzoli's ideas.*

The example given in this paragraph is an effective type of elaboration.

The conclusion to Montazzoli's response restates his thesis and adds a powerful insight: Hugo's novel is a masterpiece, a work of genius.

LITERATURE

In his memoir *Speak, Memory*, Vladimir Nabokov discusses the books he loved in childhood. A selection from the memoir appears in *Prentice Hall Literature: Timeless Voices, Timeless Themes*, Platinum.

Writing Application: Identify Support for Your Points In your response to literature, include direct quotations as well as paraphrased descriptions of events, settings, characters, and ideas.

Prewriting

13.2

Choosing Your Topic

The best topic for a response to literature is a work about which you have strong ideas. Use the following strategies to come up with a topic for your response to literature:

Strategies for Generating Topics

1. **List** Begin by listing characters from literature whom you find interesting. These characters should belong to the stories and poetry about which you have the most to say. Review your list, and choose as a topic the character or work that you find most intriguing.

Get instant help! Make your list of characters using the Essay Builder, accessible from the menu bar, on-line or on CD-ROM.

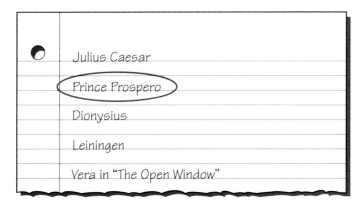

Julius Caesar

Prince Prospero

Dionysius

Leiningen

Vera in "The Open Window"

2. **Review Your Journal** In your reading journal, you may have recorded quotes from literature or themes, plots, and imagery that intrigued you. Look through your journal, and put self-sticking notes on pages that contain interesting ideas. Revisit the pages you marked, and choose one entry for your response to literature.

3. **Browse a Bookshelf** Go to the library or to a bookstore, and browse through the bookshelves to get writing ideas. Jot down titles of literature that you have read, authors you like, and literature that you would like to read. Review your notes, and choose as a topic for your response to literature a book you have already read, a comparison of two works by the same author, or a review of a book that you found while browsing.

4. **Discuss With a Peer** Discuss with a peer the books and poems you have recently read. Notice the topics you discuss the longest: Those are probably the ones for which you have the most to say. Choose one of those discussion points to form the basis of your response to literature.

TOPIC BANK

If you are having difficulty choosing a topic for your response to literature, look at these suggestions:

1. **Critical Review** Write a review of the last work you read. Because it's fresh in your mind, this piece will be a good subject for you. Freewrite until you settle on a specific aspect of the work that interests you, such as character, theme, setting, or plot.

2. **Comparison and Contrast** Choose two poems by a favorite poet. Then, compare and contrast the elements the poems have in common—speaker, theme, imagery, or structure, for example.

Responding to Fine Art

3. Study the character and setting of *Children Dancing* by Robert Gwathmey. Then, write a response to the painting in which you explore your reactions to the mood and subject matter of the work.

Responding to Literature

4. Write an analysis of "Through the Tunnel" by Doris Lessing. Discuss the central conflict in the story and the way in which the writer creates suspense to intensify the conflict. Also, analyze the way in which the point of view used enhances the story. You can find the story in *Prentice Hall Literature: Timeless Voices, Timeless Themes,* Platinum.

Children Dancing, Robert Gwathmey, Butler Institute of American Art

☑ Cooperative Writing Opportunity

5. **Book-Jacket Blurbs** In a small group, discuss works you have recently read as a class. Vote to decide on one work about which to write responses. Each group member should write one response to the literary work. Collect the group's responses, and select a passage, or blurb, from each that summarizes its meaning. Then, assign one member to design a book jacket for the work, another to select an author photo, and another to choose quotations from classmates' responses to put on the book jacket.

Narrowing Your Topic

Before you write your response to literature, narrow your topic so that you will be able to develop your ideas fully within the space limitations. Making a web is an effective way to narrow a response to literature.

Make a Web

Make a web like the one below, changing heads and categories as you see fit. Then, review your web, and choose as your narrowed topic one of the subtopics you wrote down.

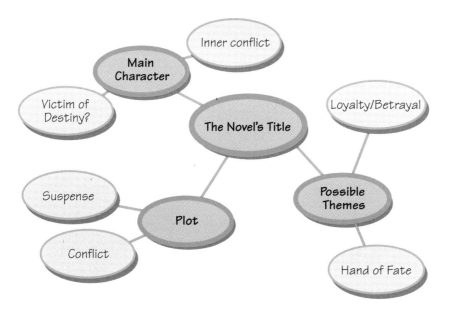

Considering Your Audience and Purpose

Responses to literature may be read by audiences of any age and may vary widely in their purpose. Choose details that will appeal to your audience and that will help you achieve your purpose.

Type of Response	Language and Details
Journal	Informal language: details that vary
Critical Review	Formal language: details that illustrate the work's strengths and weaknesses; excerpts from the work
Literary Analysis	Very formal language: details that prove your ideas about the work; excerpts from the work; excerpts from, or allusions to, other literary works

Gathering Details

Once you have a narrowed topic, gather details to support your purpose and main idea and give depth to your writing.

Use Hexagonal Writing to Gather Details

One way to ensure that you have considered all the various aspects of a literary work is to use the technique of hexagonal writing. A hexagon is a six-sided geometrical figure. With hexagonal writing, you explore six aspects (one per side) of a work of literature.

Student Work
IN PROGRESS

Name: Sheetal Wadera
Hightower High School
Missouri City, TX

Using Hexagonal Writing

Sheetal referred to her hexagonal writing figure as she gathered details for her response to literature.

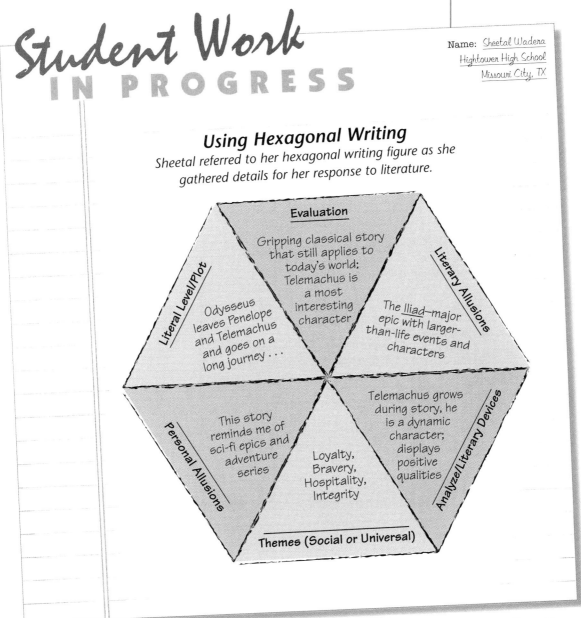

Evaluation

Gripping classical story that still applies to today's world; Telemachus is a most interesting character

Literal Level/Plot

Odysseus leaves Penelope and Telemachus and goes on a long journey . . .

Literary Allusions

The Iliad—major epic with larger-than-life events and characters

Personal Allusions

This story reminds me of sci-fi epics and adventure series

Themes (Social or Universal)

Loyalty, Bravery, Hospitality, Integrity

Telemachus grows during story, he is a dynamic character; displays positive qualities

Analyze/Literary Devices

Drafting

Shaping Your Writing

Take the details you have collected during prewriting, and organize them logically as you draft your response to literature. One way to do this is to develop a thesis statement and support it with details you've gathered.

Draft a Thesis Statement

The **thesis statement** is the main message of your essay, which you will support with various kinds of details. To come up with a thesis statement, review your notes, and answer the following:

Out of all that I have learned, the most important point I would like to make about [the work of literature] is ___?___ .

Then, use the following tips to draft your thesis statement:

- Write your thesis statement at the top of a sheet of paper.

- Refer to your prewriting notes, and list all the major details that help support your thesis statement.

- When the list is complete, decide on an organizational method that will present those details most effectively.

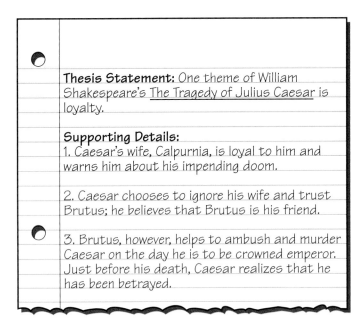

Thesis Statement: One theme of William Shakespeare's The Tragedy of Julius Caesar is loyalty.

Supporting Details:
1. Caesar's wife, Calpurnia, is loyal to him and warns him about his impending doom.

2. Caesar chooses to ignore his wife and trust Brutus; he believes that Brutus is his friend.

3. Brutus, however, helps to ambush and murder Caesar on the day he is to be crowned emperor. Just before his death, Caesar realizes that he has been betrayed.

L̲ITERATURE

The Tragedy of Julius Caesar appears in Prentice Hall Literature: Timeless Voices, Timeless Themes, Platinum.

Providing Elaboration

Cite Passages From the Work

As you draft your response to literature, cite words, lines, or passages from the work to which you are responding. Doing so will help you make your points, as well as give your readers specific examples. Enclose cited passages within quotation marks, and indicate where the passage is in the literature. If you are citing a large passage of the work, indent your left and right margins, and type the excerpt in a separate paragraph. Quotation marks are not necessary when excerpts are set off this way.

Student Work
IN PROGRESS

Name: *Sheetal Wadera*
Hightower High School
Missouri City, TX

Citing Passages From Literature
Sheetal supported her main points by citing specific passages from the Odyssey.

In ancient Greek culture, women had few legal rights, and if their husbands passed away or went to war and never returned, they were expected to remarry. Because of this, Telemachus' house was constantly overrun with suitors who wished to court his mother. Although Telemachus wanted to get rid of the suitors, he did not possess the power to do so. "For he, too, was sitting there, unhappy among the suitors, a boy, daydreaming" (19–21).

In the course of the story, Telemachus makes many moral decisions that help the readers see that he truly knows the difference between right and wrong. A prime example of this is at the beginning of the epic, when Athena is talking to Telemachus about the obnoxious suitors, and she tells him, "You need not bear this insolence of theirs; you are a child no longer" (76–77).

> Sheetal used quotations from the *Odyssey* to make her ideas clear for readers.

Revising

Revising Your Overall Structure

Make Your Introduction and Conclusion Match

Review the overall structure of your response to literature to be sure that it is clear and effective. An effective essay usually contains an introduction, a body, and a conclusion. In your introduction, be sure you have presented the main message of your response. Your conclusion should restate that main idea and reveal additional insights you may have about your topic.

▶ **REVISION STRATEGY**
Underlining Details

Read through your introduction, and underline important points you make there, as well as questions you raise. Then, read your conclusion, and underline its important details. Review your introduction and conclusion to be sure that they match. If they do not, make necessary revisions.

Student Work
IN PROGRESS

Name: *Sheetal Wadera*
Hightower High School
Missouri City, TX

Underlining Details

Sheetal underlined important details in her introduction and conclusion to make sure that her response ended where she began. She decided to add a sentence to her introduction to make her overall intent more clear.

Introduction

The *Odyssey* mainly focuses upon the character of Odysseus, telling of his wartime adventures as an epic hero. Odysseus' son, Telemachus, the secondary hero, also plays a vital role in the *Odyssey*; the reader sees him grow from a young boy to a fully grown man, and this maturity comes from the fact that Telemachus has had to learn to fend for himself during his father's absence.

In fact, tracing the growth of Telemachus during the *Odyssey* shows what qualities the ancient Greeks considered noble and admirable in a man.

Conclusion

All in all, Telemachus is a very interesting character. Not only do we see him as a young child, but as time progresses, as an intelligent young man. He plays a vital role in the *Odyssey*. His heroic actions, gestures, and thoughts make him a hero of great renown.

Revising Your Paragraphs

Polish Your Paragraphs

To be effective, a topical paragraph should have a single main idea that is supported by various types of information. An effective functional paragraph should perform a specific function, such as indicating a transition or emphasizing a point.

▶ **REVISION STRATEGY**
Using a Checklist to Revise Paragraphs

Use these questions to help you analyze and revise the topical paragraphs in your response to literature. Complete the checklist, and revise your paragraphs accordingly.

1. Does the topic sentence clearly express the main idea of the paragraph?
2. Does the paragraph contain various types of support in the form of examples, quotations, and reasons?
3. Is any of the supporting information weak, repetitive, or inappropriate?
4. Does the supporting information pertain to the main idea of the paragraph?
5. Is the supporting information presented logically? Could the supporting information be organized more effectively?
6. Do transitions connect the ideas within your paragraph?

EXAMPLE

~~In this story,~~ the narrator _{of "Axolotl"} reflects on his fascination with axolotls, which he defines as "the larval stage" (provided with gills) of a species of salamander. By the end of the first paragraph, ~~he~~ _{the narrator} has summarized the whole plot: He saw some axolotls in an aquarium, he watched them ~~a lot,~~ and thought a lot about them, and now he has become one. The plot sounds almost like a joke, like one of those cartoons in which a person and his or her pet start to look more and more alike. ~~I think Cortazar is making a point about~~ how people become what they are.

> **Learn More**
>
> To learn more about effective paragraphs, see Chapter 3.

> This correction makes the main idea of the paragraph more clear.

> This phrase was deleted to avoid unnecessary repetition.

> This sentence belongs in another paragraph, because it deals with the story's theme, not with its plot.

Revising Your Sentences

Revise for Clarity

One of the problems that can occur when writing about literature is confusion about who or what is being discussed. This is especially true when you are discussing several characters, works, themes, or writers. Read through your draft, and make sure that each sentence has a clear subject.

▶**REVISION STRATEGY**
Color-Coding Elements

Use a colored pen or highlighter to call out each character reference in your draft. Use a different color for each character. Then, locate personal pronouns that stand in for character names, and circle or highlight each using its appropriate color. If you experience confusion figuring out which color to use, the pronoun's antecedent is probably unclear. In that case, replace the pronoun with the proper noun.

Student Work
IN PROGRESS

Name: *Sheetal Wadera*
Hightower High School
Missouri City, TX

Color-Coding Characters to Check for Clarity

Sheetal used color-coding to make sure that each character reference was clear and that when she used personal pronouns, they had clear antecedents.

Unaware of his visitor's identity, Nestor invites Telemachus to join the feast of Poseidon, the blue-maned god. After the feast, Nestor he calls Telemachus and asks him who he is. Telemachus The young prince tells him that he is Odysseus' lost soldier and asks him if he knows anything about his lost father. "Nestor is full of praise for the lost soldier, and he quickly recognizes the heroic qualities of the son" (188–190). Nestor also praises Telemachus himself saying, "Your manner of speech couldn't be more like his; one would say No; no boy could speak so well" (191–192).

Grammar in Your Writing
Pronouns and Antecedents

In your response to literature, you may have used many **pronouns** to refer to characters or elements within the work. A pronoun is used in place of a noun. The noun the pronoun replaces is its **antecedent.**

Nouns and Pronouns

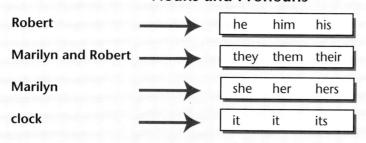

Robert	→	he	him	his
Marilyn and Robert	→	they	them	their
Marilyn	→	she	her	hers
clock	→	it	it	its

Fixing Unclear Pronouns

Because pronouns can be used in place of nouns, you can use them to help you avoid repeating a character or person's name over and over. However, when several characters are being discussed, it may be ambiguous or unclear to whom the pronoun refers. Ambiguous pronoun references can be fixed in two ways.

In the following example, the antecedent of *he* is unclear because two masculine nouns precede the masculine pronoun. The problem is eliminated by repeating Steve's name.

Unclear: Joe and Steve discussed the novel. They both enjoyed the characters and plot, but he didn't like the setting.

Clear: Joe and Steve discussed the novel. They both enjoyed the characters and plot, but Steve didn't like the setting.

In the next example, the antecedent is unclear because readers don't know whether Joe or Mike returned from vacation. The error is corrected by revising the sentence so that it is clear that Joe returned from vacation.

Unclear: Joe told Steve to read the book after he returned from vacation.

Clear: After Joe returned from vacation, he told Steve to read the book.

Find It in Your Reading Review the excerpt from the "Introduction to *The Hunchback of Notre-Dame*" on pages 278–281 of this chapter. Find three examples of pronouns, and identify their antecedents.

Find It in Your Writing Identify three examples of pronouns that refer to characters in your response to literature. If you cannot find three examples, challenge yourself to add some. Use pronouns to avoid repetition of the characters' names.

For more on pronouns and antecedents, see Chapters 16 and 23.

Revising Your Word Choice

Review your draft to be sure that you've used words correctly. Also, check your word choice, making sure that any informal words were used intentionally.

Use Formal Language

In fiction writing and journal writing, you may use informal language—language that contains conversational expressions such as slang and idioms. In an academic report, however, you should use formal English.

EXAMPLES:

SLANG: There is no way I would discourage a friend from reading the *Odyssey*. It was **way cool.**

IDIOM: When I read the *Odyssey*, it was **a wake-up call.**

FORMAL: I would never discourage a friend from reading the *Odyssey*. It was excellent.

▶ **REVISION STRATEGY**
Reading and Replacing

Read through your draft, paying particular attention to the types of words you have chosen to convey your ideas. Rewrite contractions as full words, and replace slang and idioms with more formal word choices. Also, delete instances of informal phrases such as *like, you know,* and *kind of.*

Peer Review

Work with a peer to review the level of formality of the language in your response to literature. Following are two strategies for working with peers:

- Exchange papers with a partner, and review each other's language to make sure that the level is appropriate for an academic report. Make a list of informal expressions and contractions. Help replace these with formal language.

- Read your paper aloud to a small group, and ask them to stop you whenever they hear informal English. Discuss the language and possible revisions to use formal English.

▼ **Critical Viewing**
What sorts of mistakes are you likely to catch when reading a draft aloud? **[Generalize]**

13.5 Editing and Proofreading

Proofread your response to literature carefully, looking for any errors in grammar, spelling, and punctuation.

Focusing on Mechanics

In a response to literature, you will probably refer to the authors and titles of the works you are discussing. Make sure that you spell, capitalize, and style these names and titles correctly.

Grammar in Your Writing
Styling Titles of Poems, Stories, and Novels

Use the following rules for styling titles of literary works:

- Always capitalize the first and last words in the title, including articles and prepositions. Do not capitalize articles or prepositions with fewer than four letters, unless they are the first or last word of the title.

  Of Mice and Men   John Steinbeck
  "Through the Tunnel"   Doris Lessing

- The titles of short works—such as poems, songs, and short stories—are enclosed in quotation marks.

  "The Dog That Bit People"   James Thurber
  "After Apple-Picking"   Robert Frost

- The titles of long works—such as novels, plays, and epic poetry—are set in italics or underlined. Newspaper, magazine, movie, painting, and sculpture titles are also treated this way.

  the *Iliad*   Homer
  The New York Times
  Mona Lisa   Leonardo da Vinci

Find It in Your Reading Find a book title in the excerpt from Paul Montazzoli's "Introduction to *The Hunchback of Notre-Dame*" on pages 278–281. Tell why the title is styled as it is.

Find It in Your Writing As you proofread your response to literature, check to be sure that you have written and styled all titles correctly.

For more on styling titles, see Chapter 28.

13.6 Publishing and Presenting

Once you have completed your response to literature, share it with others.

Building Your Portfolio

1. **Student Newspaper or Web Site** You could publish in a student paper or on a student Web site a review of a work of literature that has deeply affected you. First, check with the editor for submission requirements and deadlines.

2. **Book Club** Share your critique of a work of literature with a small group that meets regularly to discuss books they are reading. Prepare organized notes to which you can refer as you speak.

Reflecting on Your Writing

Pause to think about what you experienced as you wrote your response to literature. Then, answer the following questions, and put a copy of your responses in your portfolio.

- In the process of writing, what did you learn about how you value literature?

- Which strategy for prewriting, drafting, revising, or editing would you recommend to a friend?

 **Internet Tip**

To see model essays scored with this rubric, go on-line:
PHSchool.com
Enter Web Code:
eek-1001

Rubric for Self-Assessment

Use these criteria as you evaluate your response to literature:

	Score 4	Score 3	Score 2	Score 1
Audience and Purpose	Presents sufficient background on the work(s); completely achieves purpose	Presents background on the work(s); achieves purpose	Presents some background on the work(s); partially achieves purpose	Presents little or no background on the work(s); does not achieve a purpose
Organization	Presents points in logical order, smoothly connecting them to the overall focus	Presents points in logical order and connects them to the overall focus	Organizes points poorly in places; connects some points to an overall focus	Presents information in a scattered, disorganized manner
Elaboration	Supports reactions and evaluations with elaborated reasons and well-chosen examples	Supports reactions and evaluations with specific reasons and examples	Supports some reactions and evaluations with reasons and examples	Offers little support for reactions and evaluations
Use of Language	Shows overall clarity and fluency; language is appropriate; makes few mechanical errors	Shows good sentence variety; language is mostly appropriate; makes some mechanical errors	Uses awkward or overly simple sentence structures and vague evaluative terms; makes many mechanical errors	Presents incomplete thoughts; makes mechanical errors that cause confusion

13.7 *Student Work*
IN PROGRESS

FINAL DRAFT

Penelope at the loom and Telemachus, Museo Nazionale, Chiusi, Italy

◀ **Critical Viewing**
This urn displays an image of characters from Homer's *Odyssey.* Why might artists have chosen to decorate items such as urns with scenes from literature? **[Speculate]**

Telemachus
in *Homer's* Odyssey

Sheetal Wadera
Hightower High School
Missouri City, Texas

The *Odyssey* focuses mainly on the character of Odysseus, telling of his wartime travels and adventures as an epic hero. Odysseus' son, Telemachus, the secondary hero, also plays a vital role in the *Odyssey;* the reader sees him grow from a young boy to a fully grown man, and this maturity comes from the fact that Telemachus has had to learn to fend for himself during his father's absence. In fact, tracing the growth of Telemachus during the *Odyssey* shows what qualities the ancient Greeks considered noble and admirable in a man.

Sheetal reveals her thesis—the essay's main idea—in the final sentence of her introduction.

Telemachus' father, Odysseus, left home to go to war, leaving his very young son, Telemachus, and his beautiful wife, Penelope, behind. Since that fateful day, twenty years have passed, and young Telemachus has had to grow up and become sole protector of his mother and himself.

In ancient Greek culture, women had few legal rights, and if their husbands passed away or went to war and never returned, they were expected to remarry. Because of this custom, Telemachus' house was constantly overrun with suitors who wished to court his mother. Although Telemachus wanted to get rid of the suitors, he did not possess the power to do so. "For he, too, was sitting there, unhappy among the suitors, a boy, daydreaming" (19–21).

Telemachus takes his first steps toward becoming a man—and developing positive character traits—when he first visits his father's old friend Nestor, king of Pylos and a hero of the Trojan War, to tell him of the suitors' rude comments. Unaware of his visitor's identity, Nestor invites Telemachus to join the feast of Poseidon, the blue-maned god. After the feast, Nestor calls Telemachus over and asks him who he is. Telemachus tells him that he is Odysseus' lost soldier and asks Nestor if he knows anything about his lost father. "Nestor is full of praise for the lost soldier, and he quickly recognizes the heroic qualities of the son" (188–190). Nestor also

In this paragraph, Sheetal gives background information about Telemachus and his mother, Penelope.

Because this is an important event in the development of the character of Telemachus, Sheetal explains in detail what happened.

Ulysses and his son Telemachus, Kunsthistorisches Museum, Antikensammlung, Vienna, Austria

◀ **Critical Viewing** Using details in this mosaic, decide which character is Odysseus (Ulysses) and which is Telemachus, his son. **[Analyze]**

praises Telemachus outright, saying, "Your manner of speech couldn't be more like his; one would say No; no boy could speak so well" (191–192). Nestor then tells Telemachus to visit Menelaus for further news.

Obedient and determined to learn more, Telemachus arrives at Menelaus' palace, which catches the eye with shining gems and precious metals such as gold, bronze, amber, silver, and ivory. The vision is more dazzling than anything Telemachus has seen before, and he immediately senses the power and wealth that Menelaus must have. Menelaus begins to tell his young visitor old war stories, and Telemachus finds Odysseus' name mentioned many times. Although this pleases Telemachus and reminds him of his father, the tribute brings tears to his eyes. At this instant, Menelaus and Helen (the lady whose elopement with the prince of Troy started the Trojan War) recognize their guest. "Never anywhere have I seen so great a likeness in man or woman, but it is truly strange! This boy must be the son of Odysseus, Telemachus . . ." (236–240)

This paragraph helps support Sheetal's thesis. It reveals further qualities of Telemachus' character.

Telemachus also displays hospitality on several occasions. The first time we see this is when Athena appears to have been waiting. "Straight to the door he came, irked with himself, to think a visitor had been kept there waiting" (26–27). In Greek culture, it was not unusual to invite visitors to feast without knowing anything about them. In fact, it was, on many occasions, expected. Much later in the story, Telemachus is visited by a stranger. Not realizing that the beggar is his father in disguise, Telemachus says, "Friend, sit down; we'll find another chair in our own hut" (1414–1415). In Greek epic poems, one can always spare a moment to help someone or feed someone.

Throughout this response to literature, Sheetal has used formal language appropriate for her audience and purpose.

In this paragraph, Sheetal cites examples from the text of the Odyssey *to support her main point—that Telemachus displays hospitality throughout the Odyssey.*

Perhaps the most important quality displayed by the maturing Telemachus, however, is his sense of loyalty—to the memory of his father and to his mother. For example, he doesn't force his mother to choose among the raucous suitors; he respects her desires and wishes. To his father, too, Telemachus displays touching faith and loyalty. Although he was an infant when Odysseus left, his son is proud of his father and eager to preserve his reputation.

Telemachus, as portrayed by Homer, embodies many qualities prized in Greek culture. As he grows, he shows initiative and develops a keen sense of kindness and loyalty. His heroic actions, gestures, and thoughts make him a hero in his own right—one who reflects many qualities considered ideal by ancient Greek culture, and indeed, by cultures far and wide.

In her conclusion, Sheetal restates her thesis and adds a further observation about connections among cultures.

Connected Assignment
Movie Review

Just like the more formal responses to literature that you write for school, a movie review discusses strengths and weaknesses of a work. Movie critics usually begin a review by briefly summarizing the plot of the movie that is being discussed. Then, they analyze creative elements in the film and cite specific scenes or features to support their reactions. Usually, a movie review contains an opinion or recommendation for readers to view or avoid the film.

An effective movie review should do the following:
- clearly state the criteria on which the movie is being evaluated
- state a main idea and develop it, citing details from the movie
- include details that explain or illustrate ideas
- have a clear and logical organization
- make a recommendation about the movie's effectiveness and importance

Write your own movie review about a film you've seen recently. Follow the writing process suggestions as you draft.

Prewriting

Choosing Your Topic To come up with a topic for your movie review, think about the films you've seen in recent months. As an alternative, ask the local video store to print out your rental record or scan a movie book to stir up memories. Also, consider films you've seen in school as well as those viewed on recreational time. Then, choose to review a film about which you have a lot to say.

Focusing Your Response Before you begin drafting, identify your response to the movie you plan to review. Take time to pinpoint specific reasons for your positive or negative reactions. For example, you may identify weak acting as a major reason for your dislike of a movie or you may feel that a movie's special effects help it overcome a weak plot. Then, draft a statement about the movie that sums up or provides a focus for your response. Keep this focus in mind as you gather details for your movie review.

▲ **Critical Viewing** Would this movie poster be effective as a selling tool in today's market? Why or why not? **[Evaluate]**

Gathering Details After choosing your film and deciding on a focus, recall it carefully or view it several times. Jot down the key cast and crew members for accurate reference. Take notes about elements within the movie that you find especially effective or unsuccessful. You may want to prepare a chart like the one below to use as your watch the movie.

Actor's Performance:

Special Effects:

Symbolism:

Cinematography:

Soundtrack:

Drafting Invite readers into your movie review by offering your recommendation in the first paragraph. Provide any necessary background information your audience will need to understand and appreciate your review. Outline the elements you plan to discuss, and name the work's key creative forces. (In a film, these are probably the director, screenwriter, and central performers.) Briefly summarize the film's plot—without giving away the ending. In the body paragraphs, address each selected element with a general statement supported by specific examples from the film.

Revising and Editing Reread your review objectively. Make sure that you clearly indicate what is fact and what is opinion in the review. Wherever necessary, strengthen your main idea by adding supporting details. Also, review your word choice, and replace overly harsh or imprecise words with better word choices.

Publishing and Presenting Make a neat copy of your movie review, and post it in the classroom for others to read. If other classmates have written movie reviews, you may want to gather and bind them together, assembling a film anthology to share with others.

⚙ Grammar ⚙ and Style Tip

Movie reviews vary widely in tone, depending on the author's attitude toward the film. When you write your review, select words and phrases that mirror your attitude toward the movie.

Spotlight on the Humanities

Appreciating Performing Arts

Focus on Theater: Sarah Siddons

A theater review is a kind of response to literature, and a positive, glowing review is what every actor and actress desires. Considered the greatest English tragic actress of the eighteenth and nineteenth centuries, Sarah Siddons (1755–1831) made her acting debut in London in 1775 at the Drury Lane Theatre as Portia in *The Merchant of Venice* by William Shakespeare. Her performance, however, was so unsuccessful she spent the next seven years performing in smaller theaters. In 1782, she again appeared at the Drury Lane Theatre, but this time her success in Thomas Southerne's *The Fatal Marriage* made her a star. She went on to play Shakespearean roles for most of her career; her best role was that of Lady Macbeth in Shakespeare's *Macbeth*.

▲ Critical Viewing
For what role might Sarah Siddons have worn this costume? Explain. [Speculate]

Film Connection Winner of six Academy Awards, including Best Film and Best Screenplay, *All About Eve* is the story of a young actress who moves into the life of a Broadway star in a secret effort to find stardom for herself. With its sharp, witty dialogue and strong characterization, the film has become a classic since its release in 1950. The beginning and ending scenes of the film are set at a ceremony for the Sarah Siddons Awards—Broadway theater's top honors.

Art Connection Creator of a portrait of Sarah Siddons as the Tragic Muse in 1784, Sir Joshua Reynolds (1723–1792) was an influential English painter. Reynolds completed more than 2,000 portraits in his lifetime. His work was noted for its classical references, full color, and realistic representation of his subject. In 1764, he began the Literary Club in England with artists and writers such as Samuel Johnson and James Boswell.

Response to Literature Writing Activity: Review of an Awards Ceremony

The classic film *All About Eve* won six Academy Awards in 1950 and continues to place highly on "Best Ever" film lists of today. Recall or review an awards ceremony, like the Academy Awards, in which film, music, or artists are honored for their contributions. Then, write a review of that event, taking into account its script, music or dance performances, variety of presenters, and so on. Share your finished review with classmates.

Media and Technology Skills

Responding Using Technology

Activity: Share Your Impressions

Use the Internet to share your responses to literature with readers around the world. With one click of the mouse, you can share your response with a friend in another town or participate in a discussion group hosted by an author. How you use the Internet depends on the audience you want to reach.

Think About It Think of ways to share your ideas about literature. For example, you might e-mail an informal note to a friend about a poem you like. You might monitor a university's lecture series on literature via the Internet or go to an author's Web page and contribute questions or comments.

Log Onto It

- To send an e-mail, log onto your service provider. Then, copy and paste your response onto an e-mail template or attach your response to a brief e-mail note. Type in the address of the recipient, and send it off.

- Comb the newspapers for advertisements about author seminars and readings offered by bookstores and publishers. Often, these seminars and readings take place on-line. Log onto the Web site as advertised and participate as much as you want in the discussion.

Post It Electronic bulletin boards are public forums in which any computer user can read messages posted by others and respond to them. You can find bulletin boards through search engines, your Internet Service Provider, and school Web sites. Because most bulletin boards focus on a specific topic, find one that is related to your response. Keep these suggestions in mind when posting to a bulletin board:

- Read several messages and responses to evaluate the tone of the board before you add your own messages.

- Keep postings relatively short. You may want to post an edited or condensed version of your original writing.

- Use a subject heading that clearly describes your message so that readers know what to expect when they open your posting.

A Home Page of Your Own

Another way to share your views with readers on the Internet is to design your own Web literary page. Most Web pages use a computer language called HTML. You can learn the basic HTML codes fairly quickly, or use a Web design software that writes the necessary codes for you.

Here are just a few elements you might include on your home page:

- Images: Include digital photographs and/or computer artwork.
- Text: Include your stories, essays, or poems.
- Lists of favorites: Describe your favorite books, movies, songs, performers, or television shows.
- Links: Add links to your favorite Web sites.

Standardized Test Preparation Workshop

Responding to Literature-Based Prompts

This chapter explores the many ways that you can respond to a literary work. Often, standardized test questions evaluate the way you respond to literature by measuring your ability to do the following:

- Respond directly to the prompt.

- Organize your ideas so that they are clear and easy to follow.

- Develop your ideas thoroughly by using appropriate details and precise language.

- Communicate effectively by using correct spelling, capitalization, punctuation, and grammar.

Following is an example of one type of writing prompt you might find on a standardized test. Use the suggestions on the following page to help you respond. The clocks next to each stage show a suggested plan for organizing your time.

Test Tip

When writing a response to literature, don't simply summarize the piece of literature. React to it by giving opinions, examining the author's style, and connecting it to your life.

Sample Writing Situation

Read the poem "Success is counted sweetest" by Emily Dickinson. Then, respond to the prompt that follows this poem:

Success is counted sweetest

Success is counted sweetest
By those who ne'er succeed.
To comprehend a nectar
Requires sorest need.

5 Not one of all the purple Host
Who took the Flag today
Can tell the definition
So clear of Victory

As he defeated—dying—
10 On whose forbidden ear
The distant strains of triumph
Burst agonized and clear!

In "Success is counted sweetest," Dickinson communicates a message about success and failure. Write an essay identifying the poem's message and explaining how the message relates to the lives of high-school students. You may use examples and details from real life, books, movies, television shows, and from the selection you just read.

Prewriting

Allow close to one quarter of your time for prewriting.

Identify Your Response Reread the prompt and identify what, exactly, it asks you to do. Then, reread the poem and develop a response to the prompt. As you develop your response, refer to the prompt often, to be sure you don't stray from the specified task.

Gather Details for Support To gather details for your response to literature, take notes about the poem's message and the way Dickinson gets her message across. Then, include details from your own knowledge, experience, and observations.

Drafting

Allow almost half of your time for drafting.

Develop a Thesis Statement Write a thesis statement that conveys the main idea of your response, and support it with various kinds of details. As you draft, refer to your thesis statement and make sure that all your details support it.

Elaborate When writing your response, include specific descriptions from the poem. Then, elaborate on them by adding your own insights and conclusions. You may also include details that define, explain, or illustrate the points you are making.

Use Formal Language When drafting your response, use formal language. Formal language does not contain contractions, slang, or colloquial language. For example:

| Informal: | I thought the theme was a *cool idea* for a poem. |
| Formal: | The theme of the poem was an *interesting choice*. |

Revising, Editing, and Proofreading

Allow close to one quarter of your time for revising, editing, and proofreading.

Check Support Review your response for details that do not directly support your thesis statement, and remove them. Make sure that you include the title of the poem in the first line, and double-check all quotations to make sure they match the poem exactly.

Make Corrections Proofread carefully to find and correct errors in grammar, spelling, and punctuation. When making changes, place a line through text that you want eliminated and place it in brackets. Use a caret [^] to indicate places where you are adding words.

Chapter 14 Writing for Assessment

Assessment in School

Being evaluated is a part of life. For example, a music teacher may measure how much you have improved as a trombone player in the course of a year, or a track-and-field coach may assess your hurdling technique to help you prepares for an upcoming meet.

In class, evaluations help teachers assess how much students have learned and how well their students' progress compares with that of other students—in their own school and all over the nation. Teachers use various kinds of assessment tools, from pop quizzes to questions in class to essay assignments and special projects.

▲ **Critical Viewing**
What kind of test might these students be taking? How do you know? **[Analyze]**

What Is Assessment?

Assessment is evaluation. In life, people may be assessed by anyone, from parents to employers. In school, however, assessment is used to gauge the depth of students' knowledge, their ability to learn, and their problem-solving abilities.

Most educators who make assessments of students' work look for

- answers or responses that match the questions asked.
- clearly stated main points that are supported with details.
- writing that is organized logically and effectively.
- correct grammar, spelling, and punctuation.

To preview the criteria on which your essay may be evaluated, see the Rubric for Self-Assessment on page 313.

Types of Assessment

Many types of tests and essays allow teachers and other educators to assess their students' progress. Following are some assessment tools commonly used by educators:

- **Timed tests** assess students' familiarity with the tested topics.
- **Short-answer tests** require brief answers, ranging from a word or phrase to a few sentences for each question.
- **Analyses** are critical papers in which the structural components of a work are examined and evaluated.
- **Comparison-and-contrast essays** provide detailed information about the similarities and differences among two or more people, places, things, or ideas.
- **Personal essays** reveal the unique experiences and insights of the writer.

Writers in
ACTION

Emile-Auguste Chartier, renowned French philosopher, understood the importance of arriving at truths. He had the following to say about his methods:

"Every idea I get I have to deny. That's my way of testing it."

PREVIEW

Student Work
IN PROGRESS

Follow along as Tricia Bushnell, a student at Buena High School in Ventura, California, drafts and revises an essay about World War I for assessment. A completed draft appears at the end of this chapter.

Prewriting

Choosing Your Topic

You may be asked to write an essay to evaluate your under-standing of a subject. In many cases, more than one essay question is provided, and you will be asked to choose one on which to write your essay. For help with choosing a topic for an essay test, follow these guidelines:

- **Skim the Questions** Quickly read the questions, and elimi-nate those about which you have limited knowledge. One quick way to measure your knowledge is to think of at least three details that you could use immediately in answering an essay question. If you cannot easily come up with three supporting points, choose another question to answer.

- **Look for Key Words** As you read through the essay ques-tions, look for key words that reveal what your response must address. Key words can include *examine the causes, analyze, compare and contrast, distinguish between, identify,* and *evaluate.* Choose to answer the question that you feel most prepared to answer in full.

- **Identify the Format** Analyze the questions, and note the format your response will require. For example, a question may ask you to compare and contrast, trace the causes of something, or argue persuasively. If you feel especially confi-dent with any one format over the others, choose to answer the question that requires that format.

TOPIC BANK

Following are some sample essay-test questions. If you plan to practice writing for assessment, choose one of these or ask your teacher to provide you with one.

1. Explain the conditions that must exist in order for a hurri-cane to occur.

2. Which American president governed most effectively? Give reasons to support your opinion.

3. If you had a motto in life, what would it be? Explain, using examples from experience, literature, and the media.

4. Define the concept of globalization, and give examples of it in action.

5. Discuss the causes of the bubonic plague epidemics in Europe and the effects the epidemics had on people's behavior and beliefs.

Narrowing Your Response

Narrow your response by identifying your main point. To do this, note specifically what the essay question is asking of you. For example, are you going to defend a position, show the causes of something, or make a prediction? For help narrowing your topic, use the strategies that follow.

Identify Key Words

Reread the question you're answering, and find key words within it that indicate the form your response should take. Key words may include *predict, trace, compare, analyze, evaluate, support,* and *criticize.*

Once you have identified exactly what the question is asking, stay within those limits to keep your topic narrow and focused.

Match Key Words to the Thesis

To narrow your topic, find the key words in an essay question, and write a thesis statement that answers the question. Use that thesis statement as a guide when you draft your essay. This will help you to keep your topic focused and to answer effectively and completely the question that is being asked.

Elizabeth Barrett Browning
1803–1861, Field Talfourd

Emily Dickinson, artist unknown

QUESTION: Who do you predict will have a more lasting reputation as a poet: Emily Dickinson or Elizabeth Barrett Browning? Why?

THESIS: I predict that Emily Dickinson will have a more lasting literary reputation because . . .

Considering Your Audience and Purpose

Before you begin drafting, take time to identify for whom you are writing and your purpose for writing. In most assessment situations, your audience and purpose are predetermined: You will write for evaluators and teachers, and your purpose will be to show them how well you understand your subject.

To impress your audience and achieve your purpose, choose details that support your main points and use a style of language that is formal and respectful.

▲ Critical Viewing
What similarities and differences can you identify between the styles of portraits shown here?
[Compare and Contrast]

Drafting

Shaping Your Writing

Choose an Organizational Method

Take time to organize your thoughts and to plan a structure for your essay. Doing so now will cut down on the amount of revision you will have to do later.

Comparison-and-Contrast Organization Use this method of organization to show how two or more subjects are alike and different. This organizational method can take two forms: subject by subject or point by point.

Chronological Organization Use chronological organization—time order—when you're asked to trace causes and effects, examine the history of something, or tell a personal story.

Nestorian Organization Use Nestorian organization when you want to build an argument or end your paper in the strongest possible way. In this method, you lead off with your second-most important point, and present the remaining points in increasing order of importance to end with your strongest observation.

Point-by-Point Organization	Subject-by-Subject Organization
Point A	Subject A
subject A	point A
subject B	point B
Point B	point C
subject A	Subject B
subject B	point A
	point B
	point C

NESTORIAN ORGANIZATION

Introduction

Second-most persuasive point

Third-most persuasive point

Remaining points, decreasing in importance

Most persuasive point

Conclusion

Providing Elaboration

As you draft, make your writing convincing and give it depth by providing supporting details. The supporting details you choose should define, restate, explain, or illustrate your main points.

Give Supporting Details

Examples may include illustrations, instances from real life, and allusions (references) to literary works or actual experiences.

Quotations may come from a well-known person or from a literary work.

Comparisons may be drawn from the past, the present, reality, or fiction. Comparisons help your readers understand vague or unfamiliar ideas.

Personal observations may include your opinions and experiences. You might also draw upon books you've read or movies you have seen.

Student Work
IN PROGRESS

Name: *Tricia Bushnell*
Buena High School
Ventura, CA

Elaborating With Supporting Details
Tricia used various kinds of details to support the main ideas presented in her essay.

German naval policy, on the other hand, did little to influence sympathy toward Germany. While Britain had been building ties with the United States, Germany had slowly been destroying any hope for them. With the sinking of the *Lusitania*, and later the *Arabian* and the *Sussex*, it became clear that Germany was not going to follow the previous standards of war.

> This sentence reinforces the topic sentence of the paragraph.

> This factual evidence further explains German naval policy.

14.3 *Revising*

Revise your writing as best you can, given the time allotted. Following are several strategies for revising your essay.

Revising Your Overall Structure

Make the Introduction and Conclusion Match

Review your essay to be sure your introduction and conclusion match. Your introduction should state your thesis or main idea and preview the contents of the essay. Your conclusion should reinforce the ideas presented in the introduction.

▶ **REVISION STRATEGY**
Listing Main Points

Read through your introduction, and list the main points you made there. Then, list the main points that you made in your conclusion. If the majority of the main points on your lists do not match, revise either the introduction or your conclusion so that they match more closely.

The following introduction and conclusion work well together. The introduction states the main points, and the conclusion reiterates them and gives readers more to think about.

Introduction
✓ 1. Superhighways changed how we live.
✓ 2. Cars promoted urban flight.
  3. Suburbs became desirable places to live.

Conclusion
✓ 1. Cars and the development of highway systems had a huge impact on American life.
✓ 2. The rise of suburbs led to the fall of cities.
  3. Will the coming of virtual offices promote flight to exurbs?

▲ Critical Viewing
What dominant impression is revealed in this photograph? **[Analyze]**

Revising Your Paragraphs

Develop and Build Your Argument or Thesis

Your essay should build an argument or develop your thesis, or main point. Make sure that the paragraphs in your essay work together, building to your conclusion.

▶ **REVISION STRATEGY**
Locating and Ranking Main Ideas

Reread each paragraph, and jot down its main idea. Then, review the main ideas, and assign them a ranking based on their relative importance. Review your list, and switch the order of paragraphs, if necessary, to build or develop your argument or thesis.

Revising Your Sentences

Create Sentence Variety

Review your draft to be sure that your sentences begin in a variety of ways.

▶ **REVISION STRATEGY**
Checking Sentence Beginnings

Read quickly through your draft, and look at the beginnings of your sentences. If more than three sentences in a row begin the same way, rewrite or combine some of them to break up the pattern and add interest and variety to your writing.

Revising Your Word Choice

▶ **REVISION STRATEGY**
Replacing or Deleting "Empty and Hedging Words"

Locate "empty words" and "hedging words" (words that take away from meaning) in your essay, and replace or delete them. The chart at right contains words and phrases you should eliminate from your essay:

Empty Words/ Hedging Words
by way of; despite the fact that; what I mean is; in my opinion; needless to say; to the extent that; there are; the reason was that; the thing is; almost; it seems; kind of; quite; rather; somewhat; sort of; tends; nearly

Student Work
IN PROGRESS

Name: *Tricia Bushnell*
Buena High School
Ventura, CA

Deleting Empty and Hedging Words
After closely examining her draft, Tricia deleted some words that added nothing.

Although President Wilson proclaimed neutrality at the start of the war, it soon became ~~somewhat~~ clear that the U.S.'s economic heart belonged to Britain and the Allies. Impeded by the British blockade, Americans, ~~needless to say,~~ found it substantially harder to trade with Germany.

Editing and Proofreading

Misspellings indicate sloppiness or carelessness on the writer's part. Be sure you correct misspellings before you hand in your essay.

Focusing on Spelling

For Open-Book and Nontimed Essays Use a dictionary to check the spellings of words about which you are unsure. If you are working electronically, use a spell-check feature to help you catch errors. Don't, however, rely on spell-checks to catch all typographical errors. A spell-check, for instance, will not catch the mistaken use of "he" for "the" or "you" for "your."

For Timed-Test Essays If you are aware of mistakes you often make in spelling, scan your writing for such mistakes now. Otherwise, check for common errors, such as misspellings in "*i* before *e* words" and homophones such as *to, too, two; its, it's;* and *there, they're,* and *their.*

Grammar in Your Writing
Spelling *ie* and *ei* Words

Use the traditional rule for spelling words with an *ie* or *ei* combination: "Use *i* before *e* except after *c* or when sounded like *a*, as in *neighbor* or *sleigh.*"

chief   ceiling   freight   tier

The most common exception to this rule involves words that contain the *sh* sound spelled with a *c*.

ancient   conscience

Following are some more exceptions to the rule:

either   foreign   heir   height   seize   neither   forfeit   their

Find It in Your Writing Read through your essay to be sure you've correctly spelled words containing either *ei* or *ie*.

To learn more about spelling rules, see Chapter 30.

14.5 Publishing and Presenting

Building Your Portfolio

1. **Portfolio** Save your completed essay in your portfolio. Attach a small note on which you describe when and where you took this test.

2. **Guidance Counselor** Give a copy of your writing for assessment to your guidance counselor for his or her review. Then, make an appointment with the counselor to discuss how to best take advantage of your writing skills.

Reflecting on Your Writing

Take a few moments to think about writing for assessment. Then, answer the following questions, and save your responses in your portfolio.

- Were you satisfied with the question you chose to answer? Why or why not?

- If you were to coach someone on how to write effectively for assessment, what points would you emphasize? Why?

 Internet Tip

To see essays scored with this rubric, go on-line:
PHSchool.com
Enter Web Code:
eek-1001

Rubric for Self-Assessment

Use the following criteria to evaluate your writing for assessment:

	Score 4	Score 3	Score 2	Score 1
Audience and Purpose	Uses appropriately formal tone; clearly addresses writing prompt	Uses mostly formal tone; adequately addresses prompt	Uses some informal tone; addresses writing prompt	Uses inappropriately informal tone; does not address writing prompt
Organization	Presents an effective, consistent organizational strategy	Presents a clear organizational strategy with few inconsistencies	Presents an inconsistent organizational strategy	Shows a lack of organizational strategy
Elaboration	Provides several ideas to support the thesis; elaborates each idea; links all information to support thesis	Provides several ideas to support the thesis; elaborates most ideas with facts, details, or examples; links most information to thesis	Provides some ideas to support the thesis; does not elaborate some ideas; does not link some details to thesis	Provides no thesis; does not elaborate ideas
Use of Language	Uses excellent sentence and vocabulary variety; includes very few errors	Uses adequate sentence and vocabulary variety; includes few errors	Uses repetitive sentence structure and vocabulary; includes many errors	Demonstrates poor use of language; generates confusion; includes many errors

Student Work
IN PROGRESS

FINAL DRAFT

Why the United States Entered World War I

Tricia Bushnell
Buena High School
Ventura, California

Assess the relative influence of THREE of the following in the American decision to declare war on Germany in 1917.

- German naval policy
- Woodrow Wilson's idealism
- Allied propaganda
- America's claim to world power
- American economic interests

When the United States entered World War I, despite protests from Secretary of State William Jennings Bryan, America's seemingly nonchalant view of the war turned to one of excitement. Led by President Wilson's promise of "a war to end all wars," citizens of the United States quickly answered Herbert Hoover's calls for "Wheatless Wednesdays" and Victory Gardens. However, it was not Wilson's idealistic policies that persuaded the United States to enter the war on the side of the Allies; rather, it was a combination of economic ties, German naval policy, and Allied propaganda.

Although President Wilson proclaimed neutrality at the start of the war, it soon became clear that the economic heart of the United States belonged to Britain and the Allies. Impeded by the British blockade, Americans found it substantially harder to trade with Germany. Furthermore, when Germany and Britain began searching and seizing goods from American ships, Britain continued to pay for all seized items. However, the greatest economic tie came with the labors of American banker J. P. Morgan. Through his efforts, various loan agreements were made between U.S.

Tricia's thesis statement appears in the last sentence of her introduction.

Tricia's essay is clearly organized: She uses transitions, such as "furthermore" and "however" to connect the supporting details she provides.

banks and Allied powers. As a result, much of America's money lay in Allied hands; therefore, it was seemingly important that America enter the war to protect its investments.

German naval policy, on the other hand, did little to influence sympathy toward Germany. While Britain had been building ties with the United States, Germany had slowly been destroying any hope for them. With the sinking of the *Lusitania*, and later the *Arabian* and the *Sussex*, it became clear that Germany was not going to follow the previous standards of war. Germany declared unlimited submarine warfare, an idea never fathomed before. Americans were alarmed.

Further influencing American ties with the Allies was various anti-German propaganda. Commonly referred to as the "Huns," German soldiers were depicted committing violent crimes on civilians. Furthermore, Britain controlled the transatlantic cable, making it much easier for pro-British propaganda to find its way to the United States.

It seemed the Central Powers had little hope for help from the United States, and American-German economic ties appeared impossible to forge. The Americans were busy feeding on anti-German propaganda. They were all too eager to believe what they read because they were still angry over the sinking of American ships. Add to this Wilson's idealism and his 14-point plan, and the American entrance to the "Great War" on the side of the Allies was inevitable.

The conclusion to Tricia's essay sums up the main points she has already developed in the body of her writing.

▶ **Critical Viewing** Why might the sinking of a ship like the *Lusitania*, pictured, provoke outrage? **[Connect]**

Connected Assignment
Take-Home Test

Writing for assessment doesn't always take place in a controlled classroom environment. Sometimes, you will be asked to complete a test at home. A take-home test requires many of the same skills you use for an in-class test—careful time planning, clear and brief writing, attention to accuracy, and adequate supporting details. It also asks for a few added skills: You must monitor your time, stay focused, and follow guidelines about acceptable reference use.

Practice writing for a take-home test by following the writing process skills steps.

▲ Critical Viewing Do you prefer working at home as the student here is doing or working in a classroom or library? Why? [Make a Judgment]

Prewriting

Choosing Your Topic Most essay tests, at home or in school, will usually offer a choice of topics. When given a choice, focus on the topic you know most about and find most interesting.

Focusing Your Topic Even when topics are predetermined, you can focus your response on an engaging aspect of the topic. Take a few moments to prepare a topic web, on which you quickly sketch various aspects of your topic. Then, if it suits the test question, choose one specific aspect of your topic on which to focus your response.

TOPIC WEB

- USSR and US
- The Arms Race
- The Cold War
- The Iron Curtain
- Khrushchev and Nixon

Gathering Your Details Before you start drafting, follow these steps:

- Double-check the test rules.

- Assemble all allowed materials in a quiet location.

- Set a timer, if appropriate.

- Once you have set up a test environment, review what you know about the chosen topic, scanning study materials for ideas and grouping details in logical categories. Develop a thesis, and briefly outline your essay.

Drafting

State your thesis in the opening paragraph. As you elaborate with key points and supporting details, capitalize on any allowable references by including facts and quotations you might not be able to quote in a traditional test. Let the more relaxed test environment ease your writing process—walk around or speak aloud, if this will help you draft a more effective response.

Revising and Editing

Answering the Question Review your writing to make sure that you've answered the test question. If not, rework the details, as well as your introduction and conclusion, to better answer the question.

Review Organization Review the overall organization of your essay to be sure that it is consistent and effective. Move paragraphs around to better achieve your purpose or to clarify relationships among your ideas. Also, check to ensure that your introduction and conclusion "match up."

Checking Your Facts Check the accuracy of details in your writing. You may use allowed references to confirm their accuracy. Add details if your ideas need more support. Delete details that are unnecessary.

Improve the Language Review your essay to eliminate any words that may be too informal for a test situation. Also consider making these corrections to language:

- Define words that your reader may not know. The brief explanations you provide may make your essay stronger.

- Assess evaluative language. If your response requires you to express an opinion, check that you have conveyed your feelings clearly.

Grammar and Style Tip

Choose formal words and phrases to create an academic tone in your writing.

Publishing and Presenting

Type out a new copy of your writing, and review it carefully. Check to be sure that you have corrected all errors in spelling, grammar, and punctuation. Also, check to see that your paragraphs are indented and that you've correctly cited quotations or other source information.

When you are satisfied that your essay is the best it can be, hand it in. Keep a copy for your portfolio.

Spotlight on the Humanities

Recognizing the Varieties of Media

Focus on Film: *The Last Emperor*

Although the Ch'ing Dynasty may seem to you like the subject for a perfect essay-test question, such subjects may also be used as a springboard for creative work. Film director Bernardo Bertolucci released his cinematic masterpiece *The Last Emperor* in 1987. The film tells the true story of China's last emperor, Henry P'u-i (1906–1967) of the Ch'ing Dynasty, who ascended to the throne at age three. Although the young emperor was forced to renounce his throne in 1912 at five years of age, he continued to live within the walls of the Forbidden City in Peking for many years.

Dance Connection Early in the Ch'ing Dynasty, a team of dancers from the province of Fuzhou was invited to perform the Dragon Dance for the emperor in Peking. After being praised by the Ch'ing emperor for their work, they became famous throughout the country. The Dragon Dance continued to be an integral part of Chinese culture for hundreds of years. The colors of the dancing dragon are symbolic, with green suggesting great harvests, red representing excitement, and yellow symbolizing the empire. A dancing dragon is divided into nine sections and is approximately 112 feet long.

Art Connection The Ch'ing Dynasty to which the Last Emperor belonged cultivated Chinese art and culture. Artists often performed research by comparing the etchings on stone tablets and bronze vessels with the writings of ancient texts. The inscriptions helped inspire a new form of calligraphy, called *k'ao-cheng-hsueh*, which was highly defined and detailed. It allowed painters to experiment more intently with brushwork.

Assessment Writing Activity: Election Laws

Imagine the citizens of this country electing a three-year-old to be president! Fortunately, election laws in the United States specify an age requirement, but in monarchies, this is not the case. Think about the requirements you think are necessary to be president. Then, write a set of laws regarding presidential elections and the requirements needed to run for and be elected president.

The Emperor Ch'ien Lung (1736–1795) as a Young Man, Ch'ing Dynasty, Metropolitan Museum of Art

▲ **Critical Viewing** Emperor Chien Lung of the Ch'ing Dynasty is featured in this painting. What can you tell about Chinese ideas of art and beauty by looking at this painting? **[Analyze]**

Media and Technology Skills

Taking Computerized Tests

Activity: Share Test-Taking Strategies

Many tests today are conducted using computers. In some cases, you might be given a choice of taking a print test or a computerized test; in others, only the computerized version is available. Expand your test-taking strategies to include methods and approaches for taking these tests.

Think About It Review your own experiences with computerized tests or tutorials. Think about what features helped ensure your success. List three points you would like to share during a team discussion.

Discuss It Share your ideas about computerized tests with a group of peers. In addition to talking about ideas, discuss these strategies:

- **Practice.** Take a practice test or tutorial, if available. Doing so will help you to become familiar and comfortable with the test-taking process itself.

- **Read instructions and tips carefully.** Take time to read the test rules and any suggestions provided. Also familiarize yourself with the keyboard commands you may need to use.

- **Use a pen and notepad.** You may want to jot down notes, even though they will not be recorded as part of the test.

- **Ask questions.** If you are unclear about how to finish the test, ask your teacher or media center worker for assistance.

- **Print out results.** After taking a test, print out the results so that you can review them later.

- **Prepare.** You still need to know the content before you take a computerized test, so allow yourself sufficient study time to ensure that you will be ready.

Compare It Identify how computerized tests differ from print tests. During your discussion, compare related strategies for each type of test. For example, you can preview a printed test quickly by flipping through the pages to see how long it will be. Many computerized tests offer you the same ability by letting you scroll or click through the test items.

List It Summarize your discussion by making a list of your most effective test-taking strategies. Share the list with your class in a presentation. Include examples that demonstrate how each strategy helps you to succeed.

Working at the Computer

Sitting at a computer terminal for more than thirty minutes can make you feel stiff. Discomfort can distract you and prevent you from doing your best work. Follow these strategies any time you are working at the computer:

- Take time to stretch your hands and fingers every fifteen minutes.
- Relax your fingers as you take the test. Try not to clench or tense your muscles.
- Stretch your arms, legs, and fingers before the test begins. Stand up and stretch briefly every half hour.

Standardized Test Preparation Workshop

Analyzing Errors in Writing

When answering essay-test questions or other forms of assessment, pay close attention to the grammar, usage, and mechanics of your responses. Standardized tests frequently measure your ability to recognize errors in your writing. Following are some methods that will help you address some problems in spelling, punctuation, and capitalization:

- Reread sentences to check punctuation.

- When writing on a computer, use the spell-check feature.

- When a dictionary is available, look up any words that might be misspelled.

- Check for homophones—words that sound like the word you need to use but are spelled differently.

The following sample test items will give you practice with errors in writing.

Sample Test Items	Answers and Explanations

Directions: Read the following passages, and decide which type of errors, if any, appear in the underlined sections. Mark the letters for your answer. We had to go to the grocery store. <u>Mom</u>
 (1)
 <u>wanted us to pick up tomatoes lettuce and</u>
 <u>salsa for the burritos.</u>
 	
 1   **A**   Spelling error
      B   Capitalization error
      C   Punctuation error
      D   No error
	The correct answer is *C*. A comma is needed after both *tomatoes* and *lettuce* in order to punctuate the series correctly.

The burritos were done and ready to eat. <u>All</u>
 (2)
 <u>they needed now was a dab of sour creme.</u>
 	
 2   **F**   Spelling error
      G   Capitalization error
      H   Punctuation error
      J   No error
	The correct answer is *F*. The word *cream* is spelled incorrectly in the passage.

▶ **Practice 1** **Directions:** Read the following passages, and decide which type of error, if any, appears in the underlined sections. Mark the letters for your answer.

It was an easy two-pointer. "Give me the
                                                    (1)
ball!" screamed Mark again, I'm open!"

But they continued to ignore him. Here he
(2)
was, three feet away from the basket with

no one guarding him, and his teammates

acted as though he didn't exist.

Mark, insensed, couldn't figure it out.
(3)
What had he done this time to deserve

such treatment?

During the next time out, the coach,
(4)
Mr. anderson, called them all over. "Okay,

gentlemen, would someone like to explain

to me what is going on here?"

His question was met with dead silence
(5)
The players looked down at the floor.

"I'm going to get to the bottom of this,
(6)
weather you like it or not. After all, you are

grown men, not little boys, although you

can't tell from the way you are behaving!"

1 **A** Spelling error
   B Capitalization error
   C Punctuation error
   D No error

2 **F** Spelling error
   G Capitalization error
   H Punctuation error
   J No error

3 **A** Spelling error
   B Capitalization error
   C Punctuation error
   D No error

4 **F** Spelling error
   G Capitalization error
   H Punctuation error
   J No error

5 **A** Spelling error
   B Capitalization error
   C Punctuation error
   D No error

6 **F** Spelling error
   G Capitalization error
   H Punctuation error
   J No error

Workplace Writing

Workplace Writing in Everyday Life

When you complete a deposit slip at the bank or write a letter proposing your school as a site for a county competition,
you are using workplace writing skills. Workplace writing
helps people communicate with their classmates, co-workers,
customers, or club members. It also carries messages from
business to business and government to government. Effective
workplace writing can inform consumers about their purchases, advise employees of changes in company policy, move
time-linked information quickly, and even communicate
important messages from one world leader to another.

▲ Critical Viewing
What clues in this
photograph indicate
that writing is an
important workplace
skill? [Analyze]

What Is Workplace Writing?

Workplace writing includes many different written products, all of which are fact-based and geared to communicate specific information in recognizable formats. Most pieces of workplace writing are informative or persuasive in nature. The ways we publish workplace writing are changing rapidly and now include the postal service, messengers, e-mail, interoffice memos, electronic bulletin boards, and more. Effective workplace writing

- gets a message across as clearly, directly, and briefly as possible within the chosen format.
- anticipates and answers any questions the readers might have.
- addresses manageable topics and stays focused on those topics.
- is neatly formatted and effectively organized.
- contains accurate information.

Writers in
ACTION

As you move into adult life and use workplace writing more and more frequently, remember these words spoken long ago by British author and dictionary writer Samuel Johnson:

"Knowledge is of two kinds. We know a subject ourselves, or we know where we can find information upon it."

There are many rules and conventions governing workplace writing. When you don't understand them or find them unfamiliar, ask!

Types of Workplace Writing

There are several basic forms of workplace writing that you may encounter over the next few years. Others you'll get to know when you enter the work force full time. Each type of workplace writing has its own purpose and audience:

- **Business letters** are written to communicate information on business topics of interest to the writer and recipients.
- **Meeting minutes** provide a written record of the issues, facts, and opinions addressed at a meeting for the benefit of those present and other interested parties.
- **Forms and applications** must be completed in many different situations in order to provide specific factual information requested by a business or corporation.

PREVIEW
Chapter Contents

In this chapter, you will become familiar with several examples of workplace writing, including a business letter, minutes of a meeting, and forms and applications. Writing techniques accompany the examples to guide you as you practice workplace writing.

Business Letter

What Is a Business Letter?

Business letters address every type of business issue in all fields and professions, from a letter of complaint to a letter congratulating a team of employees for a job well done. An effective business letter

- includes six parts: the heading, the inside address, the salutation, the body, the closing, and the signature.

- follows one of several acceptable forms: Each part of the letter begins at the left margin when you use a *block format*. In a *modified block format*, the heading, the closing, and the signature are indented to the center of the page.

- contains formal, polite language, regardless of its content.

> In the **heading,** include your own address and the date on which the letter is sent. Including a phone number or e-mail address is optional.

Model Business Letter

In this business letter, Sam Kendra inquires about counselor jobs at a local camp.

3599 Parkview Drive
Marietta, GA 30060
(001) 376-5983

March 14, 20—

> In the **inside address,** include the name and title of the addressee, as well as the company or organization name.

Jackson Ramirez, Director
Marietta Department of Parks and Recreation
800 Turner Road
Marietta, GA 30066

Dear Mr. Ramirez:

> In the **salutation,** use the addressee's work title. If you do not have the name of a specific person within the company, use "To whom it may concern:"

I am interested in working as a counselor in your summer camp program. I attended the camp myself as a young child and had a great time. My experiences at the camp taught me important lessons that I'd like to help other youngsters learn.

Please send me some information about becoming a Parks and Recreation counselor. What are the dates and hours that the camp will run? How many counselors will you be hiring, and when do you plan to begin the process?

> In the **body** of the letter, state your purpose and include important details.

I'm eager to work as a counselor and hope you will consider me for the job. Although I've never been a counselor, I have three younger brothers and sisters, so I'm used to organizing activities for young children. I love sports and nature.

I appreciate the time you will take to answer my questions and look forward to meeting you soon.

> Depending on whom you are addressing and your purpose, decide on an appropriate **closing**. Options include "Sincerely," "Respectfully," "Regards," and "With regret."

Sincerely,

Sam Kendra

Sam Kendra

TOPIC BANK

To write a business letter that communicates successfully, choose a situation with which you are familiar. If you're having trouble coming up with your own topic, consider these possibilities:

1. **Letter About a Pet** Suppose you've just gotten a pet—an animal that you never had before. Write a letter to a local pet store, pet owners' association, or veterinarian asking for information about how to care for your pet.

2. **Letter About Computers** Many schools are changing their technology systems to include more or different kinds of computers. To help them make successful choices, they may ask for student input. Write a letter to your local school board in which you identify ways that you use computers. Make at least one suggestion about the features school computers should have.

Prewriting Identify to whom you will be writing, and jot down his or her address, company name, business title, and business address. Then, take a few moments to think about why you are writing—what you hope to achieve by writing the letter. Also, take notes on the questions you have and how you would like the recipient of the letter to respond.

Drafting As you draft, follow the format—block or modified block—that you have chosen. Provide necessary details that clearly explain why you are writing. Remember to keep a positive and appreciative tone in letters that request something, but always remain polite even in letters of complaint.

Revising Carefully review your letter. Check to be sure that you clearly state your purpose in the opening lines. The paragraphs that follow should contain only necessary information; delete details that stray from your main point. Also, review your language to be sure that you have chosen formal language.

Editing and Proofreading Begin by checking your letter's format for correctness and consistency. Then, check to be sure that you have spelled names, addresses, titles, and phone numbers correctly.

Publishing Write, type, or word-process your letter on 8 1/2 x 11 inch paper. Keep the appearance of your letter conservative to focus the reader's attention on the content. Always sign a business letter to show that you stand behind its words. Mail your neatly folded letter in a properly addressed and stamped matching envelope.

15.2 Meeting Minutes

What Are Meeting Minutes?

Meeting minutes are a written record of a meeting—of the issues discussed, the opinions expressed, and any votes taken concerning group actions. Effective meeting minutes

- note the meeting's attendees, absentees, and date and time of the meeting.
- list and summarize issues discussed at the meeting and note action itcms—steps to take to resolve issues.
- contain factual information only.

> In the heading, identify the group members, the reason for the meeting, and the date of the meeting.

Model Meeting Minutes

Tracy Mueller published the following minutes of a meeting that she attended for her school newspaper.

> Meetings usually begin with ongoing, or "old" business such as reviewing the minutes of the previous meeting.

> Title each topic, briefly summarize the discussion and opinions presented, and then describe the action items and tell who is assigned to each.

> Use features such as bulleted lists, boldface, and underlining to help readers quickly find the information they need.

> Sign meeting minutes so that group members know whom to contact to have information clarified or corrected.

Monthly Editorial Meeting: November 8, 20--

Attended: Tuong Tran, John Applebee, Doreen Rigoletti, T. J. Bairos, Paul Nathan, Suzanne Wood, Tracy Mueller
Absent: Jennie Wu

Old Business

- <u>October Meeting Minutes:</u> Minutes of last month's meeting were read. Tuong corrected the chart of closing dates, noting that February's closing date is unusual because of President's Day.

- <u>New Camera Fund:</u> We need $50 more to buy a camera. T. J. suggested that we ask the school board to fund the remaining money. A motion was made and unanimously approved to make the request at the December board meeting. John will make the presentation.

Action Item: Prepare written presentation to board. (Paul and Doreen) Present proposal to board. (John)

New Business

- <u>December Issue:</u> Staff members discussed articles planned for December in order to choose a lead story. Tracy suggested the article on vacation activities for the lead. Tuong felt we should lead with the article on ways to help others during the holidays. Everyone agreed, including Tracy, that this was the best lead.

Action Item: Write and lay out lead story. (Doreen)

Next Meeting: December 2, 20-- (Remember that this meeting will be before school, due to after-school rehearsals for holiday events.)

Respectfully submitted,

Tracy Mueller

TOPIC BANK

When taking minutes of a meeting, come prepared with notepaper, some pens, and your attention. If you'd like to practice writing meeting notes and need some help getting started, consider these possibilities:

1. **Minutes of the Club Meeting** People form clubs to enjoy common interests, such as gardening or skiing. Attend the meeting of a club you belong to, or ask permission to visit the meeting of one you don't belong to. Record and write up minutes of the meeting.

2. **Minutes of a Family or Neighborhood Meeting** Discussions by family members and neighbors about how to handle common issues such as garbage collection or late-night noise are meetings, even if they are not formally labeled this way. Get permission to record meeting minutes at one of these gatherings.

Prewriting Gather and scan handouts offered at the meeting. Then, write down the names of people present. Use short sentences or phrases to jot down the issues addressed and the views expressed. List actions agreed to, and note the people to whom they are assigned. Organize your notes in a consistent way—using people's initials to indicate various speakers, for example. Keep any handouts after the meeting for later reference.

Drafting Prepare the minutes as soon as you can after the meeting. That way, your memory will be fresh. If there was a meeting agenda, follow its organization; if not, organize your notes chronologically. As you draft, use headings, boldface, or other type features to make your organization clear.

Revising First, reread your original notes against your draft to be sure that you have left nothing out. Then, review your draft for clarity. Delete cluttering details and revise emotionally biased words to reflect a neutral tone. Add or change organizational features, such as numbered lists and bulleting, to help readers locate information easily.

Editing and Proofreading Review the minutes, and correct any spelling and grammar errors you have made. If there are any inconsistencies in your formatting, correct them now.

Publishing Print out and distribute your meeting minutes before your group has its next meeting. If group members are on-line, you may prefer to send the meeting notes to group members via e-mail.

15.3 Forms and Applications

What Are Business Forms?

Forms are preprinted documents with spaces for the user to enter specific information. Some contain directions; others assume that users will follow the labels and common conventions. Two common forms in the workplace are *fax cover sheets* and *applications.* An effectively completed form

- is accurately and completely filled out.
- is written in blue or black ink.
- contains only information that is requested on the form.

> Using letterhead or otherwise heading the page with the sender's name immediately tells readers who is sending the fax.

Model Fax Cover Sheet

A *fax* (short for facsimile) is a document that is electronically transmitted. Cover sheets tell whom the fax is for, whom it is from, and how long it is. The cover sheet should also list a phone number for the transmitter, in case the recipient has difficulty receiving or reading the fax.

YOUNGS PRINTING
45 Hook Street • Utica, NY 11581
phone 315.555.3166 • fax 315.555.2244 e-mail: young@nynet.com

Fax

FACSIMILE COVER SHEET

DATE: _10/25/20--_

TO: _Marci Conroy — c/o Hale High School_

FAX NUMBER: _315-555-5983_

FAX SOURCE TRANSMISSION NUMBER: _315-555-2244_

FROM: _Peter Dabbs_

TOTAL NUMBER OF PAGES (including this cover sheet): ___2___

REMARKS:

We'll be ready to print your newspaper by next Tuesday. I need to know how many copies you want so I can order the necessary paper stock. I've attached prices for different quantities. Call, fax, or e-mail me when you've settled on a number. Talk to you soon.

Thanks! Peter

> A fax should contain the recipient's full name and title or the name of the company, to ensure that it gets delivered.

> Note the total page count (including the cover sheet) so that recipients can tell whether all the pages have been transmitted.

> Cover sheets are usually completed by hand. Neat handwriting is a must, especially as some clarity can be lost in transmission.

Model Application

Many young people work part-time jobs to make money for school expenses or other needs. Often, potential employers will use a standard form like this one to gather basic information about job applicants.

APPLICATION FOR EMPLOYMENT   PRE-EMPLOYMENT QUESTIONNAIRE EQUAL OPPORTUNITY EMPLOYER

Kaleikini Video

Date _____ 6/8/––

Personal Information

NAME (LAST NAME FIRST) Hoskins, Jane		SOCIAL SECURITY NO. 145-01-2020		
PRESENT ADDRESS 705 Street	CITY Honolulu	STATE Hawaii	ZIP CODE 96813	
PERMANENT ADDRESS same	CITY	STATE	ZIP CODE	

PHONE NO. (001) 661-0947	REFERRED BY Lisa Du Plessis

> Forms such as this one contain limited space in which to write. When filling out an application, print neatly in small letters.

> Labels like this one ask for specific information. Be sure to read each label carefully before filling in a space.

Employment Desired

POSITION sales clerk	DATE YOU CAN START 6/15/20––	SALARY DESIRED $7/hr.
ARE YOU EMPLOYED? ☐ Yes ☑ No	IF SO, MAY WE INQUIRE OF YOUR PRESENT EMPLOYER? ☐ Yes ☐ No	
EVER APPLIED TO THIS COMPANY BEFORE? ☐ Yes ☑ No	WHERE	WHEN

> When given several options, like this, use a check mark or an X to indicate the option that is correct or preferred.

Education

	Name and Location of School	Years Attended	Did you graduate?	Subjects Studied
Grammar School	Mead Elementary	6	yes	general studies
High School	Honolulu High	2	expect to in 20––	

Former Employers

Date Month and Year	Name and Address of Employer	Salary	Position	Reason for Leaving
From 6/20/–– To 9/20/––	Honolulu Park & Rec 530 S. King Street	$6/hr.	counselor on summer arts program	summer ended
From 10/20/–– To 5/20/––	Anakua Street Theatre 5 Anakua Street	$6.50/hr.	usher candyseller	needed different hours

> Because space is limited, use standard symbols and abbreviations, such as "$" and "hr."

Connected Assignment
Phone Messages

If you're like most people, you hate missing phone calls. In the workplace, phone calls are often a key link between service providers and customers, workers and home offices, laboratories and physicians, and so on. Thus, creating phone messages—whether you compose them as the caller or record them as a message-taker—is a critical skill in the workplace and at home.

Study the suggestions below to gain practice leaving and taking phone messages. Start with leaving phone messages.

Leaving Phone Messages

Before the Call As much as possible, focus your phone calls on recognizable goals. If you wish, jot down reminders of the topics you wish to address. Be prepared to leave a message by gathering pertinent documents, such as a disputed bill or other records, near your phoning station.

▲ Critical Viewing
What information is most important in a phone message? [Assess]

Leaving the Message Introduce yourself, using your full name and company name, if appropriate. Speak slowly and clearly as you state the reason for your call and how you can be reached. Highlight any unusual contact information by repeating special telephone numbers at least once. When using a voice-mail system, follow its instructions carefully.

Following Up Before hanging up, check that your message has been accurately received. Prompt a voice-mail system to replay your message, or ask your message-taker to read back the message.

Taking Phone Messages

Before the Call Create a space near your telephone for message-taking. Keep paper and writing tools handy, perhaps using preprinted message log forms to save writing time. At home, consider posting a chalkboard or dry-erase board. If you're expecting an important call, create an optimum environment by turning off music or the television.

During the Call Be absolutely certain that you get the facts straight by listening carefully and asking the caller to repeat any confusing information. If the caller's name or company affiliation has an unusual spelling, read it back to verify accuracy. If you're using a preprinted form, check off appropriate boxes to speed your writing. Always read back the message, and ask for any necessary clarification before hanging up.

After the Call Check your message for legibility and, if necessary, rewrite it. (Make sure that you transfer information such as names, addresses, and phone numbers accurately.) Note the time of the call, and sign your name so that the phone-call recipient can ask clarifying questions.

PHONE CALL

FOR Phil Guskin   DATE 6/22/20--   TIME 3:05 AM (PM)

M rs. Candice McKenna

OF Halls Rental

PHONE 001-887-1400   EXT 60

MESSAGE She has prices for equipment rentals for sales meeting next month

	PHONED
	RETURNED YOUR CALL
X	PLEASE CALL
	WILL CALL AGAIN
	CAME TO SEE YOU
X	WANTS TO SEE YOU

SIGNED *Marianne White*

Message-takers should make every effort to be accurate. Here, the caller's name had an unusual spelling requiring careful notation.

When possible, checking off boxes limits the amount of writing necessary. Message-takers should always sign their names so that phone-call recipients can ask clarifying questions about the call.

Spotlight on the Humanities

Understanding Connections Between Art Forms

Focus on Art: Edgar Degas

Often, famous artists and sculptors are commissioned to create works of art for companies, collectors, or museums. French artist Edgar Degas (1834–1917) was part of the Impressionist movement of painters, but his emphasis on movement and the human form set him apart from his contemporaries. During the 1870's, one of his favorite themes was the female ballet dancer. Sketching a live ballet dancer as a model in his studio, he then created a series of paintings of ballet dancers onstage, in rehearsal, or offstage awaiting performance. His works, which hang in museums around the world, are favorites of both critics and the general public.

Dance Connection Ballet began in France more than 300 years ago. King Louis XIV founded the first dancing academy in 1661. Many experts view this act as a defining moment in the history of ballet. As ballet developed over the years, it was transformed from a courtly activity into a more intricate form of artistry that required special skills and training. When Edgar Degas painted his ballet dancers, ballet already enjoyed a rich heritage.

Film Connection *The Turning Point* (1977) explores the world of ballet and the intense work required by dancers to succeed in a dance career. Directed by Herbert Ross and starring Anne Bancroft and Shirley MacLaine, *The Turning Point* won Golden Globe Awards for Best Film and Best Director.

Ballet Class, Edgar Degas

▲ Critical Viewing
In what ways is this depiction of a dance rehearsal similar to and different from a rehearsal that might take place today? **[Compare and Contrast]**

Workplace Writing Application: Memo About Sculpture

Suppose you were a sculptor competing in a competition to create a work of art to adorn the entrance to a prestigious dance academy. The winning sculpture is sure to become a symbol of modern dance and will be used on promotional materials for the dance company. Write a letter proposing your ideas for the sculpture, including an introductory sketch of your work and why you think your creation should win the art contest.

Media and Technology Skills

Utilizing Business Technology

Activity: Compile a Help Tutorial

When you first start to use a new software program, you might be baffled by its many options and features. Once you are familiar with a program, however, using these functions becomes second nature. Prepare a help tutorial to share your knowledge with other students, highlighting features that you find particularly useful.

Think About It Choose a software program with which you are familiar or one that you would like to learn. Word-processing and page-layout programs are particularly helpful for workplace writing. You might also evaluate graphics utilities or database software.

Review It Use the software's on-screen Help function as well as the manual to learn or review the software's basic features. If you are using word-processing software, look for and practice these features:

- **Cut, copy, and paste:** These editing functions allow you to change written material quickly. Cut and paste allows you to move a selected item. Copy and paste allows you to place an exact copy without removing the original text.

- **Spelling check:** Many programs offer utilities to check the spelling of your text. Review how the tool works, and identify its limitations.

- **Thesaurus:** Use a thesaurus tool to identify alternative words or phrases.

- **Toolbar**: The toolbar feature, like the own shown below, makes the most common functions available at the click of a mouse.

| File | Edit | View | Insert | Format | Font | Tools | Table | Window | Work | Help | | 10:34:51 AM |

Teach It After you have learned the basic software functions, brainstorm for a list of hints and suggestions you would like to share with other students. Choose your best tips, and compile them in a Help Tutorial. Organize your ideas by topic so that readers can find the information they need quickly. Publish your tutorial as a pamphlet or brochure for your class or school computer center.

> ### Saving and Backing Up Files
>
> Save your work frequently in case of computer or power failures. Some programs allow automatic saving at desired intervals, such as every five or ten minutes. Check the Preferences, Options, or Help menu to see if this function is available.
>
> Always remember to back up your work files carefully. Store backup disks away from heat and magnetic sources.

Standardized Test Preparation Workshop

Applying Usage Rules to Writing

Writing in the workplace should be error-free and should follow the rules of grammar, usage, and mechanics. These workplace criteria are often assessed on standardized tests, which measure your ability to recognize errors in grammar, spelling, or punctuation. Use the following strategies to ensure that you avoid errors in usage:

- Check verbs to make sure that they agree with their subjects.
- Make sure that verb tense is consistent.
- Look for homophones—words that sound alike but are spelled differently.
- Fix double negatives.
- Check pronoun case to make sure that it agrees with its antecedent.

Answer the following sample test item to practice identifying usage problems.

Test Tip

Read each sentence silently to yourself several times. Each time, substitute one of the answer choices for the blank. Then, choose the word or group of words that best completes the sentence.

Sample Test Item

Answer and Explanation

Directions: Read this passage, and decide which type of error, if any, appears in the underlined section. Choose the appropriate letter for your answer.

The work-study members <u>are forming a com-</u>
(1)
<u>mitee that will elect leaders</u>.

1 **A** Spelling error

   B Capitalization error

   C Punctuation error

   D No error

The correct answer is *A*. The word *committee* is spelled incorrectly.

▶ **Practice 1** **Directions:** Read the passage, and choose the word or group of words that belongs in each space. Choose the appropriate letter for your answer.

My job interview for computer inputter went well. After ___(1)___ our common interest in sports, the job interviewer ___(2)___ to ask me questions about my skills. I ___(3)___ well in keyboarding class and was also familiar with many programs. I also told her that I will soon have extra time after school because I ___(4)___ the work study program. I ___(5)___ the job next week!

1 A discussed
  B will be discussing
  C discuss
  D discussing

2 F begins
  G began
  H was beginning
  J have begun

3 A will be doing
  B done
  C will do
  D had done

4 F join
  G will be joining
  H is joining
  J have been joining

5 A started
  B start
  C have started
  D is starting

▶ **Practice 2** **Directions:** Read the passage, and decide which type of error, if any, appears in each underlined section. Choose the appropriate letter for your answer.

Amy and Nick were elected Co-Leaders of
(1)
the school Literary Magazine. Working
(2)   (3)
together closely, their coming up with
            (4)
interesting ways to layout the magazine.

This issue promises to be the best literary
            (5)
magazine, the school has ever produced.

1 A Spelling error
  B Capitalization error
  C Punctuation error
  D No error

2 F Spelling error
  G Capitalization error
  H Punctuation error
  J No error

3 A Spelling error
  B Capitalization error
  C Punctuation error
  D No error

4 F Spelling error
  G Capitalization error
  H Punctuation error
  J No error

5 A Spelling error
  B Capitalization error
  C Punctuation error
  D No error

PART

2

Grammar, Usage, and Mechanics

Delta, 1990, Paul Giovanopoulos, Louis K. Meisel Gallery, New York

Chapter
16 Nouns, Pronouns, and Verbs

▲ Critical Viewing
What nouns can you use to name the people, places, and things in this photo? [Identify, Relate]

Every word you use can be classified as one of the eight *parts of speech*: nouns, pronouns, verbs, adjectives, adverbs, prepositions, conjunctions, and interjections.

Nouns, pronouns, and verbs form the heart of a sentence. Nouns are words that name people, places, and things. In writing about World War I, for instance, you might use nouns to name ships, planes, generals, countries, and so forth. Pronouns act as stand-ins for nouns. Instead of repeating the name each time, you may use the pronouns *he, she,* or *they.* Verbs tell something about nouns and pronouns, often by expressing some kind of action. For instance, you might write *Planes landed, and troops moved.* The words *landed* and *moved* are verbs.

The next three sections will explain these three important parts of speech.

Diagnostic Test

Directions: Write all answers on a separate sheet of paper.

Skill Check A. Identify the nouns in the following sentences. Label each *common* or *proper* and *concrete* or *abstract*. Circle any compound nouns.

1. World War I began as a local conflict between Austria-Hungary and Serbia.
2. The conflict escalated when war was declared on Russia.
3. Tension created by strong nationalism drew in other groups.
4. World War I eventually involved thirty-two nations.
5. On one side were the Allies; on the other side, the Central Powers.

Skill Check B. Identify each pronoun. Label it *personal*, *indefinite*, *reflexive*, *intensive*, *relative*, or *demonstrative*.

6. Many nations found themselves at war because of alliances they had made with other countries.
7. The war was precipitated by the assassination of Archduke Francis Ferdinand, who was heir to the Austrian throne.
8. Nationalism was one of the main factors in the war.
9. Germany, one of the primary aggressors, was itself once divided into many small principalities and kingdoms.
10. Those, however, had been united into one empire in 1871.

Skill Check C. Identify the verbs in the following sentences, and label them *action* or *linking, transitive* or *intransitive.*

11. Germany declared war on Russia on August 1, 1914.
12. The French mobilized on the same day.
13. A large-scale war appeared inevitable in Europe.
14. Concern in the United States grew as Germany employed submarine warfare.
15. American forces landed in France in 1917.

Skill Check D. Write the verb phrases in the following sentences, and underline each helping verb.

16. There had been many threats of war in Europe prior to World War I.
17. In one crisis, Germany had supported Morocco when it was agitating for independence from France.
18. This crisis was eventually settled by international conferences.
19. Austria-Hungary had annexed Bosnia and Herzegovina, and the Serbs had threatened to declare war.
20. Several diplomatic efforts had been made after the archduke was assassinated, but they had failed.

Nouns

The names people give to themselves and others, to the places where they live, and to the things that surround them are called *nouns*.

> **KEY CONCEPT** A **noun** is a word that names a person, place, thing, or idea. ■

Concrete and Abstract Nouns

Some nouns name things that can be perceived with the senses. Other nouns name qualities, characteristics, or ideas that are not known through the senses.

> **KEY CONCEPT** **Nouns** name things that can be seen and touched as well as those things that exist as concepts: ideas, qualities, and conditions. ■

The chart below shows examples of a variety of types of nouns.

CATEGORIES OF NOUNS			
People	Wilhelm	citizen	Aunt Jo
Places	beach	battlefield	Europe
Visible Things	hand	tree	lightning
Ideas	freedom	religion	friendship
Actions	decision	treatment	punishment
Conditions	health	dismay	happiness
Qualities	wisdom	strength	courage

Nouns that name people, places, or things that can be seen or recognized through any of the five senses are called *concrete nouns.* Nouns that name other things—such as ideas, actions, conditions, and qualities—are called *abstract nouns.*

Collective Nouns

Another special type of noun is used to name *groups* of people or things. Nouns of this type are called *collective nouns.*

COLLECTIVE NOUNS: community army   team   flock
               class   family   club   committee

Do not confuse collective nouns—nouns that name a collection of people or things acting as a unit—with plural nouns.

Theme: World War I

In this section, you will learn about nouns. The examples and exercises in this section are about World War I.

Cross-Curricular Connection: Social Studies

GRAMMAR IN
LITERATURE

from **In Flanders Fields**
John McCrae

Notice the concrete nouns in the following excerpt.

In Flanders *fields* the *poppies* blow
Between the *crosses, row* on *row, . . .*

▲ **Critical Viewing**
What abstract nouns does this field of poppies bring to mind?
[Connect, Respond]

Compound Nouns

Some nouns—such as *Private Jones, son-in-law,* and *baseball*—consist of two or more words acting as a unit.

▶ **KEY CONCEPT** A **compound noun** is a noun that is made up of more than one word. ■

Notice the three ways in which compound nouns are formed:

TYPES OF COMPOUND NOUNS		
Separated	Hyphenated	Combined
fire engine soap opera	rock-and-roll jack-of-all-trades	toothbrush dishwasher

▶ **Exercise 1** Classifying Nouns Identify the nouns in the following sentences, labeling each *concrete* or *abstract*. Circle each compound noun. Underline each collective noun.
1. Prewar Europe was permeated by nationalism.
2. Political and economic rivalries existed between countries.
3. My class learned that European economic expansion was chiefly centered in Africa.
4. Feeling a military threat, each nation maintained a large army even in peacetime.
5. Archduke Ferdinand was the heir-presumptive to the Austro-Hungarian throne.

▶ **Exercise 2** Writing With Nouns Write a paragraph using each of the following nouns: *soldiers, team, fund-raiser, general, bravery, victory, battlefield.*

▶ **More Practice**

Grammar Exercise Workbook
• pp. 1–4
On-line Exercise Bank
• Section 16.1
Go on-line:
PHSchool.com
Enter Web Code:
eek-1002

Common and Proper Nouns

All nouns are either *common nouns* or *proper nouns.*

> **KEY CONCEPTS** A **common noun** names any one of a class of people, places, or things. A **proper noun** names a specific person, place, or thing. ■

Proper nouns always begin with capital letters.

Common Nouns	Proper Nouns
novelist	Willa Cather, Erich Remarque
continent	North America, Africa
city	Paris, Berlin
planet	Mercury, Venus

Note About *Names of Family Members:* A noun used to describe a person's role in a family may be either common or proper, depending on how it is used. A name used simply to indicate a person's role is a common noun. A name used as a title before a personal name or as a name in direct address should be capitalized as a proper noun.

COMMON: My favorite person is my *uncle.*

PROPER: My favorite person is *Uncle* Barry.

DIRECT ADDRESS: Please, *Dad,* may I go out tonight?

> **Exercise 3** Distinguishing Between Common and Proper Nouns Identify each noun as *common* or *proper.* Supply a proper noun of the same category for each common noun. Supply a common noun of the same category for each proper noun.

1. town
2. war
3. continent
4. Wilhelm
5. League of Nations
6. England
7. country
8. general
9. battle
10. June

> **Exercise 4** Writing With Common and Proper Nouns Write a sentence using each of these words as a common noun. Then, write a sentence using each as part of a proper noun: *aunt, president, river, war, mountains.*

 **Spelling Tip**

Every proper noun begins with a capital letter. Consult a dictionary if you are unsure whether a noun is common or proper.

▼ Critical Viewing Think of some proper nouns to explain where these soldiers might be. **[Speculate]**

Section Review

GRAMMAR EXERCISES 5–9

▶ **Exercise 5** Identifying Nouns
Identify the nouns in each sentence, and label them *concrete* or *abstract*.

1. The assassination of the Austrian archduke was a result of extreme nationalism.
2. Austria issued a declaration of war against the Serbs.
3. Soon, every major power in Europe was involved in the conflict.
4. To the east, the Russians achieved several victories against the Germans.
5. The reinforcement of the German Army enabled it to drive the enemy back to Russia by 1915.
6. No decision was achieved in the east, but Russia lost many men and supplies.
7. In December 1914, the Turks began an invasion of the Russian Caucasus region.
8. Russia sought the aid of the Allies to remove some of the Turkish pressure.
9 The Allied landings at Gallipoli were failures.
10. The United States maintained its neutrality until 1917.

▶ **Exercise 6** Recognizing Kinds of Nouns Identify the nouns in each sentence, labeling each *common* or *proper*. Also, indicate whether a noun is *collective* or *compound*.

1. In 1917, the Allies began an invasion of Greece and pressured the king to abdicate.
2. After King Constantine abdicated, the government of Greece declared war on the Central Powers.
3. Besides Greece, battles took place in other areas of the Balkans, in Italy, and in the Middle East.
4. After Russia and Romania made peace

with the Central Powers, the outlook seemed ominous for the rest of the European community.
5. Allied progress in the Balkans led to the defeat of Bulgaria.
6. The Allied campaign in the Middle East also came to a successful conclusion in 1918.
7. The success of the Allied army led to the breakup of the Austro-Hungarian Empire.
8. The Czechs and the Slovaks formed a democratic state, the emperor abdicated, and an armistice was concluded.
9. The treaty of Versailles and other treaties changed the face of Europe.
10. People put their trust in the League of Nations to maintain peace.

▶ **Exercise 7** Find It in Your Reading
Read through a section of a history book about World War I. Find two examples of each of the following types of nouns: *abstract, concrete, common, proper, collective,* and *compound.*

▶ **Exercise 8** Find It in Your Writing
In a sample of your own writing, find five common nouns, one collective noun, and one compound noun. Name a proper noun that could replace each common noun. Explain whether replacing each common noun would or would not make your writing more clear.

▶ **Exercise 9** Writing Application
Write a brief account of an event that changed history in some way. Include at least two proper nouns, one compound noun, and one collective noun.

Pronouns

Repeating the same noun over and over in writing or speaking results in awkward, choppy sentences. You can avoid repeating the same noun by using substitutes called *pronouns*.

KEY CONCEPT **Pronouns** are words that act as stand-ins for nouns or for words that take the place of nouns. ■

Antecedents of Pronouns

Pronouns get their meaning from the words they stand for. These words are called *antecedents*.

KEY CONCEPT **Antecedents** are nouns (or words that take the place of nouns) for which pronouns stand. ■

In the following examples, the arrows point from the pronouns to their antecedents. In the first sentence, the pronouns *you* and *your* stand for the noun *Tom*. In the second sentence, the pronoun *it* stands for a group of words that takes the place of a noun, *Making chili for dinner.*

EXAMPLES: Tom, did *you* submit *your* article on New Mexico?

Making chili for dinner was easy, and *it* was fun.

Antecedents usually come before their pronouns, as in the examples above. Sometimes, however, this pattern is reversed:

EXAMPLE: *That* is the best book I have ever read.

Exercise 10 Identifying Pronouns and Antecedents
Identify each pronoun and its antecedent.
(1) Taos in New Mexico is famous for its art colonies. (2) The area attracts artists who are drawn to its beauty. (3) The town was settled by Spaniards in the early seventeenth century, and they called it Don Fernando de Taos. (4) Native Americans and Spaniards traded their goods in town. (5) Author D. H. Lawrence did some of his writing there in the 1920's.

Text

Get instant feedback! Exercise 10 is available on-line or on CD-ROM.

Personal, Reflexive, and Intensive Pronouns

The pronouns that you use most often to refer to yourself, to other people, and to things are called *personal pronouns*. *Reflexive* and *intensive pronouns* are formed by adding *-self* or *-selves* to some of the personal pronouns.

Personal Pronouns

Personal pronouns are used more often than any other type of pronoun.

▶ **KEY CONCEPT** **Personal pronouns** refer to (1) the person speaking, (2) the person spoken to, or (3) the person, place, or thing spoken about. ■

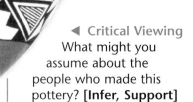

First-person pronouns refer to the person who is speaking. *Second-person pronouns* refer to the person spoken to. *Third-person pronouns* refer to the person, place, or thing spoken about.

PERSONAL PRONOUNS		
	Singular	**Plural**
First Person	I, me, my, mine	we, us, our, ours
Second Person	you, your, yours	you, your, yours
Third Person	he, him, his, she, her, hers, it, its	they, them, their, theirs

In the first example below, the antecedent of the personal pronoun is the person speaking. In the second, the antecedent of the personal pronoun is the person being spoken to. In the last example, the antecedent of the personal pronoun is the thing spoken about.

FIRST PERSON: *My* name is not George.
SECOND PERSON: When *you* left for camp, *you* forgot *your* raincoat.
THIRD PERSON: Don't judge a book by *its* cover.

Reflexive and Intensive Pronouns

Pronouns that end in -*self* or -*selves* are either reflexive pronouns or intensive pronouns.

▶ **KEY CONCEPTS** A **reflexive pronoun** ends in -*self* or -*selves* and adds information to a sentence by pointing back to a noun or pronoun earlier in the sentence. An **intensive pronoun** ends in -*self* or -*selves* and simply adds emphasis to a noun or pronoun in the same sentence. ■

The reflexive and intensive pronouns are shown in the following chart.

REFLEXIVE AND INTENSIVE PRONOUNS		
	Singular	**Plural**
First Person	myself	ourselves
Second Person	yourself	yourselves
Third Person	himself, herself, itself	themselves

A reflexive pronoun always adds information to a sentence. It cannot be left out without changing the meaning. In the first example, *himself* tells whom Michael taught. In the second, *herself* tells for whom the jeans were bought.

REFLEXIVE: Michael taught *himself* to play the guitar.

Gloria bought *herself* a new pair of jeans.

An intensive pronoun emphasizes its antecedent but does not add information to a sentence. If an intensive pronoun is removed, a sentence will still have the same meaning.

Usually, an intensive pronoun immediately follows its antecedent, as shown in the first of the following examples. Sometimes, however, an intensive pronoun is located in another part of the sentence, as shown in the second example.

INTENSIVE: The President *himself* attended the gala opening.

We spliced the cable *ourselves*.

More Practice

Grammar Exercise Workbook
• pp. 7–8
On-line Exercise Bank
• Section 16.2
Go on-line:
PHSchool.com
Enter Web Code:
eek-1002

GRAMMAR IN LITERATURE

from **The street**

Octavio Paz

In the following excerpt, personal pronouns are highlighted in blue italics.

I walk in blackness and *I* stumble and fall
and rise, and *I* walk blind, *my* feet
stepping on silent stones and dry leaves.
Someone behind *me* also stepping on
   stones, leaves:
if *I* slow down, *he* slows;
if *I* run, *he* runs, *I* turn: nobody.

Learn More

To learn more about how to use pronouns correctly, see Chapter 23, "Pronoun Usage."

▶ **Exercise 11** Identifying Personal, Reflexive, and Intensive Pronouns
Identify each pronoun and label it *personal, reflexive,* or *intensive.*
1. Have you ever been to Houston?
2. Is Daniel himself making the plans?
3. Houston is a large city, but it is not the state's capital.
4. The city was named after Samuel Houston; he was the first president of Texas when it became independent.
5. Independence itself lasted less than ten years.
6. During Texas's time as a republic, Houston was its capital.
7. The city found itself growing rapidly.
8. Not only was Samuel Houston president of the Republic of Texas, he was among the first to represent the state when it was admitted to the Union.
9. The citizens of Houston are proud of their city, its symphony, and its Museum of Fine Arts.
10. Houston has many parks, among them Hermann Park.

▲ **Critical Viewing**
How would you describe this scene in one sentence? What pronouns can replace the nouns you used? **[Assess]**

▶ **Exercise 12** Revising to Use Pronouns to Avoid Repetition
Revise this paragraph, replacing nouns with pronouns to avoid repetition. You might also combine some of the sentences.

   Paul and Robert visited Houston last spring. Paul and Robert loved spending time in Houston. Paul's uncle Richard lives in Houston. The two boys stayed at Uncle Richard's house. Uncle Richard invited Paul and Robert to come back for another visit. Paul and Robert told Uncle Richard that next winter would be an ideal time.

Demonstrative, Relative, and Interrogative Pronouns

Three other kinds of pronouns—called *demonstrative, relative,* and *interrogative* pronouns—have very special uses.

> **KEY CONCEPT** **Demonstrative pronouns** direct attention to specific people, places, or things. ■

The following chart shows the four demonstrative pronouns.

| DEMONSTRATIVE PRONOUNS ||
Singular	Plural
this, that	these, those

Demonstrative pronouns may come before or after their antecedents:

BEFORE: *That* is the ranch I would like to own.

AFTER: I hope to visit Butte and Helena. *Those* are my first choices.

One of the demonstrative pronouns, *that,* can also be used as a *relative pronoun.*

> **KEY CONCEPT** A **relative pronoun** begins a subordinate clause and connects it to the rest of the sentence. ■

RELATIVE PRONOUNS
that   which   who   whom   whose

In the following sentences, relative pronouns connect a subordinate clause (shown in blue) to a word (shown in red).

EXAMPLE: He found the cattle *that* he had lost.

Carl, *whom* we all admire, rides well.

All relative pronouns except *that* can also be interrogative pronouns.

KEY CONCEPT An **interrogative pronoun** is used to begin a question. ∎

The following chart shows the five interrogative pronouns.

INTERROGATIVE PRONOUNS				
what	which	who	whom	whose

In the following examples, notice that interrogative pronouns do not always have specific antecedents.

EXAMPLES:　*What* did you say?

Which of the answers is best?
With *whom* did you wish to speak?
Mine is blue. *Whose* is red?

Exercise 13 Recognizing Demonstrative, Relative, and Interrogative Pronouns Identify the pronoun in each of the following sentences. Then, label each *demonstrative, relative,* or *interrogative.*
　1. Butte, whose full name is Butte-Silver Bow, is in southwestern Montana.
　2. The city is situated in an area that is rich in minerals.
　3. What is the history of Butte?
　4. Butte was settled by prospectors, who came to mine gold in the 1860's.
　5. That was an activity later replaced by silver mining.
　6. Was this later replaced by copper mining?
　7. Gold, silver, and copper were the metals mined there; those brought prosperity to the area.
　8. Which is more interesting: Butte's historic district or the Copper King Mansion?
　9. The community, which was named after a nearby butte, was incorporated in 1897.
　10. We learned about energy research, tourism, medicine, and mining; these have been most important to Butte's economy.

Exercise 14 Writing With Demonstrative, Relative, and Interrogative Pronouns Write an imaginary dialogue between you and a friend, discussing an interesting place that one of you has visited. Use at least four demonstrative pronouns, three relative pronouns, and three interrogative pronouns.

Spelling Tip

Do not confuse *who's* and *whose. Who's* is always a contraction of *who is* and should never be used as a pronoun.

More Practice

Grammar Exercise Workbook
• pp. 9–10
On-line Exercise Bank
• Section 16.2
　Go on-line:
　PHSchool.com
　Enter Web Code:
　eek-1002

Complete the exercises on-line! Exercises 13 and 14 are available on-line or on CD-ROM.

Indefinite Pronouns

Indefinite pronouns also often lack specific antecedents.

> **KEY CONCEPT** **Indefinite pronouns** refer to people, places, or things, often without specifying which ones. ∎

INDEFINITE PRONOUNS			
Singular		**Plural**	**Singular or Plural**
another	much	both	all
anybody	neither	few	any
anyone	nobody	many	more
anything	no one	others	most
each	nothing	several	none
either	one		some
everybody	other		
everyone	somebody		
everything	someone		
little	something		

SPECIFIC ANTECEDENT: *Several* of the guests were late.
NO SPECIFIC ANTECEDENTS: *Everyone* ate *everything* offered.

In addition to functioning as pronouns, indefinite pronouns can also function as adjectives.

PRONOUN: *Few* are as famous as the Cleveland Orchestra.
ADJECTIVE: *Few* orchestras are as famous as this one.

> **Exercise 15** **Recognizing Indefinite Pronouns** Identify the indefinite pronouns in the following paragraph.

EXAMPLE: Did you eat any?
ANSWER: any

(1) Cleveland has several ways to attract visitors. (2) Everybody will enjoy the Rock and Roll Hall of Fame and Museum. (3) The museum is open for most of the year. (4) Something to remember is that admission is free on Wednesday evenings in the summer. (5) Anyone joining the museum receives unlimited free admission. (6) Many of the artists with exhibits at the museum do not allow their items to be photographed. (7) Not everyone likes rock-and-roll. (8) The Cleveland Ballet is popular with some. (9) More of the city's cultural institutions are found in University Circle. (10) Here are Cleveland's museums of art and natural history; each is worth a visit.

> **More Practice**

Grammar Exercise Workbook
• pp. 11–12
On-line Exercise Bank
• Section 16.2
  Go on-line:
  PHSchool.com
  Enter Web Code:
  eek-1002

Text

Get instant feedback! Exercise 15 is available on-line or on CD-ROM.

Section Review

GRAMMAR EXERCISES 16–22

▶ **Exercise 16** Identifying Pronouns and Antecedents Identify the pronoun and antecedent in each sentence. If a pronoun has no antecedent, write *none*.

1. Ithaca, which is in southcentral New York, is located on Cayuga Lake.
2. It was settled in 1789.
3. De Witt Clinton, the American statesman, made his home in Ithaca.
4. Residents of Ithaca find themselves surrounded by great natural beauty.
5. There are many cliffs and deep ravines, and their beauty is overwhelming.

▶ **Exercise 17** Identifying Personal, Reflexive, and Intensive Pronouns Identify the pronouns, and label each *personal*, *reflexive*, or *intensive*.

1. Taos, New Mexico, sits in the hills near its neighbor, Santa Fe.
2. The city itself has long been attractive to visitors from other states and countries.
3. They enjoy the beauty of the land and the spirit of the residents there.
4. At the Kit Carson Home and Museum, you can look at objects owned by Carson himself.
5. Literary buffs can occupy themselves at the D. H. Lawrence Ranch and Shrine.

▶ **Exercise 18** Recognizing Demonstrative, Relative, and Interrogative Pronouns Identify the pronouns in each sentence, and label them *demonstrative*, *relative*, or *interrogative*.

1. Visitors who come to Houston find a thriving city in southeast Texas.
2. These are often people interested in the history and culture of the area.
3. Which would you like to see: the ballet or the opera?

4. The Houston Grand Opera, whose home is in the Civic Center Complex, performs at the Gus Wortham Theater Center.
5. That is the theater of the Houston Ballet.

▶ **Exercise 19** Supplying Indefinite Pronouns Complete each sentence by adding an indefinite pronoun.

1. Has __?__ here visited Cleveland, Ohio?
2. __?__ of the attractions in Cleveland's park system include a zoo and an aquarium.
3. The Metropolitan Park System gives __?__ a chance to enjoy nature.
4. A __?__ of Cleveland's roads lead to Lake Erie.
5. Not __?__ can name __?__ of the Great Lakes.

▶ **Exercise 20** Find It in Your Reading Identify the indefinite pronouns in "The street" on page 347. Then, find an example of each type of pronoun in one or more other pieces of literature.

▶ **Exercise 21** Find It in Your Writing In your own writing, find at least one example of each of these kinds of pronouns: *personal*, *demonstrative*, *relative*, *interrogative*, and *indefinite*. Then, replace at least two nouns with pronouns.

▶ **Exercise 22** Writing Application Write a short description of a city you would like to visit. Use at least two of each type of pronoun.

Action Verbs and Linking Verbs

Nouns are necessary to name all people, places, and things. To tell something about the nouns, *verbs* are also necessary.

> **KEY CONCEPT** A **verb** is a word that expresses time while showing an action, a condition, or the fact that something exists. ■

Action Verbs

> **KEY CONCEPT** An **action verb** is a verb that tells what action someone or something is performing, has performed, or will perform. ■

In the following examples, the verbs tell what actions have been or are being performed by Hank and the horse.

ACTION VERBS: Hank *painted* the toolshed.
The horse *waited* patiently.

GRAMMAR IN
LITERATURE

from In Commemoration: One Million Volumes
Rudolfo A. Anaya

The action verbs are highlighted in the following excerpt.

I *have* always *known* there were at least a million stars. In the summer evenings when I was a child, we, all the children of the neighborhood, *sat* outside under the stars and *listened* to the stories of the old ones, los viejitos.

Theme: New Mexico
In this section, you will learn about verbs. The examples and exercises in this section are about New Mexico.

Cross-Curricular Connection: Social Studies

▼ Critical Viewing
What action verbs could you use in describing this picture? **[Describe]**

Exercise 23 Identifying Action Verbs Identify the action verb in each of the following sentences.

1. The earliest known inhabitants of New Mexico arrived around ten thousand years ago.
2. The Pueblo people inhabited adobe dwellings.
3. Nomadic Navajo and Apache peoples settled in New Mexico in the fifteenth century.
4. They attacked the Pueblo peoples, leading to four centuries of warfare.
5. Europeans learned about New Mexico in the late 1500's.

Exercise 24 Supplying Action Verbs On a separate sheet of paper, complete each sentence by supplying an action verb.

1. Spanish conquerers ___?___ control of the land from the Native Americans.
2. The United States Army ___?___ New Mexico in 1846 and claimed it for the United States.
3. The United States government ___?___ the Arizona Territory from western New Mexico.
4. In 1863, the government ___?___ the boundaries of New Mexico to their present position.
5. When people ___?___ gold and silver, mining became a major industry.

Transitive and Intransitive Verbs

An action verb can be *transitive* or *intransitive*, depending on whether or not it transfers its action to another word in the sentence.

KEY CONCEPTS A **transitive verb** takes an object. An **intransitive verb** does not direct its action to an object. ■

The word that receives the action of a transitive verb is called the *object* of the verb. The object is often a noun or pronoun.

Intransitive verbs do not have objects. The action is not directed toward any noun or pronoun in the sentence.

To find out whether a verb in a sentence is transitive or intransitive, ask *Whom?* or *What?* after the verb. If you can find an answer in the sentence, the verb is transitive. If there is no answer, the verb is intransitive

TRANSITIVE: Robert *polished* his saddle.
                Polished *what?* (saddle)

INTRANSITIVE: Linda *waited* for the wagon.
                Waited *what?* (*no answer*)

More Practice

Grammar Exercise Workbook
• pp. 13–14
On-line Exercise Bank
• Section 16.3
   Go on-line:
   PHSchool.com
   Enter Web Code:
   eek-1002

 Text

Complete the exercises on-line! Exercises 23 and 24 are available on-line or on CD-ROM.

Most action verbs can be transitive or intransitive, depending on their use in the sentence. Some action verbs, however, can only be transitive, and others can only be intransitive.

| TRANSITIVE | I *wrote* a letter from New Mexico. |
| OR INTRANSITIVE: | The secretary *wrote* quickly. |

| ALWAYS TRANSITIVE: | California grapes *rival* those of France. |
| ALWAYS INTRANSITIVE: | She *winced* at the sound of his voice. |

Consult a dictionary if you are uncertain about whether an action verb should have an object.

▶ **Exercise 25** Distinguishing Between Transitive and Intransitive Verbs Write the verb in each sentence. Then, label each *transitive* or *intransitive*. Finally, write the object of each transitive verb.

1. People call New Mexico the Land of Enchantment.
2. Tourists flock there for the beautiful scenery.
3. They also enjoy the state's unique culture.
4. The New Mexican landscape comprises four regions.
5. The Rocky Mountains extend southward into the state.
6. Western New Mexico contains part of the Colorado Plateau, a land of cliffs, canyons, and flat-topped hills.
7. Part of the Great Plains lies in the eastern part of the state's high peaks.
8. The basin and range region consists of wide valleys and high peaks.
9. The Rio Grande flows through New Mexico.
10. The Continental Divide crosses the state from north to south.

▶ Critical Viewing How would you describe this landscape? [**Analyze, Identify**]

Linking Verbs

Linking verbs link, or join, two or more words in a sentence.

More Practice

Grammar Exercise
Workbook
• pp. 15–16
On-line Exercise Bank
• Section 16.3
 Go on-line:
 PHSchool.com
 Enter Web Code:
 eek-1002

▶ **KEY CONCEPT** A **linking verb** is a verb that connects a word or words at or near the beginning of a sentence with a word or words at or near the end. ■

In the following examples, *was* connects the subject *Sam Houston* with the word *president,* and *is* connects the subject *calf* with the words *miserable and scared.* The verbs allow *president* and *miserable and scared* to help identify or describe the subjects.

LINKING VERBS: Sam Houston *was* president of Texas from 1841 to 1844.

The feverish calf *is* miserable and scared.

The above examples both use verbs that are forms of *be,* the most common linking verb. *Be* has many different forms, as shown in the following chart.

THE FORMS OF *BE*			
am	am being	can be	have been
are	are being	could be	has been
is	is being	may be	had been
was	was being	might be	could have been
were	were being	must be	may have been
		shall be	might have been
		should be	must have been
		will be	shall have been
		would be	should have been
			will have been
			would have been

Note About *Verbs Expressing Existence:* The forms of *be* do not always function as linking verbs. Instead, they express existence, usually by showing where something is located. The following examples show forms of *be* expressing existence.

EXAMPLES: Your shirt *is* in the closet.
There *are* several mistakes in that article.

Twelve other verbs may also act as linking verbs. The verbs are shown in the chart on the next page.

OTHER LINKING VERBS					
appear	feel	look	seem	sound	taste
become	grow	remain	smell	stay	turn

These verbs also allow another word in the sentence to name or describe the subject of the sentence.

EXAMPLES: He *remained* a hermit for many years.

The music *sounded* tuneless to her.

▶ **Exercise 26** Recognizing Forms of *Be* Used as Linking Verbs Write each sentence, underlining the linking verb. Then, draw an arrow to show which words are linked by the verb. If the verb does not function as a linking verb, write *none*.

EXAMPLE: New Mexico <u>could have been</u> our home.

1. New Mexico was physically larger in the last century.
2. It is a land of magnificent and varied scenery.
3. The deserts have been there for thousands of years.
4. Irrigation would be impossible without reservoirs.
5. The landscape must have been very unfamiliar to European settlers.
6. Most rainfalls in New Mexico are brief and heavy.
7. The winters are drier than the summers.
8. The state is home to a wide variety of animal life.
9. Human impact has been a negative influence on some species.
10. The state will be the subject of interest long into future decades.

▶ **Exercise 27** Identifying Other Linking Verbs Write each sentence, underlining the linking verb. Then, draw an arrow to show which words are linked by the verb.

1. Despite the dry climate, agriculture remains economically important in the state.
2. Ranching seems more profitable than farming.
3. Overgrazing appeared ruinous to the grasslands.
4. As a result, the number of cattle became smaller.
5. With improved grazing practices, the outcome looks promising.

More Practice

Grammar Exercise Workbook
• pp. 17–18
On-line Exercise Bank
• Section 16.3
   Go on-line:
   PHSchool.com
   Enter Web Code:
   eek-1002

Get instant feedback! Exercises 26, 27, 28, and 29 are available on-line or on CD-ROM.

Linking Verb or Action Verb?

Most of the verbs in the chart on page 356 can be either linking verbs or action verbs. To see whether a verb is a linking verb, substitute *am, are,* or *is* for the verb. If the substitution makes sense and connects two words, then the original is a linking verb. Otherwise, the original is an action verb.

KEY CONCEPT *Am, are,* or *is* will make sense when substituted for another linking verb in a sentence. ■

Notice how each of the verbs in these examples has been tested to see whether it is an action verb or a linking verb.

EXAMPLES: The breeze *felt* cool.
The breeze *is* cool? (linking)
Henry *felt* the sand.
Henry *is* the sand? (action)

Exercise 28 **Distinguishing Between Linking Verbs and Action Verbs** Identify each verb as either an action verb or a linking verb.

1. Reminders of the advanced cultures in New Mexico thousands of years ago remained today.
2. The Santa Fe Trail remained popular as a trading route between St. Louis and Santa Fe in the early 1880's.
3. Railroads appeared rapidly in New Mexico after the 1880's.
4. New Mexico sounds ideal for outdoor enthusiasts.
5. Chili peppers, which taste hot, are an important New Mexican crop.

Exercise 29 Supplying Linking Verbs and Action Verbs
Complete each sentence with a form of one of the following verbs: *remain, feel, grow, look, sound, appear,* or *taste.* Label each verb *linking* or *action.*

1. New Mexicans ___?___ proud of their blend of cultures.
2. At Carlsbad Caverns National Park, tourists can ___?___ at the largest underground cave system in North America.
3. The echoes in the caves ___?___ eerie.
4. The New Mexican desert ___?___ beautiful at sunrise.
5. Have you ever ___?___ chili?

▼ Critical Viewing
What actions might the inhabitants of these dwellings perform? [Infer, Interpret]

Action Verbs and Linking Verbs • **357**

Hands-on Grammar

Intransitive Verb Translator

Divide a sheet of paper into three columns. Label the first column *Subject*, the second column *Action Verb*, and the third column *What?* Then, fold the paper so the third column does not show. In the *Action Verb* column, list the following verbs: *traveled, blew, called, visited, wandered, waited, believed, asked,* and *helped.* In the *Subject* column, write a subject that makes sense with the verb. Read the sentence you have constructed.

Unfold the paper so that the third column shows. Add an object to each subject-verb combination. Before you add an object, the verb is intransitive. When you add an object, the verb becomes transitive. You may notice, however, that you cannot add an object to some of your subject-verb combinations because some verbs are always intransitive.

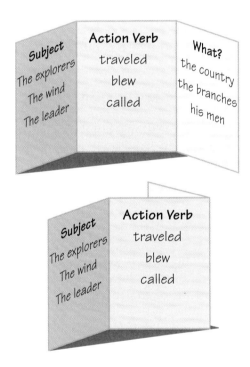

Find It in Your Reading Try this activity out with subject-verb combinations from an interesting piece of nonfiction that you read recently.

Find It in Your Writing Try the activity with subjects and verbs from a piece of your own writing.

Section 16.3 Section Review

GRAMMAR EXERCISES 30–36

Exercise 30 Identifying Transitive and Intransitive Action Verbs Identify the action verb in each sentence, and label it *transitive* or *intransitive*.

1. People often imagine New Mexico as a faraway, quiet place.
2. In fact, New Mexico has developed into a vital, vibrant, and diverse state.
3. Many interesting and unusual events have occurred in New Mexico.
4. For instance, the federal government selected Los Alamos as a site for nuclear research in 1942.
5. Some people wonder about supposed extraterrestrial landings in Roswell.

Exercise 31 Supplying Action Verbs Complete each sentence by supplying an action verb. Label the verb *transitive* or *intransitive*.

1. Taos, a small town, ___?___ national fame as an art center.
2. The Santa Fe Opera ___?___ outdoors during the summer.
3. Billy the Kid ___?___ from the Old Lincoln County Courthouse in 1881.
4. Sheriff Pat Garrett ___?___ Billy in Fort Summer, New Mexico.
5. To this day, many visitors ___?___ in the state's lakes and reservoirs.

Exercise 32 Recognizing Linking Verbs Write each sentence, underlining the linking verb. Draw an arrow showing which words are linked by the verb.

1. Santa Fe is the second-oldest city in the United States.
2. The Palace of the Governors is now the home of major museums.
3. This building had been the seat of government during the Spanish and Mexican occupations.
4. Native American and Hispanic cultures remain influential in New Mexico.
5. Native Americans seem eager to contribute to the social and economic affairs of the state.

Exercise 33 Distinguishing Between Linking Verbs and Action Verbs Complete each sentence with a form of one of the following verbs: *feel, grow, look, sound, taste, appear.* Then, label the verb *linking* or *action.*

1. Even a hot day in New Mexico ___?___ comfortable because the air is so dry.
2. Farmers in New Mexico ___?___ chili peppers, onions, and potatoes.
3. This chili ___?___ very hot and spicy.
4. When I ___?___ something spicy, I drink a big glass of water after it.
5. When the sun first ___?___, it shows off the colors of the landscape.

Exercise 34 Find It in Your Reading Choose ten verbs in a short story from your literature book. Label each action verb *transitive* or *intransitive.* Then, identify any linking verbs.

Exercise 35 Find It in Your Writing In your writing, find five examples of action verbs and five examples of linking verbs. Identify the words that are connected by the linking verbs.

Exercise 36 Writing Application Write ten sentences using these verbs, both as linking verbs and as action verbs.

taste, remain, stay, turn, become

Verb Phrases

One verb may consist of as many as four words. Acting as a unit, these words form a *verb phrase*.

> ▶ **KEY CONCEPTS**   A **verb phrase** is made up of a main verb and one or more helping verbs. Any of the many forms of *be* as well as some other verbs can be used as helping verbs. ■

Below are other verbs besides *be* that can be used as helping verbs.

HELPING VERBS OTHER THAN *BE*			
do	have	shall	can
does	has	should	could
did	had	will	may
		would	might
			must

Remember that the verb *be* can also be the main verb in a sentence. Many of the helping verbs above can be used with *be*.

Helping verbs are sometimes called *auxiliary verbs* or *auxiliaries* because they help add meaning to other verbs. Notice how helping verbs change the meaning of the sentences in the following chart.

Without Helping Verbs	With Helping Verbs
I *talk* on the telephone.	I *will talk* on the telephone.
He *returned* that book.	He *should have returned* that book.

A verb and its helping verbs are sometimes interrupted by other words, especially in questions.

UNINTERRUPTED VERB PHRASE:	The groundhog *will see* its shadow.
INTERRUPTED VERB PHRASES:	The groundhog *will* probably not *see* its shadow.
	Will the groundhog *see* its shadow?

In this section, you will learn about verb phrases. The examples and exercises in this section are about the history of Alcatraz Island.

Cross-Curricular Connection: Social Studies

◀ **Critical Viewing** Why would Alcatraz Island (shown here) make an ideal spot for a prison? **[Analyze]**

▶ **Exercise 37** Recognizing Verb Phrases Identify the verb phrase or phrases in each sentence. Do not include any words that come between the helping verb and the main verb. Indicate which verb in each phrase is the helping verb.

1. During the Civil War, the Confederacy hoped that Colonel Johnston would somehow help them bring California into the Confederacy.
2. Confederate sympathizers could not have been more wrong about Colonel Johnston.
3. He had, in fact, been born in the South.
4. However, Johnston would still do what he felt to be his duty.
5. During the Civil War, Alcatraz Island was considered the chief Union defense post of San Francisco Bay.
6. Though Johnston had been arming it for defense, no one attacked the island.
7. A group of Confederates had planned to attack the island, but the scheme was ruined after one of them had foolishly bragged of the plan in a public place.
8. How might the success of this plan have affected the outcome of the Civil War?
9. The island's weapons were never used, and by the end of the war, they had become obsolete.
10. The island was then turned into a military prison, and many Confederate sympathizers were incarcerated there.

▶ **More Practice**

Grammar Exercise Workbook
• pp. 19–20
On-line Exercise Bank
• Section 16.4
Go on-line:
PHSchool.com
Enter Web Code:
eek-1002

Text

Get instant feedback! Exercise 37 is available on-line or on CD-ROM.

Exercise 38 Supplying Helping Verbs Add a helping verb to complete each sentence.

1. Alcatraz Island __?__ become home to numerous colonies of birds.
2. The island's natural and manmade features __?__ preserved by the National Park Service.
3. The name of the island __?__ attributed to a Spanish explorer.
4. He might __?__ called it *Isla de los Alcatraces* (Island of the Pelicans) because the birds were plentiful there.
5. *Alcatraz* __?__ become the anglicized form of the original name.

Exercise 39 Writing Sentences With Verb Phrases Write a sentence in which you use each of the following verbs as the main verb in a verb phrase.

1. captured
2. imprisoned
3. isolated
4. preserved
5. visited

Exercise 40 Revising to Add Verb Phrases Revise the following paragraph so that each sentence contains a verb phrase.

(1) Alcatraz Island is in the middle of San Francisco Bay. (2) In 1933, the federal government built a maximum security prison there. (3) Today, the prison is a tourist attraction. (4) The west coast's oldest operating lighthouse is also on the island. (5) Another feature of the island is the beautiful views of the bay that it provides.

▶ Critical Viewing What verb phrases might you use to describe what it was like to be imprisoned in these quarters in Alcatraz? **[Describe]**

More Practice

Grammar Exercise Workbook
• pp. 19–20
On-line Exercise Bank
• Section 16.4
  Go on-line:
  PHSchool.com
  Enter Web Code:
  eek-1002

Section Review

GRAMMAR EXERCISES 41–45

Exercise 41 **Supplying Helping Verbs** Complete each sentence by adding a helping verb to fill each blank.

1. The army __?__ not anticipated the problems that the isolation of the island __?__ cause.
2. Prisoners __?__ work on the island, but the cost of transporting supplies __?__ becoming increasingly expensive.
3. The Great Depression __?__ contribute to the army's decision to close Alcatraz.
4. Most of the prisoners __?__ transferred to Fort Leavenworth or Fort Jay.
5. Tourists __?__ able to see the remains of Fortress Alcatraz and the disciplinary barracks.
6. The National Park Service __?__ working to make the island more accessible to tourists.
7. Visitors __?__ advised to purchase tickets well in advance.
8. The weather on the island __?__ change suddenly.
9. Tours to the island __?__ not begin until 9:30 A.M.
10. Sometimes the island __?__ closed because of adverse weather conditions.

Exercise 42 **Identifying Verb Phrases** Identify the verb phrase or phrases in each sentence. Do not include any words that interrupt the verb phrases.

1. Some visitors may find the quarter-mile walk from the dock to the cellhouse difficult.
2. They can certainly ride the electric shuttle.
3. Eating and drinking are permitted only on the dock; bottled water may also be purchased there.
4. Visitors should know that tours may be sold out up to a week in advance.

5. Alcatraz has been part of the Golden Gate National Recreation Area since 1972 and has now become one of its most popular destinations.

Exercise 43 **Find It in Your Reading** Read the following excerpt from "Diamond Island: Alcatraz," by Darryl Babe Wilson. On a separate sheet of paper, write each verb phrase. Underline the helping verb(s) in each phrase.

There was a single letter in the mailbox. Somehow it seemed urgent. The address, although it was labored over, could hardly be deciphered—square childlike print that did not complete the almost individual letters. . . . Each word pressed heavily into the paper. I could not read it but I could feel the message. "Al traz" was in the first paragraph, broken and scattered, but there. At the very bottom of the final page—running out of space—he scrawled his name. The last letter of his name, *n*, did not fit: *Gibso*.

Exercise 44 **Find It in Your Writing** Identify the verb phrases in a piece of your own writing. Underline the helping verb(s) in each verb phrase.

Exercise 45 **Writing Application** Imagine that you had to stay on an isolated island by yourself for a week. Write a description of the things that you would like to take with you. Use at least five verb phrases in your writing. Underline the helping verbs.

GRAMMAR EXERCISES 46–57

▶ **Exercise 46** Identifying Types of Nouns Identify the nouns in each sentence, and label them *concrete* or *abstract* and *common* or *proper*. Circle compound nouns, and underline collective nouns.

1. Alcatraz Island reflects various aspects of the history of California.
2. The state, which borders the Pacific Ocean, is our third largest state.
3. Its many natural resources are important to the state's economy.
4. When gold was found in 1848, it fired the imaginations of many people.
5. The discovery played an important role in the state's admission to the Union.
6. Gold was found near a sawmill outside Sacramento.
7. The ensuing Gold Rush drew prospectors from all over the world.
8. These people later became known as the Forty-niners.
9. The arrival of this group stimulated economic growth and the expansion of the railroad.
10. The nickname of California is the Golden State.

▶ **Exercise 47** Recognizing Pronouns and Antecedents Identify each pronoun and its antecedent.

1. A Spanish novel written a long time ago describes a fictional place called California. <u>That</u> may be the source of California's name.
2. The variety of climates in the state result from <u>its</u> size and location.
3. William Randolph Hearst, <u>who</u> was a journalist and publisher, lived in a lavish castle <u>that</u> <u>he</u> called San Simeon.
4. The San Andreas Fault runs through much of California. <u>It</u> causes many of the state's earthquakes.

5. California includes people <u>who</u> come from many cultural heritages.

▶ **Exercise 48** Identifying Personal, Reflexive, and Intensive Pronouns Write the pronouns in each sentence, and label them *personal*, *reflexive*, or *intensive*.

1. Major earthquakes themselves are rare, but minor tremors, landslides, and the like occur frequently.
2. Californians pride themselves on their ability to endure life on the fault.
3. Mount Whitney is located in California; it is the highest peak in the United States outside of Alaska.
4. When James W. Marshall and John A. Sutter found gold, they did not realize the impact their discovery would have.
5. The Gold Rush wore itself out almost as quickly as it began.

▶ **Exercise 49** Identifying Demonstrative, Relative, Interrogative, and Indefinite Pronouns Identify all of the pronouns. Label each *demonstrative*, *relative*, *interrogative*, or *indefinite*.

1. California has national parks that are among the most visited in the nation.
2. The General Sherman giant sequoia, which is considered the most massive tree in the world, is found in Sequoia National Park.
3. That tree has a circumference of eighty-three feet.
4. What grows in California to nearly one hundred feet high?
5. Many trees can be found in Redwood National Park; these are some of the tallest in the world.
6. All who go to California enjoy it.
7. Which does Mike prefer: the beach or

the mountains?
8 California has both of those.
9. Each of the travel agents recommends visiting the zoo in San Diego.
10. Who can go to California without visiting a movie studio?

▶ **Exercise 50** **Supplying Nouns and Pronouns** Complete the following paragraph by supplying a noun or pronoun to fill in each blank. Avoid unnecessarily repeating the same noun.

(1) Joe and __?__ want to go to California. (2) __?__ of us has ever been to __?__. (3) __?__ would probably fly into Los Angeles. (4) After visiting Hollywood and Beverly Hills, __?__ would rent a car and drive up the coast to San Francisco. (5) __?__ of our friends who have been to __?__ recommend the drive. (6) __?__ tell us that the coastal section known as Big Sur is breathtaking. (7) Huge cliffs drop suddenly into the bright blue sea, and the __?__ pounds steadily onto the rocky shore. (8) __?__ have heard that we have to drive carefully as we head up the coast, because the __?__ are windy and at times __?__. (9) Once we reached San Francisco, Joe and __?__ would visit the Golden Gate Bridge and walk throughout the __?__, admiring the architecture of __?__ buildings. (10) We would also probably take a boat out to Alcatraz. __?__ of __?__ friends who have visited the island say that the prison tour was one of the most memorable parts of __?__ trip to __?__.

▶ **Exercise 51** **Supplying Action Verbs** Complete each sentence by adding an action verb. Label it *visible* or *mental* and *transitive* or *intransitive*.

1. Many professional sports teams __?__ in California.

2. Do you __?__ their names?
3. Should we __?__ the game tonight?
4. We __?__ Redwood National Park.
5. I never __?__ such tall trees.
6. James W. Marshall __?__ gold in 1848.
7. The Gold Rush __?__ the following year.
8. The San Andreas Fault __?__ California's earthquakes.
9. Did you __?__ Death Valley?
10. Nothing much __?__ in such heat.

▶ **Exercise 52** **Identify Linking Verbs, Helping Verbs, and Verb Phrases** Identify the linking verbs and verb phrases in these sentences. List the words that each linking verb connects. Then, identify the helping verb in each verb phrase.

1. California has been a state since 1850.
2. Death Valley is the lowest point in the country.
3. Parts of Death Valley look bleak.
4. The heat can feel oppressive.
5. The temperature could not have been hotter there.
6. California's pleasant climate has been an important factor in its popularity.
7. The desert turns cold at night.
8. Despite the threat of earthquakes, California remains a popular tourist destination.
9. Can you smell the sea air?
10. California's population has grown.

▶ **Exercise 53** **Classifying Verbs** Identify the verbs and verb phrases in these sentences. Label each *action verb*, *linking verb*, or *verb phrase*.

1. California's pleasant climate draws people there.
2. Parts of the Pacific Ocean have been preserved as a habitat for blue whales.
3. Without protection, the blue whale could become extinct.
4. It is the largest mammal on Earth.

Chapter Review Exercises cont'd.

5. Such an animal's extinction would be a great loss to the planet.
6. Californians are now constructing buildings to withstand earthquakes.
7. They prepare for the threat of earthquakes.
8. Have Californians learned to live with that concern?
9. Because the state has many attractions, natural beauty, and a great climate, residents feel it is worth living with the threat of earthquakes.
10. Everyone should take precautions, however.

Exercise 54 Revising the Use of Verbs Revise five of the sentences in the previous excercise to change the type of verb that is used. For example, you might rework a sentence containing an action verb so that it contains a verb phrase.

Exercise 55 Supplying Nouns, Pronouns, and Verbs Add nouns, pronouns, and verbs to the following sentences to complete them. Label the part of speech of each word you add.

1. ___?___ famous and ordinary ___?___ have lived in California.
2. ___?___ have come from other states; ___?___ have also come from foreign countries.
3. Many people ___?___ about the famous Gold Rush when they ___?___ California history.
4. This ___?___ played an important role in California's history, because many people ___?___ west to make ___?___ fortunes.
5. Today California ___?___ known as "The Golden State" based on ___?___ history.

Exercise 56 Revision Practice: Focusing on the Use of Nouns, Pronouns, and Verbs Revise this paragraph. (1) Replace general nouns with more specific ones. (2) Replace common nouns with proper nouns where appropriate. (3) Replace proper nouns with common nouns to avoid repetition. (4) Replace nouns with pronouns where appropriate to reduce repetition. (5) Replace general verbs with more specific ones wherever possible. (6) Rework sentences where you can to replace linking verbs with action verbs.

(1) California's cities each have their own distinctive features and attractions. (2) California's capital, Sacramento, has a recreation of what Sacramento was like a century ago. (3) This old city is a popular destination for people visiting Sacramento. (4) San Francisco is known for attractions such as the Golden Gate Bridge and Chinatown, and San Francisco also features many hills and a stunningly beautiful bay. (5) San Francisco is also remembered by some people who visit San Francisco for the city's cool, breezy days. (6) Los Angeles has warmer temperatures than San Francisco, and Los Angeles is also larger than San Francisco. (7) The city is known, among other things, as the home of the movie industry. (8) Many of the people who perform in the movies and on television live in Los Angeles. (9) People who visit Los Angeles often take a tour of the places where many of the movie stars live. (10) Another popular atrraction is the shopping district in Beverly Hills.

Exercise 57 Writing Application Write an essay persuading people to visit your state. Include proper nouns to name specific places or things. Also include three action verbs, three linking verbs, and three verb phrases.

Standardized Test Preparation Workshop

Analogies

Analogy questions test your ability to determine a relationship between a given pair of words and to identify a similar relationship between the words in the second pair. Common relationships used in analogies are

Antonyms, such as fast : slow
Part-Whole or *Whole-Part,* such as buttons : sweater
Definitional/Synonyms, such as joke : humorous
Cause-Effect or *Effect-Cause,* such as rain : floods
Functional Relationship, such as artist : painting
Relationship of Degrees, such as smart : brilliant

When responding to analogies, determine the relationship between the first pair of words. Then, choose the pair that most closely reflects that relationship.

Sample Test Item

Directions: Each question below consists of a related pair of words followed by five pairs of words labeled *A* through *E*. Select the pair that *best* expresses a relationship similar to that expressed in the original pair.

LOCOMOTIVE : TRAIN ::

(A) horse : saddle

(B) tractor : plough

(C) rudder : rowboat

(D) camel : desert

(E) gasoline : automobile

Answer and Explanations

The correct answer is *E*. The relationship is functional: *A* locomotive powers a train; gasoline powers an automobile.

▷ **Practice** **Directions:** Each question below consists of a related pair of words or phrases, followed by five pairs of word or phrases labeled *A* through *E*. Select the pair that best expresses a relationship similar to that expressed in the original pair.

1 ABRIDGE : NOVEL ::
(A) interrupt : conversation
(B) rehearse : play
(C) terminate : ending
(D) punctuate : sentence
(E) abbreviate : word

2 AUDIENCE : THEATER ::
(A) crew : ship
(B) scholars : library
(C) group : society
(D) spectators : arena
(E) actors : stage

Adjectives and *Adverbs*

Nouns, pronouns, and verbs make simple communication possible. These three parts of speech can express essential ideas, such as *I need food.* For more descriptive and detailed communication, however, two other parts of speech are necessary: *adjectives* and *adverbs.*

Consider, for example, the incredible variety of birds that live in the world. Each species has unique features, abilities, and habits that make it different from every other species. Adjectives and adverbs give writers the ability to communicate these differences. In the sentence *Two majestic red-tailed hawks flew gracefully,* the adjectives *two, majestic,* and *red-tailed* provide important details about the hawks, while the adverb *gracefully* describes their action.

These two parts of speech that add description and detail to your written and spoken words are called *modifiers.* In this chapter, you will examine the ways adjectives and adverbs modify other words.

▲ **Critical Viewing** Name three adjectives to describe the mother bird and two adverbs to describe how the baby birds are crying. **[Analyze]**

Diagnostic Test

Directions: Write all answers on a separate sheet of paper.

Skill Check A. Identify all adjectives, including articles, in each of the following sentences.

1. Ostriches are the largest birds in the world.
2. Mature males may attain a height of 8 feet.
3. The birds are characterized by long, thin necks and strong legs.
4. Ostriches also have short, stubby wings, but they cannot fly.
5. The soft, fluffy feathers of the male are black and white.

Skill Check B. List the proper and compound adjectives in the following sentences, and label each one *proper* or *compound*.

6. Ostriches live on the African continent.
7. They can be found in grassland areas below the Sahara.
8. Most American students have seen ostriches only in a zoo.
9. Ostriches are the fastest two-legged animals on the planet.
10. These overgrown birds can maintain speeds of 40 miles per hour for up to 30 minutes.

Skill Check C. Identify any nouns, pronouns, or verbs used as adjectives in the following sentences. Label each appropriately.

11. Foraging ostriches eat a variety of grasses and crawling insects.
12. Like other birds, ostriches do not have any teeth.
13. They swallow most selected foods whole.
14. Ostriches consume small stones to help them digest their stomach contents.
15. These birds must also remain near a water source, as they require two gallons of water per day.

Skill Check D. In each of the following sentences, identify the adverbs and the word each adverb modifies.

16. The zoologist held an ostrich egg gently in her hands.
17. The incredibly heavy egg weighed nearly 3 pounds.
18. Female ostriches normally lay ten perfectly white eggs each season.
19. Approximately fifty eggs may be concentrated into one centrally located nest.
20. The dominant male incubates the eggs nightly, and the females incubate them daily.

Skill Check E. Identify each underlined word below as either an *adjective* or an *adverb.*

21. The ostriches stood <u>close</u> to the nest to protect their eggs.
22. Incubation is a <u>daily</u> task for the ostriches.
23. The eggs will not hatch <u>early</u>.
24. The <u>ungainly</u> birds try to chase away predators.
25. The birds are formidable because they run so <u>fast</u>.

Adjectives

Whenever you want to create a clearer picture of a person, place, or thing, you are likely to use an *adjective*.

▶ **KEY CONCEPT** An **adjective** is a word used to describe a noun or pronoun or to give a noun or pronoun a more specific meaning. ■

The way an adjective describes a word or makes it more specific is called *modification.* Modification is the act of changing something slightly. An adjective modifies a noun or pronoun by adding information that answers any of four questions about the noun or pronoun:

▶ **KEY CONCEPT** Adjectives answer the question *What kind? Which one? How many?* or *How much?* about the nouns and pronouns they modify. ■

In the following chart, the examples show adjectives that answer the four questions noted about nouns or pronouns.

QUESTIONS THAT ADJECTIVES ANSWER	
What Kind?	
large hawk	*lost* boy
metallic gleam	*purple* feather
Which One?	
that bird	*any* number
other door	*last* opportunity
How Many?	
both swans	*some* falcons
five dollars	*frequent* interruptions
How Much?	
enough birdseed	*more* fun
less effort	*adequate* space

When an adjective modifies a noun, it usually comes before the noun. Occasionally, though, the adjective may follow the noun.

Theme: Birds

In this section, you will learn how adjectives are used to modify nouns and pronouns. The examples and exercises are about different species of birds.

Cross-Curricular Connection: Science

 **Spelling Tip**

Suffixes such as *-ive, -ible,* and *-able* are often used to transform nouns into adjectives. For example, *response* becomes *responsive* or *responsible* and *reason* becomes *reasonable.*

▶ **KEY CONCEPT** An adjective may come before or after the noun it modifies. ■

BEFORE: The *large* condor is at the zoo.

AFTER: The condor at the zoo is *large*.

▶ **KEY CONCEPT** Two or more adjectives can modify one word. ■

EXAMPLE: *Several small, fuzzy* chicks were running around the farm.

Note About *a, an,* and *the*: Three adjectives—*a, an,* and *the*—are called *articles. The* is called a *definite article* because it refers to a specific noun. *A* and *an* are called *indefinite articles* because they refer to any one of a class of nouns. In the examples below, *the* refers to a specific zoo, while *an* refers to any apple.

DEFINITE: We will go to *the* zoo.

INDEFINITE: The parrot ate *an* apple.

▶ **Exercise 1** Recognizing Adjectives Write the adjectives, including articles, in each sentence below.

EXAMPLE: The swift parrot chased a small lizard.
ANSWER: The, swift, a, small

1. Parrots are found in the warm tropical areas of the planet.
2. A small number of species inhabit the cooler temperate regions.
3. The colorful birds have red, green, blue, and yellow plumage.
4. Parrots eat a wide variety of hearty seeds and nutritious fruits.
5. Parrots are monogamous, often remaining with a single mate for life.

▼ **Critical Viewing**
Name three adjectives to describe either of the parakeets in this picture. What question does each adjective answer about the parakeet? **[Analyze, Connect]**

▶ **More Practice**

Grammar Exercise Workbook
• pp. 21–22
On-line Exercise Bank
• Section 17.1
  Go on-line:
  PHSchool.com
  Enter Web Code:
  eek-1002

Nouns Used as Adjectives

Many nouns can be used as adjectives. They become adjectives when they modify other nouns and answer one of two questions about the nouns they are modifying.

KEY CONCEPT A noun used as an adjective answers the question *What kind?* or *Which one?* about a noun that follows it. ■

Noun	Adjective
pineapple	*pineapple* juice (*What kind* of juice?)
summer	*summer* habitat (*Which* habitat?)

Exercise 2 Identifying Nouns Used as Adjectives Write the noun used as an adjective in each sentence below.

EXAMPLE: The macaw perched on the top of the rock ledge.
ANSWER: rock

1. Macaws are large, noisy members of the parrot family.
2. The colorful macaws live in large flocks and roost along steep canyon walls.
3. They dig small nest holes in the relatively soft sandstone.
4. Major food sources for macaws are fruits and nuts.
5. Macaws perch among the tree branches while they eat.
6. Occasionally, they will also search the forest floor for food.
7. Because they live in the warm tropics of South America, the birds do not migrate to a winter territory.
8. Unfortunately, the macaw population is dwindling because of the actions of humans.
9. Cattle ranches are the biggest threat to the remaining habitat of the macaw.
10. The birds are also threatened by wildlife poachers.

Get instant feedback! Exercise 2 is available on-line or on CD-ROM.

More Practice

Grammar Exercise Workbook
• pp. 23–24
On-line Exercise Bank
• Section 17.1
  Go on-line:
  PHSchool.com
  Enter Web Code:
  eek-1002

▶ Critical Viewing Each part of this parrot can be named by a noun. Can any of these nouns also act as adjectives to modify another noun? Give an example. [Speculate, Identify]

GRAMMAR IN LITERATURE

from **The Widow and the Parrot**
Virginia Woolf

In the following excerpt, the adjectives in blue italics answer the questions What kind? Which one? How many? *or* How much? *about the nouns and pronouns they modify.*

She was lying in bed thinking these thoughts when a *slight* tap at the window made her start. The tap was repeated *three* times over. Mrs. Gage got out of bed as quickly as she could and went to the window. There, to her *utmost* surprise, sitting on the *window* ledge, was an *enormous* parrot. The rain had stopped and it was a *fine moonlight* night. She was greatly alarmed at first, but soon recognized the *gray* parrot, James, and was overcome with joy at his escape. . . .

Proper and Compound Adjectives

Two other types of adjectives are *proper adjectives* and *compound adjectives.*

Proper Adjectives Sometimes, proper nouns are used as adjectives or changed in form to become adjectives.

▷ **KEY CONCEPT** A **proper adjective** is a proper noun used as an adjective or an adjective formed from a proper noun. ■

Notice in the following chart that proper adjectives modify nouns by answering the questions *What kind?* or *Which one?*

Proper Nouns	Proper Adjectives
Vermont Brahms	*Vermont* cheddar (*What kind* of cheddar?) the *Brahms* symphony (*Which* symphony?)

Sometimes, proper nouns change their form when they are used as proper adjectives.

Proper Nouns	Proper Adjectives
Shakespeare Germany	*Shakespearean* play (*What kind* of play?) *German* tribes (*Which* tribes?)

Proper adjectives generally begin with a capital letter.

▶**KEY CONCEPT** A **compound adjective** is an adjective that is made up of more than one word. ∎

Most compound adjectives are hyphenated, but some are written as combined words.

Hyphenated	Combined
freeze-dried coffee *heavy-duty* boots	*farsighted* planner *underpaid* staff

If you are uncertain about the spelling of a compound adjective, consult a dictionary.

▶**Exercise 3** Recognizing Proper and Compound Adjectives
Write only the proper and compound adjectives in each sentence below, and label each. (Note: Some may be compound proper adjectives.)

EXAMPLE: Flamingos can be found in the Brazilian forests.
ANSWER: Brazilian

1. The flamingo is the name for a family of long-legged birds.
2. Scientists are fascinated by these multicolored birds.
3. Flamingos are common throughout the world, and they can be found from the African savannas to the South American mountains.
4. They are characterized by a downward-turned bill, which is used to filter underwater organisms and vegetation.
5. The largest species, called the greater flamingo, inhabits the Caribbean region.
6. The Chilean flamingo is a variety that may be found in the lowland areas of Chile and Argentina on the South American mainland.
7. The lesser flamingo is the most common type, with a worldwide population of 4 million.
8. Flamingos fashion cone-shaped nests from mud, and they generally lay one off-white egg.
9. The newborn chicks are fed by the parents for months; however, they are self-sufficient after 30 days.
10. Flamingos make their North American homes in saltwater marshes and shallow freshwater ponds.

**⚙ Grammar
⚙ and Style Tip**

Adjectives are an essential tool for writers because they add important details. However, writers should avoid using long strings of adjectives to describe every noun. The excessive use of adjectives may complicate your message or confuse your reader.

Pronouns Used as Adjectives

Just as nouns can be used as adjectives, so can certain pronouns. In fact, some personal pronouns, known as *possessive pronouns* or *possessive adjectives,* act as both pronouns *and* adjectives. Others act as either pronouns *or* adjectives.

KEY CONCEPT A pronoun functions as an adjective if it modifies a noun. ■

Possessive Pronouns or Adjectives Seven personal pronouns are known as *possessive pronouns* or *possessive adjectives.* They are pronouns because they have antecedents. They are adjectives because they modify nouns and answer the question *Which one?*

POSSESSIVE PRONOUNS OR ADJECTIVES
my   your   his   he   its   our   their
ANTECEDENT   WORD MODIFIED
The *flock* reached *its* winter feeding *grounds.*

Demonstrative Adjectives All four of the demonstrative pronouns can be used as adjectives. Unlike the personal pronouns above, they become demonstrative adjectives *instead of* pronouns. When they function as adjectives, they always come before the nouns they modify and never directly before a verb.

DEMONSTRATIVE ADJECTIVES	
this that these those	
Demonstrative Pronouns	Demonstrative Adjectives
Did the bird drop *this?*	Did the bird drop *this* feather?
Those are pretty birds.	*Those* birds are pretty.

Interrogative Adjectives Three of the interrogative pronouns become *interrogative adjectives* when they modify a noun.

INTERROGATIVE ADJECTIVES	
which what whose	
Interrogative Pronouns	Interrogative Adjectives
What happened?	*What* color is the egg?
Whose is that?	*Whose* pet is the canary?

Indefinite Adjectives Many indefinite pronouns become *indefinite adjectives* when they modify nouns. The charts below show whether they modify singular or plural nouns.

INDEFINITE ADJECTIVES		
Singular	Plural	Singular or Plural
another　　much each　　neither either　　one little	both few many several	all　　other any　　some more most

Indefinite Pronouns	Indefinite Adjectives
The parakeet ate *one*.	The parakeet ate *one* nut.
Few live in the Arctic.	*Few* birds live in the Arctic.
We saw *some* at the lake.	We saw *some* ducks at the lake.

Exercise 4 **Distinguishing Between Pronouns and Adjectives** Identify whether the underlined word in each sentence below functions as a *pronoun* or as an *adjective*. If it functions as an adjective, tell which word it modifies.

EXAMPLE:　　We watched <u>that</u> toucan fly from the perch.
ANSWER:　　　adjective (modifies toucan)

1. On a recent trip to the zoo, <u>my</u> friends and I learned about toucans.
2. <u>Those</u> are brightly colored birds known for <u>their</u> large beaks.
3. <u>That</u> toucan's beak measures more than half of <u>its</u> body length.
4. <u>Our</u> tour guide said <u>some</u> toucans may grow to be 25 inches long.
5. <u>These</u> interesting birds inhabit the tropical forests of Central and South America.
6. Only <u>one</u> species, the toucanet, lives in the mountains.
7. <u>All</u> toucans have two forward-facing toes and two backward-facing toes.
8. A <u>few</u> people in the group asked <u>what</u> foods were eaten by toucans.
9. The tour guide said <u>most</u> toucans eat small fruits and berries, but <u>several</u> eat insects and small lizards.
10. We asked <u>which</u> of the zoo's <u>many</u> birds was <u>his</u> favorite.

More Practice

Grammar Exercise Workbook
• pp. 25–26
On-line Exercise Bank
• Section 17.1
　Go on-line:
　PHSchool.com
　Enter Web Code:
　eek-1002

Get instant feedback! Exercises 4 and 5 are available on-line or on CD-ROM.

Verbs Used as Adjectives

Many words that look like verbs can function as adjectives in sentences.

▶ **KEY CONCEPT** Some verb forms, especially those ending in *-ing* and *-ed*, function as adjectives when they modify a noun. ■

Below are verbs used first as verbs and then as adjectives.

Verbs	Adjectives
The owl *was sitting* still.	The *sitting* owl was still.
The ice *melted* in the sun.	The *melted* ice was in the sun.

▶ **Exercise 5** Distinguishing Between Verbs and Adjectives
Identify whether the underlined word in each sentence below functions as a *verb* or as an *adjective.* If it functions as an adjective, tell which word it modifies.

EXAMPLE: A <u>startled</u> peacock will make a lot of noise.
ANSWER: adjective (modifies peacock)

1. The peacock, a member of the pheasant family, is known for its brilliantly <u>colored</u> feathers.
2. Only the males are <u>endowed</u> with colorful blue, gold, and green plumage.
3. The <u>camouflaged</u> females, called peahens, have drab brown-and-green feathers.
4. <u>Competing</u> males display their ornate feathers to attract mates.
5. At night, peacocks usually <u>sleep</u> in high tree branches.
6. <u>Consuming</u> small snakes and lizards, they spend their days on the ground.
7. Until recently, scientists thought that these birds <u>inhabited</u> only the forests of Southeast Asia and India.
8. The Congo peacock is a rare species that occupies a very <u>confined</u> area in central Africa.
9. Because it had eluded scientists until 1936, this bird was considered a <u>living</u> mystery when it was discovered.
10. Today, the Congo peacock is a <u>protected</u> species.

▼ **Critical Viewing**
Use *singing* as a verb and then as an adjective in sentences about this bird.
[Connect]

Adjectives • **377**

Hands-on Grammar

Turning Verbs Into Adjectives

To practice converting verb forms into adjectives, try this activity. Take several index cards, and cut out a long opening in each to create a box with two "wings," as in the model below. On one side of the card, write a verb phrase, such as *is crying, was shouting, has been forgotten,* or *was protected.* Flip the card over, and write just the participle form on the other side: *crying, shouting, forgotten, protected.*

Tape the edges of the wings of a card onto a piece of paper. In the opening, write an article and a noun spaced apart, so that a sentence such as *The child is crying* would appear. Now, bend the card to place *crying* between *the* and *child* to create the phrase *The crying child.* Create additional verb/adjective conversions. Then, extend the activity by writing a phrase after the verb form on both sides of the card. For example: Write *was shouting at his friend* on one side of a card and *shouting at his friend* on the flip side. This time, put the article and noun close together. Connecting this new card to *The child,* you can create an introductory adjective phrase such as *Shouting at his friend* to add to a longer sentence about the child.

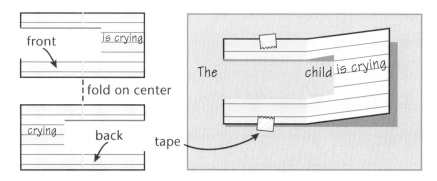

Find It in Your Reading In your reading, find examples of sentences that contain verb forms used in introductory adjective phrases. Write the sentences on your paper, and underline the verb form acting as an adjective and the noun being modified.

Find It in Your Writing Look through samples of your own writing to find sentences in which you have used *-ing* and *-ed* forms of verbs. Rewrite the sentences, changing the verbs to adjectives and expanding the sentences.

Section 17.1

Section Review

GRAMMAR EXERCISES 6–11

▶ **Exercise 6** Recognizing Types of Adjectives Identify each underlined adjective below as *article*, *proper adjective*, *compound adjective*, *possessive adjective*, *indefinite adjective*, or *demonstrative adjective*.

1. <u>The</u> kiwi is a <u>strange-looking</u> bird that can be found only in <u>some</u> areas of New Zealand.
2. While kiwis are defenseless, <u>their</u> survival has been made possible because they have no natural predators on <u>this</u> <u>South Pacific</u> island.
3. Although <u>New Zealand</u> kiwis have small, stubby wings, they are <u>earthbound</u> birds that cannot fly.
4. Long, <u>hairlike</u> feathers are <u>another</u> feature of <u>a</u> kiwi.
5. It is also the only <u>Asian</u> bird that locates food by <u>its</u> sense of smell.

▶ **Exercise 7** Recognizing Other Parts of Speech Used as Adjectives Identify any nouns, pronouns, or verbs used as adjectives in the following sentences. Write them on your paper, and label each. If none are used, write *none*.

1. The owl is a bird variety that is characterized by a large head, forward-facing eyes, and sharp claws.
2. The barn owl is the most common species in the United States.
3. The smallest species resides in the deserts of the Southwest.
4. In which places besides trees and abandoned buildings do owls make their homes?
5. The burrowing owl, for instance, may make its home in old rabbit holes.
6. Most owls are active after the evening stars have emerged.
7. They are the only birds whose eyes are located on the front of the face.
8. All owls also have excellent hearing abilities to assist their hunting efforts.
9. Rain deters hunting owls, since they cannot fly quietly with wet wing feathers.
10. Though many people dislike owls, these birds are our allies against rodents.

▶ **Exercise 8** Supplying Adjectives to Add Details Rewrite the paragraph below on your paper, supplying an adjective in each blank.

(1) The wild turkey is among the ___?___ birds in North America, much bigger than most other fowl. (2) Wild turkeys are found in ___?___ areas deep among the trees. (3) Males are ___?___ and ___?___ than females and are also more ___?___. (4) The males can also be distinguished by the wattle, a ___?___ piece of ___?___ skin that hangs from the beak. (5) The skin of the head and neck of a wild turkey is usually ___?___ in color, but it may also be a brighter shade of ___?___ or ___?___.

▶ **Exercise 9** Find It in Your Reading In the excerpt from "The Widow and the Parrot" on page 373, identify one *demonstrative adjective*, one *possessive adjective*, and one *verb form used as an adjective*.

▶ **Exercise 10** Find It in Your Writing In your own writing, find at least one example of each of the following kinds of adjectives: *proper, compound, possessive,* and *demonstrative.* Copy the sentences, and label each type of adjective.

▶ **Exercise 11** Writing Application Write a description of your favorite bird. Be sure to use precise adjectives to bring the bird to life for your readers.

Adverbs

Like adjectives, *adverbs* are used to describe or add information about other words.

▶ **KEY CONCEPT** An **adverb** is a word that modifies a verb, an adjective, or another adverb. ■

Just as adjectives answer questions about nouns and pronouns, adverbs answer questions about words they modify.

▶ **KEY CONCEPT** An adverb answers one of four questions about the word it modifies: *Where? When? In what way?* or *To what extent?* ■

An adverb modifying a verb can answer any of the four questions. An adverb modifying an adjective or another adverb, however, will answer only one question: *To what extent?*

The chart below shows adverbs answering each of the four questions. Notice the positions of the adverbs. When an adverb modifies a verb or verb phrase, it may come *before* or *after* the verb or verb phrase. Frequently, it comes *within* the verb phrase. If an adverb modifies an adjective or another adverb, it generally comes *immediately before* the adjective or adverb.

Theme: Seashells

In this section, you will learn how adverbs are used to modify verbs, adjectives, and other adverbs. The examples and exercises are about different kinds of seashells.

Cross-Curricular Connection: Science

Verbs	Adjectives
Where?	**When?**
slide *under* move *near* sit *there* slipped *between*	*often* asks sails *daily* should have answered *promptly* *soon* will depart
In What Way?	**To What Extent?**
reacted *positively* *silently* nodded left *quickly* *rudely* laughed was *cheerfully* humming	*widely* read *barely* walks researched *further* had *just* started must *not* have finished
Adverbs Modifying Adjectives	**Adverbs Modifying Adverbs**
To What Extent?	**To What Extent?**
very tall *somewhat* satisfied *frequently* absent *not* sad	*very* thoroughly *not* exactly *more* quickly *quite* definitely

◀ **Critical Viewing**
Using this photo and the information in Exercise 12, describe these cowries with phrases containing adverbs that answer each of the four questions on page 380. [Analyze]

Exercise 12 **Recognizing Adverbs** Identify the adverbs in each sentence below. Then, tell which word each adverb modifies.

EXAMPLE: The porpoise swam very rapidly.
ANSWER: very (modifies rapidly), rapidly (modifies swam)

1. Cowries are a very common variety of sea snails that are generally found in warm tropical waters.
2. They are mostly nocturnal animals, and they usually feed on algae.
3. A few species crawl slowly among corals and feed hungrily upon them.
4. These small creatures often have brilliantly colored shells.
5. For many years, cowry shells were used quite frequently by people in Africa, Asia, and Melanesia as a form of currency.

Nouns Used as Adverbs

A few words that are usually nouns can also act as adverbs.

KEY CONCEPT Nouns used as adverbs answer the question *Where?* or *When?* about a verb. ■

Some of the nouns that can be used as adverbs are *home*, *yesterday*, and *today*.

Nouns	Adverbs
The crab's *home* is under that rock.	The crab crawled *home*. (crawled *where?*)
The warm, summer *nights* cause the jellyfish to rise to the water's surface.	The jellyfish are active *nights*. (are active *when?*)

More Practice

Grammar Exercise Workbook
• pp. 27–28
On-line Exercise Bank
• Section 17.2
  Go on-line:
  PHSchool.com
  Enter Web Code:
  eek-1002

Get instant feedback! Exercise 12 is available on-line or on CD-ROM.

GRAMMAR IN
LITERATURE

from Abalone, Abalone, Abalone
Toshio Mori

Several adverbs are printed in italics in the following excerpt. An adverb that can also function as a noun is in red.

Before Mr. Abe went *away* I used to see him *quite often* at his nursery. He was a carnation grower just as I am one *today*. At noontime I used to go to his front porch and look at his collection of abalone shells.

They were lined up *side by side* against the side of his house on the front porch. I was curious as to why he bothered to collect them. It was a lot of bother polishing them.

> **Exercise 13** **Recognizing Nouns Used as Adverbs** Identify two adverbs in each sentence below, and write them on your paper. Then, circle each noun used as an adverb.

EXAMPLE: Yesterday, I casually walked to the beach and collected seashells.

ANSWER: (Yesterday,) casually

1. Weekends, I like to take my little brother to a relatively unknown stretch of seashore.
2. We carefully search the beach for shells some mornings.
3. Most days, we are seldom disappointed.
4. Today, for example, we found a dozen shells nearby.
5. My brother always races home to show our parents the assortment of cowry, cone, and conch shells that we have found.
6. Afternoons, he thoroughly cleans any sand or other debris from the shells.
7. Both of us are eagerly awaiting our trip tomorrow.
8. Sundays, we generally have the whole beach to ourselves.
9. I fully enjoy being outside in the warm sea air.
10. Unfortunately, I have to work weekdays.

✓ Spelling Tip

To form adverbs from many words ending in *y*, change the *y* to *i* and then add the suffix *-ly*. For example, *happy* becomes *happily* and *lazy* becomes *lazily*.

Adverb or Adjective?

Sometimes, the same word can be either an adverb or an adjective, depending upon how it is used in a sentence.

KEY CONCEPT Remember that an adverb modifies a verb, an adjective, or another adverb; an adjective modifies a noun or a pronoun. ■

Notice in the following examples that the adverb modifies a verb. The same word used as an adjective, on the other hand, modifies a noun.

ADVERB: The fish swam *straight* through the channel.

ADJECTIVE: The path was *straight*.

Generally, adverbs and adjectives have different forms. Many adverbs, in fact, are formed by adding *-ly* to an adjective.

Adjectives	Adverbs With *-ly* Endings
honest response	responded *honestly*
awkward movement	moved *awkwardly*

A few words ending in *-ly*, however, are adjectives.

ADJECTIVE: We found a *lovely* shell with *curly* edges.

▲ Critical Viewing If you used *lovely*, *hard*, and *underwater* in sentences about this turtle cone shell, would those words be adjectives or adverbs? Can any of them be both? [Distinguish]

Grammar and Style Tip

When using a word ending in *-ly* directly before a noun, check to make sure that it is an adjective.

▲ Critical Viewing
Write a sentence containing *best*, in which you reveal your favorite type of shell. In your sentence, is *best* functioning as an adjective or an adverb? [Connect, Analyze]

▶ **Exercise 14** **Distinguishing Between Adverbs and Adjectives** Identify each underlined word below as an *adverb* or *adjective*.

EXAMPLE: The small fish eggs were <u>barely</u> visible.
ANSWER: adverb

1. Cone snails are an unusual variety of sea snails that have <u>hard</u>, elaborately colored shells.
2. These snails are <u>quite</u> effective hunters.
3. They may feed <u>daily</u> on live or dead fish.
4. They attack their prey with <u>deadly</u> accuracy.
5. Cone snails shoot poison-tipped darts <u>straight</u> at any fish that swims within range.
6. The unwitting fish may work <u>hard</u> to escape before the snail's venom immobilizes it.
7. These <u>lovely</u> mollusks live in the warm tropical waters between Australia and India.
8. Occasionally, their empty shells are found among the <u>stately</u> palms on South Pacific islands.
9. Some of the most visually stunning varieties are spotted <u>only</u> occasionally by lucky searchers.
10. This rare shell is the <u>only</u> shell of its kind at the auction.

▶ **More Practice**

Grammar Exercise Workbook
• pp. 29–30
On-line Exercise Bank
• Section 17.2
  Go on-line:
  PHSchool.com
  Enter Web Code:
  eek-1002

Section Review

GRAMMAR EXERCISES 15–20

Exercise 15 **Recognizing Adverbs**
List the adverbs you find in each sentence below and the word each modifies.

1. The rarely studied nautilus is an extremely odd mollusk.
2. It is related most closely to squids and octopuses, but it really bears little resemblance to its relatives.
3. This unusual shellfish is entirely enclosed in a perfectly spiraled shell.
4. The nautilus also has approximately ninety tentacles that extend ominously from the opening of its shell.
5. During the day, these odd-looking shellfish usually hide quietly among the rocks on the ocean floor.
6. Nautiluses cautiously emerge after the sun has set.
7. They gradually begin to swim toward the surface and eventually reach the shallow waters of a coral reef.
8. Nautiluses feed ravenously upon crabs, which they capture easily.
9. At first light, they rapidly retreat to the relatively safe ocean floor.
10. The nautiluses' uniquely designed shells are highly prized by collectors.

Exercise 16 **Supplying Nouns Used as Adverbs** Rewrite the sentences below on your paper, supplying a noun used as an adverb to fill each blank.

1. ___?___, I regularly dive along the coral reefs.
2. ___?___, I saw a very interesting mollusk called a giant clam.
3. The 4-foot-wide creature is active ___?___ and night.
4. The incredibly heavy shell was far too big to bring ___?___.
5. ___?___, I plan to dive down to the giant clam again to show it to my cousin.

Exercise 17 **Distinguishing Between Adverbs and Adjectives** Label each underlined word below *adverb* or *adjective*.

1. Hermit crabs are <u>most</u> often found along the Atlantic coast of the United States.
2. Despite its name, many consider the hermit crab a <u>friendly</u> pet.
3. Because it lacks a <u>hard</u> shell, the young hermit crab is vulnerable to predators.
4. It works <u>hard</u> to insert its body into a discarded seashell, and then it carries the shell with it wherever it goes.
5. The crab cannot keep the same shell <u>long</u>, since it must move to a larger shell as it grows.

Exercise 18 **Find It in Your Reading** In the excerpt from "Abalone, Abalone, Abalone" on page 382, identify the words that the highlighted adverbs modify, and indicate whether each modified word is a *verb*, an *adjective*, or an *adverb*.

Exercise 19 **Find It in Your Writing** Choose a piece of writing from your portfolio, and identify five adverbs. Are there places where you can add adverbs to create a clearer picture of the action for your readers?

Exercise 20 **Writing Application** Write a short essay about something you collect or would like to collect. Include adverbs to add details to verbs, adjectives, and other adverbs.

GRAMMAR EXERCISES 21–28

▶ **Exercise 21** **Identifying Adjectives and Adverbs** Identify each underlined word below as an *adjective* or *adverb*.

1. Starfish are <u>unusual</u> creatures that can <u>often</u> be found on the <u>rocky</u> floor of the ocean.
2. The <u>average</u> starfish has <u>five</u> arms, but species have <u>sometimes</u> been found that have <u>even</u> more arms.
3. Starfish eat many small animals, but they <u>generally</u> prefer soft mollusks, <u>chewy</u> sponges, and <u>crunchy</u> corals.
4. The strong arms of a starfish can <u>easily</u> pull <u>apart</u> the <u>hard</u> shell of a clam.
5. Animals <u>seldom</u> eat starfish because they are neither <u>nutritious</u> nor tasty.

▶ **Exercise 22** **Recognizing Proper, Compound, and Possessive Adjectives** List any proper, compound, and possessive adjectives in the following sentences, and label each.

1. Sea urchins are underwater animals that are related to the starfish.
2. Their range is worldwide, and they can be found in most marine environments.
3. Its round, spine-covered body may be purple-colored or red.
4. With the exception of a species that lives near the Florida coast, sea urchins are basically harmless to people.
5. They use their beaklike mouths to scrape algae from rocks on the Atlantic Ocean bed.
6. Constant scraping against the rocks ruins the teeth of the sea urchin, but worn-down teeth are quickly replaced.
7. Sea urchins prefer colder offshore waters, but they also live near land.
8. California sea otters are members of the small group of animals that prey upon the sea urchin.

9. The once-occupied shells of sea urchins often litter American beaches.
10. If you visit the Atlantic or Pacific coast, you may see these empty shells.

▶ **Exercise 23** **Recognizing Other Parts of Speech Used as Adjectives or Adverbs** List and label nouns, pronouns, or verbs used as adjectives, as well as nouns used as adverbs, in the sentences below.

1. I saw a seahorse yesterday at an aquarium and decided to learn more about this unusual fish.
2. Here are all the facts I learned.
3. When a seahorse heads home, it swims to sea grasses near coral reefs and river estuaries.
4. The seahorse is characterized by an extended snout and a grasping tail.
5. A swimming seahorse moves by fanning its tiny fin.
6. Because they have no teeth, foraging seahorses swallow fish larvae whole.
7. Another unusual characteristic is that the male seahorse, not the female, carries the fertilized eggs.
8. Baby seahorses resemble adults at birth but take many months to mature.
9. Few animals prey upon the adult seahorse because of its hard skin.
10. Nevertheless, certain types of seahorses are on the threatened species list today because of overfishing.

▶ **Exercise 24** **Distinguishing Adverbs From Adjectives** Identify each underlined word in the items that follow as an *adjective* or *adverb*.

1. An ordinary lobster has a <u>hard</u>, segmented shell and two large claws.

2. Do not put your hands <u>close</u> to those powerful claws!
3. That diver had a <u>close</u> call when a lobster aggressively defended its territory.
4. In the <u>early</u> part of the day, most lobsters remain hidden among the rocks.
5. They usually emerge from their hiding places <u>late</u> at night.

▶ **Exercise 25** Supplying Adjectives and Adverbs in Sentences Rewrite the sentences below on your paper, supplying an adjective or adverb to fill each blank. Underline each adjective you add and circle each adverb.

1. __?__ , I learned about the __?__ odd horseshoe crab.
2. Despite __?__ name, the horseshoe crab is not __?__ a true crab.
3. It is actually a __?__ relative of spiders and scorpions.
4. Horseshoe crabs are __?__ found along __?__ shores, but __?__ species live __?__ near the Pacific.
5. One very __?__ reason for the horseshoe crab's durability is that it can live for a __?__ year without eating!
6. The crabs can also endure __?__ dramatic changes in __?__ temperature.
7. Horseshoe crabs __?__ feed nights.
8. However, some have been known to conduct their food search __?__ , too.
9. They __?__ hunt clams, oysters, and other __?__ mollusks.
10. At the beach __?__ , I will __?__ see __?__ of these __?__ animals.

▶ **Exercise 26** Revising Dull Writing by Adding Adjectives and Adverbs Revise this dull paragraph by adding adjectives and adverbs where appropriate.

(1) Oysters are valuable both as a food and as a source of pearls. (2) Pearls start out as a piece of shell or a parasite that enters an oyster's shell. (3) The oyster spreads a substance called *nacre* in layers over the invader. (4) The process happens. (5) The invader becomes enclosed in the substance, forming a pearl.

▶ **Exercise 27** Writing Application Imagine that you are exploring the ocean in a diving vessel. Write an account of your trip. Describe the things you might find, such as marine life or sunken treasure. Include adjectives and adverbs to make your description more interesting.

▶ **Exercise 28** CUMULATIVE REVIEW Parts of Speech Identify the underlined words in the following sentences as *nouns*, *pronouns*, *verbs*, *adjectives*, or *adverbs*.

1. Corals are tiny <u>shelled</u> creatures <u>that</u> play a <u>particularly</u> <u>vital</u> <u>role</u> in the ocean's ecology.
2. <u>Many</u> people <u>think</u> that corals are simply <u>underwater</u> plants, but <u>they</u> are actually animals.
3. <u>Each</u> has a tube-shaped body, which <u>is surrounded</u> at the top by a mass of <u>gently</u> <u>waving</u> tentacles.
4. The coral uses its tentacles to gather <u>minute</u> <u>particles</u> of food that <u>randomly</u> <u>drift</u> with the <u>ocean</u> current.
5. A young <u>free-floating</u> coral will attach <u>itself</u> <u>securely</u> to a rock and immediately <u>begin</u> creating a <u>hard</u> shell.
6. <u>Eventually</u>, small corals of the same species <u>form</u> a colony, which is <u>commonly</u> mistaken for <u>one</u> large organism.
7. <u>These</u> types of corals <u>often</u> contain <u>red</u>, blue, yellow, or green pigments.
8. In time, many different <u>colonies</u> of coral may create a coral reef, which serves as a <u>home</u> for thousands of <u>marine</u> animals.
9. <u>Certain</u> sea stars and <u>several</u> varieties of fish eat hard corals.
10. One <u>incredibly</u> destructive parrotfish <u>may</u> <u>consume</u> <u>five</u> tons of coral in a single <u>year</u>!

Standardized Test Preparation Workshop

Using Adjectives and Adverbs

Standardized tests often measure your understanding of grammar and usage. One way to measure this is to evaluate your understanding of modifiers. These types of questions will ask you to read a passage and choose which modifier, adjective, or adverb completes the sentence in a correct and logical way. Use the following steps when answering a question that tests these skills:

- Read the entire passage first.

- Ask yourself what type of description is needed—an adjective will tell *what kind*, *which one*, *how much*, and *how many*, and an adverb will tell *when*, *where*, *in what way*, or *to what extent* about a word in the sentence.

- Choose the modifier that will add that information and also fit the meaning of the passage.

The following sample test item will give you practice with questions that test your ability to choose the correct modifier.

Sample Test Item	Answers and Explanations
Directions: Read the passage, and choose the letter of the word or group of words that belongs in each space. Whether grown in the mounding or trailing form, the nasturtium flower, with its strong, ___(1)___ flavor, is ___(2)___ used as a tasty and attractive salad garnish.	

1 A unpleasant
  B unpleasantly
  C pungent
  D pungently
	The correct choice for the first blank is C. An adjective is needed to modify the noun *flavor*. Since the sentence indicates that the flower is edible, it is unlikely that the answer would be *unpleasant*. So the best choice is the adjective *pungent*.

2 F frequently
  G frequent
  H rarely
  J rare
	The correct choice for the second blank is F. An adverb is needed to modify the verb *is used*. Since the sentence describes positive qualities of the nasturtium flower, the adverb *rarely* is an illogical choice. So the best choice is the adverb *frequently*.

▶ **Practice 1** **Directions:** Read the passage, and choose the letter of the word or group of words that belongs in each space.

Startlingly speedy for his size, the ___(1)___ alligator climbed up the ___(2)___ bank at the edge of the everglade. He bellowed ___(3)___ , as if to announce his presence to any marsh trespassers. A ___(4)___ ibis escaped into the ___(5)___ sky.

1 **A** enormously
  B enormous
  C dainty
  D daintily

2 **F** clear
  G clearly
  H clean
  J muddy

3 **A** softly
  B softer
  C loud
  D loudly

4 **F** calm
  G calmly
  H startled
  J startling

5 **A** clear
  B clearly
  C spry
  D spryly

▶ **Practice 2** **Directions:** Read the passage, and choose the letter of the word or group of words that belongs in each space.

Fresh-baked bread ___(1)___ tops Isaac's list of ___(2)___ foods. He loves stirring the dough ___(3)___ and kneading it with his ___(4)___ hands. ___(5)___ week he bakes two loaves for his volunteer work at the nursing home.

1 **A** always
  B rarely
  C happy
  D happily

2 **F** badly
  G bad
  H lovingly
  J favorite

3 **A** softly
  B soft
  C briskly
  D brisk

4 **F** weak
  G weakly
  H powerful
  J gently

5 **A** Each
  B Last
  C Next
  D One

Chapter
18 Prepositions, Conjunctions, and Interjections

Prepositions, conjunctions, and interjections add meaning to sentences. Prepositions and conjunctions make connections and show special relationships between words. Interjections add emotion and expression to a sentence.

Whether you describe places, such as famous parks, or people, such as the Navajo, you will depend on these parts of speech to help you convey meaning effectively.

Learn how to use prepositions, conjunctions, and interjections correctly while exploring this chapter.

▲ Critical Viewing Based on this photograph, how would you compare Central Park in New York City to other parks you've visited? What prepositions and conjunctions would you use in making these comparisons? [Compare]

Diagnostic Test

Directions: Write all answers on a separate sheet of paper.

Skill Check A. Write the prepositions in the following sentences.

1. Mr. Lee's favorite park in New York City is Van Cortlandt Park.
2. This 1,100-acre Bronx park is located next to Riverdale.
3. Miles of wooded trails wind within its boundaries.
4. Apart from the woods, visitors can play baseball, cricket, or golf or relax upon its rolling green fields.
5. Many enjoy the playgrounds instead of the hiking trails.

Skill Check B. Write the complete prepositional phrases. Underline the object or objects of each preposition.

6. The Wiechquaeskeck people once lived in the area of Van Cortlandt Park.
7. According to scientists, they built their permanent settlements there about 1,000 years ago.
8. They fished along the banks of Tibbets Brook.
9. Their crops were planted upon the present-day sites of the Parade Ground and Indian Field.
10. The park's lake didn't exist when Europeans arrived in America.

Skill Check C. Label underlined words *prepositions* or *adverbs*.

11. In 1639, the Dutch West India Company purchased much of the land <u>along</u> the lower Hudson Valley from Native Americans.
12. Travel <u>through</u> it was difficult, due to unrest in the area.
13. Jacobus Van Cortlandt bought the land in the 1690's, but the wealthy Philipse family had owned it <u>before</u>.
14. He looked <u>around</u> and decided to grow crops on his land.
15. Van Cortlandt began to grow grain and to mill <u>on</u> his property.

Skill Check D. Write the conjunctions, conjunctive adverbs, and interjections in the following sentences. If the word is a conjunction, label it *coordinating, correlative,* or *subordinating.*

16. The Van Cortlandts owned the land; subsequently, they built a home and dammed Tibbets Brook.
17. Yes, you can explore both the house and the man-made lake.
18. Say, let's go to the park today, or you may prefer the museum.
19. Because it was built in 1748, it's the oldest house in the Bronx.
20. Unless I'm mistaken, their estate became parkland in 1888.

Skill Check E. Label each underlined word *subordinating conjunction, preposition,* or *adverb.*

21. Have you explored Vault Hill <u>before</u>?
22. Frederick Van Cortlandt was buried here, and this has been the family burial ground ever <u>since</u>.
23. <u>When</u> the American Revolution began, City Clerk Augustus Van Cortlandt hid New York City records from the British here.
24. <u>After</u> a time, family remains were moved to Woodlawn Cemetery.
25. <u>After</u> we explore Vault Hill, let's visit an even older burial ground.

Prepositions

Prepositions add meaning to a sentence by showing the relationship between words.

▶ **KEY CONCEPT** A **preposition** is a word that relates a noun or pronoun that appears with it to another word in the sentence. ■

Words Used as Prepositions

A preposition can affect the entire meaning of a sentence.

▶ **KEY CONCEPT** The choice of preposition affects the way the other words in a sentence relate to each other. ■

Sixty of the words most often used as prepositions are listed in the following chart.

Theme: City Parks

In this section, you will learn about prepositions. The examples and exercises in this section are about city parks.

Cross-Curricular Connection: Social Studies

FREQUENTLY USED PREPOSITIONS				
aboard	before	despite	off	throughout
about	behind	down	on	till
above	below	during	onto	to
across	beneath	except	opposite	toward
after	beside	for	out	under
against	besides	from	outside	underneath
along	between	in	over	until
amid	beyond	inside	past	up
among	but	into	regarding	upon
around	by	like	round	with
at	concerning	near	since	within
barring	considering	of	through	without

Some prepositions consist of more than one word and are called *compound prepositions*.

COMPOUND PREPOSITIONS			
according to	because of	in place of	next to
ahead of	by means of	in regard to	on account of
apart from	in addition to	in spite of	out of
aside from	in back of	instead of	owing to
as of	in front of	in view of	prior to

▶ **More Practice**

Grammar Exercise Workbook
• pp. 31–32
On-line Exercise Bank
• Section 18.1
  Go on-line:
  PHSchool.com
  Enter Web Code:
  eek-1002

GRAMMAR IN LITERATURE

from **Old Friends**
Paul Simon

The prepositions in these song lyrics by folk artist Paul Simon are highlighted in blue italics.

Old Friends,
Old Friends
Sat *on* their park bench
Like bookends.
A newspaper blown *through* the grass
Falls *on* the round toes
Of the high shoes
Of the Old Friends.

Notice how choosing different prepositions affects the relationship between words and gives each sentence a different meaning.

EXAMPLE:

We saw a squirrel $\begin{Bmatrix} \text{inside} \\ \text{near} \\ \text{within} \\ \text{next to} \end{Bmatrix}$ the *park*.

▲ **Critical Viewing**
What prepositions might you use in describing these two men? Why?
[Describe]

> **Exercise 1** **Identifying Prepositions** Identify the prepositions and compound prepositions in this paragraph.
(1) Central Park, one of America's first landscaped parks, was designed by Frederick Law Olmsted and Calvert Vaux. (2) Poor Irish and German immigrants occupied the land prior to the park's creation. (3) There was also a thriving African American community, Seneca Village, at Eighth Avenue and 82nd Street. (4) The park has been open since the late 1850's. (5) It remains extremely popular, owing to its wooded paths, baseball diamonds, green lawns, and, of course, the animals in its famous zoo.

> **Exercise 2** **Revising to See How Prepositions Affect Meaning** Revise the paragraph above, replacing the prepositions with other ones from the two facing lists. Explain how the changes in prepositions alter meaning.

⚙ **Grammar and Style Tip**

In your writing, use the correct preposition to clarify a relationship between separate things, such as location, direction, cause, or possession.

Prepositional Phrases

▶ **KEY CONCEPT** A **prepositional phrase** is a group of words that includes a preposition and a noun or pronoun, called the object of the preposition. ■

EXAMPLE: We had a picnic <u>in the</u>(park.)

In the preceding example, *park* is the object of the preposition *in*.

PREPOSITIONAL PHRASES	
Prepositions	Objects of the Prepositions
for *throughout* *between*	*you* the *school* *you* and *me*

▶ **Exercise 3** Identifying Prepositional Phrases In each sentence, identify the prepositional phrase or phrases. Write each on a piece of paper, underline the preposition, and circle its object.

1. In 1868, San Francisco selected the roughly 1,000 acres of the Golden Gate Park.
2. Few were pleased by this selection because of its windy landscape.
3. When John McLaren became superintendent in 1890, the site was suffering from neglect and overuse.
4. Under his supervision, an international exposition was held during 1894; nothing was preserved from it except the Japanese Tea Garden and a museum.
5. It has been a popular setting for a variety of gatherings.

▶ **Exercise 4** Writing Sentences With Prepositional Phrases Use each phrase in a sentence about the picture.

1. over the roadway
2. to the sky
3. beyond the bridge
4. in the distance
5. under the bridge

More Practice

Grammar Exercise Workbook
• pp. 33–34
On-line Exercise Bank
• Section 18.1
   Go on-line:
   PHSchool.com
   Enter Web Code:
   eek-1002

▼ Critical Viewing The Golden Gate Bridge is in California. What other prepositional phrases can you use in sentences about this bridge? **[Apply]**

Preposition or Adverb?

Many of the words listed as prepositions in the charts on page 392 can also be adverbs.

KEY CONCEPT Prepositions always have objects; adverbs do not. ■

If a word that can be used either as a preposition or as an adverb has an object, the word is acting as a preposition.

Prepositions	Adverbs
The smoke drifted *up* the chimney.	The dark, ugly smoke drifted *up*.
Flowers grew *along* the path.	Won't you come *along* with us?
The park is *near* our house.	We knew a park was *near*.

For a word to act as a preposition, it must have an object and be part of a prepositional phrase. In the preceding examples, notice that the adverb examples are not followed by nouns. They do not have objects.

EXAMPLE: People wandered through.

ANSWER: through (adverb)

Exercise 5 Distinguishing Between Prepositions and Adverbs Label underlined words *prepositions* or *adverbs*.
1. Hyde Park is located <u>near</u> Kensington Gardens in England.
2. Walk <u>in</u> and find a natural respite from urban London.
3. You will see horse riders trotting <u>around</u>.
4. <u>In</u> the past, the park was the hunting grounds of royalty.
5. Is the Achilles statue located <u>around</u> the park's center?

Exercise 6 Revising Sentences by Adding Objects Revise each sentence by adding an object to change the adverb to a preposition.
1. The park is near.
2. Will you walk in?
3. Stroll around and enjoy the scenery.
4. However, don't wander off.
5. The sign says "Keep off."

Section Review

GRAMMAR EXERCISES 7–12

▶ **Exercise 7** Identifying Prepositions and Prepositional Phrases Write each prepositional phrase. Then, underline each preposition and circle each object.

1. The famous Bois de Boulogne is located on the western edge of Paris.
2. It was created during the reign of Napoleon III.
3. The park was designed by Baron Georges-Eugène Haussmann.
4. According to many people, he greatly admired the large London parks, such as Hyde Park and Regents Park.
5. Napoleon wanted similar large parks for Parisians.

▶ **Exercise 8** Revising Prepositions and Prepositional Phrases Revise the following paragraph by replacing prepositions and prepositional phrases with ones that better convey the intended meaning.

(1) Have you strolled over another famous park, Boston Common? (2) It is the oldest public park from the United States. (3) The parkland was set outside in 1634. (4) It was first used for a military training ground and a cattle pasture. (5) Boston Common was enclosed on 1725, and its grounds were designed by famed architect Charles Bulfinch. (6) In the past, it was used in executions of pirates and other criminals. (7) In addition to this, the British Army camped there within the Revolution. (8) Under the park, you will see many magnificent statues and fountains. (9) A bandstand, tennis courts, and a cemetery are found among its borders. (10) In view of its historical significance, Boston Common is a fitting first stop at the famous Freedom Trail.

▶ **Exercise 9** Distinguishing Between Prepositions and Adverbs Identify each underlined word as *preposition* or *adverb*.

(1) Have you had a chance to walk <u>around</u> the Tuileries garden in Paris? (2) It is located <u>near</u> the center of the French capital. (3) The park stretches <u>on</u> a straight line from the Place de la Concorde to the Louvre. (4) Look <u>around</u> and you will see throngs of people admiring the toy boats in the square's fountain. (5) Hold <u>on</u>, I want to eat at one of the cafes within the Tuileries.

▶ **Exercise 10** Find It in Your Reading Identify the prepositions in this verse by Paul Simon. Then, rewrite the verse, replacing each preposition with a different one. Explain how the changes affect meaning.

Lost in their overcoats,
Waiting for the sunset.
The sounds of the city
Sifting through the trees,
Settle like dust
On the shoulders
Of the old friends.

▶ **Exercise 11** Find It in Your Writing Identify at least ten prepositions in a piece of your own writing. Experiment with changing the prepositions. See if any of the changes would convey your intended meaning more clearly.

▶ **Exercise 12** Writing Application Imagine spending an afternoon boating in Central Park, as pictured on page 390. Write a description of your adventure using at least five prepositional phrases.

Conjunctions and Interjections

The last two parts of speech you will learn about are *conjunctions* and *interjections*. You will use conjunctions more often than you will use interjections.

Different Kinds of Conjunctions

Unlike prepositions, which show relationships between words, conjunctions make direct connections between words.

▶ **KEY CONCEPT** A **conjunction** is a word used to connect other words or groups of words. ■

Three main kinds of conjunctions connect words: *coordinating conjunctions*, *correlative conjunctions*, and *subordinating conjunctions*.

Coordinating Conjunctions The seven *coordinating conjunctions* connect similar words or groups of words.

COORDINATING CONJUNCTIONS						
and	but	for	nor	or	so	yet

EXAMPLES: Joaquin *and* I studied Navajo weaving and cloth making.

The loom broke, *yet* the weaver continued her work.

She hung the Navajo blanket on the wall *and* then stepped back to admire it.

She wrapped herself in the blanket, *for* it had become very cold in her room.

Correlative Conjunctions *Correlative conjunctions* are similar to coordinating conjunctions. They differ only in that correlative conjunctions are always used in pairs.

CORRELATIVE CONJUNCTIONS		
both . . . and	neither . . . nor	whether . . . or
either . . . or	not only . . . but also	

EXAMPLES: He made *neither* that blanket *nor* that rug.
Both gold *and* silver bracelets were considered.
Brenda purchased *either* a Navajo bracelet *or* a Navajo blanket.

**Theme: Native
Americans**

In this section, you will learn about conjunctions and interjections. The examples and exercises in this section are about Native American culture and history.

**Cross-Curricular
Connection:
Social Studies**

▶ **More Practice**

Grammar Exercise
Workbook
• pp. 35–36
On-line Exercise Bank
• Section 18.2
Go on-line:
PHSchool.com
Enter Web Code:
eek-1002

Subordinating Conjunctions *Subordinating conjunctions* connect two complete ideas by making one of the ideas subordinate to, or less important than, the other.

FREQUENTLY USED SUBORDINATING CONJUNCTIONS			
after	because	now that	until
although	before	since	when
as	even if	so that	whenever
as if	even though	than	where
as long as	if	though	wherever
as soon as	in order that	till	while
as though	lest	unless	

The following example shows how a subordinating conjunction is used to connect related ideas.

EXAMPLE:
    subord. idea   main idea
    Because Carol practices, she is a good artist.

> **Exercise 13** **Identifying Conjunctions** Write the conjunction in each sentence. Then, label each *coordinating, correlative*, or *subordinating*.

1. Traditionally, Navajo men work as silversmiths, while the women are weavers.
2. Navajo silversmiths are among the most talented and creative in the world.
3. Even though they are immensely skilled in working silver, they are relatively new to the craft.
4. The Navajos had learned silversmithing from neighboring Mexicans before they were relocated by the government in 1864–1866, an event known as "The Long Walk."
5. In the late nineteenth century, Navajo fortunes improved, for traders recognized the market for the jewelry.
6. Trader Lorenzo Hubbell brought Mexican silversmiths to the reservation so even more Navajo men learned the craft.
7. These craftsmen would use not only Mexican but also United States coins for their raw material.
8. Whether it was a belt buckle, ring, necklace, or earring, the silversmiths' works were uniquely intricate.
9. While their silver work was already expert, the Navajos began adding their distinctive turquoise settings to jewelry in the late 1890's.
10. Neither the Navajo silversmiths nor the traders foresaw the great popularity of this jewelry.

▼ **Critical Viewing** What are two words you would use to describe this vase, and what conjunction would you use to connect the words? **[Describe]**

GRAMMAR IN
LITERATURE

from Chee's Daughter
Juanita Platero and Siyowin Miller

The conjunctions in the following excerpt are highlighted in blue italics.

The hat told the story, the big, black, drooping Stetson. It was not at the proper angle, the proper rakish angle for so young a Navajo. There was no song, *and* that was not in keeping either. There should have been at least a humming, a faint, all-to-himself "he he he heya," *for* it was a good horse he was riding, a slender-legged, high-stepping buckskin that would race the wind with light knee-urging. This was a day for singing, a warm winter day, *when* the touch of the sun upon the back belied the snow high on distant mountains.

Conjunction, Preposition, or Adverb?

After, before, since, till, and *until* can be subordinating conjunctions or prepositions. *After, before,* and *since* can also be adverbs. *When* and *where* can be subordinating conjunctions or adverbs. The part of speech of these words depends on their use within a sentence.

▶ **KEY CONCEPT** **Subordinating conjunctions** connect complete ideas. ■

The following examples show the word *before* used in three different ways.

SUBORDINATING CONJUNCTION:	She started to weave *before* she turned ten.
PREPOSITION:	The weaver starts work *before* sunrise.
ADVERB:	Have you ever watched a weaver make a blanket *before*?

▼ Critical Viewing How does this picture connect to the examples shown on the left? **[Connect]**

▶ **Exercise 14** Identifying Words as Conjunctions, Prepositions, or Adverbs Label each underlined word *subordinating conjunction, preposition,* or *adverb.*

1. Navajo women have practiced the art of weaving <u>since</u> they learned the skill from Pueblo Indians in the 1800's.
2. As with silver, traders saw the potential value of Navajo-made cloth <u>when</u> setting up shops near the reservation.
3. Navajo cloths—such as blankets, belts, rugs, and bags—have been highly prized ever <u>since</u>.
4. The Navajos used pigments collected from local vegetation <u>until</u> they started weaving for a wider audience.
5. <u>Since</u> that time, they have begun to use commercially made dyes.

▶ **Exercise 15** Writing With Conjunctions, Prepositions, and Adverbs Write three sets of three sentences using *after, before,* and *until* as conjunctions, prepositions, and adverbs.

Conjunctive Adverbs

Some words act as both conjunctions and adverbs at the same time. These words are called *conjunctive adverbs.*

▶ **KEY CONCEPT** A **conjunctive adverb** is an adverb that acts as a conjunction to connect complete ideas. ■

FREQUENTLY USED CONJUNCTIVE ADVERBS		
accordingly	finally	nevertheless
again	furthermore	otherwise
also	however	then
besides	indeed	therefore
consequently	moreover	thus

Conjunctive adverbs are often used as transitions—words that serve as links between different ideas. In the following example, notice how conjunctive adverbs work to make transitions between related ideas.

EXAMPLES: They had never been on a reservation before. *Indeed,* they had never been far away from home.

It had rained during their visit; *consequently,* the outdoor Navajo art exhibit was canceled.

The conjunctive adverb is followed by a comma.

More Practice

Grammar Exercise Workbook
• pp. 37–38
On-line Exercise Bank
• Section 18.2
  Go on-line:
  PHSchool.com
  Enter Web Code:
  eek-1002

Complete the exercises on-line! Exercises 14, 15, 16, and 17 are available on-line or on CD-ROM.

▶ **Exercise 16** Revising With Conjunctive Adverbs Revise this paragraph, adding conjunctive adverbs to connect ideas.

(1) The Navajos live in a southwestern desert country of mesas, cliffs, and canyons. This is reflected in the geometric patterns they choose for their blankets and rugs. (2) They changed their weaving styles after acquiring non-Navajo customers in the late nineteenth century. The years 1850 to 1880 are considered the "Classic Period" of weaving. (3) From the 1880's on, the Navajos adapted their weaving techniques and traditions to satisfy tourist demands. These years are referred to as the "Transitional Period." (4) Tourists preferred brighter colors. Weavers began using commercial dyes in their works. (5) Tourists also preferred rugs to blankets. Navajos began producing more rugs.

Interjections

Interjections are used mainly in speaking, not in writing.

▶ **KEY CONCEPT** An **interjection** is a word that expresses feeling or emotion and functions independently of a sentence. ■

Many feelings can be expressed by interjections, such as *ah, hey, oh, ouch, uh, well,* or *wow.* These examples show other interjections used to express different emotions.

JOY: *Hurray!* We won! EXHAUSTION: *Whew!* That was hard.

SURPRISE: *Aha!* I found the sandpainting. SORROW: She knew, *alas,* the truth.

Since interjections are independent from other words, they are set off by exclamation marks or commas.

▶ **Exercise 17** Supplying Interjections For each sentence, supply an interjection that suggests the specified emotion.

EXAMPLE: You spilled your milk on the rug. [dismay]
ANSWER: Oh, no! You spilled your milk on the rug.

1. I bought a Navajo blanket. [pleasure]
2. It was an imitation of a Navajo blanket. [anger]
3. Should I return it to the store? [hesitation]
4. The owner was a very large and threatening man. [fear]
5. He told me he would accept no returns. [acceptance]

More Practice

Grammar Exercise Workbook
• pp. 39–40
On-line Exercise Bank
• Section 18.2
 Go on-line:
 PHSchool.com
 Enter Web Code:
 eek-1002

 **Grammar and Style Tip**

Avoid interjections in your formal writing except in a special situation such as a direct quote.

Section Review

GRAMMAR EXERCISES 18–23

Exercise 18 Identifying Conjunctions Write the conjunctions in the following sentences. Then, label each *coordinating, correlative,* or *subordinating.*

1. Are you familiar with the Navajo art of sandpainting or drypainting?
2. Even though it has its roots in Navajo ceremonies, sandpainting is also a commercial art form.
3. Most scholars agree that the Navajos borrowed the idea of sandpainting and changed it to fit with their own ideas.
4. Because early sandpaintings were not permanent, there is little evidence to prove how this process occurred.
5. This sandpainting is both permanent and colorful.

Exercise 19 Identifying Different Parts of Speech Label the underlined words *conjunction, adverb, conjunctive adverb, preposition,* or *interjection.*

The first permanent sandpaintings were made in the late nineteenth century (1) <u>in order that</u> Navajo culture would be preserved. (2) <u>Wow</u>, did many Navajos object to this, but they were created anyway? (3) <u>When</u> they were published, interest in sandpaintings grew greater than (4) <u>before</u>. In 1915, Franc J. Newcomb, a trader's wife, befriended Hosteen Klah, a famous medicine man; (5) <u>consequently</u>, Newcomb amassed a large collection of sandpaintings drawn (6) <u>both</u> by her <u>and</u> by Navajos. (7) <u>Now that</u> it was filtering into non-Navajo land, artists began to use sandpainting motifs in permanent works. (8) <u>Before</u> this commercial use, however, the Navajos were careful to remove or alter certain designs. (9) <u>However</u>, despite their precautions, the acceptance of drypaintings as commercial art is still somewhat controversial, and (10) <u>yes</u>, many Navajos still do not approve.

Exercise 20 Revising With Conjunctive Adverbs Revise the following sentences using conjunctive adverbs.

1. The sandpainting is supervised by one person. Its construction is left to the most artistic.
2. Sandpaintings are difficult. Three to six men create one in about four hours.
3. It is made with colored pigments from rocks. The rocks must be collected and ground.
4. The paintings are made by sprinkling crushed rock over a floor of sand. Paintings for ceremonies are later destroyed.
5. Sandpaintings were created in Japan in the seventh century. They were created in England in the 1700's and 1800's.

Exercise 21 Find It in Your Reading Reread the excerpt from "Chee's Daughter" on page 399. List the conjunctions, and label them by type.

Exercise 22 Find It in Your Writing Choose a writing sample from your portfolio. Find any conjunctions you have used. Challenge yourself to combine three to five sentences with similar ideas by connecting them using conjunctions.

Exercise 23 Writing Application Write five sentences based on the following emotions, each using an interjection and a conjunction.

1. outrage
2. sadness
3. disapproval
4. frustration
5. relief

Hands-on Grammar

Fill In the Blanks

Cut several pieces of construction paper into strips, each about an inch wide. Then, from a different-colored sheet of construction paper, cut several dozen squares about one inch by one inch. Next, write a sentence on each of the strips. Construct the sentences so that each contains one or more prepositions or conjunctions. Then, paste the squares over all of the prepositions and conjunctions.

Write prepositions and conjunctions on all of the remaining squares. Then, with a group of classmates, experiment with placing different squares in the various sentences. Discuss how the changes in the prepositions and conjunctions affect the meaning of the sentences.

When you've finished, write a few paragraphs summing up what you learned from the activity.

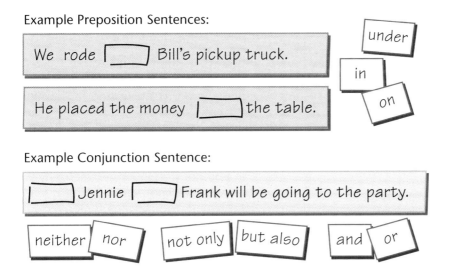

Example Preposition Sentences:

We rode ☐ Bill's pickup truck.

He placed the money ☐ the table.

under
in
on

Example Conjunction Sentence:

☐ Jennie ☐ Frank will be going to the party.

neither nor   not only but also   and or

Find It in Your Reading Try this activity with sentences from a nonfiction article that you have read recently.

Find It in Your Writing Try this activity with sentences from a piece of your own writing.

Chapter Review

GRAMMAR EXERCISES 24–32

> **Exercise 24** Identifying
Prepositional Phrases Identify each prepositional phrase in these sentences. Indicate the prepositions and the object.

1. Today, the Navajos are the largest Native American tribe inside North America.
2. The Navajos speak Apachean, a language of the Athabascan family.
3. This language has its roots in Canada.
4. The Navajos probably migrated from Canada between 900 and 1200.
5. Since their arrival in the Southwest, the Navajos have come under Pueblo influences.

> **Exercise 25** Revising Prepositions
and Prepositional Phrases Revise the following paragraph by replacing prepositions and prepositional phrases with ones that better convey the intended meaning.

1. In addition to farming, the Pueblos taught them herding.
2. Contact around the two tribes was recorded around the seventeenth century.
3. Within the eighteenth century, the Hopi lived with the Navajo.
4. The Hopi left their former dwellings despite drought and famine.
5. In spite of their extended visit and compatibility, the Pueblos influenced the Navajos in many ways.

> **Exercise 26** Classifying
Conjunctions Write the conjunctions in the sentences below, and label them *coordinating*, *correlative*, or *subordinating*.

1. The Navajo Reservation is now the area where many Navajos reside.

2. The Navajo lands are neither well irrigated nor large enough to provide a livelihood for everyone.
3. Although many live on the reservation, thousands earn their living outside of it.
4. Travel to an outside job may be the answer for some Navajos, but many have chosen to relocate.
5. Settling on irrigated lands, yet being culturally removed from the reservation, presents a difficult choice.

> **Exercise 27** Distinguishing
Between Conjunctions, Prepositions, or Adverbs Label each underlined word *conjunction*, *preposition*, or *adverb*.

1. <u>When</u> the United States was involved in World War II, several hundred Navajos made a major contribution to the Allied victory.
2. <u>Before</u> receiving help from the Navajos, the military had been worried about enemies intercepting information.
3. The military developed a code system that was foolproof, and <u>after</u> that was established, the Navajos took over.
4. This was not a code <u>in which</u> artificial words and signals were used, but simply the Navajo language.
5. <u>Since</u> the Navajo language is difficult to learn, still unwritten, and few speak it, the language was the perfect code.

> **Exercise 28** Revising to Add
Conjunctions and Prepositions to Connect Ideas Revise the following paragraphs. Combine sentences and add conjunctions and prepositions where appropriate to better connect the ideas.

(1) Using the Navajo language made Allied communication extremely secure. It

was more secure than communication had ever been during wartime. (2) The Navajo code talkers were able to perform in complete secrecy. The secrecy was maintained throughout the war. (3) The code talkers were trained in the Pacific. They were prepared to begin work.

(4) The Navajo language has survived to this day. There were pressures on the Navajo people to communicate only in English. (5) Maintaining traditional languages is important. Maintaining cultural values is also important.

> **Exercise 29** Revising Sentences With Conjunctive Adverbs Use conjunctive adverbs to make transitions between or combine the following groups of sentences.

1. The Navajo code talkers translated messages. They transmitted messages.
2. They assigned the names of birds to military terms. They translated them into Navajo.
3. The code talkers transmitted the messages. The last step was for a member of the team on the other end to translate them into English.
4. Navajo code talkers often worked in noisy command posts or combat zones. They were hunched over radio sets.
5. The Navajo code talkers' contribution was invaluable. Many believe they are greatly responsible for the victory over Japan.

> **Exercise 30** Classifying Prepositions, Conjunctions, and Interjections Label each underlined word *preposition, conjunction,* or *interjection.* If the word is a conjunction, identify it as *coordinating, correlative,* or *subordinating.* If it is a preposition, write its object.

The ancient Navajo myths and legends date back thousands of years (1) <u>but</u> still reflect the tribe's association with their surrounding environment. (2) <u>According to</u> many scholars, the story of the movement through four worlds may reflect the early history of the Navajos, (3) <u>when</u> they eventually migrated to their present location. (4) <u>Although</u> the settlement (5) <u>of</u> the Americas is still (6) <u>under</u> debate, many believe the continents were settled thousands of years ago (7) <u>as</u> bands of nomads migrated south. (8) <u>Whether</u> the Navajos first settled elsewhere or came directly to the Southwest is rarely debated, (9) <u>for</u> most archaeologists agree they probably first settled (10) <u>in</u> the Far North.

> **Exercise 31** Revising With Prepositions, Conjunctions, and Interjections Revise this paragraph, adding or replacing prepositions, conjunctions, and interjections where appropriate.

The Navajos probably first migrated on the Southwest hundreds of years ago. The new region presented a radical climate change. The early Navajo nomads probably had to alter much of their way of life. Their clothing and their dwellings were not suitable for the new environment. The fish and game were very different. New ways of finding food were needed. The greatest change that took place was in their system of beliefs. The Navajos had to adjust their cultural beliefs to reflect their new land. They also had to adjust their religious beliefs. They did this. It occurred over time. The Navajos assimilated to their new home. Their lives were changed.

> **Exercise 32** Writing Application Write a narrative about a custom or tradition that you enjoy or one that you would like to begin in your home, school, or community. Include one sentence containing two prepositions, one sentence containing two subordinating conjunctions, one sentence containing one coordinating conjunction, and one sentence containing one subordinating conjunction.

Standardized Test Preparation Workshop

Revising and Editing

Standardized tests often test your ability to connect ideas using prepositional phrases and conjunctions. Often, you will be asked to identify the best revision of a sentence or passage from among several choices. The best revision may or may not use prepositions and conjunctions to join ideas. When you approach items that require the best revision, keep the following points in mind.

- The first choice that combines ideas with a conjunction is not necessarily the best choice.
- Different conjunctions and prepositions have different meanings. Make sure you choose the revision that reflects the meaning of the original sentence or passage.

The following sample test items illustrate one of the formats used to test your ability to use prepositions and conjunctions.

Test Tip

If two choices appear to be the same, look for the small difference that distinguishes them. One of the choices is a distractor.

Sample Test Item	Answer and Explanation
Directions: Read the passage, and choose the best way to revise each underlined section. Many African cultures created music. (1) Drums and rhythms are the basis of this music. **A** Many African cultures created music, and drums and rhythms are the basis of this music. **B** Many African cultures created music based on drums and rhythms. **C** Many African cultures created rhythms. **D** Drums and rhythms are the basis of this music, but many African cultures created music.	 The best answer is *B*. Since both sentences are about African music, it is logical to combine information with the prepositional phrase *on drums and rhythms.*

Practice 1 **Directions:** Read the passage, and choose the best way to rewrite the underlined sections.

Different tones are produced. Different
(1)
drum sizes and shapes as well as hand

positions produce these tones. The
(2)
music can be quite complex. It is not

uncommon for six or seven drummers to

play in different signatures.

1 A Different tones are produced, and different drum sizes and shapes as well as hand positions produce these tones.
   B Different tones are produced by a variety of different drum sizes and shapes as well as hand positions.
   C Different tones are produced on different drum sizes and shapes as well as hand positions which produce these tones.
   D Different tones are produced, but different drum sizes and shapes as well as hand positions produce the different tones.
2 F The music can be quite complex, and it is not uncommon for six or seven drummers to play in different signatures.
   G The music can be quite complex with many different signatures.
   H The music can be quite complex, but it is not uncommon for six or seven drummers to play in different signatures.
   J The music of six or seven drummers can be quite complex.

Practice 2 **Directions:** Read the passage, and choose the best way to rewrite the underlined sections.

The drum is one of the oldest musical
(1)
instruments. And one of the most popular.

It is an instrument that is played.
(2)
By striking it with the hand,

sticks, or other objects.

1 A The drum is one of the oldest musical instruments and one of the most popular.
   B The drum is not only one of the oldest musical instruments, but also one of the most popular.
   C The drum is either the oldest musical instrument or the most popular.
   D The drum is the oldest yet most popular instrument.
2 F It is an instrument that is played by striking it with the hand or with sticks or with other objects.
   G It is an instrument that is played by striking it with the hand and with sticks or with other objects.
   H It is an instrument that is played by striking it with the hand, sticks, or other objects.
   J With the hand, it is an instrument that is played by striking it with sticks or other objects.

Cumulative Review

PARTS OF SPEECH

> **Exercise A** **Identifying Nouns and Pronouns** List the nouns in the following sentences, labeling each *compound*, *singular* or *plural*, *abstract* or *concrete*, and *common* or *proper*. Then, list the pronouns and label each *personal*, *demonstrative*, *interrogative*, *reflexive*, *intensive*, *relative*, or *indefinite*. Identify the antecedent of each pronoun.

1. The Arctic is the area near the North Pole, but it is not clearly defined.
2. The area includes the Arctic Ocean, several islands, and parts of North America, Asia, and Europe.
3. The largest areas are in Canada, Russia, and Greenland.
4. Its location, north of the Arctic Circle, gives it its name.
5. The Arctic, unlike the ice-covered plateau that is Antarctica, has a central ocean almost enclosed by land.
6. There are three landmasses, which are composed of the rock types granite and gneiss.
7. What are some rivers in the Arctic?
8. There are the Mackenzie and Yukon as well as others in the Russian Arctic.
9. The North Pole is not the coldest spot in the Arctic because the ocean warms it.
10. Oymyakon, Siberia, holds the record low temperature in the Arctic.

> **Exercise B** **Identifying Verbs** Write the verbs in the following sentences. Label the action verbs *visible* or *mental action* and *transitive* or *intransitive*. Then, label the *linking verbs*. Next, indicate any *verb phrases* and, underline *helping verbs*.

1. Ethnic groups had migrated from Asia to various parts of the Arctic.
2. The Inuit reached the Atlantic Ocean in Greenland, and the Saami lived in Norway.
3. In North America, the three main groups are the Aleuts, Native Americans, and Inuit.
4. The Aleuts inhabit the area around the Bering Sea, while Native Americans occupy the grasslands.
5. The Inuit like the areas in northern Alaska, northern Canada, and some of Greenland.

> **Exercise C** **Revising Verbs** Revise the following sentences, replacing linking verbs and verb phrases with action verbs where possible.

1. Natural materials are used by some indigenous residents for clothing, tools, and shelters.
2. Hunting and fishing are what they frequently do to gather food.
3. The time of settlement among Norse in the Arctic was in the ninth century A.D.
4. The average population of Arctic cities in North America is less than 10,000.
5. Communities of scientists have been established in Arctic regions.

> **Exercise D** **Identifying Adjectives and Adverbs** Identify the underlined words in these sentences as *adjectives* or *adverbs* and write the word each modifies.

1. Robert Edwin Peary is generally credited with leading the <u>first</u> party to the North Pole.
2. Before becoming an explorer, he <u>first</u> was a civil engineer.
3. Peary participated in the Nicaragua Canal Survey and <u>several</u> polar explorations.
4. He <u>finally</u> proved that Greenland was not a continent but an island.

5. In 1902, 1905, and 1906, Peary made <u>unsuccessful</u> attempts to reach the North Pole.

Exercise E Recognizing Prepositions, Conjunctions, and Interjections Write and label each *preposition, conjunction,* and *interjection*. Then, identify each conjunction as *coordinating, correlative, subordinating,* or as a *conjunctive adverb.*

1. Wow! Matthew Henson was an adventurous and brave person.
2. After running away from home at age 12, he traveled on a merchant ship.
3. He worked both on that ship and in a Washington, D.C., hat store.
4. Robert Peary hired him to be his valet; consequently, Henson became his translator and navigator.
5. Yes, Henson was also responsible for breaking the trail.

Exercise F Revising With Prepositions, Conjunctions, and Interjections Revise these sentences, adding and replacing prepositions, conjunctions, and interjections to precisely convey the relationships among ideas. Also, combine sentences where appropriate.

1. Henson walked ahead of Peary and the four Inuit. He may have reached the North Pole up to forty-five minutes under the rest of the party.
2. President Taft recommended Henson to a job in New York City. He wanted to recognize his work in the Arctic.
3. Was he really given a medal in the United States Congress?
4. President Eisenhower recognized Henson's achievements. He was soon forgotten.
5. In 1988, Henson was reburied on Arlington National Cemetery with full honors.

Exercise G Identifying All Parts of Speech Write this paragraph on a separate sheet of paper. Then, label each word according to its part of speech.

Before the Vikings explored the Arctic regions, the Greeks of the fourth century were aware of these regions. Some Norsemen reached Iceland, which already had a colony of Irish monks. Their voyages did not lead to the discovery of Greenland until Eric the Red landed there A.D. 982.
On April 6, 1909, Robert Edwin Peary and a small group either reached the North Pole or came very close to it. Peary made the official announcement on September 6, but Frederick Cook had announced it five days before. Experts then determined that Cook's claim was false. Peary's records were accepted, and he was given the rank of rear admiral. Scientists still debate whether Peary reached the exact location of the North Pole.

Exercise H Revising: Using Precise Language Revise the following paragraph, adding and revising words to make the paragraph more vivid and precise.

From the boat, I watched the sun set over the mountains of Alaska. The sunset was pretty, filling the sky with colors. The colors could be seen on the sea. Birds flew around the boat as the sky grew darker. The scene surrounding me made me feel good that I had decided to come on the trip.

Exercise I WRITING APPLICATION Write a brief description of a place that you would like to visit or explore. When you have finished, go through your work and identify each part of speech you have used.

Basic Sentence Parts

The Ferris wheel is a popular attraction at carnivals. Its simple rotating motion hides the fact that many gears and other essential moving parts keep the wheel going around. Similarly, you use sentences every time you speak or write, yet you may not always think about their essential parts.

Like a Ferris wheel or any other device, a good sentence functions well when its parts work together correctly. Knowing how the parts of sentences work together will give you a better understanding of how to communicate your ideas effectively.

Diagnostic Test

Directions: Write all answers on a separate sheet of paper.

Skill Check A. Write the complete subject and complete predicate in each sentence. Underline the simple subject once and the verb twice.

1. Fairs were an important part of commerce in the Middle Ages.
2. Buyers and sellers would trade commodities and merchandise.
3. Fairs improved and increased trade all over Europe.
4. Fairs for pleasure and commerce were often held together.
5. The largest fairs drew people from miles around.

Skill Check B. Write the subject of each sentence.

6. There are many fairs around the world.
7. When were these fairs established?
8. Take your brother to the fair.
9. Will Nancy be going with you?
10. Over the bridge lay the fairgrounds.

Skill Check C. Write each complement, and label it *direct object*, *indirect object*, or *objective complement*.

11. American engineer George Washington Gale Ferris invented the Ferris wheel.
12. After college, Ferris built bridges, railroads, and tunnels.
13. He eventually founded his own company.
14. He named it G.W.G. Ferris and Company.
15. Ferris showed the organizers of an 1893 exposition his plans for a 250-foot, steel-framed wheel ride.
16. The exposition organizers found his plans impressive.
17. They accepted Ferris's design.
18. Ferris promised them timely construction.
19. By selling stock in the project, he earned a profit of more than a million dollars.
20. The public considered Ferris's wheel a success.

Skill Check D. Write each complement, and label it *predicate nominative* or *predicate adjective*.

21. The most common type of fair in the United States was the agricultural fair.
22. The first United States fair, held in Massachusetts, was successful.
23. Some of the products on display were livestock, produce, and preserves.
24. The fair was quite profitable and popular among the local farmers.
25. Danbury, Connecticut, was the site of another famous fair.

Subjects and Predicates

When you are speaking to your friends, you may speak in partial sentences and still be understood. When you are writing, however, you should use complete sentences to express complete thoughts. Recognizing that every sentence must have two key parts will help you write clear, complete sentences.

Complete Subjects and Predicates

Every *sentence* that is grammatically correct consists of two parts: a *complete subject* and a *complete predicate*.

> **KEY CONCEPT** A **sentence** is a group of words with two main parts: a complete subject and a complete predicate. Together, these parts express a complete thought. ■

The complete subject includes a noun or pronoun that names the person, place, or thing that the sentence is about. The complete predicate includes a verb or verb phrase that tells something about the complete subject. The examples show that a complete subject or complete predicate may consist of only a single essential word (a noun or pronoun for the complete subject and a verb for the complete predicate). Often, however, a complete subject or complete predicate includes many other words that modify the essential words.

EXAMPLES: They | were celebrating in the streets.
COMPLETE SUBJECT | COMPLETE PREDICATE

The three clowns in the ring | tumbled.
COMPLETE SUBJECT | COMPLETE PREDICATE

> **Exercise 1** Recognizing Complete Subjects and Complete Predicates Make two columns as shown in the example. Then, write each complete subject in the first column and each complete predicate in the second column.

EXAMPLE: The fluffy squirrel chattered at us.
ANSWER:

Complete Subject	Complete Predicate
The fluffy squirrel	chattered at us.

1. Mardi Gras is celebrated in many countries.
2. The grand carnival marks the beginning of Lent.
3. Many Christians fast during Lent.
4. They indulge in merrymaking before this solemn time.
5. Food and drink are plentiful during Mardi Gras.

Theme: Carnivals

In this section, you will learn about the two main parts of sentences, subjects and predicates. The examples and exercises are about carnivals and celebrations.

Cross-Curricular Connection: Social Studies

More Practice

Grammar Exercise Workbook
• pp. 41–42
On-line Exercise Bank
• Section 19.1
  Go on-line:
  PHSchool.com
  Enter Web Code:
  eek-1002

Get instant feedback! Exercise 1 is available on-line or on CD-ROM.

Simple Subjects and Predicates

Every complete subject and complete predicate contains a word or group of words that is essential to the sentence.

▶ **KEY CONCEPTS** The **simple subject** is the essential noun, pronoun, or group of words acting as a noun that cannot be left out of the complete subject. The **simple predicate** is the essential verb or verb phrase that cannot be left out of the complete predicate. ■

In the following examples, notice that all the other words in the complete subject modify or add information to the *simple subject*. In the same way, all the other words in the complete predicate either modify the *simple predicate* or help it complete the meaning of the sentence.

	SIMPLE SUBJECT	SIMPLE PREDICATE
EXAMPLES:	*Jugs* of sweet cider	*covered* the table.
	COMPLETE SUBJECT	COMPLETE PREDICATE

	SIMPLE SUBJECT	SIMPLE PREDICATE
	Some *people*	*do* not *like* cider.
	COMPLETE SUBJECT	COMPLETE PREDICATE

Notice in the first example that the simple subject of the sentence is *jugs*, not *cider*. The object of a preposition can never be a simple subject. Notice also that in the next example, the verb phrase *do like* is split by an adverb, *not*.

Note About the Terms *Subject* and *Verb*: From this point on in this book, the word *subject* will refer to the simple subject and the word *verb* will refer to the simple predicate.

To find the subject of a sentence before the verb, ask, "What word is the sentence about?" Then, ask yourself, "What did the subject *do*?" The answer will be an action verb. If there is no answer to the second question, look for a linking verb.

EXAMPLE: The revelers marched happily through the park.
Subject: revelers *Question:* What did the revelers do? *Answer:* marched

If you find it easier to locate the verb before locating the subject, first look for an action verb or a linking verb. Then, ask *Who?* or *What?* before the verb. The answer will be the subject.

EXAMPLE: A colorful flag was hanging above the porch.
Verb: was hanging *Question:* What was hanging? *Answer:* flag

▶ **More Practice**

Grammar Exercise
Workbook
• pp. 45–46
On-line Exercise Bank
• Section 19.1
  Go on-line:
  PHSchool.com
  Enter Web Code:
  eek-1002

▶ **Exercise 2** Recognizing Simple Subjects and Simple Verbs
Write the simple subject and simple verb in each sentence.
Underline the subject once and the verb twice.

EXAMPLE: Ancient legends still fascinate us today.
ANSWER: <u>legends</u>   <u>fascinate</u>

1. Elaborate costumes abound at Mardi Gras celebrations.
2. Traditional celebrations of Mardi Gras last a full week.
3. *Mardi Gras* means "Fat Tuesday" in French.
4. The city of New Orleans is especially famous for its
   Mardi Gras festivities.
5. Spectacular fireworks end the carnival.

Compound Subjects and Verbs

The word *compound* describes a noun, adjective, or preposition with more than one part. *Airport*, for example, is a compound noun. *Compound* also describes subjects or verbs connected by conjunctions.

Compound Subjects The complete subject of a sentence
may contain two or more subjects.

▶ **KEY CONCEPT** A **compound subject** is two or more subjects that have the same verb and are joined by a conjunction
such as *and* or *or*. ∎

In the next example, the parts of the *compound subject* are
underlined once, and the verb is underlined twice.

EXAMPLE: <u>Clowns</u>, <u>balloons</u>, <u>pony rides</u>, and <u>face-painting</u>
             <u>*were offered*</u> at the carnival.

**⚙ Grammar
and Style Tip**

Compound subjects
joined with *and* take
the plural form of
a verb. Compound
subjects joined with
or take the form of
the verb that agrees
with the subject
closest to the verb.

◀ Critical Viewing
Think of a series of
actions a jester
might do, and
include them as
compound verbs in
a sentence.
[Connect]

GRAMMAR IN
LITERATURE

from **The Masque of the Red Death**
Edgar Allan Poe

The compound subject in the last sentence of this excerpt is highlighted in blue italics.

The "Red Death" had long devastated the country. . . . The scarlet stains upon the body and especially upon the face of the victim, were the pest ban which shut him out from the aid and from the sympathy of his fellow men. And the whole *seizure, progress, and termination* of the disease, were the incidents of half an hour.

Compound Verbs Sentences may also contain two or more verbs in the complete predicate.

▶ **KEY CONCEPT** A **compound verb** is two or more verbs that have the same subject and are joined by a conjunction such as *and* or *or*. ■

In the following example, the compound verb has three parts.

EXAMPLE: The <u>star</u> <u>signed</u> autograph books, <u>smiled</u> at her fans, and then <u>departed</u> in a limousine.

Sentences may also have both compound subjects and compound verbs.

EXAMPLE: <u>Megan</u> and her <u>friends</u> <u>cheered</u> and <u>shouted</u>.

Note About *Compound Verbs:* When a compound verb consists of two or more verb phrases with the same helping verb, the helping verb is often used only with the first verb.

AWKWARD REPETITION: The banjo <u>player</u> <u>was strumming</u> his banjo, <u>was stomping</u> his feet, and <u>was singing</u> enthusiastically.

HELPING VERB NOT REPEATED: The banjo <u>player</u> <u>was strumming</u> his banjo, <u>stomping</u> his feet, and <u>singing</u> enthusiastically.

▶ **Exercise 3** Recognizing Compound Subjects and Compound Verbs Write the sentence. Then, underline the words that make up each compound subject once and each compound verb twice.

EXAMPLE: Harvest <u>festivals</u> <u><u>exist</u></u> in many cultures and <u><u>appear</u></u> in many varieties.

1. Flowers, fruits, and vegetables are often used to decorate homes.
2. Harvest festivals center around a happy event, feature a special crop, or honor heroes.
3. Families and friends gather together and celebrate with traditional foods and rituals.
4. New England colonists and neighboring Native Americans celebrated the first Thanksgiving Day and shared the bountiful harvest.
5. Community events and family observances provide an opportunity for reflection, celebrate heritage, and enrich culture.

▶ **Exercise 4** Revising Sentences by Forming Compound Subjects and Compound Predicates Revise each pair of sentences by combining information to form compound subjects or verbs.

EXAMPLE: After school, the band met. Then it practiced
REVISION: After school the band met and practiced.

1. Solar calendars determine the timing of some seasonal festivals. Lunar calendars determine the timing of other seasonal festivals.
2. Chinese New Year is set by the lunar calendar. It is celebrated for a whole month.
3. Boisterous parades and colorful costumes mark the celebration of Chinese New Year. Theatrical performances mark the celebration of Chinese New Year, too.
4. A Swiss festival celebrates the end of winter. At the same time, it welcomes the advent of spring.
5. The Swiss people burn straw dummies during Homstrom. They are saying goodbye to Old Man Winter.

More Practice

Grammar Exercise Workbook
• pp. 47–48
On-line Exercise Bank
• Section 19.1
Go on-line:
PHSchool.com
Enter Web Code:
eek-1002

Get instant feedback! Exercises 3 and 4 are available on-line or on CD-ROM.

Section

19.1

Section Review

GRAMMAR EXERCISES 5–10

▶ **Exercise 5** Identifying Complete and Simple Subjects and Predicates
Make two columns. Write each complete subject in the first column and each complete predicate in the second. Underline the simple subject once and the verb twice.

1. Important festivals of respect in many countries honor the dead.
2. Such festivals have long been observed.
3. Today, people continue age-old customs honoring national heroes.
4. In the Far East, festivals of the dead include family reunions and ceremonial meals at ancestral tombs.
5. Mexicans observe *El Dia de Los Muertos* (The Day of the Dead) with offerings of flowers, pottery, food, and toys.

▶ **Exercise 6** Recognizing Subjects and Predicates Write the subject and verb in each sentence, underlining the subjects once and the verbs twice. Some may be compound.

1. The most famous annual festival in Wales is the Royal National Eisteddfod.
2. The Eisteddfod honors the finest talent in Welsh literature and music.
3. Welsh language, literature, music, and culture are promoted at the festival.
4. The history of the Eisteddfod predates the Christian era.
5. The week-long ceremony revives ancient Welsh customs, offers cultural competitions, and gives Welsh poets and musicians an opportunity to perform.

▶ **Exercise 7** Revising Sentences by Creating Compound Subjects and Compound Predicates Revise each pair of sentences by combining information to form compound subjects or verbs.

1. Cultural festivals are popular all over the world. Commemorative days are also popular all over the world.
2. Kalevala Day in Finland honors the Finnish national epic, the *Kalevala*. It also recognizes the achievements of Finnish scholar Elias Lönnrot.
3. The Salzburg Music Festival is held in Austria each year. The festival celebrates the rich legacy of some of the world's finest composers.
4. Great food is a highlight of Hawaii's annual Aloha Festival. Native entertainment is also featured.
5. Film festivals, dance celebrations, and children's carnivals crowd the calendars of many nations. They attract tourists from around the world.

▶ **Exercise 8** Find It in Your Reading
Identify the simple subject and predicate of each sentence in this excerpt from "The Masque of the Red Death."

. . . [I]n this chamber only, the color of the windows failed to correspond with the decorations. The panes here were scarlet—a deep blood color.

▶ **Exercise 9** Find It in Your Writing
Look through your writing portfolio. Find examples of sentences with a compound subject or compound verb. Identify the complete subject and predicate in each sentence.

▶ **Exercise 10** Writing Application
Write a description of your favorite holiday or feast day. Tell how you celebrate the day, what food you eat, and what activities you enjoy. In each of your sentences, underline the simple subject once and the verb twice.

Hard-to-Find Subjects

In most English sentences, a subject is followed by a verb. This section will present sentences with subjects that are not so easily found.

Subjects in Orders and Directions

▶ **KEY CONCEPT** In sentences that give orders or directions, the subject is often understood to be *you*. ■

The following chart contrasts sentences with and without the understood *you*. The subjects are underlined once and the verbs twice. Notice in the last sentence that even when a person is addressed, the subject is still understood to be *you*.

Orders or Directions	With Understood *You* Added
Dust the furniture and then wax the floor.	[You] dust the furniture and then wax the floor.
Kim, give me an apple.	Kim, [you] give me an apple.

▶ **Exercise 11** Creating Sentences With Understood Subjects Use each verb in a sentence that gives an order or a direction. Add the understood subject in parentheses in each.

1. give
2. call
3. proofread
4. ask
5. train
6. ride
7. order
8. protect
9. tie
10. offer

Subjects in Inverted Sentences

In some sentences, the usual subject-verb order is *inverted*—that is, reversed. Sentences that may be inverted in English include questions and sentences beginning with *there* or *here*. In addition, some sentences are inverted for emphasis.

Subjects in Questions Questions are often inverted.

▶ **KEY CONCEPT** In questions, the subject often follows the verb. ■

An inverted question can begin with a verb, a helping verb, or one of the following words: *how, what, when, where, who, whose,* or *why*.

To find the subject in an inverted question, rephrase the question mentally as a statement. Then, the subject and verb will fall into the usual order.

Theme: Knights and Castles

In this section, you will learn how to locate hard-to-find subjects in sentences. The examples and exercises are about knights and castles.

Cross-Curricular Connection: Social Studies

Questions	Reworded as Statements
Are we ready?	We are ready.
Do you like castles?	You do like castles.
Where was the car parked?	The car was parked where.

Note About *Questions:* Some questions are not inverted. Those beginning with an interrogative adjective or pronoun may be in the usual subject-verb order.

EXAMPLES: Which troubadour won the prize this year?
             Who cares about such nonsense?

> **Exercise 12** **Finding Subjects in Questions** Write each sentence, underlining the subject once and the verb twice.

EXAMPLE: Where was the castle located?

1. Who trained knights during the age of chivalry?
2. Where were the knights trained?
3. What were the requirements for knighthood?
4. Do knights still exist?
5. Was armor worn by all knights?
6. Which countries had a feudal system?
7. What are the dates of the Middle Ages?
8. Did you read about the Crusades?
9. How did gunpowder change knighthood?
10. Do knights fight in wars anymore?

Sentences Beginning With *There* or *Here* Two words that are often used to begin inverted sentences are *there* and *here*.

> **KEY CONCEPT** The subject of a sentence is never *there* or *here*. ■

When *there* or *here* begins a sentence, the subject usually follows the verb. As with inverted questions, mentally rephrase the sentence to find the subject.

Note About *Sentences Beginning With* There *or* Here: Some sentences beginning with *there* or *here* are not in inverted order, however. In such cases, the words *there* or *here* usually point out a specific location

EXAMPLES: There you are!
             Here the castle stands.

> **More Practice**
>
> Grammar Exercise Workbook
> • pp. 49–50
> On-line Exercise Bank
> • Section 19.2
>   *Go on-line:*
>   PHSchool.com
>   *Enter Web Code:*
>   eek-1002

✏ Spelling Tip

Because English includes words borrowed from other languages, proper spelling is often a challenge. *Chivalry,* for instance, comes from the Old French word *chevalier,* which means "knight." When in doubt, look in a dictionary for the correct spelling of tricky words.

Sentences Beginning With *There* or *Here*	Reworded With Subjects Before Verbs
There <u>is</u> my old, battered <u>suitcase</u>.	My old, battered <u>suitcase</u> <u>is</u> there.
Here <u>is</u> the <u>museum</u>!	The <u>museum</u> <u>is</u> here.

In the sentences in the chart above, *there* and *here* are adverbs; they modify the verbs and tell *where*. Occasionally, *there* is merely used to help the sentence get started and does not modify the verb. When *there* is used in this way, it is not an adverb but an *expletive*.

EXAMPLES: There <u>is</u> no <u>bridge</u> across this river.
There <u>will be</u> a drastic <u>change</u> in the weather.

In sentences where *there* is an expletive, rephrasing to find the subject may not work. To find the subject in this situation, mentally drop *there* and ask *Who?* or *What?* before the verb.

Sentences With Expletive *There*	Questions for Finding Subjects
There <u>are</u> many <u>castles</u> in England.	*Question: What* are? *Answer:* castles
There <u>may</u> not <u>be</u> any logical <u>answer</u> to that question.	*Question: What* may be? *Answer:* answer

▶ **Exercise 13**   **Finding Subjects in Sentences Beginning With *There* or *Here*** Write each sentence on your paper, underlining the subject once and the verb twice.

EXAMPLE: Here <u>is</u> my <u>book</u> about castles!

1. There are the turrets at the top.
2. Here is my favorite book on King Arthur.
3. There are many versions of the King Arthur legend.
4. There is no way of knowing the truth behind the legend.
5. There on the dresser is my copy of *Le Morte d'Arthur.*

▼ **Critical Viewing** Write three statements a tour guide might make about this castle. Start each with *there* or *here*. Underline each simple subject and verb. **[Analyze]**

420 • Basic Sentence Parts

GRAMMAR IN
LITERATURE

from **Morte d'Arthur**
Alfred, Lord Tennyson

In the following excerpt, the subject-verb order is invert-ed. Notice that, in addition to supplying emphasis, this inverted order is a feature of older language.

Then <u>spake</u> <u>King Arthur</u> to Sir Bedivere:
"<u>Hast</u> <u>thou</u> performed my mission which I gave?
What is it thou hast seen, or what hast heard?"
And answer <u>made</u> the bold <u>Sir Bedivere</u>:
"I heard the ripple washing in the reeds,
And the wild water lapping on the crag."
To whom <u>replied</u> <u>King Arthur</u>, faint and pale:
"Thou hast betrayed thy nature and thy name. . ."

Inverted Order for Emphasis Sometimes, the subject-verb order is deliberately inverted to emphasize the word or words at the end of the sentence.

▶ **KEY CONCEPT** In some sentences, the subject is placed after the verb in order to receive greater emphasis. ■

Inverted subject-verb order directs attention to the subject at the end of the sentence and adds a sense of drama or sur-prise to the sentence. Rephrased in normal subject-verb order, the sentence is less dramatic.

Notice the different dramatic impact the sentence in the chart below makes when presented in inverted order instead of in normal subject-verb order.

Inverted Word Order for Emphasis	Reworded With Subject Before Verbs
Beneath the ruined temple <u>waited</u> the deadly <u>cobra</u>.	The deadly <u>cobra</u> <u>waited</u> beneath the ruined temple.

Exercise 14 Finding Subjects in Sentences Inverted for Emphasis Write the subject of each sentence.

EXAMPLE: Behind the bookcase was hidden a secret door.
ANSWER: door

1. At his master's side rode the brave young squire.
2. Outside the castle lurked the enemy.
3. Across the moat lay safety.
4. Atop the steep hillside stood the majestic castle.
5. Through the battlements came dangerous arrows.
6. From the castle ruled the noble monarch.
7. Uncomfortable was life in the castle.
8. Along the tops of the walls and towers walked the guards.
9. Above the castle flew the colorful flags.
10. With fairness governed the beloved king.

Exercise 15 Revising Sentences by Changing Subject-Verb Order Revise the following sentences, changing them from subject-verb order to inverted order or from inverted order to subject-verb order.

EXAMPLE: A trapdoor was hidden in the floor
REVISION: Hidden in the floor was a trapdoor.

1. In the clearing near the ancient castle waited three mounted knights.
2. One of the knights sat atop a majestic steed.
3. The armed knights raced toward the castle at break-neck speed.
4. A young, inexperienced squire was standing guard at the castle wall.
5. A bright moon shone above the castle.
6. Highlighted by the light of the full moon was the squire's face.
7. Filling his eyes was a look of total fear.
8. Serving as a barrier between the attackers and the castle was a drawbridge.
9. The crank that operated the drawbridge was near the squire's hand.
10. Three frustrated knights were there outside the castle walls.

▶ Critical Viewing Write three questions you might ask this knight about jousting. Identify the simple subject and verb in each question. [Analyze]

More Practice

Grammar Exercise Workbook
• pp. 49–50
On-line Exercise Bank
• Section 19.2
  Go on-line:
  PHSchool.com
  Enter Web Code:
  eek-1002

Get instant feedback! Exercises 14 and 15 are available on-line or on CD-ROM.

Hands-on Grammar

Inverted-Sentence Cards

In most sentences, the subject comes before the verb. Sentences can be inverted, however, to show emphasis or for dramatic effect. Explore the effect of subject-verb placement with the following activity.

On each of four index cards, write *subject.* On the reverse of each card, write one of these article/noun combinations: *the king, the queen, the knight, the squire.* Next, make four cards that say *verb* on one side and have a verb on the reverse. Use these verbs: *waits, stood, spoke, reads.* Finally, make a set of cards for the adverbs and adverb phrases: *impatiently, proudly, in the castle, at the door.*

Place each set of cards in a pile so that you can read the part of speech. Choose one card from each pile and line them up in the following order: *subject, verb, adverb (or adverb phrase),* Turn the cards over to read the sentence you have created. Then, turn the cards over again to read the part of speech. While the cards are still showing the part of speech, arrange them in the following order: *adverb (or adverb phrase), verb, subject.* Flip the cards to read the new sentence. Complete these steps with the rest of the cards in each pile. (Because the first word of the sentence depends on the arrangement of cards, none of the words on your cards are capitalized. Remember that if you were writing these sentences, you would capitalize the first word of each sentence.)

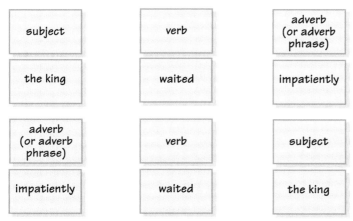

When you are finished, create a new set of cards and work with a partner to challenge each other to identify the subject in inverted sentences. Turn the cards over to check your answers. Create some inverted sentences that contain both adverbs and adverb phrases.

Find It in Your Reading Find an inverted sentences in a folk tale or a poem. Identify each part of the inverted sentence.

Find It in Your Writing Look through your portfolio to find a sentence that could be inverted for emphasis or effect. Identify the subject of the revised sentence.

Section Review

GRAMMAR EXERCISES 16–21

Exercise 16 Identifying Hard-to-Find Subjects Write the subject and verb in each sentence, underlining the subject once and the verb twice. If the subject is understood, write (*you*).

1. Do you know much about castles?
2. There were hundreds of castles built in Europe.
3. There are some still standing.
4. Where was the first castle built?
5. When was its construction completed?
6. Can you name all of the castles in Ireland?
7. Here is the article about feudalism.
8. There may not be enough information on-line.
9. Are you going to visit any castles?
10. Here we go!
11. Look at this painting of a medieval castle.
12. On the wall hung the knights' swords.
13. In the background wait the loyal squires.
14. Beneath the flapping flags strode the valiant knights.
15. On their shields appeared their crests.

Exercise 17 Rewriting Inverted Sentences to Locate Their Subjects Rewrite the following inverted sentences to put the subject before the verb. Then, underline the subject once and the verb twice.

1. Does a moat surround the castle?
2. Will our enemies use ladders to scale the walls of the castle?
3. There is the lowest wall of the castle.
4. Within the moat swim several deadly fish.
5. Here will we establish our best defense of the castle.

Exercise 18 Writing Orders, Directions, and Inverted Sentences Follow these instructions to write five sentences of your own. Underline the subject of each sentence. If the subject is understood, write (*you*).

1. Write a sentence addressing someone and giving the person an order.
2. Write a sentence that directs someone to do two things, one after the other.
3. Write a sentence that begins with *here*.
4. Write the first sentence of directions for building or cooking something.
5. Write a sentence with the order inverted for emphasis.

Exercise 19 Find It in Your Reading Identify the subject in each clause of this excerpt from *"Morte d' Arthur."*

> Then spoke King Arthur, drawing thicker breath:/"Now see I by thine eyes that this is done./Speak out: What is it thou hast heard, or seen?"

Exercise 20 Find It in Your Writing In your writing portfolio, find a question and a sentence that begins with *there* or *here*. Label the subjects of the sentences. Also, challenge yourself to rewrite one of your sentences in inverted order.

Exercise 21 Writing Application Imagine that you are a knight. Write an advertisement seeking a squire to assist you. Include one sentence that gives directions, one that asks a question, and one that begins with *there* or *here*. Identify the subjects in your sentences.

Section 19.3
Direct Objects, Indirect Objects, and Objective Complements

In addition to a verb, a complete predicate may also have one or more *complements.*

▶ **KEY CONCEPT** A **complement** is a word or group of words that completes the meaning of the predicate of a sentence. ■

This section presents three different kinds of complements used in sentences with action verbs: *direct objects, indirect objects,* and *objective complements.*

The Direct Object

Direct objects usually follow action verbs.

▶ **KEY CONCEPT** A **direct object** is a noun or pronoun that receives the action of a transitive action verb. ■

To find a direct object, ask *Whom?* or *What?* after an action verb. In the following examples, subjects are underlined once, action verbs twice, and direct objects are boxed and labeled. Notice how the direct objects answer the questions *Whom?* and *What?*

EXAMPLES:	A <u>blanket</u> of snow <u><u>covered</u></u> the $\boxed{\text{pagoda}}$. Covered *what? Answer:* pagoda
	The <u>woman</u> <u><u>is watching</u></u> the $\boxed{\text{children}}$. Watching *whom? Answer:* children

Only transitive action verbs direct their action toward someone or something—the direct object. Intransitive verbs have no direct objects.

TRANSITIVE:	The tidal <u>wave</u> <u><u>sank</u></u> the $\boxed{\text{ship}}$. Sank *what? Answer:* ship
INTRANSITIVE:	The <u>wheels</u> <u><u>sank</u></u> into the mud. Sank *what? Answer:* none

Theme: Japan
In this section, you will learn to recognize direct objects, indirect objects, and objective complements. The examples and exercises are about Japan and its culture.

Cross-Curricular Connection: Social Studies

Direct Objects in Questions When a question follows the normal subject-verb order, you can still find the direct object by asking *Whom?* or *What?* after an action verb.

EXAMPLE: Who wrote that $\overset{\text{DO}}{\boxed{\text{story}}}$?

When a question is inverted, however, the direct object will sometimes appear near the beginning, before the verb. To find the direct object, reword the question as a statement in normal word order, as shown in the following examples.

INVERTED QUESTION: Which book did you read?

REWORDED AS   You <u>did read</u> which $\overset{\text{DO}}{\boxed{\text{book}}}$.
A STATEMENT:

Compound Direct Objects When an action verb directs action toward more than one direct object, the result is a compound direct object. If there is a compound direct object in a sentence, asking *Whom?* or *What?* after the verb will give you two or more answers.

EXAMPLE: The tourists visited Japanese $\overset{\text{DO}}{\boxed{\text{temples}}}$ and $\overset{\text{DO}}{\boxed{\text{shrines}}}$.

▶ **Exercise 22** Identifying Direct Objects in Statements and Questions List the direct object or compound direct object in each sentence below.

EXAMPLE: Japanese workers spend long hours on the job.
ANSWER: hours

1. Japan owes much of its economic success to its workers.
2. Japanese workers often express loyalty and respect toward their companies.
3. They take great pride in their companies' success.
4. They work longer hours and take fewer vacations than Western workers.
5. How do Japanese companies treat their employees?
6. Large companies often offer incentives to attract and keep workers.
7. Which benefits do workers appreciate most?
8. Many workers receive free housing or medical care.
9. These benefits keep the workers happy.
10. As a result, Japanese workers produce more goods than workers in most other countries do.

More Practice

Grammar Exercise Workbook
• pp. 51–54
On-line Exercise Bank
• Section 19.3
   Go on-line:
   PHSchool.com
   Enter Web Code:
   eek-1002

Get instant feedback! Exercises 22 and 23 are available on-line or on CD-ROM.

Direct Object or Object of a Preposition? A direct object is never the noun or pronoun at the end of a prepositional phrase. Do not confuse these two sentence parts.

EXAMPLES:

DO   PREP PHRASE
I photographed the ⬚woman⬚ with the children.
Photographed *whom? Answer*: woman

PREP PHRASE   PREP PHRASE
We walked with the children through the zoo.
Walked *what? Answer*: none

▷ **Exercise 23** Identifying Direct Objects and Objects of Prepositions On your paper, indicate whether the underlined word in each sentence is a *direct object* or *object of a preposition*.

EXAMPLE: A group of tourists stood outside the <u>pagoda</u>.

ANSWER: object of a preposition

1. Many Japanese pagodas are made of <u>wood</u>.
2. They are very vulnerable to <u>fire</u>.
3. Yet these pagodas can withstand earthquakes and <u>typhoons</u>.
4. Their interlocking construction makes <u>them</u> so strong.
5. A 1,300-year-old pagoda in Nara still shows no <u>sign</u> of weakness in its structure.

▼ Critical Viewing
Add a compound direct object to complete this sentence: *When I look at this pagoda, I see . . .*
[Identify]

> **Exercise 24** **Revising by Using Direct Objects** Revise each question and answer below to form a sentence that includes a direct object or compound direct object. Underline the direct object(s).

EXAMPLE: What does Japan have? A long coastline and mountainous terrain.

ANSWER: Japan has a long <u>coastline</u> and mountainous <u>terrain</u>.

1. Who did the Japanese educate at first? Only the members of the aristocracy
2. Who later assumed the responsibility for education? Buddhist priests
3. How did this change affect education? It made it available to a larger portion of society.
4. How long did the Japanese maintain this system? Until the 1800's
5. What happened under Emperor Meiji in the late 1800's? A universal code for education was first adopted by the Japanese.

More Practice

Grammar Exercise Workbook
• pp. 51–54
On-line Exercise Bank
• Section 19.3
  Go on-line:
  PHSchool.com
  Enter Web Code:
  eek-1002

Complete the exercises on-line! Exercises 24 and 25 are available on-line or on CD-ROM.

The Indirect Object

Sentences with direct objects may have *indirect objects,* too.

> **KEY CONCEPT** An **indirect object** is a noun or pronoun that appears with a direct object and names the person or thing that something is given to or done for. ∎

To find an indirect object, first be certain that the sentence has a direct object. Then, having found the direct object, ask *To or for whom?* or *To or for what?* after the action verb.

EXAMPLES:
                    IO   DO
Liz <u>promised</u> her [sister] a [book] about Japan.
Promised *to whom?*   *Answer:* sister

                       IO   DO
We <u>should give</u> Fred's [idea] a [chance].
Should give *to what?*   *Answer:* idea

Compound Indirect Objects When there is a compound indirect object in a sentence, asking *To or for whom?* or *To or for what?* after the verb will lead to two or more answers.

EXAMPLE:
                   IO   IO
Liz <u>promised</u> her [sister] and [brother] a book.
Promised *to whom? Answer:* sister and brother

Indirect Object or Direct Object? To avoid confusing an indirect object with a direct object, remember that an indirect object almost always comes between the verb and the direct object. In a sentence in normal subject-verb order, the pattern is always verb-indirect object-direct object.

EXAMPLE: Uncle Charlie handed the bellhop a tip.
                                    IO   DO

Asking the questions for direct and indirect objects will also help you distinguish between the two kinds of complements. In the above example, the question for direct objects—handed *what?*—gives the answer *tip*. The question for indirect objects—handed *to whom?*—leads to the indirect object *bellhop*.

Indirect Object or Object of a Preposition? Do not confuse an indirect object with an object of a preposition. An indirect object is never preceded by the word *to* or *for*. Moreover, it almost never follows the direct object. In the first example below, *friends* is the object of a preposition and is located after the direct object. In the second, there is no preposition and *friends* comes before the direct object.

EXAMPLES: Angela told the news to her friends.
                                    DO   PREP PHRASE

              Angela told her friends the news.
                                 IO   DO

▲ **Critical Viewing**
Write a sentence about this performer using the word *audience* as an indirect object. What is the direct object of your sentence? [**Analyze**]

> **Exercise 25** **Recognizing Indirect Objects** Write each indirect object, including any compound indirect objects. If a sentence has no indirect object, write *none*.

EXAMPLE: They sent Mark and Elizabeth travel brochures.
ANSWER: Mark, Elizabeth

1. Mark's parents bought him plane tickets to Tokyo for his birthday.
2. He asked his boss for a leave of absence.
3. The company granted Mark eight weeks.
4. His friend lent him a suitcase large enough for his long journey.
5. As his plane lifted off, Mark felt a rush of excitement and nervousness.
6. While away, Mark wrote his parents a letter every week.
7. He told them about the culture and people of Japan.
8. A guide gave him a complete tour of the city.
9. Mark visited Tokyo's financial and commercial centers.
10. When Mark returned, he showed his friends pictures of Tokyo.

The Objective Complement

A third kind of complement, one that generally comes after a direct object, is called an *objective complement.*

▶ **KEY CONCEPT** An **objective complement** is an adjective or noun that appears with a direct object and describes or renames it. ■

Objective complements do not occur often. They are used only with verbs such as *appoint, name, make, think,* or *call.*

An objective complement can be found only in a sentence that has a direct object. To determine whether a word is an objective complement, say the verb and the direct object and then ask *What?* The following examples illustrate the method you should use to locate objective complements.

EXAMPLES:
                          DO   OC
            Ben <u>called</u> his dog Rover.
            Called dog *what? Answer:* Rover

                                    DO   OC   OC
            The <u>beautician</u> <u>made</u> Ann's hair short and curly.
            Made hair *what? Answer:* short and curly

The objective complement in the last example is compound.

▶ **Exercise 26** Recognizing Objective Complements Write the objective complement in each sentence, including all parts of any compound objective complements.

EXAMPLE: Mr. Matsuto made his reply very short.
ANSWER: short

1. The Japanese consider the emperor the symbol of their nation.
2. They once thought their emperor sacred and inviolable.
3. Japan's 1947 constitution declared the emperor's position ceremonial.
4. The constitution named the prime minister head of state.
5. In 1989, Japan declared Akihito emperor.
6. The people considered his marriage to a commoner symbolic of Japan's democracy.
7. Japan's limited land and large population make the country densely populated.
8. Limited space makes housing development difficult.
9. In spite of the overcrowding, the Japanese find their homeland a paradise.
10. The Japanese call their country the "land of the rising sun."

Spelling Tip

Note the difference between *complement* and *compliment:* A *complement* is something that completes or brings to perfection. A *compliment* is an expression of courtesy or praise.

Section 19.3 Section Review

GRAMMAR EXERCISES 27–32

Exercise 27 Recognizing Direct Objects Write the direct object in each sentence, including all parts of any compound direct objects.

(1) Japanese comprise 99 percent of the population of Japan. (2) The small remainder includes Koreans, Chinese, and Ainu. (3) The Ainu represent the aborigines of Japan. (4) They once inhabited the northernmost islands of Japan. (5) They possessed distinct biological characteristics. (6) After World War II, however, Japanese culture almost fully assimilated the Ainu. (7) Metropolitan areas now dominate the Japanese landscape. (8) Its people have created an industrialized urban society with relatively few resources. (9) Nearly all citizens speak Japanese. (10) In addition to speaking the official language, many Japanese also know some English.

Exercise 28 Recognizing Complements Used With Action Verbs Write and label each *direct object*, *indirect object*, and *objective complement*.

1. The Japanese named their country *Dia Nihon*, which means "origin of the sun."
2. The Treaty of Versailles made the Caroline Islands a part of Japan.
3. I showed my father the cities of Yokohama and Osaka on the map.
4. The rugged mountains and rocky soil of Japan make farming difficult.
5. Kirisawa wrote some of the Japanese ideogrammatic alphabet on the chalkboard for the class.
6. The University of Tokyo granted the foreign students a scholarship.
7. Our hosts offered us sushi for lunch.
8. At the Japanese festival, I ate blowfish.
9. The prime minister of Japan appoints legislators and cabinet members.
10. Frank sent me his book of Japanese architecture.

Exercise 29 Writing Sentences With Complements Complete each sentence by adding the complement(s) indicated in parentheses, plus needed modifiers.

1. Frances painted ___?___. (direct object)
2. The Japanese musician played ___?___. (compound direct object)
3. Anna's friend wrote ___?___. (indirect object and direct object)
4. Charlie bought ___?___. (compound indirect object and direct object)
5. Andrew considered ___?___. (direct object and objective complement)

Exercise 30 Find It in Your Reading In a newspaper, find an article about another country. Label any *direct objects*, *indirect objects*, and *objective complements* in the article.

Exercise 31 Find It in Your Writing In your own writing, find five direct objects and two indirect objects. Also, note whether you have used objective complements in any of your compositions.

Exercise 32 Writing Application Japan exports many products, such as automobiles and electronics, to the United States. Write a description of an item in your home that may have been imported from another country, and discuss how it works. Include and label two *direct objects*, one *indirect object*, and one *objective complement* in your description.

Subject Complements

In this section, you will see linking verbs followed by other kinds of complements, called *subject complements*.

▶ **KEY CONCEPT** A **subject complement** is a noun, pronoun, or adjective that appears with a linking verb and tells something about the subject of the sentence. ■

A subject complement will almost always be found *after* a linking verb. The two kinds of subject complements are known as *predicate nominatives* and *predicate adjectives*.

The Predicate Nominative

The word *nominative* comes from the Latin word *nomen* meaning "name." The words *noun* and *pronoun* are also derived from *nomen*. A *predicate nominative* names or identifies the subject of a sentence.

▶ **KEY CONCEPT** A **predicate nominative** is a noun or pronoun that appears with a linking verb and renames, identifies, or explains the subject of the sentence. ■

A subject and a predicate nominative are two different words for the same person, place, or thing. Acting as an equal sign, the linking verb joins these two parts and equates them.

In the examples, subjects are underlined once, linking verbs twice, and predicate nominatives are boxed and labeled.

EXAMPLES: That <u>painting</u> of the shoreline <u><u>is</u></u> a $\overset{\text{PN}}{\boxed{\text{masterpiece}}}$.
(*Masterpiece* explains *painting*.)

The new <u>lifeguard</u> at the pool <u><u>will be</u></u> $\overset{\text{PN}}{\boxed{\text{Sue}}}$.
(*Sue* renames *lifeguard*.)

Their first <u>choice</u> <u><u>was</u></u> $\overset{\text{PN}}{\boxed{\text{you}}}$.
(*You* identifies *choice*.)

Like other sentence parts, predicate nominatives may be compound.

EXAMPLES: Most <u>people</u> at the beach <u><u>were</u></u> $\overset{\text{PN}}{\boxed{\text{sunbathers}}}$ or
$\overset{\text{PN}}{\boxed{\text{surfers}}}$. (*Sunbathers* and *surfers* name *people*.)

The new <u>lifeguard</u> <u><u>may be</u></u> either $\overset{\text{PN}}{\boxed{\text{Sue}}}$ or $\overset{\text{PN}}{\boxed{\text{Celia}}}$.
(*Sue* or *Celia* renames *lifeguard*.)

Theme: Beaches and Tides

In this section, you will learn about predicate nominatives and predicate adjectives. The examples and exercises are about beaches and tides.

Cross-Curricular Connection: Science

▶ **More Practice**

Grammar Exercise Workbook
• pp. 55–56
On-line Exercise Bank
• Section 19.4
Go on-line:
PHSchool.com
Enter Web Code:
eek-1002

GRAMMAR IN LITERATURE

from **The Marginal World**
By Rachel Carson

Predicate nominatives in this passage are highlighted in blue italics. Note also that the subject and verb are inverted in the last sentence.

The edge of the sea is a strange and beautiful *place*. All through the long history of Earth it has been an *area* of unrest where waves have broken heavily against the land, where the tides have pressed forward over the continents, receded, and then returned. For no two successive days is the shoreline precisely the same.

▷ **Exercise 33** Recognizing Predicate Nominatives Write the predicate nominative in each sentence, including all parts of any compound predicate nominatives.

EXAMPLE: This beach is a good site for fishing and an excellent place for diving.

ANSWER: site place

1. Beaches are strips of land bordering an ocean or another body of water.
2. Some of our favorite beaches are barrier beaches.
3. Barrier beaches are generally elongated islands or sandbars.
4. The beach at Coney Island, in New York, is a barrier beach.
5. Beaches along the islands of Hawaii are the main attraction for tourists.
6. Waves, tides, and the wind will always be a beach's worst enemy.
7. These elements are the primary cause of erosion.
8. Sand dunes are one result of winds and tides.
9. White sand on a beach is the product of coral and limestone deposits.
10. High tides and storms are cause for alarm for beach residents.

▼ **Critical Viewing**
Complete this sentence: *This rocky coastline would be a great . . .* What is the predicate nominative in your sentence? **[Analyze]**

The Predicate Adjective

The other kind of subject complement is called a *predicate adjective*. With a linking verb, it describes the subject.

> **KEY CONCEPT** A **predicate adjective** is an adjective that appears with a linking verb and describes the subject of the sentence. ■

In each of the following examples, you can see that the linking verb joins the subject to a word that describes the subject. These descriptive words are predicate adjectives.

EXAMPLES: A trip to the beach <u>will be</u> fun.
P.A.

My sunburn <u>feels</u> hot and painful.
P.A.

> **Exercise 34** Recognizing Predicate Adjectives Write the predicate adjective in each sentence, including all parts of any compound predicate adjectives.

1. In the cloudless sky, the moon appeared luminous.
2. The moon is closer to the Earth than the sun is.
3. Its gravitational pull on the Earth is stronger.
4. The Earth's oceans are responsive to the pull of the moon.
5. The gravitational pull of the moon is great and constant
6. Tides are higher at certain times of the day because of the moon's pull.
7. Marine life is plentiful at the edge of the sea.
8. These forms of life must be hardy and adaptable.
9. The fronds of seaweed were smooth and gleaming.
10. The delicate shells on the shore looked unreal.

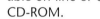

<Text>

Get instant feedback! Exercise 34 is available on-line or on CD-ROM.

> **More Practice**

Grammar Exercise Workbook
• pp. 55–56
On-line Exercise Bank
• Section 19.4
  Go on-line:
  PHSchool.com
  Enter Web Code:
  eek-1002

▶ Critical Viewing Write two sentences containing predicate adjectives to describe the beach and the sunset in this photograph. [**Analyze**]

Section Review

GRAMMAR EXERCISES 35–40

Exercise 35 Recognizing Subject Complements Write and label the predicate nominatives or predicate adjectives in each sentence,

1. Shorelines are home to tidal pools.
2. The environments of tidal pools are unique and delicate.
3. The current is the source of a rich supply of nutrients along beaches.
4. Tidal pools are natural basins in sand.
5. Creatures in tidal pools are adaptable.
6. They are strange and beautiful forms of life.
7. Buffeting waves and frequent submersion are dangerous to them.
8. Suction-cup feet are the only protections of a starfish.
9. Rocks and boats are often host to marine animals like barnacles.
10. Seaweed is quite resilient.

Exercise 36 Supplying Subject Complements in Sentences Write a subject complement or compound subject complement to complete each sentence.

1. The waves that crashed on the shore were __?__ .
2. The foam felt __?__ and __?__ .
3. The sun was a giant orange __?__ in the sky.
4. Tides are a good __?__ of energy.
5. A dam can be an essential __?__ for capturing this energy.
6. Dams can be __?__ , but they are worth the money.
7. The 50-foot tides in the Bay of Fundy in Canada are the __?__ in the world.
8. Birds flying over the bay were __?__ and __?__ .
9. The beach is a good __?__ to play or relax.
10. The most unusual thing I saw in the water was a __?__ .

Exercise 37 Revising Sentences by Using Subject Complements Revise each sentence below so that it includes a predicate nominative or predicate adjective.

1. We took a refreshing morning walk along the beach.
2. We saw a rocky and craggy shoreline.
3. A distant boat seemed to be a tiny speck on the horizon.
4. Our dinner consisted of fresh fish and vegetables.
5. The beach at night has a mysterious quality.

Exercise 38 Find It in Your Reading Identify the predicate nominative and predicate adjective in this excerpt from *The Marginal World*.

. . . Water and air were pallid. Across the bay the moon was a luminous disc in the western sky, suspended above the dim line of the distant shore. . . .

Exercise 39 Find It in Your Writing Look through your writing portfolio. Find two examples of predicate nominatives and two examples of predicate adjectives. Label the complements, and underline the subject once and the linking verb twice in each sentence.

Exercise 40 Writing Application Write a description of a day at a beach or park. Include a predicate nominative, a compound predicate nominative, and two predicate adjectives in your description.

GRAMMAR EXERCISES 41–47

▶ **Exercise 41** Identifying Basic
Sentence Parts Write each of the following sentences on your paper. Draw a
vertical line separating the complete subject from the complete predicate. Underline
each simple subject once and each verb
twice. Then, identify the function of any
italicized complement.

1. Surfing became a popular water *sport*
   in the 1960's.
2. The sport is *popular* today in the
   United States, Australia, and Japan.
3. A person participating in this sport
   rides *waves* in the ocean.
4. The surfer lies, kneels, or stands on a
   surfboard.
5. People in Hawaii gave *surfing* its start
   hundreds of years ago.
6. They made *themselves* wooden boards.
7. Today's boards are *compositions* of
   polyurethane wrapped in fiberglass.
8. Surfers call boards under 8 feet in
   length *short boards.*
9. The beaches of Hawaii are the most
   famous surfing *locations* in the world.
10. All forms of surfing require exact *tim-
    ing* and quick *reflexes.*
11. The most popular form of surfing is
    stand-up.
12. The surfer paddles the *board* out
    beyond the breaking waves.
13. He or she stands and rides a *wave*
    toward the shore.
14. Annual surfing competitions in Hawaii,
    California, and Australia are *exciting.*
15. Bodysurfing and windsurfing are other
    aquatic *sports.*

▶ **Exercise 42** Identifying Hard-to-
Find Subjects On your paper, write the
following sentences. Underline each subject once and each verb twice. If a subject
is understood, write (*you*).

1. Do you play beach volleyball?
2. Here is the only available volleyball net
   on the beach.
3. Are there enough players for a game?
4. Where are the rest of your friends?
5. Gather your friends to form a team.
6. There are no open spots left on the
   beach.
7. Here is my favorite place to play
   volleyball.
8. There are never enough people with
   whom to play.
9. Would you like to play against us?
10. Which ball would you prefer to use?
11. On the beach are some annoying
    insects.
12. Along the Atlantic coast from Canada
    to Argentina is found the common
    sand flea.
13. Avoid this freaky critter.
14. With a sudden leap comes the sand flea.
15. On almost any kind of decaying veg-
    etable or animal matter feast these
    tiny creatures.

▶ **Exercise 43** Identifying
Complements Write and label any
direct objects, indirect objects, objective
complements, predicate nominatives, or
predicate adjectives you find in the following sentences.

1. Carol spent her childhood at the beach.
2. Studying marine life is her passion.
3. As a high-school student, she studied
   biology avidly.
4. In college, Carol focused her studies
   on marine biology.
5. Now, Carol supervises marine biolo-
   gists and researchers in the navy.
6. She recently bought herself a small
   cottage at the shore.
7. She proudly showed her mother and
   father the place.

8. They gave her a housewarming present during their visit.
9. They considered the cottage lovely.
10. Carol felt thrilled by their response.
11. Next to the cottage, she has planted some flowers.
12. She gives the flowers water every day in the summer.
13. She has outlined the flower bed with many different kinds of shells.
14. Friends gave her their nicest shells.
15. She calls her garden "my cozy posies."

▶ **Exercise 44** **Adding Basic Parts to Complete Sentences** Complete each sentence with a noun, pronoun, or adjective. Identify the use of the word in the sentence as a *subject, direct object, indirect object, predicate nominative,* or *predicate adjective.*

1. My favorite summer ___?___ is swimming.
2. Jen bought ___?___ a new swimsuit.
3. The sky looks ___?___ and ___?___ this morning.
4. Bring your ___?___ to the beach.
5. This is a good ___?___ for sailing.
6. My father and ___?___ rented a ___?___ for the day.
7. My father's ___?___ taught ___?___ sailing.
8. His sailing skills were ___?___.
9. We still had ___?___, however.
10. The lake water felt ___?___ and ___?___.

▶ **Exercise 45** **Writing Sentences With Objective Complements** Add an objective complement of the type indicated to each of the following sentences.

1. We named our pet starfish (noun).
2. The dock master considered his staff (adjective).
3. Unanimously, the beach club members appointed me (noun).

4. The hurricane left the shoreline (adjective) and (adjective).
5. I called Dave a powerful (noun) and a fine (noun).

▶ **Exercise 46** **Revising Sentences by Adding Complements** Revise the following sentences by following the directions in parentheses.

1. Jacques bought a goldfish. (Add an indirect object.)
2. The fish was bright orange. (Add another predicate adjective.)
3. They bought for the goldfish (Add a direct object.)
4. The most interesting thing in the bowl was (Add a predicate nominative.)
5. The goldfish gave a lot of pleasure. (Add an indirect object.)
6. We named the fish. (Add an objective complement.)
7. In the last few weeks, Jacques has bought many for his aquarium. (Add a compound direct object.)
8. Keeping fish has become a favorite of his. (Add a predicate nominative.)
9. Keeping fish can be very (Add a compound predicate adjective.)
10. All of Jacques friends consider him (Add an objective complement.)

▶ **Exercise 47** **Writing Application** Write a description of a marine animal that you have seen at the beach, at an aquarium, or on film. Underline the subject of each sentence once, the verb twice, and circle each complement. Include at least one sentence in inverted order.

Standardized Test Preparation Workshop

Recognizing Appropriate Sentence Construction

Knowing how to use the basic parts of a sentence correctly is the foundation for good writing. Every sentence must contain a subject (the *who* or *what* that performs the action) and a verb (the action the subject is performing) and express a complete thought. If one of these parts is missing, it is an incomplete sentence.

Standardized tests measure your ability to identify complete sentences. When answering these test questions, check each group of words for a subject and a verb, and then determine whether it expresses a complete thought. Also, make sure that the sentence is not really two sentences placed together incorrectly.

The following question will give you practice with the format used for testing your knowledge of basic sentence parts.

Test Tips

- Remember that a verb can either follow or come before its subject. Also, a form of *be* can act as the main verb of a sentence.
- Watch out for answer choices that are really two sentences run together with no punctuation or with just a comma separating them.

Sample Test Item	Answer and Explanation
Directions: Choose the letter of the best way to rewrite each underlined section. If the underlined section needs no change, choose "Correct as is." In 1769, the first automobile was built. (1) By Nicholas Cugnot. He was a French military officer. **A** In 1769, the first automobile was built by a French military officer. Nicholas Cugnot. **B** In 1769, Nicholas Cugnot, a French military officer, built the first automobile. **C** In 1769, Nicholas Cugnot built the first automobile, he was a French military officer. **D** Correct as is	The correct answer is *B*. The sentence provides all of the information from the original without introducing either an incomplete sentence (as in *A*) or incorrectly running together two sentences (as in *C*).

Practice 1 **Directions:** Choose the letter of the best way to write each underlined section. If the underlined section needs no change, choose "Correct as is."

In a head-on crash. A car's driver and
(1)
passengers can be thrown forward. And

seriously injured. To protect those inside
(2)
most new cars have airbags. Airbags pop
(3)
out of the steering wheel. Or the dashboard.

They inflate instantly with nitrogen gas.

1 A In a head-on crash, a car's driver and passengers can be thrown forward. And seriously injured.

B In a head-on crash. A car's driver and passengers can be thrown forward they can be seriously injured.

C In a head-on crash, a car's driver and passengers can be thrown forward and seriously injured.

D Correct as is

2 F To protect those inside. Most new cars have airbags.

G Most new cars have airbags. This is to protect those inside.

H Most new cars have airbags, this is to protect those inside.

J Correct as is

3 A Airbags pop out of the steering wheel or dashboard. They inflate instantly. With nitrogen gas.

B Airbags pop out of the steering wheel or dashboard and inflate instantly with nitrogen gas.

C Airbags inflate instantly with nitrogen gas and they pop out of the steering wheel or dashboard.

D Correct as is

Practice 2 **Directions:** Choose the letter of the best way to write each underlined section. If the underlined section needs no change, choose "Correct as is."

An airbag system contains three things.
(1)
Electronic sensors, an inflator, and the bag

itself. The sensors in the system are set. To
(2)
ignore collisions. When the cars are going

less than ten to fourteen miles per hour.

In a crash, the bag becomes fully inflated.
(3)
In one twentieth of a second.

1 A An airbag system contains electronic sensors, an inflator, and the bag itself.

B An airbag system contains three things. The three things are electronic sensors, an inflator, and the bag itself.

C An airbag system contains. Electronic sensors, an inflator, and the bag itself.

D Correct as is

2 F The sensors are set to ignore collisions. When the cars are going less than ten to fourteen miles per hour.

G The sensors are set to ignore collisions. The cars are going less than ten to fourteen miles per hour.

H The sensors are set to ignore collisions when the cars are going less than ten to fourteen miles per hour.

J Correct as is

3 A In a crash. The bag becomes fully inflated in one twentieth of a second.

B In a crash, the bag becomes fully inflated in one twentieth of a second.

C The bag becomes fully inflated in a crash.

D Correct as is

Phrases
and Clauses

Louvre Museum, Paris, France

The preceding chapters have described the simple building blocks of grammar, including the various parts of speech and the basic sentence parts. This chapter will focus on two additional elements—phrases and clauses—that function in specific ways in sentences.

A **phrase** is a group of words, without a subject and verb, that functions in a sentence as one part of speech. A **clause** is a group of words with its own subject and verb. Some clauses can stand by themselves as complete sentences; others can function only as parts of sentences.

Phrases and clauses add important pieces of information to your writing. In a composition about France, for instance, your phrases and clauses might add information about the culture, social groups, politics, and economics of the country.

As you have seen in previous chapters, sentences are a mixture of subjects, verbs, and modifiers that work together to communicate an idea. In this chapter, you will learn how various phrases and clauses can be incorporated into sentences to enrich the quality of your writing.

▲ **Critical Viewing**
The glass pyramid became part of the Louvre in 1988. What is its effect placed in front of the museum's original buildings? **[Analyze]**

Diagnostic Test

Directions: Write all answers on a separate sheet of paper.

Skill Check A. List the prepositional phrases, appositives, and appositive phrases in the following sentences, and label each. For each item that you list, identify the word it modifies or renames.

1. The Eiffel Tower, France's most recognizable structure, is a Paris landmark.
2. The tower was built for the Paris World's Fair of 1889.
3. Alexandre Gustave Eiffel, an engineer, was the tower's designer.
4. The tower is made of wrought iron and exceeds 984 feet in height.
5. The Eiffel Tower attracts thousands of visitors each year.

Skill Check B. Identify and label the infinitive phrase, gerund phrase, or participial phrase in each sentence. Identify the word modified by each participial phrase, and identify the function of each gerund and infinitive phrase.

6. Fontainebleau is a large chateau located southeast of Paris.
7. Constructing the chateau was the idea of King Francis I.
8. Many well-known artists were hired to decorate the ornate interior of the building.
9. Fontainebleau was looted during the French Revolution, but Napoleon managed to restore the palace to its former glory.
10. The republican government, assuming control of the chateau in 1871, made it a national monument.

Skill Check C. Write the subordinate clause in each sentence, and then tell whether it is an adjective, an adverb, or a noun clause. If a clause is elliptical, write the missing word or words.

11. Versailles is more famous than any other palace in Europe.
12. The enormous building, which has 1,300 rooms, was constructed on the site of a small hunting lodge.
13. Although more than 30,000 craftsmen labored on the palace, it still took longer than forty years to complete.
14. King Louis XIV, who ruled France for much of the seventeenth century, moved the royal court to Versailles in 1682.
15. Whoever visits the palace will be overwhelmed by the sheer size and beauty of the building.

Skill Check D. 16–20 For each adjective and adverb clause in Skill Check C, identify the word it modifies. Tell how each noun clause functions in its sentence.

Phrases

There are several kinds of *phrases,* among them preposi- tional phrases, appositive phrases, participial phrases, gerund phrases, and infinitive phrases. In this section, you will learn how phrases can be used to add meaning and variety to your sentences.

Prepositional Phrases

A **prepositional phrase** is a group of words made up of a preposition and a noun or pronoun, called the object of the preposition. *Over their heads, until dark,* and *after the baseball game* are all examples of prepositional phrases. Sometimes, a single prepositional phrase may have two or more objects joined by a conjunction. *Between the window and the wall* and *with the wind and freezing rain* are examples of preposi- tions followed by compound objects. (See Chapter 18 to review prepositions.)

In this section, you will learn how prepositional phrases modify other words by functioning either as adjectives or as adverbs within sentences.

Adjective Phrases

A prepositional phrase that acts as an adjective is called an *adjective phrase.*

▶ **KEY CONCEPT** An **adjective phrase** is a prepositional phrase that modifies a noun or pronoun by telling *what kind* or *which one.* ■

The following chart contrasts adjectives with adjective phrases.

Adjectives	Adjective Phrases
A *beautiful* French painting hung in the palace.	A French painting *of great beauty* hung in the palace.
Mary took a *boxed* lunch.	Mary took lunch *in a box.*

A prepositional phrase that answers the question *What kind?* or *Which one?* will be an adjective phrase. In the first sentence on the right in the chart, for example, the question *What kind of painting?* is answered by *of great beauty.*

Adjective phrases usually modify nouns functioning as subjects, direct objects, indirect objects, or predicate nominatives.

Theme: France

In this section, you will learn to use prepositional, appositive, and verbal phrases. The examples and exercises in this section are about France.

Cross-Curricular Connection: Social Studies

🔵 **Learn More**

To review basic information about prepositions, turn to Chapter 18.

MODIFYING A SUBJECT: The mansion *across the road* has been abandoned.

MODIFYING A
DIRECT OBJECT: Let's take a picture *of the Eiffel Tower.*

MODIFYING AN
INDIRECT OBJECT: They gave the students *on the bus* a tour.

MODIFYING A
PREDICATE NOMINATIVE: France is a country *with many charms.*

A sentence may often have a series of two or more adjective phrases. When this happens, each succeeding phrase may modify the object of the preceding phrase.

EXAMPLE: We bought tickets *for the trip to Paris.*

The adjective phrase *for the trip* describes *tickets*. The adjective phrase *to Paris* modifies *trip.*

More than one adjective phrase may describe the same noun.

EXAMPLE: The painting *of the palace in the museum* is old.

▶ **Exercise 1** Identifying Adjective Phrases Write each sentence, underlining the adjective phrase or phrases in each. Then, draw an arrow from each phrase to the word it modifies.

EXAMPLE: France has miles of coastline.

ANSWER: France has miles <u>of coastline</u>.

1. France is the second-largest country in Europe.
2. The capital city of France is Paris.
3. Lyon, Toulouse, and Marseille are three other major cities in France.
4. The nickname of France is *L'Hexagone.*
5. The country borders two major bodies of water: the Atlantic Ocean and the Mediterranean Sea.
6. The Pyrenees Mountains along the southern border separate France and Spain.
7. One border country to the east of France is Switzerland.
8. North of France is the tiny principality of Luxembourg.
9. France controls a group of islands in the Pacific.
10. A rough estimate of the country's population is sixty million.

▶ **More Practice**

Grammar Exercise
Workbook
• pp. 57–58
On-line Exercise Bank
• Section 20.1
 Go on-line:
 PHSchool.com
 Enter Web Code:
 eek-1002

Get instant feedback! Exercise 1 is available on-line or on CD-ROM.

Adverb Phrases

A prepositional phrase can also act as an adverb.

▶ **KEY CONCEPT** An **adverb phrase** is a prepositional phrase that modifies a verb, an adjective, or an adverb by pointing out *where, when, in what way,* or *to what extent.* ■

The following chart shows that adverb phrases function in a similar way to single-word adverbs.

Adverbs	Adverb Phrases
She ran *swiftly.*	She ran *with speed.*
They were happy *there.*	They were happy *at the French cafe.*

If a prepositional phrase is an adverb phrase, it will answer the question: *Where? When? In what way?* or *To what extent?* In the first example on the right in the chart, the question *Ran in what way?* is answered by *with speed,* an adverb phrase.

Unlike an adjective phrase, which almost always follows the word it modifies, an adverb phrase may either follow the word it modifies or be located elsewhere in the sentence.

EXAMPLES: An alpine village vanished *during the avalanche.*

During the avalanche, an alpine village vanished.

Like single-word adverbs, adverb phrases can modify verbs, adjectives, or adverbs.

MODIFYING
A VERB: The runner dashed *past the spectators.*

MODIFYING
AN ADJECTIVE: The Loire Valley is rich *in historical buildings.*

MODIFYING
AN ADVERB: The French exchange student arrived late *for class.*

Like adjective phrases, two or more adverb phrases may modify the same word.

EXAMPLE: *In the afternoon,* we walked *to Notre Dame.*

▶ Speaking and Listening Tip
Many of the examples and exercises in this section contain names of French places and people, which may be unfamiliar or seem difficult to pronounce. Get together with a classmate who is studying French, and let him or her help you practice French pronunciation.

More Practice

Grammar Exercise
Workbook
• pp. 57–58
On-line Exercise Bank
• Section 20.1
Go on-line:
PHSchool.com
Enter Web Code:
eek-1002

> **Exercise 2** Identifying Adverb Phrases Write each sentence, underlining the adverb phrase or phrases in each. Then, draw an arrow from each phrase to the word it modifies.

EXAMPLE: France is situated above the Iberian Peninsula.

ANSWER: France is situated <u>above the Iberian Peninsula</u>.

1. France's geography is marked by various natural formations.
2. Several large rivers cut across the country.
3. Without a doubt, the Seine River is the most important French river.
4. It flows through Paris and empties into the English Channel.
5. The Rhone, Loire, and Rhine rivers are also important to France.
6. Two impressive mountain ranges exist within French territory.
7. The French Alps rise majestically near France's southwestern boundary.
8. Europe's second-highest peak is located within this mountain range.
9. Cable cars carry skiers high up the mountain.
10. The Pyrenees Mountains stretch along the Spanish border.

▲ **Critical Viewing** In what ways might a winter-sports enthusiast react to skiing on Mont Blanc, the highest peak in the Alps? Use a prepositional phrase in your answer. **[Infer]**

Appositives and Appositive Phrases

The term *appositive* comes from a Latin verb meaning "to put near or next to."

Appositives

Using **appositives** in your writing is an easy way to give additional meaning to nouns and pronouns.

> **KEY CONCEPT** An **appositive** is a noun or pronoun placed next to another noun or pronoun to identify, rename, or explain it. ■

As the next chart shows, appositives generally follow immediately after the words they identify, rename, or explain.

APPOSITIVES

Some French villagers, the *old-timers*, prefer to travel the dirt roads.

Her greatest attribute, *charm,* was not enough.

Notice that commas are used because these appositives are *nonessential.* In other words, they could be omitted from the sentences without altering the basic meanings of the sentences.

Some appositives, however, are not set off by any punctuation because they are *essential* to the meaning of the sentence.

EXAMPLE: The artist *Monet* was a great French painter.

Note About Terms: Sometimes, the terms *nonrestrictive* and *restrictive* are used in place of *nonessential* and *essential.*

Exercise 3 Identifying Appositives Write the appositive in each sentence. Then, write the word each appositive renames.

EXAMPLE: Jacques, our guide, told us about French people.
ANSWER: guide (Jacques)

1. Sixty million people, France's population, are dispersed throughout the country.
2. Many rural people, farmers, are moving to urban areas.
3. Today, nearly one sixth of the population is located near Paris, the capital.
4. The most mountainous area, the southeast, has experienced a large decline in population in recent years.
5. France has a lower population growth rate than its neighbor Germany.

Appositive Phrases

When an appositive is accompanied by its own modifiers, it is called an *appositive phrase.*

KEY CONCEPT An **appositive phrase** is a noun or pronoun with modifiers, placed next to a noun or pronoun to add information and details. ■

The modifiers within an appositive phrase can be adjectives, adjective phrases, or other groups of words functioning as adjectives.

More Practice

Grammar Exercise Workbook
• pp. 59–60
On-line Exercise Bank
• Section 20.1
  Go on-line:
  PHSchool.com
  Enter Web Code:
  eek-1002

Text

Get instant feedback! Exercise 3 is available on-line or on CD-ROM.

APPOSITIVE PHRASES

France was invaded during World War II, *the most terrible war the world has known.*

Amethyst, *a purple birthstone,* is the gem for February.

Fred explained numismatics, *the hobby of coin collecting.*

Appositives and appositive phrases may follow nouns or pronouns used in almost any role within a sentence.

WITH A SUBJECT:	Ernest Hemingway, *a famous author,* wrote in a terse style.
WITH A DIRECT OBJECT:	The chef prepared *escargots, a snail dish.*
WITH AN INDIRECT OBJECT:	I brought my brother, *a boy of six,* a souvenir from the Louvre.
WITH AN OBJECTIVE COMPLEMENT:	I chose the color purple, *an unusual color for a house.*
WITH A PREDICATE NOMINATIVE:	My favorite food was cassoulet, *a hearty stew.*
WITH THE OBJECT OF A PREPOSITION:	Store the onions in the cellar, *a cool, dry place.*

Appositives and appositive phrases may also be compound.

EXAMPLE:	Armand, both *his schoolmate* and *his confidant,* was always welcome in the house.

When appositives or appositive phrases are used to combine sentences, they help to eliminate unnecessary words. The following examples show how two sentences may be joined.

TWO SENTENCES:	Marseille is located on the Mediterranean Sea. The city is an important French seaport.
COMBINED:	Marseille, *an important French seaport,* is located on the Mediterranean Sea.

> ### ⚙ Grammar and Style Tip
>
> One good way to streamline your writing is to combine sentences using an appositive phrase. For instance, in the second example, the sentence could have started as two choppy sentences: The chef prepared *escargots. Escargots* is a snail dish.

▶ **Exercise 4** Combining Sentences With Appositive Phrases
Combine each pair of sentences by turning one of them into
an appositive phrase.

EXAMPLE: Marie is a Sorbonne student. She is well educated.

ANSWER: Marie, a Sorbonne student, is well educated.

1. France's educational system is one of Europe's best. It is
   subsidized by the government.
2. Children are required to attend school until they reach
   early adulthood. That is generally sixteen years of age.
3. *Écoles* educate children six through ten years old. *Écoles*
   are French primary schools.
4. *Lycées* are attended by students between the ages of
   eleven and eighteen. *Lycées* are French secondary schools.
5. Jean-Luc attends a religious school, as do nearly one fifth
   of the students in France. Jean-Luc is a tenth grader.
6. A large number of French students take the *baccalauréat*.
   It is a difficult college-entrance exam.
7. After passing the test, students are eligible to attend college
   for free for one year. The year is their freshman year.
8. Students are given licenses after three years of study. The
   licenses are degrees similar to a bachelor's degree.
9. Some students choose alternative post-high-school paths.
   The paths may be technical schools or trade schools.
10. France also offers its most ambitious students the option to
    attend specialized institutions called *grandes écoles.* Those
    students are mainly business, science, and engineering
    majors.

More Practice

Grammar Exercise
Workbook
• pp. 59–60
On-line Exercise Bank
• Section 20.1
  Go on-line:
  PHSchool.com
  Enter Web Code:
  eek-1002

Complete the exercise
on-line! Exercise 4 is
available on-line or
on CD-ROM.

The Panthéon, Paris

◀ **Critical Viewing**
The Panthéon
contains the remains
of illustrious French
citizens—among
them, writer Victor
Hugo and scientist
Marie Curie. How
might this building
serve to inspire the
university students
who pass by each
day? Answer using
an appositive
phrase. [**Relate**]

Verbal Phrases

When a verb is used as a noun, an adjective, or an adverb, it is called a *verbal.* Although a verbal does not function as a verb, it still retains two characteristics of verbs: It can be modified in different ways, and it can have one or more complements. A verbal with modifiers or a complement is a *verbal phrase.*

Participles

Many of the adjectives you use are actually verbals known as *participles.*

KEY CONCEPT A **participle** is a form of a verb that can act as an adjective. ■

The most common kinds of participles are *present participles* and *past participles.* These two kinds of participles can be distinguished from each other by their endings. Present participles end in *-ing* (*frightening, entertaining*). Past participles usually end in *-ed* (*frightened, entertained*), but many have irregular endings such as *-t* or *-en* (*burst, written*).

The following chart shows participles modifying nouns within sentences.

Present Participles	Past Participles
Limping, the hiker favored his *aching* ankle.	*Confused,* Nan returned to her *interrupted* work.

Notice that participles answer the adjective question *What kind?* or *Which one?* about the nouns or pronouns that they modify.

EXAMPLES: Irma's *shining* eyes betrayed her excitement.
What kind of eyes? *Answer: shining* eyes
The *shattered* window needs replacement.
Which window? Answer: the *shattered* window

Note About *Being* and *Having:* Participles also have a present perfect form.

EXAMPLE: *Having decided,* Madeleine acted quickly.
Being greeted by his friends, François shakes hands all around.

 **Learn More**

For information about irregular verb endings, turn to Chapter 22.

GRAMMAR IN LITERATURE

from **Two Friends**
Guy de Maupassant

Notice the highlighted past and present participles in this selection.

Reassured, they started to fish.

Opposite them Marante Island, *deserted*, hid them from the other bank. The little building which had housed a restaurant was shut up and looked as if it had been abandoned for years.

M. Sauvage caught the first gudgeon. Morissot got the second, and from then on they pulled in their lines every minute or two with a silvery little fish *squirming* on the end, a truly miraculous draught.

> **Exercise 5** Identifying Present and Past Participles Write the participle in each sentence. Then, label it *present* or *past*.
> 1. The established form of government in France is democracy.
> 2. The last adopted constitution of France was written in 1958.
> 3. According to the constitution, the people are represented by two large governing bodies.
> 4. The 577-member National Assembly is responsible for all proposed legislation.
> 5. The smaller group of elected officials, the Senate, must either ratify or veto the Assembly's legislation.

> **Exercise 6** Supplying Participles Complete each sentence by supplying the *present* or *past participle*, as indicated, of each word in parentheses.
> 1. The ___?___ Public elects a president to a seven-year term. (vote—present)
> 2. ___?___ elections determine the new members of the Assembly and the Senate. (stagger—past)
> 3. The ___?___ president must also select a Council of Ministers. (designate—past)
> 4. The prime minister holds one of the most ___?___ posts in the government. (tax—present)
> 5. The French president serves as the commander in chief of the country's ___?___ forces. (arm—past)

More Practice

Grammar Exercise Workbook
• pp. 61–66
On-line Exercise Bank
• Section 20.1
  Go on-line:
  PHSchool.com
  Enter Web Code:
  eek-1002

Get instant feedback! Exercises 5, 6, and 7 are available on-line or on CD-ROM.

Verb or Participle?

It is easy to confuse a participle acting as part of a verb phrase with a participle acting as an adjective because they share the endings *-ing* and *-ed*.

▷ **KEY CONCEPTS** A **verb** shows an action, a condition, or the fact that something exists. A **participle** acting as an adjective modifies a noun or a pronoun. ■

The following chart shows verbs and then participles as adjectives. Notice that as verbs, the words tell what someone or something does or did. The participles, however, describe someone or something.

Verbs	Participles
The dog is *snarling* at the plumber. (What is the dog doing?)	The *snarling* dog attacked the plumber. (*Which* dog?)
The mimes *delighted* their audience. (What did the mimes *do?*).	*Delighted,* the audience applauded. (*What kind* of audience?)

▷ **Exercise 7** Distinguishing Between Verbs and Participles
Identify each underlined word as a *verb* or *participle.* If it is a participle, write the word it modifies.

EXAMPLE: The French people have experienced <u>increasing</u> prosperity since the 1940's.

ANSWER: participle (prosperity)

1. Until World War II, France <u>based</u> its economy mainly on agriculture.
2. Today, the country has a very <u>diversified</u> economy.
3. France is a <u>leading</u> industrial power in the world.
4. It is a major producer of <u>advanced</u> electronics and other high-tech devices.
5. The government is <u>playing</u> an important role in the European Union.

▼ Critical Viewing
Use a participle as an adjective in a sentence describing two features of the French countryside depicted in this photograph. [Describe]

Participial Phrases

Participles may be parts of *participial phrases.*

▶ **KEY CONCEPT** A **participial phrase** is a participle modified by an adverb or adverb phrase or accompanied by a complement. The entire phrase acts as an adjective. ■

The following examples show different ways that participles may be expanded into phrases.

EXAMPLES: *Traveling quickly,* we saw much of the French countryside.

The tourist, *confused by the signs,* got lost.

Scanning the French dictionary, Ann found the words for "entrance" and "exit"—*entrée* and *sortie.*

Participial phrases are punctuated according to their use within a sentence. The following chart contrasts nonessential and essential participial phrases. In the sentences on the left, the participial phrases could be removed without altering the basic meaning of the sentence. However, if you remove the participial phrases from the sentences on the right, the meaning of the sentences will not be the same.

Nonessential Phrases	Essential Phrases
There is Craig, *standing by the bus stop.*	The boy *standing by the bus stop* is Craig.
Painted in 1497, the mural is Leonardo's masterpiece.	The mural *painted in 1497* is almost beyond repair.

In the first sentence on the left in the chart, *standing by the bus stop* merely adds information about *Craig,* who has already been identified. In a similar sentence on the right, however, the same phrase is essential for the identification of *boy,* because there could be many different boys in view. In the second sentence on the left, *painted in 1497* is an additional description of *mural.* In the sentence on the right, the phrase is essential. It identifies the mural that is being discussed.

 **Spelling Tip**

Notice that many French words—even some commonly used in English—have accent marks. Watch for accents on words such as *résumé, café,* and *entrée* and on names such as *André* and *Renée.*

▶ **KEY CONCEPT** Participial phrases can often be used to combine information from two sentences into one. ■

TWO
SENTENCES: We were exhausted by the climb up Mont Blanc.
We rested by the side of the trail.

COMBINED: Exhausted by the climb up Mont Blanc, we rested by the side of the trail.

▶ **Exercise 8** Recognizing Participial Phrases Write the participial phrase in each sentence. Then, write the word the participial phrase modifies. Finally, label the phrase *essential* or *nonessential.*

1. Pioneering in different fields, the French have been leaders in the scientific world.
2. The French government, having supported scientific research for more than 350 years, has made many advances possible.
3. In 1635, the Royal Garden became one of the first scientific research centers sponsored by a government.
4. King Louis XIV, known as the Sun King, founded the Royal Academy of Science.
5. Revered as the father of modern chemistry, Antoine Lavoisier gave much to science.

▶ **Exercise 9** Combining Sentences With Participial Phrases Combine each pair of sentences by turning one into a participial phrase.

1. Marie Curie helped found the field of nuclear chemistry. She did so studying radioactive elements.
2. French researchers have also achieved numerous medical breakthroughs. They have been striving to improve the quality of life.
3. During the eighteenth century, Marie François Xavier Bichat conducted research. It focused on the study of human anatomy.
4. Another French researcher, Louis Pasteur, invented several vaccines. He invented them for a world plagued by disease.
5. Pasteur devoted his life to scientific study. He made many other crucial discoveries.

▶ **More Practice**

Grammar Exercise Workbook
• pp. 61–66
On-line Exercise Bank
• Section 20.1
  Go on-line:
  PHSchool.com
  Enter Web Code:
  eek-1002

▲ **Critical Viewing** Use a participial phrase in a sentence comparing one aspect of Marie Curie's laboratory with an aspect of a modern one. **[Compare and Contrast]**

Gerunds

Many nouns ending in *-ing* are actually verbals known as *gerunds*. Gerunds are not difficult to recognize once you realize that they always end in *-ing* and always function as nouns.

KEY CONCEPT A **gerund** is a form of a verb that acts as a noun. ■

The following examples show some of the ways gerunds may be used as nouns.

GERUNDS	
Subject	*Eating* is my favorite pastime in France.
Direct Object	The French people make *visiting* a pleasure.
Indirect Object	Mr. Mendoza's lecture gave *traveling* a new dimension.
Predicate Nominative	One Frenchman's favorite activity is *debating*.
Object of a Preposition	Their well-behaved dog showed signs of careful *training.*
Appositive	Brady's profession, *advertising*, is very competitive.

▼ Critical Viewing
Describe a structure in the United States that is as recognizable as the Eiffel Tower to people around the world. Use a gerund in your response. **[Relate]**

Exercise 10 Identifying Gerunds Write the gerund in each sentence. Label each one *subject, direct object, indirect object, predicate nominative, object of a preposition,* or *appositive.*

EXAMPLE: She gave fencing her best effort.
ANSWER: fencing (indirect object)

1. Nearly one third of the French population is involved in some type of athletic training.
2. This is remarkable, because the schools focus mainly on learning.
3. Jogging, running, and walking are practiced by hundreds of thousands of French people every day.
4. Rugged individual sports—climbing and hiking—are popular all over France.
5. Skiing is another widely enjoyed individual sport.

Verb, Participle, or Gerund?

Words ending in *-ing* may be either parts of verb phrases, participles acting as adjectives, or gerunds.

▶ **KEY CONCEPT** Words ending in *-ing* that act as nouns are gerunds. They do not have helping verbs like verbs ending in *-ing*, nor do they act as adjectives, as participles do. ■

The following chart shows the same word functioning in sentences as a verb, a participle, and a gerund.

Verb	Participle	Gerund
Kevin is yawning at his desk.	The yawning boy was very tired.	Yawning is contagious.

▶ **Exercise 11** Distinguishing Between Verbs, Participles, and Gerunds Identify each underlined word as a *verb*, *participle*, or *gerund*.

EXAMPLE: The French have been <u>increasing</u> the national literacy rate for the last fifty years.

ANSWER: verb

1. <u>Reading</u> is a popular pastime throughout France.
2. <u>Reading</u> newspapers and magazines, the commuter waited for the metro.
3. French people are <u>reading</u> more periodicals than ever.
4. Articles written in both English and French are strong <u>selling</u> points for many magazines.
5. <u>Selling</u> magazines is a difficult task in the competitive French market.
6. One of France's oldest newsmagazines, *L'Express* is <u>selling</u> well after many years of publication.
7. The <u>leading</u> daily newspapers include *Le Monde, Le Parisien,* and *Le Figaro.*
8. *The New York Times* and *The Washington Post* are <u>leading</u> the way for other English-language papers in France.
9. <u>Publishing</u> books is an ever-expanding industry in France.
10. Ironically, authors are <u>publishing</u> more comic books today than many other types of books.

▶ **More Practice**

Grammar Exercise Workbook
• pp. 67–68
On-line Exercise Bank
• Section 20.1
  Go on-line:
  PHSchool.com
  Enter Web Code:
  eek-1002

Get instant feedback! Exercises 10 and 11 are available on-line or on CD-ROM.

Gerund Phrases

Like participles, gerunds may be joined by other words to make *gerund phrases.*

▶ **KEY CONCEPT** A **gerund phrase** is a gerund with modifiers or a complement, all acting together as a noun. ■

The following examples show just a few of the ways that gerunds may be expanded into gerund phrases.

GERUND PHRASES	
With adjectives:	*His constant, angry ranting* made Napoleon difficult to tolerate.
With an adjective phrase:	*Arguing about grades* will get you nowhere.
With an adverb:	*Answering quickly* is not always a good idea.
With a prepositional phrase:	Many places in France prohibit *walking on the grass.*
With an object of a preposition:	Pierre was incapable of *reciting the poem.*
With indirect and direct objects:	The French teacher tried *giving her students praise.*

Note About *Gerunds* and *Possessive Pronouns:* Always use the possessive form of a personal pronoun in front of a gerund.

INCORRECT: We never listen to *him boasting.*
CORRECT: We never listen to *his boasting.*

▶ **Exercise 12** Identifying Gerund Phrases Write the gerund phrase or phrases in each sentence. Label each one *subject, direct object,* or *object of a preposition.*
1. Making movies is a big business in France.
2. An average year for the French film industry entails producing roughly 150 movies.
3. Only India and the United States are known for making more movies than France.
4. Viewing American movies is a popular French pastime, but the French try promoting their own films.
5. Government restrictions limit the showing of American films to one third of the nation's theaters.

Text

Get instant feedback! Exercises 12 and 13 are available on-line or on CD-ROM.

▶ **More Practice**

Grammar Exercise Workbook
• pp. 60–70
On-line Exercise Bank
• Section 20.1
Go on-line:
PHSchool.com
Enter Web Code:
eek-1002

◀ Critical Viewing
What might be some of the reasons for the popularity of Notre Dame, the Gothic cathedral in the middle of Paris? Use at least one gerund phrase in your response. [Speculate]

▶ **Exercise 13** **Revising to Form Gerund Phrases** Revise each sentence, changing the underlined words to a gerund phrase. You may have to add or change words to keep the meaning of the sentence.

EXAMPLE: Construction of *Notre Dame de Paris* began in 1163 <u>when the cornerstone was laid.</u>

ANSWER: Construction of *Notre Dame de Paris* began in 1163 with the laying of the cornerstone.

1. <u>To complete the cathedral</u> was no small task
2. <u>To gaze at Gothic architecture</u> makes our thoughts ascend.
3. Gothic architects and artisans worked <u>to craft</u> the rose windows of stained glass.
4. <u>To build it</u> took teams of workers eighty-seven years.
5. No expense was spared <u>to erect</u> a church that would reflect the prestige of Paris.

Infinitives

The third and last kind of verbal is the *infinitive.*

KEY CONCEPT An **infinitive** is a form of a verb that generally appears with the word *to* and acts as a noun, an adjective, or an adverb. ■

The next chart shows examples of infinitives acting as nouns. When infinitives function as nouns in sentences, they can be used in almost as many ways as gerunds are.

INFINITIVES USED AS NOUNS	
Subject	To understand requires maturity and acceptance.
Direct Object	The peasants of France decided to rebel.
Predicate Nominative	The French soldier's only hope was to surrender.
Object of a Preposition	Our flight from Paris was about to leave.
Appositive	You have only one choice, to stay.

Unlike gerunds, infinitives can also act as adjectives and adverbs.

INFINITIVES USED AS MODIFIERS	
Adjective	The children showed a willingness *to cooperate.*
Adverb	During the war, the French people struggled *to resist.* Some people were unable *to fight.*

Exercise 14 Writing Sentences With Infinitives Write sentences on the subject of another country, using infinitives according to the instructions given.

1. Use *to visit* as an adverb.
2. Use *to watch* as a subject.
3. Use *to ride* as the object of a preposition.
4. Use *to eat* as a predicate nominative.
5. Use *to return* as an appositive.

More Practice

Grammar Exercise Workbook
• pp. 71–72
On-line Exercise Bank
• Section 20.1
Go on-line:
PHSchool.com
Enter Web Code:
eek-1002

Exercise 15 Identifying Infinitives Write the infinitive in each sentence. Then, label each *subject, direct object, predicate nominative, object of a preposition, appositive, adjective,* or *adverb.*

EXAMPLE: Museums are my favorite places to visit.

ANSWER: to visit (adjective)

1. France has a large number of interesting museums to visit.
2. Almost every museum contains numerous priceless works of art for the visitor to admire.
3. Since many museums were in disrepair, the government decided in 1956 to renovate them.
4. To modernize was the ultimate goal of the government program.
5. Constructed originally as a fortress by King Philippe August, the Louvre was intended to defend Paris from its enemies.
6. To explore France's most important museum requires several full days.
7. Massive crowds during the 1980's left the museum with only one option, to expand.
8. American architect I. M. Pei was hired to design a new entrance.
9. To enter the Louvre through the enormous glass pyramid is a most awesome experience.
10. To economize, visitors can buy a three-day pass for the Louvre and other French museums.

🖥 **Internet Tip**

To learn more about the Louvre's history and collections, go to its official Web site at **http://www.louvre.fr/** Choose the **English** option.

◄ Critical Viewing What features of this Louvre gallery make viewing its art an enjoyable experience for visitors? Use an infinitive phrase in your response. **[Evaluate]**

Prepositional Phrase or Infinitive?

The difference between a prepositional phrase and an infinitive is easy to recognize once you are aware of it.

KEY CONCEPTS A prepositional phrase always ends with a noun or pronoun. An infinitive always ends with a verb. ■

Notice the difference between the prepositional phrase and the infinitive in the following chart.

Prepositional Phrase	Infinitive
The French soldier listened *to the command.*	A general's purpose in the army is *to command.*

Note About *Infinitives Without* To: Sometimes infinitives do not include the word *to.* When an infinitive follows one of the eight verbs listed here, the *to* is generally omitted.

dare	help	make	see
hear	let	please	watch

EXAMPLES: She doesn't dare *go* without permission.
Did you hear the French vocalist Edith Piaf *sing* on that old recording?

Exercise 16 **Distinguishing Between Prepositional Phrases and Infinitives** Write the infinitive or the prepositional phrase beginning with *to* in each sentence. Then, label each *prepositional phrase* or *infinitive.*

EXAMPLE: When I am in Paris, I like to drive.
ANSWER: to drive (infinitive)

1. To travel is very easy in France.
2. There are many different ways to tour.
3. In Paris, the subway is a good place to start.
4. The subway will take you to every part of the city.
5. You can travel easily from the fancy Sixteenth District to the Latin Quarter, where students hang out.
6. You will want to buy a book of tickets good for ten rides.
7. Outside of Paris, high-speed trains can take travelers to cities in several parts of the country.
8. These trains can accelerate to speeds of more than 200 miles per hour.
9. Travelers are also able to take high-speed trains as far as Amsterdam, Holland.
10. Trains to most European cities leave Paris often.

Journal Tip

This section has provided information on France and French culture. Go back and take notes in your journal on some topics that have interested you. You can review them later to find a subject for a report or research paper.

Infinitive Phrases

Infinitives also can be joined with other words to form phrases.

▶ **KEY CONCEPT** An **infinitive phrase** is an infinitive with modifiers, complements, or a subject, all acting together as a single part of speech. ■

INFINITIVE PHRASES	
With an adverb:	Jeffrey's entire family likes *to rise early*.
With adverb phrases:	*To skate on the ice* without falling was not easy for him.
With a direct object:	He hated *to leave the city of Lyon*.
With indirect and direct objects:	They promised *to show us the slides* from their trip to France.
With subject and complement:	I would like her *to determine her own goals*.

▶ **Exercise 17** Revising Sentences to Change Participles and Gerunds to Infinitives Rewrite each sentence, changing the participles and gerunds to infinitives.

EXAMPLE: One of my favorite activities is watching the French cooking show on Channel four.

ANSWER: One of my favorite activities is to watch the French cooking show on Channel four.

1. Eating in France is eating well.
2. Many French people prefer dining at home.
3. They browse among the small shops and markets, looking for the freshest ingredients.
4. Many French people learn cooking with herbs and spices.
5. Making a delicious meal with little money is a notable ability of French people.
6. Tempting travelers, each part of the country offers regional specialties.
7. Choosing among the wide variety of cooking styles in France is a difficult task.
8. The object of one style, *haute cuisine*, is preparing rich, elaborately presented meals.
9. The object of the style known as *nouvelle cuisine* is making light dishes without the heavy cream of *haute cuisine*.
10. The aim of all French cuisine is preparing food that is not only delectable but also attractively served.

More Practice

Grammar Exercise Workbook
• pp. 71–74
On-line Exercise Bank
• Section 20.1
  Go on-line:
  PHSchool.com
  Enter Web Code:
  eek-1002

Get instant feedback! Exercises 16 and 17 are available on-line or on CD-ROM.

Section Review

GRAMMAR EXERCISES 18–27

> **Exercise 18** Identifying Adjective and Adverb Phrases Write the sentences, underlining each prepositional phrase. Identify each as either an *adjective phrase* or an *adverb phrase*.

1. Charlemagne was an influential figure in French history.
2. During the Middle Ages, he became the first true ruler of France.
3. In 771, Charlemagne inherited the territory of his father and brother.
4. He soon initiated a long series of wars against rival factions throughout western Europe.
5. Around this time, he also provided military aid to the Pope in Rome.
6. For a reward, the Pope gave Charlemagne the title of Holy Roman Emperor.
7. By the year 800, Charlemagne ruled over the majority of western Europe.
8. He founded his permanent capital of Aix-la-Chapelle in present-day western Germany.
9. Charlemagne imposed upon his subjects an intelligent system of laws and government.
10. He also established a number of crude educational centers among the monasteries under his control.

> **Exercise 19** Revising a Paragraph to Combine Sentences Using Appositives and Appositive Phrases Revise this paragraph, combining short sentences by using appositives and appositive phrases.

Joan of Arc was the national heroine of France. She saved the country from English rule during the Hundred Years' War. She was born in Domremy in 1412. Domremy was a small town in northeastern France. Joan believed she had a divine mission.

The mission was the liberation of France. Charles VII allowed her to lead his soldiers into battle against the English. Charles VII was the French king. After several important victories, Joan was captured by the Burgundians. The Burgundians were England's allies. The English executed Joan for the act of opposing the laws of the church. Such an act is called heresy.

> **Exercise 20** Supplying Participles Depending on the context of the sentence, supply either the present or past participle of the verb in parentheses. Then, label each participial phrase *essential* or *nonessential*.

1. The French author Voltaire is one of the most (admire) writers of the eighteenth century.
2. He was born with the (give) name François Marie Arouet in Paris in 1694.
3. (Serve) time in prison at age twenty-four, Arouet changed his name to Voltaire.
4. The young man was already a (respect) writer by this time.
5. (Achieve) popular and critical acclaim in 1718, the drama *Oedipe* is regarded as Voltaire's first major success.
6. In addition to being a writer, Voltaire was also an (aspire) philosopher.
7. (Rebel) against intolerance, censorship, and injustice, he founded a reformist group (call) the *Philosophes*.
8. This group of intellectuals attempted to change society by presenting (oppose) views of (accept) theories.
9. In all of his work, Voltaire offers his readers material (distinguish) by wit and intelligence.
10. The author of countless letters, plays, poems, and essays, he was clearly a master of the (write) word.

Exercise 21 Identifying Gerunds and Gerund Phrases Write the gerund or gerund phrase in each sentence. Identify the function of each as *subject, direct object, indirect object, predicate nominative, object of a preposition,* or *appositive.*

1. In 1642, the French king Louis XIV began the difficult task of ruling.
2. As he was only four years old, the running of France was left to his mother and her counselor until Louis was older.
3. After the death of his mother's counselor, Louis instituted a new policy: governing without a prime minister.
4. One of Louis's obsessions was expanding the power and influence of France.
5. Louis made conquering the Netherlands and defeating the English his priorities.

Exercise 22 Distinguishing Between Verbs, Participles, and Gerunds Identify each underlined word as *verb, participle,* or *gerund.*

1. Conquering Europe was the goal of French emperor Napoleon Bonaparte.
2. His conquering armies defeated the united forces of Europe in many battles.
3. French soldiers were conquering enemy armies for more than fifteen years.
4. After attacking Russia in 1812, Napoleon's army was forced to retreat.
5. In less than a year, France and allied European forces were fighting again.

Exercise 23 Writing Sentences With Verbal Phrases Write sentences about a political or military leader, using verbal phrases as instructed.

1. Use *leading* as a subject.
2. Use *inspired* as a predicate adjective.
3 Use *to continue* as a direct object.
4. Use *forgetting* as the object of the preposition *without.*
5. Use *to remember* as a subject.

Exercise 24 Identifying Infinitives and Infinitive Phrases Write the infinitive or infinitive phrase in each of the following sentences. Label each *subject, direct object, predicate nominative, object of a preposition, appositive, adjective,* or *adverb.*

1. Charles de Gaulle was to lead France through World War II and the difficult post-war years.
2. In the 1930's, De Gaulle thought the French army was unprepared for the war it was about to fight.
3. After the French government surrendered in 1940, De Gaulle felt he had but one choice, to escape.
4. He resolved to form a new French government in England.
5. For the remainder of the war, he continued to command the resistance groups and the Free French army.

Exercise 25 Find It in Your Reading In the excerpt from "Two Friends" on page 450, identify each highlighted participle as *present* or *past,* and name the word that the participle modifies.

Exercise 26 Find It in Your Writing In the compositions in your portfolio, find an example of an adjective and adverb phrase, an appositive, a participle, a gerund, and an infinitive. If you cannot find an item, challenge yourself to add it in an appropriate place in your writing.

Exercise 27 Writing Application Imagine that you are going to host a French exchange student. Write a brief letter telling the student about your school and town and what to bring to this country for the visit.

Clauses

Every clause contains a subject and a verb. However, not every clause can stand by itself as a complete thought.

> **KEY CONCEPT** A **clause** is a group of words with its own subject and verb. ■

Independent and Subordinate Clauses

The two basic kinds of clauses are the *independent clause* and the *subordinate clause.*

> **KEY CONCEPT** An **independent clause** can stand by itself as a complete sentence. ■

Independent clauses are used in several different ways.

STANDING ALONE:	That woman teaches Latin.
WITH ANOTHER INDEPENDENT CLAUSE:	Mudslides will engulf these hillside villas, *and some will be ruined.*
WITH A SUBORDINATE CLAUSE:	Brian asked to be excused from studying *because he was ill.*

> **KEY CONCEPT** A **subordinate clause,** although it has a subject and verb, cannot stand by itself as a complete sentence; it can only be part of a sentence. ■

EXAMPLE: The woman *to whom I introduced you* teaches Latin.

This sentence contains the subordinate clause *to whom I introduced you*, which appears in the middle of an independent clause.

EXAMPLE: *Unless the rain stops soon*, mudslides will engulf these hillside villas.

In this sentence, the subordinate clause, *unless the rain stops soon*, precedes the independent clause.

EXAMPLE: Brian asked *that he be excused.*

Here, the subordinate clause follows the independent clause.

Like phrases, subordinate clauses can function as adjectives, adverbs, and nouns in sentences.

Theme: Ancient Rome

In this section, you will learn about adjective, adverb, and noun clauses. The examples and exercises in this section are about Ancient Rome.

Cross-Curricular Connection: Social Studies

🌐 Learn More

To find out how different combinations of clauses determine different types of sentences, see Chapter 21.

> **Exercise 28** Recognizing
> **Independent and Subordinate**
> **Clauses** Write and label the
> independent and subordinate
> clauses in these sentences.
> 1. The luxury of baths, which we
>   have come to associate with Rome,
>   was imported from the East.
> 2. The earliest Roman literature,
>   which contained translations
>   from Greek classics, was based
>   on Greek models.
> 3. Roman boys, who received better
>   training than the girls did, were
>   taught the Greek classics.
> 4. The Greeks were conquered by
>   Rome, but culturally the Greeks were the conquerors.
> 5. Romans were proud of their civilization, although much of
>   it was Greek in origin.

▲ Critical Viewing
What might some
of the figures on
these ancient coins
represent? Answer
using a sentence
with a subordinate
clause. **[Speculate]**

Adjective Clauses

One way to add description and detail to a sentence is by
using an *adjective clause.*

> **KEY CONCEPT** An **adjective clause** is a subordinate
> clause that modifies a noun or pronoun by telling *what kind*
> or *which one.* ∎

Most often, adjective clauses begin with one of the relative
pronouns: *that, which, who, whom,* or *whose.* Sometimes,
however, adjective clauses may begin with a *relative adverb,*
such as *before, since, when, where,* or *why.* All of these words
relate the clause to the word it modifies.

> **KEY CONCEPT** An adjective clause begins with a relative
> pronoun or a relative adverb. ∎

In the chart on the next page, the adjective clauses are
italicized. Arrows indicate the noun or pronoun modified by
each clause. These are adjective clauses because they answer
the questions *What kind?* and *Which one?* Notice also that the
first three clauses begin with relative pronouns and the last
two begin with relative adverbs.

ADJECTIVE CLAUSES

Anyone *who reads about ancient Rome* will find it very interesting.

I finished reading the book *that you loaned me.*

We gave the story, *which we found fascinating,* a second read.

Spring is thc time *when peepers make their shrill evening sound.*

Our trip to Italy ended with a visit to the town *where my parents were born.*

Like appositives and participial phrases, adjective clauses can often be used to combine information from two sentences into one. Using adjective clauses to combine sentences can indicate the relationship between ideas as well as add detail to a sentence.

TWO SENTENCES: This statue represents a Roman soldier. He is dressed for battle.

COMBINED: This statue represents a Roman soldier who is dressed for battle.

Adjective clauses, like appositive and participial phrases, are set off by punctuation only when they are not essential to the meaning of a sentence. The chart on the following page contrasts nonessential and essential adjective clauses.

Notice that in the sentences on the left, omitting the adjective clauses would not change the basic message. However, if you were to take away the adjective clauses on the right, the message would not be complete. (See Chapter 28 for more about punctuating adjective clauses.)

▶ **Critical Viewing** What elements of this sculpture suggest the subject's status as a soldier? Use a sentence with an adjective clause in your answer. **[Analyze]**

Nonessential Clauses	Essential Clauses
One of Dickens's best characters is Charles Darnay, *who appears in Dickens's novel about the French Revolution.*	The novel *that everyone must read by Monday afternoon* promises to be very exciting.
Jean McCurdy, *who studied three hours every evening for a month*, won the statewide competition.	A student *who studies regularly* usually finds test-taking easy.

In the sentences on the left, the commas indicate that the clauses give additional information. In the sentences on the right, the lack of commas shows that the clauses are needed to identify the words they modify. Read the contrasting sentences aloud. Notice that you naturally pause before and after the nonessential clauses and that your voice drops as you read them. Realizing this should help you recognize clauses in your own writing that need to be set off with commas.

> **Exercise 29** Identifying Adjective Clauses and the Words They Modify Write the adjective clause in each sentence. Then, write the word or words the adjective clause modifies. Finally, label the clause *nonessential* or *essential*.

EXAMPLE: The Roman Empire, which achieved greatness, had humble beginnings.

ANSWER: which achieved greatness; The Roman Empire (nonessential)

1. The Punic Wars, a name derived from the Latin word for *Phoenician*, were fought between Rome and Carthage.
2. The first war, which made Rome a naval power, ended in 241 B.C.
3. A second war that was fought between the two powers began in 218 B.C.
4. The Carthaginians, who were led by Hannibal, marched on Italy but failed to completely conquer the Romans.
5. The third Punic War, which resulted in ruin for Carthage, removed any serious threat to Rome's supremacy.
6. Slaves and gold that reached Rome from the new territories kindled the idea that conquest was profitable.
7. The city that began as a republic was becoming an empire.
8. The Romans conquered Gaul, now known as France.
9. The Greeks, who looked on the Romans as barbarians, were instrumental in shaping Roman culture.
10. The period of relative stability that Roman rule brought to its conquered territories was known as *pax romana* (Roman peace).

> **More Practice**
>
> Grammar Exercise Workbook
> • pp. 75–76
> On-line Exercise Bank
> • Section 20.2
>   Go on-line:
>   PHSchool.com
>   Enter Web Code:
>   eek-1002

Get instant feedback! Exercise 29 is available on-line or on CD-ROM.

Relative Pronouns

Relative pronouns function in two ways.

▶ **KEY CONCEPT** **Relative pronouns** connect adjective clauses to the words they modify and act as subjects, direct objects, objects of prepositions, or adjectives in the clauses. ■

To tell how a relative pronoun is used within a clause, separate the clause from the rest of the sentence, and find the subject and verb in the clause.

THE USES OF RELATIVE PRONOUNS WITHIN CLAUSES
As a Subject

A structure *that is built on a good foundation* is built to last.
    Clause: that is built on a good foundation.
    Subject: that   *Verb:* is built
    Use of relative pronoun: subject

As a Direct Object

My brother-in-law, *whom my sister met at college,* is a poet.
    Clause: whom my sister met at college
    Reworded clause: my sister met whom at college
    Subject: sister   *Verb:* met
    Use of relative pronoun: direct object

As an Object of a Preposition

This is the book *about which I read enthusiastic reviews.*
    Clause: about which I read enthusiastic reviews.
    Reworded clause: I read enthusiastic reviews about
                which
    Subject: I   *Verb:* read
    Use of relative pronoun: object of a preposition

As an Adjective

The senator *whose opinion was in question* spoke to the press.
    Clause: whose opinion was in question
    Subject: opinion   *Verb:* was
    Use of relative pronoun: adjective

Note About *Understood Words:* Sometimes in writing and in speech, a relative pronoun is left out of an adjective clause. The missing word, though simply understood, still functions in the sentence.

EXAMPLES: The legendary heroes [*whom*] *we studied* were
                great men and women.
                The suggestions [*that*] *they made* were ignored.

Grammar **and Style Tip**

Although adding adjective and adverb clauses to your sentences can make your writing more interesting, be careful not to make your sentences too long. Too many long sentences can be just as distracting as too many short, choppy ones.

Relative Adverbs

Unlike a relative pronoun, a relative adverb has only one use within a clause.

KEY CONCEPT **Relative adverbs** connect adjective clauses to the words they modify and act as adverbs in the clauses. ■

The following chart shows an adjective clause introduced by a relative adverb.

More Practice

Grammar Exercise Workbook
• pp. 75–76
On-line Exercise Bank
• Section 20.2
  Go on-line:
  PHSchool.com
  Enter Web Code:
  eek-1002

THE USE OF RELATIVE ADVERBS WITHIN CLAUSES

Pat yearned for the day *when she could walk without crutches.*

    Clause: when she could walk without crutches
    Reworded clause: she could walk when without crutches
    Subject: she   *Verb:* could walk
    Use of relative adverb: adverb

Exercise 30 **Recognizing the Uses of Relative Pronouns and Relative Adverbs** Write the adjective clause in each sentence, circling the relative pronoun or relative adverb. Then, label the use of the relative pronoun within the clause *subject, direct object, object of a preposition, adjective,* or *adverb.*

EXAMPLE: The first great ruler ⓣhat we learned about was Julius Caesar.

ANSWER: that we learned about (object of a preposition)

1. Julius Caesar, about whom Shakespeare later wrote a play, was renowned as the conqueror of Gaul.
2. Rome, which was expanding quite rapidly, was undergoing a great deal of turmoil at home.
3. Julius Caesar, whose seven years in Gaul removed him from much of the intrigue, was a talented politician.
4. The army, which Caesar commanded ably, was devoted to him.
5. Julius Caesar claimed to be defending the republic at the moment when he and his army marched on Rome in 49 B.C.

▲ Critical Viewing How well do you think this sculpture represents real human qualities? Answer using an adjective clause. [Evaluate]

Exercise 31 Combining Sentences With Adjective Clauses
Turn each pair of sentences into a single sentence with an adjective clause. Then, underline each adjective clause, and draw an arrow from it to the word or words it modifies.

1. Caesar fought a civil war for four years after his march on Rome. He challenged those who might oppose him.
2. Julius Caesar was not a vicious conqueror. He made friends with his former enemies.
3. He was made dictator for life. This would be a position similar to that of a monarch.
4. Romans felt a monarchy would violate their ideals. They placed a high value on tradition.
5. Caesar's enemies united against him. They assassinated him in 44 B.C.

Adverb Clauses

Subordinate clauses can also act as adverbs.

KEY CONCEPT **Subordinate adverb clauses** modify verbs, adjectives, adverbs, or verbals by telling *where, when, in what way, to what extent, under what condition,* or *why.* ■

KEY CONCEPT All adverb clauses begin with subordinating conjunctions. ■

The following chart shows some of the most common subordinating conjunctions.

SUBORDINATING CONJUNCTIONS		
after	even though	unless
although	if	until
as	in order that	when
as if	since	whenever
as long as	so that	where
because	than	wherever
before	though	while

Recognizing these subordinating conjunctions will help you identify adverb clauses. In the next chart, the adverb clauses are italicized. Arrows point to the words modified by each clause. The first answers the question *When?*, the second adverb clause answers the question *Where?*, and so on. The last two adverb clauses are different because they provide information that a single adverb cannot. The next-to-last adverb clause answers the question *Under what condition?* The question *Why?* is answered by the last adverb clause in the chart.

More Practice

Grammar Exercise Workbook
• pp. 75–76
On-line Exercise Bank
• Section 20.2
Go on-line:
PHSchool.com
Enter Web Code:
eek-1002

Text

Complete the exercise on-line! Exercise 31 is available on-line or on CD-ROM.

ADVERB CLAUSES
Modifying a Verb
When you finish your book about Rome, you should then begin your report.
Modifying an Adjective
Tricia seemed happy *wherever she was.*
Modifying an Adverb
Faster *than the eye could follow,* the race car sped away.
Modifying a Participle
Laughing *until he gasped for breath,* Fred could not speak.
Modifying a Gerund
Driving a car *if you do not have a license* is illegal.
Modifying an Infinitive
We decided to remain in our seats *so that we could watch the movie again.*

▼ **Critical Viewing**
Using an adverb clause, describe characteristics of this sculpture that are not unlike men's features today.
[Compare]

Whether an adverb clause appears at the beginning, middle, or end of a sentence can sometimes affect the meaning.

EXAMPLES: *Before the year was over,* Caesar made plans to march into Rome.

Caesar made plans to march into Rome *before the year was over.*

Like adjective clauses, adverb clauses can be used to combine the information from two sentences into one. The combined sentence shows a close relationship between the ideas.

TWO SENTENCES: It was storming. They did not launch the attack.

COMBINED: *Because it was storming,* they did not launch the attack.

▶ **Exercise 32** Identifying Adverb Clauses and the Words They Modify Write the adverb clause in each sentence. Then, write the word or words each adverb clause modifies.

EXAMPLE: After Caesar was killed, his nephew Octavius
              gained power.
ANSWER: After Caesar was killed (gained)

1. Because he was Caesar's nephew, Octavius hunted Caesar's assassins after his death.
2. After he fought in Egypt and returned to Rome, he became emperor in all but name.
3. He was fortunate that the army had supported him.
4. Acting as if he himself were emperor, he was treated as one.
5. Since he was given the honorary title of Augustus, he has been known as Caesar Augustus.

Elliptical Adverb Clauses

Sometimes, words are omitted in adverb clauses, especially in those clauses that begin with *as* or *than* and are used to express comparisons. Such clauses are said to be *elliptical.*

▶ **KEY CONCEPT** An **elliptical clause** is a clause in which the verb or subject and verb are understood but not actually stated. ■

Even though the subject or the subject and the verb have been left out of an elliptical clause, they still function to make the clause express a complete thought. In the following examples, the understood words have been added in brackets. The sentences are alike except for the words *he* and *him.* In the first sentence, *he* is a subject. In the second sentence, *him* functions as a direct object. The use of each word is easy to see when the omitted words are noted.

VERB UNDERSTOOD: She resembles their father more *than he*
                     [*does*].
SUBJECT AND VERB   She resembles their father more *than*
UNDERSTOOD: [*she resembles*] *him.*

When you read or write elliptical clauses, mentally include the omitted words. Doing this should help clarify the meaning you intend.

🔲 **Research Tip**

Look for information about Roman emperors under "Ancient Rome" or under the names of particular rulers: "Julius Caesar," "Caesar Augustus," "Tiberius," "Nero," "Marcus Aurelius," and so on.

Exercise 33 Recognizing Elliptical Adverb Clauses Write each sentence, adding the missing words in any elliptical clause. Then, underline the complete adverb clause in each sentence, and circle the words you have added.

EXAMPLE: Roman emperors were treated more like gods than men.

ANSWER: Roman emperors were treated more like gods than (they were treated like) men.

1. Caesar Augustus was considered as divine as his uncle.
2. Rome's territories increased more under Augustus' rule than under his uncle's.
3. His successors expanded the empire even farther than he.
4. They depended on the army as much as Caesar Augustus.
5. The empire as we know it owes as much to his successors as to Caesar Augustus.

Exercise 34 Combining Sentences With Adverb Clauses Turn each pair of sentences into a single sentence with an adverb clause. Then, underline each adverb clause.

EXAMPLE: Rome was hard to rule. It was a large bureaucracy.

ANSWER: Rome was hard to rule because it was a large bureaucracy.

1. The nature and government of Rome resulted from Caesar Augustus. They evolved gradually.
2. Many emperors appointed their heirs. Control of the empire would be hereditary.
3. There were twelve emperors in the century following Augustus' death. Only four were related to him.
4. Augustus' line ended in A.D. 68. Nero, the last emperor related to him, died in A.D. 68.
5. The Senate might endorse or appoint a successor. Real power remained with the army.

Exercise 35 Writing Sentences With Adverb Clauses Write sentences about a historical era using adverb clauses, as indicated below.
1. Use *although* in a clause modifying a verb.
2. Use *if* in a clause modifying a gerund.
3. Use *as much as* in an elliptical clause.
4. Use *whenever* in a clause modifying an adjective.
5. Use *while* in a clause modifying a participle.

More Practice

Grammar Exercise Workbook
• pp. 77–78
On-line Exercise Bank
• Section 20.2
  Go on-line:
  PHSchool.com
  Enter Web Code:
  eek-1002

Get instant feedback! Exercises 32, 33, 34, and 35 are available on-line or on CD-ROM.

Noun Clauses

Subordinate clauses can also act as nouns.

KEY CONCEPT A **noun clause** is a subordinate clause that acts as a noun. ■

A *noun clause* acts in almost the same way as a single-word noun does in a sentence.

KEY CONCEPT In a sentence, a noun clause may act as a subject, direct object, indirect object, predicate nominative, object of a preposition, or appositive. ■

The chart on the following page contains examples of the various functions of noun clauses.

Learn More

To review basic sentence parts, turn to Chapter 19.

GRAMMAR IN
LITERATURE

from Julius Caesar
William Shakespeare

Act IV, Scene iii, Brutus' tent

In these lines, the noun clauses are highlighted in blue. In Brutus' last speech, notice that the word that, *introducing the noun clause, is understood.*

CASSIUS. *That you have wronged me* doth appear in this:
You have condemned and noted Lucius Pella
For taking bribes here of the Sardians;
Wherein my letters, praying on his side,
Because I knew the man, was slighted off.

BRUTUS. You wrong yourself to write in such a case.

CASSIUS. In such a time as this it is not meet
That every nice offense should bear his comment.

BRUTUS. Let me tell you, Cassius, *you yourself
Are much condemned to have an itching palm,
To sell and mart your offices for gold
To undeservers.*

Introductory Words

Noun clauses frequently begin with the words *that, which, who, whom,* or *whose,* the same words that are used to begin adjective clauses. *Whichever, whoever,* or *whomever* may also be used as introductory words in noun clauses. Other noun clauses begin with the words *how, if, what, whatever, where, when, whether,* or *why.*

KEY CONCEPT Introductory words may act as subjects, direct objects, objects of prepositions, adjectives, or adverbs in noun clauses, or they may simply introduce the clauses. ■

Note in this chart that the introductory word *that* in the last example has no function except to introduce the clause.

NOUN CLAUSES	
Subject	*Whoever is last* must pay a penalty.
Direct Object	Please invite *whomever you want.*
Indirect Object	His manner gave *whoever met him* a shock.
Predicate Nominative	Our problem is *whether we should stay here or leave.*
Object of a Preposition	Use the money for *whatever purpose you choose.*
Appositive	The occupied country rejected our plea *that orphans be cared for by the Red Cross.*

Exercise 36 **Identifying Noun Clauses** Write the noun clause in each sentence. Then, label the clause *subject, direct object, indirect object, predicate nominative, object of a preposition,* or *appositive.*

EXAMPLE: Whoever was Roman felt it a great honor.
ANSWER: Whoever was Roman (subject)

1. In the beginning, a Roman citizen was whoever was born in Rome.
2. Later, what was necessary was to be born in Roman territory.
3. Citizenship was available only to whoever was free-born.
4. Romans often made whomever they conquered slaves.
5. Romans often let conquered peoples do whatever they wanted as long as taxes were paid.

More Practice

Grammar Exercise Workbook
• pp. 78–79
On-line Exercise Bank
• Section 20.2
  Go on-line:
  PHSchool.com
  Enter Web Code:
  eek-1002

Get instant feedback! Exercise 36 is available on-line or on CD-ROM.

NOUN CLAUSES	
Direct object:	*Whatever he accomplished* would be satisfactory.
Adjective:	The little girl could not decide *which flavor of ice cream she would like.*
No function in clause:	The officials determined *that the polls had been rigged.*

Most words that begin noun clauses may also introduce adjective or adverb clauses. To decide whether a clause acts as a noun, look at the role of the clause in the sentence. In the following examples, all three subordinating clauses begin with *where,* but only the first is a noun clause because it functions in the sentence as a direct object.

NOUN CLAUSE: Caesar told his soldiers *where they would gather for battle.*

ADJECTIVE CLAUSE: They took the soldier to a tent *where a doctor examined his wound.*

ADVERB CLAUSE: She lives *where the weather is warm all year.*

Note About *Introductory Words:* The introductory word *that* is often omitted from a noun clause. In the following example, the understood word *that* is in brackets.

EXAMPLE: The secretary suggested [*that*] *you leave your name.*

▶ **Exercise 37** Recognizing the Uses of Introductory Words
Write the introductory word from each noun clause in Exercise 36. Then, label the use of each within the clause *subject, direct object, object of a preposition, adjective, adverb,* or *a word with no function.*

EXAMPLE: Whoever was Roman felt it to be a great honor.
ANSWER: Whoever (subject)

▲ Critical Viewing
Many aspects of present-day stadiums resemble the Roman Colosseum. Using a noun clause, describe one or two of them. **[Relate]**

Hands-on Grammar

Noun Clause Flip-and-Folds

Practice with a Noun Clause Flip-and-Folds to learn how to vary your sentences by using noun clauses in various positions. Begin with several narrow strips of paper about 4" long. On one strip, print WAS THAT WE WON THE CONTEST. On another strip, print IT WAS GOOD NEWS. On a third strip, print WE HEARD THE. Now begin making sentences. Put the first two strips together, beginning with IT WAS . . . ; cover up the WAS at the beginning of the second strip. You will have a sentence in which THAT WE WON THE CONTEST is an appositive.

> IT WAS GOOD NEWS   THAT WE WON THE CONTEST

Next, fold under IT WAS on the first strip, uncover WAS on the second strip, and use THE from the third strip. The noun clause is now a predicate noun.

> THE GOOD NEWS   WAS THAT WE WON THE CONTEST

Next, add WE HEARD THE to form these variations—one making the clause a direct object, and the other, again, an appositive:

> WE HEARD THAT WE WON THE CONTEST

> WE HEARD THE GOOD NEWS THAT WE WON THE CONTEST

Now, flip the two strips, fold under WAS on the noun clause strip, and fold under IT on the other strip. Note that the noun clause becomes the subject of the sentence.

> THAT WE WON THE CONTEST WAS GOOD NEWS

When you have finished, make other strips to flip and fold. Try these sentence parts: WE KNOW / WE TALK ABOUT / WHO WON THE CONTEST / IT WAS OUR FRIEND / WHEN WE WON THE CONTEST. Add other sentence parts that you can flip and fold to make noun clauses. Be on the lookout for some constructions that may actually be adjective clauses.

Find It in Your Reading Find examples of noun clauses in a story or article. For each one, identify its function in the sentence.

Find It in Your Writing Review a piece of writing from your portfolio. Combine two pairs of sentences using noun clauses.

Section Review

GRAMMAR EXERCISES 38–45

▶ **Exercise 38** Recognizing
Independent and Subordinate Clauses
Identify the independent and subordinate
clause in each sentence.

1. The ruins of many of the Romans'
   great buildings are still standing.
2. Later civilizations used stones from the
   Roman ruins when they wanted to build.
3. This scavenging, which occurred in
   many countries, has reduced the available information about the Romans.
4. The ruins of the city itself, which are
   dotted throughout present-day Rome,
   are most amazing.
5. Ruins can also be found in other
   European cities that were once a part
   of the Roman Empire.

▶ **Exercise 39** Identifying Adjective
Clauses, the Words They Modify, and
Introductory Words Write the adjective
clause in each sentence and the word
the clause modifies. Circle each relative
pronoun or adverb, and label its use
*subject, direct object, object of a preposition,
adjective,* or *adverb.* Finally, label the
clause *essential* or *nonessential.*

1. Ancient Rome, which had a million
   inhabitants at its zenith, was the
   supreme city of the empire.
2. A Roman aqueduct that was built in
   Spain still carries water to the city of
   Segovia.
3. Romans, whose concerns were unifor-
   mity and tradition, built or added on
   to cities.
4. Each city had temples, baths, theaters,
   and a forum, which served as a meeting place.
5. The Romans, who were fond of their
   comforts, had indoor heating and
   plumbing.

6. The things that wealthy Romans took
   for granted fell into disuse for many
   centuries after the Romans' fall.
7. Virgil, whom later cultures respected,
   was perhaps the most famous Roman
   writer.
8. He is a writer about whom much has
   been said in praise.
9. Virgil moved to Rome when his father's
   farm was confiscated.
10. The poet, whose greatest work was the
    Aeneid, died before he could give it the
    final revision.

▶ **Exercise 40** Identifying Noun
Clauses Write the noun clause in each
sentence. Label the clause *subject, direct
object, indirect object, predicate nominative,
object of a preposition,* or *appositive.*

1. Historians observe that the Roman
   Empire was attacked by many tribes.
2. The British Isles were the site where
   invading barbarians wiped out most
   traces of the Romans.
3. One fact became clear: that the Roman
   bureaucracy could no longer support
   the empire.
4. Whoever wanted to avoid paying taxes
   moved to the country.
5. Whatever group invaded a particular
   area often assumed Roman adminis-
   trative duties.
6. Roman armies often consisted of
   soldiers from whatever groups were
   living in a particular region.
7. Romans maintained whatever traditions
   they could.
8. Many people believed that the empire
   was still an entity.
9. Today's civilization owes whoever
   promoted Roman ideals a great debt.
10. We should remember onc fact: that
    much of our language and culture
    comes from the Romans.

> **Exercise 41** **Supplying Relative Adverbs** Supply a logical relative adverb to complete each sentence. Then, write the word or words it modifies. Finally, add the missing words in the elliptical clauses.

1. In the third century A.D., the Romans encountered trouble __?__ they turned.
2. Barbarian tribes wanted to cross the frontier __?__ they could settle in Roman lands.
3. Trying appeasement __?__ they resorted to war, the Romans hoped to avoid fighting.
4. Refortifying towns __?__ they could be protected against raids was common.
5. Taxes had to be raised __?__ these defenses could be built.
6. Economic recession was soon widespread __?__ were the crushing taxes.
7. The Goths crossed into Roman territory earlier __?__ the Franks.
8. To repel the invaders, Romans collected more taxes __?__ before.
9. As a ruler, the emperor Aurelian was better __?__ others.
10. One of his successors, Diocletian, divided the empire so that it came to resemble two empires more __?__ one.

> **Exercise 42** **Revising to Combine Sentences Using Adjective and Adverb Clauses** Turn each pair of sentences into one with an adjective or adverb clause. Underline each clause, and indicate the word or words it modifies.

1. Diocletian appointed a co-emperor. The co-emperor had the same powers as he did.
2. Diocletian laid more emphasis on the divine status of the emperor. He was less tolerant of Christianity.
3. Under Diocletian, the army increased in size. Conscription was reintroduced.

4. Later, Constantine gained control. He then reunited the divided empire under one ruler.
5. He ordered his soldiers to wear a Christian symbol on their shields. He wanted to see whether the God of the Christians would help him win a battle.
6. Tolerance of Christianity was promoted. Persecution was only a sporadic occurrence.
7. Christianity became officially protected. It was able to grow and develop within the empire.
8. Constantine built a new city called Constantinople. It then remained an imperial capital for a thousand years.
9. In A.D. 380, the emperor Theodosius came to power. He then forbade worship of the old pagan gods.
10. Constantinople and the East were progressing. The West was declining.

> **Exercise 43** **Find It in Your Reading** In the excerpt from *Julius Caesar* on page 474, identify the function of the highlighted noun clause in each sentence.

> **Exercise 44** **Find It in Your Writing** Look through your writing portfolio. Find an example of each of the three types of subordinate clauses—adjective, adverb, and noun. If you cannot find an example of a particular type of clause, find a place where you can add such a clause to a piece of writing.

> **Exercise 45** **Writing Application** Choose a period in ancient history that you would like to visit. Write a description of what you think life would be like for you in that time. Include at least one adjective clause, one adverb clause, and one noun clause.

Chapter Review

GRAMMAR EXERCISES 46–52

▶ **Exercise 46** Identifying Adjective, Adverb, and Appositive Phrases Write and label each adverb and adjective phrase. Identify the word or words it modifies. Write each appositive phrase and the word or words it renames.

1. Ancient Rome produced many writers and scholars of great renown.
2. Their influence was felt long after the decline of the Roman Empire.
3. Italian culture is indebted to Roman learning.
4. During the Middle Ages, Italian universities were considered models for other universities.
5. The earliest universities were intended for the training of clergy and administrators.
6. Latin, the Romans' language, was the language of the universities.
7. Italy was the center of a great change in education and culture.
8. The Renaissance, a flowering of art and culture, was inspired by classical antiquity.
9. The belief seemed justified by the Italian artists, Michelangelo, Raphael, and Leonardo da Vinci.
10. Their excellence in several areas—painting, sculpture, and architecture—led to the end of religious domination of culture.

▶ **Exercise 47** Distinguishing Between Participles, Verbs, and Gerunds Identify each underlined word in the following sentences as a *participle*, *verb*, or *gerund*. For each participle, tell whether it is *past* or *present*, and write the word or words it modifies.

1. In the first half of the twentieth century, Italy was struggling for power in Europe.
2. Desiring recognition, the country fought in both world wars.
3. In the first war, Italy was on the winning side, but siding with the losers in the second war led to much turmoil.
4. After World War II, voting in general elections revealed that a majority favored the formation of a republic.
5. The reigning king, Humbert, abdicated, leaving the country.

▶ **Exercise 48** Identifying Gerund, Participial, and Infinitive Phrases Identify each underlined phrase as either *gerund*, *participial*, or *infinitive*. If participial or infinitive, write the word or words it modifies. If gerund or infinitive, tell how it functions in the sentence.

1. Deciding to start in the country's capital, many tourists begin their trip to Italy in Rome.
2. Careful planning is necessary when visiting Rome.
3. Everyone looks forward to visiting the former center of civilization.
4. Having room for fifty thousand people, the Colosseum was the arena where Romans went to be entertained.
5. Being able to look at an ancient Roman interior is a good incentive for going to the Pantheon.
6. Looking almost anywhere in Rome reveals how the modern city is built on the ruins of Rome.
7. To visit some of the oldest ruins in Rome, walk two blocks from the Pantheon.
8. It is easier to travel in the Vatican City by shuttle bus than it is to walk.

9. <u>To call St. Peter's Cathedral impressive</u> is an understatement.
10. No modern Roman building is allowed <u>to be taller than St. Peter's</u>.

▶ **Exercise 49** **Identifying Adjective, Adverb, and Noun Clauses** Write the subordinate clause in each sentence, and identify it as *adjective, adverb,* or *noun.* For each adjective or adverb clause, name the word or words it modifies.

1. Florence, which was the birthplace of the Renaissance, has the best collection of Renaissance art in Europe.
2. Michelangelo, whose work includes the magnificent statue *David,* lived and worked for a time in Florence.
3. The people whom he lived with, the Medicis, were rulers of Florence.
4. Florence was the city that commissioned *David* from Michelangelo.
5. The Uffizi Gallery, where the best paintings in Italy are found, is in Florence.
6. Siena enjoyed status as a major military power until Florence defeated it.
7. As a result, the town has more Gothic art than it has Renaissance art.
8. The National Picture Gallery offers prime examples of Gothic Sienese art, even though most tourists prefer to see Renaissance art.
9. Milan's art is not as grand as that of other Roman cities, although its church is the third largest in Europe.
10. Before the day is over, we must look at Da Vinci's *Last Supper.*

▶ **Exercise 50** **Revising a Paragraph to Combine Sentences Using Clauses** Revise this paragraph, using clauses to combine short sentences. Underline your new clause, and label it.

Siena is convenient to Florence. It does not have any major attractions. The cathedral in Florence has a magnificent dome.

It is not as large as the one in St. Peter's Basilica. Michelangelo planned St. Peter's dome. He admitted it could never be as fine as the dome in Florence. The Palazzo Vecchio is a Florentine landmark. It was once the home of the Medicis. The Uffizi Gallery has the greatest collection of Italian paintings anywhere. There are works by Da Vinci, Raphael, Botticelli, and Michelangelo there.

▶ **Exercise 51** **Writing Application** Write a short essay about a place or an attraction in Italy that you would like to see. Tell why this place interests you. Include adjective, adverb, participial, and gerund phrases to add details. Also, include one adjective and one adverb clause. Label each of these items.

▶ **Exercise 52** **CUMULATIVE REVIEW Parts of Speech and Basic Sentence Parts** Identify each underlined item as a *subject, verb, direct object, indirect object, predicate nominative,* or *predicate adjective.*

1. We found <u>Milan</u> less magnificent than Rome or Florence.
2. <u>Do</u> people in Milan care more about soccer than about art?
3. Locals give their <u>team</u> the greatest support.
4. Milan is an industrial <u>city</u>.
5. It is more <u>famous</u> for fashion than for antiquities.
6. The City Tower of Siena offers tourists a three-hundred-step <u>climb</u>.
7. From the top is <u>one</u> of the best views in Italy.
8. The Uffizi Gallery is not a very large <u>museum</u>.
9. The square <u>contains</u> statues of great Italians.
10. Would <u>you</u> like to visit Fiesole?

Standardized Test Preparation Workshop

Recognizing Appropriate Sentence Construction

On standardized tests, questions that measure your ability to use phrases and clauses reveal your understanding of basic sentence construction and style. A phrase is a group of words that acts as a unit without a subject and a verb; a clause is a group of words that contains a subject and verb. When faced with these types of questions, first read the entire passage to get an idea of the author's purpose. Focus on the underlined group of words, and note any ways they might be combined without changing the meaning. Then, choose a revision that uses a phrase or clause to combine like ideas without changing the meaning or author's message. The following test items will give you practice with these types of questions.

Test Tip

Watch for repetition in consecutive sentences. Often, the correct answer eliminates the repetition by combining the sentences with a phrase or clause or by forming a compound subject or verb while maintaining the sense of the original sentences.

Sample Test Item

Directions: Read the passage, and choose the letter of the best way to rewrite the underlined sentences.

Ian bought a flexible airline ticket for his (1) upcoming vacation. Its flexibility means that he will be able to stop in several places.

1 A Ian just bought a flexible airline ticket for his upcoming vacation, and this means he can stop in several places.

B Ian bought an airline ticket for his upcoming vacation. He will stop in more than one place because it is flexible.

C For his upcoming vacation, Ian bought a flexible airline ticket, and this means he can stop in several places.

D For his upcoming vacation, Ian bought a flexible airline ticket, which will let him stop in several places.

Answer and Explanation

The correct answer is *D*. This revision combines the two sentences, successfully eliminating extra words and repetition while keeping the sense of the original. Choices *A* and *C* are awkward because there is no clear antecedent for the word *this*. Choice *B* moves words around without actually combining the sentences. It also leaves *it* without a clear antecedent.

▶ **Practice 1** **Directions:** Read the passage, and choose the letter of the best way to rewrite the underlined sentences.

There are two places Ian wants to visit.
(1)
The places are Hong Kong and New

Zealand. The flight leaves from New York.
             (2)
There is a one-day stopover in Alaska. From
                                      (3)
Alaska, the flight continues to Hong Kong.

In Hong Kong, Ian will spend a week.

1 A Hong Kong and New Zealand are two of the places Ian wants to visit.

   B Two places Ian wants to visit are Hong Kong and New Zealand.

   C There are two places, Hong Kong and New Zealand, that Ian wants to visit.

   D Ian wants to visit two places, and they are Hong Kong and New Zealand.

2 F The flight leaves from New York and has a one-day stopover in Alaska.

   G The flight leaves from New York, and there is a one-day stopover in Alaska.

   H The flight leaves New York, and then it stops over in Alaska for one day.

   J The flight leaves New York and has a stopover of one day in Alaska.

3 A From Alaska, the flight continues to Hong Kong, and Ian will spend a week there.

   B Ian will spend a week in Hong Kong after arriving there from Alaska.

   C From Alaska, the flight continues to Hong Kong, where Ian will spend a week.

   D The flight continues to Hong Kong; Ian will spend a week in Hong Kong.

▶ **Practice 2** **Directions:** Read the passage, and choose the letter of the best way to rewrite the underlined sentences.

After a week in Hong Kong, Ian will be
(1)
ready to move on. New Zealand is his next

stop. He is interested in the Maoris. The
                                      (2)
Maoris were the first known people in New

Zealand. It will be quite a journey. It will
                              (3)
be one that Ian most likely will never forget.

1 A After Hong Kong, Ian will be ready to move on to his next stop, and that will be New Zealand.

   B Once Ian has spent a week in Hong Kong, he'll be ready to move on to New Zealand.

   C After Hong Kong, Ian will be ready for New Zealand—the next stop.

   D After a week in Hong Kong, Ian will be ready to move on to New Zealand.

2 F Ian is interested in the Maoris, who were the first known people in New Zealand.

   G Called the Maoris, New Zealand's first people are of interest to Ian.

   H Ian is interested in the Maoris because they were the first known people in New Zealand.

   J Ian is interested in the Maoris, and they were New Zealand's first people.

3 A It will most likely be quite a journey that Ian will never forget.

   B Ian will most likely never forget the journey.

   C It will be quite a journey, and Ian will never forget it most likely.

   D It will be quite a journey, one that Ian most likely will never forget.

Effective Sentences

When we first learn to talk, we start by speaking single
words. Then, we begin grouping words together to form
sentences. It is at this point that we are able to start communicating in a meaningful way. Putting words together into
sentences—nouns or pronouns accompanied by verbs to
express complete thoughts—is the first step toward being
an effective communicator, both as a speaker and as a writer.
In this chapter, you will learn basic sentence functions and
structures—ways in which you can vary sentence structures
to make your writing more clear and interesting—and some
of the types of errors that can occur in your sentences.

Diagnostic Test

Directions: Write all answers on a separate sheet of paper.

Skill Check A. Label each sentence *declarative, interrogative, imperative,* or *exclamatory.*

1. Have you ever wanted to visit Antarctica?
2. Make sure to dress as warmly as you can for that adventure.
3. What an amazing animal a penguin is!
4. How can the penguin survive in such a frigid environment?
5. Their bodies are well adapted to life in subfreezing temperatures.

Skill Check B. Combine these sentences using the method indicated.

6. Antarctica was not discovered until the early 1800's. This was mostly because of its remoteness. (turn a sentence into a phrase)
7. Captain James Cook was the first explorer to cross the Antarctic Circle. He was on a mission from the British navy. (join with a relative pronoun)
8. Cook circumnavigated Antarctica. He never actually sighted the continent. (join with a comma and a coordinating conjunction)
9. Cook studied deposits of rocks in icebergs at sea. Cook concluded that a barren southern continent existed. (use a compound verb)
10. Cook reported his findings. Explorers from several other countries began their own search for the southern continent. (join with subordinating conjunction)

Skill Check C. Rewrite the following sentences to be more direct or to vary their beginnings as indicated in parentheses.

11. A Russian expedition sailed around Antarctica and discovered some offshore islands in 1821. (prepositional phrase)
12. The first known landing on Antarctica was by John Davis, who was an American explorer and whose main interest was commerce. (appositive)
13. James Weddell, traveling farther south than any other explorer, discovered the sea that bears his name. (participial phrase)
14. It was in the 1840's, at which time Antarctica's status as a continent was finally established. (Be more direct.)
15. One determined explorer, James Ross, was an explorer from Britain who sailed into a gulf that is now called the Ross Sea. (Be more direct.)

Skill Check D. Label each of the following items *fragment, run-on,* or *misplaced modifier.* Then, rewrite the item so that it is correct.

16. Many expeditions in the late 1800's and early 1900's.
17. One scientific expedition became caught on the ice, its members spent the winter of 1897–1898 stranded there.
18. Ernest Shackleton led a British expedition before turning back because of exhausted supplies to within 97 miles of the South Pole.
19. The Norwegian Roald Amundsen and a party of four reached the South Pole using dogs to pull their sleds on December 14, 1911.
20. Arrived five weeks before a British expedition led by Robert Scott.

The Four Functions of a Sentence

Sentences can be classified according to what they do. The four types of sentences in English are *declarative, interrogative, imperative,* and *exclamatory.*

Declarative sentences are the most common type. They are used to "declare," or state facts.

▶ **KEY CONCEPT** A **declarative sentence** states an idea and ends with a period. ■

DECLARATIVE: Hot-air balloons are flown mainly for recreation. Recently, adventurers succeeded in flying around the world in a hot-air balloon.

Interrogative means "asking." An *interrogative sentence* is a question.

▶ **KEY CONCEPT** An **interrogative sentence** asks a question and ends with a question mark. ■

INTERROGATIVE: Have you ever flown in a hot-air balloon? Do you think you would enjoy the experience?

▶ **Exercise 1** Identifying Declarative and Interrogative Sentences Write each of the following sentences on your paper. Identify each as declarative or interrogative, and punctuate it correctly.
1. Have you ever been to a balloon festival
2. We went to one in Albuquerque last year
3. Although I had heard about such festivals, I wondered what I would see there
4. When we arrived, the balloons were still on the ground
5. Next year, do you think you might go

Theme: Balloons

In this section, you will learn about the four types of sentences. The examples and exercises are about balloons.

Cross-Curricular Connection: Science

▶ Critical Viewing Write a sentence comparing these festive balloons to the kinds of balloons used in a balloon festival. **[Compare and Contrast]**

The word *imperative* is related to the word *emperor*, a person who gives commands. *Imperative sentences* are like emperors: They give commands.

KEY CONCEPT An **imperative sentence** gives an order or a direction and ends with either a period or an exclamation mark. ■

Most imperative sentences start with a verb. In this type of imperative sentence, the subject is understood to be *you*.

IMPERATIVE: Follow the directions carefully.
                Wait for me!

Notice the punctuation at the end of these examples. In the first sentence, the period suggests that a mild command is being given in an ordinary tone of voice. The exclamation mark at the end of the second sentence suggests a strong command, one given in a loud voice.

To *exclaim* means to "shout out." *Exclamatory sentences* are used to "shout out" emotions, such as happiness, fear, delight, and anger.

KEY CONCEPT An **exclamatory sentence** conveys strong emotion and ends with an exclamation mark. ■

EXCLAMATORY: She's not going to make that balloon trip without me!
                  I have been waiting for the opportunity all my life!

Exercise 2 Identifying Imperative and Exclamatory Sentences Write each of the following sentences on your paper. Add the correct punctuation to the end of each sentence. Label imperative sentences *I* and exclamatory sentences *E*.
1. Tell me about the festival
2. What an amazing sight it was
3. I have never seen so many balloons
4. Wait until next year
5. Come with us, and you'll see what I mean

Exercise 3 Writing the Four Types of Sentences Write a paragraph to one of your friends encouraging him or her to participate in some type of adventure with you. Use each of the four types of sentences at least once. Identify each type you have used.

More Practice

Grammar Exercise Workbook
• pp. 81–84
On-line Exercise Bank
• Section 21.1
  Go on-line:
  PHSchool.com
  Enter Web Code:
  eek-1002

Complete the exercises on-line! Exercises 1, 2, and 3 are available on-line or on CD-ROM.

Section Review

GRAMMAR EXERCISES 4–9

▶ **Exercise 4** Classifying Sentences by Function Label each sentence *declarative, interrogative, imperative,* or *exclamatory.*

1. Did you know that the Four Corners Hot-Air Balloon Fiesta is held in late May?
2. What I didn't know is that the International Balloon Fiesta is held in October.
3. Last year's festival was fantastic!
4. Which festival did you attend?
5. When you go to next year's festival, take lots of pictures.
6. Have you ever gone up in a balloon?
7. Miranda said it was the most exciting experience she's ever had.
8. What a thrill that would be!
9. Let me know if you decide to do it.
10. Maybe I'll try it, too.

▶ **Exercise 5** Supplying Appropriate Punctuation for Sentences Punctuate each sentence according to its function.

1. The Montgolfier brothers were the first to experiment with hot-air balloons
2. When they began experimenting in the 1700's, no one else had yet been successful
3. Who do you think their first passengers were
4. Even if you don't know, take a guess
5. A duck, a rooster, and a sheep were the first passengers
6. That's crazy
7. Balloon flights soon became a fad in Europe
8. Which was more popular, the hot-air balloon or the hydrogen-gas balloon
9. Look at this picture of the Montgolfier brothers
10. How daring they were

▶ **Exercise 6** Writing Sentences to Fit Functions Write a sentence that revises or answers each of the sentences below. The sentence you write should have the function indicated in parentheses.

1. Who first experimented with hot-air balloons? (declarative)
2. Is that the most amazing thing you've ever heard? (exclamatory)
3. I hope to learn more about ballooning. (interrogative)
4. Jacques Alexandre Charles and the Roberts brothers launched the first hydrogen balloon. (interrogative)
5. Will you tell me more? (imperative)

▶ **Exercise 7** Find It in Your Reading Skim through a travel magazine to find at least two examples of each of the four types of sentences. You can find your examples in advertisements and in articles.

▶ **Exercise 8** Find It in Your Writing Review a short story or a piece of autobiographical writing from your portfolio. Find at least one example of each type of sentence. Check to see that you have punctuated each correctly.

▶ **Exercise 9** Writing Application Write a brief narrative about a group of people your age who take part in an unusual adventure, such as a ballooning expedition. You can include dialogue. Try to use each type of sentence at least twice in your story.

Section 21.2 *Sentence Combining*

Books written for very young readers present information in short, direct sentences. While this makes the book easy to read, it doesn't make it enjoyable or interesting to mature readers. Writing that is to be read by mature readers should include sentences of varying lengths and complexity to create a flow of ideas. One way to achieve sentence variety is to combine sentences—to express two or more related ideas or pieces of information in a single sentence.

EXAMPLE: We went to the South Pole.
               We met scientists.

               We went to the South Pole and met scientists.
               We met scientists at the South Pole.
               We met scientists when we went to the South Pole.

▶ **KEY CONCEPT** Sentences can be combined by using a compound subject, a compound verb, or a compound object. ■

EXAMPLE: Moira enjoyed learning about Antarctic exploration.
                      Tom enjoyed learning about Antarctic exploration.

COMPOUND SUBJECT: Moira and Tom enjoyed learning about Antarctic exploration.

EXAMPLE: Lisa raced her dog sled.
                      Lisa won a prize.

COMPOUND VERB: Lisa raced her dog sled and won a prize.

EXAMPLE: Scott rode the icebreaker.
                      Scott rode the snowmobile.

COMPOUND OBJECT: Scott rode the icebreaker and the snowmobile.

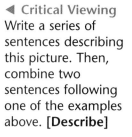

◀ **Critical Viewing** Write a series of sentences describing this picture. Then, combine two sentences following one of the examples above. **[Describe]**

▶ **Exercise 10** Combining Sentences Using Compound Verbs, Subjects, and Objects Combine each pair of sentences in the way that makes the most sense. Identify what you have done to combine them.

EXAMPLE: Milly chopped ice with a pick. She also used an axe.

ANSWER: Milly chopped ice with a pick and an axe. (compound objects)

1. Sir Edmund Winterbottom was an explorer. So was his son, Cecil.
2. They wanted to go on an adventure together. They decided to visit the South Pole.
3. Their trip took months of preparation. Their trip took detailed planning.
4. Long underwear had to be purchased. Then, warm coats had to be bought.
5. They would travel to the southern tip of South America. They would fly from there to the American Antarctic outpost.
6. The Winterbottoms also needed a guide. They required transport across the ice.
7. Following months of preparation, they were ready to go. They were excited.
8. Sir Edmund packed a large bag. Cecil did, too.
9. Their guide met them at the outpost with provisions. He also met them with his dog-sled team.
10. Within minutes, they had their equipment packed. They were off!

▶ **KEY CONCEPT** Sentences can be combined by joining two independent clauses to form a compound sentence. ▪

Use a compound sentence when combining ideas that are related but independent. Compound sentences are formed by joining two independent clauses either with a comma and a conjunction or with a semicolon.

EXAMPLE: The wind chilled the tundra. The snow battered my face.

COMPOUND   The wind chilled the tundra, and the snow
SENTENCE: battered my face.

EXAMPLE: The snowstorm lasted for hours. The wind and the snow mingled with the air.

COMPOUND   The snowstorm lasted for hours; the wind and
SENTENCE: the snow mingled with the air.

▶ **More Practice**

Grammar Exercise Workbook
• pp. 85–86
On-line Exercise Bank
• Section 21.2
  Go on-line:
  PHSchool.com
  Enter Web Code:
  eek-1002

Complete the exercises on-line! Exercises 10 and 11 are available on-line or on CD-ROM.

▷ **Exercise 11** Forming Compound Sentences by Joining Independent Clauses Combine the following sentences using the method given in parentheses.

EXAMPLE: (semicolon) The South Pole is very cold. Ice is everywhere.

ANSWER: The South Pole is very cold; ice is everywhere.

1. (semicolon) The South Pole is a point at the southern end of the Earth's axis. It rests in central Antarctica.
2. (comma and conjunction) It is often associated with the magnetic South Pole. They are 1,600 miles apart.
3. (comma and conjunction) The magnetic poles change location with time, a phenomenon known as polar wandering. The direction of wandering has been observed to reverse.
4. (semicolon) Compasses do not work at the magnetic poles. The magnetic field at these poles is vertical.
5. (comma and conjunction) As for the South Pole, a Norwegian explorer named Roald Amundsen reached it first. He did so on December 14, 1911.
6. (comma and conjunction) Today, people actually live at the South Pole part of the year doing scientific research. Amundsen's feat was herculean for its day.
7. (semicolon) Antarctica is the coldest continent on Earth. It holds the record for the lowest temperature ever recorded: –128.6° F.
8. (semicolon) The interior of Antarctica is a windy polar desert. Average precipitation is less than two inches each year.
9. (comma and conjunction) Coastal areas of the Antarctic are milder. Precipitation in those regions averages up to eight inches per year.
10. (comma and conjunction) The precipitation that falls on the South Pole is always in the form of snow. It usually is the byproduct of cyclones.

▲ **Critical Viewing** Write two separate sentences describing this penguin. Then, combine the sentences to form a compound sentence. [Describe]

▷ **KEY CONCEPT** Sentences can be combined by changing one of them into a subordinate clause. ■

Use a compound sentence when you are combining sentences to show the relationship between ideas. The subordinating conjunction will help readers understand the relationship.

EXAMPLE: We were frightened. We thought there might be an avalanche.

COMBINED WITH A SUBORDINATE CLAUSE: We were frightened because we thought there might be an avalanche.

Exercise 12 Combining Sentences Using Subordinating Clauses Using the subordinating conjunction or relative pronoun in parentheses, combine these pairs of sentences.

1. (although) Antarctica's total area in summer is about 5.5 million square miles. It does not always stay the same size.
2. (because) During the winter, Antarctica nearly doubles in size. A large amount of sea ice forms at its periphery.
3. (which) The true boundary of Antarctica is not the coastline of the continent but the Antarctic Convergence. It is a sharply defined zone at the southern ends of the Atlantic, Indian, and Pacific oceans.
4. (where) Colder waters flowing north from Antarctica mix with warmer waters moving south. The convergence is defined.
5. (because) A measurable physical difference in the ocean occurs at this point. The water surrounding the Antarctic continent is considered an ocean unto itself.
6. (even though) Antarctica has no native population. Scientific and support staffs reside there usually for no more than one year at a time.
7. (whose) The first person born in Antarctica was Emilio Palma. His father was an Argentine naval officer.
8. (which) Ninety-five percent of the surface of Antarctica is covered by ice. Antarctica contains 70 percent of Earth's freshwater supply.
9. (since) It has a thick ice cover. It has the highest average elevation of all the continents.
10. (although) The lowest point on the continent appears to be the Bentley Subglacial Trench, which is 8,200 feet below sea level and is covered by 9,840 feet of ice. Lower points may exist.

Exercise 13 Combining Sentences Using Subordinating Conjunctions or Relative Pronouns Using a subordinating conjunction or relative pronoun of your choice, combine the following pairs of sentences.

1. Seven nations—Argentina, Australia, Chile, France, Great Britain, New Zealand, and Norway—once declared territorial claims to parts of the Antarctic. The continent was uninhabited.
2. The Antarctic Treaty was signed in 1961. Their claims were renounced in the interests of international cooperation and scientific research.
3. Future economic development of the Antarctic landmass is unlikely. It is so icebound.
4. Extensive resources have yet to be harvested from the continental shelf. The technology is in development.
5. However, marine life in the Antarctic waters is being economically developed. It is plentiful.

More Practice

Grammar Exercise Workbook
• pp. 85–86
On-line Exercise Bank
• Section 21.2
Go on-line:
PHSchool.com
Enter Web Code:
eek-1002

Get instant feedback! Exercises 12, 13, and 14 are available on-line or on CD-ROM.

▶ **KEY CONCEPT** Sentences can be combined by changing one of them into a phrase. ■

Change a sentence into a phrase when you are combining sentences in which one of the sentences just adds detail.

EXAMPLES: My dog-sled team races tomorrow. We race on the tundra of the Antarctic.
My dog-sled team races tomorrow on the tundra of the Antarctic.

My dog-sled team races tomorrow on the tundra of the Antarctic. The Antarctic is one of the most inhospitable places on Earth.
My dog-sled team races tomorrow on the tundra of the Antarctic, one of the most inhospitable places on Earth.

▶ **Exercise 14** Combining Sentences With Phrases Combine the following pairs of sentences by changing one to a phrase.

1. Antarctica was once a central, tropical region of Gondwanaland. Gondwanaland was an ancient supercontinent on Earth.
2. Gondwanaland broke apart many years ago. It broke from the force of shifts in the Earth's plates.
3. The supercontinent split to form the separate continents in the current Southern Hemisphere. It split during the late Mesozoic era.
4. Antarctica consists of two main geologic areas. These areas are East Antarctica and West Antarctica.
5. East Antarctica is covered by massive layers of ice. The ice is thousands of meters thick.
6. West Antarctica appears to be a continuation of the Andes Mountains. The Andes are in South America.
7. Glaciologists and geologists speculate that without its ice cover, West Antarctica would be an island archipelago. An island archipelago is a sea containing a large group of islands.
8. Despite its frozen landscape, West Antarctica is home to Mount Erebus. Erebus is a 12,448-foot volcano.
9. The two areas are separated by the Transantarctic Mountains. The mountain range is running across the entire continent.
10. Within these mountains are many coal deposits and fossil remains. The remains come from the time that Antarctica had a tropical climate.

▼ Critical Viewing
Write a sentence about this photo in which you include the phrase *rising above the thick ice*.
[Describe]

Sentence Combining • 493

Hands-on Grammar

Folding in Phrases

You can practice what you have learned about combining sentences with phrases by doing the following activity.

Cut out several long, narrow strips from a legal size (8 1/2" by 14") piece of paper. On each strip, write one of the following pairs of related sentences:

Antarctica is a cold, white continent. It is covered almost entirely by ice and snow.

One animal that thrives in Antarctica is the southern elephant seal. It is the largest seal in the world.

Mount Erebus is Antarctica's most active volcano. It occasionally spurts volcanic rock over the island on which it sits.

In 1911, Norwegian explorer Roald Amundsen won the race to the South Pole. His victory was by a five-week margin.

Now combine the sentence pairs by folding over the paper to cover up the first few words of the second sentence that come before the phrase you want to connect to the first sentence. For example, by covering up *It is* on the second sentence of the first pair, you would be able to read: *Antarctica is a cold, white continent covered almost entirely by ice and snow.*

Read your combined sentences aloud to be sure they make sense. Then, write some new pairs of sentences of your own on additional strips of paper, and test your classmates' ability to combine them.

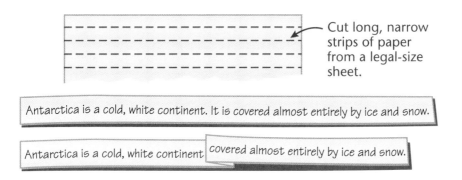

Cut long, narrow strips of paper from a legal-size sheet.

Antarctica is a cold, white continent. It is covered almost entirely by ice and snow.

Antarctica is a cold, white continent covered almost entirely by ice and snow.

Find It in Your Reading Select a long sentence from one of your textbooks. Split it into several shorter sentences that the writer may have combined.

Find It in Your Writing Look through your portfolio for paragraphs that contain several short sentences in a row. Combine the sentences using one of the ways you have learned in this chapter.

Section Review

GRAMMAR EXERCISES 15–20

Exercise 15 Combining Sentences Using Compound Parts Combine each pair of sentences by creating a compound subject, verb, or object.

1. I watched a program about the South Pole. My dad saw it with me.
2. The show focused on exploration. It also highlighted elements of the climate.
3. The geography of Antarctica was mentioned. Also, its wildlife was discussed.
4. The program started on Monday. It concluded on Tuesday.
5. We found the program interesting. It was also intellectually stimulating.

Exercise 16 Combining Clauses and Phrases Combine each pair of sentences by creating a compound sentence, forming a complex sentence, or changing one sentence into a phrase.

1. The soil in the interior of Antarctica is very dry. The area receives only two inches of snow each year.
2. The soil is so dry. Some geologists call it a "polar desert."
3. Rainfall and snowfall are heavier in some areas. These areas are along the coasts.
4. Icy winds make the continent seem even colder. They blow across Antarctica throughout the year.
5. The largest ice shelf in Antarctica is the Ross Ice Shelf. It is the size of Texas.
6. Antarctica is isolated from the rest of the world. It has avoided problems found on other continents.
7. The ice there is the purest in the world. It is untainted by industrial pollution.
8. Residents obtain the water they need. They do this by melting ice and snow.
9. The climate is so cold. Few insects live on the mainland of Antarctica.
10. Few animals live on the mainland. The Antarctic Ocean abounds with wildlife.

Exercise 17 Revising a Paragraph by Combining Sentences Using phrases, combine pairs of sentences in the following passage.

Antarctica was not discovered until the early 1800's. This delay occurred because of its remoteness. The ancient Greeks first theorized about the existence of Antarctica. They were advanced in geography. They believed that the Southern Hemisphere must have large continents. These continents existed to balance those in the Northern Hemisphere. In 1772, British explorer James Cook sailed as far south as he could. Cook searched for the southern continent. Huge ice blocks prevented him from reaching Antarctica. He did spot many whales and seals. Groups of hunters arrived in the area. They arrived soon after Cook's voyage. Several hunters reached the continent. This occurred a few years later.

Exercise 18 Find It in Your Reading Select a long sentence from a story or textbook. Determine what ideas the writer has combined in the sentence and what method was used to combine ideas.

Exercise 19 Find It in Your Writing Revise a piece of writing from your portfolio. Combine at least five pairs of sentences, using different techniques.

Exercise 20 Writing Application Imagine that you were an early explorer of Antarctica. Write several short sentences from the journal you kept. Then, combine some of the sentences.

Varying Sentences

Vary your sentences to produce a rhythm, to achieve an effect, or to emphasize key points or connections among ideas. There are many ways that you can achieve sentence variety.

Vary Sentence Length

You have already learned that you can combine several short, choppy sentences to form a longer sentence. However, having too many long sentences in a row is as uninteresting as having too many short ones. When you want to emphasize a point or surprise a reader, insert a short, direct sentence to interrupt the flow of long sentences. Look at this example:

The viola, which evolved from medieval fiddles, is first depicted in early sixteenth-century drawings and literature. Like most instruments of the Renaissance, it was built in a range of sizes. Played standing up, the largest violas were the specialties of Italian masters. <u>One such master was Antonio Stradivari.</u>

Some sentences contain only one idea and cannot be broken up. It may be possible, however, to state the idea in a shorter sentence. Other sentences contain two or more ideas and might be shortened by breaking up the ideas.

> **Exercise 21** **Making Simpler Sentences** In the following items, break up long sentences into two or more sentences or restate long sentences in a simpler, more direct way.
> 1. Plucked lutes include the banjo and guitar as well as the Arabic *oud*, from which the name of the European lute is derived.
> 2. The neck of a lute may be a short elongation of the body, as in the Chinese *pipa*, or it may be a separate element fastened to or piercing the body.
> 3. Frequently, the neck incorporates a fingerboard, which may have frets, against which the strings can be pressed to alter their sound.
> 4. The technique of bowing is not as old as that of plucking, and fiddles, or bowed lutes, such as the violin or viol, arrived in Europe from Asia only in the Middle Ages.
> 5. The violin and its relatives, at first associated with country dance music and considered inferior to the quieter, more sedate viol, became dominant during the 1700's.

Theme: Musical Instruments

In this section, you will learn ways to vary sentence lengths and beginnings to make your writing more interesting. The examples and exercises are about different musical instruments.

Cross-Curricular Connection: Music

More Practice

Grammar Exercise Workbook
• pp. 87–88
On-line Exercise Bank
• Section 21.3
  Go on-line:
  PHSchool.com
  Enter Web Code:
  eek-1002

Complete the exercises on-line! Exercises 21 and 22 are available on-line or on CD-ROM.

GRAMMAR IN
LITERATURE

from **Like the Sun**
R. K. Narayan

The writer has used both long and short sentences in this passage to make the writing more interesting.

. . . A drummer and a violinist, already seated on a Rangoon mat, were waiting for him. The headmaster sat down between them like a professional at a concert, cleared his throat and began an alapana, and paused to ask, "Isn't it good Kalyani?" Sekhar pretended not to have heard the question. The headmaster went on to sing a full song composed by Thyagaraja and followed it with two more. All the time the headmaster was singing, Sekhar went on commenting within himself, He croaks like a dozen frogs, He is bellowing like a buffalo. Now he sounds like loose window shutters in a storm.

▼ **Critical Viewing**
Write two sentences, one long and one short, to compare the sound of a violin to that of a guitar or a bass. [**Compare**]

✿ **Grammar and Style Tip**

One way to test how smoothly your sentences flow is to read them aloud. By reading your work aloud in a lively way, you will be able to identify when your sentence structure falls flat, grows boring, or does not provide the necessary interest for the subject matter. Reading your work aloud also helps you catch some of the common sentence errors discussed later in this chapter.

▶ **Exercise 22** Revising a Paragraph to Improve Sentence Variety Rewrite this paragraph, breaking up long sentences into two or more simple sentences or restating long sentences more simply.

  Just as mechanical inventions served European music when the fully developed keyboard arose in the Middle Ages, so electrical engineers have offered twentieth-century musicians innovative ways of producing and controlling sounds. Since the 1930's, electric amplification has altered the technique of popular singers and instrumentalists. Electric organs have mostly influenced popular music, but since the mid-1960's, synthesizers have been important tools of composers of many music styles. Except in the manipulations of sound used in rock music, however, amplification, like broadcasting and recording, serves chiefly to disseminate music rather than to create it. With the electric guitar, such amplification replaced the sound box and stimulated new musical effects; the long-term implications of sound production cannot yet be predicted.

Varying Sentence Openers and Structures

Another way to produce sentence variety is to avoid starting each sentence in the same way. Consider these options:

START WITH A NOUN: The piano is a difficult instrument to learn.

START WITH AN ADVERB: Surprisingly, the piano is a difficult instrument to learn.

START WITH A PARTICIPLE: Having played the piano, I know it is a difficult instrument to learn.

START WITH A PREPOSITIONAL PHRASE: For many young musicians, the piano is difficult to learn.

You can also vary sentence beginnings by reversing the traditional subject-verb order.

EXAMPLES:

    S   LV COMP
The pipers are here.

COMP LV   S
Here are the pipers.

    S   V   ADV. PHRASE
The parade came around the corner.

    ADV. PHRASE   V   S
Around the corner came the parade.

Exercise 23 Revising to Vary Sentence Openers Follow the instructions in parentheses to revise each sentence.
1. (Start with an adverb.) All drums are separately classified as part of the membranophone family of instruments.
2. (Start with a prepositional phrase.) A drum has one or two heads for sound resonance.
3. (Start with a participle.) The heads of a drum stretched across a frame are usually made of plastic or animal skin.
4. (Start with a prepositional phrase.) Cylindrical drums vary in size from huge basses to shallow snares.
5. (Start with an adverb.) The snare's intense, crisp sound surprisingly makes up for its lack in size.

Exercise 24 Revising to Invert Sentences Rewrite each sentence, reversing the traditional subject-verb order.
1. The orchestra enters from backstage.
2. The conductor is here.
3. Rehearsal is held in the auditorium.
4. The instruments remained silent before the concert.
5. The sound of a violin is beautiful.

More Practice

Grammar Exercise Workbook
• pp. 89–92
On-line Exercise Bank
• Section 21.3
  Go on-line:
  PHSchool.com
  Enter Web Code:
  eek-1002

Complete the exercises on-line! Exercises 23 and 24 are available on-line or on CD-ROM.

Section 21.3 Section Review

GRAMMAR EXERCISES 25–31

Exercise 25 Revising to Simplify Long Sentences In these items, break up long sentences into simple sentences or restate them more simply.

1. The xylophone, whose name comes from the Greek *xylon,* meaning "wood," is a percussion instrument consisting of a series of wooden bars that are struck with mallets to produce sounds.
2. Xylophones were developed in Southeast Asia by the fourteenth century, and they arrived and took root as folk instruments in Central Europe about 1500.
3. In Africa, where the xylophone was imported from Madagascar, its use spread throughout the continent; the xylophone became a prominent instrument in African music.
4. Africans who had been enslaved introduced the xylophone to Latin America, where it is known as a *marimba.*
5. By the nineteenth century, performers had popularized the xylophone in western Europe, and its first orchestral use was in *Danse Macabre* (1874) by the French composer Camille Saint-Saëns.

Exercise 26 Varying Sentence Openers Rewrite this sentence five times, each time beginning with one of the sentence parts listed below: *The members of the orchestra tuned their instruments.* (1) an adverb; (2) a prepositional phrase; (3) a participial phrase; (4) a different prepositional phrase; (5) a different adverb

Exercise 27 Revising Sentences by Inverting Subject-Verb Order Revise each sentence using an inverted structure.

1. The parade marches down the street.
2. The people along the curb are smiling and waving.
3. The brass instruments shine in the sun.
4. The shofar sounded low and mournful.
5. The orchestra is here.

Exercise 28 Revising Sentences in Several Ways Revise the paragraph below by varying sentence length, sentence beginnings, or word order.

A glass harmonica was invented by Benjamin Franklin. It is known as the Franklin harmonica and consists of a set of glass bowls, graduated in size to produce distinct pitches, and the bowls are fine-tuned by filling them with different amounts of water. The Franklin harmonica was popular in the early 1800's. Mozart and Beethoven were intrigued by the instrument. The pieces they wrote for the instrument are still performed occasionally.

Exercise 29 Find It in Your Reading Find a paragraph in a magazine article that illustrates strong sentence variety. Present your example to the class.

Exercise 30 Find It in Your Writing Make at least five revisions in a piece of your own writing to improve sentence variety.

Exercise 31 Writing Application Write a review of a concert by the school band or by your favorite band. Use sentences of different lengths, and vary the way your sentences begin or their subject-verb order to provide more interesting reading.

Avoiding Sentence Problems

Fragments, run-on sentences, and misplaced modifiers can all make your writing confusing. Being able to recognize the parts of sentences and different kinds of clauses and phrases can help you avoid certain errors in your writing.

Recognizing Fragments

Some groups of words, even though they have a capital at the beginning and a period at the end, are not complete sentences. They are *fragments*.

▶ **KEY CONCEPT** A **fragment** is a group of words that does not express a complete thought but is punctuated as if it were a sentence. ■

A fragment is only *part* of a sentence, but a sentence always has a subject *and* a verb. A fragment does not always have both parts. It can be a group of words with no subject. It can be a group of words that includes a possible subject but no verb. It can be a group of words with a possible subject and only part of a possible verb. It can even be a subordinate clause standing alone.

▼ **Critical Viewing** What happens if only part of an orchestra arrives for a concert? How does that compare to a sentence fragment? **[Compare]**

FRAGMENTS

To hear the orchestra play.
Listened carefully and happily.
The tuba in the marching band.
The parade coming around the bend.
When the band played.

You will usually be able to tell whether a group of words expresses a complete thought. One trick is to read the words aloud. This will help you hear whether or not some part is missing.

In the chart below, words have been added to the preceding fragments to make complete sentences. Read each italicized fragment; then read the sentence. Can you hear the difference? What part is missing in the fragment?

COMPLETED SENTENCES

We went *to hear the orchestra play.*
We *listened carefully and happily.*
I play *the tuba in the marching band.*
The parade was *coming around the bend.*
When the band played, I didn't recognize the song.

Each of the preceding examples needed one or more new parts. The first needed both a subject and a verb. The second needed only a subject. The third became complete when a subject and a verb were added. The fourth became complete when a helping verb was added. The final example needed a complete independent clause to go with the subordinate clause.

▶ **Exercise 32** Recognizing Sentence Fragments Write *F* for each item that is a fragment and S for complete sentences.

1. Consists of woodwind, brass, and percussion instruments.
2. Originally a section in ancient Greek theaters.
3. Located between the stage and the audience.
4. Dancers and instrumentalists used this area.
5. In a modern theater.
6. The part reserved for musicians called the orchestra pit.
7. The term *orchestra* now designates an area of seating in an auditorium.
8. The string section in four parts.
9. The double basses often duplicate the cello part an octave lower.
10. The number of instruments can vary.

Text

Get instant feedback! Exercise 32 is available on-line or on CD-ROM.

▶ **More Practice**

Grammar Exercise Workbook
• pp. 93–94
On-line Exercise Bank
• Section 21.4
Go on-line:
PHSchool.com
Enter Web Code:
eek-1002

Correcting Phrase Fragments

A phrase by itself is a fragment. It cannot stand alone because it does not have both a subject and a verb.

▶ **KEY CONCEPT** A phrase should not be capitalized and punctuated as if it were a sentence. ■

Three types of phrases—prepositional, participial, and infinitive—are often mistaken for sentences. A *phrase fragment* can be changed into a sentence in either of two ways. The first way is to add the phrase fragment to a nearby sentence. This example shows a prepositional phrase following a sentence.

FRAGMENT: The musicians took their places. *On the stage.*

You can correct this fragment simply by attaching the phrase to the preceding sentence.

ADDED TO The musicians took their places
NEARBY SENTENCE: *on the stage.*

You can correct other fragments simply by attaching them to the beginning of a sentence. The participial phrase fragment in the next example can easily be corrected in this way.

FRAGMENT: *Waiting for silence.* The conductor held his baton in the air.

ADDED TO *Waiting for silence,* the conductor held
NEARBY SENTENCE: his baton in the air.

Sometimes, however, you may not be able to correct a phrase fragment by adding it to a nearby sentence. Then, you will need to use the second way to change a phrase fragment into a sentence: Correct the fragment by adding to the phrase whatever is needed to make it a complete sentence. Often this method requires adding a subject or a verb.

CHANGING PHRASE FRAGMENTS INTO SENTENCES

Phrase Fragments	Complete Sentences
By the conductor.	The seating of an orchestra is determined *by the conductor.*
Listening to the opera.	*Listening to the opera,* I found myself swept away.
To play an instrument.	I would like *to play an instrument.*

◄ **Critical Viewing**
The timpani is sometimes called a kettledrum. Explain why in a complete sentence. [**Make a Judgment**]

Exercise 33 Revising to Change Phrase Fragments Into Sentences Use each of the following phrase fragments in a sentence. You may use the phrase at the beginning, at the end, or in any other position in the sentence. Check to see that each of your sentences contains a subject and a verb.

EXAMPLE: Arriving at the music hall.

ANSWER: Arriving at the music hall, the performers tuned their instruments.

1. Accompanied by other musicians.
2. Into the night air.
3. To the left of the conductor.
4. Behind the strings section.
5. Playing the kettledrum.
6. Hearing the glockenspiel.
7. With a harp or piano.
8. Feeling the pounding of the bass drum.
9. Without brass instruments.
10. Reserving two orchestra seats.

More Practice

Grammar Exercise Workbook
• pp. 93–94
On-line Exercise Bank
• Section 21.4
  Go on-line:
  PHSchool.com
  Enter Web Code:
  eek-1002

Complete the exercise on-line! Exercise 33 is available on-line or on CD-ROM.

Correcting Clause Fragments

All clauses have subjects and verbs, but some cannot stand alone as sentences.

▶ **KEY CONCEPT** A subordinate clause should not be capitalized and punctuated as if it were a sentence. ■

Subordinate clauses do not express complete thoughts. Although a subordinate adjective or adverb clause has a subject and a verb, it cannot stand by itself as a sentence. Like phrase fragments, *clause fragments* can usually be corrected in either of two ways:

1. Attach the fragment to a nearby sentence.

FRAGMENT:	The class enjoyed the concert. *That was held in the auditorium.*
ADDED TO A NEARBY SENTENCE:	The class enjoyed the concert *that was held in the auditorium.*

2. Add an independent clause to the fragment.

CHANGING CLAUSE FRAGMENTS INTO SENTENCES	
Clause Fragments	**Complete Sentences**
That we heard.	I bought a recording of the music *that we heard.* The music *that we heard* is now on CD.
When the orchestra played.	People got up to dance *when the orchestra played.* *When the orchestra played,* people got up to dance.

▶ **Exercise 34** Revising Clause Fragments to Form Sentences
Rewrite each fragment to make it a complete sentence.
1. Who directed the orchestra.
2. That was performed last week.
3. As the band played on.
4. That you like to hear.
5. That can be pleasing.
6. When the trombone player began.
7. That she described.
8. After we played a concert last week.
9. Who told me about the concert.
10. While the musicians tuned their instruments.

Correcting Run-on Sentences

Unlike a fragment, a *run-on sentence* is an overcrowded sentence—one that has too much information.

▶ **KEY CONCEPT** A **run-on** is two or more complete sentences that are not properly joined or separated. ∎

Two Kinds of Run-on Sentences

There are two kinds of run-on sentences. One kind is made up of two sentences run together without any punctuation between them. This type of run-on is called a *fused sentence.* The other consists of two or more sentences separated only by a comma. This is called a *comma splice.*

RUN-ONS	
With No Punctuation	**With Only a Comma**
I go to concerts often Mozart is my favorite composer.	A clarinet has an almost cylindrical tube, an oboe has a conical pipe.

▼ Critical Viewing
Write a sentence comparing the appearance or sound of these three instruments. Make sure your sentence is not a run-on. **[Compare]**

▶ **Exercise 35** Recognizing Run-on Sentences
On your paper write *S* if the item is a sentence and *RO* if the item is a run-on.

EXAMPLE: Bells vibrate at their rim gongs vibrate at their center. (RO)

1. Musical instruments around the world vary in purpose and design they can be made from natural or human-made materials.
2. Any tool that can expand the scope of musical sounds—such as clapping, stamping, whistling, and singing—is a musical instrument.
3. Sound arises from vibrations transmitted by waves to the ear, some vibrations are simply noise.
4. Regular vibrations produce tones that can be pleasing to the ear, the faster the vibrations, the higher the pitch that is perceived.
5. Some pipe organs encompass the full audible range of pitch, more than ten octaves most instruments have a much more limited range.

Correcting Run-on Sentences

Using End Marks Properly used, an end mark splits a run-on into two shorter but complete sentences. Which end mark you use depends upon the function of the sentence.

RUN-ON: Many instruments were improved in the nineteenth century the piano was made with a cast-iron frame, which allowed a greater range of sounds.

CORRECTED SENTENCES: Many instruments were improved in the nineteenth century. The piano was made with a cast-iron frame, which allowed a greater range of sounds.

RUN-ON: Have you heard the new song, I heard it yesterday.

CORRECTED SENTENCES: Have you heard the new song? I heard it yesterday.

Using Commas and Coordinating Conjunctions
Sometimes, the two parts of a run-on are related and should stay in the same sentence. In that case, the run-on can be changed into a compound sentence. Use a comma and a coordinating conjunction to combine two independent clauses into a compound sentence. To separate the two clauses properly, it is necessary to use both a comma and a coordinating conjunction. A comma by itself is not enough.

RUN-ON: The oldest instrument family consists of idiophones, they are also the most widespread of instruments.

CORRECTED SENTENCE: The oldest instrument family consists of idiophones, and they are also the most widespread of instruments.

RUN-ON: I would like to play an instrument, I do not have musical ability.

CORRECTED SENTENCE: I would like to play an instrument, but I do not have musical ability.

Using Semicolons You can sometimes use a semicolon to punctuate the two parts of a run-on when the ideas expressed in the two parts are closely related.

RUN-ON: Idiophones range in complexity from hollowed logs to cast-bronze bells, the family dates back to the Stone Age.

CORRECTED SENTENCE: Idiophones range in complexity from hollowed logs to cast-bronze bells; the family dates back to the Stone Age.

▲ Critical Viewing Write two sentences about the sound of this instrument. Then, combine your sentences without forming a run-on. **[Describe]**

> **Exercise 36** Revising to Correct Run-ons Rewrite each of the following run-ons using any of the three methods described in this section.

1. Some instruments produce a tone with no identifiable pitch the triangle is one such instrument.
2. The greater the power of audio waves, the louder their sound, some electronically amplified music can reach a painful, ear-damaging intensity.
3. The tone color of the sound is influenced by the presence of the overtones in the sound wave, the perception of timbre is affected by the duration and location of the sound.
4. Musical sounds are caused by three components, the first component is the vibrating substance, such as a violin string, set into motion by bowing or striking.
5. The second component is the reflector, amplifier, or resonator connected to the vibrating substance, the third is the device that alters or varies the sound, such as a key, valve, or fret.

More Practice

Grammar Exercise Workbook
• pp. 95–96
On-line Exercise Bank
• Section 21.4

Go on-line:
PHSchool.com
Enter Web Code:
eek-1002

Recognizing Misplaced Modifiers

Misplaced Modifiers A phrase or clause that acts as an adjective or adverb should be placed close to the word it modifies. Otherwise, the meaning of the sentence may be unclear. A modifier placed too far away from the word it modifies is called a *misplaced modifier.* Because they are misplaced, such phrases and clauses seem to modify the wrong word in a sentence.

MISPLACED MODIFIER: Nancy marched in the parade *with a smile* on her face.

The misplaced modifier is the phrase *with a smile.* It sounds as though the parade has a smile. The sentence needs to be reworded to put the modifier closer to *Nancy.*

CORRECTED SENTENCE: *With a smile* on her face, Nancy marched in the parade.

MISPLACED MODIFIER: *Playing the trumpet,* the parade was enjoyable.

In this sentence, *playing the trumpet* should modify a person. Instead, it incorrectly modifies *parade.* The sentence needs to be rewritten to include the name of the musician.

CORRECTED SENTENCE: *Playing the trumpet,* Elizabeth enjoyed the parade.

Exercise 37 Recognizing Misplaced Modifiers Some of the sentences in the following exercise are correct, but most of them contain a misplaced modifier. Read each sentence carefully, and check the placement of the modifiers. If the sentence is correct, write *C* on your paper. If the sentence contains a misplaced modifier, write *MM*.

EXAMPLE: Touring extensively around the world, people love the Vienna Philharmonic Orchestra. (MM)

1. Zubin Mehta was born in Bombay, India, into a musical family.
2. His father from 1955 to 1959 served as associate concertmaster of the Halle Orchestra in Manchester, England.
3. As a child, Mehta studied piano and violin.
4. In Vienna, Austria, Mehta left India and medical studies at age eighteen to study conducting.
5. At his musical studio in Vienna, Mehta studied with Hans Swarowsky.
6. Organized by the Royal Liverpool Orchestra, Mehta won the first conductor's competition.
7. Including a one-year engagement as assistant to the resident maestro, Mehta benefited from the prizes of the competition.
8. Working for a number of prominent orchestras, his career soon expanded.
9. Appointed music director for the Los Angeles Philharmonic and the Montreal Symphony, Mehta became the first conductor to head two major North American orchestras simultaneously.
10. Mehta replaced Pierre Boulez as music director of the New York Philharmonic, receiving much critical acclaim.

▲ Critical Viewing
Use the phrase *looking up from their music* in a sentence about this picture. Make sure that the modifier is not misplaced. [Connect]

More Practice

Grammar Exercise Workbook
• pp. 97–98
On-line Exercise Bank
• Section 21.4
  Go on-line:
  PHSchool.com
  Enter Web Code:
  eek-1002

Get instant feedback! Exercise 37 is available on-line or on CD-ROM.

Revising Sentences
With Misplaced Modifiers

Among the most common misplaced modifiers are prepositional phrases, participial phrases, and adjective clauses. All
are corrected in the same way—by placing the modifier as
close as possible to the word it modifies.

First, consider a misplaced prepositional phrase. This error
usually occurs in a sentence with two or more prepositional
phrases in a row.

MISPLACED: *With their new instruments* in the auditorium, the
             orchestra practiced.

The misplaced modifier should be moved closer to *orchestra*.

CORRECTED: *With their new instruments*, the orchestra prac-
             ticed in the auditorium.

Participial phrases are sometimes used at the beginning of
sentences. When such a phrase is used this way, it must be
followed immediately by a word that it can logically modify.

MISPLACED: *Raising their bows*, the signal from the conductor
             was their cue.

Who or what is raising their bows? The sentence needs to be
rewritten to put a word such as *violinists* next to the modifier.

CORRECTED: *Raising their bows*, the violinists waited for the
             signal from the conductor.

A misplaced adjective clause should also be moved closer to
the word it modifies. In the following sentence, the clause is so
far away from *music* that it seems to modify *weeks* or *searching*. The sentence needs to be rearranged.

MISPLACED: I found the music after several weeks of

             searching *that the conductor recommended.*

CORRECTED: After several weeks of searching, I found the

             music *that the conductor recommended.*

> **Exercise 38** Revising Sentences to Correct Misplaced
Modifiers Rewrite the sentences in the following exercise to
eliminate the misplaced modifiers. In each rewritten sentence,
underline the modifier that was misplaced in the original.
Then, draw an arrow pointing from the modifier to the word
it modifies.

EXAMPLE: Richard planned to meet Rachel before the con-
            cert at Radio City Music Hall at a restaurant.

ANSWER: Richard planned to meet Rachel <u>at a restaurant</u>
            before the concert at Radio City Music Hall.

1. Gustav Mahler was an Austrian composer and conductor
   whose works influenced many twentieth-century composers living in the nineteenth century.
2. After studying at the Vienna Conservatory, the assistant
   conductor at Bad Hall in Austria was named Mahler.
3. Mahler subsequently held posts in several European cities
   with opera companies.
4. Becoming artistic director of the Imperial Opera in Vienna,
   Vienna became a great operatic center because of Mahler.
5. Mahler moved to New York City, where he conducted the
   Metropolitan Opera and the New York Philharmonic,
   another city known for opera.
6. Mahler composed four numbered symphonies after years
   of conducting that included solo voices with or without
   chorus.
7. Mahler was the musical heir of Beethoven, Bruckner, and
   Wagner in his symphonies.
8. Achieving great fame, twentieth-century music was greatly
   influenced by Mahler.
9. Experimenting with the traditional system of keys
   and chords, most of his symphonies end in a
   key different from the initial key.
10. Leaving an unfinished tenth symphony,
    Mahler's death took place in Vienna
    in 1911.

More Practice

**Grammar Exercise
Workbook**
• pp. 99–102
On-line Exercise Bank
• Section 21.4
Go on-line:
PHSchool.com
Enter Web Code:
eek-1002

Text

Complete the exercise
on-line! Exercise 38 is
available on-line or
on CD-ROM.

▶ Critical Viewing Write a sentence
about this picture that includes the
participial phrase *holding a baton*. Make
sure that the modifier is not misplaced.
[Connect]

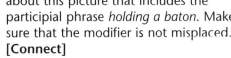

Section
21.4

Section Review

GRAMMAR EXERCISES 39-44

▶ **Exercise 39** Revising Fragments to Form Sentences Change each of the following fragments into a sentence. Check to see that each of your sentences contains an independent clause.

1. The marching band fun to watch.
2. Before the music started.
3. When the opera starts.
4. With a piano solo.
5. The musicians starting to play.
6. Bagpipes and loudly playing drums.
7. Marching down Main Street.
8. To buy a saxophone.
9. After the open-air concert.
10. Three friends singing with the chorus.

▶ **Exercise 40** Revising to Eliminate Run-on Sentences Identify and eliminate run-ons from the following items. If a sentence is correct, write *correct*.

1. The score is the musical notation for a multipart composition, the music that is to be performed by each voice or instrument is written on a separate staff.
2. A full score shows the music for all of the instruments all of the staves are aligned one above another.
3. The individual musicians are given separate parts these parts show only the music for their particular instrument.
4. Until the early thirteenth century, all European music was circulated in complete scores, and performers read from these scores.
5. The use of these scores was abandoned in the thirteenth century, this was done for reasons of space.

▶ **Exercise 41** Revising a Paragraph to Eliminate Sentence Errors Revise the following paragraph, correcting any fragments, run-ons, or misplaced modifiers.

The piano is a stringed keyboard musical instrument, it is sometimes called the pianoforte. Predecessors of the piano, keyboard players performed on clavicords or harpsicords prior to the eighteenth century. By varying the touch of the fingers, the sound of the piano can be intensified. Unlike with earlier keyboard instruments. A harpsichord maker of Florence, Italy, the first piano was built by Bartolomeo Cristofori. Little did he know. That his invention would have such an impact on both concert and popular music. Today, pianos sit in concert halls and homes all around the world, millions of children and adults take piano lessons every day.

▶ **Exercise 42** Find It in Your Reading In this sentence from "Like the Sun," identify how the writer has avoided creating a run-on sentence.

Sekhar paused for a moment outside the headmaster's room to button up his coat; that was another subject the headmaster always sermonized about.

▶ **Exercise 43** Find It in Your Writing Carefully review a piece of your own writing for fragments, run-ons, or misplaced modifiers. Correct any errors you find.

▶ **Exercise 44** Writing Application Pick a musical instrument, and write a description of how the instrument sounds. Proofread your description carefully to make sure it contains no fragments, run-ons, or misplaced modifiers.

Chapter Review

GRAMMAR EXERCISES 45–50

▶ **Exercise 45** Identifying and Punctuating the Four Functions of Sentences Identify each sentence as *declarative, interrogative, imperative,* or *exclamatory.* Then, write the end mark for each sentence.

1. Will you come to the concert with me
2. The school orchestra is performing
3. Bring your jacket; the concert is on the great lawn
4. Have you been to an outdoor concert before
5. This orchestra is quite good
6. I wish I could join
7. Your sister may want to come
8. Ask her if she is free Friday night
9. The weather should be clear
10. What fun it will be

▶ **Exercise 46** Combining Short Sentences Combine the pairs of sentences using the method indicated in parentheses.

1. My sister plays the accordion. She also sings in a band. (compound verb)
2. I used to play the accordion. I was not very good. (semicolon)
3. I have always wanted to play a musical instrument well. I have never taken lessons. (comma and coordinating conjunction)
4. Our mother plays the harp. She also plays the lute. (compound object)
5. My father does not play any instruments. He appreciates people who have musical ability. (form a subordinate clause)
6. He has other special talents, though. One of his talents is sketching. (phrase)
7. I went to a concert last weekend. I carefully studied the styles of different performers. (form a subordinate clause)

8. My sister would like to play professionally. We are sure that she is good enough. (comma and coordinating conjunction)
9. I will learn to play an instrument this semester. I'll learn the piano. (phrase)
10. I cannot play soccer after school. I have piano practice. (form a subordinate clause)

▶ **Exercise 47** Varying Sentence Length and Beginnings Rewrite each sentence. Break the sentence into two sentences; rewrite it in a simpler, more direct way; or vary the beginning of the sentence.

1. The woodwind family of instruments contains both wood and metal instruments, despite its name.
2. The woodwind tube, which is long and narrow, is sometimes attached to a flexible reed, and, when it is played, the reed vibrates.
3. The air column vibrating within the instrument may be shortened or lengthened by covering finger holes or pushing keys, which affects the pitch of the tone that the instrument produces.
4. You can lengthen the column of air, and that action, if it is taken by a player, will make the tone lower.
5. The contrabassoon is the longest woodwind in the orchestra, and it is providing the deepest tones.

▶ **Exercise 48** Revising to Eliminate Sentence Errors Copy the following passage on a separate sheet of paper. Revise, eliminating any fragments, run-ons, or misplaced modifiers.

Conductors gesture silently to direct the orchestra with their hands or a baton. Generally, the right hand is used to indicate the tempo the left hand indicates both the entry of a different instrument and changes in volume. The right hand moves in commonly recognized patterns for groups of two, three, four, or more beats per measure, these patterns have in common a downward movement on the first beat. Sometimes called the downbeat.

Conductors of instrumental ensembles generally use a baton that contains many different performers. The modern conductor appeared only during the nineteenth century. A professional responsible for total music interpretation. In earlier times, the conductor, often one of the performers, functioned mainly as the time beater. Conductors of small choral ensembles that performed the polyphonic music of the Renaissance beat time with their hands or by tapping with a roll of paper or a rod, in the Baroque Era, harmonies provided by a keyboard player were an essential feature of most music. The conductor kept the ensemble together with a steady background beat on the keyboard who was often also the composer. During the nineteenth century, conductors separated themselves from the ensemble, standing in front of it to direct; they also began using the baton.

Exercise 49 Revision Practice: **Writing Effective Sentences** Copy the following passage on a separate sheet of paper. Revise, combining sentences or revising sentences as needed. Correct all errors in sentence structure.

The Vienna Philharmonic Orchestra, one of the most renowned classical music ensembles in the world. It was originally formed by musicians from the Vienna State Opera, the members of the opera joined together to establish a professional concert orchestra capable with the highest degree of competence of playing the most difficult new works. They gave their first performance as the Vienna Philharmonic Orchestra on March 28, 1842, at the Grosser Redoutensaal. Then, Vienna's main concert hall. The conductor, German composer and conductor Otto Nicolai. At first, concerts took place sporadically they were further disrupted by Austria's Revolution of 1848. German pianist, violinist, and composer Carl Eckert conducted a few concerts during the 1850's, the orchestra did not play on a regular basis until 1860.

The Vienna Philharmonic moved to Karntnertortheater in 1860. It remained until the opening of the Musikverein in 1870. Its first permanent conductor was Austrian conductor Felix Dessoff. He was director of the orchestra from 1860 to 1875. He introduced the music of Hungarian-born composer Franz Lizst. He also introduced the work of German composers Richard Wagner and Johannes Brahms. Other early conductors of the Vienna Philharmonic include Austro-Hungarian conductor Hans Richter. Austrian composer and conductor Gustav Mahler. During Mahler's tenure as artistic director that the Vienna Philharmonic gained international prominence. There have been many notable conductors including the American Leonard Bernstein of the Vienna Philharmonic.

Exercise 50 Writing Application Write a review of a concert or musical performance you have attended recently. Focus on varying the length and structure of your sentences, and proofread carefully to eliminate any fragments, run-on sentences, or misplaced modifiers.

Standardized Test Preparation Workshop

Revising and Editing Sentences

Whether writing an e-mail or an essay for a test, you must use sentences correctly and effectively to communicate logically. Because this skill is so important, it is often evaluated on standardized tests. When choosing the most effective sentence from the list of answer choices, use the following strategies:

Test Tip

Read each answer silently to yourself to help you pick out fragments or run-ons. Then, choose the sentence that best answers the question.

- Avoid choosing run-on sentences in which two or more complete sentences are written as a single sentence.

- Identify and avoid any sentence fragments in your choices. Fragments do not express a complete thought.

- Determine whether you can combine several short sentences into one longer one.

- Be sure all modifiers are placed near the words they modify.

- Make sure your choice presents all of the important information without changing the meaning of the original.

Sample Test Item	Answer and Explanation
Sandor has written an essay for chorus class. You have been asked to read the essay and offer suggestions for improving it. When you finish reading this passage, answer the multiple-choice question that follows. 1 Gioacchino Rossini produced several notable 2 operas. In the early 1800's. He was a 3 composer from Italy.	
1 What is the BEST way to combine the sentences in lines 1–3? (*"Gioacchino. . . Italy."*) **A** Gioacchino Rossini produced several notable Italian operas in the early 1800's. **B** In the early 1800's, Italian composer Gioacchino Rossini produced several notable operas. **C** Gioacchino Rossini, who was an Italian composer; created notable operas in the 1800's. **D** In Italy in the early 1800's. Gioacchino Rossini produced several notable operas.	The correct answer is *B.* Choice B correctly combines the important elements of all of the sentences and eliminates the fragment error.

Practice 1 *Steven has written an essay for history class and has asked you to review it for him. When you finish reading the passage below, answer the multiple-choice questions that follow.*

1 The time was in the 1720's. Colonists
2 who were living in South Carolina.
3 Petitioned England. They wanted forts
4 built to their south. The forts were needed
5 to provide protection from the Spanish
6 in Florida, this was so the colonists.
7 could maintain their trade which was
8 active, and it was with the nearby Indians.

1 What is the BEST way to combine the sentences in lines 1–4? (*"The . . . south."*)

A In the 1720's, colonists who were living in South Carolina. Petitioned England, They wanted forts built to their south.

B In the 1720's in South Carolina, and colonists wanted forts built to their south, and they petitioned England.

C In the 1720's, colonists living in South Carolina petitioned England to build forts to their south.

D In the 1720's, colonists petitioned England, and they wanted forts built in South Carolina to their south.

2 What is the BEST way to rewrite the sentences in lines 4–8? (*"The . . . Indians."*)

F The forts were needed to provide protection from the Spanish in Florida so the colonists could maintain their active trade with the nearby Indians.

G The forts were needed to provide protection. From the Spanish in Florida. So the colonists could maintain their active trade with the nearby Indians.

H The forts were needed to provide protection from the Spanish in Florida and from the nearby Indians.

J The forts were providing protection from the Spanish in Florida, and the colonists were trading actively with the nearby Indians.

Practice 2 *Ashley has written a report for a social studies course. You have been asked to review it. When you finish reading the passage below, answer the multiple-choice questions that follow.*

1 Soon after the first real trains appeared.
2 Some began building ones that were
3 miniature in size who were engineers.
4 These trains were not toys, and they
5 were detailed models, and they were
6 built to try out ideas. For real trains.

1 What is the BEST way to combine the sentences in lines 1–3? (*"Soon . . . engineers."*)

A Soon after the first real trains appeared, some engineers that were miniature in size began building ones.

B Soon after the first real trains appeared, some engineers began building trains, and they were miniature in size.

C Soon after the first real trains appeared. Ones that were miniature in size were built by some engineers

D Soon after the first real trains appeared, some engineers began building miniature ones.

2 What is the BEST way to combine the sentences in lines 4–6? (*"These . . . trains."*)

F These trains were not toys, they were detailed models, they were built to try out ideas for real trains.

G These trains were not toys; they were detailed models built to try out ideas for real trains.

H These trains were toys and detailed models, and they were built to try out ideas for real trains.

J These trains were not toys. They were detailed models. They were built to try out ideas. The ideas were for real trains.

Cumulative Review

PHRASES, CLAUSES, AND SENTENCES

Exercise A **Recognizing Basic Sentence Parts** Copy the following sentences, underlining each simple subject once and each simple predicate twice. Circle the complements and label each *direct object, indirect object, objective complement, predicate nominative,* or *predicate adjective.* Then, identify the function of each sentence as *declarative, imperative, interrogative,* or *exclamatory.*

1. Which continent surrounds the South Pole?
2. Antarctica is mostly circular, with one long arm reaching toward South America.
3. We call the two large indentations the Ross and Weddell seas.
4. The real boundary of Antarctica is the Atlantic Convergence, beyond the end of the continent.
5. There is 70 percent of the world's fresh water in the ice.

Exercise B **Revising to Combine Sentences** Rewrite the following sentences according to the directions in parentheses. In your new sentences, underline each simple subject once and each simple predicate twice. Circle each subject complement.

1. Whales live in the waters around Antarctica. There are also shrimplike animals in the water. (combine by forming a compound subject)
2. Antarctica has two main geographic areas; one is East Antarctica. West Antarctica is the other. (combine by forming a compound predicate nominative)
3. Some of the deposits covering East Antarctica are igneous. Other deposits are sedimentary. (combine by forming a compound predicate adjective)
4. The Transantarctic Mountains contain coal deposits. There are fossils in the Transantarctic Mountains. (combine by forming a compound direct object)
5. Mount Erebus rises above West Antarctica. It could erupt some day. (combine by forming a compound verb)

Exercise C **Identifying Phrases and Clauses** Label each phrase in the following sentences *prepositional phrase, appositive phrase, participial phrase, gerund phrase,* or *infinitive phrase.* Label each clause *adjective clause, adverb clause,* or *noun clause.*

1. Richard Byrd, an American explorer, author, and aviator, is known for his expeditions to the Antarctic.
2. Making his first flight over the North Pole brought Byrd recognition, which included a medal from the government.
3. What Byrd did the next year was to fly an airplane.
4. Assisted by Bernt Balchen, Bertrand Acosta, and George Noville, Byrd flew from New York to France.
5. Byrd established Little America, a base on the Bay of Whales, when he made his first expedition to the Antarctic.
6. In 1929, he was the first to fly over the South Pole.
7. After he extensively mapped Antarctica, Byrd retired from the navy with the rank of rear admiral.
8. Researching in several fields, Byrd spent five months alone on Antarctica when he was on his second expedition.
9. There were four flights, which resulted in many discoveries, during the third expedition.

10. The fourth expedition was intended to explore and to map more territory.

Exercise D
Revising to Combine Sentences Rewrite the following sentences according to the instructions in parentheses.

1. On December 14, 1911, Roald Amundsen reached the South Pole. He was the first person to do so. (combine by forming an adjective clause)
2. Amundsen lived in Antarctica for more than a year. He was a Norwegian explorer. (combine by forming an appositive phrase)
3. He was a success. The weather conditions were very favorable. (combine by forming an adverb clause)
4. Amundsen also had a great deal of knowledge. He was familiar with polar conditions. (combine by forming a prepositional phrase)
5. He had another ability. Amundsen could endure great physical stress. (combine by forming an infinitive phrase)
6. Robert Scott had set his goal. He hoped to be the first man to reach the South Pole. (combine by forming a gerund phrase)
7. He succeeded on January 18, 1912. He found Amundsen's tent and flag. (combine by forming a participial phrase)
8. His group of five people suffered on the return trip. They did not survive. (combine by forming an adjective clause)
9. Scott entered the Royal Navy at the age of 14. He commanded the National Antarctic Expedition. (combine by forming an appositive phrase)
10. He left England in 1901. Then, Scott established a base on McMurdo Sound in Antarctica. (combine by forming a participial phrase)

Exercise E
Revision Practice: Writing Effective Sentences Revise the following passage, combining sentences or revising sentences as needed. Correct all errors in sentence structure.

Mount Erebus, an active volcano on the eastern coast of Ross Island. The mountain, who named it after one of his two vessels, was discovered by Sir James Ross. Sir Ernest Henry Shackleton established his winter quarters there and used it as a base. succeeded in climbing Mount Erebus. Shackleton joined the British merchant navy. In 1901 he sailed with Robert Scott. In 1908, he commanded the mission to reach the South Pole he came close to his goal. He attempted to cross the Antarctic continent. Shackleton wanted to travel from the Ross Sea to the Weddell Sea. Another explorer did this many years later. It was a 12-member British team called the Commonwealth Trans-Antarctic Expedition. The Ross Sea is actually an extension of the Pacific Ocean. It is free of ice in the summer; therefore, the shoreline serves as a departure site for expeditions.

Exercise F
Writing Application Write a short description of a place you would like to see from the air. Make your writing interesting by varying your sentence lengths and structures. Avoid sentence errors. Underline each simple subject once and each simple verb twice. Then, circle at least three phrases and three clauses.

▲ Critical Viewing
Think of the present
and past tense forms
of three verbs that
describe actions you
do with money. How
do the two tenses
vary in form?
[Connect, Contrast]

Having a good command of the English language requires a thorough understanding of how to use verbs. Verbs can help you explain when actions occur and how the time of one action relates to the time of another. Some verbs follow predictable rules to show a change in tense or form. Others follow irregular patterns that you must memorize.

Just as the nations of Europe now use a standard currency to facilitate the exchange of goods and services, the rules of verb usage facilitate the exchange of information. By following these rules, you can communicate more effectively.

This chapter shows how verbs are formed and how they are used to indicate the time when an action occurs. It also illustrates how verbs are used to indicate who is performing an action.

Diagnostic Test

Directions: Write all answers on a separate sheet of paper.

Skill Check A. Identify the tense of each verb in italics. Then, tell whether the form is *basic* or *progressive.*

1. My aunt and uncle *are running* a financial planning business.
2. They *have taught* many people how to save and use money well.
3. They *used* their own savings to start their business.
4. Next month, they *will hold* a financial planning seminar for teens.
5. I *have been studying* economics in school and plan to attend their seminar.
6. My aunt thinks most people *are relying* too heavily on credit.
7. My aunt and uncle *had done* the same thing when they were young.
8. They *had been struggling,* but now they are helping other people with similar problems.
9. Because I have been following their advice, they expect that my investments *will be growing* in the future.
10. By the time I graduate from high school, I *will have been employing* their system for four years.

Skill Check B. Write the four principal parts of the following verbs.

11. save
12. deposit
13. cost
14. spend
15. grow

Skill Check C. Choose the correct form of the verb in parentheses.

16. People have long (striven, strove) to earn or raise money.
17. People have also (did, done) many unusual things to earn money.
18. In dance marathons in the 1930's, people danced to win cash prizes until they (grown, grew) weak.
19. Others have (swam, swum) or have (ran, run) great distances to win money.
20. Whenever people's bank accounts have (shrank, shrunk), they have (hit, hitted) upon new schemes to raise money.

Skill Check D. Identify the verb in each sentence below as *active* or *passive.*

21. Mexicans call their currency the *peso.*
22. The currency of China is known by the Chinese as the *yuan.*
23. Banks often exchange one form of currency for another.
24. The *euro* now serves as the currency of numerous European nations.
25. The U.S. dollar has been used for many years as the prevailing currency of international trade.

Verb Tenses

In writing and speaking, the different *tenses* of verbs are used to express time.

▶ **KEY CONCEPT** A **tense** is a form of a verb that shows the time of an action or a condition. ■

The Six Tenses of Verbs

Verbs have six tenses, each of which can be expressed in two different forms—*basic* and *progressive.*

THE BASIC AND PROGRESSIVE FORMS OF THE SIX TENSES	
Present	She *writes* about U.S. currency for a living.
Past	She *wrote* an article about coin collecting last year.
Future	She *will write* a book about old coins next year.
Present Perfect	She *has written* for the best magazines.
Past Perfect	She *had written* her first article by the time she was eighteen.
Future Perfect	She *will have written* two books by July.
Present Progressive	She *is writing* a newsletter about rare coins now.
Past Progressive	She *was writing* her weekly column.
Future Progressive	She *will be writing* a new book soon.
Present Perfect Progressive	She *has been writing* for years.
Past Perfect Progressive	She *had been writing* speeches when her first book on coins was published.
Future Perfect Progressive	By the end of the year, she *will have been writing* about different forms of currency for a decade.

Theme: The Currency of the World

In this section, you will learn to recognize and use the six tenses of verbs in both their basic and progressive forms. The examples and exercises are about money around the world.

Cross-Curricular Connection: Social Studies

> **Exercise 1** Identifying Verb Tenses Using the chart on page 520, identify the tense of each verb in italics.

EXAMPLE: He *has been bartering* services for products.
ANSWER: present perfect progressive

1. Money *serves* as a convenient medium of exchange.
2. People *have used* money for many centuries.
3. Previously, people often *bartered* for goods and services.
4. This mode of exchange *had been serving* people for centuries when a simpler way of doing business was devised.
5. Soon, people *were using* shells and furs to make purchases.
6. Some cultures also *minted* coins from precious metals.
7. By the twentieth century, much of the world *had implemented* standard coins and paper money.
8. Today, we *are utilizing* a wide variety of means of exchange.
9. Imagine how we *will be buying* items in the year 3000.
10. By then, people *will have been conducting* business with one another for more than 4,000 years.

▲ Critical Viewing
Write a series of sentences about the use of cash machines. Use three different verb tenses. **[Apply]**

EXPRESSING TIME THROUGH VERB TENSES		
Past	Existing or happening in the past	James collected old Spanish doubloons.
Past Perfect	Existing or happening before a specific time in the past	James had collected stamps until then.
Present	Existing or happening now	James now collects U.S. silver dollars.
Present Perfect	Existing or happening sometime before now	He has collected that particular coin for several years.
Future	Existing or happening in the future	He will collect coins for a long time.
Future Perfect	Existing or happening before a specific time in the future	By the time he is sixty years old, he will have collected coins for most of his life.

> **More Practice**

Grammar Exercise Workbook
• pp. 107–112
On-line Exercise Bank
• Section 22.1
Go on-line:
PHSchool.com
Enter Web Code:
eek-1002

Get instant feedback! Exercise 1 is available on-line or on CD-ROM.

> **Exercise 2** Identifying the Uses of Tense Identify the tense and time indicated by the italicized verb in each sentence.

EXAMPLE: People *have used* many metals to make coins.

ANSWER: present perfect; existing or happening some time before the present

1. American currency generally *has featured* pictures of past presidents.
2. George Washington's face *appears* on the quarter and the one-dollar bill.
3. The symbols and pictures that appear on coins and paper currency *have varied* from culture to culture.
4. The Greeks *were producing* coins with pictures of gods and goddesses on them in ancient times.
5. The ancient Romans *decorated* their coins with portraits of Roman emperors.

▼ Critical Viewing
Which of the sentences in Exercise 2 do you think this coin illustrates? Why? **[Connect]**

> **Exercise 3** Writing Sentences in Different Tenses Rewrite each sentence, supplying the verb in the tense indicated.

EXAMPLE: Massachusetts (become—past) the first American colony to mint coins.

ANSWER: Massachusetts became the first American colony to mint coins.

1. At first, the British (try—past progressive) to prevent the American colonies from printing their own money.
2. The British government (hope—past perfect progressive) to make the colonists trade exclusively with England.
3. Despite the restrictions, the colonists (manage—past perfect) to purchase goods from foreign traders.
4. By 1690, the colony of Massachusetts (issue—past progressive) its own coins and paper money.
5. Our class (examine—future) several colonial coins during a field trip to a museum next week.

> **Exercise 4** Revising Verb Tense Rewrite each sentence, correcting the tense of the italicized verb.
1. Until the twentieth century, coins used in the Islamic world *will contain* few pictures of people.
2. In the past, Islamic countries *adorn* their coins with inscriptions from the Koran, their holy book.
3. Today, in some countries, people *lobbied* to get new symbols and faces on their currency.
4. In the future, new faces *appear* on U.S. currency.
5. By 2300, people *had used* coins for nearly 3,000 years.

Get instant feedback! Exercises 2, 3, and 4 are available on-line or on CD-ROM.

> **More Practice**

Grammar Exercise Workbook
• pp. 113–120
On-line Exercise Bank
• Section 22.1
  Go on-line:
  PHSchool.com
  Enter Web Code:
  eek-1002

The Four Principal Parts of Verbs

Tenses are formed from *principal parts* and helping verbs.

KEY CONCEPT A verb has four principal parts: the present, the present participle, the past, and the past participle. ■

The chart below lists the principal parts of two verbs.

THE FOUR PRINCIPAL VERB PARTS			
Present	Present Participle	Past	Past Participle
walk	walking	walked	walked
run	running	ran	run

The first principal part is used to form the present and future tenses. To form the present, an *-s* or *-es* is added whenever the subject is *he, she, it,* or a singular noun (*he walks, Paul runs*). To form the future tense, the helping verb *will* is added (*he will walk, Paul will run*).

The second principal part is used with various helping verbs to produce all six of the progressive forms (*he is walking, Paul was walking,* and so on).

The third principal part is used to form the past tense (*he walked, Paul ran*).

The fourth principal part is used with helping verbs for the three perfect tenses (*he has walked, Paul had run,* and so on).

Regular Verbs

Most of the verbs in the English language, including the verb *walk,* are regular.

KEY CONCEPT The past and past participle of a **regular verb** are formed by adding *-ed* or *-d* to the present form. ■

The past and past participle of regular verbs have the same form. In the chart at the top of the next page, *have* is in parentheses in front of the past participle to remind you that this verb form is a past participle only if it is used with a helping verb.

Notice that the final consonant is sometimes doubled to form the present participle (ski*pp*ing) as well as the past and the past participle (ski*pp*ed). Notice also that the final *e* may be dropped in forming the present participle (typing).

PRINCIPAL PARTS OF REGULAR VERBS			
Present	Present Participle	Past	Past Participle
wash	(is) washing	washed	(have) washed
help	(is) helping	helped	(have) helped
type	(is) typing	typed	(have) typed
print	(is) printing	printed	(have) printed
issue	(is) issuing	issued	(have) issued
plot	(is) plotting	plotted	(have) plotted

Exercise 5 Identifying Principal Parts of Regular Verbs
Identify the principal part used to form each verb in Exercise 2 on page 522. The first one is done as an example below.

EXAMPLE: American currency generally *has featured* pictures of past presidents.

ANSWER: featured (past participle)

Irregular Verbs

Although most verbs are regular, a number of very common verbs, such as *run,* are irregular.

KEY CONCEPT The past and past participle of an **irregular verb** are not formed by adding *-ed* or *-d* to the present form. ■

The past and the past participle of irregular verbs are formed in various ways. Some common irregular verbs are shown in the charts that follow. Whenever you are in doubt about the principal parts of an irregular verb, use a dictionary to check them.

THE FOUR PRINCIPAL PARTS OF IRREGULAR VERBS			
Present	Present Participle	Past	Past Participle
lay	laying	laid	(have) laid
bring	bringing	brought	(have) brought
begin	beginning	began	(have) begun
fly	flying	flew	(have) flown
cost	costing	cost	(have) cost
pay	paying	paid	(have) paid
lose	losing	lost	(have) lost
sell	selling	sold	(have) sold
spend	spending	spent	(have) spent

IRREGULAR VERBS WITH THE SAME PRESENT, PAST, AND PAST PARTICIPLE

Present	Present Participle	Past	Past Participle
bid	bidding	bid	(have) bid
burst	bursting	burst	(have) burst
cost	costing	cost	(have) cost
cut	cutting	cut	(have) cut
hit	hitting	hit	(have) hit
hurt	hurting	hurt	(have) hurt
let	letting	let	(have) let
put	putting	put	(have) put
set	setting	set	(have) set
shut	shutting	shut	(have) shut
split	splitting	split	(have) split
spread	spreading	spread	(have) spread
thrust	thrusting	thrust	(have) thrust

IRREGULAR VERBS WITH THE SAME PAST AND PAST PARTICIPLE

Present	Present Participle	Past	Past Participle
bring	bringing	brought	(have) brought
build	building	built	(have) built
buy	buying	bought	(have) bought
catch	catching	caught	(have) caught
get	getting	got	(have) got or gotten
hang	hanging	hung	(have) hung
hold	holding	held	(have) held
keep	keeping	kept	(have) kept
lay	laying	laid	(have) laid
lead	leading	led	(have) led
leave	leaving	left	(have) left
lose	losing	lost	(have) lost
pay	paying	paid	(have) paid
sell	selling	sold	(have) sold
send	sending	sent	(have) sent
sit	sitting	sat	(have) sat
sleep	sleeping	slept	(have) slept
stand	standing	stood	(have) stood
stick	sticking	stuck	(have) stuck
strike	striking	struck	(have) struck
teach	teaching	taught	(have) taught
win	winning	won	(have) won
wring	wringing	wrung	(have) wrung

Technology Tip

The present participle can be used as a key word to locate information on the Internet. For instance, typing the word *flying* will lead you to Web sites that have information about flying airplanes and other related topics.

IRREGULAR VERBS THAT CHANGE IN OTHER WAYS

Present	Present Participle	Past	Past Participle
arise	arising	arose	(have) arisen
began	beginning	began	(have) begun
blow	blowing	blew	(have) blown
break	breaking	broke	(have) broken
choose	choosing	chose	(have) chosen
come	coming	came	(have) come
do	doing	did	(have) done
draw	drawing	drew	(have) drawn
drink	drinking	drank	(have) drunk
drive	driving	drove	(have) driven
eat	eating	ate	(have) eaten
fall	falling	fell	(have) fallen
fly	flying	flew	(have) flown
freeze	freezing	froze	(have) frozen
give	giving	gave	(have) given
go	going	went	(have) gone
grow	growing	grew	(have) grown
know	knowing	knew	(have) known
lie	lying	lay	(have) lain
ride	riding	rode	(have) ridden
ring	ringing	rang	(have) rung
rise	rising	rose	(have) risen
run	running	ran	(have) run
see	seeing	saw	(have) seen
shake	shaking	shook	(have) shaken
shrink	shrinking	shrank	(have) shrunk
sing	singing	sang	(have) sung
sink	sinking	sank	(have) sunk
slay	slaying	slew	(have) slain
speak	speaking	spoke	(have) spoken
spring	springing	sprang	(have) sprung
steal	stealing	stole	(have) stolen
stride	striding	strode	(have) stridden
strive	striving	strove	(have) striven
swear	swearing	swore	(have) sworn
swim	swimming	swam	(have) swum
take	taking	took	(have) taken
tear	tearing	tore	(have) torn
throw	throwing	threw	(have) thrown
wear	wearing	wore	(have) worn
write	writing	wrote	(have) written

More Practice

Grammar Exercise Workbook
• pp. 113–120
On-line Exercise Bank
• Section 22.1
Go on-line:
PHSchool.com
Enter Web Code:
eek-1002

▶ **Exercise 6** Using the Principal Parts of Irregular Verbs
Choose the correct form of the verb in parentheses.
1. The Chinese emperor Shi Huangdi (holded, held) the reigns of power in China around 220 B.C.
2. He (seeked, sought) ways to strengthen his country.
3. To protect China's northern border, Shi Huangdi had (drew, drawn) up plans for a huge stone wall.
4. Then, he had (put, putted) 300,000 workers to the task of constructing the wall.
5. Once the wall had been (build, built), Shi Huangdi turned to the country's economy.

▶ **Exercise 7** Supplying the Correct **Principal Parts of Irregular Verbs** Rewrite each sentence, supplying the correct principal part of the verb given in parentheses.
1. He ___?___ out an order requiring all Chinese to use the same currency, a round coin with a square hole in the middle. (send)
2. A common currency ___?___ it easier for one region of China to trade goods with another. (make)
3. Eight hundred years later, the Chinese ___?___ the first people to use paper money. (become)
4. When Marco Polo visited in the 1200's, he ___?___ that the Chinese were using paper money instead of coins. (see)
5. Polo had ___?___ to European leaders about this practice after he had returned to Italy. (speak)

▶ **Exercise 8** Revising to Correct the Use of Irregular Verbs
Revise this paragraph, correcting any errors in the use of irregular verbs.

The Chinese begun issuing paper money around A.D. 600. Even after they had heard about Chinese paper money from Marco Polo, Europeans remained unconvinced. They keeped wondering how a piece of paper could have value. It wasn't until the 1600's that banks in Europe choosed to issue paper bills, called bank notes, to their customers. When depositors took bank notes to their banks, they could be given gold or silver coins in exchange. The idea of government-issued paper money had not catched on until the 1800's.

▲ Critical Viewing
Use two different irregular verbs in describing this photograph of the Great Wall of China. [Describe]

Conjugating the Tenses

With the principal parts of verbs and helping verbs, you can form all the tenses.

> **KEY CONCEPT** A **conjugation** is a complete list of the singular and plural forms of a verb in a particular tense. ■

For each tense, there are three singular forms and three plural forms that correspond to the first-, second-, and third-person forms of personal pronouns.

To conjugate the six tenses in their basic forms, you need only three of the principal parts: the present, the past, and the past participle. To conjugate the six tenses in their progressive forms, you need the present participle and a form of the verb *be*.

CONJUGATION OF THE BASIC FORMS OF *PAY*		
	Singular	**Plural**
Present		
First Person Second Person Third Person	I pay you pay he, she, it pays	we pay you pay they pay
Past		
First Person Second Person Third Person	I paid you paid he, she, it paid	we paid you paid they paid
Future		
First Person Second Person Third Person	I will pay you will pay he, she, it will pay	we will pay you will pay they will pay
Present Perfect		
First Person Second Person Third Person	I have paid you have paid he, she, it has paid	we have paid you have paid they have paid
Past Perfect		
First Person Second Person Third Person	I had paid you had paid he, she, it had paid	we had paid you had paid they had paid
Future Perfect		
First Person Second Person Third Person	I will have paid you will have paid he, she, it will have paid	we will have paid you will have paid they will have paid

CONJUGATION OF THE PROGRESSIVE FORMS OF *PAY*

	Singular	Plural
Present Progressive		
First Person Second Person Third Person	I am paying you are paying he, she, it is paying	we are paying you are paying they are paying
Past Progressive		
First Person Second Person Third Person	I was paying you were paying he, she, it was paying	we were paying you were paying they were paying
Future Progressive		
First Person Second Person Third Person	I will be paying you will be paying he, she, it will be paying	we will be paying you will be paying they will be paying
Present Perfect Progressive		
First Person Second Person Third Person	I have been paying you have been paying he, she, it has been paying	we have been paying you have been paying they have been paying
Past Perfect Progressive		
First Person Second Person Third Person	I had been paying you had been paying he, she, it had been paying	we had been paying you had been paying they had been paying
Future Perfect Progressive		
First Person Second Person Third Person	I will have been paying you will have been paying he, she, it will have been paying	we will have been paying you will have been paying they will have been paying

Note About *Be:* The verb *be* is highly irregular. The following conjugation of the first two tenses lists the forms.

PRESENT: I am   we are
             you are   you are
             he, she, it is they are

PAST: I was   we were
             you were   you were
             he, she, it was they were

▶ **Exercise 9** Conjugating the Basic Forms of Verbs
Conjugate the basic forms of the five verbs below.

EXAMPLE: spend (conjugated with *we*)

ANSWER: present: we spend   present perfect: we have spent

past: we spent   past perfect: we had spent

future: we will spend   future perfect: we will have spent

1. stop (conjugated with *she*)
2. cost (conjugated with *it*)
3. collect (conjugated with *they*)
4. sell (conjugated with *we*)
5. choose (conjugated with *I*)

▶ **Exercise 10** Conjugating the Progressive Forms of Verbs
Conjugate the progressive forms of the five verbs below.

EXAMPLE: spend (conjugated with *we*)

ANSWER: present progressive: we are spending
past progressive: we were spending
future progressive: we will be spending
present perfect progressive: we have been spending
past perfect progressive: we had been spending
future perfect progressive: we will have been spending

1. study (conjugated with *they*)
2. put (conjugated with *he*)
3. lend (conjugated with *you*)
4. forget (conjugated with *I*)
5. strive (conjugated with *we*)

▶ **Exercise 11** Supplying the Correct Tense of Verbs On your paper, write each sentence, using the indicated form for each verb in parentheses.
1. Until recently, most coins (contain) precious metals like gold or silver. (past perfect)
2. However, the number of coins in circulation today greatly (exceed) the world's supply of precious metals. (present)
3. Making gold coins (become) impractical. (present perfect)
4. It is likely that the value of old silver and gold coins (rise) in the future. (future)
5. For that reason, more people than ever (seek) to collect old coins. (future progressive)

▲ **Critical Viewing**
How does this coin compare with those we use today? What verb forms did you use in making your comparison? **[Compare]**

Get instant feedback! Exercises 9, 10, and 11 are available on-line or on CD-ROM.

▶ **More Practice**
Grammar Exercise Workbook
• pp. 113–120
On-line Exercise Bank
• Section 22.1
Go on-line:
PHSchool.com
Enter Web Code:
eek-1002

Hands-on Grammar

Top-Ten List of Irregular Verbs

Complete the following activity to prepare a reference that you can use to remind you how to conjugate irregular verbs that you find especially troublesome.

Brainstorm with classmates to come up with a list of irregular verbs that have at times caused problems in your writing. One of you should record the verbs on the chalkboard or on a piece of paper.

Review the list of verbs, and choose the ten that you find most difficult to conjugate. Then, make a folding chart like the one below, in which you list the present, past, future, present perfect, past perfect, future perfect, present progressive, past progressive, future progressive, present perfect progressive, past perfect progressive, and future perfect progressive tenses of each verb.

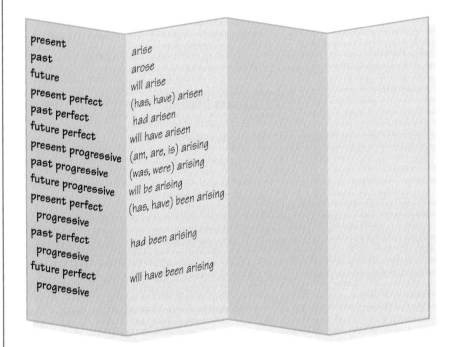

Find It in Your Reading Scan through stories and essays you have read recently to help you come up with verbs to include on your list.

Find It in Your Writing Look through your portfolio to find examples of irregular verbs. Then, add them to your chart or, if necessary, compile a second chart.

Section Review

GRAMMAR EXERCISES 12–22

Exercise 12 Identifying Verb Tenses and Forms On your paper, label the tense and form of each verb in italics.

1. People *have been collecting* coins for hundreds of years.
2. People *call* coin collectors *numismatists*.
3. Coin collecting *has been rising* in popularity with the advent of the Internet.
4. Before being able to use the Internet, collectors often *had traveled* great distances to examine and buy coins.
5. Thanks to the Internet, numismatists can now *purchase* coins in faraway places with a click of a button.

Exercise 13 Identifying the Uses of Tense Label the tense and the time of the italicized verb in each sentence.

1. A second industry *has grown* alongside the development of national currencies.
2. Counterfeiting has been a major problem for banks and governments since the first coins and bills *were produced*.
3. Counterfeiters often *use* sophisticated methods to make fake money.
4. In some nations, counterfeit currency *had reduced* public confidence in the value of the country's currency.
5. By using new technology, the U.S. government *has thwarted* many recent attempts to counterfeit U.S. currency.
6. The government *changed* the design of the twenty-dollar bill to make it more difficult for counterfeiters to copy.
7. Many years ago, the U.S. government *had begun* to use special paper on which to print its money.
8. This unique paper *has* microscopic threads embedded in it.
9. It is certain that the world's governments *will use* new methods to deter counterfeiters in the future.

10. It is hoped that by the next millennium, governments *will have succeeded* in eradicating counterfeit currency.

Exercise 14 Revising to Correct Verb Tense Revise the following paragraph, correcting errors in verb tense.

A coin's condition influences its value. The value of coins changed with time. A rare penny that is worth thousands of dollars to collectors today is worth just one cent at one time. To help establish the value of a coin, numismatists establish five gradations to rank the condition of coins. It is possible that years from now, the change in your pocket has become valuable.

Exercise 15 Recognizing Principal Parts of Verbs Identify the principal part of each verb in italics.

1. Although most countries have their own currency, many *conduct* business using the U.S. dollar.
2. In the past, this situation *helped* to keep the value of the dollar stable.
3. At this very moment, people throughout the world *are making* business deals based on the U.S. dollar.
4. Improvements in international trade regulations and communication *have made* such transactions possible.
5. People *have bought* products from foreign businesses through the Internet without needing to convert currencies.

Exercise 16 Using the Principal Parts of Verbs Choose the principal part that is correct in each sentence on the next page.

532 • Verb Usage

1. Many books have been (wrote, written) on the value of money worldwide.
2. Writers have (gave, given) much thought to this topic.
3. Economists have long (knew, known) that the value of money fluctuates.
4. They have (threw, thrown) new light on that which gives money value.
5. For example, a dollar (buyed, bought) more in the 1920's than it does today.
6. Many of our grandparents have (saw, seen) prices double, triple, or even quadruple in their lifetimes.
7. Things that had (took, taken) five cents to purchase many years ago, now may cost several dollars.
8. In that sense, the value of a dollar has (shrank, shrunk) over the years.
9. As prices for goods have risen, the value of money has (fell, fallen).
10. All is not bad news, however. Along with rising prices, people's incomes have also (grew, grown).

▶ **Exercise 17** Supplying Correct Verb Forms Supply the correct principal part of the verb in parentheses.

1. Some economists have ___?___ that coins and bills will slowly be replaced by other forms of currency. (claim)
2. Indeed, fewer people than ever before are ___?___ cash today to purchase goods and services. (use)
3. These days, people routinely ___?___ goods and services with credit cards, debit cards, and checks. (buy)
4. This ___?___ not always ___?___ the case. (be)
5. Until recently, people had ___?___ most purchases with cash. (make)

▶ **Exercise 18** Revising to Correct the Use of Irregular Verbs Revise this passage, correcting errors in verb usage.

Today, many transactions occur without the exchange of coins or paper money. This happen most often in wealthy countries when large amounts of money are involved. However, many employees are also payed by having funds deposited directly into their accounts. Experts speculate that in the future, very few people will be relying on cash to conduct business transactions. They speculate that once computer technology becomes common throughout the world, coins and paper money will have became obsolete. By 2010, we will have saw many changes.

▶ **Exercise 19** Conjugating the Basic and Progressive Forms of Verbs Conjugate the following verbs in both the basic and progressive forms.

1. earn (conjugate with *I*)
2. keep (conjugate with *you*)
3. go (conjugate with *they*)
4. tell (conjugate with *he*)
5. fly (conjugate with *we*)

▶ **Exercise 20** Find It in Your Reading Label the tense and form of each italicized verb in this excerpt from "Civil Peace" by Chinua Achebe.

. . . Jonathan *thought* he *heard* even more voices now than before and *groaned* heavily. His legs *were sagging* under him and his throat *felt* like sandpaper.

▶ **Exercise 21** Find It in Your Writing Choose a paragraph from one of your compositions. Circle each verb or verb phrase, and identify its tense and form.

▶ **Exercise 22** Writing Application In this section, you learned about the history of currency. Write about the history of something else that interests you. Use at least three different tenses. Circle each verb, and identify its tense.

Active and Passive Voice

In addition to using verbs to show the time that something happened, you can show whether the subject is performing or receiving the action. You can do this by changing the *voice* of a verb. You can show voice only with action verbs.

> **KEY CONCEPT** **Voice** is the form of a verb that shows whether the subject is performing the action. ■

There are two voices in English: *active* and *passive.*

> **KEY CONCEPTS** A verb is **active** if its subject performs the action. A verb is **passive** if its action is performed upon the subject. ■

Differences Between Active and Passive Voice

Any action verb, with or without a direct object, can be in the active voice. In these examples, the subject is doing the action.

ACTIVE VOICE: Ken *bought* a set of paints.
My sister *drives* to art school.

Most action verbs can also be used in the passive voice. A passive verb is made from a form of *be* and the past participle of a transitive verb (one that can have a direct object). In the first example below, Ken is still the performer; yet the word *Ken* is now the object of the preposition *by* and not the subject of the sentence. In the second example, *sister* is still the subject, but the person doing the action is not identified.

PASSIVE VOICE: A set of paints *was bought* by Ken.
My sister *was driven* to art school.

> **Exercise 23** Distinguishing Between the Active and Passive Voices Identify each verb or verb phrase as *active* or *passive.*
> 1. Many prominent nineteenth-century artists *lived* in France.
> 2. The Frenchman Auguste Rodin *is cherished* by art lovers.
> 3. Rodin's birthday, November 12, *is celebrated* by admirers.
> 4. Surprisingly, Rodin *did* not *grow* up in an artistic family.
> 5. His father *worked* as a police official.
> 6. Early success *was* not *experienced* by Rodin.
> 7. He *was denied* entrance to the finest art school in Paris.
> 8. Despite this setback, Rodin *persevered.*
> 9. He *pursued* sculpture on his own.
> 10. He also *worked* for other sculptors.

Get instant feedback! Exercises 23 and 24 are available on-line or on CD-ROM.

More Practice

Grammar Exercise Workbook
• pp. 121–124
On-line Exercise Bank
• Section 22.2
Go on-line:
PHSchool.com
Enter Web Code:
eek-1002

Using Voice Correctly

To write well, you must know when to use the active voice and when to use the passive voice. There are no firm rules, but here are some suggestions:

KEY CONCEPT Use the active voice whenever possible. ■

Good writing is crisp and direct. Sentences with active verbs are less wordy and more direct than those with passive verbs. Notice that both sentences below report the same information, but the sentence in the active voice is shorter and more direct.

ACTIVE VOICE: Esteban *sketched* the bowl of apples.
PASSIVE VOICE: The bowl of apples *was sketched* by Esteban.

There are, of course, times when it is more appropriate to use the passive voice. Use the passive voice to point out the receiver of an action whenever the performer is not important or not easily identified.

KEY CONCEPT Use the passive voice to emphasize the receiver of an action rather than the performer of an action. ■

Placing a word at or near the beginning of a sentence helps emphasize its importance. When you want to stress the importance of the receiver of an action, then it is proper to use the passive voice.

PASSIVE VOICE: Maria *was given* an art award by a museum official.
                     The damaged statue *was placed* downstairs.

Exercise 24 Revising Sentences in the Passive Voice Rewrite each sentence below, changing it from passive to active voice.
1. The art exhibit was seen by our whole family.
2. A review of the exhibit had been read by us before we went.
3. Tickets for the exhibit were purchased by my mother.
4. The Internet was used by her to make the purchase.
5. Each work in the exhibit was painted by an Impressionist artist.

▼ Critical Viewing
Think of two sentences concerning the creation of this painting, one in the active voice and one in the passive voice. Which sentence is shorter and more direct? [Connect, Contrast]

Tiberius and Agrippina, Peter Paul Rubens

GRAMMAR IN LITERATURE

from **My Left Foot**
Christy Brown

In this passage, writer and artist Christy Brown describes events after his difficult birth. Notice the active voice verbs (in blue) and passive voice verbs (in red) in the passage.

After my birth mother *was sent* to recuperate for some weeks and I *was kept* in the hospital while she was away. I *remained* there for some time, without name, for I *was*n't *baptized* until my mother was well enough to bring me to church.

It was my mother who first *saw* that there was something wrong with me. I was about four months old at the time. She *noticed* that my head *had* a habit of falling backward whenever she *tried* to feed me.

▶ **Exercise 25** Revising to Use the Active Voice On your paper, rewrite the following paragraph, changing at least four uses of the passive voice to the active voice. If you have chosen to leave any sentence in the passive voice, explain your reason.

EXAMPLE: The sculpture was honored with a blue ribbon.
ANSWER: Keep in passive voice because performer of action is unidentified.

(1) The mid-twentieth century has been heralded by many art scholars as an exciting era for innovative art. (2) Jasper Johns, one of the most interesting artists of that era, worked in the United States in the 1950's. (3) Audiences and critics were thrilled by Johns's bold paintings. (4) Exploring a new direction, he painted such ordinary objects as numerals and the letters of the alphabet. (5) Thick layers of paint were used by Johns on his paintings. (6) The texture of his creations was intensified by this technique. (7) In the late 1950's, he incorporated actual objects into his paintings. (8) Objects like rulers and compasses were attached by him to his paintings. (9) Johns is considered by many art scholars to be one of the most influential American artists of the twentieth century. (10) Many of his works are exhibited in prominent art museums and galleries around the world.

▶ **More Practice**

Grammar Exercise
Workbook
• pp. 121–124
On-line Exercise Bank
• Section 22.2
  Go on-line:
  PHSchool.com
  Enter Web Code:
  eek-1002

Complete the exercise on-line! Exercise 25 is available on-line or on CD-ROM.

Section 22.2 Section Review

GRAMMAR EXERCISES 26–31

Exercise 26 Distinguishing Between the Active and Passive Voices
On your paper, identify the voice of the verb in each of the following sentences.

1. In the 1960's, Andy Warhol was noticed by the art world for his silk-screen prints of ordinary objects.
2. Common objects, such as soup cans and soft-drink bottles, were often depicted in these prints.
3. This seemingly defiant approach to art defined the Pop Art movement.
4. Warhol also made silk-screen prints of famous celebrities.
5. Warhol's reputation as an innovator was established by these prints.

Exercise 27 Using the Passive and Active Voices Identify the voice of the italicized verb in each sentence. Then, rewrite the sentence, changing the voice from active to passive or passive to active.

1. The works of Leonardo da Vinci *have inspired* viewers for hundreds of years.
2. Da Vinci *had been heralded* by his peers in Italy as a talented artist.
3. Modern critics *have praised* him as a superb painter, sculptor, architect, and scientist.
4. He *is remembered* best by art lovers for *The Last Supper* and the *Mona Lisa.*
5. *The Last Supper was painted* by Da Vinci on one wall of a dining hall of a monastery.
6. Many people *have described* the *Mona Lisa* as a masterpiece.
7. The work *depicts* a beautiful woman.
8. A sense of mystery *is captured* in the woman's smile.
9. The work also *displays* great technical mastery.
10. By the early 2000's, Da Vinci's works *will have been admired* by people for nearly five hundred years.

Exercise 28 Revising to Use the Active Voice Rewrite this paragraph, changing several uses of the passive voice to the active voice. Explain why you have left any sentence in the passive voice.

(1) The fourteenth and fifteenth centuries are described by art historians as a time of revival in European art and culture. (2) This period has often been called the Renaissance, or "rebirth." (3) Prior to the Renaissance, European art had been marked by a long period of inactivity. (4) The sculptor Donatello is considered by critics and historians to be one of the greatest Renaissance artists. (5) A golden era in sculpture was signaled by Donatello's completion of a statue of David in 1435.

Exercise 29 Find It in Your Reading Make a photocopy of a magazine article about one of the fine arts. Highlight all of the verbs in the active voice in one color and all of the verbs in the passive voice in another color.

Exercise 30 Find It in Your Writing In a piece of your own writing, find at least five sentences in the passive voice. Rewrite these sentences in the active voice.

Exercise 31 Writing Application Write a brief description of a work of art that you or one of your friends created. Use both active and passive voice verbs. Circle each verb, and identify its voice. Explain your use of the passive voice.

Chapter Review

GRAMMAR EXERCISES 32–40

Exercise 32 Identifying the Tenses of Verbs Identify the tense and form of each verb or verb phrase in italics.

1. Painters today *have* a great choice of subjects to depict.
2. Over the years, artists *have painted* various objects and people.
3. Before the 1600's, most European artists *had focused* on religious subjects.
4. Dutch artists in the 1600's *were experimenting* with new subject matter.
5. They *developed* genre painting, in which they *focused* on realistic depictions of scenes from ordinary life.
6. This shift in subject matter *had represented* a radical break from tradition.
7. For the first time, artists *were devoting* attention to the lives of ordinary people.
8. Even today, many artists *are working* in this tradition.
9. Artists *will paint* ordinary life as long as that subject matter continues to intrigue them.
10. By the year 2100, genre painting *will have aroused* the interest of painters and viewers for nearly 500 years.

Exercise 33 Supplying Principal Parts of Verbs Rewrite each sentence, supplying the correct principal part of the verb in parentheses.

1. One of the most important developments in twentieth-century painting has ___?___ Abstract Expressionism. (be)
2. Abstract Expressionism ___?___ the public's attention in the 1940's. (catch)
3. It ___?___ out of earlier artistic attempts to express emotions. (grow)
4. Until then, most artists had ___?___ ways to depict how objects really looked or seemed. (seek)

5. In contrast, Abstract Expressionist painters are ___?___ to express the emotional aspects of things. (strive)

Exercise 34 Revising the Usage of Irregular Verbs Revise this paragraph, correcting errors in verb usage.

Abstract Expressionists maked their creations by using bold colors and lines. Unlike painters from other schools who taked a lot of time to work over tiny details in their paintings, the Abstract Expressionists often flinged paints at a canvas as if they were in a frenzy. Jackson Pollock and Willem de Kooning were two Abstract Expressionists who become prominent artists. These artists do what few before them had dared to do.

Exercise 35 Conjugating the Basic and Progressive Forms of Verbs Conjugate the basic and progressive forms of the following verbs in the *present, past, future, present perfect, past perfect,* and *future perfect* tenses.

1. arrange (conjugate with *I*)
2. spread (conjugate with *it*)
3. draw (conjugate with *we*)
4. buy (conjugate with *you*)
5. shake (conjugate with *they*)

Exercise 36 Supplying the Correct Tenses of Verbs Write the indicated form for each verb in parentheses.

1. Present perfect—Artists (be) the subject of many feature films.
2. Past—In *The Agony and the Ecstasy,* Charlton Heston (portray) the Renaissance artist Michelangelo.

3. Present—The film (show) Michelangelo's total devotion to painting the ceiling of the Sistine Chapel.
4. Past perfect—The Dutch Impressionist painter Vincent van Gogh (serve) as a favorite subject of other popular films.
5. Present progressive—Today, many people (relate) painting to film.
6. Present perfect—Filmmakers often (view) the film frame as a canvas.
7. Present progressive—Many of today's films (feature) sophisticated effects.
8. Present perfect progressive—Promising young artists (create) these effects.
9. Future—Many future artists (express) their ideas with computer graphics.
10. Future progressive—By creating dazzling effects with computers, many young people (demonstrate) that art is not limited to canvas.

▶ **Exercise 37** Distinguishing Between Active and Passive Voices
Identify whether the verb in each sentence is in the *active* or *passive* voice.

(1) The earliest known paintings were created by cave dwellers thousands of years ago. (2) These cave dwellers lived in Europe. (3) Pictures of wild animals were drawn by them on cave walls. (4) The cave dwellers depicted deer, horses, and other animals in earth pigments. (5) Every year, thousands of visitors are drawn to a cave in Lascaux, France, to see these early paintings.

▶ **Exercise 38** Revising to Use the Active Voice Revise this paragraph, replacing passive voice verbs with active voice verbs where appropriate.

(1) Artists don't always start young. (2) Talent is shown by some artists after they have lived a full life. (3) Grandma Moses was noticed by art experts when she was in her seventies. (4) In the 1940's, her career was launched by art critics.

(5) Before then, she had lived a quiet life as a farmer's wife. (6) Rural scenes had been painted by her for her own pleasure. (7) Recognition from art experts quickly transformed her into a celebrity. (8) Her work was praised by experts for its simple depiction of rural life. (9) Many of her paintings have been purchased by museums and collectors. (10) Many amateur artists have been inspired by Grandma Moses' career.

▶ **Exercise 39** Revising to Improve Verb Usage Revise this passage, correcting verb usage and changing the passive voice into the active voice where appropriate.

Artists have seeked to make portraits and sculptures of people for thousands of years. The earliest known artistic representations of individuals are statues of ancient Egyptian rulers from around 2700 B.C. During the Middle Ages, portraits of rulers, nobles, and important church officials were generally drawed by artists. Later, they begin to focus on ordinary people. By the eighteenth century, portrait painting had became an established art form. Many artists, then and now, have make their living by painting portraits. The invention of photography has affected portrait painting. Today, an individual usually sit for a photograph, rather than a painting. Yet, a special impression is created by a portrait that has been did in oils. The art of portrait painting will continuing for many years to come.

▶ **Exercise 40** Writing Application
Write a real or made-up history of a painting or an artist. Use verbs in several different tenses and both voices in your paragraph.

Standardized Test Preparation Workshop

Standard English Usage: Using Verbs

Many standardized tests assess your ability to apply the rules of verb usage. You may be given a passage that contains a series of blanks and asked to choose words to fill in the blanks. Often, the choice of words will involve selecting the correct form of a verb. When choosing a verb, first read the sentence silently to yourself, and determine when it is taking place. Then, choose a verb that indicates the same point in time or tense of the sentence.

The following test items will give you practice with the format of questions that test verb usage.

Test Tip

Read the sentence silently to yourself several times. Each time, substitute one of the answer choices in place of the blank. Eliminate those choices that sound awkward or change the meaning of the sentence.

Sample Test Items

Directions: Read the passage, and choose the letter of the word or group of words that belongs in each space.

After serving as an ambulance driver during World War I, Ernest Hemingway ___(1)___ time in Paris, along with many other writers, including Ezra Pound and F. Scott Fitzgerald. These writers ___(2)___ known as the "Expatriates" because they had intentionally chosen to live outside the United States.

1 A spend

 B had spent

 C spent

 D spended

2 F became

 G become

 H are

 J have been

Answers and Explanations

The correct answer is C. The passage is clearly set in the past, so the appropriate choice is the past tense of the verb *spend*. *Spend* is an irregular verb, and its past tense is *spent*, not *spended*.

The correct answer is F. Again, because the passage describes events from the past, a past tense verb is called for. *Became* is the past tense of the verb *become*.

▶ Practice 1

Directions: Read the passage, and choose the letter of the word or group of words that belongs in each space.

The United States __(1)__ from World War II as the most powerful nation on Earth. Proud of the part they __(2)__ in defeating the Axis, Americans now __(3)__ life to return to normal. Soldiers and sailors __(4)__ home, the rationing of scarce goods ended, and the nation __(5)__.

1 A emerges
  B had emerged
  C emerged
  D will emerge

2 F had played
  G played
  H play
  J would have played

3 A want
  B wanted
  C had wanted
  D would want

4 F were coming
  G come
  H came
  J had come

5 A had prospered
  B would prosper
  C prospered
  D prospers

▶ Practice 2

Directions: Read the passage, and choose the letter of the word or group of words that belongs in each space.

Real and lasting gains __(1)__ in civil rights after World War II. Those gains __(2)__ largely from the courageous actions of Martin Luther King, Jr., and other civil rights leaders of the 1950's and 1960's. One of the movement's major breakthroughs __(3)__ the passage of legislation that protected the voting rights of all Americans. Today, there __(4)__ many African Americans in political office. This situation would not __(5)__ without the efforts of Martin Luther King, Jr., and others.

1 A was made
  B were made
  C had been made
  D were maked

2 F were the result
  G resulting
  H had resulted
  J resulted

3 A is
  B were
  C was
  D are

4 F are
  G were
  H have been
  J will be

5 A be occurring
  B have occurred
  C occur
  D have occur

Pronoun Usage

At one time in the history of the English language, the forms of both nouns and pronouns were changed to indicate how they were being used in a sentence. Today, nouns change form only to show possession: A noun is made possessive by adding an apostrophe and an *s* (a *woman's* dress) or just an apostrophe (the two *boys'* gloves).

Pronouns in modern English still have different forms depending on how they are used in a sentence. This chapter will explain the various forms of pronouns and their uses.

The rules of proper pronoun usage have developed over time to help us communicate more effectively and efficiently. Whether you are writing about modern times or about America in the "Roaring Twenties," you need to use pronouns correctly in order to communicate.

▲ **Critical Viewing**
Describe the actions of both people in the picture, using such pronouns as *he, she, him, her, his, they,* and *their.*
[Analyze]

Diagnostic Test

Directions: Write all answers on a separate sheet of paper.

Skill Check A. Write the pronouns in each sentence, and identify the case for each as *nominative*, *objective*, or *possessive*.

1. They danced a popular dance from the 1920's.
2. The author dedicated his book on the Jazz Age to her.
3. We saw pictures of fancy dresses worn in the 1920's.
4. Grandfather remembers his best friend from way back then.
5. "The happiest people were we children," he recalled.

Skill Check B. Identify the case of each underlined pronoun in the following sentences, and tell how it is used in the sentence.

6. <u>Her</u> grandmother lived during the 1920's.
7. <u>She</u> is extremely happy that we are interested in <u>her</u> stories.
8. She enjoys telling <u>me</u> her stories.
9. The two biggest fans of the 1920's are she and <u>I</u>.
10. Talking to her fascinates <u>me</u>.

Skill Check C. Indicate the correct pronoun to complete the following sentences.

11. One of (me, my) favorite heroes of the 1920's is Charles Lindbergh.
12. (His, His') adventures were followed by people from all over the world.
13. His quest was known for (it's, its) difficulty.
14. Do you know where (you're, your) ancestors were in the 1920's?
15. I am sure that (their, they're) experiences are very interesting.

Skill Check D. Choose the correct pronoun in parentheses, and identify its function in the sentence or clause.

16. I know (who, whom) gave her the article about 1920's fashion.
17. She is not sure (who, whom) they are featuring next.
18. To (who, whom) did she lend her book?
19. Do you know (who, whom) made the first solo flight across the Atlantic Ocean?
20. Give it to (whoever, whomever) wrote this report on famous aviators.

Skill Check E. Choose the correct pronoun in parentheses. Then, write any words or phrases that are understood to precede or follow the pronoun.

21. I know more about the fads of the 1920's than (she, her).
22. The speaker knows less about the 1920's than (I, me).
23. The films of the 1920's are as familiar to his grandmother as (he, him).
24. No living silent film star is as respected as (she, her).
25. This collection of photographs from the 1920's is more precious to me than (they, them).

Case

Case is a term used to describe the different forms of nouns and pronouns.

▶ **KEY CONCEPT** Case is the form of a noun or a pronoun that indicates its use in a sentence. ■

The Three Cases

Both nouns and pronouns have three cases:

▶ **KEY CONCEPT** The three cases are the *nominative*, the *objective*, and the *possessive*. ■

The following chart shows the uses of each of these three cases.

Case	Use in Sentence
Nominative	Subject or Predicate Nominative
Objective	Direct Object, Indirect Object, Object of a Preposition, or Object of a Verbal
Possessive	To Show Ownership

Using the correct case of nouns is seldom a problem because the form changes only in the possessive case.

NOMINATIVE: The old *car* would not start.

OBJECTIVE: We could not start the old *car.*

POSSESSIVE: The old *car's* battery needed to be replaced.

In the first sentence, *car* is the subject. In the second sentence, *car* is the direct object. The form changes only in the *possessive* case, by adding an apostrophe and an *s.*

In contrast to nouns, personal pronouns have different forms for all three cases.

Nominative	Objective	Possessive
I	me	my, mine
you	you	your, yours
he, she, it	him, her, it	his, her, hers, its
we	us	our, ours
they	them	their, theirs

**Theme:
Roaring Twenties**

In this section, you will learn about the three cases of pronouns and their uses and forms. The examples and exercises in this section are about the Roaring Twenties.

Cross-Curricular Connection: Social Studies

GRAMMAR IN LITERATURE

from **A Visit to Grandmother**

William Melvin Kelley

Notice the pronouns in the nominative case (in red) and objective case (in blue) in this excerpt. How is each pronoun used?

. . . So *I* stood on the porch and watched GL hitching that horse up to the white folks' buggy. For a while there, the animal was pretty quiet, pawing a little, but not much. And *I* was feeling a little better about riding with GL behind that crazy-looking horse. *I* could see how GL was happy *I* was going with *him*. *He* was scurrying around that animal buckling buckles and strapping straps, all the time smiling, and that made *me* feel good.

▲ **Critical Viewing**
Write three sentences describing both the man holding the horse and the women in the carriage. Use *he, him, she, her, they,* or *them* in your sentences. **[Analyze]**

Exercise 1 Identifying Case Write the case of each under-lined pronoun. Then, indicate its usage.

EXAMPLE: The reporter told the truth about <u>them</u>.
ANSWER: objective (object of a preposition)

1. <u>Our</u> ancestors lived through the 1920's, a remarkable period in history.
2. If <u>you</u> had been alive in the 1920's, you would have witnessed many exciting events.
3. The people of the 1920's saw <u>their</u> world change rapidly.
4. <u>They</u> enjoyed benefits brought about by advances in commerce and technology.
5. Many of <u>them</u> heard the world's first radio broadcast.
6. Other innovations in science and business amazed and excited <u>them</u>.
7. These advances brought about great prosperity for many Americans and <u>their</u> descendants.
8. Such advances in technology gave <u>them</u> a sense of optimism for the future.
9. The beneficiaries of their optimism are <u>we</u>.
10. Reading about events of the 1920's and studying <u>them</u> can offer many insights into modern times.

▶ **More Practice**

Grammar Exercise Workbook
• pp. 125–126
On-line Exercise Bank
• Section 23.1
 Go on-line:
 PHSchool.com
 Enter Web Code:
 eek-1002

The Nominative Case

There are two major uses of pronouns in the nominative case:

> **KEY CONCEPT** Use the nominative case when a pronoun is used as the *subject* of a verb or as a *predicate nominative*. ■

The chart below illustrates these two uses.

More Practice

Grammar Exercise Workbook
• pp. 127–128
On-line Exercise Bank
• Section 23.1
  Go on-line:
  PHSchool.com
  Enter Web Code:
  eek-1002

NOMINATIVE PRONOUNS	
Subject	*She* is the conductor of the band. *I* want to learn more about the music of the 1920's. *They* danced the Charleston while we sat.
Predicate Nominative	The famous historian is *she.* It is *I.* Our closest friends have always been *they.*

Nominative Pronouns in Compounds When using a compound subject or a compound predicate nominative, check the case by mentally removing the other part of the compound or by mentally inverting the sentence.

COMPOUND SUBJECT:	Marie and *I* watched a film about the 1920's. (*I* watched a film about the 1920's.) Beth and *he* will learn more about that time from his grandmother. (*He* will learn more about that time from his grandmother.)
COMPOUND PREDICATE NOMINATIVE:	The winners were Tim and *she.* (Tim and *she* were the winners.) The best dancers are Kay and *I.* (Kay and *I* are the best dancers.)

Nominative Pronouns With Appositives Appositives sometimes follow a pronoun in order to rename it or identify it. If a pronoun used as a subject or predicate nominative is followed by an appositive, the nominative case is still used.

SUBJECT:	*We* musicians love music of the 1920's.
PREDICATE NOMINATIVE:	The ones with the most spirit are *we* sophomores.

> **Exercise 2** Identifying Pronouns in the Nominative Case

Choose the nominative case pronoun that completes each sentence.

1. (We, Us) Americans have always enjoyed sports.
2. Fiercely devoted sports fans are (we, us).
3. My great-grandfather and (I, me) often talk about sports heroes from the 1920's.
4. My great-grandfather was obsessed with sports in the 1920's when (he, him) was a young boy.
5. (I, Me) have learned much about Babe Ruth and Red Grange from him.
6. His first heroes in baseball and football were (they, them).
7. My great-grandfather described a time when (he, him) saw Babe Ruth smack a home run.
8. His brother and (he, him) went to that game together.
9. He said that the most excited fans in the stadium were (they, them).
10. "(He, Him) and I almost caught that baseball," he recalled.

> **Exercise 3** Using Pronouns in the Nominative Case Write a nominative pronoun to complete each sentence. Then, identify how the pronoun is used in the sentence.

1. My friends and ___?___ have been learning about the Roaring Twenties.
2. Did ___?___ know that the Roaring Twenties closely followed World War I?
3. ___?___ Americans were excited by the return of peace and improvements in our economy.
4. Many Americans supported the Republican party, and ___?___ elected Warren G. Harding president in 1920.
5. It was ___?___ who became the twenty-ninth president of the United States.

▼ Critical Viewing Describe your impression of these two political leaders. Use *I, he,* and *they* in your sentences. **[Describe]**

President
Warren G. Harding

Vice-President
Calvin Coolidge

> **Exercise 4** Revising to Correct Errors in Pronoun Usage

Revise the following sentences to correct errors in pronoun usage. If a sentence is correct, write *correct.*

1. I learned that him and his wife were from Ohio.
2. My friends and me are interested in learning more about Harding.
3. Harding appointed many friends to government positions. Some of they became involved in several scandals.
4. Harding served as president until August 1923, when he died of a heart attack in San Francisco, California.
5. Calvin Coolidge was vice president, so Harding's successor was he.

The Objective Case

The objective case is used with the objects of verbs and prepositions as well as with the objects of verbals.

▶ **More Practice**

Grammar Exercise Workbook
• pp. 127–128
On-line Exercise Bank
• Section 23.1
Go on-line:
PHSchool.com
Enter Web Code:
eek-1002

▶ **KEY CONCEPT** Use the objective case when a pronoun is used as the object of any verb, preposition, or verbal. ■

The chart below illustrates the uses of objective pronouns.

OBJECTIVE PRONOUNS	
Use	**Examples**
Direct Object	I baked *them* yesterday. Our teacher praised *her*.
Indirect Object	Give *him* the good news. Alice gave *us* the poster from the 1920's.
Object of Preposition	Between *us*, there are no secrets. Walk beside *them*.
Object of Participle	Racing *her*, he crashed into an antique car. The girl chasing *them* was her sister.
Object of Gerund	Dad likes helping *me* with my homework. Warning *them* was my primary concern.
Object of Infinitive	To tell *them* clearly, he had to shout. He wants to ask *me* about my visit.

Objective Pronouns in Compounds Errors with objective case pronouns most often occur in compounds. To check yourself, mentally remove the other part of the compound.

EXAMPLES: Our history teacher praised John and *her*.
(Our history teacher praised *her*.)

The project was assigned to Charles and *him*.
(The project was assigned to *him*.)

Take special care to use the objective case after the preposition *between*.

INCORRECT: This matter is between *you* and *I*.

CORRECT: This matter is between *you* and *me*.

▼ **Critical Viewing** Write three sentences about this flapper. Use a pronoun in a different case in each sentence. **[Analyze]**

Objective Pronoun With Appositives If an appositive appears after a pronoun used as an object, make sure that you use an objective pronoun.

DIRECT OBJECT: The musical entertained *us* girls.

INDIRECT OBJECT: The club gave *us* leaders an award.

OBJECT OF A
PREPOSITION: All of *us* history students were
nervous about the assignment.

▶ **Exercise 5** Identifying Pronouns in the Objective Case
Choose the pronoun in the objective case to complete each sentence. Then, identify how the pronoun is used in the sentence.

EXAMPLE: The orchestra plans to join (him, he) later.
ANSWER: him (object of infinitive)

1. To (we, us) historians, the 1920's is often known as the Roaring Twenties or the Jazz Age.
2. For Americans in the 1920's, the Jazz Age promised (they, them) great hope and excitement.
3. With stock holdings enriching (they, them), many Americans achieved wealth beyond their wildest dreams.
4. The independent, glamourous flappers of the 1920's are role models for some of (we, us) modern women.
5. Studying (they, them) holds special meaning for today's independent women.

▶ **Exercise 6** Supplying Pronouns in the Objective Case
Write an objective pronoun to complete each sentence. Then, identify how the pronoun is used in the sentence.

EXAMPLE: My parents gave ___?___ an antique watch for my birthday.
ANSWER: me (indirect object)

1. My aunt questioned my sisters and ___?___ about the 1920's.
2. She then gave ___?___ the novel *This Side of Paradise* (1920) by F. Scott Fitzgerald.
3. She enjoys suggesting books to ___?___.
4. Between my sisters and ___?___, we have read enough books to fill a small library.
5. It is easy to get my aunt to start talking; it is stopping ___?___ that is sometimes hard.

⊛ Technology Tip

The spell-check function on most word-processing programs will recognize *it's* and *its* as correctly spelled words. It is up to you to recognize that *it's* means *it is* or *it has* and that *its* shows ownership.

The Possessive Case

The possessive case of pronouns is used to show possession before nouns and before gerunds. Some possessive pronouns are also used by themselves.

KEY CONCEPT Use the possessive case before nouns to show ownership. ■

EXAMPLES: *My* report on the Roaring Twenties is almost done.
Their suggestions have been very helpful.

KEY CONCEPT Use the possessive case before gerunds. ■

EXAMPLES: *Your* asking questions made me focus.
I did not appreciate *his* writing in my book.

KEY CONCEPT Use certain possessive pronouns by themselves to indicate possession. ■

EXAMPLES: That book is *hers*, not *his*.
Is this movie poster *yours* or *mine*?

Sometimes, possessive pronouns are incorrectly spelled with an apostrophe. Spellings such as *your's, our's, their's,* and *her's* are incorrect. In addition, do not confuse the possessive pronouns *its, your,* and *their* (which do not contain apostrophes) with the contractions *it's, you're,* and *they're.*

POSSESSIVE PRONOUN: Which 1920's song is your favorite?

CONTRACTION: *You're* expected to dress up for the party.

Exercise 7 Using Pronouns in the Possessive Case Choose the correct word in parentheses.
1. Each era has (it's, its) distinct fashion trends.
2. Have you ever thought about how (your, you're) great-grandparents may have dressed in the 1920's?
3. Some clothing in the 1920's was similar to (ours, our's).
4. Flappers wore skirts that revealed (they're, their) knees.
5. Those long pearl necklaces were (hers, her's).
6. (They're, Their) choosing to dress that way was a clear break with tradition.
7. (Your, You're) going to enjoy our 1920's fashion show.
8. (Its, It's) scheduled for next Friday evening.
9. I found several suits from the 1920's; (they're, their) in the closet backstage.
10. Back then, men often wore (they're, their) hair parted in the middle.

More Practice

Grammar Exercise Workbook
• pp. 129–130
On-line Exercise Bank
• Section 23.1
Go on-line:
PHSchool.com
Enter Web Code:
eek-1002

Get instant feedback! Exercise 7 is available on-line or on CD-ROM.

Section Review

GRAMMAR EXERCISES 8–13

Exercise 8 Identifying Case Write the case of each of the underlined pronouns in the following sentences. Then, write its use.

1. Historians believe that studying the past will help <u>us</u> in the future.
2. In the 1920's, enterprising business-men and <u>their</u> associates amassed fortunes.
3. Their investments in oil, railroads, and steel brought great wealth to <u>them</u>.
4. Their wealth won <u>them</u> status and fame.
5. The principal investors in the stock market were <u>they</u>.

Exercise 9 Identifying Pronouns in the Objective Case Choose the correct pronoun in parentheses to complete each sentence. Then, identify its case.

1. <u>They</u> used (their, they're) wealth to influence politicians.
2. (They, Their) having so much wealth and power made poor people jealous.
3. Bill and (me, I) read novels by some prominent writers of the 1920's.
4. The novelists wrote about rich people and sometimes criticized (they, them).
5. Our teacher said that (us, we) should learn more about the 1920's economy.

Exercise 10 Revising to Correct Pronoun Usage Revise this paragraph, correcting errors in pronoun usage.

(1) The people of the 1920's experienced many exciting events. A number of techno-logical breakthroughs were witnessed by they. (2) Many of them thrilled at seeing new forms of entertainment. (3) Like the people of today, the people of the 1920's often spent they're Saturday afternoons at movie theaters. (4) On some of those Saturdays, them watched the films of Charlie Chaplin. (5) Its him who created the character of the little tramp with the funny walk. (6) People all around the world soon fell in love with he and his antics. (7) Two of the first international movie stars were him and Al Jolson. (8) Although Chaplin's early films did not feature dialogue, they were often accompanied by dramatic music. (9) Fortunately, Chaplin's films have survived to the present and still give many of we great enjoyment. (10) Watching them, your certain to laugh out loud.

Exercise 11 Find It in Your Reading In this passage from "A Visit to Grandmother," identify at least one pro-noun in each of the three cases, and tell how it is used.

She let him go, and fell back into her chair, grabbing the arms. Her hands were as dark as the wood, and seemed to become part of it.

Exercise 12 Find It in Your Writing In your portfolio, find five sen-tences containing pronouns in all three cases. Check that you have used the pro-nouns correctly. Write down each pronoun, its case, and its use in the sentence.

Exercise 13 Writing Application Imagine that you are interviewing a per-son who lived in the United States during the 1920's. Make a list of questions and responses from your interview. Try to use pronouns in all three cases in your tran-script of the interview.

Special Problems With Pronouns

Choosing the correct form of a pronoun is not always a matter of choosing the form that sounds correct. For example, would it be correct to say, "I can run faster than her"? Though the sentence may sound correct to you, it is wrong because an objective pronoun (*her*) is used when a nominative pronoun (*she*) is needed. Several words are understood in the sentence, which reads, in full, "I can run faster than she (can run)."

This section will discuss two special pronoun problems: the proper uses of *who* and *whom* and the related forms *whoever* and *whomever*, as well as the use of pronouns in clauses where some words are omitted but understood.

Theme: Mars
....
In this section, you will learn about special problems with pronouns. The examples and exercises in this section are about Mars.
....
Cross-Curricular Connection: Science

Using *Who* and *Whom* Correctly

Knowing when to use *who* or *whom* and the related forms *whoever* and *whomever* is less confusing if you understand how the words are used.

KEY CONCEPT *Who* and *whoever* are nominative case pronouns. *Whom* and *whomever* are objective case pronouns. ■

The chart below shows the forms of these pronouns and their uses in sentences.

Case	Pronoun	Use in Sentence
Nominative	who, whoever	Subject or Predicate Nominative
Objective	whom, whomever	Direct Object, Object of a Verbal, or Object of a Preposition
Possessive	whose, whosever	To Show Ownership

The following pages focus on the nominative and objective pronouns, as the possessive case rarely causes problems.

Note About *Whose*: Do not confuse the contraction *who's*, which means "who is," with the possessive pronoun *whose*.

POSSESSIVE PRONOUN: *Whose* satellite went into orbit?

CONTRACTION: *Who's* our first contestant tonight?

The Nominative Case: *Who* and *Whoever* The nominative case is used for subjects and for predicate nominatives.

▶ **KEY CONCEPT** Use *who* or *whoever* for the subject of a verb. ■

EXAMPLES: *Who* is the person directing the Mars study?
I know *who* had the best science project.
He chose *whoever* volunteered for the space project.

In the last two sentences, *who* and *whoever* are the subjects of subordinate clauses. You can be sure you are using the correct case in a subordinate clause by determining the use of the pronoun. Consider the pronoun in the following sentence:

EXAMPLE: I will accept help from *whoever* will offer it.

The first step in checking the case of the pronoun is to isolate the subordinate clause. In this example, the subordinate clause is *whoever will offer it*, a noun clause acting as the object of the preposition *from*.
The next step is to see how the words in the subordinate clause are used. The verb in the clause is *will offer*; the direct object is *it*. *Whoever* is the correct pronoun because it acts as a subject and, therefore, must be in the nominative case.

▶ **KEY CONCEPT** Use *who* or *whoever* for a predicate nominative. ■

EXAMPLE: The culprit is *who*?

A problem may arise when the pronoun is the predicate nominative in a subordinate clause.

EXAMPLE: The police do not know *who* the culprit is.

To see whether the pronoun is correct, first isolate the subordinate clause (*who the culprit is*). Next, determine each word's use within the clause. Because this clause is inverted, put it into normal word order: *The culprit is who.* You can now see that the subject is *culprit*, the verb is *is*, and *who* is the predicate nominative of the linking verb. Because predicate nominatives require the nominative case, *who* is correct.

The planet Mars has a polar icecap.

▲ **Critical Viewing** Write two questions about this picture using the word *who* or *whom* in each. **[Analyze]**

The Objective Case: *Whom* and *Whomever* The objective case of these pronouns is used for direct objects of verbs, objects of verbals, and objects of prepositions.

KEY CONCEPT Use *whom* and *whomever* for the direct object of a verb or the object of a verbal. ■

In this example, *whom* is the object of the infinitive *to see.* Check the pronoun's case by mentally rewording the sentence.

EXAMPLE:　　*Whom* did you expect to see?
　　　　　　　(You did expect to see *whom*?)

Pronouns in the objective case also occur in the subordinate clauses of complex sentences.

EXAMPLES:　　We asked *whom* they chose to go into space.
　　　　　　　You can select *whomever* you want.

To see whether the correct pronouns have been used, first isolate the subordinate clause (*whom they chose, whomever you want*). Next, put the clauses in normal word order: *they chose whom; you want whomever.* It now becomes clear that the subjects are *they* and *you* and that the correct direct objects are *whom* and *whomever.*

KEY CONCEPT Use *whom* or *whomever* for the object of a preposition. ■

Whom is the object of a preposition in both examples below.

EXAMPLES:　　From *whom* did you receive the message?
　　　　　　　Whom did you receive the message from?

If the pronoun is used to connect the clauses of a complete sentence, it is necessary to check the pronoun's case more carefully. Look at these two sentences with adjective clauses.

EXAMPLES:　　I spoke to the astronaut with *whom* we had dined.
　　　　　　　I spoke to the astronaut *whom* we had dined with.

In the first sentence, the objective pronoun immediately follows its preposition, *with.* In the second sentence, the pronoun and the preposition are separated by many words. To check the case, isolate the subordinate clause: *whom we had dined with.* Next, put the clause in the normal word order: *We had dined with whom.* The clause has a subject (*we*), a verb (*had dined*), and a prepositional phrase (*with whom*). *Whom* is the correct pronoun because the objective case is required for the object of a preposition.

More Practice

Grammar Exercise
Workbook
• pp. 131–132
On-line Exercise Bank
• Section 23.2
　Go on-line:
　PHSchool.com
　Enter Web Code:
　eek-1002

GRAMMAR IN LITERATURE

from **Invasion From Mars**
Howard Koch

Notice the use of who *in the following excerpt.*

. . . Due to the unusual nature of this occurrence, we have arranged an interview with the noted astronomer, Professor Pierson, *who* will give us his views on this event.

Exercise 14 Using *Who* and *Whom* Correctly in Questions and Clauses Choose the correct pronoun in each sentence, and identify the case of the pronoun.

1. (Who, Whom) has not wondered whether there is life on other planets?
2. From (who, whom) can we learn about plans to send a satellite to Mars?
3. The person most likely to be able to answer that question is (who, whom)?
4. If you could take a trip to Mars, (who's, whose) the person you would like most to accompany you?
5. Someday, such a trip may become possible. In the meantime, (whoever, whomever) is interested in Mars can learn more about it from books, magazines, and the Internet.

Exercise 15 Revising to Correct the Use of *Who* and *Whom* Revise the following sentences to correct errors in the use of *who* and *whom*. If a sentence is correct, write *correct*.

1. Cherie asked whomever she saw about the reddish planet in the sky.
2. Indeed, Mars is close enough to us that it is visible to whoever wants to search for it even without a telescope.
3. To who did you remark that it takes 687 Earth days for Mars to revolve around the sun?
4. Whom did you ask?
5. In whose book did you see a photograph of Mars?

▼ Critical Viewing Use *who* in a sentence about astronauts on Mars. Use *whom* in a sentence about the people watching them. **[Draw Conclusions]**

Use Pronouns Correctly in Elliptical Clauses

In an *elliptical clause*, some words are omitted because they are understood. Sentences with elliptical clauses are often used to draw comparisons. Such sentences are usually divided into two parts connected by *than* or *as: Fran is smarter than he,* or *Tom is as happy as I.* In selecting the case of the pronoun, you must know what the unstated words are.

KEY CONCEPT In elliptical clauses beginning with *than* or *as,* use the form of the pronoun that you would use if the clause were fully stated. ■

The case of the pronoun depends upon whether the omitted words belong before or after the pronoun. In the examples below, the omitted words are supplied in brackets.

WORDS LEFT OUT AFTER PRONOUN:	Jo is as interested in space exploration as *he.*
	Jo is as interested in space exploration as he [is].
WORDS LEFT OUT BEFORE PRONOUN:	We gave Scott the same telescope as *her.*
	We gave Scott the same telescope as [we gave] her.

If the omitted words come *after* the pronoun, use a nominative pronoun because it is the subject of the omitted verb. If the omitted words come *before* the pronoun, use an objective pronoun because the pronoun will be an object, generally the direct object or indirect object of the omitted verb or the object of a preposition.

Often, the entire meaning of the sentence depends on the case of the pronoun. Compare, for example, the meaning of the following sentences when the nominative pronoun is changed to an objective pronoun.

WITH A NOMINATIVE PRONOUN:	Stan taught us more about the solar system than *she.*
	Stan taught us more about the solar system than she [did].
WITH AN OBJECTIVE PRONOUN:	Stan taught us more about the solar system than *her.*
	Stan taught us more about the solar system than [he taught] her.

Always follow the steps in the chart on the next page when you choose a pronoun in an elliptical clause.

Technology Tip

You can learn more about space exploration by visiting various government Web sites. Type *space program* or *NASA* into your browser.

CHOOSING A PRONOUN IN ELLIPTICAL CLAUSES

1. Consider the choices of pronouns: nominative or objective.
2. Mentally complete the elliptical clause.
3. Base your choice on what you find.

Exercise 16 Identifying the Correct Pronoun in Elliptical Clauses Rewrite each sentence, choosing one of the pronouns in parentheses and correctly completing the elliptical clause.

EXAMPLE: She is more knowledgeable about satellites than (I, me).

ANSWER: She is more knowledgeable about satellites than I am.

1. Astronauts who have traveled to outer space probably know more about Mars and the solar system than (we, us).
2. The desire to explore new frontiers is more pressing to them than (we, us).
3. Much of the exploration of Mars has been undertaken by machines that can travel far longer in outer space than (we, us) humans.
4. These machines are accurate and efficient; however, they aren't as expressive or emotional as (we, us) humans.
5. The desire to be an astronaut is much greater in (she, her) than (he, him).

Exercise 17 Using the Correct Pronoun in Elliptical Clauses Complete each sentence by choosing an appropriate pronoun and completing the elliptical clause.

EXAMPLE: Joanne writes more often than ___?___.

ANSWER: Joanne writes more often than I do.

1. Young children think about Mars more often than ___?___.
2. I wish I had as much imagination as ___?___.
3. The possibility of living on other planets seems more real to them than ___?___.
4. I don't think I'm nearly as imaginative as ___?___.
5. According to this science-fiction writer, problem-solving skills are more highly developed in Martians than ___?___.

More Practice

Grammar Exercise Workbook
• pp. 131–132
On-line Exercise Bank
• Section 23.2
Go on-line:
PHSchool.com
Enter Web Code:
eek-1002

Get instant feedback! Exercises 16 and 17 are available on-line or on CD-ROM.

Hands-on Grammar

Pronoun Fold-Over

Cut construction paper into strips that are each about an inch wide. Then, write sentences on each strip. Each sentence should contain half of a compound predicate. Leave a blank in each compound predicate where a pronoun would appear.

With a group of classmates, fold over each strip so that the first part of the compound predicate is hidden. Only the blank where the pronoun will appear should show. Hiding the first half of the compound predicate should help the members of your group identify which pronoun case to use to complete each sentence. Write down the pronouns in the blank spaces. Then, share your answers with classmates.

Use these sentences to create additional strips:

The only ones who attended were Bill and ___?___.

The winners were Mrs. Simmons and ___?___.

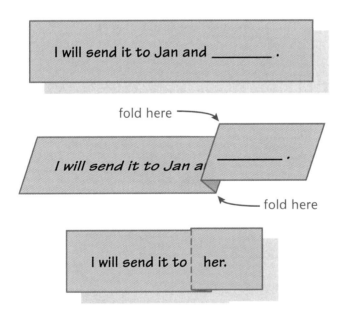

To extend this activity, create strips with sentences in which you leave out the first word of a compound subject.

Find It in Your Reading Find five sample sentences containing compound predicates or compound subjects in a work of narrative nonfiction. Include these sentences in the strips you make.

Find It in Your Writing Try the activity above with five sentences from a piece of your own writing.

Section 23.2 Section Review

GRAMMAR EXERCISES 18–23

Exercise 18 Using *Who* and *Whom* in Questions Choose the pronoun in parentheses that completes each question.

1. The first person to walk in space was (who, whom)?
2. From (who, whom) did we learn about the atmosphere on Mars?
3. Do you know (who, whom) is preparing a science project on Mars?
4. Is that the person (who, whom) I should interview?
5. With (who, whom) should I check my facts before I submit my paper?

Exercise 19 Using *Who* and *Whom* Correctly in Clauses Write the subordinate clause in each sentence. Then, identify how the form of *who* or *whom* is used.

1. I wonder (whose, who's) idea it was to name Mars after the Roman god of war.
2. The person was clearly someone (who, whom) knew a lot about mythology.
3. (Whoever, Whomever) gave Mars its name felt that the planet's red color was symbolic of blood and war.
4. No matter (who, whom) we asked, we could not find out how the names of Mars' moons were chosen.
5. I forget from (who, whom) we learned that Phobos and Deimos were sons of Ares, the Greek god of war.

Exercise 20 Using Pronouns Correctly in Elliptical Clauses Rewrite each sentence, choosing the correct pronoun and completing the elliptical clause.

1. Ancient people may have been more imaginative than (we, us).
2. Space was more a world of mystery for them than (you and I, you and me).

3. We modern people no longer believe, as (they, them), that Earth is the center of the universe.
4. We now know far more about outer space and the solar system than (they, them).
5. The concept of space exploration is far more familiar to us than (they, them).

Exercise 21 Find It in Your Reading Explain why the playwright used *who* instead of *whom* in this sentence from *Invasion From Mars.*

. . . Incredible as it may seem, both the observations of science and the evidence of our eyes lead to the inescapable assumption that those strange beings who landed in the Jersey farmlands tonight are the vanguard of an invading army from the planet Mars.

Exercise 22 Find It in Your Writing Look through your portfolio and find at least five sentences in which you have used *who* or *whom.* Check to see that you used the pronouns correctly.

Exercise 23 Writing Application Imagine that you have met an alien life form. Write questions that you would ask. Use some of the following pronouns and phrases in your questions. Include at least two elliptical clauses in your questions.

1. more advanced than [pronoun]
2. whoever
3. as smart as [pronoun]
4. whom
5. than [pronoun]

GRAMMAR EXERCISES 24–32

▶ **Exercise 24** Identifying Case On your paper, write each pronoun you find in this paragraph. Then, tell whether it is *nominative*, *objective*, or *possessive*.

(1) We humans have wondered for many centuries what exists in the universe that surrounds us. (2) People who gaze into the night sky may wonder if beings on other planets are staring back at them. (3) In recent years, our efforts to learn what lies on other planets have begun to bear fruit. (4) In 1971, we Americans gained much information about Mars from the *Mariner 9* spacecraft, a robot probe. (5) That year, *Mariner 9* orbited Mars and sent us photographs of that mysterious planet. (6) The photographs impressed whoever saw them. (7) American scientists sent another satellite to Mars in 1997, and it was an even bigger success. (8) *Pathfinder* sent us Earthlings more than 16,000 photographic images of the surface of Mars. (9) Our attempts to land on Mars again in 1999 have proved less successful. (10) We on Earth lost touch with two Martian landers as they approached their destinations.

▶ **Exercise 25** Adding Nominative Pronouns to Sentences On your paper, write a nominative pronoun to complete each sentence below. Then, tell its use.

1. The first people to examine my science project on Mars were ___?___.
2. My father and ___?___ arrived soon after the exhibition hall opened.
3. ___?___ praised my model of Mars and its two orbiting moons.
4. Everyone ___?___ saw the project thought ___?___ deserved an *A*.
5. After my presentation, my brother and ___?___ went out with our parents to celebrate.

▶ **Exercise 26** Adding Objective Pronouns to Sentences On your paper, rewrite each sentence, adding an objective pronoun in the blank. Then, tell its use.

1. My older brother gave ___?___ a lesson on astronomy.
2. Although we share few other hobbies between ___?___, he insists that I learn about space exploration.
3. Challenging ___?___ is useless.
4. He is the one person against ___?___ I can never win an argument.
5. To appease ___?___, I agreed to read a book on colonizing Mars.

▶ **Exercise 27** Adding Possessive Pronouns or Contractions to Sentences On your paper, rewrite each sentence, supplying a possessive pronoun or a contraction to fill the blank.

1. Earthlings could not live comfortably on Mars because ___?___ atmosphere is too dense with carbon dioxide.
2. ___?___ a fact that the average temperature on Mars is −80°F.
3. Through ___?___ study of photographs taken by telescope, scientists have discovered craters on Mars.
4. The scientists believe ___?___ the result of meteor landings on the planet.
5. ___?___ probably wondering whether we on Earth will ever travel to Mars.
6. ___?___ a question that may be answered in the near future.
7. ___?___ a major study of life on Mars being conducted currently.
8. Astronomers have studied photographs taken by a Martian lander. The findings in this book are ___?___.
9. I wonder ___?___ idea it was to put this photo of Mars on the cover.
10. ___?___ going to purchase the book?

> **Exercise 28** Revising to Correct Errors in the Use of *Who* and *Whom* and Nominative and Objective Pronouns
Revise this paragraph, correcting errors in pronoun usage.

(1) Two astronomers who have studied Mars have now published their findings. The scientists are named Wendy Smith and William Yung. (2) Him and her are scientists who we respect. (3) Their research is certain to impress whomever reads their book. (4) My brother and I showed it to whomever him and me saw in the college library. (5) The person to who the book is dedicated was my favorite professor.

> **Exercise 29** Using Pronouns in Elliptical Clauses Change each underlined pronoun from the objective to the nominative, and vice versa. Be sure to complete each elliptical clause.

1. Janice enjoys seeing movies about Mars more than <u>I</u>.
2. She is more fascinated by outer space than <u>he</u>.
3. She spends more time visiting museums than <u>them</u>.
4. She believes that space beings can talk with each other better than <u>us</u>.
5. I think she would enjoy being the friend of a Martian more than <u>I</u>.

> **Exercise 30** Revising to Use Pronouns to Eliminate Repetition
Revise this passage, inserting pronouns where appropriate to eliminate repetition. In addition, correct any errors in pronoun usage.

Mars has two moons. The two moons' names are Phobos and Deimos. Phobos is the larger moon. Phobos is also closer to Mars than Deimos is. The name *Phobos* comes from Greek mythology. Phobos was the son of Ares, the Greek god of war. Deimos was Phobos' brother. My sister read an interesting fact about he. My sister told the fact to me. The orbits of Mars and Phobos may lead to Mars and Phobos crashing into each other in 50 million years.

My brother told my sister that my brother was not worried about the crash. "I don't plan to be around in 50 million years," my brother said.

Some scientists believe that Phobos and Deimos started out as asteroids. Jupiter pushed Phobos and Deimos toward Mars. Then, Phobos and Deimos began to orbit Mars.

> **Exercise 31** Writing Application
Imagine that you are part of a crew traveling to Mars. Describe yourself and the other space travelers. Use pronouns in all three cases in your paragraph, and include either *who* or *whom* in at least one sentence. Underline the pronouns that you use.

> **Exercise 32** CUMULATIVE REVIEW Verb Usage and Pronoun Usage Rewrite this paragraph, correcting any errors.

(1) On Halloween night 1938, many Americans were tuned to they're radios. (2) What they heared frightened they and they're friends. (3) It will have been a radio dramatization of a play about an invasion by Martians. (4) Whom could have thought it was real? (5) Hundreds of people called the police, who's phones didn't stop ringing. (6) Some people packed suitcases and begun evacuating their homes. (7) The broadcast had putted some people into a state of panic. (8) Others listened to the broadcast more carefully than them. (9) They would realize that the events aren't real. (10) They may just have set down and had a good laugh.

Standardized Test Preparation Workshop

Pronoun Usage

Standardized tests measure your knowledge of the rules of standard grammar, such as correct pronoun usage. Some questions may test your ability to use the three cases of personal pronouns correctly. When answering these questions, determine what type of pronoun is needed in the sentence—*nominative, objective,* or *possessive.* Also, consider the rules for special problems with pronouns, such as use in *compound structures, appositives, elliptical clauses* and the use of *who* and *whom,* before choosing a pronoun. The following test item will give you practice with the format of questions that test your knowledge of pronoun usage.

Test Tip

Before choosing a pronoun for an elliptical clause beginning with *than* or *as,* mentally complete the clause using an objective or a nominative pronoun. Base your choice on the pronoun that does not change the meaning of the sentence.

Sample Test Items

Directions: Read the passage, and choose the letter of the word or group of words that belongs in each space.

Yes, the surprise party you heard about for Larry and ___(1)___ is true. So you and ___(2)___ can't tell anyone.

1 A I
   B her
   C she
   D we

2 F he
   G I
   H me
   J we

Answers and Explanations

The correct answer is *B*. Since the sentence requires a word that is the object of a preposition, an objective case pronoun is the correct choice. Therefore, the pronoun *her* best completes the compound object of the preposition *for*.

The correct answer is *G*. Because the missing pronoun is part of a compound subject, the nominative *I* is correct.

▶ **Practice 1** **Directions:** Read the passage, and choose the letter of the word or group of words that belongs in each space.

It has always been ___(1)___ policy to accept returns within 90 days. A refund for any item returned after 90 days must be approved by ___(2)___ in writing. It is ___(3)___ , the customer's, responsibility to seek written approval for the refund. Otherwise, ___(4)___ cannot give you a guarantee. The manager, Mrs. Rajani, would be happy to speak with you regarding this matter. Please feel free to contact ___(5)___ .

1 A their
  B her
  C our
  D his

2 F he
  G we
  H him
  J us

3 A our
  B you
  C your
  D his

4 F they
  G we
  H he
  J you

5 A her
  B we
  C she
  D they

▶ **Practice 2** **Directions:** Read the poem, and choose the letter of the word or group of words that belongs in each space.

If you were ___(1)___ ,
And I were you,
With ___(2)___ would ___(3)___
Be talking to?
If our garden were ___(4)___
And their garden were ours,
Which of ___(5)___
Would plant the flowers?

1 A me
  B I
  C she
  D they

2 F what
  G who
  H whom
  J whose

3 A him
  B me
  C us
  D we

4 F theirs
  G their
  H they
  J them

5 A we
  B us
  C her
  D him

Tornado Bahamas, Winslow Homer

When you speak, you automatically use words that agree with other words. You might say, for example, "The twister moves fast." You know you must add an *-s* to *move* when the subject is *twister* to make the verb agree with the subject.

Agreement is the match—the "fit"—between words or grammatical forms. Because grammatical agreement is not always obvious, you need to study some sentences more closely than others.

In the first section of this chapter, you will learn to make a subject agree with its verb. The second section focuses on agreement between pronouns and their antecedents.

▲ **Critical Viewing**
Describe how you think the wind would sound and feel if you were in the scene depicted above. Use verbs that agree with the subjects in your sentences. **[Describe]**

Diagnostic Test

Directions: Write all answers on a separate sheet of paper.

Skill Check A. Choose the verb in parentheses that agrees with the subject of each sentence.

1. Thunderstorms (is, are) dangerous because of lightning.
2. If the right conditions (exists, exist), thunderstorms can become tornadoes.
3. Nebraska and Kansas, located in the region known as Tornado Alley, (has, have) been hit by many tornadoes.
4. A tornado in a southeastern state—such as Florida, South Carolina, or Georgia—(is, are) often caused by a hurricane.
5. A tornado or a hurricane (is, are) a frightening weather phenomenon.
6. Tornadoes occur when cold, dry polar air and warm, moist tropical air (meets, meet).
7. Each occurrence of a tornado (is, are) studied by a team of scientists.
8. The team (examines, examine) the atmospheric conditions and the damage caused by the tornado.
9. On the Internet, there (is, are) photos showing how tornadoes form.
10. Mathematics (is, are) important to scientists who must use formulas to determine the dimensions and speed of a tornado.
11. Two thirds of a town in Kansas (was, were) destroyed during one tornado.
12. Most of the damage could be fixed, but some buildings (was, were) damaged beyond repair.
13. Every one of the townspeople (has, have) been helping to rebuild.
14. Many (believes, believe) that within a year, much of the damage will be mended.
15. One hundred thousand dollars (is, are) the cost of the repairs.

Skill Check B. Choose the correct pronoun in each sentence.

16. John and Pam are studying earth science, a subject (you, they) need for a career in weather forecasting.
17. One of John's favorite teachers is (his, their) physics teacher.
18. Both John and Alfredo will be taking (his, their) tests today.
19. Every student feels (he or she, they) will do well on the test.
20. After I study for a test, I want to reward (me, myself).

Skill Check C. Revise the following sentences to correct problems in pronoun reference.

21. Alfredo told John he was sure he'd pass the test.
22. When the boys entered the classroom he each sat down.
23. On the test, they asked how tornadoes are formed.
24. Nearly every tornado gets their force from strong vertically spinning winds.
25. John and myself knew almost all the answers.

Subject and Verb Agreement

For a subject and verb to agree, both must be singular or both must be plural. In this section, you will learn how to distinguish between singular and plural subjects, how to make verbs agree with compound subjects, and how to deal with problems of agreement with special subjects.

Singular and Plural Subjects

When making a verb agree with its subject, you need to identify the subject and determine its number.

▶ **KEY CONCEPTS** A singular subject must have a singular verb. A plural subject must have a plural verb. ■

SINGULAR SUBJECT
AND VERB: <u>Thunder</u> usually <u>follows</u> lightning.

PLURAL SUBJECT
AND VERB: <u>We</u> <u>are</u> about to get our umbrellas.

▶ **Exercise 1** Making Verbs Agree With Their Subjects
Choose the verb in parentheses that agrees with the subject of each sentence.
1. Tornadoes (leaves, leave) a trail of destruction.
2. Meteorologists (uses, use) special instruments to measure the speed of tornado winds.
3. Tornado winds (races, race) at around 240 miles per hour.
4. In just a few minutes, a twister (roars, roar) past.
5. In that brief period, it (is, are) able to level buildings.

▶ **KEY CONCEPT** A phrase or clause that interrupts a subject and its verb does not affect subject-verb agreement. ■

EXAMPLES: The <u>destruction</u> of tornadoes <u>is</u> devastating.
             The community <u>members</u> who experience the devastation <u>help</u> each other.

In the first example, the singular subject *destruction* takes the singular verb *is*. Even though the plural noun *tornadoes* is closer to the verb, it is the object of a preposition and does not affect subject and verb agreement. In the second sentence, the plural subject *members* agrees with the plural verb *help* even though they are separated by an adjective clause that causes the singular noun *devastation* to be closer to the verb.

Theme: Wind

In this section, you will learn about subject and verb agreement. The examples and exercises in this section are about tornadoes and hurricanes.

Cross-Curricular Connection: Science

Grammar and Style Tip

Remember that in grammar, the concept of number refers to the two forms of a word: singular and plural. Singular words indicate one; plural words indicate more than one.

GRAMMAR IN LITERATURE

from **Uncoiling**
Pat Mora

The subjects and verbs agree in the following excerpt from this poem by Pat Mora. The subjects are printed in red, and the verbs are in blue.

She *sighs* clouds,
head thrown back, eyes closed, roars
and rivers *leap*,

boulders *retreat* like crabs
into themselves.

She *spews* gusts and thunder, . . .

Exercise 2 Making Separated Subjects and Verbs Agree

Choose the verb in parentheses that agrees with the subject of each sentence.

1. A tornado occurring over a lake or an ocean (is, are) a waterspout.
2. A waterspout with winds of less than 50 miles per hour usually (lasts, last) longer than a tornado does.
3. A ship's crew members sailing on the ocean (fears, fear) waterspouts.
4. Water around waterspouts (churns, churn).
5. Small vessels caught in a storm (tosses, toss) violently from side to side.

Exercise 3 Correcting Subject and Verb Agreement

Revise the following passage, correcting all errors in subject-verb agreement. Not every sentence contains an error.

Scientists from the National Weather Service gathers weather information from all parts of the country. If the information indicates a tornado, a warning of severe weather conditions are issued. The movements of the tornado shows where it will strike. People living in that area evacuate. Putting storm cellars under homes also provide an excellent source of shelter. On hearing news of a tornado, members of a family heads for the shelter. Often, a supply of water and canned goods is kept there. When the powerful winds of the tornado passes, the people feel safe leaving the shelter. Usually, a broadcast on radio or TV announce the all-clear. What signs of the storm's fury remains?

More Practice

Grammar Exercise Workbook
• pp. 133–134
On-line Exercise Bank
• Section 24.1
  Go on-line:
  PHSchool.com
  Enter Web Code:
  eek-1002

Text

Get instant feedback! Exercises 1, 2, and 3 are available on-line or on CD-ROM.

Compound Subjects

A compound subject has two or more subjects, usually joined by *or* or *and*. Use the following rules when making compound subjects agree with verbs.

Subjects Joined by *and* Only one rule applies to compound subjects connected by *and:* Whether the parts of the compound subject are all singular, all plural, or mixed, the verb is usually plural.

▶ **KEY CONCEPT** A compound subject joined by *and* is generally plural and must have a plural verb. ■

TWO SINGULAR SUBJECTS: A <u>thunderstorm</u> and a <u>tornado</u> <u>hit</u> the town.

TWO PLURAL SUBJECTS: <u>Thunderstorms</u> and <u>tornadoes</u> <u>appear</u> on the radar screen.

A SINGULAR SUBJECT AND A PLURAL SUBJECT: Luckily, the <u>tornado</u> and the <u>thunderstorms</u> often <u>miss</u> our area.

There are two exceptions to this rule. If the parts of a compound subject are thought of as one item or the word *every* or *each* precedes the compound subject, then the verb is singular. Note the number of the subjects and verbs in the following examples:

EXAMPLES: The best <u>detection</u> and specialized tornado <u>equipment</u> <u>is</u> Doppler radar.
<u>Each tornado</u> and <u>thunderstorm</u> <u>demonstrates</u> nature's power.
<u>Every weather center</u> and <u>emergency network</u> in the United States <u>issues</u> warnings for severe weather.

Singular Subjects Joined by *or* or *nor* When both parts of a compound subject connected by *or* or *nor* are singular, a singular verb is required.

▶ **KEY CONCEPT** Two or more singular subjects joined by *or* or *nor* must have a singular verb. ■

EXAMPLE: A <u>tornado</u> or <u>hurricane</u> <u>causes</u> terrible damage.

▲ **Critical Viewing** Imagine that you are the person who took this picture. Write two sentences, one with a singular subject and one with a plural subject, that describe this situation. Make sure that each verb agrees with its subject. **[Speculate]**

Plural Subjects Joined by *or* or *nor* When both parts of a compound subject connected by *or* or *nor* are plural, a plural verb is required.

▶ **KEY CONCEPT** Two or more plural subjects joined by *or* or *nor* must have a plural verb. ■

EXAMPLE: Neither <u>tornadoes</u> nor <u>hurricanes</u> <u>cause</u> as many deaths as lightning storms.

Subjects of Mixed Number Joined by *or* or *nor* If one part of a compound subject is singular and the other is plural, the verb agrees with the subject that is closer to it.

▶ **KEY CONCEPT** If one or more singular subjects are joined to one or more plural subjects by *or* or *nor*, the subject closest to the verb determines agreement. ■

EXAMPLES: Neither <u>David</u> nor my <u>parents</u> <u>are frightened</u> by thunderstorms.
Neither my <u>parents</u> nor <u>David</u> <u>is frightened</u> by thunderstorms.

▶ **Exercise 4** **Choosing Verbs That Agree With Compound Subjects** Choose the verb in parentheses that agrees with the subject of each sentence.
1. *Cyclone* and *typhoon* (is, are) other names for a type of storm that North Americans call a hurricane.
2. Meteorologists and other scientists (describes, describe) hurricanes as rotating storms from the tropical ocean.
3. Dull-red sunsets or a high barometric reading (predicts, predict) a potential hurricane brewing at sea.
4. In modern times, the radio or television (allows, allow) people to learn about a hurricane before it strikes.
5. Both strong winds and heavy rainfall (is, are) typical during hurricanes.
6. Late summer and early fall (is, are) hurricane season.
7. A moist, tropical region at high risk for hurricanes (is, are) the Caribbean Islands.
8. Neither Hurricane Andrew nor Hurricane Mitch (was, were) a mild hurricane.
9. Either Hurricane Camille or Hurricane Mitch (holds, hold) the record for the lowest barometric pressure ever recorded.
10. During one hurricane, four adults and a child (was, were) trapped in a building, but they were safely rescued in the end.

▶ **More Practice**

Grammar Exercise Workbook
• pp. 135–136
On-line Exercise Bank
• Section 24.1
Go on-line:
PHSchool.com
Enter Web Code:
eek-1002

Get instant feedback! Exercise 4 is available on-line or on CD-ROM.

Confusing Subjects

Some kinds of subjects have special agreement problems:

Inverted Sentences Foremost among confusing subjects are the hard-to-find subjects that come after the verbs. A sentence in which the subject comes after the verb is said to be inverted. Subject and verb order is usually inverted in questions.

▶ **KEY CONCEPT** A verb must still agree in number with a subject that comes after it. ■

EXAMPLE: At the top of the hill <u>are</u> two light-
             ning <u>rods</u>.
             (Two lightning rods are at the top of
             the hill.)

Check to make sure the verb agrees with the subject by mentally rewording the sentence so that the subject comes first.

The words *there* and *here* often signal an inverted sentence. These words never function as the subject of the sentence.

EXAMPLES: There <u>are</u> the satellite <u>photos</u> of the hurricane.
             Here <u>is</u> the revised <u>information</u> on the storm.

Note About *There's* and *Here's*: Both of these contractions contain the singular verb *is: there is* and *here is.* They should not be used with plural verbs.

CORRECT: There<u>'s</u> only one <u>hurricane</u> expected this week.
             There <u>are</u> two <u>hurricanes</u> expected next week.

▲ **Critical Viewing**
Write a sentence beginning with the word *there* that describes this photograph. [Describe]

▶ **Exercise 5** Making Subjects and Verbs Agree in Inverted Sentences Choose the item in parentheses that agrees with the subject of each sentence.
1. (There's, There're) usually a series of warnings before a hurricane.
2. Causing the greatest losses (was, were) Hurricane Floyd.
3. On the radar (glows, glow) traces of a hurricane track.
4. Where on these radar screens (is, are) the eye of the hurricane?
5. Here (is, are) the flashlights and candles in case the lights go out during the storm.

▶ **More Practice**

Grammar Exercise
Workbook
• pp. 137–138
On-line Exercise Bank
• Section 24.1
  Go on-line:
  PHSchool.com
  Enter Web Code:
  eek-1002

Subjects of Linking Verbs Subjects with linking verbs may also cause agreement problems.

▶ **KEY CONCEPT** A linking verb must agree with its subject, regardless of the number of its predicate nominative. ■

EXAMPLES: The strong <u>winds</u> <u>are</u> one reason we expect a tornado.
One <u>reason</u> we expect a tornado <u>is</u> the strong winds.

In the first example, the plural verb *are* agrees with the plural subject *winds*, although the predicate nominative *reason* is singular. In the next example, the singular subject *reason* takes the singular verb *is*, although the predicate nominative *winds* is plural.

Collective Nouns Collective nouns—such as *audience*, *class*, *club*, and *committee*—name groups of people or things.

▶ **KEY CONCEPTS** A collective noun takes a singular verb when the group it names acts as a single unit. A collective noun takes a plural verb when the group it names act as individuals with different viewpoints. ■

SINGULAR: The weather <u>club</u> <u>plans</u> to track the tornado.
PLURAL: The weather <u>club</u> <u>have</u> split the responsibilities of tracking the tornado.

Nouns That Look Like Plurals Some nouns that end in -*s* appear to be plural but are actually singular in meaning. For example, nouns that name branches of knowledge, such as *civics* and *economics*, and those that name single units, such as *molasses* or *mumps*, take a singular verb.

▶ **KEY CONCEPT** Use singular verbs to agree with nouns that are plural in form but singular in meaning. ■

SINGULAR: <u>Physics</u> <u>requires</u> skill in mathematics.
The <u>news</u> today <u>reports</u> good weather.

When words such as *ethics*, *politics*, and *acoustics* do not name branches of knowledge but indicate characteristics, their meanings are plural. Similarly, such words as *eyeglasses*, *pliers*, and *scissors*, though they name single items, generally take plural verbs.

PLURAL: The <u>acoustics</u> in the weather center <u>are</u> terrible.
The <u>scissors</u> <u>are</u> in the top drawer.

Indefinite Pronouns Some indefinite pronouns are always singular, some are always plural, and some may be either singular or plural. Prepositional phrases that interrupt the subject and verb do not affect agreement.

> **KEY CONCEPTS** Singular indefinite pronouns take singular verbs. Plural indefinite pronouns take plural verbs. ■

SINGULAR: anybody, anyone, anything, each, either, every, everybody, everyone, everything, neither, nobody, no one, nothing, somebody, someone, something
PLURAL: both, few, many, others, several

SINGULAR: <u>Everyone</u> on the rescue squad <u>has left</u> for the day.
PLURAL: <u>Many</u> of the houses <u>were damaged</u> during the storm.

> **KEY CONCEPT** The pronouns *all, any, more, most, none,* and *some* usually take a singular verb if the antecedent is singular, and a plural verb if it is plural. ■

SINGULAR: <u>Some</u> of the area <u>is ruined</u> due to the hurricane.
PLURAL: <u>Some</u> of the cars <u>are</u> beyond repair

> **Exercise 6** Making Verbs Agree With Indefinite Pronouns
Choose the item in parentheses that agrees with the subject of each sentence.
1. Everyone studying tornadoes (has, have) learned some amazing facts.
2. Using a computer program, each of us (was, were) assigned an imaginary tornado to track.
3. Many (finds, find) the assignment exciting and informative.
4. A few in the class (is, are) frightened by the strength of the twister.
5. Some of the students (researches, research) the effects of tornadoes in certain areas of the country.

Titles of Creative Works and Names of Organizations
Plural words in the title of a creative work or in the name of an organization do not affect subject-verb agreement.

> **KEY CONCEPT** A title or the name of an organization is singular and must have a singular verb. ■

EXAMPLES: *<u>Dealing With Severe Weather Conditions</u> <u>is</u>*
a useful reference.
<u>Weather Services</u> <u>is</u> a helpful agency.

Amounts and Measurements Most amounts and measurements, although they appear to be plural, actually express single units or ideas

KEY CONCEPT A noun expressing an amount or measurement is usually singular and requires a singular verb. ■

EXAMPLES: Two hundred million dollars is the cost in property damage from the tornado.
Two miles was our distance from the tornado.
Three quarters of the town was destroyed.
Half of the trees were uprooted.

In the first three examples, the subjects take singular verbs. *Two hundred million dollars* is one sum of money; *two miles* is a single distance; and *three quarters* is one part of a town. In the last example, *half* refers to a number of individual trees and therefore takes a plural verb.

Exercise 7 Making Verbs Agree With Confusing Subjects
Choose the item in parentheses that agrees with the subject of each sentence.
1. Tornadoes (is, are) a good reason for extreme caution.
2. Each tornado (has, have) unique characteristics.
3. Most (looks, look) like a funnel.
4. Many (approaches, approach) without warning.
5. One sign of approaching turbulent weather (is, are) thunder clouds.
6. Experiencing the most tornadoes (is, are) the middle of the country.
7. Each year, a series of tornadoes (causes, cause) damage to the region of the United States known as Tornado Alley.
8. *Beware the Twisters* (is, are) a book about the destruction caused by tornadoes.
9. In 1968, three million dollars (was, were) the cost of the damage caused by a tornado that passed through Tracy, Minnesota.
10. All meteorologists in the agency (rates, rate) tornadoes.
11. Physics (is, are) a science meteorologists use to measure a tornado.
12. At the center of a tornado (appears, appear) areas of low pressure.
13. (There's, There are) lots of activity in the tornado's core.
14. Some areas of a tornado (is, are) illuminated by lightning.
15. The news occasionally (contains, contain) reports about people who have seen the core, or center, of a tornado.

More Practice

Grammar Exercise Workbook
• pp. 137–138
On-line Exercise Bank
• Section 24.1
Go on-line:
PHSchool.com
Enter Web Code:
eek-1002

 Text

Get instant feedback! Exercises 6 and 7 are available on-line or on CD-ROM.

Hands-on Grammar

Inverted-Sentence Wheel

Practice inverting sentences and finding the subject.

1. Cut out a cardboard circle with a diameter of 5". Make four holes in it, as shown in the illustration. They should be about 1/4" from the edge of the circle.
2. Cut out four smaller cardboard circles—1" to 1-1/2" in diameter. Make a small hole in each circle.
3. Unfold four paper clips, as shown. Put the paper clips through the holes in the big circle, and then attach a small circle to the other end of each paper clip.
4. Tape a paper circle, 3-1/2" in diameter, to the middle of the large circle. That is the verb wheel.
5. On one of the small cardboard circles, write *two marbles.* Write *under the table* on the circle that is opposite. Then, write *the marble* on another small cardboard circle. On the opposite circle, write *under the table.* On the paper circle in the center, write the verbs *are* and *is* twice, as shown.
6. Turn the wheel so that a verb is upright. Then, read the sentence from top circle to bottom circle. Which is the subject? Spin the wheel so that the other verb is upright and read the sentence. Has the subject changed place in the sentence?

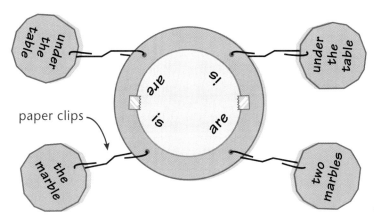

7. Illustrate the following sentences with your wheel:
   On the table is the vase.   *Cookie crumbs are under the table.*
   The vase is on the table.   *Under the table are cookie crumbs.*

Find It in Your Reading In a story or textbook that you are reading, find other examples of sentences with inverted word order. Illustrate those sentences on your wheel.

Find It in Your Writing Review a piece of writing from your portfolio. If you have used inverted word order in any of your sentences, check to be sure that the verb agrees with the subject.

Section
24.1

Section Review

GRAMMAR EXERCISES 8–15

Exercise 8 **Making Subjects Agree With Their Verbs** Choose the verb in parentheses that agrees with the subject of each sentence.

1. Rain during thunderstorms (falls, fall) quite rapidly.
2. Loud claps of thunder (shakes, shake) the house.
3. Lightning bolts (flashes, flash) across the sky.
4. Heavy rains or fast-melting snow (causes, cause) floods in many parts of the world.
5. Either too much rain or too much snow (makes, make) the level of rivers rise.
6. Rising rivers (means, mean) trouble.
7. Towns in the flood zone (is, are) in great danger.
8. A city or vacation spot located near the ocean (is, are) in danger of a tidal wave.
9. People (evacuates, evacuate) these areas before the storm hits.
10. Neither the Western Hemisphere nor the Eastern Hemisphere (is, are) immune to flooding.

Exercise 9 **Choosing Verbs for Inverted Sentences and Indefinite Pronouns** Choose the verb in parentheses that agrees with the subject of the sentence.

1. In the spring months (begins, begin) tornado season.
2. Most (occurs, occur) at this time of year due to weather patterns.
3. Often at the end of a hot, humid day (appears, appear) the thunderclouds.
4. Each cloud that produces tornadoes (is, are) different from regular clouds.
5. (Does, Do) people hear any thunder?
6. There (is, are) often rumbles of thunder before a tornado hits.

7. Each of the dark clouds (seems, seem) ready to burst.
8. At the bottom of the cloud (twists, twist) rounded cloud masses.
9. Everybody in the shelters (fears, fear) the powerful funnel.
10. Some of the most violent winds (uproots, uproot) trees and even overturn railroad cars.

Exercise 10 **Choosing the Correct Linking Verb** Choose the verb in parentheses that agrees with the subject of the sentence.

1. Severe weather conditions (is, are) a threat.
2. In Florida, one reason for building strong houses (is, are) hurricanes.
3. Hurricanes in early fall (is, are) a danger in the Southeast.
4. The responsibility of meteorologists (is, are) weather alerts.
5. These warnings (is, are) the key to saving lives during such storms.

Exercise 11 **Making Verbs Agree With Confusing Subjects** Choose the verb in parentheses that agrees with the subject of the sentence.

1. The news (includes, include) many stories of severe storms.
2. Tornadoes (represents, represent) one type of weather disaster.
3. In 1977, in the Midwest, there (was, were) millions of dollars of destruction from a tornado that lasted seven hours.
4. About 340 miles (was, were) the distance traveled by this tornado.
5. Most tornadoes (does, do) not last that long.

Section Review Exercises cont'd.

6. *Tornadoes* by Michael Allaby (is, are) a reference book on the subject.
7. Another natural disaster nearly everyone (fears, fear) is a tsunami.
8. A tsunami is a series of waves that (occurs, occur) in an ocean or other large body of water.
9. Most people in North America (calls, call) tsunamis *tidal waves.*
10. Earthquakes on the sea floor (is, are) a major cause of tsunamis.
11. About 12 to 23 inches (is, are) the height of the typical tsunami when it begins at sea.
12. As they approach the shore, some tsunamis (reaches, reach) a height of 100 feet.
13. There (was, were) several destructive tsunamis during the 1990's.
14. Sometimes, politics (causes, cause) a delay in aid to the regions that are affected by tsunamis.
15. Not one of the towns (has, have) received money to make repairs.

▶ **Exercise 12**   Revision Practice: Agreement   Copy the paragraph on a separate sheet of paper. Revise it to correct all errors in subject-verb agreement.

Physics play an important role in predicting the weather. The science of weather studies and predictions are called meteorology. Both atmospheric occurrences and geographic location affects weather forecasts. Each of the weather forecasts depend on complex technology. Atmospheric pressure or wind require careful measurement. Twelve hours are the amount of advance time needed for short-range forecasts. For long-range predictions, mathematics create important numerical models. These models, along with a supercomputer, makes accurate forecasts possible. Neither the computers nor the math truly predict the weather. There's sometimes sudden changes in weather patterns.

▶ **Exercise 13**   Find It in Your Reading   Read the following excerpt from Pat Mora's poem "Uncoiling." Then, write all the verbs that agree with the subject, and indicate whether they are singular or plural.

With thorns, she scratches
  on my window, tosses her hair
  dark with rain,
snares lightning, cholla, hawks,
  butterfly
swarms in the tangles.

▶ **Exercise 14**   Find It In Your Writing   Review a draft from your portfolio, written in the present tense. Underline each subject once and each verb twice. Make sure your subjects and verbs agree.

▶ **Exercise 15**   Writing Application   Use each of the items below as the subject of a sentence. Provide verbs for each sentence that agree with the subjects provided. Underline all the subjects once and all the verbs twice.

1. All of the trees
2. Thunder and lightning
3. All of the tornadoes
4. One of the houses
5. Two thirds of the town
6. Storms at sea
7. The path of most hurricanes
8. Spaghetti and meatballs
9. Rain or snow
10. Neither he nor she

Section 24.2 Pronoun and Antecedent Agreement

Antecedents are the nouns (or the words that take the place of nouns) for which pronouns stand. In this section, you will learn how to make a pronoun agree with its antecedent.

Agreement Between Personal Pronouns and Antecedents

The following rule is the basis for pronoun and antecedent agreement:

▷ **KEY CONCEPT** A personal pronoun must agree with its antecedent in number, person, and gender. ■

The grammatical number of a pronoun indicates whether it is *singular* or *plural*. *Person* indicates whether the pronoun is first person (the one speaking), second person (the one spoken to), or third person (the one spoken about). Some nouns and pronouns also indicate *gender*—masculine, feminine, or neuter.

In the following example, the pronoun *his* and the antecedent *Byron* are both singular, in the third person, and masculine.

EXAMPLE: *Byron* completed *his* trip to India.

Agreement in Number Making personal pronouns agree with their antecedents in number is usually a problem only when the antecedent is a compound.

▷ **KEY CONCEPT** Use a singular personal pronoun with two or more singular antecedents joined by *or* or *nor*. ■

EXAMPLE: Neither *Tim* nor *Ike* liked *his* flight to India.

▼ **Critical Viewing** The Taj Mahal was built by Shah Jahan as a mausoleum for his favorite wife. Write two sentences describing the Taj Mahal. Make sure that your personal pronouns agree with their antecedents. **[Describe]**

▶ **KEY CONCEPT** Use a plural personal pronoun with two or more antecedents joined by *and*. ■

EXAMPLE: *Darlene and Carol* liked *their* flights to India.

Agreement in Person and Number A personal pronoun and its antecedent will not agree if there is a shift in either person or number in the second part of the sentence.

▶ **KEY CONCEPT** When dealing with pronoun-antecedent agreement, take care not to shift either person or gender. ■

SHIFT IN PERSON: *Michelle* is studying Hindi, a language *you* will find useful while living in India.

CORRECT: *Michelle* is studying Hindi, a language *she* will find useful while living in India.

SHIFT IN NUMBER: Either *Tim* or *Ed* brought *their* map.
CORRECT: Either *Tim* or *Ed* brought *his* map.

Note About *Generic Masculine Pronouns:* Historically, a masculine pronoun (*he, his, him, himself*) has been used to refer to a singular antecedent whose gender is not specified. Today, however, many writers prefer to use both the masculine and feminine pronouns (*he or she, him or her, his or her, himself or herself*) instead of the generic masculine form. When using two pronouns becomes awkward, rewrite the sentence.

▶ **KEY CONCEPT** When gender is not specified, use both the masculine and the feminine pronouns or rewrite the sentence. ■

EXAMPLES: A *guest* might thank *his or her* host with a gift.
          Guests might thank *their* host with a gift.

▶ **Exercise 16** Supplying Personal Pronouns to Agree With Their Antecedents Choose the correct pronoun in each sentence.

EXAMPLE: Visitors to India need ____?____ passports.
ANSWER: their

1. Marge and Susan took ____?____ vacation in India last month.
2. Marge decided to spend ____?____ time touring Agra.
3. The Taj Mahal is well known for ____?____ beauty.
4. Neither Marge nor Susan forgot ____?____ camera.
5. Susan told me that both of them missed ____?____ families.

Text

Get instant feedback! Exercises 16 and 17 are available on-line or on CD-ROM.

▶ **More Practice**

Grammar Exercise Workbook
• pp. 139–140
On-line Exercise Bank
• Section 24.2
Go on-line:
PHSchool.com
Enter Web Code:
eek-1002

Agreement With Indefinite Pronouns

When you write a sentence with a personal pronoun that has an indefinite pronoun as its antecedent, make sure that the two pronouns agree. (See page 572 for indefinite pronouns.)

KEY CONCEPTS Use a singular personal pronoun when the antecedent is a singular indefinite pronoun. Use a plural personal pronoun when the antecedent is a plural indefinite pronoun. ■

SINGULAR: *One* of the men rode *his* elephant.
PLURAL: *All* of the men rode *their* elephants.

With an indefinite pronoun that can be either singular or plural, agreement depends on the word to which the indefinite pronoun refers. In the first example below, the pronoun *some* refers to the singular noun *village*. In the second example, *some* refers to the plural noun *villagers*.

EXAMPLES: *Some* of the village had lost *its* charm.
             Some of the villagers expressed *their* displeasure.

Exercise 17 Making Personal Pronouns Agree With Indefinite Pronouns Choose the correct pronoun in each sentence.

1. Many visitors to India begin (his, their) vacations in Bombay.
2. All of the students enjoyed (his or her, their) visit to that city.
3. One of Bombay's best features is (its, their) pleasant climate.
4. Some of the city's appeal is (its, their) blend of old and new.
5. Both students knew (his, their) trip would be great.
6. Neither of them had developed (his or her, their) photographs of the city.
7. One of the girls finally let me see (her, their) pictures.
8. Every Indian city has (its, their) own charm.
9. Both Bombay and New Delhi face challenges because of (its, their) large populations.
10. However, either Bombay or New Delhi will delight and surprise (its, their) visitors.

▼ Critical Viewing Write a sentence about this picture using this phrase: *Neither the boy nor his elephant . . .* [Infer]

Pronoun and Antecedent Agreement • 579

Using Reflexive Pronouns

Reflexive pronouns end in *-self* or *-selves* and refer to an antecedent earlier in the sentence.

KEY CONCEPT A reflexive pronoun must agree with an antecedent that is clearly stated. ■

POOR: The tour guide brought the good news to Peter and *myself*.

CORRECT: The tour guide brought the good news to Peter and *me*.

Exercise 18 Correcting Misuse of Reflexive Pronouns
Correct the sentences that misuse reflexive pronouns. If a sentence contains no error, write *correct*.
1. Karen and myself studied India in our social studies class.
2. Tom said that Paula and himself had learned about India.
3. It was Billy and myself who remembered that Gandhi was assassinated in 1948.
4. During the fight for independence, Gandhi wore simple garments he had spun himself.
5. The results were a surprise to the teachers and ourselves.

Four Special Problems in Pronoun Agreement

When you use personal pronouns, make sure that they have antecedents that are clearly defined. Problems can occur when the antecedent is unstated or unclear or when the personal pronoun refers to the wrong antecedent.

KEY CONCEPT A pronoun must agree with an antecedent that is either clearly stated or clearly understood. ■

VAGUE: The *movie* about India was disappointing because *they* never made the characters seem realistic.

CLEAR: The *movie* about India was disappointing because *it* never made the characters seem realistic.

CLEAR: The movie about India was disappointing because *the director* never made the characters seem realistic.

In the preceding example, the meaning of the sentence is vague because there is no antecedent for the pronoun *they*. The sentence can be made clear by replacing *they* with a personal pronoun or a noun that agrees with the antecedent *movie*.

More Practice

Grammar Exercise Workbook
• pp. 141–142
On-line Exercise Bank
• Section 24.2
  Go on-line:
  PHSchool.com
  Enter Web Code:
  eek-1002

Get instant feedback! Exercise 18 is available on-line or on CD-ROM.

> **KEY CONCEPT** A personal pronoun should always refer to a single, obvious antecedent. ■

AMBIGUOUS: I put a postcard in the book, but I lost *it*.
CLEAR: I put a postcard in the book, but I lost the book.
             I can't find the postcard that I put in the book.

In the first example, the pronoun *it* is ambiguous because *it* can refer to either *postcard* or *book*.

> **KEY CONCEPT** A personal pronoun should always be close enough to its antecedent to prevent confusion. ■

DISTANT: Charlie asked Ralph questions about the map of India. Ralph tried to help, but, even more confused, he asked the teacher.

CLEAR: Charlie asked Ralph questions about the map of India. Ralph tried to help him, but, even more confused, Charlie asked the teacher.

In the example above, the pronoun *he* is too far from its antecedent, *Charlie*. The passage is much clearer if the word *Charlie* is repeated. You could also reword the passage to move the pronoun closer to its antecedent.

> **KEY CONCEPT** Use the personal pronoun *you* only when the reference is truly to the reader or the listener. ■

INCORRECT: During colonial rule in India, you weren't allowed the same privileges as many British citizens.
CORRECT: During colonial rule in India, Indian citizens weren't allowed the same privileges as many British citizens.

▲ **Critical Viewing**
Write two or three sentences describing some of the carving on this tenth-century Indian temple. Use *they* and *it* in your sentences and make sure that the antecedents are clear. **[Describe]**

Exercise 19 Recognizing Proper Usage Identify the sentence in each pair that better follows the conventions of English usage of pronouns. Explain your choices.

1. (A) The film we watched about India was informative because it explained Hinduism, Buddhism, Islam, and other religions.
   (B) The film we watched about India was informative because they explained Hinduism, Buddhism, Islam, and other religions.

2. (A) The next time it is shown, you should see it.
   (B) The next time they show it, you should see it.

3. (A) India has one of the largest Muslim populations in the world, even though they are a minority in it.
   (B) India has one of the largest Muslim populations in the world, even though Muslims are a minority there.

4. (A) Jane told Andrea that Indonesia has the largest Muslim population in the world, but Andrea wanted to confirm the information.
   (B) Jane told Andrea that Indonesia has the largest Muslim population in the world, but Andrea wanted to confirm it.

5. (A) Each of the students completed their assignment on the culture of India.
   (B) Each of the students completed his or her assignment on the culture of India.

Exercise 20 Correcting Special Problems in Pronoun Agreement Revise the following paragraph, correcting all errors in pronoun and antecedent agreement.

Mohandas K. Gandhi led Indians to independence from British rule. It made him famous. He promoted passive resistance, which you can use to change society. Sit-ins and boycotts are often involved in it. Gandhi was soon joined in his struggle by Jawaharlal Nehru. He was a much younger man. Gandhi taught passive resistance; he believed it would win them their freedom. When Gandhi became the leader of the Indian National Congress, he persuaded them that they needed to adopt his plan. Under this plan, one way you resisted British rule was by not paying your taxes. They also did not attend British schools or courts. Many of them gave up good jobs because they had to deal with the British. Gandhi and his followers believed passionately in the movement for independence, and they achieved it—especially when millions of Indians had joined it.

More Practice

Grammar Exercise Workbook
• pp. 143–144
On-line Exercise Bank
• Section 24.2
  Go on-line:
  PHSchool.com
  Enter Web Code:
  eek-1002

Text

Complete the exercises on-line! Exercises 19 and 20 are available on-line or on CD-ROM.

Section Review

GRAMMAR EXERCISES 21–26

▶ **Exercise 21** Supplying Personal Pronouns That Agree With Their Antecedents Use an appropriate personal pronoun to complete each sentence.

1. We heard the ancient story of Rama from __?__ Indian friend Ved.
2. Rama was loved by the people of the kingdom for __?__ kind nature.
3. Sadly, Dasrath, Rama's father, had to send __?__ son into exile.
4. While in exile, Rama worried about __?__ wife Sitia.
5. Hanuman, a flying monkey general, found Sitia and told __?__ that help was on the way.
6. Each region of India has __?__ own fashions.
7. Some Indian women like colorful skirts that swirl as __?__ walk.
8. An Indian may wear __?__ traditional clothes every day.
9. Most women in India wear __?__ saris every day.
10. Red is the color of joy and celebration, so brides usually wear __?__.

▶ **Exercise 22** Using Reflexive Pronouns Correctly Rewrite each sentence, correcting the misused reflexive pronouns. If a sentence contains no error, write *correct*.

1. Ms. Shinh prepared ourselves and her other class to study Indian history.
2. Andy and myself reviewed the notes about the Indus valley.
3. Neither Anna nor Liz gave herself enough time to study.
4. This book on Sanskrit, India's ancient language, is meant for myself, not John.
5. Manita told the class that her sister and herself had come from New Delhi.

▶ **Exercise 23** Revising to Eliminate Errors in Pronoun Agreement Rewrite these sentences, correcting any vague pronoun-antecedent agreement.

1. During the 1700's, the British came to India to trade with the Indians, but they ended up ruling them.
2. The British built a railway system in India that linked parts of it.
3. The British told the Indians that the improvements were important to them.
4. In 1947, after years of protest, they finally won their freedom from them.
5. In 1950, India became a republic with a constitution; it is still in force.

▶ **Exercise 24** Find It in Your Reading Read this excerpt from Rabindranath Tagore's "The Cabuliwallah"; then, list each pronoun and its antecedent. List the narrator as the antecedent of "I."

I cannot tell what my daughter's feelings were at the sight of this man, but she began to call him loudly. Ah, I thought, he will come in, and my seventeenth chapter will never be finished!

▶ **Exercise 25** Find It in Your Writing Review a piece of your writing, and be sure that all the personal pronouns have clear antecedents. If you find pronouns with vague or missing antecedents, make the necessary revisions.

▶ **Exercise 26** Writing Application Write five sentences about a country you have studied. Include at least five pronouns, and provide clear antecedents.

Chapter Review

GRAMMAR EXERCISES 27–33

Exercise 27 **Making Separated Subjects and Verbs Agree** Choose the verb in parentheses that agrees with the subject of each sentence.

1. Old people in India (commands, command) great respect.
2. White hair on old people (is, are) considered a sign of age and wisdom.
3. Each of the children (is, are) taught from a young age to respect their elders.
4. Often, children from a middle-class or wealthy home (is, are) spoiled for as long as possible.
5. Younger siblings in a large family (is, are) watched by older brothers or sisters.

Exercise 28 **Making Verbs Agree With Their Subjects** Choose the verb in parentheses that agrees with the subject of each sentence.

1. Hustle and bustle (does, do) not always rule an Indian's life.
2. Leisure time and entertaining (is, are) important, too.
3. Often, family members or a friend (drops, drop) by unexpectedly for a visit.
4. Neither food nor beverages (is, are) denied those who arrive.
5. Either a homemade sweet or a spicy treat (is, are) customarily offered.
6. Only about half of India's villages (has, have) electricity.
7. Anyone living in one of these villages (works, work) hard for a living.
8. (There's, There're) farmers who use oxen to plow their fields.
9. Although almost every one of the village farmers (wants, want) a tractor, many cannot afford one.
10. Both the practicing of old traditions

and an attention to the daily routine (is, are) a part of village life.

Exercise 29 **Revising Sentences to Eliminate Errors in Subject-Verb Agreement** Rewrite each sentence to correct errors in subject-verb agreement.

1. More than one billion people lives in India.
2. A popular image of India are its bustling cities.
3. However, the majority of Indians lives away from urban centers.
4. Ilay Cooper's *Arts and Crafts of India* illustrate a number of traditional works from the countryside.
5. The slopes of a hill or the bottom of a valley are home to many villagers.
6. Both warmth and affection is shown to dear friends.
7. Indians believe that simplicity and modesty is admirable qualities in a person.
8. Great wealth or intelligence are not a reason to boast.
9. Offering help and giving support to someone in need comes naturally to most Indians.
10. Neither monsoon rains nor a light shower keep Indians from celebrating independence day on August 15.

Exercise 30 **Making Personal Pronouns Agree With Their Antecedents** Write an appropriate personal pronoun to complete each sentence.

1. My uncle wrote to me about __?__ visit to India.
2. He met an Indian family, and __?__ invited him to dinner.
3. The wife made __?__ own fresh bread, called *naan*.

4. The husband said that ___?___ wife's *naan* was the best.

5. She also served *laddoo*, a sweet that gets ___?___ flavor from cardamom seeds.

6. My uncle said that on entering most Indian homes, ___?___ had to take off ___?___ shoes.

7. He also learned that in traditional families, parents arrange ___?___ children's marriages.

8. Young people count on ___?___ parents to make a good match for ___?___.

9. When a woman gets married, she may go to live with ___?___ husband's family.

10. My uncle noticed that an Indian child is respectful toward ___?___ parents.

▶ **Exercise 31** **Revising to Eliminate Errors in Agreement** Rewrite each sentence, making the change indicated in parentheses and adjusting other parts of the sentence as necessary to maintain agreement.

1. All Indian students are taught to respect their teachers. (Change "All Indian students" to "Each Indian student.")

2. Every student rises when his or her teacher walks into the room. (Change "his or her" to "their.")

3. Most city schools require their students to wear uniforms. (Change "require" to "requires.")

4. Few children dare to misbehave in school. (Change "Few children" to "Almost no child.")

5. One of the boys had to have his parents meet with the teacher. (Change "One" to "Two.")

6. Nearly all students want to have their parents send them to school. (Change "Nearly all students" to "Nearly every student.")

7. Some of the girls have to care for their younger brothers. (Change "have" to "has.")

8. Many schools teach their students three languages: English, Hindi, and a regional language. (Change "Many schools" to "Almost every school.")

9. Each student spends many hours at his or her studies. (Change "Each student" to "We.")

10. I am going to enjoy my Hindi class next year. (Change "I" to "You.")

▶ **Exercise 32** **Writing Application** In approximately ten sentences, write a dialogue among three people discussing their first day in a new school. Use both nouns and pronouns to clarify who says what to whom, and underline every pronoun and its antecedent. In addition, underline every subject and verb. Be sure that all agree.

▶ **Exercise 33** **CUMULATIVE REVIEW Verb Usage, Pronoun Usage, and Agreement** Rewrite the following paragraph, correcting errors in verb and pronoun usage and subject-verb and pronoun-antecedent agreement.

How many of you has read Tagore's story "The Cabuliwallah"? It took place in Calcutta, India, where you will find many interesting stories. It was about a young girl who makes friends with a man much older than her. He is a peddler who comes to their house. The girl was Mini, and the man is Rahmun, and the friendship between her and him lasts just a short time. Mini and her father found that Rahmun is a person who they like. Each of his quaint jokes amuse them. However, one day Rahmun will have been arrested, and they send him away. At the time of his' return eight years later, he has been almost forgotten by Mini's father and herself.

Standardized Test Preparation Workshop

Making Words Agree

Your knowledge of the rules of subject and verb agreement is frequently tested on standardized tests. When checking a sentence for errors, first identify the subject. Next, identify the type of subject: singular, plural, or compound. Then, apply the rules of agreement to make sure that the verb in the sentence agrees with the subject.

The following questions will give you practice with different formats used for items that test knowledge of subject-verb agreement.

Test Tip

If a phrase falls between the subject and the verb, the verb must agree with the subject, not with the noun in the phrase.

Sample Test Item	Answers and Explanations

Directions: Identify the underlined words and phrases in the following sentence that contain an error.
 	
Josh and his sisters remembers the words
    (A)   (B)   (C)
 	
to the song. No errors.
   (D)   (E)
	The correct answer is *B*. The compound subject of the sentence is *Josh and his sisters*. When singular and plural subjects are joined by *and*, the verb is plural. Therefore, *B, remembers*, the singular form of the verb, contains the error.

Choose the revised version of the following sentence that eliminates all errors in grammar, usage, and mechanics. Josh and his sisters remembers the words to the song. **A.** Josh, nor his sisters remembers the words to the song. **B.** Neither Josh and his sisters remember the words to the song. **C.** Neither Josh nor his sisters remember the words to the song. **D.** Either Josh or his sisters remember the words to the song.	The correct answer is *C*. The compound subject of the sentence is *neither Josh nor his sisters*. When singular and plural subjects are joined by *or* or *nor*, the verb must agree with the subject closest to it. In this case, the subject *sisters* is plural, so the plural verb *remember* should be used in the sentence.

Practice 1 **Directions:** Identify which underlined words and phrases in each of the following sentences contains an error.

1 The days is becoming shorter as
  (A)   (B)
December approaches. No error
  (C)   (D)   (E)

2 The dog with the brown spots
  (A)   (B)
become nervous during a thunder
  (C)   (D)
storm. No error
  (E)

3 Grandpa play golf just like a pro.
  (A)   (B)   (C)   (D)
No error.
  (E)

4 Either Pamela or Sofia tallies the
  (A)   (B)   (C)
votes every week. No error.
  (D)   (E)

5 Jorge and Leora only speaks
  (A)   (B)   (C)
Spanish with their mother.
  (D)
No error.
  (E)

Practice 2 **Directions:** Choose the revised version of each numbered sentence that eliminates all errors in grammar, usage, and mechanics.

1 As long as humans has walked the Earth, herbs have been used for both medicinal and healing purpose.

  A As long as humans has walked the Earth, herbs have been used for both medicinal and healing purposes.
  B As long as humans have walked the Earth, herbs have been used for both medicinal and healing purposes.
  C As long as humans having walked the Earth, herbs having been used for both medicinal and healing purpose.
  D As long as humans have walked the Earth, herbs has been used for both medicinal and healing purposes.

2 To this day, many medicines is derived from some type of plant. One of the most commonly used medicines, aspirin, originally come from white willow or willow bark.

  F To this day, many medicines is derived from some type of plant. One of the most commonly used medicines, aspirin, originally comes from white willow or willow bark.
  G To this day, many medicines are derived from some type of plant. One of the most commonly used medicines, aspirin, originally come from white willow or willow bark.
  H To this day, many medicines are derived from some type of plant. One of the most commonly used medicines, aspirin, originally came from white willow or willow bark.
  J To this day, many medicines is derived from some type of plant. One of the most commonly used medicines, aspirin, originally came from white willow or willow bark.

▲ **Critical Viewing**
Compare the number of different types of musical instruments in the picture. Use the word *more* or *most* in your comparison. **[Identify]**

Adjectives and adverbs are important parts of speech that help writers make their sentences livelier, clearer, and more interesting and complete. What modifiers could a writer use to describe the sound of an unusual stringed instrument such as a sitar, a lute, or a hurdy-gurdy? The different sounds of these instruments make their music unique and colorful. Similarly, a carefully chosen adjective or adverb often turns an ordinary sentence into a superior one.

Modifiers are also important because they are used to make comparisons. For instance, if you wanted to compare the wide range of instruments in the world, you might use various forms of adjectives and adverbs to show similarities and differences in their sizes, shapes, and sounds.

In the first section of this chapter, you will learn rules for writing the forms of adjectives and adverbs used to make comparisons. In the second section, you will learn how to avoid a number of common usage problems involving comparisons.

Diagnostic Test

Directions: Write all answers on a separate sheet of paper.

Skill Check A. Identify the degree of each underlined modifier as *positive, comparative,* or *superlative.*

1. The sitar is the <u>most prominent</u> musical instrument in India.
2. It is <u>more difficult</u> to play than a guitar.
3. The <u>earliest</u> sitars were crafted more than 800 years ago.
4. It may take twenty years of practice to become a <u>skillful</u> sitar player.
5. My neighbor plays the instrument <u>more competently</u> than I do.

Skill Check B. Write the comparative and superlative form of each modifier.

6. rhythmic
7. loud
8. classical
9. quietly
10. far

Skill Check C. Write the appropriate form of the underlined modifier to complete each sentence.

11. The lute is <u>more difficult</u> to play than the mandolin, but the sitar is the ___?___ of all to play.
12. The musical traditions of northern and southern India contain <u>many</u> similarities but even ___?___ differences.
13. In general, Western musicians have taken <u>little</u> interest in Indian music and even ___?___ in Korean music.
14. The untrained musicians played <u>badly</u> in the morning and even ___?___ in the afternoon when they were tired.
15. Some scales are <u>simple</u> to play, and this one is the ___?___ of all.

Skill Check D. Write the appropriate comparative or superlative degree of the modifiers in parentheses.

16. A hurdy-gurdy produces a (strong) sound than a lute.
17. Compared to the hurdy-gurdy and the lute, a sitar has the (distinctive) sound.
18. This pumpkin must be (dry) before it can be used to make a sitar.
19. The sitar has the (many) frets of all stringed instruments.
20. Of Sandra, Jacques, and me, I handle the instrument the (confidently).

Skill Check E. Rewrite each sentence, correcting the unbalanced or illogical comparison.

21. Ensembles of classical musicians are more common in India than amateur musicians.
22. The sitar's chords are more varied than the tambura.
23. The Yugoslavian tambura has a longer neck than any lute.
24. It resembles an Indian instrument more than any stringed instrument from Eastern Europe.
25. The Turks introduced this instrument in Yugoslavia, Greece, and everywhere in Europe.

Degrees of Comparison

Most adjectives and adverbs have three forms, called *degrees*, that are used to modify and make comparisons.

Recognizing Degrees of Comparison

Each of the three degrees of comparison has a name: the *positive*, the *comparative*, and the *superlative*.

KEY CONCEPT Most adjectives and adverbs have three different forms to show degrees of comparison—the *positive*, the *comparative*, and the *superlative*. ■

There are different ways to form the *comparative* and *superlative* degrees of adjectives and adverbs. Notice, for example, how the forms of the adjectives and adverbs in the following chart are changed to show the degrees of comparison.

DEGREES OF ADJECTIVES		
Positive	Comparative	Superlative
simple impressive good	simpler more impressive better	simplest most impressive best
DEGREES OF ADVERBS		
soon impressively well	sooner more impressively better	soonest most impressively best

Exercise 1 Recognizing Degrees of Comparison Identify the degree of each underlined modifier.

EXAMPLE: Josef is the <u>best</u> player in the orchestra.

ANSWER: superlative

1. The accordion is a <u>small</u>, hand-held instrument.
2. It resembles an <u>earlier</u> German instrument, the handaoline.
3. Cyril Demian invented an <u>early</u> accordion in 1829.
4. The <u>oldest</u> accordions had only ten melody buttons.
5. Modern accordions have <u>more</u> melody and bass buttons.
6. These enable it to produce the <u>widest</u> range of notes.
7. The piano accordion is the <u>most familiar</u> type of accordion.
8. <u>Pianolike</u> keys are on the right side of the instrument.
9. Many people like the accordion <u>better</u> than the concertina.
10. The concertina has been used <u>most often</u> in folk music.

Theme: Unusual Musical Instruments

In this section, you will learn how to use adjectives and adverbs correctly to make comparisons. The examples and exercises in this section are about old or unusual musical instruments.

Cross-Curricular Connection: Music

More Practice

Grammar Exercise Workbook
• pp. 145–146
On-line Exercise Bank
• Section 25.1
  Go on-line:
  PHSchool.com
  Enter Web Code:
  eek-1002

Get instant feedback! Exercises 1 and 2 are available on-line or on CD-ROM.

Regular Forms

Modifiers can be either regular or irregular, depending on how their comparative and superlative degrees are formed. Two rules govern the formation of regular modifiers. The first rule applies to modifiers with one or two syllables.

> **KEY CONCEPTS** Use *-er* or *more* to form the comparative degree and *-est* or *most* to form the superlative degree of most one- and two-syllable modifiers. ■

The more common method for forming the comparative and superlative degrees of one- and two-syllable modifiers is to add *-er* and *-est* to the modifier rather than to use *more* and *most.*

| EXAMPLES: | loud | louder | loudest |
| | shiny | shinier | shiniest |

More and *most* are used with one- and two-syllable modifiers when adding *-er* and *-est* would sound awkward.

| EXAMPLES: | famous | more famous | most famous |

The comparative and superlative degrees of all adverbs that end in *-ly*, regardless of the number of syllables, are formed with *more* and *most.*

| EXAMPLES: | evenly | more evenly | most evenly |

> **KEY CONCEPT** Use *more* and *most* to form the comparative and superlative degrees of all modifiers with three or more syllables. ■

| EXAMPLES: | difficult | more difficult | most difficult |

Note About Comparisons With *Less* and *Least*: *Less* and *least*, the opposite of *more* and *most*, are also used to form the comparative and superlative degrees of most modifiers.

EXAMPLES:	tall	less tall	least tall
	hopeless	less hopeless	least hopeless
	ambitious	less ambitious	least ambitious

> **Exercise 2** **Writing Sentences Using Degrees of Comparison** Write sentences using the modifiers and degrees given below. Use *less* or *least* in one or more sentences.

1. charming (comparative)
2. funny (comparative)
3. bold (superlative)
4. beautifully (superlative)
5. educated (comparative)

⚙ Grammar ⚙and Style Tip

When choosing the degree of a modifier, be careful to avoid excessive exaggerations, which may hurt your writing. Try not to use a superlative modifier when all you really need is one in the comparative degree.

▶ **Exercise 3** Supplying Comparative and Superlative **Modifiers** Write each sentence on your paper. Use the form that is specified in parentheses for the underlined modifier.

EXAMPLE: That is one of the <u>small</u> instruments I have ever seen. (superlative)

ANSWER: That is one of the smallest instruments I have ever seen.

1. Some types of bagpipes are <u>simple</u> than others. (comparative)
2. I learned that the Highland pipe can play <u>many</u> notes. (comparative)
3. The Irish *uilleann* pipe is the <u>complicated</u> version. (superlative)
4. As you may know, bagpipes are played <u>often</u> in Scotland (superlative)
5. Some Irish pipers play <u>expressively</u> than Scots pipers. (comparative)

Irregular Forms

The comparative and superlative degrees of a few commonly used adjectives and adverbs are formed in unpredictable ways.

▶ **KEY CONCEPT** The irregular comparative and superlative forms of certain adjectives and adverbs must be memorized. ■

Notice in the following chart that the form of some irregular modifiers differs only in the positive degree. The modifiers *bad, badly,* and *ill,* for example, all have the same comparative and superlative degrees *(worse, worst).*

IRREGULAR MODIFIERS		
Positive	**Comparative**	**Superlative**
bad	worse	worst
badly	worse	worst
far (distance)	farther	farthest
far (extent)	further	furthest
good	better	best
ill	worse	worst
late	later	last *or* latest
little (amount)	less	least
many	more	most
much	more	most
well	better	best

▶ **More Practice**

Grammar Exercise Workbook
• pp. 147–148
On-line Exercise Bank
• Section 25.1
  Go on-line:
  PHSchool.com
  Enter Web Code:
  eek-1002

Get instant feedback! Exercises 3 and 4 are available on-line or on CD-ROM.

💡 **Spelling Tip**

Irregular modifiers are not the only modifiers with tricky spelling changes. Remember that some regular modifiers are changed in different ways when adding *-er* or *-est;* for example, *happy, happier, happiest.*

▶ **KEY CONCEPTS** *Bad* is an adjective. Do not use it to modify an action verb. *Badly* is an adverb. Do not use it after a linking verb. ■

INCORRECT: Keith plays the bassoon *bad.*

CORRECT: Keith plays the bassoon *badly.*

INCORRECT: Keith feels *badly.*

CORRECT: Keith feels *bad.*

Note About *Good* and *Well*: Like *bad*, *good* is an adjective and cannot be used as an adverb after an action verb. It can, however, be used as an adjective after a linking verb.

INCORRECT: Jennifer plays the oboe *good.*

CORRECT: This oboe seems *good.*

Well is generally an adverb. Like *badly*, it can be used after an action verb.

CORRECT: Jennifer plays the oboe *well.*

When *well* is used to mean "healthy," it is an adjective. Thus, *well* can also be used after a linking verb.

CORRECT: Jennifer should be *well* soon.

▶ **Exercise 4** **Forming Comparative and Superlative Degrees of Irregular Modifiers** Write the appropriate form of the underlined modifier to complete each sentence.

EXAMPLE: My singing is <u>bad</u> today, but it was ___?___ yesterday.

ANSWER: worse

1. Your voice sounds <u>good</u>, but a kazoo makes it sound ___?___.
2. I play it <u>better</u> when I hum, but you say it is ___?___ when you talk into the kazoo.
3. Kazoos are used <u>little</u> as a children's toy, ___?___ in blues music, and ___?___ in a classical orchestra.
4. Usually it sounds <u>much</u> like buzzing, but sometimes it sounds ___?___ like quacking.
5. My harmonica-playing sounds <u>bad</u> and my kazoo-playing sounds ___?___, but my zobo playing is certainly the ___?___.

▲ **Critical Viewing** Compare this oboe to a flute in at least three different ways. Which modifiers would you use? **[Compare and Contrast]**

Degrees of Comparison • **593**

GRAMMAR IN
LITERATURE

from **Like the Sun**
R. K. Narayan

Notice the highlighted regular form of modifiers in all three degrees in the passage.

. . . The headmaster had gone *nearly* hoarse, when he paused to ask, "Shall I go on?" Sekhar replied, "Please don't, sir; I think this will do. . . ." The headmaster looked *stunned*. His face was beaded with perspiration. Sekhar felt the *greatest* pity for him. But he felt he could not help it. No judge delivering a sentence felt *more pained* and help-less. Sekhar noticed that the headmaster's wife peeped in from the kitchen, with *eager* curiosity. The drummer and the violinist put away their burdens with an air of relief. . .

▶ **Exercise 5** Supplying Irregular Modifiers Write an appropriate degree of an irregular modifier to complete each sentence. Use the chart on page 592 if you need help.

EXAMPLE: Suffering from a throbbing headache, the musician is not feeling ___?___ today.

ANSWER: well

1. This store has the ___?___ selection of antique instruments in the state.
2. I have been able to find ___?___ nineteenth-century English woodwinds here than in a store in England.
3. The price I was quoted for a five-key clarinet was the ___?___ of all the stores I visited.
4. Even though I had to travel ___?___ to get here than to a local store, it was worth the trip.
5. This bassoon, made in 1880, has a ___?___ sound than a modern bassoon.
6. I wish that I did not play the bassoon so ___?___.
7. I have received ___?___ training on the instrument than my sister.
8. She has been taking lessons for ___?___ years than I.
9. She can play at least seven instruments very ___?___.
10. Yet she is not the ___?___ bit conceited.

More Practice

Grammar Exercise Workbook
• pp. 147–148
On-line Exercise Bank
• Section 25.1
 Go on-line:
 PHSchool.com
 Enter Web Code:
 eek-1002

▼ **Critical Viewing** What qualities of this instrument make it seem older than a guitar? Use modifiers in your answers. **[Judge]**

Section 25.1

Section Review

GRAMMAR EXERCISES 6–12

▶ **Exercise 6** Recognizing Modifiers
Underline the modifier in these phrases.

1. most common lyre
2. played more skillfully
3. larger instrument
4. earliest versions
5. more decorated style

▶ **Exercise 7** Recognizing Degrees of Comparison Identify the degree of each underlined modifier.

1. You will have a <u>better</u> understanding of the Chinese *qin* if you know about zithers.
2. Zithers are among the <u>most common</u> stringed instruments in the world.
3. The *qin*'s strings are stretched over a <u>curved</u> board.
4. It features several melody strings and even <u>more numerous</u> accompaniment strings.
5. The *qin* is <u>more traditional</u> in China than a lute or a fiddle.

▶ **Exercise 8** Forming the Comparative and Superlative Degrees
Rewrite the underlined modifier in the degree indicated in parentheses.

1. The stronger the vibrations of the player's lips, the <u>loud</u> the sound from a horn. (comparative)
2. The <u>simple</u> type of horn is made from an animal horn. (superlative)
3. These instruments are <u>commonly</u> used in religious rituals. (superlative)
4. Horns made from shells are <u>little</u> used as musical instruments. (comparative)
5. Adding finger holes on the side gives it a <u>wide</u> range of notes. (comparative)

▶ **Exercise 9** Revising to Eliminate Errors in Modifiers Revise this paragraph, eliminating errors in forms and degrees of modifiers.

The *sheng* is one of the more old Chinese instruments. It is more popularist in China. It has a low pitch than the *chi*. Chinese instruments are used often in religious ceremonies than on other occasions. Archaeological digs have unearthed some of the better musical artifacts ever found.

▶ **Exercise 10** Find It in Your Reading Identify the degree of the underlined modifiers in this passage from R. K. Narayan's "Like the Sun."

. . . He felt very <u>unhappy</u> that he could not speak <u>more soothingly</u>. Truth, he reflected, required as much strength to give as to receive.

▶ **Exercise 11** Find It in Your Writing Look through your writing portfolio for examples of sentences containing modifiers in the comparative or superlative degree. You might also rewrite some of your sentences that contain positive modifiers so that they express comparisons.

▶ **Exercise 12** Writing Application
Write five sentences of your own using the modifier and degree given below.

1. deep (superlative)
2. talented (comparative)
3. musical (superlative)
4. well (positive)
5. highly (comparative)

Making Clear Comparisons

In this section, you will learn the correct uses of the comparative and superlative degrees. You will also learn how to change an illogical comparison into a logical comparison.

Using Comparative and Superlative Degrees

There are two simple rules that govern the use of the comparative and superlative degrees:

▶ **KEY CONCEPTS** Use the comparative degree to compare two people, places, or things. Use the superlative degree to compare three or more people, places, or things. ■

Notice in the examples below that specific numbers need not be mentioned. The context of the sentence indicates whether two or more than two things are being compared.

COMPARATIVE: Oil paintings are *more effective* than watercolors. My sketch is *more detailed* than his.

SUPERLATIVE: We bought the *most expensive* painting of all. This exhibit has the *largest* number of early works in the city.

Note About *Double Comparisons:* Do not add both *-er* and *more* or *-est* and *most* to a regular modifier. In addition, do not add any of these endings or words to an irregular modifier.

INCORRECT: That sailboat is *more faster* than the other. John's technique is *more better* than mine.

CORRECT: That sailboat is *faster* than the other. John's technique is *better* than mine.

▶ **Exercise 13** Supplying the Comparative and Superlative Degrees Write the appropriate comparative or superlative degree of the modifier in parentheses.

EXAMPLE: Alfred is the (young) of all the students.
ANSWER: youngest

1. Mary Cassatt was one of the (early) American Impressionists.
2. She used (bright) colors than many of her contemporaries.
3. Her revolutionary style in an art world dominated by men made it (difficult) for her to get her work displayed.
4. Mary Cassatt's (good) works are of families, especially mothers and daughters.
5. She lived (comfortably) in France than in the United States.

Theme: The Art of Mary Cassatt
....
In this section, you will learn the correct uses of the comparative and superlative degrees of adjectives and adverbs. The examples and exercises in this section are about the art of American painter Mary Cassatt.
....
Cross-Curricular Connection: Art

Text

Get instant feedback! Exercise 13 is available on-line or on CD-ROM.

▶ **More Practice**

Grammar Exercise Workbook
• pp. 149–150
On-line Exercise Bank
• Section 25.2
Go on-line:
PHSchool.com
Enter Web Code:
eek-1002

Making Logical Comparisons

Some comparisons are illogical—they do not make good sense. In order to write logical comparisons, you must make sure you do not mistakenly compare two unrelated items and that you do not unintentionally compare something with itself.

Balanced Comparisons Sometimes, when you are in a hurry, you may compare two or more unrelated items. It is then necessary to rephrase the sentence so that the comparison is properly balanced.

KEY CONCEPT Make sure that your sentences compare only items of a similar kind. ∎

Because an unbalanced comparison is illogical, it may be unintentionally humorous. The way the examples below are written, the paintings of an artist are being compared not to paintings but to another artist.

UNBALANCED: We prefer Auguste Renoir's paintings to Mary Cassatt.

CORRECT: We prefer Auguste Renoir's paintings to Mary Cassatt's.

UNBALANCED: Critics considered the *paintings of Mary Cassatt* to be more emotional than *James Whistler.*

CORRECT: Critics considered the *paintings of Mary Cassatt* to be more emotional than *those of James Whistler.*

Child in a Straw Hat, Mary Cassatt

▶ Critical Viewing Write three statements about this painting that include the word *than.* [Analyze]

▶ **Exercise 14** **Making Balanced Comparisons** Rewrite each sentence, correcting the unbalanced comparison.

EXAMPLE: Cassatt's paintings were as detailed as Degas.
ANSWER: Cassatt's paintings were as detailed as Degas's.

1. Cassatt's later use of color was more vibrant than earlier.
2. Some of her works were more successful than her fellow painters.
3. Degas's friendship was more meaningful to her than Seurat.
4. Cassatt's earlier paintings were more relaxed than later.
5. An Impressionist's brush strokes are looser than an Expressionist.
6. Cassatt preferred outdoor light to a studio.
7. She posed her subjects more realistically than Picasso.
8. Her woodcuts were more influenced by Japanese art than France.
9. For Cassatt, Europe's artistic community was more accepting than America.
10. Americans' appreciation for modern art was less developed than Europeans.

Ballerine, Edgar Degas

▲ **Critical Viewing** What similarities do you see between this painting by Edgar Degas and the one by Mary Cassatt on page 597? **[Compare]**

Other and Else in Comparisons An illogical comparison can also be caused by failing to use the words *other* or *else.*

▶ **KEY CONCEPT** When comparing one within a group to the rest of the group, make sure that your sentence contains the word *other* or the word *else.* ■

Adding *other* or *else* in this type of comparison will prevent comparing something with itself. For instance, because Monet was an Impressionist, he cannot be compared to all Impressionists. He must be compared to all *other* Impressionists. Similarly, since Elizabeth works in the studio, she cannot be compared to *anyone* in the studio; she must be compared to *anyone else.*

ILLOGICAL: Monet's paintings became *more popular than those of any* Impressionist.

LOGICAL: Monet's paintings became *more popular than those of any other* Impressionist.

ILLOGICAL: Elizabeth has worked in the art studio *longer than anyone.*

LOGICAL: Elizabeth has worked in the art studio *longer than anyone else.*

💡 **Spelling Tip**

When making comparisons, don't confuse the word *than* with the word *then. Then* is an adverb that shows time. *Than* is a conjunction that links items in a comparison.

▶ **Exercise 15** Revising *Other* and *Else* in Comparisons
Revise each sentence, correcting the illogical comparison.

EXAMPLE: Richard is more talented than anyone in class.

ANSWER: Richard is more talented than anyone else in class.

1. Mary Cassatt produced more prints than any American artist of her time.
2. Her printmaking was more influenced by the art of Japan than that of any country.
3. When Cassatt and several artist friends attended an exhibition of Japanese prints in Paris, she was more impressed than anyone in the group.
4. Cassatt returned to the exhibit more often than anyone.
5. She began to concentrate on printmaking more than on any art form.

▶ **Exercise 16** Writing Clear Comparisons Rewrite each sentence on your paper, completing the comparison in a balanced and logical way.

EXAMPLE: Sherilyn's paintings of horses are more realistic than ___?___.

ANSWER: Sherilyn's paintings of horses are more realistic than Barry's.

1. For many people, yellow creates a happier feeling than any ___?___.
2. Many people prefer orange paint to blue because they feel orange is ___?___ than blue.
3. I have always considered green to be the ___?___ color of all.
4. Compared to green, black is a ___?___ and ___?___ color.
5. I believe purple is ___?___ than either red or blue.
6. I prefer the color ___?___ more than anyone ___?___ in ___?___.
7. The ___?___ color of all is ___?___.
8. If I were going to choose the ___?___ color of all for my room, it would be ___?___.
9. People who wear red clothes are ___?___ than people who wear black clothes.
10. I feel the ___?___ comfortable when I am wearing ___?___ clothes.

More Practice
Grammar Exercise Workbook
• pp. 150–151
On-line Exercise Bank
• Section 25.2
Go on-line:
PHSchool.com
Enter Web Code:
eek-1002

▼ **Critical Viewing**
Make some comparisons of yellow to other colors. Use *-er*, *more*, *-est*, or *most* in your comparisons. **[Compare and Contrast]**

Hands-on Grammar

Comparison Flip Test

Use a Comparison Flip Test to learn when the word *other* is needed to complete a comparison. First, print this partial sentence across the middle of a sheet of paper: *I like* [leave 1-1/2" space] *better than . . .*

Next, cut out six 3" squares, and draw a 1" x 1-1/2" rectangle in from the middle of the left edge. On each rectangle, print a different category with the word *any.* Examples: *any city, any food, any sport,* and so on. Around the rectangle, print five examples of the category— five cities, five foods, and so on. Then, cut out the rectangles, turn them over, and print *any other* plus the category. (See illustration.)

Now, cut out six 1-1/4" squares. On one side of each, print one example of one of the categories: *Miami, pizza,* and so on. On the other side, print something that is different from or opposite the category: *the country, plain water,* and so on. Then, do the flip test.

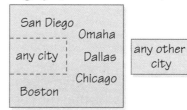

Place the 3" square at the end of your sentence, and fit the rectangle appropriate to the category in the cut-out section. Then, in the space between the words *I like* and *better than,* place the 1" square that corresponds to the category. If the item showing on the 1" square matches the category of items on the 3" square, you must flip the rectangle so that the *any other* side is facing up, because you are comparing something with others in the same category. If the item showing on the 1" square does not match the category, flip the rectangle so that the *any* side is facing up. Go on making comparisons by changing categories and flipping squares and rectangles to see when you need *any other* or when just *any* makes sense.

Find It in Your Reading Look in ads for "better than," "faster than," "more than," and so on, and see if the comparisons are correct.

Find It in Your Writing Review a piece of your writing to be sure your comparisons are logical and complete. Correct any that are not.

Section 25.2 *Section Review*

GRAMMAR EXERCISES 17–22

Exercise 17 Using Comparative and Superlative Forms Correctly
Choose the correct comparative or superlative form in each sentence.

1. Which painter do you like (better, best), Degas or Renoir?
2. Of all Impressionist painters, I consider Pissaro the (more, most) interesting.
3. Renoir was a (more intense, more intenser) artist than many of his peers.
4. However, the scenes he painted are often the (more, most) cheerful of all.
5. Of Degas, Cassatt, and Renoir, Degas was the (older, oldest).
6. He was also the (more, most) original of the three.
7. Of his paintings of horses and ballerinas, which do you prefer (more, most)?
8. Cassatt painted (slower, more slower) than Degas.
9. Of the work of all Impressionists, her paintings seem (more, most) peaceful.
10. Cassatt's paintings are much admired, but her prints are even more (famous, famouser).

Exercise 18 Supplying Correct Degrees of Modifiers Write the appropriate comparative or superlative degree of the modifier in parentheses.

1. Renoir focused on light (well) than many of the other Impressionists.
2. He used light to make skin, fabrics, and textures the (brilliant) parts of his paintings.
3. Renoir earned (much) money by painting portraits than by any other means.
4. His subjects are the (expressive) of all the Impressionists.
5. Renoir suffered for many years from arthritis, and at the end of his life it grew even (bad).

Exercise 19 Revising to Clarify Comparisons Revise each sentence to correct unbalanced or illogical comparisons.

1. Degas's focus was more on people than Renoir.
2. The techniques he used in painting ballet dancers were more sophisticated than his fellow painters.
3. His sketches of horse racing came earlier than dancers.
4. Cassatt was friendlier with Degas than anyone in the Impressionist group.
5. Cassatt's paintings were more inventive than any woman painter of her time.

Exercise 20 Find It in Your Reading In this excerpt from "What Makes a Degas a Degas?" is the author using a comparative or superlative modifier? What is he comparing?

The results of Degas's experiments could have been executed much more quickly had he used pastels instead of oils. What Degas wanted, however, was to make paint look spontaneous.

Exercise 21 Find It in Your Writing Look through your portfolio for examples of comparisons. Check to see that your comparisons are clear and logical.

Exercise 22 Writing Application Write a comparison of the work of two painters, musicians, or actors. Make sure that you use comparative and superlative modifiers correctly and that your comparisons are clear.

GRAMMAR EXERCISES 23–30

Exercise 23 Recognizing Positive, Comparative, and Superlative Degrees
Identify the degree of each underlined modifier.

1. The harp is one of the <u>oldest</u> instruments.
2. Today's harps are <u>more</u> sophisticated than ancient ones.
3. Impressionists considered the harp to be the <u>most expressive</u> instrument.
4. With the harp, it was <u>easy</u> to create rippling tones that sounded like water.
5. Composer Claude Debussy gave the harp a <u>greater</u> role within the orchestra.
6. His style was <u>more modern</u> than that of many of his contemporaries.
7. <u>Most</u> of Debussy's innovations dealt with harmonies.
8. A <u>dreamy</u> quality characterized his compositions.
9. Debussy created chamber works <u>late</u> in his career.
10. *Nocturnes* is one of his <u>more widely</u> known compositions.

Exercise 24 Forming Irregular Comparative and Superlative Degrees
Write the correct form of the underlined modifier to complete each sentence.

1. The fame of many modern composers has spread <u>far</u>, but Debussy's has spread even ___?___.
2. Béla Bartók was influenced <u>little</u> by Franz Liszt and even ___?___ by Richard Strauss.
3. Bartók studied <u>many</u> Turkish songs and even ___?___ Hungarian songs.
4. Bartók's violin concertos are <u>good</u>, but his string quartets are ___?___.
5. When first performed, this concerto was greeted <u>badly</u> by critics and even ___?___ by the audience.

Exercise 25 Supplying the Comparative and Superlative Degrees
Write the appropriate degree of the modifier in parentheses.

1. Gregorian chants are the (good) known of all types of Medieval music.
2. Pope Gregory I was (active) in the composition of church music than earlier religious leaders.
3. Early forms of chant involved just a melody line, while (late) forms involved a two-part harmony.
4. This two-part harmony was the (early) step toward the development of multi-part music in Europe.
5. Multi-part harmonies were (difficult) to compose but (satisfying) to hear than simple melodies.

Exercise 26 Revising to Eliminate Errors in Comparisons Revise each sentence to correct unbalanced or illogical comparisons.

1. The music of the Renaissance was smoother than Medieval times.
2. John Dunstable's style was more graceful than Francesco Landini.
3. The influence of composers from Holland was greater than France.
4. In the seventeenth century, the popularity of instrumental music was greater than vocal music.
5. Johann Sebastian Bach's compositions were more sophisticated than Vivaldi and other composers.
6. In the eighteenth century, Vienna was more important as a classical music center than any European city.
7. More classical composers gathered in Vienna than anywhere.
8. The works of Haydn and Mozart are better known than Salieri.
9. Giuseppe Verdi's operas were more

concerned with human relationships than anything.

10. Richard Wagner created operas that were longer and more dramatic than any composer.

▶ **Exercise 27** **Revising Sentences to Eliminate Errors With Modifiers**
Revise the following sentences, correcting any errors in the use of modifiers. If a sentence is correct, write *correct*.

1. I have been studying the oboe for a long time than anyone in my family.
2. I think the oboe has a more clearer sound than any instrument.
3. Compared to a bassoon, an oboe is lighter and higher pitched.
4. My cousin is the more talented of the three musicians in my family.
5. He plays the clarinet smoothlier than anyone else I have ever heard.
6. He played few wrong notes as a child and even few today.
7. He has been practicing two compositions and plans to perform the one he knows the most thoroughly.
8. The first time I tried the piece, I played it badly, but now I can play it better.
9. Performing my own composition at the festival has been my most exciting musical experience ever.
10. I received a warm reception than anyone who performed at the festival.

▶ **Exercise 28** **Revising a Paragraph to Eliminate Errors With Modifiers**
Revise the following paragraph, correcting any errors in the usage of modifiers.

Jean Sibelius from Finland is his country's famousest composer. He is more linked to Finnish nationalism than anyone. Born in 1865, Sibelius took up the violin early than any instrument. He thought at first about becoming a violinist, but he was most interested in composing. Sibelius's early compositions were more influenced by Russian composers than Finland. By the time he reached his thirties, however, Sibelius had developed an original style than before. Turning to Finnish themes, he created his more memorable work. By 1900, Finns were intent on becoming independent from Russia than in previous years. Sibelius's *Finlandia* debuted that year and created more controversy in Finland than any composition. Despite being banned by the Czar of Russia, *Finlandia* soon became the important symbol of Finnish independence.

▶ **Exercise 29** **Writing Application**
Imagine that you are a music reviewer for a magazine. Write a brief article comparing three different songs or albums. Use comparative and superlative forms of modifiers in your review and make sure that your comparisons are clear and logical.

▶ **Exercise 30** **CUMULATIVE REVIEW Correcting Errors in Verb, Pronoun, and Modifier Usage and Agreement** Rewrite the following paragraph, correcting errors in usage and agreement.

(1) The first instrument I ever play was the triangle. (2) My kindergarten teacher ask the other kids and I to choose instruments from a collection that was setting in the back of the room. (3) The others choosed drums or horns, but I pick the triangle. (4) I seen it shining brightly than the other instruments. (5) I was also impress by it's shape and tone. (6) While the triangle is an easy instrument to play, they are hard to play good. (7) There is many ways to play a triangle, but I knew only one way to play—loud. (8) I striked the instrument over and over without any sense of rhythm. (9) Certainly no one in the class played louder than me. (10) After much practice, us musicians learned to play together better.

Standardized Test Preparation Workshop

Standard English Usage: Modifiers

Standardized test questions often measure your ability to use modifiers correctly. This may be done by testing your ability to choose the correct form of comparison to complete a sentence. Use the following strategies to help you determine which form to use in a sentence:

- If no comparison is being made, use the **positive form** of the modifier.

- If one thing or action is compared to another thing or action, use the **comparative form** of the modifier—ending in *-er* or preceded by *more*.

- If one thing or action is being compared to more than one other thing or action, use the **superlative form** of the modifier—ending in *-est* or preceded by *most*.

- Be aware that some modifiers have **special forms,** such as *good, bad, much,* and *many.*

> ### Test Tip
> Be careful not to choose a double comparison, such as *more younger* to complete a sentence. The correct form is *younger.*

Sample Test Items

Directions: Read the passage, and choose the word or group of words that belongs in each space.

Although San Diego is a growing city; it is still much ____(1)____ than Los Angeles. Its climate is one of the ____(2)____ in the United States.

1 A more small

  B most small

  C smaller

  D smallest

2 F more beautiful

  G beautifuller

  H beautifullest

  J most beautiful

Answers and Explanations

The best answer is C. San Diego is being compared to one other city, so a comparative form is needed. Because *small* is a short word, its comparative is formed simply by adding *-er.*

The best answer is J. San Diego's climate is being compared to all United States climates; therefore, a superlative form is needed. Because *beautiful* is a three-syllable word, *most* is used to form the superlative. Note that choices *G* and *H* are neither correct forms nor proper words.

Practice 1 **Directions:** Read the passage, and choose the word or group of words that belongs in each space.

Fifteen museums make San Diego's Balboa Park one of the nation's ___(1)___ cultural complexes. Its Spanish Revival buildings remind visitors of an ___(2)___ era. The buildings were ___(3)___ decorated than had been seen previously. Two international expositions held in San Diego were ___(4)___ to the park's development. It now offers the ___(5)___ entertainment opportunities in the city.

1 **A** larger
  B more large
  C largest
  D large

2 **F** earliest
  G earlier
  H more early
  J most early

3 **A** more highly
  B highlier
  C highliest
  D most highly

4 **F** most crucial
  G crucialer
  H more crucial
  J crucial

5 **A** more diverse
  B diversest
  C most diverse
  D diverser

Practice 2 **Directions:** Read the passage, and choose the word or group of words that belongs in each space.

Almost nothing could be ___(1)___ than a day at the San Diego Zoo. I know I had one of the ___(2)___ times ever! The zoo is acknowledged as one of the ___(3)___ in the entire world. As famous as the zoo is for the variety of exhibits, it has often received even ___(4)___ recognition for its work with endangered giant pandas. The birth of a baby panda at the zoo was a ___(5)___ achievement.

1 **A** interestinger
  B more interesting
  C interestingest
  D most interesting

2 **F** goodest
  G best
  H better
  J good

3 **A** most fine
  B finer
  C finest
  D more fine

4 **F** more great
  G greater
  H greatest
  J great

5 **A** more significant
  B most significant
  C significant
  D less significant

Miscellaneous Problems in Usage

Throughout history, women have achieved stunning success in many different fields. For example, Hildegard von Bingen delighted contemporaries with her writings and musical compositions in the twelfth century, and Amelia Earhart became a flying sensation in the twentieth century. These women strove for excellence in their chosen fields, and their successes inspire others.

Success in many fields requires, among other things, accurate and effective use of language. In this chapter, you will study some usage problems that have not been presented earlier. In the first section of this chapter, you will learn how to form negative sentences correctly. In the second section, you will study troublesome words and expressions.

▲ **Critical Viewing**
Marie Curie, pictured above, is renowned for her research in radioactivity. Use negative sentences to compare her laboratory to modern laboratories with which you are familiar. **[Distinguish]**

Diagnostic Test

Directions: Write all answers on a separate sheet of paper.

Skill Check A. Choose the word in parentheses that makes each sentence negative without forming a double negative.

1. In earlier times, people assumed that women couldn't do (nothing, anything) outside the domestic sphere.
2. They thought women didn't have (no, any) leadership abilities.
3. It was also believed that women (had, hadn't) scarcely the strength or intelligence of their male counterparts.
4. Susan B. Anthony (was, wasn't) but one woman we remember for her achievements.
5. She (was, wasn't) hardly the only person to work for women's suffrage, but only Anthony is commemorated on U.S. currency.

Skill Check B. Choose the correct expression to complete each sentence.

6. Oftentimes, girls weren't (learned, taught) the same skills and lessons as boys.
7. Rather (than, then) science, math, or literature, girls studied cooking, sewing, and caring for the family.
8. (Being that, Because) they were often denied learning opportunities, their successes are that much more remarkable.
9. Women often had to make (their, there) own opportunities.
10. In ancient Egypt, Hatshepsut ruled as regent (due to, because of) her stepson's young age.
11. Within a few years, she had herself crowned pharaoh (so, so that) she could rule in her own right.
12. In more recent times, Marie Curie won an unprecedented (too, two) Nobel Prizes.
13. Her work, (which, who) dealt with radiation, advanced scientific research in the field of radioactivity.
14. Elizabeth I of England (adapted, adopted) to the requirements of sovereignty with strength and resolve.
15. (Beside, Besides) leading in peacetime, she also proved herself a strong leader in wartime.
16. In the twentieth century, Rosa Parks, an African American living in the South, refused to move (further, farther) back in the bus so that a white person could sit up front.
17. She inspired thousands and had a powerful (affect, effect) on the civil rights movement.
18. Eileen Collins (already, all ready) knew how to fly before she became an astronaut.
19. Harriet Tubman guided slaves (among, between) bondage in the South and freedom in the North.
20. (Them, Those) women, and many others, have inspired countless generations to strive to achieve their own dreams.

Negative Sentences

At one time, it was correct to use several negative words in one sentence. It was correct, for example, to say, "Father *didn't* tell *nobody nothing*." Today, however, only one negative word is used to make the entire sentence negative. The above sentence can be restated correctly in one of three ways: "Father *didn't* tell anybody anything," "Father told *nobody* anything," or "Father told *nothing* to anybody."

Recognizing Double Negatives

A **double negative** is the use of two negative words in a sentence when only one is needed.

▶ **KEY CONCEPT** Do not write sentences with double negatives. ■

The following chart gives examples of double negatives and the two ways each can be corrected.

CORRECTING DOUBLE NEGATIVES	
Double Negatives	**Corrections**
She *couldn't* fix *nothing*.	She *couldn't* fix *anything*. She could fix *nothing*.
Ellen *didn't* have *no* training.	Ellen *didn't* have *any* training. Ellen had *no* training.
She *wouldn't* ask *no one* for help.	She *wouldn't* ask *anyone* for help. She asked *no one* for help.

▶ **Exercise 1** Avoiding Double Negatives Choose the word in parentheses that correctly completes each sentence.
1. No one (couldn't, could) tell Marie Curie that women were inferior in science.
2. She grew up in Poland, not (nowhere, anywhere) close to France, where she did her most famous work.
3. Marie wasn't as interested in (nothing, anything) as much as she was in radioactivity.
4. She and her husband won the 1903 Nobel Prize for Physics, but not without (no, some) help from Antoine Becquerel, who shared the award.
5. A woman hadn't (never, ever) before won a Nobel Prize.

💡 **Spelling Tip**

To make a helping verb negative, just add *n't* to the end of the verb or follow it with the word *not*. Watch out for some exceptions: *Can't* and *won't* lose some letters when put into the negative form, and *cannot* is spelled as one word.

Forming Negative Sentences Correctly

Negative sentences are formed correctly in one of three ways:

Using One Negative Word: The most common way to make a sentence negative is with a single negative word—such as *no, not, none, nothing, never, nobody,* or *nowhere*—or with the contraction *n't* added to a helping verb.

▶ **KEY CONCEPT** Do not use two negative words in the same clause. ■

Using two of these negative words in the same clause will create a double negative.

DOUBLE NEGATIVE: She *wouldn't never* learn that by herself.
CORRECT: She *wouldn't* ever learn that by herself.
                          She *would* never learn that by herself.

Using *But* in a Negative Sense: When *but* means "only," it usually acts as a negative.

▶ **KEY CONCEPT** Do not use *but* in its negative sense with another negative. ■

DOUBLE NEGATIVE: He *hadn't but* one hero.
CORRECT: He had *but* one hero.
                          He had only one hero.

Using *Barely, Hardly,* and *Scarcely:* These words have a negative sense and should not be used with other negative words.

▶ **KEY CONCEPT** Do not use *barely, hardly,* or *scarcely* with another negative. ■

DOUBLE NEGATIVE: She *hadn't barely* mastered the new language.

CORRECT: She had *barely* mastered the new language.

DOUBLE NEGATIVE: He *couldn't hardly* see beyond that hill.
CORRECT: He could *hardly* see beyond that hill.

DOUBLE NEGATIVE: It *hadn't scarcely* started to rain.
CORRECT: It had *scarcely* started to rain.

▲ Critical Viewing
Marie Curie is admired for her research in radioactivity, among other things. Write several sentences about a person whom you admire. Use the words *but, barely, hardly,* and *scarcely* in your sentences.
[Support]

▶ **Exercise 2** Avoiding Problems With Negatives Choose the word in parentheses that makes each sentence negative without creating a double negative.

EXAMPLE: There (isn't, is) scarcely a more famous female aviator than Amelia Earhart.

ANSWER: is

1. Amelia Earhart hardly liked (anything, nothing) as much as flying.
2. Nobody (could, couldn't) keep her on the ground.
3. Before she became the first woman to break the speed record while crossing the Atlantic alone, some people thought women wouldn't (ever, never) be good pilots.
4. That (was, wasn't) but one aviation record that Earhart broke.
5. She disappeared during an attempt to fly around the world, and to this day no one (doesn't know, knows) for certain what happened on that last flight.

▶ **Exercise 3** Revising Sentences to Correct Double Negatives Rewrite each sentence, correcting the double negative.

EXAMPLE: Harriet Tubman didn't allow nothing to stop her from helping others.

ANSWER: Harriet Tubman allowed nothing to stop her from helping others.

1. Born into slavery, Harriet Tubman wasn't never supposed to enjoy the freedom of her white masters.
2. She didn't have no real childhood.
3. When still a young woman, she escaped to the North, but she didn't scarcely take any time to enjoy her new freedom.
4. Harriet didn't think nobody should be a slave.
5. She felt she didn't have but one choice: to return to the South to guide others to freedom.
6. No one wasn't able to stop her, and she never lost one person on her eighteen trips on the Underground Railroad.
7. She wouldn't let no one turn back once they had started.
8. Tubman didn't never stop fighting for freedom: During the Civil War, she served as a nurse, scout, and spy for the Union army.
9. She didn't hardly restrict herself to just one cause: She also fought for women's rights, raised money for schools for black people, and established a home for poor and elderly black people.
10. Harriet Tubman couldn't abide no injustices.

More Practice

Grammar Exercise Workbook
• pp. 153–154
On-line Exercise Bank
• Section 26.1
  Go on-line:
  PHSchool.com
  Enter Web Code:
  eek-1002

Complete the exercises on-line! Exercises 2 and 3 are available on-line or on CD-ROM.

Section Review

GRAMMAR EXERCISES 4–9

▶ **Exercise 4** Avoiding Double Negatives Choose the word in parentheses that makes each sentence negative without forming a double negative.

1. In the 1840's, medical schools didn't want (nothing, anything) to do with female applicants.
2. Elizabeth Blackwell (would, wouldn't) never give up, however, and on her thirtieth try, she was accepted by Geneva College.
3. She (had, hadn't) barely gotten her degree when she traveled to Europe to gain practical experience in hospitals.
4. When she returned, no one in the medical community (would, wouldn't) trust her.
5. She wouldn't acknowledge (no, any) resistance and opened a hospital to serve poor women and children.

▶ **Exercise 5** Revising Sentences to Avoid Problems With Negatives Rewrite each sentence, correcting the double negative.

1. Aung San Suu Kyi didn't promote no violence in her struggle for freedom from the military government in Burma.
2. Her father, who was assassinated when Aung San Suu Kyi was only two, didn't want no one to live under oppression, and she continued his struggle.
3. While living in India, she didn't ignore none of the methods and teachings of Mohandas Gandhi, the nonviolent protest leader.
4. She couldn't hardly win a military battle, so she gave speeches, visited the people, and started a new political party based on democratic ideals.
5. The government couldn't do nothing to stem her popularity, so they placed her under house arrest for more than ten years.

▶ **Exercise 6** Revising a Paragraph to Correct Double Negatives Rewrite the following, correcting all double negatives.

When she wasn't barely a teenager, Joan of Arc heard the voices of saints. They told her that no one but she couldn't rid France of the invading English. First, she convinced the French king that she wasn't telling no lies when she claimed she could restore his kingdom. Charles VII believed he hadn't but one choice: to trust Joan. It didn't take scarcely ten days to break the English siege of Orleans. The English couldn't do nothing to defeat her. Joan wouldn't take no rest until Charles VII was crowned at Rheims. She didn't allow nobody to attack the king as she led him through enemy territory. In Paris, however, she couldn't do nothing to prevent her own capture. The English didn't want no more trouble from Joan, so they sentenced her to death.

▶ **Exercise 7** Find It in Your Reading Locate an article on a famous woman in a newspaper, a magazine, or one of your textbooks. Find at least two examples of negative sentences. Explain why the negatives are used correctly.

▶ **Exercise 8** Find It in Your Writing In your own writing, find five examples of negative words. Check to make sure that you have not included any sentences with double negatives.

▶ **Exercise 9** Writing Application Write about a woman whom you admire. Include three negative sentences. Be sure to avoid double negatives and to form all negative sentences correctly.

Common Usage Problems

This section presents an alphabetical list of forty-five usage problems that sometimes cause confusion in writing and speaking.

▶ **KEY CONCEPT** Study the items in this glossary, paying particular attention to similar meanings and spellings. ■

(1) a, an The article *a* is used before consonant sounds; *an* is used before vowel sounds. Words beginning with *h, o,* or *u* can have either a consonant sound or a vowel sound.

(2) accept, except *Accept* is a verb meaning "to receive." *Except* is a preposition meaning "other than" or "leaving out."

VERB: Settlers of the western frontier *accepted* the harsh realities of frontier life.
PREPOSITION: They easily found all the natural resources they needed *except* water and wood.

(3) adapt, adopt *Adapt* means "to change." *Adopt* means "to take as one's own."

EXAMPLES: Easterners quickly learned to *adapt*.
            Newcomers *adopted* the customs of neighbors.

(4) affect, effect *Affect*, almost always a verb, means "to influence." *Effect* may be used as a noun or as a verb. As a noun, it means "result." As a verb, it means "to bring about" or "to cause."

VERB: Natural disasters *affected* the farmers' success.
NOUN: Settlers knew the *effects* of nature and tried to combat them.
VERB: The tractor *effected* a drastic change in farming.

(5) ain't *Ain't* was originally a contraction of *am not*, but it is no longer considered standard English.

(6) all ready, already *All ready*, two separate words used as an adjective, is an expression meaning "ready." *Already*, an adverb, means "even now" or "by or before this time."

ADJECTIVE: The cowboys were *all ready* for the cattle drive.
ADVERB: Many of them had *already* driven cattle north.

Theme: Westward Expansion

In this section, you will learn about forty-five common usage problems. The examples and exercises in this section are about the people who took part in the westward expansion of the United States during the 1800's.

Cross-Curricular Connection: Social Studies

(7) all right, alright *Alright* is a nonstandard spelling. Make sure you use the two-word form.

NONSTANDARD: Business was *alright* if the town was located near some form of transportation.

CORRECT: Business was *all right* if the town was located near some form of transportation.

(8) all together, altogether *All together* means "together as a single group." *Altogether* means "completely" or "in all."

EXAMPLES: Cowhands had to work *all together* to transport cattle over long distances.
They would fail *altogether* if they worked alone.

(9) among, between Both of these words are prepositions. *Among* always implies three or more. *Between* is generally used only with two things.

EXAMPLES: Cows were branded so that the owners could pick out their cows from *among* a crowd.
Cowboys could transport the cows *between* the ranch and the railroad.

(10) anxious This adjective implies uneasiness, worry, or fear. Do not use it as a substitute for eager.

LESS ACCEPTABLE: The cowboys were *anxious* to reach the next town.

PREFERRED: The cowboys were *eager* to reach the next town.
The ranchers were *anxious* about cattle thieves.

(11) anywhere, everywhere, nowhere, somewhere Never end these adverbs with an *-s*.

NONSTANDARD: At first, ranchers didn't use fences, so cattle could wander *anywheres*.

CORRECT: At first, ranchers didn't use fences, so cattle could wander *anywhere*.

(12) as to *As to* is awkward. Replace it with *about*.

NONSTANDARD: Miners had no worries *as to* the land.

CORRECT: Miners had no worries *about* the land.

Technology Tip

If you are using the spell-check feature of a word-processing program, keep in mind that it will not pick up as errors words such as *all right, alright, all together*, and *altogether*.

(13) at Do not use *at* after *where*. Simply eliminate it.

NONSTANDARD: They didn't care *where* they were *at* as long as they found precious metals.

CORRECT: They didn't care *where* they were as long as they found precious metals.

(14) awhile, a while *Awhile* is an adverb that means "for a while." It is never preceded by a preposition. *A while* is an article and a noun, usually used after prepositions such as *for* or *after*.

ADVERB: The miners stayed *awhile* and worked the mine.

NOUN: After *a while*, a boom town would grow up to serve the needs of the miners.

(15) bad, badly *Bad* is an adjective that means "incorrect," "ill," or "undesirable." *Badly* is an adverb that means "in a bad way" or "poorly."

ADJECTIVE: Miners papered their walls with newspapers to insulate themselves from a *bad* winter.

ADVERB: Compared to today's insulation, the paper worked *badly*.

▲ Critical Viewing
Using the words *bad* and *badly*, write a movie scene using this photograph as inspiration.
[Speculate]

▷ **Exercise 10** Avoiding Usage Problems 1–15 Choose the correct expression to complete each sentence.
1. For (awhile, a while) ships and stagecoaches were the only means to deliver mail from the East to California.
2. In 1860, a California senator and a Missouri businessman (adapted, adopted) a plan to provide faster mail delivery.
3. The pony express delivered mail (among, between) St. Joseph, Missouri, and Sacramento, California.
4. At first, no one had any idea (as to, about) the exact time it would take a rider to travel from Missouri to California.
5. The service employed about eighty riders (altogether, all together) to deliver the mail.
6. Riders endured (bad, badly) weather and the threat of attacks by Indians.
7. After a rider covered at least 75 miles, he reached a station where another rider was (all ready, already) waiting.
8. The new rider would (accept, except) the leather saddlebag and continue along the route.
9. The fate of the pony express (ain't, isn't) a happy one.
10. The new transcontinental telegraph had a major (affect, effect) on the pony express, quickly shutting it down.

▷ **More Practice**

Grammar Exercise Workbook
• pp. 155–156
On-line Exercise Bank
• Section 26.2
  Go on-line:
  PHSchool.com
  Enter Web Code:
  eek-1002

Get instant feedback! Exercise 10 is available on-line or on CD-ROM.

(16) because Do not use *because* after the word *reason*. Say "The reason . . . that" or reword the sentence.

NONSTANDARD: *The reason* miners moved so often is *because* they were always searching for a major strike.

CORRECT: *The reason* miners moved so often is *that* they were always searching for a major strike. Miners moved so often *because* they were always searching for a major strike.

(17) being as, being that Do not use either expression. Use *because* or *since* instead.

(18) beside, besides *Beside* means "close to" or "at the side of." *Besides* means "in addition to."

EXAMPLES: Tombstone, Arizona, developed *beside* a mine. *Besides* mines, towns were started near transportation centers and major shipping points.

(19) bring, take *Bring* means "to carry from a distant place to a nearer one." *Take* means the opposite: "to carry from a near place to a more distant place."

EXAMPLES: Cowboys would *bring* cattle over thousands of miles to a town with a train station. The trains would then *take* the cattle to the East, where they would be sold for food.

(20) different from, different than *Different from* is preferred.

LESS ACCEPTABLE: A transportation town was *different than* a mining town because it was usually more permanent.

PREFERRED: A transportation town was *different from* a mining town because it was usually more permanent.

(21) doesn't, don't *Doesn't* is the correct verb form for third-person singular subjects. *Don't* is used with all other subjects.

NONSTANDARD: A town *don't* thrive without townspeople. It *don't* seem very prosperous. He *don't* want to stay if there is no work.

CORRECT: A town *doesn't* thrive without townspeople. It *doesn't* seem very prosperous. He *doesn't* want to stay if there is no work.

(22) done *Done*, the past participle of *do*, should always follow a helping verb.

NONSTANDARD: Merchants *done* the job of supplying farmers, miners, and cowhands.

CORRECT: Merchants *have done* the job of supplying farmers, miners, and cowhands.

(23) due to *Due to* means "caused by" and should be used only when the words *caused by* can logically be substituted.

NONSTANDARD: *Due to* the lack of natural resources, towns were often established in groups.

CORRECT: The establishment of towns in groups was *due to* the lack of natural resources.

(24) farther, further *Farther* refers to distance. *Further* means "to a greater degree or extent" or "additional."

EXAMPLES: The *farther* away a town was from transportation, the harder it was for people to get supplies.
The area around Virginia City, Nevada, was *further* developed to supply resources to the city.
Virginia City needed *further* support to survive.

(25) fewer, less *Fewer* is used with objects that can be counted. *Less* is used with qualities or quantities that cannot be counted.

EXAMPLES: *fewer* stagecoaches, *fewer* horses, *fewer* supplies
less land, *less* wood, *less* communication

(26) gone, went *Gone* is the past participle of *go*. It should be used as a verb only with a helping verb. *Went* is the past tense of *go* and is never used with a helping verb.

NONSTANDARD: Easterners *gone* west to find a better life.
They *could have went* to a major eastern city to make a better life for themselves.

CORRECT: Easterners *had gone* west hoping to find a better life.
Easterners *went* west to find a better life.
They *could have gone* to a major eastern city to make a better life for themselves.

(27) in, into *In* refers to position. *Into* suggests motion.

POSITION: People often traveled west *in* wagons.
MOTION: They loaded their supplies *into* a covered wagon.

> **⚙ Grammar and Style Tip**
>
> Vary your vocabulary to make your writing more interesting. Explore new words and expressions, but always check for correct usage.

(28) irregardless Putting *ir-* on this word makes it a double negative. Use *regardless* instead.

NONSTANDARD: People settled in the West, *irregardless* of the dangers.

CORRECT: People settled in the West, *regardless* of the dangers.

(29) just When you use *just* to mean "no more than," place it right before the word or phrase it logically modifies.

LESS ACCEPTABLE: Since there was little wood, houses were *just* made of sod.

PREFERRED: Since there was little wood, houses were made of *just* sod.

(30) kind of, sort of These expressions should not be used to mean "rather" or "somewhat."

NONSTANDARD: Travel was *kind* of slow.

CORRECT: Travel was *rather* slow.

▼ **Critical Viewing**
Write a description of this painting, correctly using one of the two words listed in each of the usage problems 24–27. [**Interpret**]

Exercise 11 Avoiding Usage Problems 16–30 Choose the correct expression to complete each sentence.

1. Pony express riders carried the mail (irregardless, regardless) of bad weather, rough terrain, or danger.
2. They (gone, went) about 75 miles a day.
3. Teenagers (did, done) much of the riding.
4. They were chosen (due to, because of) their light weight.
5. Horses traveled (fewer, less) miles per day than the riders.
6. The mail was carried (in, into) special leather saddlebags.
7. (Beside, Besides) letters, pony express riders also carried small packages.
8. The mail traveled much (farther, further) in a day with the pony express than on a ship or stagecoach.
9. The service (just lasted, lasted just) a year and a half.
10. The reason it closed down is (that, because) the transcontinental telegraph service had opened for business two days earlier.

(31) lay, lie *Lay* means "to put or set (something) down." Its principal parts—*lay, laying, laid,* and *laid*—are usually followed by a direct object. *Lie* means "to recline." Its principal parts—*lie, lying, lay,* and *lain*—are never followed by a direct object.

LAY: *Lay* the luggage on top of the stagecoach.
        The driver is *laying* the bags in the back compartment.
        The passengers *laid* their handbags on the seats.
        The bags were jostled about and no longer rested where the driver had *laid* them.

LIE: Passengers had to sleep in the stagecoach and were not able to *lie* down.
        The handbag is *lying* on the floor at her feet.
        The child *lay* down across her parents' laps.
        She had *lain* there throughout the night.

(32) learn, teach *Learn* means "to acquire knowledge." *Teach* means "to give knowledge to."

EXAMPLES: A person *learned* many different skills in order to survive in the West.
             Settlers *taught* newcomers how to manage in the new terrain.

More Practice

Grammar Exercise Workbook
• pp. 155–156
On-line Exercise Bank
• Section 26.2
  Go on-line:
  PHSchool.com
  Enter Web Code:
  eek-1002

Text

Get instant feedback! Exercise 11 is available on-line or on CD-ROM.

(33) leave, let *Leave* means "to allow to remain." *Let* means "to permit."

NONSTANDARD: Cowboys *leave* the cattle wander over great tracts of land.
They *let* calves with the mothers, even if the father belongs to a different herd.

CORRECT: Cowboys *let* the cattle wander over great tracts of land.
They *leave* calves with the mothers, even if the father belongs to a different herd.

(34) like *Like* is a preposition and should not be used in place of the conjunction *as*.

NONSTANDARD: Crime in the West was widespread, *like* it was in the East.

CORRECT: Crime in the West was widespread, *as* it was in the East.

(35) of Do not use the preposition *of* in place of the verb *have*. *Of* after *outside, inside, off*, or *atop* is also undesirable in formal writing. Simply eliminate it.

NONSTANDARD: A single sheriff would *of* watched over a group of towns.

CORRECT: A single sheriff would *have* watched over a group of towns.

LESS ACCEPTABLE: One judge held court *inside* of a restaurant.
PREFERRED: One judge held court *inside* a restaurant.

(36) only Be sure to place *only* in front of the word you mean to modify.

EXAMPLES: *Only* one cowboy wanted to go to town today. (No one else wanted to go to town.)
One cowboy *only* wanted to go to town. (He did not want to do anything else.)

(37) seen *Seen* is a past participle and can be used as a verb only with a helping verb.

NONSTANDARD: The judge *seen* a number of criminals.
CORRECT: The judge *has seen* a number of criminals.

⊘ Learn More

To learn how your mastery of English usage is tested on standardized tests, see the Standardized Test Preparation Workshop for this chapter on pages 626–627.

(38) set, sit *Set* means "to put (something) in a certain place." Its principal parts—*set, setting, set,* and *set*—are usually followed by a direct object. *Sit* means "to be seated." Its principal parts—*sit, sitting, sat,* and *sat*—are never followed by a direct object.

SET:	*Set* the tools in the barn.
	He is *setting* the plow in the backyard.
	His wife *set* the food on the table.
	She had *set* the plates out earlier.
SIT:	They brought a rocking chair from the East to *sit* in.
	She is *sitting* in it right now.
	She *sat* in it whenever they stopped.
	Her mother had *sat* in that chair before her.

(39) so *So* is a coordinating conjunction. It should be avoided when you mean "so that."

LESS ACCEPTABLE:	Townsfolk formed vigilante groups *so* they could enforce the law as they saw fit.
PREFERRED:	Townsfolk formed vigilante groups *so that* they could enforce the law as they saw fit.

(40) than, then Use *than* in comparisons. *Then,* an adverb, usually refers to time.

EXAMPLES:	The telegraph was faster *than* the pony express.
	The transcontinental telegraph was installed, and *then* the pony express went out of business.

(41) that, which, who Use these relative pronouns correctly. *That* and *which* refer to things; *who* refers only to people.

EXAMPLES:	The wagon *that* carried the food for a cattle drive was called the chuck wagon.
	The person *who* took care of the extra horses on a cattle drive was called a wrangler.

(42) their, there, they're *Their,* a possessive pronoun, always modifies a noun. *There* can be used either as an expletive at the beginning of a sentence or as an adverb. *They're* is a contraction of *they are.*

PRONOUN:	Farmers spent all *their* time working the land.
EXPLETIVE:	*There* are many obstacles to a good harvest.
ADVERB:	The fields over *there* will be planted tomorrow.
CONTRACTION:	*They're* deciding what crops to plant this year.

(43) them Do not use *them* as a substitute for *those*.

NONSTANDARD: *Them* horses are extremely fast.
CORRECT: *Those* horses are extremely fast.

(44) to, too, two *To*, a preposition, begins a phrase or an infinitive. *Too*, an adverb, modifies adjectives and other adverbs. *Two* is a number.

PREPOSITION: *to* the homestead, *to* the miner
INFINITIVE: *to* dig, *to* plow
ADVERB: *too* dry, *too* quickly
NUMBER: *two* fields, *two* cows

(45) when, where Do not use *when* or *where* directly after a linking verb. Do not use *where* in place of *that*.

NONSTANDARD: A barn raising is *when* farmers could socialize with their neighbors.
A general store is *where* they got supplies.
He heard *where* the square dance was held after harvest time.

CORRECT: A barn raising allowed farmers to socialize with their neighbors.
A farmer could get supplies at a general store.
He heard *that* the square dance was held after harvest time.

▶ **Exercise 12** Revising a Paragraph to Correct Usage
Problems 31–45 Rewrite the following paragraph, correcting the errors in usage. Not every sentence contains an error.

(1) Even though life in the West was difficult, settlers would leave some time to enjoy themselves. (2) Homesteaders often combined they're work and play. (3) They might travel too a neighbor's farm to help with harvesting a crop or husking corn. (4) A barn raising was when farmers could do some work and have some fun. (5) The men at a house or barn raising were divided into teams so the work would go faster and be more fun. (6) The teams would lie down the floor together and then each take responsibility for building a different wall. (7) This was a good way to learn newcomers some of the skills needed to survive in the West. (8) Women might set with their neighbors at a quilting bee. (9) Traveling vaudeville shows would set up outside of several towns each year. (10) One farmer seen the famous performers Buffalo Bill, Annie Oakley, Edwin Booth, and Laura Keene.

▶ **More Practice**

Grammar Exercise
Workbook
• pp. 155–156
On-line Exercise Bank
• Section 26.2
  Go on-line:
  PHSchool.com
  Enter Web Code:
  eek-1002

Get instant feedback!
Exercise 12 is available on-line or on CD-ROM.

Hands-on Grammar

Illustrating Usage Problems on Index Cards

Work on common usage problems by creating illustrations that represent each word's proper usage. In the examples below, *in* and *into* are illustrated with paper airplanes and garbage cans showing that *in* refers to position and *into* suggests motion. *Bring* and *take* are illustrated with drawings and arrows showing that *bring* means "to carry from a distant place to a nearer one," while *take* means "to carry from a near place to a more distant one."

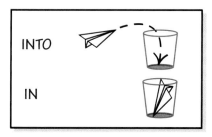

Each of the ten word pairs below represents a common usage problem. Using the common-usage glossary on pages 612–621, illustrate each word. Don't worry about making detailed drawings—just make sure they clearly illustrate the main difference between the proper usage of the two words. Use one index card for each word pair, and use the same side of the index card to illustrate both words.

After you have completed your illustrations, practice the correct usage of each word. Working with a partner, take turns selecting index cards at random, studying the illustrations, and forming sentences that use each word correctly. Refer to the common-usage problems glossary to check your answers.

1. among, between
2. fewer, less
3. lay, lie
4. beside, besides
5. leave, let
6. that, which, who
7. set, sit
8. learn, teach
9. accept, except
10. farther, further

Find It in Your Reading In textbooks or magazines, find examples of the words above used correctly in sentences. Write the example sentences on the backs of the appropriate index cards.

Find It in Your Writing Look through pieces of writing in your writing portfolio for examples of the words above used correctly in sentences. Write the example sentences on the back of the appropriate index cards. If you cannot find examples of any of the words, challenge yourself to write new sentences on the backs of the cards using the words correctly.

Section 26.2 Section Review

GRAMMAR EXERCISES 13–19

Exercise 13 Supplying *a* or *an* Correctly Complete each expression with *a* or *an*.

1. occurrence
2. usual amount
3. heirloom
4. urban outfit
5. hard-packed trail

Exercise 14 Avoiding Usage Problems Choose the correct expression to complete each sentence.

1. Life in the West favored those who could (adapt, adopt) to many jobs.
2. A well-rounded man could (except, accept) any kind of job to survive.
3. If he were paid (bad, badly) at one occupation, he could move on to another.
4. He could move about freely (like, as) the birds did.
5. George Jackson, (who, which) is credited with discovering gold in the Rockies, also worked as a roustabout, farmhand, miner, and businessman.
6. Buffalo Bill Cody is a famous jack-of-all-trades, (too, two).
7. After his father died when Bill was eleven, he worked for (awhile, a while) as a messenger for a freight company.
8. (Being as, Because) war broke out in 1861, Bill joined the Union army.
9. In 1872, Bill embarked on a career very (different from, different than) any of his previous occupations.
10. As a showman, he traveled much (further, farther) than ever before.

Exercise 15 Revising Sentences to Correct Usage Errors Rewrite each sentence, correcting the error in usage.

1. The life of a cowboy was kind of lonely.
2. On long cattle drives, cowboys spent all day setting in the saddle.
3. They had to keep the cattle altogether for the entire ride.
4. On these drives, cowboys laid down under the stars to go to sleep.
5. At home on the range, cowboys just didn't watch over the cattle.
6. They also would of had to do repairs.
7. The installation of fences effected relations with the ranchers' neighbors.
8. Tension between cattle ranchers and farmers was all ready strained.
9. Everyone was anxious to help.
10. Range wars erupted everywheres across the West.

Exercise 16 Writing Sentences Using Troublesome Words Correctly use each word in an original sentence.

1. accept
2. further
3. like
4. which
5. altogether
6. just
7. awhile
8. lay
9. set
10. effect

Exercise 17 Find It in Your Reading In a newspaper, find five examples of words discussed in this section. Explain why each is used correctly.

Exercise 18 Find It in Your Writing In your own writing, find three examples of words discussed in this section. Check to make sure that your usage of the words is correct. If not, revise your work.

Exercise 19 Writing Application Write an essay telling what you would and would not like about life in the Old West. Be sure to avoid all the usage errors described in this section.

Chapter Review

GRAMMAR EXERCISES 20–25

▶ **Exercise 20** Avoiding Double
Negatives Choose the word in parentheses that makes each sentence negative without forming a double negative.

1. Today's ranchers and their families aren't (nowhere, anywhere) near as isolated as their counterparts in the Old West.
2. A hundred years ago, cowboys didn't (never, ever) go to town except on paydays.
3. Because we have automobiles, we don't have to wait for (no, any) special opportunities.
4. In addition, the roads (aren't, are) rarely in as poor condition as they were in the past.
5. Now children can ride buses to school; they don't have to stay home (any, no) more.
6. With advances in technology, no one (doesn't have, has) to rely solely on his or her own resources.
7. Nothing (can, can't) replace horses, but alternatives like jeeps and helicopters are sometimes used as well.
8. Since the 1940's, the price of land has risen, so ranchers can't waste (none, any) of their land.
9. They (could, couldn't) scarcely afford to leave any parcel of land unused.
10. They rotate the grazing fields so that no field (doesn't become, becomes) exhausted of all nourishment.

▶ **Exercise 21** Avoiding Usage
Problems Choose the correct expression to complete each sentence.

1. (Farther, Further) settlement of western lands and the growth of transportation and communication ended the period of time called the Old West.

2. No time in our history is more exciting (than, then) this one.
3. However, some legends that (bad, badly) distorted history sprang up.
4. Pecos Bill, for example, supposedly (learned, taught) broncos how to buck.
5. Many who had lived in the West were (anxious, eager) to capture its essence for posterity.
6. (Besides, Beside) his many other classics, Mark Twain wrote a novel about his experiences as a reporter in the West.
7. Anyone who (seen, has seen) the paintings of Frederic Remington can easily imagine the frontier.
8. The Old West has influenced many artists (who, which) grew up after the heyday.
9. Thomas Hart Benton and Georgia O'Keeffe have used western backgrounds in (their, they're) paintings.
10. Filmmakers and novelists have (adopted, adapted) the tales of the Old West for their own stories.
11. *Oklahoma!*, one of the most popular American musicals, recounts the (affects, effects) of the range wars between ranchers and homesteaders.
12. There (isn't, ain't) any way to single out the most famous writers of westerns, but Louis L'Amour and Larry McMurtry are two of the most popular.
13. Western movies were (kind of, rather) popular from the 1920's through the 1950's.
14. Works in the 1990's portrayed a West (different from, different than) that seen in older works.
15. (Them, Those) later works, like the movies *Unforgiven* and *Dances With Wolves*, often showed the West in a less heroic light.

> **Exercise 22** **Revising Sentences to Correct Usage Problems** Rewrite each sentence, correcting the error in usage.

1. Being as westerns were very popular in the first half of the twentieth century, many actors became famous by playing cowboys.
2. When taken altogether, there were quite a few men who became famous as television and movie cowboys.
3. Clint Eastwood, John Wayne, Gene Autry, and Roy Rogers are between the most famous cowboy stars.
4. Gene Autry was all ready a successful singer of cowboy songs when he made his first movie.
5. He became a popular actor due to his roles as a singing cowboy.
6. Even though he did alright as an actor and singer, he decided to branch out into business, too.
7. He wasn't only successful as an actor; his businesses did well, too.
8. Roy Rogers was another popular movie cowboy who became a successful businessman, to.
9. Rogers's wife, Dale Evans, played an heroine in many of his movies.
10. Them two were quite a pair.

> **Exercise 23** **Revising a Paragraph to Correct Double Negatives and Other Usage Problems** Rewrite the following paragraph, correcting all fifteen usage errors.

(1) Three years after the transcontinental telegraph made the pony express obsolete, post office officials established they're first railway post office. (2) Clerks sorted mail while traveling into special train cars. (3) Towns could erect posts besides a train track and hang their mail in a pouch from the top. (4) Catcher arms attached to the train cars would snatch the mail bags off of the posts. (5) This was quicker then stopping to pick up the mail. (6) Too deliver mail, the clerks would toss mail sacks onto the train platforms of a town. (7) Letters and packages could be sent anywheres in the United States. (8) The airplane was the next advance to effect the postal system. (9) At first, mail who was sent by air was more expensive. (10) The plan to deliver mail via guided missile failed all together on its first attempt. (11) Irregardless, the post office continued to experiment with new ways to improve service. (12) In the 1970's, private mail services were established so people could choose how to send their parcels. (13) The reason private services started is because the rates for the government's postal services had continued to rise. (14) In the latter half of the twentieth century, computer technology adopted to send messages electronically from one computer to another for personal use. (15) E-mail has almost eliminated private correspondence, like the telegraph eradicated the pony express.

> **Exercise 24** **Using Troublesome Words Correctly** Write twenty sentences —two sentences for each of the following pairs of words. Be sure the words are used correctly.

1. badly, bad
2. than, then
3. all together, altogether
4. farther, further
5. affect, effect
6. adopt, adapt
7. lie, lay
8. learn, teach
9. set, sit
10. gone, went

> **Exercise 25** **Writing Application** Imagine that you live in the Old West. Write a letter describing the place and your experiences to someone who has never been there.

Standardized Test Preparation Workshop

Standard English Usage

Standardized tests frequently test your mastery of standard English usage. Some items focus on choosing the correct word to fill in a blank; others may test your ability to avoid or correct double negatives.

The following questions will give you practice with a format that is used to assess your understanding of standard English usage.

Test Tip

When looking for the best word or group of words to complete a sentence, read the whole sentence, trying each answer choice in turn.

Sample Test Item

Answer and Explanation

Directions: Read the passage, and choose the word or group of words that belongs in the space. Mark the letter for your answer.

When I was on the trip, I never went ___(1)___ that didn't interest me.

1 **A** everywhere
  B nowhere
  C anywhere
  D no place

The correct answer is C. The word *anywhere* completes the sentence according to the conventions of standard English usage and makes sense in the space. This choice also avoids a double negative, which would be created by using *nowhere*.

> **Practice 1** **Directions:** Read the passage, and choose the word or group of words that belongs in each space.

Michael was __(1)__ to marry Janine as soon as they could arrange it. He was __(2)__ to settle down, have children, and grow old with her. This desire was no __(3)__ the wishes of his best friend, George. __(4)__ for George, there was no longer __(5)__ to share his dream.

1 **A** anxious
  B desirous
  C most eager
  D eager

2 **F** already
  G all ready
  H unready
  J readier

3 **A** different from
  B different than
  C different
  D different then

4 **F** Accept
  G Expect
  H Except
  J Excepting

5 **A** no one
  B anyone
  C nobody
  D anything

> **Practice 2** **Directions:** Read the passage, and choose the word or group of words that belongs in each space.

When he was a younger man, Michael had __(1)__ higher expectations for himself. It wasn't just __(2)__ who could turn a block of wood into a rocking horse with a set of carving tools. He knew he could succeed as an artist, and Janine knew it __(3)__. __(4)__ that, he vowed to love her forever. Nothing could __(5)__ change his mind about her.

1 **A** kind of
  B sort of
  C somewhat
  D somewhere

2 **F** everyone
  G someone
  H no one
  J anyone

3 **A** two
  B too
  C to
  D besides

4 **F** Because of
  G Because
  H Being
  J Since

5 **A** never
  B not
  C ever
  D evermore

Cumulative Review

USAGE

Exercise A Using Verbs and Pronouns Choose the correct word or group of words that makes each sentence correct. For each verb or verb phrase, label its tense and voice. For each pronoun, identify its case.

1. Sequoyah (was, is) a Native American (who, whom) was also known by (his, its) English name, George Guess.
2. (He, It) developed a system of writing for the Cherokees (who, that) could then (published, publish) books and newspapers.
3. The giant sequoia trees and Sequoia National Park in California (is, are) named after (he, him).
4. Many species (had been, are being) eliminated by the glaciers, and now only three of (it, them) survive.
5. The Petrified Forest in Arizona (consisted, consists) of extinct species.
6. The giant sequoia (has been, had been) growing on the Sierra Nevada mountains, where most of (their, its) groves (is, are) protected in national parks.
7. The branches (are, had been) covered by (their, its) scalelike leaves.
8. By counting (their, its) rings, we know that some trees (had, have) lived for thousands of years.
9. The General Sherman Tree is in Sequoia National Park, and (he, it) (stands, has been standing) approximately 275 feet tall.
10. The coast redwood, similar to (its, his) cousin the giant sequoia, (grew, grows) to great sizes.
11. Unlike most conifer trees, (it, they) produces sprouts after it (has been, will be) cut down.
12. The dawn redwood is a deciduous tree, a characteristic that distinguishes it from (its, their) relatives (who, that) are evergreen trees.
13. Fossil specimens of the dawn redwood (are, were) identified in 1941, and some in (its, their) family were found afterward in China.
14. Ancient redwood trees (are, were) protected in Redwood National Park, and (they, it) include the world's tallest tree.
15. (It, They) (was standing, stands) close to 370 feet tall.

Exercise B Making Words Agree Choose the correct word or group of words that makes each sentence correct.

1. Death Valley (contains, contain) the (lower, lowest) point in the Western Hemisphere.
2. (Much, More) of the valley (lies, lie) below sea level.
3. This area is also one of the (hot, hottest) regions in the world.
4. Yearly rainfall (measure, measures) (less, least) than 2 inches.
5. Sand and dust storms that last for (many, more) hours (is, are) common.
6. The valley (is, are) (almost, most) entirely enclosed by mountains.
7. The Panamint Range to the west (rises, rise) to a (maximum, most maximum) altitude at Telescope Peak.
8. On the (most eastern, eastern) side (is, are) the Amargosa Range.
9. Sand and salt (forms, form) the (high, higher) portions of the valley.
10. The (low, lowest) parts of the valley floor (is, are) salt flats.
11. The valley and surrounding mountains (is, are) included in Death Valley National Park.
12. It is the (larger, largest) contiguous park of all national parks in the United States.

13. There (is, are) (most, more) than 900 plant species there.
14. Desert shrubs and grasses (grows, grow) (sparsely, more sparsely) on the slopes around the valley floor.
15. A (few, less) species of desert reptiles (live, lives) in Death Valley.

Exercise C Revising a Paragraph to Eliminate Errors in Agreement Rewrite the following paragraph, correcting any errors in agreement.

The Appalachian Mountains runs along the eastern part of North America. It have different names in different places. For example, the Green Mountains, Alleghenies, Blue Ridge, and Great Smokies is all part of the Appalachian Mountains. The Appalachians are lowest and least rugged than the Rocky Mountains. The most high Appalachian peak is Mt. Mitchell in North Carolina, which is 6,684 feet. Still, early settlers had a hardest time crossing this heavily forested mountains.

Exercise D Revising Sentences to Correct Miscellaneous Problems in Usage Rewrite the following sentences, correcting negative sentences and other common usage problems.

1. The Sierra Nevada mountain range is in California accept for a small part in Nevada.
2. Being that Mount Whitney is the highest point in the continental United States, it is the highest point in the Sierra Nevadas.
3. Mount Whitney isn't hardly the only notable mountain of the High Sierra.
4. Williamson peak rises further than North Palisade, Russell, and Tyndall peaks.
5. These peaks lay along the western part of the southeastern portion of the range.

6. There isn't but one block of the Earth's crust in the Sierra Nevada.
7. Kings Canyon National Park has a higher canyon wall then any others in the United States.
8. Devils Postpile National Monument isn't nothing more than one notable rock formation.
9. Muir Woods National Monument ain't located in the Sierra Nevada mountains.
10. Yosemite National Park contains a most unique region of the range.

Exercise E Revising a Paragraph to Correct Usage Errors Rewrite the following paragraph, correcting the usage errors.

Juan Cabrillo was a Portuguese explorer whom served Spain. He travel to Mexico with Hernán Cortés. Once they're, he than sailed northward in the Pacific Ocean. In 1542, he will discover San Diego Bay. After leaving them, he discovered islands including the Channel Islands. Much years later, Alcatraz Island was discovered by Juan Manuel de Ayala. Santa Catalina, San Clemente, and San Nicolas ain't inside the national park. The park contains San Miguel, Santa Rosa, Santa Cruz, Anacapa, and Santa Barbara, to. There aren't but animals and birds living on the islands. Them include brown pelicans, seals, and sea lions.

Exercise F Writing Application
Write a description of the geographic features that make up the region in which you live. Make your writing interesting by varying your sentence lengths and structures. Try to avoid sentence errors and common usage problems. Be sure that the words in your sentences follow rules of agreement and that your modifiers are used correctly.

Although you wouldn't remember it, you probably started using capital letters when you learned the alphabet. Without your realizing it, capital letters most likely continue to catch your attention when you look at advertisements, headlines, and road signs, among other things. Capital letters also serve an important role in writing. Through capitalization, writers indicate important words or signal a new thought.

Many rules govern the use of capitalization. This chapter will introduce you to the most widely accepted rules, showing you when and where to capitalize letters in your writing.

▲ Critical Viewing
In what ways would you use capitalization if you were writing a description of this mountain?
[Describe]

Diagnostic Test

Directions: Write all answers on a separate sheet of paper.

Skill Check A. Copy each of the underlined words below, and tell whether it is a *proper noun* or a *proper adjective.*

1. the <u>Swiss</u> countryside
2. the <u>Rocky Mountains</u>
3. <u>Yellowstone National Park</u>
4. the <u>Australian</u> continent
5. explorer <u>David Livingstone</u>

Skill Check B. Write the words that should be capitalized in each of the following sentences.

6. the himalayas of asia are the highest mountain range in the world.
7. they are located between the indus river and the brahmaputra river.
8. these majestic mountains were formed millions of years ago when the indian subcontinent collided with the eurasian landmass.
9. the majority of the greatest peaks can be found in the countries of tibet, nepal, and india.
10. the tallest himalayan peak is mt. everest, which is situated approximately 80 miles from nepal's capital of kathmandu.
11. it was named for sir george everest, a british surveyor who was the first to establish its location and height.
12. the enormous mountain was successfully scaled in 1953 by members of an expedition led by col. john hunt of great britain.
13. on may 29, 1953, edmund hillary of new zealand and a nepalese guide, tenzing norgay, were the first men to stand on the summit.
14. since that time, everest has been climbed by several international teams, including the italians, the japanese, and, in 1963, an american expedition.
15. for more information on this region of the world, read the books *geography of the himalayas* and *in exile from the land of snows.*

Skill Check C. Proofread the following paragraph, and correct all errors in capitalization.

Few people can claim to have stood on top of the world—And only one man can claim to have been there first. That person is sir Edmund Hillary. although he shares the glory of his achievement with his climbing partner, tenzing norgay, hillary was the first person to reach the Summit of mount Everest in nepal, 29,028 feet above Sea Level—the highest spot on earth. Hillary has said of himself, "i've moved from being a child who dreamed a lot and read a lot of books about adventure, to actually getting involved in things like mountaineering. . . ." These are humble words for a man who has climbed the swiss alps and conquered eleven different peaks of more than 20,000 Feet in the himalayas of tibet and nepal.

Using Capitals for First Words

Capital letters work as a visual clue to the reader by making certain words stand out more prominently on a page.

Theme: Geography

In this chapter, you will learn about capitalization. The exercises and examples are about geography.

Cross-Curricular Connection: Geography

Sentences

Always signal the start of a new idea by capitalizing the first word in a sentence.

▶ **KEY CONCEPT** Capitalize the first word in declarative, interrogative, imperative, and exclamatory sentences. ■

Note that each of the following sentences is complete. Each contains both a subject and a verb and makes sense by itself.

DECLARATIVE: Alberto visited the Grand Canyon last summer.
INTERROGATIVE: Did you mail the monthly bills?
IMPERATIVE: Get a stamp out of the drawer.
EXCLAMATORY: This letter says I've won a trip to Niagara Falls!

▶ **KEY CONCEPT** Capitalize the first word in interjections and incomplete questions. ■

EXAMPLES: Fantastic! Ouch! Darn!

EXAMPLES: When? For Maria? How much?

▶ **KEY CONCEPT** Capitalize the first word of a complete sentence following a colon. If a list follows a colon, it is not a complete sentence and, therefore, no capital letter is used. ■

SENTENCE
FOLLOWING COLON: We saw what was in the valley: It was a beautiful waterfall.
LIST FOLLOWING COLON: The mail carrier delivered our mail: two letters, a package, and a card.

Quotations

▶ **KEY CONCEPT** Capitalize the first word in a quotation if the quotation is a complete sentence. ■

EXAMPLE: "Mountains are earth's undecaying monuments."
                                    —Nathaniel Hawthorne

Even when the quotation appears with a "he said/she said" expression, a capital letter is still used to begin the quotation.

EXAMPLE: "It's awfully hot in the canyon," the man said.

If a "he said/she said" expression occurs in the middle of quoted material that is one continuous sentence, only the first word of the quotation gets a capital letter.

EXAMPLE: "If you visit her," Liz said, "please tell me."

If a "he said/she said" expression sits between two complete sentences, both sentences receive capital letters.

EXAMPLE: "Our family vacations are great
            fun!" Arleen exclaimed. "We are
            going camping this year."

When a portion of a quotation that is not a complete sentence is contained within a longer sentence, do not capitalize the first word of the quoted part of the sentence.

EXAMPLE: Mark Twain, who saw pony express riders in
            action, said that a rider was "usually a little
            bit of a man."

If the quoted fragment shifts to the beginning of the sentence, the first word should then be capitalized.

EXAMPLE: "Usually a little bit of a man" is the way Mark
            Twain described a Pony Express rider.

▲ Critical Viewing
What are three different capitalization rules that you might use in writing about this waterfall? **[Connect]**

Poetry

▶ **KEY CONCEPT** Capitalize the first word in each line of most poetry even if the line does not begin a new sentence. ■

EXAMPLE: Falling upon earth,
            Pure water spills
            From the cup   —Bashō

I and O

These words always require capitalization.

▶ **KEY CONCEPT** Capitalize *I* and *O* throughout a sentence. ■

EXAMPLES: "Eureka! I have found it. "—Archimedes
            "O Romeo, Romeo! Wherefore art thou Romeo?"
                                            —Shakespeare

Exercise 1 Using Capitals for First Words Copy the following items, adding the missing capitals. Some items may require more than one capital letter.

1. central Australia is home to Ayers Rock.
2. my teacher said, "surprisingly, Ayers Rock is the largest single rock formation in the world."
3. wow! the red sandstone monolith rises 1,143 feet above the surrounding terrain.
4. seventy million years ago, the rock appeared much different from the way it does today: it was a small island surrounded by an inland sea.
5. did you know that Ayers Rock is called Uluru by the aboriginal people of Australia?

Exercise 2 Writing a Postcard Using Capital Letters for First Words Imagine that you are on a trip to Australia or another distant tourist destination. Write a postcard to a friend, describing some of your experiences. Use each of the rules for capitalizing first words at least once in your postcard.

More Practice

Grammar Exercise Workbook
• pp. 157–158
On-line Exercise Bank
• Chapter 27
Go on-line:
PHSchool.com
Enter Web Code:
eek-1002

▼ Critical Viewing If you were to write a few sentences describing the Australian landscape shown here, what would you write? What capitalization rules would you use? **[Describe]**

Using Capitals for Proper Nouns

A **proper noun** is a noun that names a specific person, place, or thing.

▶ **KEY CONCEPT** Capitalize all proper nouns, including each part of a person's name. ■

The given or first name, the initials standing for a name, and the surname or last name all receive capital letters.

EXAMPLES: Chester Worth, Maria A. Lopez

If a surname begins with *Mc, O',* or *St.,* the letter following it is capitalized.

EXAMPLES: McGregor, O'Mara, St. John

The capitalization of names beginning with *de, D', la, le, Mac, van,* or *von* will vary.

EXAMPLES: De Mello, de Mello

▶ **KEY CONCEPT** Capitalize the proper names of animals. ■

EXAMPLES: Rin-Tin-Tin, Sylvester, Fido

▶ **KEY CONCEPT** Capitalize geographical names. ■

Capitalize the names of streets, towns, cities, counties, states, provinces, countries, continents, valleys, mountains, rivers, and oceans. If a place can be found on a map, you should normally capitalize it.

EXAMPLES: Strokes Avenue, Galapagos Islands, Red Sea

The sun and the moon are not capitalized.
When a compass point is used simply to show direction, it is not capitalized. A specific location is capitalized.

EXAMPLES: We headed northwest.
             My cousin lives in the Southwest.

▶ **Exercise 3** **Capitalizing Names** Write the names below on a separate sheet of paper, inserting capital letters where appropriate.

1. sydney, australia
2. hawaiian islands
3. the pacific northwest
4. mr. ed
5. lassie

▶ **KEY CONCEPT** Capitalize the names of monuments, buildings, and meeting rooms. ■

The following chart shows examples of monuments, buildings, and meeting rooms:

SPECIFIC PLACES	
Monuments and Memorials	Washington Monument, Lincoln Memorial
Buildings	Smithsonian Institution, Superdome, the Actors' Conservatory Theater
School and Meeting Rooms	Room 20B, Laboratory C, Oval Office

Do not capitalize the words *theater, hotel,* and *university* unless they are part of a proper name.

EXAMPLES: The theater is one of the oldest buildings in town.
The Fallon House Theater is in an old ghost town.

The word *room* is capitalized only if it refers to a specific room and is combined with a name, letter, or number.

EXAMPLE: The geology exam will be given in Room 46.

▶ **KEY CONCEPT** Capitalize the names of specific events and periods of time. ■

SPECIAL EVENTS AND TIMES	
Historic Events	Stone Age
Historic Periods	War of 1812
Documents	Gettysburg Address, Homestead Act
Days and Months	Monday, April
Holidays and Religious Days	Labor Day, Good Friday
Special Events	Kentucky Derby

▶ **KEY CONCEPT** Do not capitalize the seasons. ■

EXAMPLE: We felt a winter chill in the air as we reached the mountaintop.

> **KEY CONCEPT** Capitalize the names of various organizations, government bodies, political parties, nationalities, and languages. ■

SPECIFIC GROUPS AND LANGUAGES	
Clubs	Rotary Club, Lynbrook Speech Club, Lions Club
Organizations	League of Women Voters, American Cancer Society, United Farm Workers
Institutions	University of Miami, Marymount General Hospital
Businesses	Fresh Food Corporation, Unlimited Knowledge, Inc.
Government Bodies	Senate of the United States, Houses of Parliament, Department of Defense
Political Parties	Republicans, Whigs
Nationalities	American, French, Russian, Mexican
Languages	English, Spanish, French, Yiddish

> **KEY CONCEPT** Capitalize references to religions, deities, and religious scriptures. ■

Each religion has a set of words referring to the important and sacred beliefs it holds. The major religious groups to which you are likely to refer in your writing include Christianity, Judaism, Buddhism, Islam, Confucianism, and Hinduism.

CHRISTIANITY: God, Lord, Father, Son, Holy Spirit, Bible, books of the Bible (Exodus, Kings, Romans)

JUDAISM: God, Lord, Prophets (Moses, Abraham), Torah, Talmud

EASTERN RELIGIONS: Buddhism (Buddha, Tripitaka); Islam (Allah, Koran); Hinduism (Brahma, Vedas)

This list is not complete. Other religious references that you encounter must also be capitalized. These include any pronoun references made to the deity in Christian or Jewish writings.

When writing about mythological gods and goddesses, capitalize the proper names of gods and goddesses, but do not capitalize the words *god* and *goddess.*

EXAMPLES: the god Pluto, the goddess Athena

> **KEY CONCEPT** Capitalize the names of awards. ■

Notice in the following examples that the word *the* is not capitalized.

EXAMPLES: the Kevin E. Morris Scholarship; the Nobel Peace Prize; the Academy Awards; the Oscar; Eagle Scout

> **KEY CONCEPT** Capitalize the names of specific types of air, sea, space, and land craft. ■

When capitalizing the names of air, sea, space, and land craft, do not capitalize the word *the* preceding a name unless the word is part of the official name.

AIR:	Boeing 747		SPACE:	*Sputnik I*
SEA:	*Lusitania*		LAND:	the Model T

More Practice

Grammar Exercise Workbook
• pp. 159–160
On-line Exercise Bank
• Chapter 27
  Go on-line:
  PHSchool.com
  Enter Web Code:
  eek-1002

Text

Get instant feedback! Exercises 4, 5, and 6 are available on-line or on CD-ROM.

> **Exercise 4** Using Capitals in Sentences With Proper Nouns
Copy the following sentences, adding the missing capitals.
1. The sahara stretches 3,200 miles across the northern portion of africa.
2. The desert begins at the atlantic ocean and extends to the red sea.
3. The northern edge of the desert terminates in the atlas mountains, a dramatic scene that has been photographed from satellites such as landsat.
4. During the ice age, north africa was a land of shallow lakes and rich vegetation.
5. By the time of the roman empire, the region had completely turned to desert.

> **Exercise 5** Proofreading to Correct Errors in the Capitalization of Proper Nouns Rewrite this paragraph, adding or eliminating capital letters where appropriate.
(1) The Sahara is the largest desert in the World. (2) The Desert covers large sections of several countries, including morocco, algeria, tunisia, libya, and egypt. (3) Although the desert is generally flat, the snow-capped mount Tahat rises above the swirling sands of the central sahara. (4) A small group of Nomadic muslims, people called bedouins, travel throughout the desert. (5) The majority of the Desert Population, however, is confined to cities, such as luxor, ghat, and reggane.

▲ Critical Viewing What proper nouns might apply to this picture? **[Speculate]**

Using Capitals for Proper Adjectives

A proper noun used as an adjective or an adjective formed from a proper noun is called a *proper adjective*.

KEY CONCEPT Capitalize most proper adjectives. ∎

EXAMPLES: Swiss government, American people, Gothic style

Proper adjectives used in popular expressions are exceptions.

EXAMPLES: french fries, venetian blinds

Adjectives referring to culture or climate that derive from capitalized terms for regions are also generally lowercase.

EXAMPLES: artic wind (but *the Artic*), western pioneers (but *the West*)

KEY CONCEPT Capitalize brand names used as adjectives. ∎

EXAMPLES: Timetrue watches, Hercules luggage

KEY CONCEPT Do not capitalize prefixes attached to proper adjectives unless the prefix refers to a nationality. ∎

EXAMPLES: pre-Mayan architecture, Indo-European

KEY CONCEPT In a hyphenated adjective, capitalize only the proper adjective. ∎

EXAMPLE: Spanish-speaking Americans

Exercise 6 Using Capital Letters for Proper Adjectives Copy the sentences and add any missing capitals.
1. The european continent is dominated by the massive peaks of the Alps.
2. They were formed millions of years ago as a result of a collision between the eurasian and african landmasses, which forced the rock to rise.
3. Today, the Alps exist within the borders of France, Switzerland, Italy, and Austria.
4. french-speaking, german-speaking, and italian-speaking peoples inhabit the area.
5. The tallest of the Alps are taller than the tallest of the Rocky Mountains of the american West.

▼ Critical Viewing
What is a proper adjective you might use in describing this ship? [Describe]

Using Capitals for Titles

Capital letters are used to indicate titles of people and works of art and literature.

Titles of People Titles used before names and in direct address require capitalization.

▶ **KEY CONCEPT** Capitalize a person's title when it is used with the person's name or when it is used in direct address in place of a person's name. ■

TITLE:	Professor Scott gave an interesting lecture.
IN PLACE OF A NAME:	Your lecture, Professor, was very interesting.
GENERAL REFERENCE:	My history professor is late.

The titles of government officials may require capitalization in certain cases.

▶ **KEY CONCEPT** Capitalize titles of government officials when they are followed by a proper name or when used in direct address. ■

In the United States, titles such as supervisor, mayor, governor, congressman, congresswoman, senator, judge, and ambassador are used for different government officials. Officials of other countries also have titles. All of these are capitalized when they are used before a proper name or in direct address. General references, however, usually omit the capital.

PRECEDING A PROPER NAME:	Mayor Martin Hanley will speak.
IN DIRECT ADDRESS:	Will you speak tonight, Mayor?
IN A GENERAL REFERENCE:	The mayor works on the budget.

▶ **Critical Viewing** This illustration depicts a former justice of the Supreme Court, Thurgood Marshall. How would you use capitals when writing his name and title? **[Connect]**

▶ **KEY CONCEPT** Capitalize titles of certain high government officials if they refer to the incumbent even when the titles are not followed by a proper name or used in direct address. ■

EXAMPLES: The President returned from his trip early.
He will meet with the Queen of England today.
The Supreme Court of the United States has eight justices and a Chief Justice.

▶ **KEY CONCEPT** Capitalize important words in compound titles, but not prefixes and suffixes added to the title. ■

EXAMPLES: Lieutenant Governor, ex-Senator Jorgenson

▶ **KEY CONCEPT** Capitalize titles showing family relationships when they refer to a specific person unless they are preceded by a possessive noun or pronoun. ■

EXAMPLES: Did Uncle John find this stone in the cave?
Anne's uncle climbed Mount Everest.

▶ **KEY CONCEPT** Capitalize abbreviations of titles before and after names. ■

The most common abbreviations found before and after names include *Mr., Mrs., Ms., Jr.,* and *Sr.*

EXAMPLES: Mr. Kevin Peterson, Jr.,   Mrs. Ann Sikorski

▶ **Exercise 7** Using Capitals for Titles of People Copy the sentences below that need capitals, adding the missing capitals. If a sentence does not need additional capitalization, write *correct*.

1. While exploring northeastern Wyoming in 1875, a team of surveyors led by colonel Richard Dodge discovered an unusual rock formation, which they named Devil's Tower.
2. Several years after its discovery, senator Francis Warren campaigned to protect it.
3. In 1906, president Theodore Roosevelt, jr., designated Devil's Tower as the first national monument.
4. A popular destination for rock climbers, Devil's Tower was first scaled in 1893 by mr. William Rogers and mr. Willard Ripley.
5. In the 1990's, secretary of the interior Bruce Babbitt banned rock climbing at the site during June.

▶ **More Practice**

Grammar Exercise Workbook
• pp. 161–162
On-line Exercise Bank
• Chapter 27
Go on-line:
PHSchool.com
Enter Web Code:
eek-1002

Get instant feedback! Exercise 7 is available on-line or on CD-ROM.

KEY CONCEPT Capitalize the first word and all other key words in the titles of books, periodicals, poems, stories, plays, paintings, and other works of art. ∎

BOOK: *Heart of Darkness*
PERIODICAL: *Better Homes and Gardens*
POEM: "Flower in the Crannied Wall"
STORY: "A Visit to Grandmother"
PLAY: *How to Succeed in Business Without Really Trying*
PAINTING: *The Artist's Daughter With a Cat*
SONG: "This Land Is Your Land"

As you look at the preceding examples, there are a number of things to notice. First, articles—the words *a, an,* and *the*—are capitalized only when they are the first word of the title. Second, conjunctions and prepositions shorter than four letters are capitalized only when they are the first word in the title. Third, adjectives, nouns, pronouns, verbs, and adverbs are all considered key words and are always capitalized. When capitalizing a subtitle, the same rule is used.

EXAMPLE: *Language: A Reflection of People and Culture*

KEY CONCEPT Capitalize titles of courses when the courses are language courses or when the courses are followed by a number. ∎

WITH CAPITALS: Latin II, English, California History 1A
WITHOUT CAPITALS: mathematics, history, home economics

Exercise 8 **Capitalizing Titles of Things** Write the following titles, adding the missing capitals. Underline the titles that are printed in italics.

EXAMPLE: Play: *fiddler on the roof*
ANSWER: Fiddler on the Roof

1. class: psychology 101
2. newspaper: *the new york times*
3. painting: *starry night*
4. statue: *the thinker*
5. story: "the lottery"

More Practice

Grammar Exercise
Workbook
• pp. 161–162
On-line Exercise Bank
• Chapter 27
  Go on-line:
  PHSchool.com
  Enter Web Code:
  eek-1002

Get instant feedback!
Exercise 8 is available
on-line or on CD-ROM.

Hands-on Grammar

Capitalization Card

Create a capitalization reference card that you can keep in your notebook, and refer to it any time you are unsure of a capitalization rule. Start by reviewing the chapter and noting all of the different types of items that are capitalized. Then, draw lines on a piece of paper to divide it into squares. Draw as many squares as you need to cover each of the types of items that are capitalized. Use both sides of the card. Categories might include countries, cities, and corporations.

List the categories in alphabetical order in the boxes you've created. Add examples beneath each of the categories. Once you've finished, keep the card you have created in your notebook.

BOOK TITLES	BUILDING NAMES	BUSINESSES
All Creatures Great and Small	Space Needle	Prentice Hall
CITIES	**CLUBS**	**COUNTRIES**
Miami, Florida	Rotary Club	England

Find It in Your Reading Look through your history book to find examples of words that fit into the various categories. Then, as you continue reading in various subjects, add other examples you come across.

Find It in Your Writing Consult your capitalization card whenever you are working on a piece of writing and are unsure about a capitalization rule.

Chapter Review

GRAMMAR EXERCISES 9–16

Exercise 9 Using Capitalization **With First Words** Copy the following items, adding the missing capitals. Some items may require more than one capital.

1. the Japanese island of Honshu is dominated by Mount Fuji, the tallest mountain in the country.
2. were you aware that the mountain, which many people consider sacred, is actually an extinct volcano?
3. the article made this observation: mount Fuji has been dormant for hundreds of years; the last eruption occurred in 1707.
4. "the cone-shaped mountain rises 12,387 feet above sea level," the geologist explained. "because it is so cold at this altitude, Mount Fuji's peak is usually covered with snow."
5. its head reaches above the clouds, it surveys the mountains all around; it hears the thunder far below— fuji, o highest of mountains!
   —traditional Japanese song

Exercise 10 Using Capitals for **Proper Nouns** Copy the following items, adding the missing capitals.

1. The largest waterfall in the world is victoria falls.
2. It is located in africa, along the border of zambia and zimbabwe.
3. Between january and april, nearly 75 million gallons of water flow into batoka gorge every minute.
4. This waterfall was discovered in november 1855 by david livingstone, a minister of the presbyterian church.
5. Livingstone, who had been sent to the region by the london missionary society, stumbled upon the falls while following the zambezi river.

Exercise 11 Proofreading: **Correcting Errors in Capitalization of First Words and Proper Nouns** Revise the following paragraph, adding and removing capitals as needed.

(1) David Livingstone named the enormous waterfall He discovered after queen Victoria, the reigning monarch of england. (2) the founder of the british south africa company, cecil Rhodes, arranged for the construction of a bridge that spans the Gorge directly in front of the falls. (3) rhodes, who also founded the de beers mining company, is perhaps best known for instituting the rhodes scholarship at Oxford university. (4) Today, Tourists wishing to visit the falls can stay at the masuwe lodge or the Masaka Sun hotel, both of which have western foods, such as bubbles cola and smith cookies. (5) other points of interest in the area include Victoria Falls national park and Livingstone game park.

Exercise 12 Using Capitalization **With Proper Adjectives** Copy the sentences below that need capitals, adding the missing capitals. If a sentence does not need additional capitalization, write *correct*.

1. Iceland is a large island that lies 500 miles off the northwest coast of Scotland, just south of arctic waters.
2. The island's remarkably diverse environment, a combination of volcanoes, glaciers, and hot springs, is so unusual that the apollo astronauts trained there for their lunar landings.
3. Although Iceland was discovered by irish explorers in the eighth century, norse adventurers were the first to

inhabit the island.

4. Over time, the island was settled by various scandinavian and celtic groups.
5. Because of these affiliations, most icelandic people are very pro-norwegian.

> **Exercise 13** **Using Capitalization With Titles of People** Copy the sentences below that need capitals, adding the missing capitals. If a sentence does not need additional capitalization, write *correct.*

1. In 1923, superintendent Doane Robinson, head of the South Dakota Historical Society, began planning the massive stone monument known as Mount Rushmore.
2. Initially, Robinson envisioned that the carving would contain the images of notable western figures, such as general George Custer and chief Sitting Bull.
3. The artist who was hired to create the carving, Gutzon Borglum, persuaded Robinson to feature four famous presidents instead.
4. By 1925, senator Peter Norbeck and congressman William Williamson had secured permission for Borglum to begin working in Haney National Forest.
5. On June 15, 1927, president and mrs. Calvin Coolidge participated in the formal dedication of the site; however, it would take Borglum more than Fourteen years to complete the monument.

> **Exercise 14** **Capitalizing Titles** Copy the following titles, and add capitals where necessary. Underline titles that are printed in italics.

1. book: *into thin air*
2. play: *the glass menagerie*
3. magazine: *national geographic*
4. song: "sound of silence"
5. poem: "if—"

> **Exercise 15** **Proofreading: Applying All the Rules of Capitalization** Copy the following paragraph, correcting each error in capitalization.

One of the greatest natural wonders of north America is Niagara falls. It is situated on the Niagara river, about halfway between lake Erie and lake Ontario. The river actually forms part of the United States-canadian border. Niagara falls consists of two waterfalls, the Horseshoe Falls and the American Falls. The Horseshoe is on the Canadian Side of the border in the province of ontario. The American falls is on the united states side in the state of New York. Niagara falls was formed about 12,000 years ago, after the last great ice sheet melted from the region. Indian Tribes lived in the Niagara falls area long before the first europeans arrived. The name *Niagara* comes from the Iroquois Indian word *Onguiaahra,* meaning "the strait." The first written account of the falls was published in 1683. Louis Hennepin, a roman catholic missionary who traveled with the French Explorer René-Robert Cavelier, wrote, "these waters foam and boil in a fearful manner. they thunder continually."

> **Exercise 16** **Writing Application** Use the following directions to write five sentences of your own, using capitals wherever necessary.

1. Write a sentence in which you name the title of a book and its author.
2. Write a sentence that includes the names of two different states and their capitals.
3. Write a sentence about a famous battle and the two sides that participated in it.
4. Write a sentence about the day of the week and the month.
5. Write a sentence that names two of your favorite songs.

Standardized Test Preparation Workshop

Proofreading

Standardized tests often measure your understanding of the rules of capitalization. One way in which tests do this is by giving you a passage to proofread and identify the types of errors, including capitalization, spelling, and punctuation. The following sample items will help you practice proofreading for errors.

Test Tip

Look not only for words that are not capitalized and should be, but also for words that are capitalized and should not be.

Sample Test Items

	Answers and Explanations
Directions: Read the passage and decide which type of error, if any, appears in each underlined section. On the day after the incident, the organization released the following comments: "<u>it is</u> (1) <u>our firm belief that we took all of the necessary measures to ensure our passengers'</u> <u>safety.</u> <u>Valueright airlines is relieved that no</u> (2) <u>one was injured."</u>	
1 A Spelling error B Capitalization error C Punctuation error D No error	The correct answer for item 1 is *B*. The word *It* should be capitalized, since it begins a complete sentence following a colon.
2 F Spelling error G Capitalization error H Punctuation error J No error	The correct answer for item 2 is *G*. The word *airlines* should be capitalized, since it is part of the company's name.

▶ Practice 1 **Directions:** Read the following passage and decide which type of error, if any, appears in each underlined section.

The Rocky mountains received two feet of
(1)
snow Monday. The national weather service
                        (2)
has warned that additional snow could be

coming later in the week. Given the
                              (3)
tremendous amount of snow that has fallen

this winter; avalanches are expected in

certain Areas. Skiiers have been warned
(4)   (5)
not to venture into restricted areas under

any circumstances.

1 A Spelling error
  B Capitalization error
  C Punctuation error
  D No error

2 F Spelling error
  G Capitalization error
  H Punctuation error
  J No error

3 A Spelling error
  B Capitalization error
  C Punctuation error
  D No error

4 F Spelling error
  G Capitalization error
  H Punctuation error
  J No error

5 A Spelling error
  B Capitalization error
  C Punctuation error
  D No error

▶ Practice 2 **Directions:** Read the following passage and decide which type of error, if any, appears in the under-lined section.

Shakespeare's great tragedies include *the*
(1)
Tragedy of Macbeth, the Tragedy of Romeo

and Juliet, and *king Lear.* Many scholars
(2)
consider "Hamlet" to be his finest work,
(3)
however. In this great tragedy, the Title
                (4)
Character struggles with questions about

the meaning of life as he looks to avenge
                        (5)
his Father's death.

1 A Spelling error
  B Capitalization error
  C Punctuation error
  D No error

2 F Spelling error
  G Capitalization error
  H Punctuation error
  J No error

3 A Spelling error
  B Capitalization error
  C Punctuation error
  D No error

4 F Spelling error
  G Capitalization error
  H Punctuation error
  J No error

5 A Spelling error
  B Capitalization error
  C Punctuation error
  D No error

When Beethoven wrote the "Moonlight Sonata" more than 150 years ago, he included in his music not only the notes he wanted played but also *how* he wanted them played. Through the use of accepted music notation, he left precise instructions on the tempo, the mood he wanted to convey, the loudness and softness, and the rests. By following Beethoven's instructions, today's musicians are able to play that piece almost exactly as Beethoven played it himself.

Just as a composer must do more than set down notes on paper, a writer must do more than set down words on paper. Just as a composer must tell musicians how to play the music, so a writer must tell readers how the words are to be read. To give the reader this information, a writer uses a set of standard marks called *punctuation*.

▲ **Critical Viewing**
How is the musical notation in this piece like punctuation in a sentence? [**Compare**]

Diagnostic Test

Directions: Write all answers on a separate sheet of paper.

Skill Check A. Write the following sentences, using proper end marks to punctuate them.

1. Did Beethoven write the "Moonlight Sonata" in 1801
2. Oh Wasn't it called the Piano Sonata No 14
3. It is only sixteen minutes long
4. What a great figure-skating performance was choreographed to that sonata
5. Play the "Moonlight Sonata" on the piano

Skill Check B. Write the following sentences, inserting commas where necessary.

6. When I was in third grade I first heard the song "Moondance."
7. My mother thinks "Blue Moon" "Moon River" and "It's Only a Paper Moon" are better songs.
8. "Obviously when we bought the album" said Larry "we knew there would be many famous songs."
9. I hope the album will arrive in Albany New York before June 21 2001.
10. I wanted to share my favorite song "Shine On Harvest Moon" with them.

Skill Check C. Write the following sentences, inserting colons and semicolons where necessary.

11. Van Gogh painted my two favorite pieces *Starry Night* and *Sunflowers.*
12. *The Night Sky* is not very realistic nevertheless it is beautiful.
13. *The Sleeping Gypsy* is dominated by a few subjects the lion, the gypsy, and the moon.
14. Michelle's birthstone is a diamond Debra's is an opal.
15. Warning If taken internally, consult a physician immediately.

Skill Check D. Write the following sentences, inserting quotation marks where necessary.

16. Have you ever been to the Prado? he asked.
17. It is filled with wonderful Spanish art, he continued.
18. Goya, Velázquez, and El Greco he said are all there.
19. Perhaps you should take me there, I suggested.
20. Have you read The Road Not Taken by Robert Frost?

Skill Check E. Write the following sentences, inserting apostrophes, hyphens, and dashes where necessary.

21. My favorite book growing up I still like to read it every now and then! was *Goodnight Moon.*
22. I scored twenty five points in my last basketball game.
23. Have you ever spent much time with a two year old?
24. It is my oldest sisters favorite movie.
25. Really, I havent seen it yet.

End Marks

Just as every sentence must begin with a capital letter, so it must end with an end mark. The three end marks are the *period* [.], the *question mark* [?], and the *exclamation mark* [!]. These marks clearly indicate to a reader that he or she has arrived at the end of a thought. End marks also indicate the emotion or tone of a sentence. In this section, you will have the opportunity to review the more common uses of end marks and to study some of their other functions.

Basic Uses of End Marks

The period has three basic uses:

> **KEY CONCEPT** Use a period to end a declarative sentence, a mild imperative, and an indirect question. ■

A *declarative sentence* is a statement of fact or opinion.

STATEMENT OF FACT: The moon is a satellite of the Earth.
STATEMENT OF OPINION: The moon looks pretty tonight.

An *imperative* gives a direction or command. An imperative often begins with a verb.

MILD IMPERATIVE: Look through the telescope.

Some declarative sentences include an *indirect question.*

DIRECT QUESTION: Is the moon smaller than the Earth?
INDIRECT QUESTION: I asked whether the moon was smaller than the Earth.

Theme: Space Travel
In this section, you will learn about periods, question marks, and exclamation marks. The examples and exercises are about space travel.

Cross-Curricular Connection: Science

◀ **Critical Viewing** This is a view of the Earth from the moon. Imagine that you are standing on the moon, and write two exclamatory sentences about the view. **[Speculate]**

KEY CONCEPT Use a question mark to end a direct question, an incomplete question, or a statement intended as a question. ■

A *direct question* demands an answer; it stands as a direct request. All direct questions must end with a question mark.

DIRECT QUESTIONS:	Did you see the full moon? How far away is the moon?

In some cases, only a portion of the question is written out and the rest is simply understood. When this occurs, place a question mark at the end of the incomplete question.

INCOMPLETE QUESTIONS:	Where? What color? How much?

Sometimes, a question is phrased as if it were a declarative sentence. Use a question mark to show that the sentence is a question.

STATEMENTS INTENDED AS QUESTIONS:	You saw that? The Earth has one satellite?

Because some sentences express a great amount of emotion, another end mark was developed—the exclamation mark.

KEY CONCEPT Use an exclamation mark [!] to end an exclamatory sentence, a forceful imperative sentence, or an interjection expressing strong emotion. ■

An *exclamatory sentence* shows strong emphasis or emotion. Use an exclamation mark at the end of an exclamatory sentence.

EXCLAMATORY SENTENCES:	A man landed on the moon! That shuttle cost millions of dollars!

A strongly worded imperative that demonstrates forcefulness or strong emotion will also take an exclamation mark.

STRONG IMPERATIVE:	Don't touch those wires!

Strong interjections should also be followed by an exclamation mark.

STRONG INTERJECTIONS:	Breathtaking! Ouch! Oh!

Sometimes, a strong interjection may appear before a short exclamatory sentence. If this occurs, you may use either a comma or an exclamation mark after the interjection.

WITH A COMMA:	Goodness, that thunder was loud!
WITH AN EXCLAMATION MARK:	Goodness! That thunder was loud!

> **Exercise 1** Using the Period, Question Mark, and Exclamation Mark Copy the following items, adding the necessary periods or question marks.

1. The moon's diameter is about one fourth the size of the Earth's
2. Is it true that there is no atmosphere on the moon
3. The moon travels around the Earth at approximately 2,300 miles per hour
4. That is really fast
5. The pull of gravity is only one-sixth that of the Earth's
6. Did you see the footage on television of Neil Armstrong's moon landing
7. You can see only half the moon's entire surface at any one time
8. Is there a new moon tonight
9. Look There's a full moon
10. When the moon is full, it is farther away from the sun than it is when it is a new moon

Other Uses of End Marks

> **KEY CONCEPT** Most abbreviations end with a period. ■

| ABBREVIATIONS WITH PERIODS: | Mrs. | Jr. | Ave. | Capt. | Wash. |
| | M.D. | R.N. | A.M. | ft. | |

| ABBREVIATIONS WITHOUT PERIODS: | FBI | FL | kg | L |

> **KEY CONCEPT** Use a period after numbers and letters in outlines. ■

EXAMPLE:
    I. Our Solar System
      A. Earth
        1. moon
      B. Pluto
        1. Charon

> **Exercise 2** Proofreading for End Marks Proofread the following sentences, inserting end marks where necessary.

1. When I was ten, I was 4 ft 9 in tall
2. Did they arrive at 9:00 A.M. or P.M.
3. Mr Roth is our band teacher
4. We have a holiday in honor of Martin Luther King, Jr
5. Watch out, Capt Reid, that coffee cup is leaking

Learn More

For an abbreviations reference, see Abbreviations on page 868.

Get instant feedback! Exercises 1 and 2 are available on-line or on CD-ROM.

More Practice

Grammar Exercise Workbook
• pp. 163–164
On-line Exercise Bank
• Section 28.1
Go on-line:
PHSchool.com
Enter Web Code:
eek-1002

Section
28.1 *Section Review*

GRAMMAR EXERCISES 3–7

▶ **Exercise 3** **Using End Marks** Copy all of the following sentences, adding all necessary end marks.

1. Early observers thought that the dark spots on the moon were oceans
2. This is why they are called *mares*, the Latin word for "sea"
3. Are there oceans on the moon
4. No, there are not
5. The moon is so bright tonight
6. There are mountains and craters on the moon
7. The highest ranges have peaks almost as tall as the Himalayas
8. What is the origin of the moon's craters
9. Some craters show signs of being volcanic in origin
10. Most resulted from impacts with meteorites or asteroids

▶ **Exercise 4** **Proofreading to Correct End Marks** On a separate sheet of paper, copy the following passage. Proofread the passage, correcting and adding end marks as needed.

In the mid-twentieth century, people began to travel in space On April 12, 1961, a cosmonaut from the USSR made a single orbit around the Earth Alan B Shepherd completed a 300-mile flight, but John H Glenn, Jr was the first person from the United States to orbit the Earth. Glenn orbited the Earth on Feb 20, 1962 Wow That must have been a thrill

Since then, many spaceflights have been launched from the John F Kennedy Space Center in Florida Who would have believed how far the technology would advance. Today, astronauts from the United States and cosmonauts from the former Soviet Union often work together on research Have you ever seen a picture of the space station in which they work It's quite a feat of engineering

▶ **Exercise 5** **Find It in Your Reading** Read the following from "Leiningen Versus the Ants." Tell why you think the writer uses an exclamation mark.

The Brazilian rose heavily to his feet. "I've done my best," he gasped. "Your obstinacy endangers not only yourself, but the lives of your four hundred workers. You don't know these ants!"

▶ **Exercise 6** **Find It in Your Writing** Look through your portfolio. Find examples of sentences that you have ended with a period, a question mark, or an exclamation mark. Explain why you used each mark.

▶ **Exercise 7** **Writing Application** Write sentences of your own using the following directions.

1. Write a question about schoolwork, and then rephrase it as an indirect question.
2. Write a declarative sentence about something you like.
3. Rewrite your declarative sentence so that it can end with an exclamation mark.
4. Write a strong imperative you have heard from your teacher.
5. Write a statement intended as a question to get information from a friend about a book he or she has read.

Commas

The comma [,] tells the reader to take a short pause before continuing the sentence.

The comma is used more than any other internal punctuation mark. As a result, many errors are made in its use. This section presents rules to help you use the comma correctly—to separate basic elements and to set off added elements in sentences.

Commas With Compound Sentences

A compound sentence is two or more independent clauses joined by one of the following coordinating conjunctions: *and, but, for, nor, or, so,* or *yet.* A comma is needed to separate the independent clauses.

▶ **KEY CONCEPT** Use a comma before the conjunction to separate two independent clauses in a compound sentence. ■

Always check to make sure that you have written two complete sentences joined by a coordinating conjunction before you insert a comma.

EXAMPLES: We read about Mexico, and then we wrote our report on it.

Storm clouds were gathering overhead, so we brought the lawn chairs inside.

The most common error that writers make with this rule is to insert a comma automatically when they see a conjunction. Remember, however, that coordinating conjunctions can also join compound subjects, compound verbs, prepositional phrases, and clauses. When they are used in one of these ways, no comma is required.

COMPOUND SUBJECT:	The parents and the teachers meet tonight.
COMPOUND VERB:	Tourists swim and play sports when they visit Mexico.
TWO PREPOSITIONAL PHRASES:	I hit the golf ball into the water and then into a sand trap.
TWO SUBORDINATE CLAUSES:	My brothers enjoy books only if they are relatively short and only if they offer a lot of action.

> **Exercise 8** Using Commas in Compound Sentences If a comma is needed in one of the following sentences, write the word before the comma, the comma, and the conjunction following the comma. If no comma is needed, write *correct*.

EXAMPLE: I practice my Spanish daily but I still make mistakes.

ANSWER: daily, but

1. Mexico's full name is the United Mexican States and it is known as *Estados Unidos Mexicanos* in Spanish.
2. The capital is Mexico City and it is also Mexico's largest city.
3. The United States is to Mexico's north and Belize and Guatemala are to its south.
4. The Tropic of Cancer goes through Mexico so the area to the south can be extremely hot.
5. In parts of the country, the temperature can go as high as 120 degrees Fahrenheit yet as low as 32 degrees Fahrenheit.
6. Some southern parts of Mexico can receive up to sixty inches of rain a year but most of the country is much drier.
7. It is hotter in Monterey than in Mexico City but not much hotter.
8. The wide temperature range gives Mexico an extremely varied plant life but rainfall affects it, too.
9. The north is desertlike but cacti grow there and yucca and mesquite as well.
10. Wolves are found in the north and in the mountain forests, along with bears and jaguars.

> **More Practice**

Grammar Exercise Workbook
• pp. 165–170
On-line Exercise Bank
• Section 28.2
  Go on-line:
  PHSchool.com
  Enter Web Code:
  eek-1002

Get instant feedback! Exercise 8 is available on-line or on CD-ROM.

◀ Critical Viewing Make a statement about the contrast between rural and urban areas of Mexico. Use two independent clauses. Identify where you would place the comma. Then, revise the sentence so that a comma is not required. [Analyze]

Commas With Series and Adjectives

Series Whenever a series of words, phrases, or clauses occurs in a sentence, you will need to insert commas.

▶ **KEY CONCEPT** Use commas to separate three or more words, phrases, or clauses in a series. ■

Grammar and Style Tip

When showing a contrast, use opposing series of adjectives to create parallel structure.

WORDS: I read the articles, extracts, and books for my final exam.

PREPOSITIONAL PHRASES: Mexico had been ruled by the Spanish, by the Mexicans, and by the French.

CLAUSES: The bank filled quickly with people who transferred their accounts, who cashed checks, and who opened safe-deposit boxes.

Some writers omit the last comma in a series. This is permissible as long as the writer follows a consistent pattern. In your own work, however, you will find that the full use of commas generally works better. This is especially true in those cases where the last comma is needed to prevent confusion.

CONFUSING: Streams of people, honking geese and souvenir vendors swarmed outside the hotel.

ALWAYS CLEAR: Streams of people, honking geese, and souvenir vendors swarmed outside the hotel.

Commas are not needed when all the items in a series have already been separated by conjunctions (usually *and* or *or*).

EXAMPLE: I cut and chopped and diced onions until I cried.

Commas should also be avoided within pairs of items that are used together so frequently that they are thought of as a single item. Notice in the following example that commas separate the pairs but not the items in the pairs.

EXAMPLE: I asked for ham and eggs, coffee and cream, and bread and butter.

GRAMMAR IN
LITERATURE

from **Work That Counts**
Ernesto Ruelas Inzunza

In the following passage, commas are used to separate the names of birds listed as items in a series.

. . . Five species of swallows, scissor-tailed flycatchers, white-winged and mourning doves, wood storks, white pelicans, cormorants, and white-faced and white ibises are also among the list of more than 220 species of migratory birds recorded at Veracruz.

Adjectives Use commas to divide adjectives of equal rank. Such adjectives are called *coordinate adjectives.*

> **KEY CONCEPT** Use commas to separate **coordinate adjectives**—adjectives of equal rank. ■

To determine whether adjectives in a sentence are of equal rank, ask yourself two questions: First, can you put an *and* between the adjectives and still have the sentence retain its exact meaning? Second, can you switch the adjectives and still have a sentence that sounds grammatically correct? If the answer to the two test questions is yes, you have adjectives of equal rank and a comma should be placed between them.

EXAMPLES: The country's wild, beautiful scenery is an attraction for tourists.

She left detailed, precise instructions for the substitute.

In these examples, *wild* and *beautiful* and *detailed* and *precise* qualify as coordinate adjectives.

> **KEY CONCEPT** Do not use commas to separate **cumulative adjectives**—adjectives that must stay in a specific order. ■

EXAMPLES: Colonial Mexico had rigid social classes.

In a few short hours, we will be finished.

Try putting an *and* between these adjectives or changing their order. The sentences do not make sense. These adjectives must stay in the order in which they are written. Therefore, no comma is used to separate them.

> **Exercise 9** Separating Items in a Series Copy each sentence that needs commas, adding the necessary commas. For sentences that need no commas, write *correct*.

EXAMPLE: Mexican cooking uses tomatoes chilies and lots of spices.

ANSWER: Mexican cooking uses tomatoes, chilies, and lots of spices.

1. Reptiles found in Mexico include turtles iguanas rattlesnakes and lizards.
2. Both sea and game birds are numerous.
3. Corn cotton fruits wheat beans coffee tomatoes and rice are grown in Mexico.
4. Natural resources in Mexico include petroleum silver copper gold lead and zinc.
5. Plant and animal life vary with climatic zone altitude and precipitation.
6. Mexican culture is a mixture of Native American North American and Spanish influences.
7. Native American groups included the Maya the Aztec and the Toltec.
8. Evidence suggests that a hunting people existed in 13,000 B.C. that crop cultivation developed around 8000 B.C. and that the first major civilization in Mexico was the Olmec.
9. The Aztecs reached the height of their power by the fifteenth century and were intellectually and artistically advanced.
10. The Spaniards heard of the Aztecs' wealth wanted to take their gold and sent a large invading army in 1519.

> **Exercise 10** Using Commas With Adjectives For each of the following phrases, write *cumulative* if the adjectives are cumulative and require no comma. If the adjectives are equal in rank, write the adjectives, inserting the comma.

EXAMPLE: a vivid beautiful scene
ANSWER: a vivid, beautiful scene

1. spicy hot food
2. several distinct cultural groups
3. rigid social classes
4. hot humid climate
5. earliest advanced civilizations
6. small native minority
7. bleak arid landscape
8. rich complex history
9. varied native fauna
10. distinctive regional character

More Practice

Grammar Exercise Workbook
• pp. 165–166
On-line Exercise Bank
• Section 28.2
Go on-line:
PHSchool.com
Enter Web Code:
eek-1002

Text

Get instant feedback! Exercises 9, 10, and 11 are available on-line or on CD-ROM.

Commas After Introductory Material

▷ **KEY CONCEPT** Use a comma after an introductory word, phrase, or clause. ■

	KINDS OF INTRODUCTORY MATERIAL	
Words	Introductory Words	No, I will not go to Mexico with you.
	Nouns of Direct Address	Cindy, could you hold this picture of Mexico?
	Common Expressions	Of course, we can get that printed for you.
	Introductory Adverbs	Obviously, the student had tried. Hurriedly, she hid the present she had wrapped.
Phrases	Prepositional Phrases	In the deep recesses of the couch, I found the watch I had lost.
	Participial Phrases	Jumping over the fence, the horse caught its back hoof.
	Infinitive Phrases	To get to the appointment on time, the man left early.
Clauses	Adverb Clauses	When the steaks were medium rare, we took them off the grill.

▷ **Exercise 11** Proofreading for Commas After Introductory Material Copy the following passage on a separate sheet of paper. Add commas after introductory material as needed.

When the Spaniards decided to conquer Mexico they appointed Hernán Cortés to lead the army. Soon after landing in Mexico Cortés found someone who could speak Aztec. Having learned of discord in the Aztec Empire Cortés convinced some natives to join him. At the time that all of this was happening Montezuma was the leader of the Aztec Empire. During his march to the Aztec capital Cortés was in communication with Montezuma. Reaching the capital in November of 1519 Cortés took Montezuma hostage. In the following year Cortés had to return to the coast of Mexico. In his absence his deputy mistreated and killed many Aztecs. After Cortés returned from the coast a battle was fought in which Montezuma was killed. Taking the capital in 1521 the Spaniards ultimately ended Aztec power.

▷ **More Practice**

Grammar Exercise Workbook
• pp. 167–168
On-line Exercise Bank
• Section 28.2
  Go on-line:
  PHSchool.com
  Enter Web Code:
  eek-1002

Commas With Parenthetical and Nonessential Expressions

Commas are often used within a sentence to set off parenthetical and nonessential expressions.

Parenthetical Expressions A parenthetical expression is a word or phrase that interrupts the general flow of a sentence. Study the following list of common parenthetical expressions.

NOUN OF DIRECT ADDRESS:	Don, Mrs. Burke, my son, sweetheart
CONJUNCTIVE ADVERBS:	also, besides, furthermore, however, indeed, instead, moreover, nevertheless, otherwise, therefore, thus
COMMON EXPRESSIONS:	by the way, I feel, in my opinion, in the first place, of course, on the other hand,
CONTRASTING EXPRESSIONS:	not that one, not there, not mine

▲ **Critical Viewing**
In a sentence about the condition of these ruins, include a parenthetical comment about the grass. [**Describe**]

KEY CONCEPT Use commas to set off parenthetical expressions. ■

Two commas are used to enclose the entire parenthetical expression when the expression is located in the middle of the sentence.

NOUN OF DIRECT ADDRESS:	We will go, Marge, as soon as your father arrives.
CONJUNCTIVE ADVERB:	The boys, therefore, decided to go to Acapulco.
COMMON EXPRESSION:	The flowers, in my opinion, have never looked healthier.
CONTRASTING EXPRESSIONS:	It was here, not there, that we found the answer.

If one of these expressions is used at the end of the sentence, however, only one comma is necessary.

EXAMPLE: We will go as soon as your father arrives, Marge.

Essential and Nonessential Expressions Because commas are used only with nonessential expressions, writers must learn to distinguish between essential and nonessential material. (The terms *restrictive* and *nonrestrictive* are sometimes used to refer to the same types of expressions.)

An *essential* expression is a word, phrase, or clause that provides essential information in a sentence: information that cannot be removed without changing the meaning of the sentence. In the following example, the clause following *boy* tells *which* boy the writer means. Thus, it provides essential information in the sentence.

KEY CONCEPT Do not use commas to set off essential expressions. ■

EXAMPLES: The boy who is holding the book is going to Mexico.

The famous dramatist Ben Jonson wrote these comedies.

Because the clauses in the sentences above are essential expressions, they are not set off with commas.

Nonessential expressions provide additional, but not essential, information in a sentence. If you remove nonessential material from a sentence, the remaining sentence will still contain all the necessary information required by the reader.

EXAMPLES: Joe Warren, who is holding the book, is going to Mexico.

Ben Jonson, a famous dramatist, wrote these comedies.

In the first example, the boy is specifically named, and the information contained in the clause provides only an additional fact. Thus, this clause is nonessential.

Once you have decided whether or not an expression is essential, you can apply this rule:

KEY CONCEPT Use commas to set off nonessential expressions. ■

When applying this rule, be alert for three types of word groups: appositives, participial phrases, and adjective clauses. They often serve as either essential or nonessential expressions. Check them carefully to avoid committing comma errors. Study the chart on the next page until you feel confident that you can tell the difference between essential expressions and nonessential expressions.

Learn More

To learn more about essential and nonessential expressions, see Chapter 20.

ESSENTIAL AND NONESSENTIAL EXPRESSIONS

Appositive	Essential	My friend Joanne went to the University of Indiana.
	Nonessential	Joanne, my friend, went to the University of Indiana.
Participial Phrase	Essential	The teacher wearing a blue dress took the students on the field trip.
	Nonessential	Mrs. Goff, wearing the blue dress, took the students on the field trip.
Adjective Clause	Essential	The hotel that we enjoyed the most had three swimming pools and lighted tennis courts.
	Nonessential	The Royal Tahitian Hotel, which was our favorite, had three swimming pools and lighted tennis courts.

▶ **Exercise 12** Setting Off Parenthetical Expressions
Copy each of the following sentences, inserting any commas necessary to set off parenthetical expressions. If no change is necessary, write *correct.*

EXAMPLE: The Spanish conquest of Mexico was in fact quite complex.

ANSWER: The Spanish conquest of Mexico was, in fact, quite complex.

1. The first Spanish viceroy of Mexico Antonio de Mendoza was appointed in 1535.
2. This appointment it appears established a Spanish colonial government in Mexico for almost three hundred years.
3. Moreover the Spaniards had sixty-one viceroys in Mexico.
4. Mexico you know was called New Spain then.
5. A series of expeditions adding land to Spain's territory increased the power of Spain in the Americas.
6. New Spain included present-day Texas and New Mexico and California.
7. The viceregal system was not in fact always a fair one.
8. Native Americans who were supposed to be free were treated like slaves.
9. The most powerful institution in colonial Mexico was in all probability the Roman Catholic Church.
10. The people who occupied positions of power were from the Spanish-born minority who enjoyed power out of proportion to their numbers.

More Practice

Grammar Exercise Workbook
• pp. 167–168
On-line Exercise Bank
• Section 28.2
  Go on-line:
  PHSchool.com
  Enter Web Code:
  eek-1002

Get instant feedback! Exercises 12 and 13 are available on-line or on CD-ROM.

> **Exercise 13** Distinguishing Between Essential and Nonessential Expressions If one of the following sentences contains an essential expression needing no additional commas, write *essential*. If the sentence contains a nonessential expression, copy the sentence and add the necessary commas.

EXAMPLE: Those who tried to institute reforms sometimes succeeded but more often failed.

ANSWER: essential

(1) Spain attempted reforms which proved largely ineffectual to help the condition of Native Americans. (2) Their failure due to the fact that distance made enforcement difficult kept the Native Americans in misery. (3) The inefficiency and corruption that were so prevalent in the colonial government greatly disturbed Spain. (4) Spain tried reforms in the eighteenth century that could not eliminate the problem. (5) Resentment of the Mexican-born population which was inflamed by European ideas of freedom continued to grow. (6) The most immediate and perhaps most important cause of the Mexican War for Independence was the occupation of Spain by Napoleon. (7) Independence which took more than ten years to achieve was formally proclaimed in August 1821. (8) Peace long missing in Mexico did not last long. (9) Mexico a country that was not used to democracy continued to have problems. (10) Antonio Lopez de Santa Anna who was elected president in 1833 was to have an impact on both Mexico and the United States.

GRAMMAR IN
LITERATURE

from Work That Counts
Ernesto Ruelas Inzunza

In the following sentence, notice that the word Jeros *is essential, and the phrase* who is new to hawk watching *is nonessential. The writer sets off the nonessential phrase (highlighted in blue italics) with commas.*

After sunset, I finally have time to sit peacefully and tell my friend Jeros, *who is new to hawk watching,* the story of the discovery of the River of Raptors.

Other Uses of the Comma

Commas are used in the following situations:

With Locations Whenever you are citing a specific place, check to see whether a comma is required.

> **KEY CONCEPT** When a geographical name is made up of two or more parts, use a comma after each item. ■

EXAMPLES: I traveled from Taos, New Mexico, to Tijuana, Mexico.
This cheese was shipped from Montigny, Moselle, France, by my friend Robert.

With Dates Dates containing numbers require commas.

> **KEY CONCEPT** When a date is made up of two or more parts, use a comma after each item except in the case of a month followed by a day or a month followed by a year. ■

EXAMPLES: On Friday, April 17, we will have a special meeting.
We will discuss the class trip to Monterey on November 11, 2001.
February 1980 was one of the wettest months on record.

If the parts of a date have already been joined by prepositions, no comma is needed.

EXAMPLE: The city's new mass-transit system ran its first train on June 11 of 1974.

With Titles Use a comma with titles that follow a name.

> **KEY CONCEPT** When a name is followed by one or more titles, use a comma after the name and after each title. ■

EXAMPLE: I noticed that Jeremy McGuire, Sr., is a partner in this firm.

A similar rule applies with some business abbreviations:

EXAMPLE: She worked for Heller and Ramirez, Inc., for a year.

With Addresses Addresses consisting of two or more parts need commas to separate the parts.

▶ **KEY CONCEPT** Use a comma after each item in an address made up of two or more parts. ■

EXAMPLE: Katie Wedel's new address is 160 11th Street, Anytown, Missouri 63131.

If this address were on an envelope, most of the commas would be omitted.

Mahoney
260 Broadway
Anytown, NY 10960

stamp

Katie Wedel
160 11th Street
Anytown, MO 63131

Avoid using commas if prepositions join parts of an address.

EXAMPLE: Katie Wedel lives on 11th Street in Anytown.

With Salutations and Closings You will need to use commas in the openings and closings of many letters.

▶ **KEY CONCEPT** Use a comma after the salutation in a personal letter and after the closing in all letters. ■

SALUTATIONS: Dear Rupert,   Dear Aunt Dolly,
CLOSINGS: Sincerely,   In appreciation,

▶ Critical Viewing What punctuation is used on this sign? In what situation would a comma be required with this street name? [Apply]

With Numbers Certain numbers also need commas.

Learn More

For a more detailed explanation of punctuating quotations, see Section 28.4.

> **KEY CONCEPT** With numbers of more than three digits, use a comma after every third digit from the right. ■

EXAMPLES: The projected complex would house 1,245 people.

The company has sold 498,362,719 jelly beans.

There are several exceptions to this rule: ZIP Codes, phone numbers, page numbers, serial numbers, years, and house numbers do not have commas.

ZIP CODE: 26413
TELEPHONE NUMBER: (612) 555-3702
PAGE NUMBER: page 1047
HOUSE NUMBER: 18364 Lamson Road
SERIAL NUMBER: 173 55 2007

With Omissions Sometimes, you will purposely omit a word or phrase from a sentence; this omission results in an elliptical sentence. For clarity, you should insert a comma where the words have been left out.

> **KEY CONCEPT** Use a comma to indicate the words left out of an elliptical sentence. ■

In the following example, the omitted word is clearly understood. The comma serves as a visual clue to the reader that an omission exists.

EXAMPLE: The man walked quickly and the woman, slowly.

With Direct Quotations Commas also set off direct quotations.

> **KEY CONCEPT** Use commas to set off a direct quotation from the rest of the sentence. ■

EXAMPLES: The guest asked, "Do you know of any nearby grocery stores that are open all night?"
"If you don't mind a little drive," the host said, "you will find one about three miles down the road."
"Oh, that will be perfect," the guest replied.

For Clarity You will occasionally run across a sentence structure that may be confusing without a comma. By inserting a comma, you can reduce the confusion and prevent misreading.

▶ **KEY CONCEPT** Use a comma to prevent a sentence from being misunderstood. ■

UNCLEAR: She studied French and Mayan art.
CLEAR: She studied French, as well as Mayan art.

Note About the *Careless Use of Commas:* Generally, you should not use a comma unless you have a rule clearly in mind. Study the following examples of the careless overuse of commas, and avoid such use in your own writing.

MISUSED WITH ADJECTIVE AND NOUN:	The Mexican, Aztecs came from farther north.
CORRECT:	The Mexican Aztecs came from farther north.
MISUSED WITH COMPOUND SUBJECT:	We watched as the man, and woman executed some fancy dance steps.
CORRECT:	We watched as the man and woman executed some fancy dance steps.
MISUSED WITH COMPOUND VERBS:	The dancers leaped, and twirled around the stage.
CORRECT:	The dancers leaped and twirled around the stage.
MISUSED WITH PREPOSITIONAL PHRASES:	The dancers bowed to the audience, and to the conductor.
CORRECT:	The dancers bowed to the audience and to the conductor.
MISUSED WITH SUBORDINATE CLAUSES:	I won't forget that you gave me the ticket, and that I thoroughly enjoyed the performance.
CORRECT:	I won't forget that you gave me the ticket and that I thoroughly the performance.

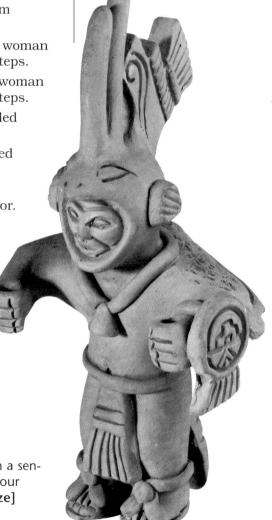

▶ **Critical Viewing** Use the verbs *wears* and *dances* in a sentence about this sculpture of an Aztec warrior. Does your sentence require a comma? Why or why not? **[Analyze]**

Exercise 14 Using Commas in Other Situations Copy the following sentences, adding the necessary commas.
1. On April 21 1836 the Mexicans were defeated by Texans.
2. The Texans' victory occurred at San Jacinto Texas.
3. America had territorial ambitions in Texas and California so in 1846 they declared war on Mexico.
4. United States troops occupied northern Mexico and in 1847 Mexico City.
5. In February of 1848 a large part of Mexican territory became part of the United States.
6. This loss occurred on February 2 1848.
7. "Santa Anna" according to the encyclopedia "was compelled to resign after the war."
8. Again Mexico suffered internal dissension and in 1854 a revolution.
9. June 1863 saw French troops reach Mexico and cause the current government officials to flee.
10. Porfirio Díaz a general was dictator of Mexico from 1877 to 1911.

Exercise 15 Correcting the Careless Use of Commas
Some of the commas have been used incorrectly in the following sentences. Rewrite each sentence, removing any incorrect commas. Write *correct* if the sentence requires no additions or alterations.

EXAMPLE: I knew that I was right, and that Chichén Itzá was Mayan.

ANSWER: I knew that I was right and that Chichén Itzá was Mayan.

1. Díaz led a rebellion in 1871, and in 1877, to become leader of Mexico.
2. He fought, and struggled to gain power.
3. He rebelled against President Juárez, and against his successor, Tejada.
4. After ruling for over thirty years, he lost power to Francisco Madero.
5. Emiliano Zapata, and Pancho Villa refused to recognize Madero's authority.
6. Madero's assassination, rival leaders, and foreign intervention all contributed to turmoil in Mexico.
7. Finally, things began to improve in the twenties.
8. Mexico, and the United States, began to work more closely.
9. Leaders searched for ways to improve Mexico's economic prosperity, and the prosperity of all its citizens.
10. The country, like all countries, still has problems, but it is struggling to solve them.

More Practice

Grammar Exercise Workbook
• pp. 169–170
On-line Exercise Bank
• Section 28.2
Go on-line:
PHSchool.com
Enter Web Code:
eek-1002

Get instant feedback! Exercises 14 and 15 are available on-line or on CD-ROM.

Section Review

GRAMMAR EXERCISES 16–24

Exercise 16 Using Commas in Compound Sentences If a comma is needed in one of these sentences, write the word before the comma, the comma, and the word after the comma. If no comma is needed, write *correct.*

1. Mexico is a federal republic and it has jurisdiction over several islands.
2. The Sierra Madre contains the highest peaks in Mexico and it is a volcanic range.
3. Mexico is not exempt from earthquakes nor are they always mild.
4. A serious earthquake struck and killed more that 7,000 people in 1985.
5. The country is also prone to hurricanes and these can be quite devastating.

Exercise 17 Separating Items in a Series Copy each sentence that needs commas, inserting them as required. If no comma is needed, write *correct.*

1. Mexico can be roughly divided into the *tierra caliente tierra templada* and *tierra fría.*
2. In English, this means "the hot land" "the temperate land" and "the cold land."
3. The climate is governed by latitude and elevation.
4. The country includes coastal plains a central plateau and volcanic peaks.
5. Some of Mexico's rivers are the Grijalva the Usumacinta and the Conchos.

Exercise 18 Proofreading for Commas With Series, Adjectives, and Introductory Material Copy the following passage on a separate sheet of paper. Add or delete commas as needed.

When people think of Mexico today they think of its tourist attractions. These attractions include ancient ruins beautiful beaches rural villages and exciting urban areas. Obviously there is much to see in Mexico.

In order to reach Acapulco you must travel quite far south. Historically it is a good harbor port and a tourist resort. Tourists flock to Acapulco to relax to enjoy the sun and to visit the interesting historical sites.

Exercise 19 Setting Off Parenthetical Expressions Copy each of the following sentences, inserting commas as necessary.

1. Mexico City the capital is also the cultural center of the country.
2. Octavio Paz a Mexican writer won the prestigious Nobel Prize for Literature in 1990.
3. Mayans and Aztecs in fact were highly advanced in art and science.
4. Mayans it is said excelled at painting and sculpture.
5. Mexican folk arts such as weaving and pottery are world renowned.

Exercise 20 Distinguishing Between Essential and Nonessential Expressions If a sentence contains an essential expression needing no commas, write *essential.* If it contains a nonessential expression, insert the commas where needed.

1. Mexico City is home to several museums that display the country's past.
2. The National Museum of Anthropology which is in Mexico City is devoted to Mayan and other artifacts.
3. The museum that is in Chapultepec Castle is concerned with Mexico's history since the Spanish conquest.

4. Another museum that has an important archaeological collection is in Yucatan.
5. Mexico is a country whose cultural glory is not all in the past.
6. Some Mexican actors who have achieved world fame are Cantinflas and Dolores Del Rio.
7. Architecture so popular with Native Americans is still a flourishing art.
8. A group of dancers that specializes in Mexican folk dances tours the world.
9. Some folk dances which predate the Spanish conquest still survive today.
10. Mexico where sports are popular has hosted the Olympic Games and the World Cup.

▶ **Exercise 21** Other Uses of Commas Remove incorrectly used commas or add them where necessary.

1. Mexico's area is approximately 756066 square miles.
2. I told my pen pal that my address is 23 Deer Park Lane Omaha Nebraska 27103.
3. She said "I will write to you very soon."
4. He studied Aztec, and Mayan culture.
5. Spanish, and other languages, are spoken in Mexico.
6. Some of Mexico's peaks are almost 19000 feet high.
7. Mayans were famous for their architecture and for their sculpture.
8. Europeans are the smallest minorities in Mexico.
9. Mexico, and the United States share a common border.
10. He is going to Acapulco Mexico for his vacation this year.

▶ **Exercise 22** Find It in Your Reading Explain the reason for each of the commas in the following excerpt from "Work That Counts."

. . . At eight this morning, as Jeros and I climbed the observation tower, about forty-five Swainson's hawks were just taking off from the nearby canyon where they had spent the night. Shortly afterward, we saw hundreds of them turning circles in the thermal columns of hot air, effortlessly gaining altitude. By eleven, the Swainson's had joined smaller numbers of broad-winged hawks and turkey vultures, forming long streams of migrants. Such large flocks, totaling more than 20,000 birds at times, can take up to thirty minutes to pass overhead. Resembling myriad moving organisms in a plankton sample, the raptors filled our binoculars' field of view. We watched the avian river continue north until it disappeared.

▶ **Exercise 23** Find It in Your Writing In your portfolio, look for examples of cumulative and coordinate adjectives. Make sure that you have used commas correctly in each example.

▶ **Exercise 24** Writing Application Write five sentences of your own using the following instructions.

1. Use at least three adjectives to describe your best friend.
2. Write a compound sentence with two independent clauses, each containing information about a place you would like to visit.
3. Write a sentence listing at least three things you like about the place where you live.
4. Write your address as it would appear on an envelope and in a sentence.
5. Write a sentence about a movie you have seen in which a character uses the expression *by the way.*

Section 28.3 Semicolons and Colons

The semicolon [;] is a punctuation mark that serves as the happy medium between the comma and the period. It signals the reader to pause longer than for a comma but to pause without the finality of a period. The colon [:] is used primarily to point ahead to additional information. It directs the reader to look farther.

The first part of this section will cover the rules that govern the use of semicolons. The second part will present the ways in which you can use colons.

Using the Semicolon

The semicolon is used to separate independent clauses that have a close relationship to each other. A semicolon is also used to separate independent clauses or items in a series that already contain a number of commas.

Using the Semicolon With Independent Clauses
Semicolons are most often used between independent clauses.

▷ **KEY CONCEPT** Use a *semicolon* to join independent clauses that are not already joined by the conjunction *and, but, for, nor, or, so,* or *yet.* ■

Two sentences joined by a conjunction need a comma before the conjunction.

EXAMPLE: My mother works in a school, but she does not teach.

Because the semicolon is stronger than the comma, it replaces both the comma and the conjunction. Notice in the following example that the second independent clause of two clauses joined by a semicolon starts with a lowercase letter. Do not use a capital following a semicolon unless the word following a semicolon would call for a capital in any position.

EXAMPLE: My mother works in a school; she does not teach.

Do not use a semicolon to join unrelated independent clauses. Use a semicolon to join only those that are closely related.

INCORRECT: My aunt and uncle have five children; it will snow today.

CORRECT: My aunt and uncle have five children; they have two boys and three girls.

In this section, you will learn about semicolons and colons. The examples and exercises are about friends, relatives, neighbors, and acquaintances.

Cross-Curricular Connection: Social Studies

Sometimes, the independent clauses will share a similar structure as well as a similar meaning.

EXAMPLE: Before today, my uncle was out of work; tomorrow, he starts a new job.

Notice that both sentences center around a shared subject—work. The sentences are also similar to each other in structure. This is a situation in which to use a semicolon.

Occasionally, independent clauses may set up a contrast:

EXAMPLE: My sister excels at art; I can barely draw a straight line.

So far, the discussion has concentrated on using a semicolon to join two independent clauses. However, if there are more than two independent clauses, you can still use semicolons:

EXAMPLE: Joe's grandparents were not born in this country; they emigrated here from Italy; they settled comfortably in Boston.

Independent clauses also need a semicolon when they are joined by a conjunctive adverb or a transitional expression.

▶ **KEY CONCEPT** Use a semicolon to join independent clauses separated by either a conjunctive adverb or a transitional expression. ■

Conjunctive adverbs are adverbs used as conjunctions to connect independent clauses. Common conjunctive adverbs are *accordingly, also, besides, consequently, furthermore, however, indeed, instead, namely, nevertheless, otherwise, similarly, therefore,* and *thus.* Transitional expressions are expressions that connect one independent clause with another. Transitional expressions include *as a result, at this time, first, for instance, in fact, on the other hand, second,* and *that is.*

CONJUNCTIVE ADVERB: A cloudless blue sky dawned that morning; nevertheless, rain was expected.

TRANSITIONAL EXPRESSION: We needed to fit the whole family around the dinner table; as a result, Dad pulled out the extra leaf.

Because words used as conjunctive adverbs and transitions can also interrupt one continuous sentence, use a semicolon only when there is an independent clause on each side of the conjunctive adverb or transitional expression.

INCORRECT: The team was; consequently, disqualified.

CORRECT: The team was, consequently, disqualified.

Using the Semicolon to Avoid Confusion The semicolon can also be used to avoid confusion in sentences that contain other internal punctuation; for example, two independent clauses that contain their own internal punctuation.

▶ **KEY CONCEPT** Use semicolons to avoid confusion when independent clauses already contain commas. ■

When a sentence consists of two independent clauses joined by a coordinating conjunction, the tendency is to place a comma before the conjunction. However, when one or both of the sentences also contain commas, a semicolon may be used before the conjunction to prevent confusion.

EXAMPLE: My cousins borrowed my favorite album, a recording of a jazz concert; but they returned it safely.

The semicolon also helps avoid confusion in a series of items containing their own internal punctuation. A series generally has several items separated only by commas.

▼ Critical Viewing
Do you think the boys in the picture are friends or relatives? Explain your answer.
[Speculate]

Snap the Whip, Winslow Homer

KEY CONCEPT Use a semicolon between items in a series if the items themselves contain commas. ■

EXAMPLE: We visited the Averills, who live in Wisconsin; the Wilsons, friends in Michigan; and the Garcias, former neighbors now living in North Dakota.

You will use the semicolon in a series most commonly when the items contain either nonessential appositives, participial phrases, or adjective clauses.

APPOSITIVES: I sent notes to Mr. Nielson, my science teacher; Mrs. Jensen, my history instructor; and Mrs. Seltz, my coach.

PARTICIPIAL PHRASES: I developed a terrible headache from listening to my cat, meowing at the door; my dog, howling at the neighbors; and my sister, babbling on the phone.

ADJECTIVE CLAUSES: The car that I bought has spare tires, which are brand new; a stereo, which has just been installed; and a great engine, which has been newly tuned.

Notice that commas are used to separate the nonessential material from the word or words to which they refer or that they modify. The semicolons separate the complete items in the series.

Exercise 25 Using the Semicolon With Independent Clauses Decide where a semicolon is needed in each of the following sentences. Write the word that goes before the semicolon, the semicolon, and the word that goes after it.

EXAMPLE: I once had a red yo-yo my sister had a green one.
ANSWER: yo-yo; my

1. Genealogy is the history of the descent of a family from an ancestor the family tree gives information about the family.
2. The earliest known ancestor is placed at the top of a family tree direct descent can be traced easily.
3. Genealogy is a very popular pastime it can also be a challenging profession.
4. Genealogy is useful in the validation of wills it can ensure the fair distribution of property if a dispute occurs.
5. One practical use of genealogy is found in the medical field physicians can search genealogical records for family histories of unusual diseases.

More Practice

Grammar Exercise Workbook
• pp. 171–172
On-line Exercise Bank
• Section 28.3
  Go on-line:
  PHSchool.com
  Enter Web Code:
  eek-1002

Get instant feedback! Exercises 25 and 26 are available on-line or on CD-ROM.

GRAMMAR IN LITERATURE

from **Mothers and Daughters**
Tillie Olsen and Julie Olsen Edwards

Semicolons are used here to avoid confusion in a series.

Here are daughters and mothers of every shape and human hue; in every age and stage from mother and infant, to old daughter and old, old mother; and here is the family resemblance in face, expression, stance, body.

▼ **Critical Viewing**
How do semicolons prevent words from becoming as jumbled as these birthday candles? **[Connect]**

▶ **Exercise 26** Using Semicolons With Internal Punctuation

Copy each sentence, adding semicolons where they are needed to avoid confusion. Also, add necessary commas.

EXAMPLE: For my mother's birthday I baked cookies which were made with raisins muffins which were made with dates and a cake.

ANSWER: For my mother's birthday, I baked cookies, which were made with raisins; muffins, which were made with dates; and a cake.

1. Jane heard loud poorly played piano music the shouts of her sisters Mary Tina and Carol and the television announcer's voice.
2. The dinner table laden with food looked inviting and the happy hungry family sat down eagerly to the birthday dinner.
3. On the table were turkey which was made with gravy noodles which were cooked in butter and ham which was baked with honey.
4. Jane's family had invited several neighbors—Mr. Jensen who lived next door Laura Wilson Jane's friend and Mr. and Mrs. Wilson Laura's parents.
5. Air travel was a topic of conversation among Mr. Jensen an airline pilot Laura a model-plane enthusiast and Mr. and Mrs. Wilson airline customer-service agents.

Using the Colon

The colon acts mainly as an introductory device. It is also used in several special situations.

Using Colons as Introductory Devices To use the colon correctly as an introductory device, you must be familiar with the different items it can introduce.

KEY CONCEPT Use a colon before a list of items following an independent clause. ■

EXAMPLE:　We must bring the following items to the family reunion: potato salad, a grill, and a blanket.

As shown in this example, the independent clause before a list often includes a phrase such as *the following* or *the following items.* You should familiarize yourself with these phrases, because they often indicate the need for a colon. Of course, you should not depend on these phrases alone to signal the need for a colon. The most important point to consider is whether or not an independent clause precedes the list. If it does, use a colon.

EXAMPLE:　I bought my father several gifts: a shirt, a tie, and a pair of shoes.

Colons can also be used to introduce certain quotations:

KEY CONCEPT Use a colon to introduce a quotation that is formal or lengthy or a quotation that does not contain a "he said/she said" expression. ■

Often, a formal quotation requiring a colon will consist of more than one sentence. However, your best guideline for inserting a colon should be the formality of the quotation. The more formal the quotation, the more likely you will need a colon. Do not use a colon to introduce a casual quoted remark or dialogue, even if more than one sentence is used.

COLON:　The speaker began with these words: "I have never been so honored in all my life."

COMMA:　As Ann left the room, she called, "I really must hurry. I don't want to be late."

▲ Critical Viewing Finish this statement: *The gift in the box might be one of the following items . . .* Where will you place the colon? Where will you use commas? **[Speculate]**

EXAMPLES: Dad walked angrily to the door and then turned: "Your excuses are weak. You have gone too far this time."

Teresa stood up slowly: "I think I'll go home. It's been a long day."

A colon can also serve as an introductory device for a sentence that either amplifies or summarizes what has preceded it:

KEY CONCEPT Use a colon to introduce a sentence that summarizes or explains the sentence before it. ■

EXAMPLES: The garage attendant provided me with one piece of advice: He said to check my water level often until I could get my car in for the needed repairs.

His tuna casserole lacked a rather vital ingredient: He forgot the tuna!

Notice that a capital letter follows the colon because the words following make a complete sentence.

KEY CONCEPT Use a colon to introduce a formal appositive that follows an independent clause. ■

Using a colon, instead of a comma, to introduce an appositive that follows an independent clause gives additional emphasis to the appositive.

EXAMPLE: I missed one important paragraph lesson: writing the topic sentence.

When you are using colons in sentences, always check to be sure that an independent clause comes before the colon.

INCORRECT: We decided to: see an old movie.

CORRECT: We decided to see an old movie: *An American in Paris.*

INCORRECT: Our tour took us by: the rose gardens, the Japanese park, and the hanging gardens.

CORRECT: Our tour took us by some beautiful spots: the rose gardens, the Japanese park, and the hanging gardens.

Although an independent clause must precede a colon, it is not necessary that the words following the colon be an independent clause. An appositive composed of a word or short phrase may, for example, follow a colon.

EXAMPLES: From the jeep, I looked out over the dry grass and saw the king of beasts: a lion.

I have the best friend in the world: my sister.

You could successfully argue that a comma would also be appropriate where the colon is inserted. However, the colon provides a slightly more dramatic effect.

Special Uses of the Colon The colon has several specialized functions that you will probably encounter in your reading and writing:

Among the special situations that require the use of a colon are references to time, volume and page numbers, chapters and verses in the Bible, book subtitles, business letter salutations, and labels that are used to introduce important ideas. Study the examples that are given in the following chart; it shows how the colon is used in each of these special situations.

SPECIAL SITUATIONS REQUIRING COLONS	
Numerals Giving the Time	5:22 A.M. 7:49 P.M.
References to Periodicals (Volume Number: Page Number)	*Forbes* 4:8
Biblical References (Chapter Number: Verse Number)	Genesis 1:5
Subtitles for Books and Magazines	*Fixing Hamburger: One Hundred Ways to Prepare Delicious Meals*
Salutations in Business Letters	Dear Mr. Biggs: Ladies: Dear Sir:
Labels Used to Signal Important Ideas	**Warning:** Cigarette smoking can be hazardous to your health. Note: This letter must be postmarked no later than the tenth of this month.

▶ **Exercise 27** Understanding the Use of the Colon Copy the following sentences, adding colons where necessary. Capitalize the first word if a complete sentence follows the colon.

1. I have one project for myself this summer to chart my family tree.
2. To begin, I will need some important information my mother's maiden name, my grandparents' dates of birth and marriage, and the year the family came to America.
3. Before long, I will have found just what I need my grand-father's birth certificate.
4. It is time to do the research off to City Hall!
5. My grandmother gave me sound advice "know your roots."
6. My sister scorned the advice and my project "why do all that work?"
7. There is a simple explanation for my sister's attitude she is too young to understand.
8. I have found all of the papers I need birth and death certificates, marriage licenses, and immigration records.
9. I made a startling discovery my great-grandparents were born in China!
10. I am proud of my work this summer the genealogical search for my ancestry.

▶ **Exercise 28** Using Colons for Special Writing Situations
Copy each of the following items, adding the necessary colons. Underline any titles that appear in italics.

1. My family tree is entitled "The Gens One Hundred Years and Growing."
2. I used an interesting book for my research, *Finding Your Roots Tracing Your Family History.*
3. There was also a helpful article in *Time* 147 34.
4. I began my research at 8 30 A.M. today.
5. I carefully hurried past a sign that read "Warning Stairs may be slippery."

More Practice

Grammar Exercise Workbook
• pp. 173–174
On-line Exercise Bank
• Section 28.3
  Go on-line:
  PHSchool.com
  Enter Web Code:
  eek-1002

▶ Critical Viewing In a sentence about this picture, use a colon to set off a list of interesting features of this building on Ellis Island. [**Describe**]

Hands-on Grammar

Semicolon Connections

Often, the choice between using a conjunction or a semicolon to connect clauses is a stylistic one. Explore the effects of each choice with the following activity.

Write the following sentence on a strip of colored paper. Cut on either side of the subordinating conjunction. Turn over the piece you have cut, and write a large semicolon on the other side of the piece. Next, flip the card to read the sentence with the subordinating conjunction; then, with the semicolon. Determine which version gives an indication of the relationship between events.

> We left because we were tired.

> We left ; we were tired

Write and cut sentence strips using the conjunctions *therefore, if, after, unless, as,* and *where.* (For this activity, place the subordinate clause at the end of the sentence rather than at the beginning.) Discuss with a partner how the meaning of the sentence is affected when you change the conjunction to a semicolon.

Next, complete sentence strips for compound sentences that contain coordinating conjunctions. Cut the coordinating conjunctions out to make flip sections with semicolons on the other side. (Keep the comma that precedes the conjunction with the conjunction rather than with the sentence.) Again, discuss with a partner when a semicolon is more effective and when the comma and conjunction are more effective.

> The evidence is clear, and it cannot be denied

> The evidence is clear ; it cannot be denied

Find It in Your Reading Look for compound and complex sentences in a short story. Use the Semicolon Connections activity to evaluate the author's choice of conjunction or semicolon.

Find It in Your Writing Look for compound and complex sentences in your writing. Identify one place where you have used a semicolon to connect clauses. If you cannot find one, challenge yourself to revise at least one sentence to include one.

Section Review

GRAMMAR EXERCISES 29–33

Exercise 29 Using Semicolons and Colons Correctly Copy each of the following sentences, adding semicolons and colons where necessary.

1. Many Americans wish to discover their roots most families can be traced back to the time of their arrival.
2. Tracing the family's country of origin is usually difficult it can also become expensive.
3. My mother gave me a book, *Tracing Your Irish Ancestors A Few Simple Steps.*
4. She would like me to learn more about the place our family came from County Kerry in Ireland.
5. Genealogical research in Britain and Ireland is relatively easy records are well kept and accessible.
6. Other records may have been lost language is often a barrier.
7. We will be visiting relatives in Ireland next summer It is a place I can't wait to see!
8. I know exactly where to start my research the library.
9. The library opens at 10 00 Saturday morning.
10. It closes at 3 00 P.M.

Exercise 30 Revising to Combine Sentences With Semicolons and Colons
On a separate sheet of paper, revise the following paragraph. Use semicolons and colons as appropriate to combine clauses or to set off lists.

Genealogy is a major hobby around the world. Its popularity is increasing in the United States. The great surge in interest here started in the 1930's. Then, it increased somewhat after World War II. People engage in genealogical research for a variety of reasons. Some are curious. Some hope to establish a legal right to property, which may require proof of family connections. Some seek membership in lineage societies, which are becoming increasingly popular.

On a family tree are listed the names of relatives. The relatives listed include the following parents, grandparents, great-grandparents and so on. Information is recorded for each person on the tree. The information usually recorded is as follows date and place of birth, marriage, death, and names of children.

Exercise 31 Find It in Your Reading Read the following excerpt from "The Way to Rainy Mountain," and tell why the author used a semicolon in this case.

. . . They could find no buffalo; they had to hang an old hide from the sacred tree.

Exercise 32 Find It in Your Writing In a selection in your writing portfolio, find two related independent clauses that are linked by a comma and coordinating conjunction. Rewrite the sentence so that the clauses are joined by a semicolon instead.

Exercise 33 Writing Application
Interview an older member of your family. In a detailed, well-developed essay, tell an interesting story about your family or describe one of your family's time-honored traditions. If you use direct quotations, remember to punctuate your work correctly. Use at least three semicolons and three colons in your essay.

Quotation Marks and Underlining

Writers try to provide support for their ideas and arguments. Direct quotations can provide that support. They can also make short stories and novels more interesting. Learn the rules for the use of quotation marks. This section will discuss the use of underlining as well as quotation marks to indicate different types of titles, names, and words.

Direct Quotations

This section will take a close look at direct quotations to help clarify any uncertainties you may have regarding the way to punctuate them.

> **KEY CONCEPT** A direct quotation represents a person's exact speech or thoughts and is enclosed in quotation marks [" "]. ∎

DIRECT QUOTATION: "High school is closer to the core of the American experience than anything else I can think of."—Kurt Vonnegut, Jr.

Do not confuse direct quotations with indirect ones.

> **KEY CONCEPT** An indirect quotation reports only the general meaning of what a person said or thought and does not require quotation marks. ∎

INDIRECT QUOTATION: Kurt Vonnegut, Jr., wrote that being in high school was a true part of the American experience.

An indirect quotation rephrases someone else's words. The words are not the exact words of the speaker. In a direct quotation, the words of the speaker are quoted exactly.

All direct quotations must be indicated by quotation marks. There are various ways a writer may present a direct quotation. One way is to quote an uninterrupted sentence. Another way is to present a quoted phrase within an otherwise complete sentence. Writers may also use an introductory, concluding, or interrupting expression with a quotation.

To enclose a sentence that is an uninterrupted direct quotation, double quotation marks [" "] are placed around the quoted material. Of course, each complete sentence of any quotation begins with a capital letter.

EXAMPLE: "The past is but the beginning of a beginning."
—H. G. Wells

**Theme:
Science Fiction**

In this section, you will learn about using quotation marks, italics, and underlining. Many of the examples and exercises are about science fiction.

Cross-Curricular Connection: Literature

Sometimes, you will insert only a quoted phrase into a sentence. You must set off this fragment with quotation marks also. Notice in the following examples that the first word of a phrase or fragment is capitalized only when it falls at the beginning of a sentence or when it would be capitalized regardless of its position in a sentence.

EXAMPLES: In writing about history, H. G. Wells called it "a race between education and catastrophe."

"A race between education and catastrophe" is the way H. G. Wells referred to history.

Generally, you will wish to add a "he said/she said" expression to a quotation to show who is speaking. Use the following rule for a "he said/she said" expression that comes before the quotation.

▶ **KEY CONCEPT** Use a comma or colon after an introductory expression. ■

INTRODUCTORY   H. G. Wells wrote, "The past is
EXPRESSION: but the beginning of a beginning."

If you do not use a "he said/she said" expression in your introduction to a quotation or if the introductory phrase takes a more formal tone, use a colon instead of a comma before the quotation.

EXAMPLE: The professor held up a book: "Today, we will discuss Jules Verne's work *Around the World in Eighty Days.*"

▶ **KEY CONCEPT** Use a comma, a question mark, or an exclamation mark after a quotation followed by a concluding expression. ■

CONCLUDING   "The past is but the beginning
EXPRESSION: of a beginning," wrote Wells.

▲▼ Critical Viewing
Use these pictures to illustrate a scientific principle. [**Connect**]

When a direct quotation is interrupted by a "he said/she said" expression, quotation marks enclose both parts of the quotation.

▶ **KEY CONCEPT** Use a comma after part of a quoted sentence followed by an interrupting expression. Use another comma after the expression. ■

INTERRUPTING
EXPRESSION: "The past," wrote Wells, "is but the beginning of a beginning."

Two quoted sentences may also be interrupted.

▶ **KEY CONCEPT** Use a comma, question mark, or exclamation mark after a quoted sentence that comes before an interrupting expression. Use a period after the expression. ■

EXAMPLE: "What does writing teach?" Ray Bradbury asked. "First and foremost, it reminds us that we are alive."

▶ **Exercise 34** **Indicating Direct Quotations** Copy each sentence that needs quotation marks, adding the necessary marks. If no quotation marks are needed, write *correct*.

EXAMPLE: Mary Shelley wrote I beheld the wretch—the miserable monster whom I had created.

ANSWER: Mary Shelley wrote, "I beheld the wretch— the miserable monster whom I had created."

1. Mr. Phileas Fogg lived, in 1872, at No. 7, Saville Row, Burlington Gardens.—Jules Verne
2. Verne wrote that Phileas Fogg was an Englishman.
3. One of his questions was Was Phileas Fogg rich?
4. You are a Frenchman, I believe, asked Phileas Fogg, and your name is John?
5. Then, the new servant responded, Jean, if monsieur pleases.
6. Mr. Fogg told him that the name Passepartout was preferable.
7. He must have traveled everywhere, at least in the spirit.—Jules Verne
8. You are well recommended to me; I hear a good report of you, said Phileas Fogg.
9. Then, Fogg told Passepartout that his watch was four minutes slow.
10. I have a natural aptness for going out of one business into another, confided Jean Passepartout.

🜲 **Grammar**
🜲 and **Style Tip**

Vary the way you indicate the speaker of a quotation. Sometimes, introduce the quotation with an indication of the speaker; sometimes, indicate the speaker following the quotation; and sometimes, interrupt the quotation.

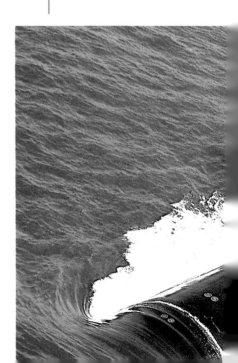

Exercise 35 **Indicating and Capitalizing Quotations** Copy the following sentences, making the necessary corrections in punctuation and capitalization. In two of the sentences, the quote has been underlined so that you can identify it.

EXAMPLE: space—the final frontier announced Captain Kirk these are the voyages of the starship *Enterprise*.

ANSWER: "Space—the final frontier," announced Captain Kirk. "These are the voyages of the starship *Enterprise*."

1. the year 1866 was marked by a strange event begins Verne's *20,000 Leagues Under the Sea.*
2. sea-going ships have been encountering an 'enormous thing' Verne continues a long spindle-shaped object.
3. this was described as infinitely larger and quicker than a whale.
4. but it did exist said Verne's narrator there was now no denying the fact.
5. some characters in the book said that they would not believe it existed unless they had seen it . . . with their own scientific eyes.
6. as for dismissing it as a myth wrote Verne this was no longer possible.
7. the monster came into fashion in all the big cities said the narrator.
8. it was sung about in cafes continued the narrator jeered at in the newspapers, acted out in the theaters.
9. the 'monster subject' inflamed people's minds.—Jules Verne
10. after some encounters with ships, the narrator said the problem took on a different complexion.

More Practice

Grammar Exercise Workbook
• pp. 175–176
On-line
Exercise Bank
• Section 28.4

Go on-line:
PHSchool.com
Enter Web Code:
eek-1002

▼ **Critical Viewing** With a partner, exchange two or three sentences about this picture. Write down what was said. Use capitals and quotation marks as needed. **[Apply]**

Other Punctuation Marks With Quotation Marks

Whether to place punctuation inside or outside the quotation marks presents a problem for some writers. Four basic rules, once learned, will help clear up most of the confusion.

KEY CONCEPT Always place a comma or a period inside the final quotation mark. ■

EXAMPLES: "I enjoy Jack Finney's work," said Elaine.

"The future," C. S. Lewis believed, "is something which everyone reaches at the rate of sixty minutes an hour."

Note in the second example that the quotation is split, but this makes no difference in the placement of the comma. It still goes inside the quotation marks.

KEY CONCEPT Always place a semicolon or colon outside the final quotation mark. ■

EXAMPLES: One repair person said, "I can't do it for less than eighty dollars"; another indicated he could fix it for half that price!

She listed the ingredients for "an absolutely heavenly salad": spinach, mushrooms, hard-boiled eggs, and bacon.

KEY CONCEPT Place a question mark or exclamation mark inside the final quotation mark if the end mark is part of the quotation. ■

EXAMPLES: The reader asked, "How will the story end?"

The TV announcer exclaimed, "You just won the $10,000 jackpot!"

▶ **KEY CONCEPT** Place a question mark or an exclamation mark outside the final quotation mark if the end mark is not part of the quotation. ■

EXAMPLES: Did you hear that speaker when he said, "Just use your imagination to write science fiction"?

I was thrilled when they said, "And for president, Debbie Schmidt"!

With question marks and exclamation marks, only one mark is needed. In the following, the quotation is a question and the sentence is a statement. No period, however, is needed.

EXAMPLE: My mother asked, "Did you feed the animals?"

▶ **Exercise 36** **Adding Other Punctuation Marks** Copy the following sentences, adding any needed commas, colons, semi-colons, or end marks.

EXAMPLE: The young child shouted gleefully, "I believe in time travel"

ANSWER: The young child shouted gleefully, "I believe in time travel!"

1. Was it in *The Time Machine* that H. G. Wells wrote, "The Time Traveller, for so it will be convenient to speak of him"
2. He asked, "You have all heard what they have to say about this Fourth Dimension"
3. "The thing the Time Traveller held in his hand was a glittering metallic framework," wrote Wells, "scarcely larger than a small clock, and very delicately made"
4. The Time Traveller said "It is my plan for a machine to travel through time"
5. The Psychologist in *The Time Machine* exclaimed, "Of all the wild, extravagant theories"
6. The narrator said, "I am absolutely certain there was no trickery" then the time machine vanished.
7. Then, the Medical Man asked, "Do you seriously believe that that machine has travelled into time"
8. "Into the future or the past," responded the Time Traveller, "I don't, for certain, know which"
9. Did you believe it when the Time Traveller said, "I intend to explore time"
10. The characters agreed, "None of us quite knew how to take it"

▶ **More Practice**

Grammar Exercise Workbook
• pp. 177–180
On-line Exercise Bank
• Section 28.4
Go on-line:
PHSchool.com
Enter Web Code:
eek-1002

Get instant feedback! Exercise 36 is available on-line or on CD-ROM.

▶ **Exercise 37** Adding Quotation Marks and Other
Punctuation Marks Copy the following sentences, adding the
necessary quotation marks and punctuation.

EXAMPLE: Did you say Let's meet after the first showing of
             Somewhere in Time?

ANSWER: Did you say, "Let's meet after the first showing of
             Somewhere in Time"?

1. Does Mary Shelley's *Frankenstein* begin I am by birth a
   Genevese
2. So soon as the dazzling light vanished says the narrator
   the oak had disappeared
3. He acknowledges that Destiny was too potent
4. Her immutable laws had decreed my utter and terrible
   destruction said the Monster
5. He added It is with considerable difficulty that I remember
   the original era of my being
6. Did you realize who spoke the lines A strange multiplicity
   of sensations seized me
7. I saw, felt, heard, and smelt all at the same time continued the Monster
8. By degrees he said I remember, a stronger light pressed
   upon my nerves
9. Upon spotting the village, he exclaimed How miraculous
   did this appear
10. The teacher asked Do you know who the Monster is

◀ Critical Viewing
What information
might this girl be
reading that would
surprise or amaze
someone from the
nineteenth century?
[Deduce]

Quotation Marks
in Special Situations

Several special situations may occur when you write direct quotations. These include dialogues, quotations of more than one paragraph, and quotations within other quoted material.

First, consider the use of quotation marks when writing a dialogue—a direct conversation between two or more people. Use quotation marks to enclose the directly quoted conversation, and begin a new paragraph for each change of speaker.

KEY CONCEPT When writing dialogue, begin a new paragraph with each change of speaker. ■

EXAMPLE: The station attendant shouted from behind the hood, "You're a quart low on oil, Mrs. Lowell. Would you like me to put some in for you?"
"Yes, thank you," she replied.
"What kind of oil do you use in the car?"

In cases where one quotation consists of several paragraphs of quoted material, remember the following rule:

KEY CONCEPT For quotations longer than a paragraph, put quotation marks at the beginning of each paragraph and at the end of the final paragraph. ■

EXAMPLE: "Experts are noticing a change in the types of food Americans are buying. More fast foods, such as TV dinners and canned meals, are being purchased by food shoppers.
"Many people who used to spend a great deal of time preparing meals now work outside their homes. Researchers conclude that this is the reason more fast foods are being purchased.
"People need well-balanced meals. They now buy meals that can be prepared quickly. Thus, people today must spend more time at work and less time in the kitchen."

Occasionally, you may need to indicate a quotation contained within another quotation.

KEY CONCEPT Use single quotation marks for a quotation within a quotation. ■

EXAMPLE: The fund-raiser concluded, saying, "As we try to raise money for this worthy cause, let us not forget that old English proverb that says, 'Where there's a will, there's a way.' "

GRAMMAR IN
LITERATURE

from **Through the Tunnel**
Doris Lessing

Notice how the following dialogue is punctuated. How can you tell who is speaking?

"Have a nice morning?" she asked, laying her hand on his warm brown shoulder a moment.
"Oh, yes, thank you," he said.
"You look a bit pale." And then, sharp and anxious, "How did you bang your head?"

▷ **Exercise 38** Proofreading for Punctuation and Capitalization The following dialogue has no paragraphing, quotation marks, capitalization, or punctuation. Each number indicates a new speaker. Copy the dialogue, starting new paragraphs and adding the necessary quotation marks, capitalization, and punctuation.

(1) science fiction is not a modern invention said the speaker these subjects have been written about since ancient times what is the oldest example of science fiction that you can recall (2) tara raised her hand and said *the twilight zone* is pretty old (3) yes agreed the speaker can anyone think of any books (4) i used to read jules verne's books like *from the earth to the moon* said michael (5) jules verne wrote a great deal of early science fiction said the speaker enthusiastically other books were *journey to the center of the earth* and *off on a comet* (6) what about *star trek* said someone (7) yes *star wars* is my favorite another voice exclaimed (8) one at a time said the speaker attempting to control the crowd these are all great examples they are all similar because they are about the future and scientific and technological developments (9) another speaker added science fiction began in ancient times and still continues today ray bradbury said the whole history of mankind is nothing but science fiction he also said that science fiction is a combination of our dreams and our accomplishments (10) how do you feel about science fiction do you enjoy it asked tara

Underlining and Other Uses of Quotation Marks

In printed material, italics and quotation marks are used to set some titles, names, and words apart from the rest of the text. In handwritten or typed material, italics are not available, so underlining is used instead. Quotation marks, on the other hand, are used in both printed and handwritten materials.

This section gives rules for using underlining and quotation marks as well as rules for titles and names that require neither.

Underlining You should use underlining in your writing or typing to highlight titles of long written works and other major artistic works. You will also need to indicate certain names and foreign expressions by underlining them. In addition, you can use underlining to indicate words you want to emphasize.

▶ **KEY CONCEPT** Underline or italicize the titles of long written works and the titles of publications that are published as a single work. ■

Following are examples of titles you should underline:

TITLES OF WRITTEN WORKS THAT ARE UNDERLINED	
Titles of Books	<u>Dune</u> by Frank Herbert
Titles of Plays	<u>A Raisin in the Sun</u> by Lorraine Hansberry <u>The Man Who Came to Dinner</u> by Moss Hart
Titles of Periodicals	<u>Galaxy Science Fiction</u> <u>Journal of American History</u>
Titles of Newspapers	<u>The New York Times</u> the Palm Beach <u>Post</u> the Chicago <u>Sun-Times</u>
Titles of Long Poems	<u>Idylls of the King</u> by Alfred, Lord Tennyson <u>Gilgamesh</u>

Notes About *Newspaper Titles:* The portion of the title that should be underlined will vary from newspaper to newspaper. *The New York Times* should always be fully capitalized and underlined. Other papers, however, can usually be treated in one of two ways: *The Los Angeles Times* or the Los Angeles *Times.* Unless you know the true name of a paper, choose one of these two forms and use it consistently.

Many media presentations and pieces of artwork also require underlining.

KEY CONCEPT Underline the titles of movies, television and radio series, paintings, sculpture, and lengthy works of music. ■

MOVIE: <u>It's a Wonderful Life</u>, dir. Frank Capra

SERIES: <u>NOVA</u>, PBS

PAINTING: <u>The River</u>, Claude Monet

SCULPTURE: <u>The Minute Man</u>, Daniel Chester French

MUSIC: <u>The Water Music</u>, George Friedrich Handel

▼ **Critical Viewing**
In a research paper about Charles Lindbergh and this plane, how would you set off the name of the plane? [**Apply**]

▶**KEY CONCEPT** Underline the names of individual air, sea, space, and land craft. ■

AIR:	the <u>Spirit of St. Louis</u>
SEA:	the S.S. <u>Seagallant</u>
SPACE:	<u>Millenium Falcon</u>
LAND:	the <u>De Witt Clinton</u>

If a *the* precedes the name, do not underline or capitalize it because it is not considered part of the official name. Note also that a specific name given to a group of vehicles (for example, the Explorer spaceships) is capitalized but not underlined.

▶**KEY CONCEPT** Underline foreign words not yet accepted into English. ■

EXAMPLES: It is <u>verboten</u> to leave the building without permission. (German: forbidden)
Everyone said that the <u>coq au vin</u> was delicious. (French: chicken cooked in wine)

Because the process of accepting words and phrases into the English language is a continuous one, you cannot always be certain whether a phrase is still considered foreign. Check those doubtful phrases in the dictionary. If the word or phrase is not in the dictionary, you can generally consider it foreign. If it is in the dictionary, it will either be labeled with the name of the foreign language, in which case you should underline it, or it will be given standard treatment as an English word, in which case you should not underline it.

Certain other words need underlining because they are being used in a special way.

▶**KEY CONCEPT** Underline numbers, symbols, letters, and words used to name themselves. ■

NUMBERS:	When I say the number <u>three</u>, you start running.
SYMBOLS:	Is that an <u>!</u> at the end of that sentence?
LETTERS:	Is that first letter a <u>G</u> or an <u>S</u>?
WORDS:	She wrote the word <u>fluid</u>, but she meant <u>fluent</u>.

⚙ **Grammar and Style Tip**

In much formal writing, numbers are written out as words. In newspaper articles—especially sports articles—numerals are often used. When you are writing, use one method of presentation for numbers. Do not switch back and forth between numerals and spelled-out words

▶ **KEY CONCEPT** Underline words that you wish to stress. ■

EXAMPLE: We will need a <u>minimum</u> of six dollars for the trip.

Although the underlining of the word in this example clarifies the meaning of the sentence, do not overdo underlining for emphasis. In most cases, you should rely on precise word selection to convey your meaning and emphasis.

▶ **Exercise 39** Underlining Titles, Names, and Words Write and underline titles, names, or words that require underlining. If a sentence needs no correction, write *correct.*

1. The movie Planet of the Apes was released in 1968.
2. Reviews were published in The New York Times and many other papers.
3. The Planet of the Apes soundtrack was by Jerry Goldsmith.
4. Charlton Heston wrote about starring in the movie in An Actor's Life.
5. He had a small role in the sequel Beneath the Planet of the Apes.
6. Rod Serling, creator of The Twilight Zone series, wrote the screenplay for Planet of the Apes.
7. We thought we could see the movie in Radio City Music Hall.
8. The magazine Starlog has published many articles about the series.
9. The word apes was used to include the many species in the movies.
10. The surprise ending of the first movie was greeted as a true coup de théâtre.

Quotation Marks With Titles

Quotation marks are used to set off certain titles.

▶ **KEY CONCEPT** Use quotation marks around the titles of short written works. ■

SHORT STORY: "Nightfall" by Isaac Asimov
CHAPTER FROM A BOOK: "Five Days in a Mine" from *Kids With Courage*
SHORT POEM: "Mowing" by Robert Frost
ESSAY TITLE: "Style" by Maya Angelou
ARTICLE TITLE: "How to Organize Your Life"

More Practice

Grammar Exercise Workbook
• pp. 179–180
On-line Exercise Bank
• Section 28.4
  Go on-line:
  PHSchool.com
  Enter Web Code:
  eek-1002

Get instant feedback! Exercises 39 and 40 are available on-line or on CD-ROM.

Technology Tip

When writing about a particular work, use the search feature of a word-processing program to help you find every instance of the title. Make sure that you have correctly used quotation marks or underlining to set off the title.

▶ **KEY CONCEPT** Use quotation marks around the titles of songs, episodes in a series, and parts of a long musical composition. ■

EPISODE: "The Iran File" from *60 Minutes*

SONG TITLE: "Swing Low, Sweet Chariot"

PART OF A   "E.T. Phone Home"
LONG MUSICAL   from *E.T., The Extra
COMPOSITION: Terrestrial* soundtrack

Occasionally, you may refer to a title of one long work contained in a larger work. Singly, each title would require underlining; when used together, another rule applies:

▶ **KEY CONCEPT** Use quotation marks around the title of a work that is mentioned as part of a collection. ■

EXAMPLE: "Plato" from *Great Books of the Western World*

▶ **Exercise 40** **Using Quotation Marks With Titles** From each of the following sentences, copy the title and enclose it in quotation marks.

EXAMPLE: The story Euphio Effect is about the addictive quality of television.

ANSWER: "Euphio Effect"

1. The short poem Ozymandias by Shelley addresses some science-fiction themes.
2. Swift wrote science fiction and essays like A Modest Proposal.
3. Edgar Allan Poe ventured into science fiction with stories like The Tell-Tale Heart.
4. Bradbury's short story There Will Come Soft Rains was set thirty-five years into the future.
5. The Day the World Ended is the opening chapter of one of Kurt Vonnegut's books.

▲ **Critical Viewing** What type of musical composition might this orchestra be playing? Would you use underlining or quotation marks when writing the title of such a work? **[Speculate]**

Titles Without Underlining or Quotation Marks

Some titles require neither underlining nor quotation marks.

KEY CONCEPT Do not underline or place in quotation marks the names of the Bible, its books, divisions, or versions or other holy scriptures, such as the Koran. ■

EXAMPLE: He received a Bible as a gift.

KEY CONCEPT Do not underline or place in quotation marks the titles of government charters, alliances, treaties, acts, statutes, or reports. ■

EXAMPLES: the Declaration of Independence
Civil Rights Act

Exercise 41 Punctuating Different Types of Titles Copy the titles, enclosing them in quotation marks or underlining them. If neither quotation marks nor underlining is needed, write *correct*.

1. I listened to the Binary Sunset track on the Star Wars: A New Hope soundtrack.
2. A different soundtrack also includes music from Close Encounters of the Third Kind.
3. Here They Come! is an exciting piece from Star Wars.
4. Shadows of the Empire is a book set between the movies The Empire Strikes Back and Return of the Jedi.
5. Han Solo and The Princess is a short romantic composition by John Williams.
6. My essay Leia Through the Trilogy will have to be revised after the release of the first trilogy.
7. Nick submitted the poem A Jedi Knight to Amazing Stories for publication.
8. It was the source of the chapter My Time With Yoda in the book we are trying to write.
9. I thought we could model it after a long poem like Byron's The Prisoner of Chillon.
10. He thought a short poem like Poe's Dream Within a Dream was more inspiring.

More Practice

Grammar Exercise Workbook
• pp. 179–180
On-line Exercise Bank
• Section 28.4
  Go on-line:
  PHSchool.com
  Enter Web Code:
  eek-1002

 Text

Get instant feedback! Exercise 41 is available on-line or on CD-ROM.

Section
28.4

Section Review

GRAMMAR EXERCISES 42–47

Exercise 42 Punctuating Quotations Copy the following sentences, adding the appropriate quotation marks and other punctuation marks. Quoted phrases are underlined.

1. I thought C. S. Lewis wrote only children's books said Ryan
2. In a letter about *The Lion, the Witch, and the Wardrobe,* Lewis wrote Let us suppose that there were a land like Narnia
3. A frequent question is Why is my set of Narnia books numbered in the wrong order
4. So perhaps it does not matter very much in which order anyone reads them—C. S. Lewis
5. He wrote many scholarly essays about a variety of topics the teacher explained

Exercise 43 Punctuating Different Types of Titles Copy the titles, enclosing them in quotation marks or underlining them.

1. Kurt Vonnegut's book Welcome to the Monkey House includes the short story A Long Walk to Forever.
2. Some of the stories were originally published in magazines like The Atlantic Monthly or The Magazine of Fantasy and Science Fiction.
3. In 1970, he wrote a play called Happy Birthday, Wanda June.
4. The New York Times called Vonnegut "a laughing prophet of doom."
5. In his novel Cat's Cradle, the chapter called Nice, Nice, Very Nice introduces the reader to one of Bokonon's songs.

Exercise 44 Using Quotation Marks and Underlining Copy the following sentences, adding the appropriate quotation marks and properly punctuating any titles. The quoted phrase is underlined.

1. Roger Ebert writes E.T. is a movie full of surprises
2. It is a variation of the story The Wizard of Oz.
3. During the movie, E.T. watches an episode of Tom and Jerry and reads the Buck Rogers comic strip.
4. He also watches an old science-fiction movie called This Island Earth.
5. During the movie, Gertie hears the bedtime story Peter Pan.

Exercise 45 Find It in Your Reading Look through several movie, music, and book reviews to find examples of different kinds of titles and how they are set off. Then, look in these reviews for direct quotations and how they are punctuated. Copy the titles and quotations on a separate sheet of paper. Note the source of each.

Exercise 46 Find It in Your Writing Find a selection in your portfolio that has quoted material in it. Make sure that you have punctuated correctly with quotation marks.

Exercise 47 Writing Application Write a brief descriptive paragraph about your favorite science-fiction story. Include a quotation from one of your favorite characters. Be sure to properly punctuate your titles and quotations.

Dashes, Parentheses, and Hyphens

Commas, dashes, and parentheses all perform a similar function—that of separating certain words, phrases, and clauses from the rest of the sentence. To use these marks effectively, a writer must become acquainted with their different qualities. The comma is the most common mark and, therefore, draws the least attention to itself. The dash sets off material more dramatically. Parentheses set off technical or explanatory material clearly from the rest of the sentence.

This section will focus on the uses of the dash, parentheses, and hyphens, giving you rules to follow in using them.

Dashes

The dash, a long horizontal mark made above the writing line [—], functions to set off material in three basic ways:

KEY CONCEPT Use dashes to indicate an abrupt change of thought, a dramatic interrupting idea, or a summary statement. ■

In the following chart, examples illustrate the three basic uses of the dash.

USES OF THE DASH	
To indicate an abrupt change of thought:	I cannot believe how many free throws my brother missed—oh, I don't even want to think about it!
To set off interrupting ideas dramatically:	The slam dunk—which must be the most spectacular shot in basketball—makes a great addition to any highlight film. Next Saturday—do you have to work that day?—we want you to play basketball with us.
To set off a summary statement:	Point guard, shooting guard, small forward, power forward, and center—deciding which of these positions to play took me a full five minutes. To see his jersey hanging from the rafters—this was his greatest dream.

It may help you to know that words such as *all, these, this,* and *that* frequently begin a summary sentence preceded by a dash.

> **Theme: Basketball**
> In this section, you will learn about using dashes, parentheses, and hyphens. The examples and exercises are about basketball, past and present.
> **Cross-Curricular Connection: Physical Education**

Although nonessential appositives and modifiers are usually set off with commas, dashes are sometimes used.

▷ **KEY CONCEPT** Use dashes to set off a nonessential appositive or modifier when it is long, when it is already punctuated, or when you want to be dramatic. ■

APPOSITIVE: The cause of her happiness—winning the lead in the school play—pleased her parents.

MODIFIER: The drum major—who wore a white hat, a gold cape, and blue boots—led the band at the game.

Notice how the examples in the following charts each meet at least one of the three criteria in the rule.

USING DASHES WITH NONESSENTIAL APPOSITIVES	
Reasons for Use	**Examples**
Length	The selfish player—an egomaniac more concerned with his own statistics than his team—will not pass the ball.
Internal Punctuation	Some of the players on the team—for example, Karen, Susan, and Maria—always play well under pressure.
Strong Emphasis	The upsets—three games against superior teams—were totally unexpected.

Nonessential modifiers are generally set off only when they have internal punctuation or when strong emphasis is desired.

USING DASHES WITH NONESSENTIAL MODIFIERS	
Internal Punctuation	The coach—who, for some reason known only to himself, decided to take the star player out of the game—has no fans.
Strong Emphasis	Lara's three-point shot—which she has mastered so well that even a professional could take lessons from her—is helping us beat formidable teams.

You may recall that a parenthetical expression consists of words or phrases that are inserted into a sentence but have no essential grammatical relationship to it. Parenthetical expressions are often enclosed by dashes.

Grammar and Style Tip

Use dashes sparingly. As an alternative to commas, they can add emphasis and variety to your writing. If overused, however, they will lose their impact.

KEY CONCEPT Use dashes to set off a parenthetical expression when it is long, already punctuated, or especially dramatic. ■

Short parenthetical expressions do not need dashes.

EXAMPLE: I will, I think, go.

If the parenthetical expression is long or contains its own punctuation, you may want to set it off with dashes:

EXAMPLE: Their amazing winning streak—they won by two points Monday, by one point yesterday, and by one point today—cannot last long.

Use dashes if the parenthetical expression is a question or an exclamation:

EXAMPLE: After Karen hit the improbable shot at the buzzer—can you believe the ball swooshed in?— the fans carried her away on their shoulders.

Enclose a parenthetical expression in dashes if you want it to stand out from the rest of the sentence:

EXAMPLE: At the first practice of the season—the coach actually told us that we would hate every minute of every practice—he made us run for two hours.

Although the dash has many uses, be careful not to overuse it. Using an occasional dash adds sentence variety and interest; putting dashes in too often will make your thoughts seem confused and disjointed.

Exercise 48 Using the Dash On your paper, copy the following sentences, adding one or two dashes in each.

1. The rules of basketball I don't even want to think how many there are! have changed over the years.
2. Basketball enjoyed by people all over the world was invented in 1891 by James Naismith in Springfield, Massachusetts.
3. To create a game suited for indoor play this was Naismith's goal.
4. Naismith thought his game such a fantastic game would be appropriate for indoor play in the wintertime.
5. Many star basketball players for example, Dr. J, Oscar Robertson, and Michael Jordan often practiced a skill until they could execute it flawlessly.

More Practice

Grammar Exercise Workbook
• pp. 181–182
On-line Exercise Bank
• Section 28.5
Go on-line:
PHSchool.com
Enter Web Code:
eek-1002

Get instant feedback! Exercise 48 is available on-line or on CD-ROM.

Parentheses

Parentheses set off supplementary material not essential to the understanding of the sentence. Though not as dramatic as the dash, parentheses are the strongest separator you can use.

Rules for Using Parentheses The following rules will help you determine when using parentheses is appropriate:

▷ **KEY CONCEPT** Use parentheses to set off asides and explanations only when the material is not essential or when it consists of one or more sentences. ■

Note that you can take out all the material in parentheses in the following examples without altering the meaning:

EXAMPLES: The coaches will look at each player's skills (passing, shooting, and rebounding) when deciding which players to recruit for the all-star team. Nancy perfected her passing (only after years of practice) and will now start as her team's point guard.

We will pick up the new uniforms tomorrow. (The salesperson promised that she would have them ready.) By tomorrow night, we should be wearing our new jerseys.

▷ **KEY CONCEPT** Use parentheses to set off numerical explanations such as dates of a person's birth and death and around numbers and letters marking a series. ■

EXAMPLES: James Naismith invented the game of basketball at the request of Luther H. Gulick (1865–1918), who was his employer.

One half of the team's members (6) caught the flu just before the championship game.

You need to raise at least twenty thousand dollars ($20,000) to send the team to play the exhibition game in China.

Go to the sporting goods store and pick up these items: (1) basketball, (2) water bottle, (3) towels, and (4) bandages.

Who played in the NBA first: (a) Larry Bird, (b) Nate Archibald, or (c) Shaquille O'Neal?

In following these rules, be careful not to overuse parentheses. As with the dash, overuse can lead to choppy, unclear prose—something every good writer wants to avoid.

▼ Critical Viewing
Use a parenthetical comment about a nonessential element in a statement about this picture. **[Describe]**

Capitalizing and Punctuating With Parentheses

Several guidelines will help you punctuate and capitalize the material in parentheses.

KEY CONCEPT When a phrase or declarative sentence interrupts another sentence, do not use an initial capital or end mark inside the parentheses. ■

EXAMPLE: A frankfurter (my grandmother tasted one for the first time last summer) provides a delicious snack at a basketball game.

However, if the sentence is exclamatory or interrogative, the rule changes.

KEY CONCEPT When a question or exclamation interrupts another sentence, use both an initial capital and an end mark inside the parentheses. ■

EXAMPLE: College basketball games (These have featured some remarkable personalities!) reach millions of viewers every March through television.

There is another rule for sentences between sentences:

KEY CONCEPT With any sentence that falls between two complete sentences, use both an initial capital and an end mark inside the parentheses. ■

EXAMPLE: We drove to the high-school basketball championship. (It took more than five hours.) The high level of play surpassed our expectations.

Apply this rule for commas, semicolons, colons, and end marks:

KEY CONCEPT In a sentence that includes parentheses, place any punctuation belonging to the main sentence after the parenthesis. ■

EXAMPLES: Our shooting guard had an amazing season (averaging 45 points per game)!

The powerful center set several scoring records (22, to be exact), and he helped his team capture three championship titles.

More Practice

Grammar Exercise Workbook
• pp. 183–184
On-line Exercise Bank
• Section 28.5
  Go on-line:
  PHSchool.com
  Enter Web Code:
  eek-1002

> **Exercise 49** Using Parentheses On your paper, copy the following sentences, adding the necessary parentheses.

EXAMPLE: Pete Maravich Have you ever seen him play? displayed remarkable passing skills.

ANSWER: Pete Maravich (Have you ever seen him play?) displayed remarkable passing skills.

1. Michael Jeffrey Jordan Wasn't he the greatest basketball player ever? was born on February 17, 1963, in Brooklyn, New York.
2. After a stellar high-school career it must have been spectacular Jordan earned an athletic scholarship to attend the University of North Carolina.
3. Jordan He had such an amazing career! played the guard position at the University of North Carolina.
4. When did Jordan first win a college championship: a 1982, b 1983, or c 1984?
5. Jordan left college after his junior year. He was that good! He then began his career as a professional basketball player.

> **Exercise 50** Using Capitals and Punctuation With Parentheses On your paper, copy each sentence, making the necessary changes in capitalization and punctuation. If no corrections are needed, write *correct.*

EXAMPLE: When I finished the workout (what a tough one it was) I took a shower.

ANSWER: When I finished the workout (What a tough one it was!), I took a shower.

1. Shooting (do you know how to shoot a jump shot?) is one of the most important skills in basketball.
2. You can improve your jump shot (It's one of basketball's most effective offensive weapons!) only by practicing.
3. The jump shot (It's the most commonly used shot in competitive basketball today) takes much practice to perfect.
4. Your shooting form (So much depends on your mechanics.) is extremely important.
5. Maybe you can become a better shooter (you'd better hope so!) with practice.

▼ Critical Viewing
Add a parenthetical statement to the following sentence: *One of the players is my neighbor.* **[Apply]**

Hyphens

The hyphen is often mistaken for the dash. You should note that the hyphen is shorter than the dash.

Hyphens are used to divide certain numbers and parts of words, to join some compound words, and to divide words at the ends of lines. This section will focus on the rules governing the appropriate use of the hyphen.

With Numbers Some numbers written out as words require hyphens to separate the parts of the number:

KEY CONCEPT Use a hyphen when writing out the compound numbers *twenty-one* through *ninety-nine.* ■

EXAMPLE: The star of the team scored *forty-seven* points!

KEY CONCEPT Use a hyphen with fractions used as adjectives. ■

EXAMPLE: The recipe calls for *one-half* cup of mushrooms.

In the preceding example, the fraction functions as an adjective. If it were used as a noun, the hyphen would then be omitted.

EXAMPLE: *Three fourths* of the junior varsity team came to the practice.

With Word Parts Some word parts require the use of a hyphen:

KEY CONCEPT Use a hyphen after a prefix that is followed by a proper noun or an adjective. ■

EXAMPLE: The school's basketball season started in *mid-September.*

KEY CONCEPT Use a hyphen in words with the prefixes *all-, ex-, and self-,* and in words with the suffix *-elect.* ■

EXAMPLES: all-star   self-addressed
              ex-teacher   senator-elect

Always check to make sure that a complete word joins the prefix or suffix. When these prefixes and suffixes combine with only part of a word, no hyphen is needed.

INCORRECT: ex-ecutive
CORRECT: executive

With Compound Words Hyphens are used with some compound words:

KEY CONCEPT Use a hyphen to connect two or more words that are used as one word unless the dictionary gives a contrary spelling. ■

The use of hyphens in compound words is a matter of changing style. The dictionary should always be your authority on this matter. Three examples, hyphenated in most dictionaries, follow.

EXAMPLES: merry-go-round   crow's-feet   off-season

KEY CONCEPT Use a hyphen to connect a compound modifier that comes before a noun. ■

EXAMPLES: The clouds cast a *grayish-blue* tint on the water.

The *well-prepared* team played with confidence.

If a compound modifier comes after the noun, however, the hyphen is dropped.

BEFORE: We got the pizza from an *all-night* deli.
AFTER: A deli open *all night* delivered the pizza.

If, however, the dictionary shows the compound modifier with a hyphen, the word remains hyphenated regardless of its position in the sentence.

EXAMPLES: We water-skied behind a *jet-propelled* boat.

Our ski boat was *jet-propelled.*

KEY CONCEPT Do not use hyphens with compound modifiers that include words ending in *-ly* or with compound proper adjectives or compound proper nouns acting as adjectives. ■

INCORRECT: The *badly-damaged* car sat in the body shop.
CORRECT: The *badly damaged* car sat in the body shop.
INCORRECT: The *North-American* continent has many mountains.
CORRECT: The *North American* continent has many mountains.

> **💡 Spelling Tip**
>
> Most words that end in *ball*—for example, *baseball, basketball, football,* and *volleyball*—describe a particular sport. They are spelled without a hyphen or a space.

For Clarity Certain letter combinations may cause a reader to misread a passage. Inserting a hyphen can prevent this.

KEY CONCEPT Use a hyphen within a word when a combination of letters might otherwise be confusing. ■

EXAMPLES: *co-op*   versus   *coop*
            re-lay versus   *relay*

   Unusual combinations of words can also be made clearer with hyphens.

KEY CONCEPT Use a hyphen between words to keep the reader from combining them erroneously. ■

EXAMPLES: a new *car-buyer*   versus   a *new-car* buyer
            three-point margins   versus   three *point-margins*

Exercise 51 Using Hyphens in Numbers, Word Parts, and Words On your paper, rewrite the sentences, adding necessary hyphens. Use a dictionary when in doubt. If no hyphen is needed, write *correct*.

EXAMPLE: The politician congratulated the senator elect.
ANSWER: The politician congratulated the senator-elect.

1. The history of basketball is filled with many all star players.
2. Some players have been self proclaimed stars; some have been legitimate stars.
3. Many players have become famous because of their offensive ability.
4. Moses Malone—a powerful center with a body like a tank—became famous because of his mind boggling rebounding.
5. Although he was not an ex marine, he often appeared to possess the posture of a soldier.
6. He displayed awe inspiring prowess when going after rebounds.
7. He routinely grabbed twenty six or twenty seven rebounds in a game when others felt lucky to grab ten.
8. He quickly set all time rebounding records.
9. Moreover, from the beginning of his career, he displayed the self assurance of a veteran.
10. Not surprisingly, he won numerous fans, including thousands from the non English speaking world.

More Practice

Grammar Exercise Workbook
• pp. 185–186
On-line Exercise Bank
• Section 28.5
  Go on-line:
  PHSchool.com
  Enter Web Code:
  eek-1002

Get instant feedback! Exercises 51 and 52 are available on-line or on CD-ROM.

Exercise 52 **Using Hyphens to Avoid Ambiguity** On your paper, copy the sentences, adding hyphens to make each sentence clear.

EXAMPLE: We had to relay the wood floor.

ANSWER: We had to re-lay the wood floor.

1. The coaches who attended the awards ceremony were dressed so neatly that it was obvious that they had repressed their suits for the event.
2. The organizers decided to repair presenters and coaches.
3. Unfortunately, one of the coaches could not resign a promising point guard for his team.
4. The point guard was semi literate and had failed his classes.
5. Another coach was elated about a twelve year old boy he had spotted playing at a local playground.
6. The boy was apparently a selftaught basketball prodigy who played as if he were nineteen years old.
7. When I asked him how to prepare for next season, he gave me a selfhelp book on strength training.
8. The coauthor of the book is a famous sportswriter from the Midwest.
9. The writer claims that basketball is considered to be a semiinfectious disease in her state.
10. After I left the ceremony, I could not reenter the arena because I no longer had my standing room ticket.

▶ Critical Viewing What hyphenated words might you use in a written description of this picture? [Connect]

Using Hyphens at the Ends of Lines

"To divide or not to divide?" This question comes up again and again when a writer reaches the end of a line of writing. In such a situation, you must decide whether to put one last word on the line, drop the word down to the next line, or divide it. The decision should be based on certain rules. The most important rule is the one regarding syllables.

KEY CONCEPT If a word must be divided, always divide it between syllables. ■

If you are in doubt about how to divide a word into syllables, check a dictionary. It will show, for example, that the word *intricately* has four syllables, *in tri cate ly,* and it can be divided as in the following example:

EXAMPLE: The coach's plan was a model of intri-
             cately plotted teamwork.

Always place the hyphen at the end of the first line—never at the start of the next line.

INCORRECT: The fans and players will continue to sup
             -port this coach as long as he wins.

CORRECT: The fans and players will continue to sup-
             port this coach as long as he wins.

Prefixes and suffixes provide a natural place for division.

KEY CONCEPT If a word contains word parts, it can almost always be divided between the prefix and the root or the root and the suffix. ■

PREFIX: ex-tend   out-side   mis-fortune
SUFFIX: hope-less   four-some   fif-teen

If the suffix is composed of only two letters, however, avoid dividing the word between the root and suffix.

▶ **Critical Viewing** Identify three multisyllable words based on this picture. Between what letters in each word could you use a hyphen at the end of a line? [**Apply**]

In addition to avoiding a two-letter suffix, there are a number of other words that should not be divided. Be on the lookout for one-syllable words that sound like two-syllable words or look as if they are long enough to be two syllables. Do not divide them.

INCORRECT: lod-ge   clo-thes   thro-ugh
CORRECT: lodge   clothes   through

Each of these examples consists of only one syllable; therefore, dividing them is inappropriate. You will also need to watch divisions that result in a single letter standing alone.

> **KEY CONCEPT** Avoid dividing a word so that a single letter stands alone. ■

INCORRECT: stead-y   a-ble   e-vict
CORRECT: steady   able   evict

> **KEY CONCEPT** Avoid dividing proper nouns and proper adjectives. ■

The following divisions have traditionally been considered undesirable.

INCORRECT: We recently hired Sylvia Rodri-
              guez.

              I just finished eating a Mexi-
              can banana.

You may occasionally need to divide a word that already contains a hyphen.

> **KEY CONCEPT** Divide a hyphenated word only after the hyphen. ■

If you use the word *apple-pie* as an adjective, you would hyphenate it. When dividing the word at the end of a line, divide it only at the hyphen.

INCORRECT: Plans for a strong team appeared to be in ap-
              ple-pie order.

CORRECT: Plans for a strong team appeared to be in apple-
              pie order.

🗹 Spelling Tip

The spell-check feature in most word-processing programs will not recognize uncommon family names and may highlight them as incorrect. Double-check your spelling of proper nouns.

KEY CONCEPT Avoid dividing a word so that part of the word is on one page and the remainder is on the next page. ■

Often, chopping up a word in this way will confuse your readers or cause them to lose their train of thought.

Exercise 53 Using Hyphens to Divide Words In the sentences below, if a word has been divided correctly, write *correct.* If not, divide the word correctly or write it as one word if it cannot be divided.

EXAMPLE: Have you given much tho-
                      ught to this problem?

ANSWER: Have you given much thought to this problem?

1. Do you want to play basketball with my teammates?
2. We play basketball ever-
   y Saturday morning.
3. The star of our team (Did you know we had a star?) is my sister-in-law.
4. Do you know how much of the world's population enjoys playing basketball?
5. Millions of people enjoy watching or playing basketball.
6. Some people like to play basketball indoors; others like playing outdoors.
7. Basketball has long been dominated by powerful centers.
8. Wilt Chamberlain was one of basketball's most dominant centers.
9. Did you and your friends know that Wilt Chamberlain once scored 100 points in a professional game?
10. He did so against the New York Knicker-
    bockers in 1962.

Exercise 54 Using Hyphens in Written Work On a piece of looseleaf paper with the margins marked, copy a paragraph from your social studies textbook. Use the margin guidelines to keep the margins of your report even. Break words as necessary to stay within the margin guidelines.

More Practice

Grammar Exercise Workbook
• pp. 185–186
On-line Exercise Bank
• Section 28.5
  Go on-line:
  PHSchool.com
  Enter Web Code:
  eek-1002

 Text

Complete the exercises on-line! Exercises 53 and 54 are available on-line or on CD-ROM.

Section 28.5

Section Review

GRAMMAR EXERCISES 55–60

Exercise 55 Using the Dash On your paper, copy the following sentences, adding one or two dashes in each.

1. Basketball which has long been thought to be an urban game is extremely popular in the suburbs.
2. Modern players are much more muscular it's rare to see a lanky player anymore than players from the past.
3. This does not mean that basketball is a game only for giants thank goodness!
4. People of average height less than six feet tall have had basketball careers.
5. Tyrone "Muggsy" Bogues who enjoyed a stellar career at Wake Forest University in the late 1980's and went on to play professionally stands just five feet three inches tall.

Exercise 56 Using Parentheses On your paper, rewrite the following sentences using the necessary parentheses and capitalization.

1. Earvin Johnson did you know that he was called Magic Johnson? was one of the best point guards in basketball.
2. Johnson My dad saw him play was born in 1959 in Lansing, Michigan.
3. He starred as the point guard perhaps the most important position on the team of the Michigan State team.
4. By the time he retired in 1991, he had won numerous All-Star honors 12.
5. When did Magic Johnson first lead his professional team to a world championship: a 1980, b 1981, or c 1982?

Exercise 57 Using Hyphens in Numbers, Word Parts, and Words Rewrite the sentences that need hyphens. Use a dictionary when in doubt. If no hyphen is needed, write *correct.*

1. Wilt Chamberlain was one of the most intimidating players in basketball.
2. He was a perennial allstar during his long professional basketball career.
3. An ex high school standout, he enjoyed a stellar college career at the University of Kansas.
4. Chamberlain played for three seasons with the University of Kansas team— that university had well trained teams.
5. During his long career, he demon strated great self discipline.

Exercise 58 Find It in Your Reading Explain the use of hyphens in the excerpt from "Rare Air: Michael on Michael."

. . . And teams played me one-on-one at North Carolina. They never double-teamed me.

Exercise 59 Find It in Your Writing Look through your portfolio. Find examples of hyphens, parentheses, and dashes you have used. Explain why you used each mark.

Exercise 60 Writing Application Imagine that a talent scout has come to watch you play a sport. Write five sentences that you would want to say following the game. Use the guidelines below.

1. Use ex-teacher in a question.
2. Use the word second-class in a sentence about the sport.
3. Use a dash to set off a statement.
4. Use parentheses to set off an interrupting idea.
5. Use the dash to indicate an abrupt change of thought.

Section 28.6 Apostrophes

Insects comprise the largest class of animals on the planet. They are social animals, and they are extremely organized. So, too, are the rules governing apostrophes.

Though the apostrophe ['] is classified as a punctuation mark and not as a letter, its misuse can result in the misspelling of many words. The apostrophe serves two purposes: to show possession and to indicate missing letters. In most cases, you must place the apostrophe between the letters of the word, not before or after it. Thus, misplacement of the apostrophe leads to spelling errors. This section will provide you with rules so that you can use the apostrophe correctly.

Theme: Bugs

In this section, you will learn about the use of apostrophes. The exercises and examples are about insects and other bugs.

Cross-Curricular Connection: Science

GRAMMAR IN LITERATURE

from **Leiningen Versus the Ants**
Carl Stephenson

Some of the apostrophes in this excerpt indicate missing letters in contractions. Those words are marked in blue. The apostrophe in the red word indicates possession.

"Listen, lads!" he shouted. "You're frightened of those beggars, but I'm proud of you. There's still a chance to save our lives—by flooding the plantation from the river. . . ." Leiningen then remembered the paralyzing effect of ants' venom.

Apostrophes With Possessive Nouns

An apostrophe must be used to indicate possession or ownership with nouns.

With Singular Nouns As shown in the examples, the following rule applies to most singular nouns:

▶ **KEY CONCEPT** Add an apostrophe and *s* to show the possessive case of most singular nouns. ■

EXAMPLES:
The wing of the *insect* becomes the *insect's* wing.

The sections of the *ant* become the *ant's* sections.

The mandibles of the *cockroach* become the *cockroach's* mandibles.

The legs of the *centipede* become the *centipede's* legs.

The eye of the *fly* becomes the *fly's* eye.

The forelegs of a *mantis* become a *mantis's* forelegs.

When a singular noun ends in *s*, as in the last example, you can still follow this style in most cases. Ancient and classical names are the exception.

EXAMPLE: Zeus' thunderbolt.

With Plural Nouns Showing possession with plural nouns ending in *s* or *es* calls for a different rule:

▶ **KEY CONCEPT** Add an apostrophe to show the possessive case of plural nouns ending in *s* or *es*. ■

EXAMPLES:
The wings of the *bees* become the *bees'* wings.
The tracks of the *caterpillars* become the *caterpillars'* tracks.
The larvae of the *moths* become the *moths'* larvae.

▲ Critical Viewing
In a complete sentence that contains the possessive of *insect,* identify and describe three features of this insect. **[Describe]**

Not all plural nouns end in *s* or *es*, however. Another rule will help you form the possessive case of these nouns:

KEY CONCEPT Add an apostrophe and *s* to show the possessive case of plural nouns that do not end in *s* or *es*. ■

EXAMPLES: The books of the *men* become the *men's* books.

The songs of the *people* become the *people's* songs.

With Compound Nouns Sometimes, you will find that a noun showing ownership consists of several words.

KEY CONCEPT Add an apostrophe and *s* (or just an apostrophe if the word is a plural ending in *s*) to the last word of a compound noun to form the possessive. ■

This rule refers to names of businesses and organizations, names with titles, and hyphenated compound nouns.

APOSTROPHES WITH COMPOUND NOUNS	
Businesses and Organizations	The Good Earth's menu the Lions Clubs' motto
Names With Titles	the Secretary of Defense's visit Edward VIII's abdication
Hyphenated Compound Nouns Used to Describe People	my father-in-law's glasses the secretary-treasurer's pen

With Expressions Involving Time and Amounts If you use possessive expressions involving time or amounts, you will need to use an apostrophe.

KEY CONCEPT To form possessives involving time or amounts, use an apostrophe and *s* or just an apostrophe if the possessive is a plural ending in *s*. ■

TIME: a day's journey   six years' time
AMOUNT: one quarter's worth   fifty cents' worth

To Show Joint and Individual Ownership When two nouns are involved, take care to show ownership accurately.

▶**KEY CONCEPT** To show joint ownership, make the final noun possessive. ■

EXAMPLES: Roger and Jeremy's ant farms
(They share the same ant farms.)

the husband and wife's car
(They share one car.)

▶**KEY CONCEPT** To show individual ownership, make each noun possessive. ■

EXAMPLES: Roger's and Jeremy's ant farms
(Each has his own ant farm.)

the husband's and wife's cars
(Each owns a separate car.)

Checking Your Use of the Rules Often, confusion results over the application of the various rules because writers forget to determine whether they are writing about a singular noun or a plural noun. First, determine whether the owner is singular or plural. Then, consider the word before the apostrophe you are going to add. If you place the apostrophe correctly, the letters to the left of the apostrophe should spell out the owner's complete name. Look at the checking technique in this chart:

CHECKING THE USE OF APOSTROPHES		
Incorrect	**Explanation**	**Correction**
Jame's car	The owner is not *Jame,* but *James.*	James's car
one boys' book	The owner is not *boys,* but *boy.*	one boy's book
two girl's lunches	The owner is not *girl,* but *girls.*	two girls' lunches

Exercise 61 Using Apostrophes With Single-Word Possessive Nouns Copy the underlined nouns, which may be singular or plural, putting them into the possessive form when necessary. For sentences that do not require possessive forms, just write the underlined word.

EXAMPLE: <u>Insects</u> sizes can vary tremendously.
ANSWER: Insects'

1. The <u>insects</u> class is the largest in the world.
2. The <u>class</u> distribution is all over the world.
3. Insects outnumber all other animal <u>species</u>.
4. Some <u>moths</u> wingspans can be twelve inches.
5. A stick <u>insect</u> length can also be twelve inches.

Exercise 62 Using Apostrophes With Compound Nouns Copy the underlined nouns, putting them into the possessive form.

EXAMPLE: I share my sister-in-law fear of insects.
ANSWER: sister-in-law's

1. <u>Life-cycle</u> lengths vary from insect to insect.
2. The <u>seventeen-year locust</u> maturation period is from thirteen to seventeen years.
3. The <u>jaws</u> function in an insect is to crush food.
4. Some insects live in a highly organized society, with the <u>leader</u> role being taken by the queen.
5. My <u>entomological society</u> rules for membership are strict.

Exercise 63 Using Apostrophes to Show Joint and Individual Ownership From each of the following sentences, copy the underlined words, changing them to show joint or individual ownership as the instructions indicate.

1. <u>Plant and insect</u> relationships are often necessary to the plant. (joint)
2. <u>Bee and ant</u> organizations are quite complex. (individual)
3. <u>Wasps and termites</u> social interactions are also quite unique. (individual)
4. Some <u>wasps and flies</u> maturation period is a matter of days. (individual)
5. Certain insects live by one of two methods; <u>parasitism and predation</u> features are quite different. (individual)

More Practice

Grammar Exercise Workbook
• pp. 187–188
On-line Exercise Bank
• Section 28.6
  Go on-line:
  PHSchool.com
  Enter Web Code:
  eek-1002

Text

Get instant feedback! Exercises 61, 62, and 63 are available on-line or on CD-ROM.

Apostrophes With Pronouns

Some pronouns showing ownership require an apostrophe:

KEY CONCEPT Use an apostrophe and *s* with indefinite pronouns to show possession. ■

EXAMPLES:
another's	nobody's	one's
anyone's	someone's	everybody's

If you form a two-word indefinite pronoun, add the apostrophe and the -*s* to the last word only.

EXAMPLES: nobody else's   one another's

Possessive personal pronouns do not need an apostrophe.

KEY CONCEPT Do not use an apostrophe with the possessive forms of personal pronouns. ■

With the words *yours, his, hers, theirs, its, ours,* and *whose,* no apostrophe is necessary. These already show ownership.

EXAMPLES: Looking at the butterfly collections, I decided *yours* far outdistanced the other entries.
Its beautiful colors drew everyone's notice.

Pay special attention to the possessive forms *whose* and *its* because they are easily confused with the contractions *who's* and *it's.* Just remember that *whose* and *its* show possession.

PRONOUNS: *Whose* wallet is this?

Its chimes rang out clearly.

Who's and *it's,* on the other hand, are contractions of the words *who is* and *it is.* They both require apostrophes to indicate the missing letters.

CONTRACTIONS: *Who's* responsible for naming insects?

It's up to whoever discovers a new species to name it.

▼ Critical Viewing
What possessive pronoun would you use to refer to the colony of these insects? [Apply]

▶ **Exercise 64** Proofreading for Correct Use of Apostrophes

On a separate sheet of paper, rewrite each sentence. Correct any errors in the use of apostrophes.

EXAMPLE: That hive is her's.

ANSWER: That hive is hers.

1. A parasite finds it's nourishment in other living creatures.
2. A social hierarchy is usually led by a queen, and all the offspring are her's.
3. Workers are usually male, and their's is the responsibility to keep the society going.
4. Some ants take over others colonies and use them for workers.
5. The eyes of an insect are on its head.
6. Some insect societies are almost as complex as our's.
7. My fear of insects is greater than yours.
8. I thought this was your ant farm, but it must be some-one's else.
9. An insect has a nervous system who's center is a nerve cord running from the head to the abdomen.
10. An insect's heart is not as complicated as your's or mine's.

▶ **More Practice**

Grammar Exercise Workbook
• pp. 187–188
On-line Exercise Bank
• Section 28.6
Go on-line:
PHSchool.com
Enter Web Code:
eek-1002

▼ **Critical Viewing**
Identify two possessive nouns suggested by this picture. What possessive pronouns could take the place of these nouns? **[Apply]**

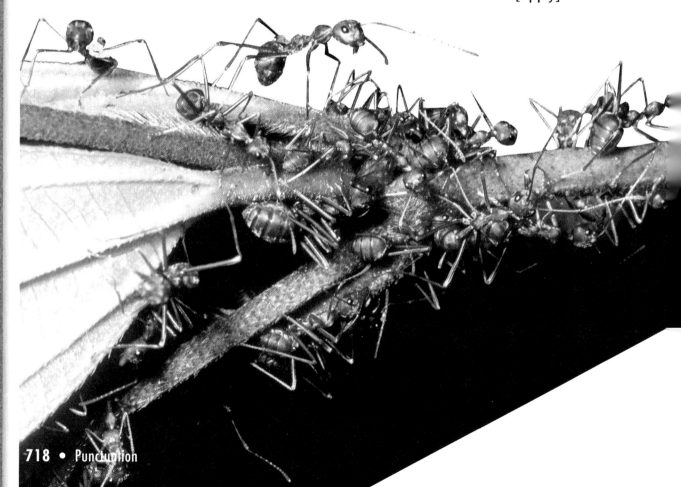

Apostrophes With Contractions

The meaning of a contraction is implied by its name. It is a word contracted in size by the removal of some letter or letters and the insertion of an apostrophe to indicate the missing letters. This leads to the following basic rule for contractions:

▶ **KEY CONCEPT** Use an apostrophe in a contraction to indicate the position of the missing letter or letters. ■

Contractions With Verbs Verbs are often used in a contracted form. Look at the following chart, noticing how often these verb contractions are used in common speech patterns.

COMMON CONTRACTIONS WITH VERBS		
Verbs with *not*	are not = aren't do not = don't	was not = wasn't were not = weren't
Pronouns with *will*	I will = I'll you will = you'll	she will = she'll they will = they'll
Pronouns and nouns with the verb *be*	I am = I'm you are = you're	who is = who's Mark is = Mark's
Pronouns with *would*	I would = I'd he would = he'd	we would = we'd they would = they'd

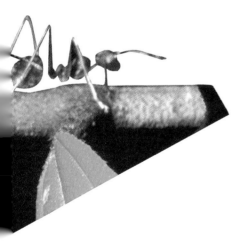

One special contraction changes letters as well as drops them: *Will not* becomes *won't* in the contracted form.

Try to avoid most verb contractions in formal writing. They tend to make your style more informal than you may wish.

INFORMAL: He's promised that he'll hide the beetle if we're still afraid of it.

FORMAL: He has promised that he will hide the beetle if we are still afraid of it.

Contractions With Years In writing about years, insert an apostrophe in places where a number is left out.

EXAMPLES: Decathlon Champion of '75
the snowstorm of '03

Contractions With *o', d', and l'* These letters followed by the apostrophe make up the abbreviated form of the words *of the* or *the* as spelled in several different languages.

EXAMPLES:　　o'clock　　　d'Angelo
　　　　　　　O'Sullivan　　l'Abbé

As you can see, these letters and apostrophes are combined most often with surnames.

Contractions With Dialogue When writing dialogue, you may want to keep the flavor of the speaker's individual speaking style. Therefore, use any contractions the speaker might use. You may also want to include a regional dialect or a foreign accent. Because speech often includes pronunciations with omitted letters, you should insert apostrophes to show those changes.

EXAMPLES:　　C'mon—aren't you comin' fishin'?
　　　　　　　'Tis a fine spring morn we're havin'.
　　　　　　　That li'l ant is aworkin' hard!

As with most punctuation, overuse reduces the effectiveness and impact, so watch the overuse of the apostrophe with contractions—even in dialogue.

▶ **Exercise 65** **Apostrophes With Contractions** If a contraction is underlined in the following paragraph, write the original two words. If two words are underlined, write the contraction they would form.

EXAMPLE:　　Aren't people who study insects called entomologists?

ANSWER:　　Are not

(1) Insects <u>do not</u> have lungs but a network of tubes to carry air through the body. (2) They are invertebrates, which means that they <u>haven't</u> got a backbone. (3) <u>They've</u> been found on land and in most types of water. (4) Insect predators <u>cannot</u> live without feeding on other insects. (5) Most species <u>don't</u> grow in the same way people do. (6) <u>They are</u> able to reach adulthood by metamorphosis. (7) Insects that are scavengers <u>will not</u> eat living plants or animals. (8) Some parasitic insects are so small that you <u>would not</u> be able to see them without a microscope. (9) An <u>insect's</u> often distinguished by its three body parts. (10) My friend studies insects and says that <u>it's</u> an interesting field.

More Practice

Grammar Exercise
Workbook
• pp. 189–190
On-line Exercise Bank
• Section 28.6
　Go on-line:
　PHSchool.com
　Enter Web Code:
　eek-1002

Get instant feedback! Exercises 65 and 66 are available on-line or on CD-ROM.

Special Uses of the Apostrophe

An apostrophe is also used to show the plural of numbers, symbols, letters, and words used to name themselves.

▷ **KEY CONCEPT** Use an apostrophe and *s* to write the plurals of numbers, symbols, letters, and words used to name themselves. ■

EXAMPLES: There are two *8*'s in that number.
You need two more *?*'s.
Her *b*'s and *d*'s all look the same.
A's and *an*'s cause confusion.

▷ **Exercise 66** Using the Apostrophe in Special Cases Copy the following sentences, adding an apostrophe and an *s* to numbers, symbols, letters, and words whenever necessary. Underline all items in italics.

EXAMPLE: On my last report card, I got all *A* and *B*.
ANSWER: On my last report card, I got all <u>A</u>'s and <u>B</u>'s.

1. On my two papers on insects, I got *95*.
2. I might get *100* on my next papers.
3. I spelled beetle with too many *e*.
4. I must have written twenty *entomology* in that paper.
5. People in their *20* generally have a lot of energy.
6. Europeans put an extra line in their *7* to show that they are different from their *1*.
7. Insect abdomens are segmented into *10* or *11*.
8. Insect legs are usually arranged in *2*.
9. Is it all right to use *&* in my paper, or should I spell out the word?
10. She is allergic to bees, so she has two *Rx* in case she gets a bee sting.

▶ Critical Viewing Describe the appearance of this bug. What possessive noun did you use? **[Apply]**

Section Review

GRAMMAR EXERCISES 67–72

Exercise 67 Using Apostrophes With Single-Word and Compound Possessive Nouns Put each underlined word into the possessive if necessary. If not, write *correct*.

1. An <u>insect</u> circulatory system is quite simple.
2. The <u>heart</u> function is to keep the body cavity filled with blood.
3. The <u>walls</u> of the heart contract to force the blood out.
4. The <u>Department of the Environment</u> concerns about the loss of habitats are well founded.
5. My <u>brother-in-law</u> hobby is butterfly collecting.

Exercise 68 Using Apostrophes to Show Ownership Put each of the underlined words in the correct possessive form as indicated in parentheses.

1. The <u>antennae and eyes</u> function is to send stimuli to the insect's brain. (individual)
2. <u>Butterflies and moths</u> physical characteristics are similar. (individual)
3. <u>Compound eyes and simple eyes</u> uses in an insect are different. (individual)
4. <u>Moths and butterflies</u> metamorphoses are complete metamorphoses. (joint)
5. Some <u>beetles and flies</u> form of metamorphosis is known as hypermetamorphosis. (joint)

Exercise 69 Using Apostrophes Correct the use of apostrophes in the underlined words.

1. <u>His'</u> butterfly collection is quite extensive.
2. I believe <u>your's</u> is quite interesting, too.

3. A lepidopterist is someone <u>who's</u> interest is butterflies and moths.
4. A butterfly spends <u>it's</u> larval stage as a caterpillar.
5. <u>Its</u> very hungry during this stage.
6. <u>Who's</u> bug cage is that?
7. At 7 <u>oclock</u>, the fly will lay her eggs.
8. <u>Jame's</u> cricket has six legs.
9. <u>Nobodys</u> butterfly hatched early.
10. It is nothing compared to <u>their's</u>.

Exercise 70 Find It in Your Reading Read the following excerpt from "Leiningen Versus the Ants." Explain the use of each apostrophe.

. . . The planter's chin jutted; they hadn't got him yet, and he'd see to it they never would. While he could think at all, he'd flout both death and the devil.

Exercise 71 Find It in Your Writing Look through your portfolio. Find examples of apostrophes in contractions and for possession. Make sure that you used apostrophes correctly.

Exercise 72 Writing Application Write five sentences of your own using the following guidelines.

1. Write a sentence that distinguishes *who's* from *whose*.
2. Write two sentences that distinguish joint and individual ownership using forms of *my friend and I*.
3. Write a sentence using *will not* as a contraction.
5. Write a sentence using the possessive of *complete sentence*.

Chapter

28 Chapter Review

GRAMMAR EXERCISES 73–81

> **Exercise 73** **Using End Marks**
Write the proper end mark for each of the following sentences.

1. What beautiful colors on those dragonflies
2. Are there fossils of damselflies and dragonflies
3. The tiny openings in their outer skeletons are called spiracles
4. Hey Those compound eyes are enormous
5. Look at that dragonfly warming in the sun

> **Exercise 74** **Using Commas**
Rewrite the following sentences, adding commas where necessary.

1. Where there are hollow trees honeybees make their hives.
2. Beekeepers used to keep bees in baskets but now they use wooden boxes.
3. Bees store nectar honey and pollen in honeycombs.
4. The queen the drone and the worker make up the three castes in the honeybee community.
5. During their six weeks of life worker bees build the honeycomb clean the hive feed the young and defend the colony.
6. They are armed with straight barbed stingers.
7. The worker bees produce royal jelly a protein-rich substance from special glands.
8. This is fed to the larvae but after the first three days larvae are fed bee bread a mixture of pollen and honey.
9. Queen bees however are fed royal jelly for the duration of their development.
10. The stages of development that make up the complete metamorphosis are egg larva pupa and adult.

11. The worker bees use small soft lumps of wax to build the honeycomb.
12. Returning to the hive bees use either the round dance or the wagging dance to communicate.
13. Bees use different movements to communicate distance direction and location of food.
14. Pollen baskets filled by bees using small brushes on their hind legs carry pollen.
15. The study of insects which I find fascinating is called entomology.

> **Exercise 75** **Using Semicolons and Colons** Rewrite the following sentences, adding semicolons and colons where necessary.

1. Fireflies are actually beetles they are not really flies.
2. The light flashes steadily It is a code that sends messages.
3. Other insects use their sense of smell to find mates however, fireflies use light.
4. Each species seems to have its own signal it can be recognized by all members of the group.
5. A code is a complicated combination of speed and brightness It is like a visual Morse Code.
6. Carnivorous fireflies are found in one genus Photuris.
7. They will mimic the signals of other species as a result, they attract unsuspecting prey.
8. Female fireflies lay their eggs soon after mating at this time, they fly to damp areas near water.
9. Eggs pass from the insect's body through a tube the ovipositor.
10. There are several varieties of fireflies the pyralis, the insect-eating fireflies, and the glowworms.

Chapter Review • **723**

Chapter Review Exercises cont'd.

▶ **Exercise 76** Using Quotation Marks and Underlining Copy the following sentences, using capitalization, punctuation marks, quotation marks, and underlining where appropriate. Quoted phrases are underlined so that you will know where they begin and end.

1. Did Muhammad Ali say float like a butterfly, sting like a bee
2. In his book The Lord of the Flies, William Golding wrote ralph wept for the end of innocence.
3. Golding's play The Brass Butterfly was published in 1958.
4. Isn't Papillon, the French word for butterfly, the name of a movie starring Steve McQueen and Dustin Hoffman I asked
5. Robert Schumann, himself a composer of works including Papillons, exclaimed about Chopin hats off, gentlemen—a genius
6. Puccini's opera, Madame Butterfly, was initially a failure until Puccini revised it.
7. I didn't know The Flight of the Bumble Bee is a song from an opera called Tsar Saltan said Steve.
8. Rudolf Friml was an American composer he added who wrote the operetta called The Firefly.
9. Really exclaimed my sister my favorite book is The Very Lonely Firefly
10. Also, A Bug's Life and Beetlejuice are two of my favorite movies she told me.

▶ **Exercise 77** Using Dashes, Parentheses, and Hyphens Copy the following sentences, adding dashes, parentheses, and hyphens where necessary.

1. Butterflies and moths Did you know they make up an order called Lepidoptera? have many similarities and differences.
2. Some of their habits for example, flying by day or flying by night distinguish the two groups of insects.

3. Most butterflies are brightly colored while many moths are dull colored.
4. Butterflies have scale covered wings.
5. Moths rest with their wings flattened at least, some of them do.
6. The bodies of butterflies and moths have three main divisions: 1 head, 2 thorax, and 3 abdomen.
7. The body parts are made from a material called *chitin* pronounced kite-in.
8. Moth antennae they can sometimes be hairlike and sometimes featherlike differ from butterfly antennae which have a knob at the ends.
9. The butterfly proboscis which is used to feed on nectar in the flowers remains coiled up under the head.
10. Of the types of butterflies and moths 160,000 more than three quarters are moths.

▶ **Exercise 78** Using Apostrophes Write the proper form of the word or words that require apostrophes in the following sentences. If a sentence is correct, write *correct*.

1. These insects usually lay thousands of eggs.
2. Butterflies and moths larvae contain the cells that produce adult insects.
3. A caterpillars first meal is its own eggshell.
4. It contains nutrients essential to the insects growth.
5. All caterpillars skin is very flexible.
6. The caterpillars head contains a brain and sense organs.
7. A hawkmoths caterpillar feeds on the bed straw plant.
8. The goat moths caterpillar lives in an apple tree, eating the trees wood for almost four years.
9. Moths dont eat holes in your clothes; their larvae do.
10. The caterpillars spinnerets produce silk threads, which make up the cocoon.

▶ **Exercise 79** Proofreading
Sentences for Punctuation Copy the
following sentences, and use all of the
rules of punctuation to add or correct the
punctuation marks. Quoted phrases are
underlined so that you will know where
they begin and end.

1. In Lewis Carrolls, Alices Adventures in
   Wonderland, the Caterpillar says <u>I
   don't see</u>
2. The pupa the third, major stage in a
   butterfly or moths life transforms the
   caterpillar into an adult
3. A butterfly pupa chrysalis seems lifeless, in fact extensive changes are taking place: within the cocoon
4. Inside the shell the caterpillar is as
   Ben Franklin wrote, <u>snug / As a bug
   in a rug</u>
5. Cocoons change in order to survive
   They adapt their color and size to
   blend in with the surroundings
6. While the flambeaus chrysalis is
   rugged looking an owl butterflys
   appearance resembles a fragile dead
   leaf
7. Do the giant swallowtail once called
   the Orange Dog and the great mormon
   look like pieces of wood
8. The head; wings; abdomen; and thorax
   can be seen through the chrysalis Did
   you know some are bright pink while
   they develop over several weeks
9. Arthur Twidles illustrations including
   one called A Collector at Work decorate
   his book "Beautiful Butterflies of the
   Tropics".
10. The term butterfly may come from the
    butter colored fly; the name for one of
    the first butterflies to appear each
    spring in Europe
11. Moses Harris published an early work
    on butterflies The Aurelian in 1766
12. Butterflies are protected by law: Some
    countries forbid collecting and scien-
    tists must obtain a permit in order to
    study rare species

13. Moths that cannot see red light are
    attracted to smelly sugary liquids and
    will feed at night
14. Male butterflies and day flying moths
    are brightly colored but the females
    are much duller
15. <u>Remember</u> as James Gleick wrote <u>a
    butterfly stirring the air today in
    Peking can transform storm systems
    next month in New York</u>

▶ **Exercise 80** Proofreading a
**Passage for Punctuation and
Capitalization** On a separate sheet of
paper, copy the following passage. Correct
capitalization and punctuation.

have you ever considered an insect for a
pet? most people—and i used to agree with
them—would rather walk, over hot coals,
than spend time in a room with a bug. mr.
janus, my science teacher; changed my
mind. My Science Class at lakeview high
school in northridge, pennsylvania, raised
monarch butterflies. monarchs fly south to
mexico in early november. mr. janus used
to say, "not all insects are nasty, biting
creatures. the butterfly is a graceful and
delicate thing" My whole class enjoyed the
project and we learned a lot from Mr.
Janus.

▶ **Exercise 81** Writing Application
Write a summary of a movie or a book
you have recently enjoyed. Include one or
two direct quotations as well as the title of
the work and the titles of similar works.

Standardized Test Preparation Workshop

Revising, Editing, and Proofreading

Standardized tests often include items that measure your ability to revise, edit, and proofread. These sections may be set up as individual items, or you may be given a hypothetical peer-review situation. The following items will give you practice with both formats.

Test Tip

If several choices seem to correct an error, examine each more closely. One choice probably introduces a new error and should be eliminated.

Sample Test Items	Answers and Explanations

Directions: Choose the best way to write each underlined section. If the underlined section needs no change, mark the choice "Correct as is."
 	
 "Look" she called, "up there"!
 (1)
 	
 1 A "Look she called, "up there."
  B "Look," she called, "up there!"
  C "Look"! she called "up there."
  D Correct as is
	
	 The correct answer is *B*. As a part of the direct quotation, the exclamation mark belongs before the quotation mark. All other punctuation in this passage is correct.

Directions: You have been asked to read and critique a classmate's essay. Read the essay, and think about the suggestions you would make. Then, answer the multiple-choice questions that follow.
 	
 1 The science teacher directed the students;
 2 parents, and other guests to look at the
 3 migrating birds.
 	
 1 What is the BEST change to make to line1?
  A Capitalize *science.*
  B Change the semicolon to a comma.
  C Delete the semicolon.
  D Change *students* to *student's.*
	
	 The correct answer is *B*. Items in this series should be separated by commas, not semi-colons.

▶ **Practice 1** **Directions:** Choose the best way to write each underlined section. If the underlined section needs no change, mark the choice "Correct as is."

Last call for flight 1233 to Washington
(1)
D.C announced the ticket agent, "The
(2)
345 PM. flight to Washington, D.C. will be

leaving the gate immediately"!

1 A "Last call for flight 1233 to Washington D.C" announced the ticket agent.

 B "Last call for flight 1233 to Washington, D.C" announced the ticket agent.

 C "Last call for flight 1233 to Washington, D.C.," announced the ticket agent.

 D Correct as is

2 F "The 3:45 PM flight to Washington, D.C., will be leaving the gate immediately!"

 G "The 3:45 P.M. flight to Washington, D.C., will be leaving the gate immediately!"

 H "The 3:45 PM flight to Washington, D.C., will be leaving the gate immediately!"

 J Correct as is

▶ **Practice 2** **Directions:** After having each student write an essay about a cultural event, your English teacher has asked the class to exchange papers and critique each other's essays. You have received Beth's essay. As you read her composition, think about what suggestions you would make. Then, answer the multiple-choice questions that follow.

1 Joy Brandt of the Carolina Book Festival
2 announced "The nominees this year are
3 among the best ever we are very excited
4 to have such distinguished candidates".

1 What is the BEST way to rewrite lines 1–4?

 A Joy Brandt, of the Carolina Book Festival, announced, The nominees this year are among the best ever." We are excited to have such distinguished candidates."

 B Joy Brandt, of the Carolina Book Festival, announced, "The nominees this year are among the best ever. We are excited to have such distinguished candidates".

 C Joy Brandt, of the Carolina Book Festival, announced, "The nominees this year are among the best ever. We are excited to have such distinguished candidates."

 D Joy Brandt, of the Carolina Book Festival, announced, The nominees this year are among the best ever. We are excited to have such distinguished candidates."

Cumulative Review

MECHANICS

▶ **Exercise A** Using Capitalization

Copy all the items in the following sentences that require capitalization, adding the missing capitals.

1. james russell lowell was the editor of the magazine *the atlantic monthly.*
2. before and after the american civil war, he called for stories emphasizing local color.
3. george washington cable, a writer from the south, had served in the confederate army.
4. in new orleans, louisiana, he began to write for the new orleans *times-picayune* newspaper.
5. cable's stories about creole life, descendants from the french or spanish settlers, in scribner's magazine, made him famous in the united states and great britain.
6. his novels include *old creole days* and *the creoles of louisiana.*
7. joel chandler harris created the character of uncle remus.
8. he learned local dialects working on *the countryman,* a newspaper published by a southern plantation owner.
9. the stories contain animals like brer rabbit that act like humans.
10. harris's stories provide a record of oral african american folk tales from the southeastern united states.
11. francis hopkinson smith was both a painter and a writer.
12. the book *colonel carter of cartersville* presents a picture of life in the confederacy.
13. kate chopin depicted louisiana's cajun and creole cultures.
14. two of her short-story collections, *bayou folk* and *a night in acadie,* were published in the 1890's.
15. her last novel, *the awakening,* was both her most famous and most controversial.

▶ **Exercise B** Using End Marks, Commas, Semicolons, and Colons

Write the following sentences, inserting end marks, commas, semicolons, and colons where necessary.

1. Sarah Orne Jewett wrote short stories about people in a New England state Maine
2. Was her most famous collection *The Country of the Pointed Firs* written in 1896
3. Hey I also enjoyed *Deephaven A Country Doctor* and *The Life of Nancy*
4. Bret Harte was born in Albany New York however he moved to California
5. Did he write "The Luck of Roaring Camp" "The Outcasts of Poker Flat" and "Plain Language from Truthful James" for the magazine he edited *Overland Monthly*
6. These are classics of regional American literature his works are noted for their tales of life in mining towns
7. Through connections he became a United States consul in Krefeld Germany subsequently he was transferred to Glasgow Scotland
8. While in these positions he continued to write including two successful stories "An Ingénue of the Sierras" and "A Protégée of Jack Hamlin's"
9. Joaquin Miller the pen name of Cincinnatus Hiner Miller lived with Native Americans edited a newspaper became a judge and wrote poetry
10. Yes He settled in California and he incorporated the local color of the American West into his poetry

▶ **Exercise C** Using All the Rules of Punctuation Write the following sentences, inserting end marks, commas, semicolons, colons, quotation marks, underlining, dashes, parentheses, hyphens, and apostrophes where necessary.

1. The book whose full title is Poems of Sidney Lanier, Edited by His Wife contains works previously published in magazines like The Century Magazine Scribner's Magazine and Lippincott's Magazine
2. Sidney Laniers 1842 1881 best known poem is The Marshes of Glynn
3. Is that the poem written in 1879 that reads Beautiful glooms, soft dusks in the noon-day fire
4. After serving in the Confederate army performing as a flutist in a Baltimore Maryland orchestra and lecturing on English literature Lanier became renowned for his poetrys musical quality
5. Yes Lanier certainly lived his life in a different fashion from that of another famous poet of that era Emily Dickinson
6. Emily Dickinson Can you believe that most of her poetry wasnt published until four years after her death was born in Amherst Massachusetts
7. Her poems how very personal and profound they are include the themes of love death and immortality.
8. Didnt Dickinson 1830 1886 live her life mostly in seclusion
9. Most of Dickinsons pocms are numbered rather than named and No 254 reads 'Hope' is the thing with feathers—
10. A three volume edition of her letters to friends was published in 1955 more than seventy years after her death

▶ **Exercise D** Proofreading Dialogue for Capitalization and Punctuation On a separate sheet of paper, rewrite the following dialogue, inserting the proper capitalization, punctuation, and indentation. (Each new speaker is indicated by an asterisk.)

* hey joanna have you ever heard of the humorists christine asked *dont you mean comedians replied joanna *no ted was telling me about writers like josh billings petroleum v nasby and artemus ward *well joanna commented their names certainly are funny. they were all very creative pseudonyms used by the writers who satirized people and politics using local dialects *that sounds very effective joanna said were these pieces written in *yes these writers were able to influence public opinion interrupted christine nasbys writing was published in newspapers like the *findlay jeffersonian* and the *toledo blade* *were these normal articles or opinions *Christine explained david ross locke wrote letters from the character nasby, an adopted persona during the civil war the letters helped the side of the north after the war he turned his attention to causes like temperance and womens rights *can we still read any of this writing today joanna asked *nasby's letters were published in books like *the nasby papers* and there is also the collection called *josh billings, his sayings* *carlos who had just entered the room asked hey are you talking about artemus ward the character created by charles farrar browne *not yet said christine but that is a similar story ward was a traveling showman who wrote with horribly incorrect spelling and grammar

▶ **Exercise E** WRITING APPLICATION
Write a brief first-person narrative that includes dialogue in which you and a friend discuss a book, a movie, or a television show that was made in America. Be sure to follow all the rules of capitalization and punctuation.

Sentence Diagraming Workshop

Subjects, Verbs, and Modifiers

To diagram a sentence with just a subject and a verb, draw a horizontal line, place the subject on the left, the verb on the right, and then draw a vertical line to separate the subject from the verb.

EXAMPLE:
$$\overset{S}{\text{Kathleen}} \overset{V}{\text{laughed.}}$$

Kathleen	laughed

When you diagram adjectives, place them on slanted lines directly below the nouns or pronouns they modify. Similarly, place adverbs on slanted lines directly below the verbs, adjectives, or other adverbs they modify.

EXAMPLE:
$$\overset{\text{ADV}}{\text{Quite}}\ \overset{\text{ADJ}}{\text{hesitant,}}\ \overset{\text{ADJ}}{\text{my}}\ \text{sister}\ \overset{\text{ADV}}{\text{did not answer}}\ \overset{\text{ADV}}{\text{quickly.}}$$

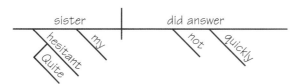

Orders and directions whose subjects are understood to be *you* are diagramed in the usual way, with parentheses around the understood subject. Inverted sentences also follow the usual subject-verb order in a diagram. The capital letter shows which word begins the sentence.

EXAMPLES:

ORDER
Stand up.

QUESTION
How are you?

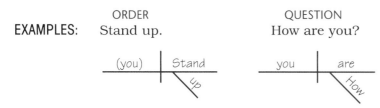

Usually when *there* or *here* begins a sentence, it will function as an adverb modifying the verb. In this case, it should be diagramed on a slanted line below the verb.

Sometimes, however, *there* is used simply to get the sentence started. In this case, it is an expletive. Diagram an expletive by placing it on a short horizontal line above the subject. Diagram interjections and nouns of direct address in the same way.

EXAMPLES: EXP There was a storm. INT N of DA Alas, my friend, you lost.

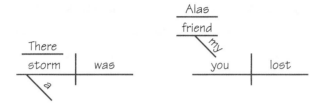

Exercise 1 Diagraming Subjects, Verbs, and Modifiers

Correctly diagram each sentence.

1. Mr. Ricardo, come here.
2. The ship wandered quite aimlessly.
3. Swallows soared overhead.
4. The beautiful white waterfall thunderously cascaded down.
5. There should be a parade today.

Adding Conjunctions

Conjunctions are diagramed on dotted lines drawn between the words they connect. In the example, coordinating conjunctions are used to join both adjectives and adverbs.

EXAMPLE: CONJ CONJ The small but fierce dog barked loudly and steadily.

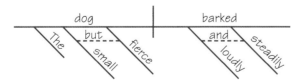

Conjunctions that connect compound subjects and compound verbs are also written on dotted lines drawn between the words they connect. Notice in the example on the next page how the horizontal line of the diagram is split so that each part of a compound subject or verb appears on a line of its own. Notice also the position of the correlative conjunctions *neither* and *nor.*

EXAMPLE:

CONJ   CONJ   CONJ
Neither Amanda nor Lisa wrote or called.

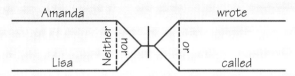

When a modifier modifies both parts of a compound subject or verb, however, it is placed under the main line of the diagram. In the example below, the adverb *confidently* modifies both parts of the compound verb, so it is placed under the main line.

EXAMPLE:

ADV   ADJ   ADJ
Confidently, the children and their parents

ADV   ADV
walked in and sat down.

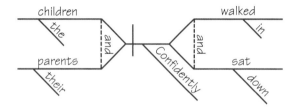

Exercise 2 Diagraming Sentences With Conjunctions

Correctly diagram each sentence.

1. Wood can be painted or varnished.
2. Must pork and bacon be cooked thoroughly?
3. The unusual and colorful kite soared gracefully and slowly dipped.
4. Two obviously unhappy children and their desperately uncomfortable parents fidgeted anxiously and waited very impatiently.
5. The mechanical toy frog will not only croak but also jump far.

Complements

In a diagram, a direct object is positioned on the main horizontal line after the verb. A short vertical line is added to separate it from the verb. An indirect object is placed on a horizontal line extended from a slanted line directly below the verb.

EXAMPLES:

DO   IO   DO
Sue wore a gold chain.   I gave Ted advice.

Because an objective complement helps complete the meaning of a direct object, they are placed side by side. A short slanted line is added to separate the direct object from the objective complement.

EXAMPLE: The President named him Chief of Staff.

Both predicate nominatives and predicate adjectives are also placed on the main horizontal line after the verb. A short, slanted line is used to separate them from the verb.

EXAMPLES: My dog is a spaniel.   We felt grouchy.

As the following example shows, compound complements are diagramed by splitting the lines on which they appear. Conjunctions are placed on dotted lines drawn between the words they connect.

EXAMPLE: We showed Ellie and Tom the zoo and the museum.

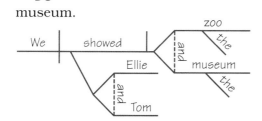

▶ **Exercise 3** Diagraming Complements Correctly diagram each sentence.
1. The irritable little boy pushed his food away.
2. This remarkable but true story taught Sally and me something.
3. His shy and cautious manner gave June and me courage.
4. The fresh, clean mountain air felt wonderful.
5. Her husband is a friend and a companion.

Prepositional Phrases

The diagram for a prepositional phrase has a slanted line for the preposition and a horizontal line for the object of the preposition. Modifiers are placed on slanted lines below the horizontal line. Adjective phrases are placed directly below the noun or pronoun they modify. Adverb phrases are placed directly below the verb, adjective, or adverb they modify.

EXAMPLE: The child *with the red ball* skipped *up the hill.*

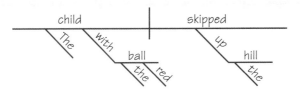

An adjective phrase that modifies the object of the preposition of another prepositional phrase goes below the other phrase.

EXAMPLE: I had salad *with pineapple in it.*

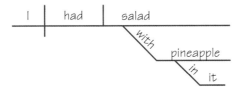

A prepositional phrase with a compound object is diagramed in the same way as the other compound parts of a sentence. The following example shows an adjective phrase that modifies a direct object.

EXAMPLE: We need a house *with three bedrooms and a den.*

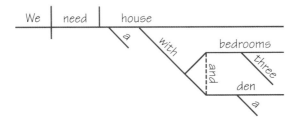

> **Exercise 4** **Diagraming Prepositional Phrases** Correctly diagram each sentence.
> 1. They flew in a private airplane across the Rockies.
> 2. Water trickled down Mark's neck.
> 3. Select a detergent for clothing with greasy stains and ground-in dirt.
> 4. Without much hope, Becky argued for more time.
> 5. Corina lives in an apartment with a balcony.

Appositives and Appositive Phrases

An appositive is placed in parentheses beside the noun or pronoun it identifies, renames, or explains. Any adjectives or adjective phrases included in an appositive phrase are placed directly beneath the appositive.

APPOSITIVE PHRASE

EXAMPLE: Harriet Danby, *her friend for many years*, is a lawyer.

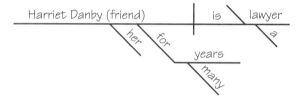

> **Exercise 5** **Diagraming Appositives and Appositive Phrases** Correctly diagram each sentence.
> 1. Gladys was a pianist, a very talented performer.
> 2. I know the author of that book, one of the top bestsellers.
> 3. The rat, a rodent, has one pair of upper incisors.
> 4. Mario prepared the meal, a lavish feast with six courses.
> 5. Their staircase, a spiral flight of steps, needs repair.

Participles and Participial Phrases

Because participles act as adjectives, they are placed directly beneath the noun or pronoun they modify. Unlike adjectives, however, participles are positioned partly on a horizontal line that extends from the slanted line. An adverb or adverb phrase that modifies a participle is placed below it. When a participle has a complement, the complement is also placed in its normal position, on the horizontal line with the participle, separated from the participle by a short vertical line. See the example on the next page.

PARTICIPIAL PHRASE

EXAMPLE: *Carefully reviewing books for children,* Russell stays busy.

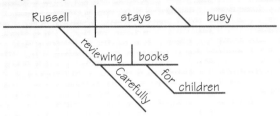

Exercise 6 **Diagraming Participles and Participial Phrases**
Correctly diagram each sentence.
1. He held a basket brimming with goodies.
2. Going without sleep, many volunteers worked into the night.
3. This deserted island offers peace and tranquillity.
4. From the beehive came a loud buzzing noise.
5. Stalling without warning, the car caused a traffic jam.

Gerunds and Gerund Phrases

A gerund that acts as a subject, direct object, or predicate nominative is diagramed on a pedestal above the main horizontal line of the diagram. Modifiers and complements that are part of a gerund phrase are added to the diagram in the usual way. Notice the shape of the line on which the gerund rests.

GERUND PHRASE

EXAMPLE: The lease forbids *keeping any pets on the premises.*

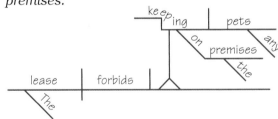

A gerund or gerund phrase that acts as an indirect object or an object of a preposition is placed on a line slanting down from the main horizontal line.

GERUND PHRASE

EXAMPLE: His lecture gave *traveling to South America* new dimensions.

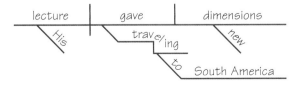

A gerund or gerund phrase that acts as an appositive is placed on a pedestal, in parentheses, next to the noun or pronoun it accompanies. The example below shows a diagram containing an appositive modifying a direct object.

GERUND PHRASE

EXAMPLE: We mastered one sport, *playing tennis.*

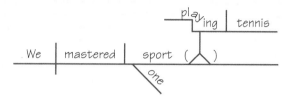

> **Exercise 7** **Diagraming Gerunds and Gerund Phrases**
> Correctly diagram each sentence.
> 1. His favorite activity was hiking through the woods.
> 2. Achieving the position of senator will be very difficult.
> 3. Their ability to harmonize made songwriting exciting.
> 4. Clark's fear, injuring his elbow, kept him on the bench.
> 5. All of Jill's friends like helping her with her projects.

Infinitives and Infinitive Phrases

Infinitives and infinitive phrases can act as nouns, adjectives, or adverbs. An infinitive acting as a noun is generally diagramed on a pedestal just as a gerund is, but the line on which the infinitive rests is simpler.

INFINITIVE PHRASE

EXAMPLE: She wanted *to show us her stamp collection.*

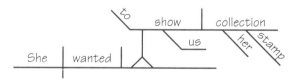

If an infinitive phrase has a subject, add it at the left.

INFINITIVE PHRASE

EXAMPLE: We asked her *to stay.*

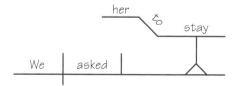

An infinitive acting as an adjective or adverb is diagramed much as a prepositional phrase is.

INFINITIVE

EXAMPLE: Beth was proud *to try.*

When an infinitive in a sentence does not include the word *to,* add it to the sentence diagram in parentheses.

INFINITIVE PHRASE

EXAMPLE: Clancy helped me *climb the ladder to the attic.*

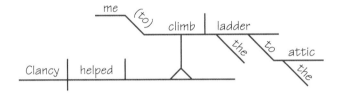

> **Exercise 8**   Diagraming Infinitives and Infinitive Phrases
Correctly diagram each sentence.
1. Gordon's greatest accomplishment was to write a novel about etiquette during the sixteenth century.
2. Her mother let Susan go to the movies.
3. To focus on just one problem would be advisable.
4. Her inclination was to tell him the truth about his idea.
5. The person to see about tickets has left.

Compound Sentences

To diagram a compound sentence, just diagram each independent clause separately. Then, join them at the verbs with a dotted line on which the conjunction or semicolon is placed.

INDEPENDENT CLAUSE

EXAMPLE: *A gentle breeze blew across the lake,* and

INDEPENDENT CLAUSE
the raft floated inland.

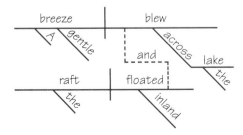

> **Exercise 9** **Compound Sentences** Diagram each sentence.
>
> 1. His temperature is high, but he remains alert.
> 2. Should I plant this cherry tree in that corner, or would you prefer it near the fence?
> 3. The steak was perfect, and the salad was excellent, but the dessert was too sweet.
> 4. Joan has little sense of her own worth; she never asserts herself.
> 5. Yesterday, we cleaned the attic and filled boxes with useless items; later, we went to the dump.

Complex Sentences

Complex sentences have an independent clause and one or more adjective, adverb, or noun clauses. Each clause is placed on a separate horizontal line.

Adjective Clauses To diagram a sentence with an adjective clause, first diagram the independent clause. Then, diagram the adjective clause beneath it. Connect the two clauses with a dotted line that extends from the modified noun or pronoun in the independent clause to the relative pronoun or relative adverb in the adjective clause. The position of the relative pronoun changes depending on its function in the adjective clause. In the following example, the relative pronoun is acting as the direct object of the adjective clause.

ADJECTIVE CLAUSE

EXAMPLE: My friend *whom you met yesterday* just called.

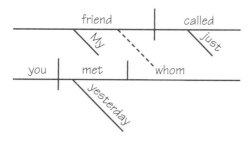

When a relative pronoun acts as an object of a preposition or as an adjective or when a clause is introduced by a relative adverb, the dotted line must be bent to connect the clauses.

ADJECTIVE CLAUSE

EXAMPLE: I need time *when I can study.*

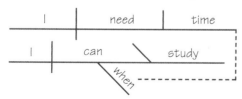

Adverb Clauses The main difference between a diagram for an adjective clause and one for an adverb clause is that the subordinating conjunction for an adverb clause is written on the dotted line. This line extends from the modified verb, adjective, adverb, or verbal in the main clause to the verb in the adverb clause.

ADVERB CLAUSE

EXAMPLE: To look *before you leap* is good advice.

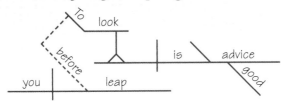

Noun Clauses When diagraming a sentence with a noun clause, first diagram the independent clause. Then, place the entire noun clause on a pedestal extending upward from the position the noun clause fills in the sentence. Notice that the pedestal meets the noun clause at the verb.

NOUN CLAUSE

EXAMPLE: *Whatever you decide* is fine with me.

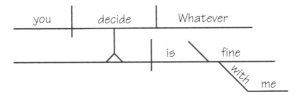

When an introductory word in a noun clause has no function in the clause, it is written alongside the pedestal.

NOUN CLAUSE

EXAMPLE: The question, *whether Jonas is truly sorry*, will be revealed in the next episode.

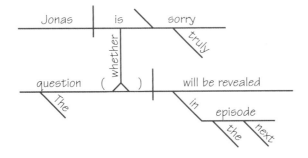

▷ **Exercise 10** Diagraming Complex Sentences Correctly diagram each sentence.
1. Barbara McClintock is a scientist whom I greatly admire.
2. He drives as if he were in a race.
3. They told us that they would be late.
4. We hope to complete this job while time remains.
5. The side lawn is the place where we always played croquet.

Compound-Complex Sentences

To diagram a compound-complex sentence, begin by diagraming and connecting each of the independent clauses just as you would if you were diagraming a compound sentence. Then, diagram and connect each subordinate clause.

ADVERB CLAUSE

EXAMPLE: *When we bought our microwave oven,* we considered that brand, but we decided *that it was too expensive.*

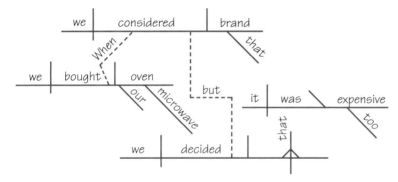

▷ **Exercise 11** Diagraming Compound-Complex Sentences Correctly diagram each sentence.
1. Because it rained, we missed the game that had been scheduled, but we still had a good time.
2. We waited until the plane landed, and then we rushed to the gate where the passengers would enter.

Academic
and Workplace
Skills

Chapter 29

Speaking, Listening, Viewing, and Representing

Speaking, listening, viewing, and representing are all unique forms of communication used for conveying and receiving information. Speaking and listening both use language to represent ideas. Therefore, understanding language is the key to developing good speaking and listening skills.

Forms of viewing and representing also use language to convey information, but always in combination with visual representations. Learning how to interpret these visual representations and seeing how they work with language to present meaning is the first step in improving your viewing and representing skills.

All together, speaking, listening, viewing, and representing are the building blocks of communication and of one's view of the world.

▲ **Critical Viewing**
Which of these students is speaking? Which is listening most attentively? Explain your choices. **[Infer]**

Speaking
and Listening Skills

In school, good speaking and listening skills are essential for success. Learning how to take part in group discussions and how to give a well-prepared oral presentation are two activities that require good speaking skills.

Critical listening skills are important also. Learning how to become a critical listener will enable you to understand and evaluate the most important points in a speaker's message.

Speaking in a Group Discussion

In school, you will most likely participate in a number of *group discussions,* or informal meetings used to openly discuss ideas. These group discussions will focus on subjects you are studying or activities being planned. To get the most from a group discussion, you have to learn to participate in it.

Communicating Effectively Effective communication means thinking before speaking. Plan the points you want to make and how you will express them. Organize these points in a logical order. Think of examples or supporting facts to illustrate your points. Also, remember to speak clearly, pronouncing words slowly and carefully.

Asking Questions Get in the habit of asking questions. Asking questions can help you clarify your understanding of another speaker's ideas. Questions can also be used to call attention to possible errors in the speaker's points or areas of confusion.

Making Relevant Contributions The information or ideas you choose to contribute should be related to the topic being discussed. When you do contribute, clearly show how your ideas are connected to the topic.

▶ **Exercise 1** Policy Discussion With three to five other students, hold a fifteen-minute group discussion about the benefits and drawbacks of a particular school policy. After the discussion, write a brief journal entry about how you used the strategies above as you participated.

▶ **More Practice**

Academic and Workplace Skills Activity Book
• p. 1

Speaking in Public

Giving a presentation in front of an audience is *public speaking.* By learning more about speeches and speechmaking, you can improve your public-speaking skills.

Understanding Different Types of Speeches

There are four kinds of speeches: informative, persuasive, entertaining, and extemporaneous. To make your speech more effective, use language—informal, standard, or technical—that suits your purpose and is appropriate for the audience.

▶ **KEY CONCEPT** Choose the kind of speech you will give and the language you will use by thinking about your purpose and what your audience is like. ■

- An **informative speech** explains an idea, a process, or an object. Facts must be presented in a clear, organized way. Also, in an informative speech, technical language may be used to more accurately describe the topic.

- A **persuasive speech** is usually spoken in standard English; it tries to make the audience agree with the speaker's position or to take some action. Opinions need to be supported by statements or facts.

- An **entertaining speech**, spoken both in standard and informal language, offers the audience an enjoyable experience. Entertaining passages may be included in other kinds of speeches to offer variety or to provide emphasis.

- An **extemporaneous speech** is an informal speech given to suit an occasion, event, or audience and does not rely on a prepared manuscript but on the speaker's knowledge and ability to improvise.

▲ Critical Viewing
Do you think this athlete is giving a prepared speech or an extemporaneous speech? Explain. **[Deduce]**

▶ **Exercise 2** Listing Speech Topics and Audiences List two possible topics and the intended audience for each of the four types of speeches discussed on this page.

Preparing and Presenting a Speech

Once you know what kind of speech you will give and have chosen an appropriate topic, you will need to gather and organize information and practice your speech before you present it.

▷ **KEY CONCEPT** To prepare your speech, research your topic, cite reliable sources, and organize your thesis. ■

Gather Valid Proof From Reliable Sources Research the subject using the library or other reliable sources to find valid proof, or conclusive evidence, to support your claims. Research is especially important when preparing an informative or persuasive speech.

Use Appropriate Appeals to Support Your Arguments The evidence you use to support your claims should be appropriate to your topic. For example, if you are writing a persuasive speech on the benefits of a healthy diet, it would be appropriate to research and cite evidence from nutritional experts, but not from the founder of a fast-food chain.

Present a Clear Thesis To help you organize and develop your thesis, make an outline. Begin your outline with any necessary background material. Arrange information in a rational sequence. Include logical points to support your message. Then, transfer this information to index cards to which you can refer while presenting your speech.

▷ **KEY CONCEPT** When presenting your speech, use rhetorical forms of language and verbal and nonverbal strategies. ■

Use Rhetorical Strategies Let the audience know your important points by repeating key words and phrases. Keep your speech lively and interesting by using active verbs and colorful adjectives. Create a sense of rhythm in your speech through the use of parallel phrases or parallel series of words.

Use Verbal and Nonverbal Strategies Vary the pitch of your voice and the rate at which you speak, and use movements, gestures, and facial expressions to emphasize key points of your message.

▷ **Exercise 3** Presenting a Persuasive Speech Prepare a persuasive speech on a topic that interests you. Follow the steps on this page to prepare and present your speech to your classmates.

⊛ Technology Tip

Practice your speech by recording it on an audio- or videotape. Play it back to analyze how you sound and look. Use the evaluation tips on page 748 to discover ways to improve your speech and delivery.

▷ **More Practice**

Academic and Workplace Skills Activity Book
• p. 2

Evaluating a Presentation or Performance Evaluate works by your peers. These include presentations, such as original essays or narratives. They also include performances, such as interpretations of poetry and individual or group performances of scripts. The main purpose of the evaluation is to determine which techniques and skills were successful and which need more work. A secondary purpose is to apply the successful techniques and skills to improve your own presentations and performances.

KEY CONCEPT An effective speaker uses verbal and non-verbal techniques to gain and hold an audience's attention. ■

TIPS FOR EVALUATING A SPEECH

- Did the speaker introduce the topic clearly?
- Did the speaker support main ideas with appropriate details?
- Did the speaker establish eye contact?
- Did the speaker's gestures and movements reinforce the message?
- Did the speaker project loudly enough?
- Did the speaker vary voice, pitch, and speaking rate?
- Did the speaker pronounce all words clearly and correctly?

Improving Your Own Presentations and Performances When you evaluate another speaker's presentation or delivery, you identify the reasons you, as a listener, did or did not find the presentation effective. Keep these reasons in mind as you practice your next presentation. If you found your attention wandering because the speaker never varied his or her position or made eye contact, then be sure to vary your position as you speak and to make eye contact with your audience.

Exercise 4 Evaluating a Presentation or Performance Use the suggestions on this page to evaluate a presentation or performance given in class. Comment on the skills that the person used effectively, and give specific examples of how the skills were used. Be tactful in pointing out any problems the speaker displayed. Give your completed evaluation to the person.

> **Research Tip**
>
> Ask your librarian for help in finding information on giving presentations, such as speeches or dramatic performances. Also, look for presentations and performances on audio- and videotape, and study the techniques used by the presenters or performers.

Listening Critically

There's a lot more to listening than just hearing words. Listening involves active participation. Listening critically involves evaluating and making judgments about what you hear.

> **KEY CONCEPT** A critical listener takes an active role in the information he or she hears. ■

Learning the Listening Process One reason to become a better listener is to acquire new ideas and information on which to build your knowledge. Understanding the listening process will bring you one step closer to becoming a critical listener.

Focus Your Attention Give the speaker your undivided attention so you can fully understand the information you hear. If you are planning to attend a formal presentation or speech on a particular topic, acquire more information about the topic before attending. This will increase your interest and make it easier for you to focus your attention.

Interpret the Information When you are listening to a speaker, you have to analyze what you are hearing. Some information will be more important than other information. It is up to you to be selective in what you will try to remember. Use the following suggestions to guide you:

- Listen for words and phrases that are emphasized or repeated.

- Test your understanding of important statements by rephrasing them in your own words.

- Take notes and summarize ideas in writing.

- Be alert to nonverbal signals, such as tone of voice, gestures, and facial expressions. Often, body language is as important a part of the communication process as verbal language.

- Find a meaningful pattern in which to combine present and past information.

Respond to the Speaker's Message After the speaker has finished speaking, respond to the information you heard. Think about whether you feel the speaker has made valid points and supported them well. Jot down questions you still have after listening. If possible, ask questions to clarify the speaker's message.

> **Exercise 5** **Using the Listening Process** Apply the listening strategies on this page to a lecture by your teacher or a presentation or a performance by one of your peers.

⊙ Technology Tip

To improve your ability to interpret information, listen to tape recordings of classroom lectures. Ask your teachers for permission before taping. Practice your listening skills, using the techniques on this page, while you play the tapes at home.

> **More Practice**
>
> Academic and Workplace Skills Activity Book
> - p. 3

Using Different Types of Listening Part of being a critical listener is knowing how to adjust your listening according to the situation. There are four main types of listening: *critical, empathic, appreciative,* and *reflective.*

Types of Listening		
Type	**How to Listen**	**Situation**
Critical	Listen for facts and supporting details to understand and evaluate the speaker's message.	Informative or persuasive essays, class discussions, announcements
Empathic	Imagine yourself in the other person's position, and try to understand what he or she is thinking.	Conversations with friends or family
Appreciative	Identify and analyze aesthetic or artistic elements, such as character development, rhyme, imagery, and descriptive language.	Oral presentations of a poem or short story and dramatic performances
Reflective	Ask questions to get information, and use or reflect on the speaker's responses to form new questions.	Class or group discussions

Asking Different Types of Questions Use different types of questions to get the information you want to know.

- An **open-ended** question allows the person you are asking to make choices about the kinds of information used in the response. Use follow-up questions to clarify specific points. An example of an open-ended question is "Why are you the best candidate for class president?"

- A **closed** question leads to a specific response and must be answered with a yes or a no. Sometimes, you may want to explore the reasons for the answer by asking an open-ended follow-up question.

- A **fact** question is aimed at getting a particular piece of information and must be answered with facts: "How many votes did you receive in the election?" Follow-up questions may help you pinpoint the source of information.

▷ **Exercise 6** Using Different Types of Listening For one week, keep a "listening log." Jot down examples of ways you have used each of the types of listening. Remember that you may use more than one type of listening for the same situation.

▷ **Exercise 7** Using Different Types of Questions Work with a classmate on this exercise. Have your classmate choose a topic in which he or she is interested and knowledgeable. Then, ask two open-ended, two closed, and two fact questions to learn about that topic. Record the person's responses, and then switch roles.

Evaluating Your Listening Improve your listening skills by evaluating them. Use the following strategies to guide you:

Rephrase and Repeat Statements Test your understanding of the speaker's statements by rephrasing and then repeating them. If necessary, ask questions to improve your paraphrase.

Compare and Contrast Interpretations Compare your interpretation of a speaker's message with that of a classmate's. Before discussing with your classmate, jot down a brief summary of the speech or presentation and any questions you have. Then, compare your notes with your partner's.

Research Points of Interest or Contention Use the library or other references to learn more about the topic or to check questionable facts in the speaker's presentation.

▷ **Exercise 8** Evaluating Your Listening Skills Working with another classmate, use the skills listed above to evaluate how well you listen to a lecture by a teacher, a presentation by a classmate, or a story told by one of your friends. Afterward, write an evaluation describing how well you listened and the areas in which you need to improve.

Technology Tip

Practice your critical listening skills by listening to campaign speeches at school and in local elections and by listening to commentary on current events on television.

Viewing Skills

Visual representation is an important and effective way to communicate. Television programs, textbooks, Web sites, and works of art are common types of media that use images to add to your view of the world. In this section, you will learn how to interpret information from visual sources.

Interpreting Maps and Graphs

Finding information in maps and graphs involves understanding the features contained within them.

▶ **KEY CONCEPT** Determine your purpose for reading the map or graph, and then find the information to fulfill this purpose. ■

Maps A *map* can show climate, population density, changes over historical periods, battles in a war, the relative heights of landforms, or weather patterns, among many other types of information. To interpret a map, (1) determine the type and purpose of the map; (2) read the title, captions, and labels, and examine the distance scale and other symbols; (3) relate the information on the map to any written information accompanying it.

🔖 **Research Tip**

Browse through atlases to see the many uses that maps have. Note the features of each map and the various symbols used to communicate information.

Members of the European Union

Azimuthal Equal Area Projection

0   250   500 Miles

0   250 500 Kilometers

FINLAND

SWEDEN

North Sea

IRELAND   DENMARK

UNITED KINGDOM

NETH. GERMANY

BELGIUM

ATLANTIC OCEAN

LUX.

FRANCE   AUSTRIA

PORTUGAL   SPAIN   ITALY

GREECE

Members by:

1957

1973

1986

2000

◀ Critical Viewing
What is the purpose of this map? **[Analyze]**

Graphs

Graphs present numerical information in visual form and compare two or more sets of related information. Study the following three types of commonly used graphs.

Line Graph A *line graph* shows changes over a period of time. A line connects points, which appear as dots at intersections on the graph. Each dot represents a number or a quantity of something. To interpret a line graph, (1) read the labels to see what the data represent and the time interval for which the data are being recorded, (2) read both the horizontal axis (left-to-right line) and the vertical axis (bottom-to-top line) that make up the two axes of the graph, and (3) compare and contrast the data.

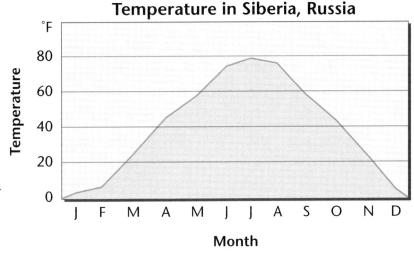

Bar Graph A *bar graph* compares and contrasts quantities. The height or length of each bar shows what numbers it represents. To interpret a bar graph, (1) match the label of each bar on the horizontal axis to the number that the bar reaches on the vertical axis, (2) note the labels to see what each bar represents and why the two bars are being compared, and (3) compare and contrast the data.

◄▲ Critical Viewing
What can you learn about Siberia from these two graphs? **[Synthesize]**

Pie Graph A *pie graph* shows the relationship of parts to a whole. The graph is a circle that represents 100 percent of something. Each part stands for a portion, or percentage, of the whole. To interpret a pie graph, (1) look at the numbers that go with each part, (2) match the parts to the key to see what each represents, and (3) use the numbers and parts to make comparisons.

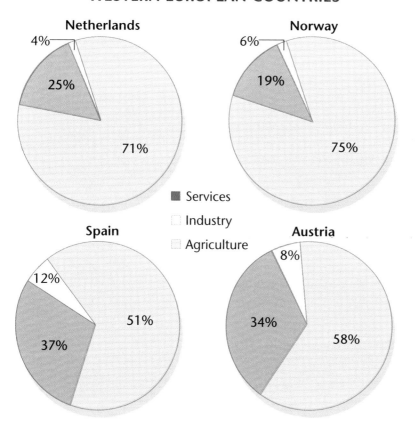

THE LABOR FORCE IN SELECTED WESTERN EUROPEAN COUNTRIES

Netherlands
4%
25%
71%

Norway
6%
19%
75%

■ Services
▢ Industry
▢ Agriculture

Spain
12%
51%
37%

Austria
8%
34%
58%

◀ Critical Viewing
Which country has the largest agricultural labor force? **[Identify]**

▸ **Exercise 9** Reading Information Visually Use the tips you have just read to interpret the map and the graphs in this section. Write an explanation of the information presented in each. Then, decide what conclusions can be drawn from them.

More Practice

Academic and Workplace Skills Activity Book
• pp. 4–5

Viewing Information Media Critically

To be an informed consumer of information, it is important that you learn to critically evaluate what you see and hear in the media. Applying critical viewing skills to the various forms of news media will help you to understand events and issues and to formulate your own opinions.

KEY CONCEPT Learn to identify and evaluate the different kinds of information found in nonprint media. ■

Recognizing Kinds of Information Media Much of the information you receive comes to you from visual media, particularly television. The quality and relevance of this information depends on the type of program being viewed.

The following chart describes several forms of nonprint information media.

NONPRINT INFORMATION MEDIA			
Form of News Media	**Topic(s)**	**Coverage and Content**	**Point of View**
Nightly News	Current events or news	Brief summaries illustrated by video footage	Presents information objectively
Documentary	One topic of social interest	Story shown through narration and video footage	Expresses controversial opinions
Interview	Topics of social interest	Conversation of questions and answers	Presents opinions of interviewee
Television Newsmagazine	Covers a variety of topics	Feature with hosts and footage, meant to entertain and inform	Emphasizes stories that grab a viewer's attention
Commercial	Products, people, and ideas	Short message of images and slogans	Presents information to sell something or to persuade

Evaluating and Critiquing Persuasive Techniques

When you view any form of media, you should be aware of persuasive techniques used to misrepresent information and possibly distort your understanding of a message or an event.

Glittering generalities are lofty, broad statements that seek to appeal to a wide audience. The statement, "The best is yet to come if we all do our part" "glitters" with positive words and ideas, but it offers no real insight. Note glittering generalities, and examine them to find out what they really mean.

Bandwagon appeals are statements that use a form of peer pressure as their support. A bandwagon appeal suggests that you should take a certain action or think in a certain way because many others do.

Symbols are images that stand for or embody the qualities of another thing. For example, an advertisement for a car may include symbols of wealth, power, and prestige in addition to showing the actual car. Including these symbols suggests that the car is also a symbol of these qualities and that owning the car will make you feel wealthy, powerful, and important.

Deconstructing Information From the Media First, determine the kind of media program you are watching. Then, use your knowledge of persuasive techniques combined with the following strategies to deconstruct—break down into pieces—the images and language of the media you are viewing.

- Be aware of the purpose and limitations of the program you are watching. Find out who wrote or sponsored the program.

- Separate **facts** (proven statements) from **opinions** (beliefs). Use resources to check questionable information.

- Watch for **bias**—presenting a subject from one point of view.

- Note the kinds of images shown and their emotional impact.

- View the complete program before reaching your own conclusions about issues, people, and information.

 **Learn More**

For more information about methods of persuasion, see Chapter 7. For information on how advertisements persuade, see Chapter 8.

Exercise 10 Identifying Persuasive Techniques in Advertisements Find examples of glittering generalities, bandwagon appeals, and symbols in advertising. Choose your examples from electronic and print media. Write a brief explanation of the persuasive technique used in each advertisement.

More Practice

Academic and Workplace Skills Activity Book
- p. 6

Interpreting Fine Art

Paintings, drawings, sculpture, and photographs are all examples of fine art. To enrich your understanding and enjoyment of these works, you must interpret the various elements that make up the artwork.

▷**KEY CONCEPT** In works of art, meaning is communicated through elements of design. ■

Interpreting Elements of Design To help you interpret a work of art, consider the following questions:

- Does the work present definable objects or is it abstract—not showing any particular objects?

- What shapes, lines, and colors do you see?

- What mood, theme, or message does the work convey?

- Which areas are darkest, and which are lightest? What does the contrast of light and dark areas suggest?

- How do all the individual elements work together to create a feeling or an idea?

Dancers, Pink and Green, Edgar Degas, Metropolitan Museum of Art

▷**Exercise 11** Responding to Fine Art Interpret the painting *Dancers, Pink and Green*, by Edgar Degas, by answering the questions listed above. Write your answers in a notebook, along with any other observations. Share your impressions in an open discussion with your classmates.

🗓 **Research Tip**

Spend some time in the library viewing books and slides of fine art. Which artists and works of art do you prefer? Make notes in your journal about why they appeal to you.

💿 **Technology Tip**

Great art museums are waiting for you on the Internet. Enter the name of the museum in a search engine to find the URL (address) of the museum's Web site.

Representing Skills

Graphic organizers, multimedia presentations, and performances are ways in which you can express yourself to the world. In this section, you will learn how to prepare your own visual representations.

Creating Visual Aids

For large amounts of information or complex ideas, it is helpful to organize the material into a visual aid, such as a graphic organizer, map, or diagram. These visual aids can also help you present information to others and to organize and remember information when you study.

▷ **KEY CONCEPT** Graphic organizers make information easier to comprehend and remember. ■

Use these strategies to construct your own visual aid:

- **Use Text Descriptions** Note the headings and subheadings that are used to organize the text. You can use headings to develop a concept map or an idea web, which will present these categories in visual form.

- **Determine the Text Structure** Consider the structure of the text when you choose a visual aid to display the information. For texts that show comparison and contrast, a Venn diagram may be the best choice. A flowchart is a good way to display cause-and-effect relationships. Problems and solutions can be shown in charts or diagrams. Main ideas and supporting details lend themselves to an outline. Chronological events can be represented on a timeline.

- **Identify Your Purpose** Is the purpose of the visual aid to help you study or to present information to others? Your answer will determine what information to include and which visual aid to use. Visual aids used for studying can be simple webs, charts, tables, or outlines. Visual aids used for presentations should be designed with an audience in mind. They should be appealing to the viewer and easy to understand.

- **Study Effective Graphics** Notice the effective use of graphics in textbooks, newspapers, and magazines. How are these graphics used to support the information in the text? For example, a graph may show information to support a viewpoint or to prove an argument.

Learn More

For more information about text structures, see the following "Exposition" chapters: "Comparison and Contrast," Chapter 9; "Cause and Effect," Chapter 10; "Problem and Solution," Chapter 11.

Following are descriptions of various types of visual aids and examples of how they are used.

Charts, Graphs, and Tables These visual aids can be used to present survey statistics, results of experiments or research, and other complex information. A table outlining a feudal society, for example, would show the people occupying the highest ranks (kings, emperors, and lesser rulers) at the top and those of lower ranks (merchants, peasants, and craftsmen) at the bottom.

Diagrams, Maps, and Illustrations These drawings show the features of an object, place, or process. For example, you might make a drawing, like the one below, of how a volcano erupts.

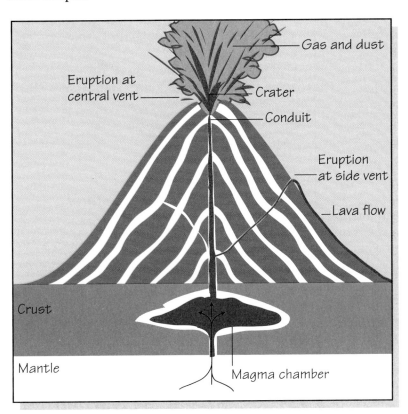

▶ **Exercise 12** **Creating Visual Aids From Textbooks** Choose a chapter from your math, science, or social studies textbook. Make a graphic organizer to represent a concept or group of facts in the chapter. Explain why you chose that particular type of visual aid and how it helps to clarify the information.

Technology Tip

Explore the table, graph, and graphics features on a computer, including changing text into graph and table form, merging text and pictures, and drawing capabilities.

▶ **More Practice**

Academic and Workplace Skills Activity Book
• p. 8

Using Formatting

There are many formatting techniques on most word processors that can aid you in making visual representations like the flyer shown here. Remember that the features you use should match the purpose of the text.

- Type styles have different effects on the viewer. Letters and characters can be italic (slanted), bold (dark type), or a combination of the two. They can also be shadowed or outlined and printed in a range of colors.

- Different effects can be produced by indenting and spacing the text. Information can be presented in bulleted lists or, when information has to appear in a certain order, numbered lists.

- Parts of the text can be shaded or colored for effect or to call attention to the information. Borders can be added to make information stand out or for decoration.

- Graphics can be added to attract the viewers and to give them an idea of what kind of information they can expect to read.

Have Rake, Will Travel

Buried in Autumn Leaves?

HARD-WORKING, DEPENDABLE
HIGH-SCHOOL STUDENT WILL RAKE YOUR LAWN

- Have own rake and leaf blower
- Will rake leaves from lawn and shrubbery
- Will bag leaves and take them to curb
- Reasonable rates
- Satisfaction guaranteed
- Available most weekdays 3:15 P.M. – 6:30 P.M. and weekends

*Call or e-mail
Tom Wilson*
Tel. 101-555-3377 or
twilson@rakeleaves.com

Exercise 13 Using Formatting to Design a Brochure
Use the tips on formatting and design to prepare a flyer or brochure that promotes a school sport or club. When your flyer is complete, ask a classmate to evaluate your use of various formatting and design features.

Technology Tip

Consult the software manual, Help feature, or toolbar to explore the possibilities for formatting, using the software on your computer.

Working With Multimedia

Some kinds of information are most effectively presented with sounds and visuals. When preparing a multimedia presentation, consider using an overhead projector, a slide projector, a video-tape player, or an audiocassette player. These can enhance your presentation with still images, moving images, recorded voices, music, graphic organizers, and art.

Giving a Multimedia Presentation Although almost any kind of media can be used in a multimedia presentation, you should consider the topic, the audience, and the available equipment before you choose which media to use.

Use the following suggestions to help you prepare and give a multimedia presentation:

- Outline your oral report, and decide which parts will be more effective if presented through visual and aural media.

- Choose forms of media that suit your topic. If your topic is American life during World War II, you might play popular music of that time as a background and show slides of women workers in defense industries to illustrate the changes in society resulting from the war.

- Use media selections evenly throughout your presentation, not just at the beginning or end.

- Make sure all visual images can be seen by the entire audience. Small images can be photocopied and enlarged before being shown on an overhead projector.

- Rehearse your presentation with the multimedia equipment. Become familiar with making adjustments to the equipment.

- Before the presentation, double-check your equipment to make sure everything is in working condition.

- Have a backup plan in case your equipment fails. You might have copies of illustrations or graphic organizers to give to the audience.

Technology Tip

Use a search engine to find Web sites with graphics you can print or download and use in your multimedia presentation.

▶ **Exercise 14** Preparing and Giving a Multimedia Presentation Look through some of your past speeches and reports. Choose one, and prepare a plan for enhancing it with multimedia selections. Outline your presentation, including the media you will use and the order of presentation. Practice a few times, and then present it to your classmates.

▶ **More Practice**

Academic and Workplace Skills Activity Book
- p. 10

Producing a Video

Video cameras allow individuals to record their experiences and express their ideas through the medium of film. In addition to operating the camera, video artists must learn to edit the tape to produce the effects they want.

KEY CONCEPT A video can inform, entertain, persuade, or serve all three purposes. ■

Making a Video The process of making a video is similar to making a film, although on a smaller scale. First, you must write out a story or list of scenes meant to convey a message. This document is the beginning of a *shooting script.* Include descriptions of settings, narration or dialogue between characters, and costumes and props needed. Decide on *camera angles,* or positions, for each shot or sequence of shots.

Use the shooting script to make a *storyboard* that illustrates a clear sequence of events. A storyboard looks like a cartoon strip, with each important shot planned and illustrated.

Select locations for shooting, and get permission to use them. Cast the roles, and rehearse. Write out a shooting schedule listing each scene, when and where it will be shot, and who is in it. Film the scenes, and store the video in a safe place.

Edit the video to produce the effect you want. You might cut to make action happen more quickly, to move from one location to another, or to insert flashbacks or new material. You may also decide to reshoot some scenes.

Tips for Videotaping

- Hold the camera steady. Learn to use all the features of the equipment.

- Use shooting techniques such as **panning** (moving the camera to the left or right), **zooming** (adjusting from a distant to a close view or from a close view to a distant one), **fading** (increasing or decreasing image intensity), and **cutting** (moving directly from one shot to another).

- Be sure to shoot enough film. It is always easier to cut than to reshoot.

Exercise 15 Producing a Video Produce a five-minute documentary or story video. You may work with a partner. Write out a shooting script. On your storyboard, plan the scenes you will shoot. Then, select locations, cast actors, rehearse, and film your video. After editing, present your video to your classmates.

More Practice

Academic and Workplace Skills Activity Book
• p. 11

Performing or Interpreting

In an oral interpretation, the performer communicates his or her personal conception of a written work.

> **KEY CONCEPT** Performers use voice and gestures and their own personal insights to communicate the meaning of a text. ■

Preparing a Performance or Interpretation It is best to choose a poem or story that has personal meaning for you and that you think the audience will appreciate. Write the text out and highlight the ideas and phrases you wish to emphasize. Decide on the mood you wish to achieve. Experiment with different ways of reading the text aloud to achieve the desired effect. Use tone of voice and pitch to express emotions. Use gestures and other body language to convey meaning and mood. Set the scene through background music, props, and costumes, if appropriate. Rehearse in front of a mirror and then before friends and family. Ask for their feedback to improve your performance.

> **Exercise 16** **Interpreting a Poem** Choose a poem you would like to interpret for an audience. Make notes on key words and ideas and the emotions and meanings you wish to convey. Practice reading the poem aloud and get feedback from listeners. Then, interpret the poem for your class.

> **More Practice**
>
> Academic and Workplace Skills Activity Book
> • p. 12

Reflecting on Your Speaking, Listening, Viewing, and Representing

Review the skills covered in this chapter. Write a journal entry evaluating your experiences using these skills. Use the following questions as a starting point:

- How might effective speaking and listening benefit me in the different areas of my life—school, work, hobbies, friends, and family?

- How have I improved my ability to critically evaluate information from the media?

- What have I learned from producing visual presentations and/or interpreting literature through performing?

Standardized Test Preparation Workshop

Interpreting Graphic Aids

Items that measure your ability to read not only text but also visuals are included on some standardized tests. Interpreting graphic aids means understanding the visual representation of information. You use this skill to read textbooks, news articles, directions, and surveys. On a test, a chart, map, or graph, as well as text on a particular topic, may be provided. The graphic often presents statistical information or shows categories of information that can be compared or measured. The text often provides context or shows the significance of the information.

The items that follow will give you practice with a format in which these items might appear. To respond to the questions or sentence completions, read and analyze both the graphic aid and the text.

Test Tip

Before answering the question, look at the visual and the text. Then, evaluate the answer choices to locate the one that is correct according to the information from both sources.

Sample Test Item	Answer and Explanation

Directions: Read the passage on the next page. Answer the question below.
 	
1 What types of foods were probably missing from a sailor's diet?
 	
  A vegetables
 	
  B meat
 	
  C fruits
 	
  D bread
	The correct answer is C. The text explains that many sailors contracted the disease scurvy. The chart tells you that a deficiency of citrus fruits causes scurvy. By putting together the information from the chart and the text, you can draw the conclusion that the sailors were probably not getting enough fruit.

> **Practice** **Directions:** Read the passage and answer the questions that follow.

Vitamins are chemical compounds that the human body requires in small amounts in order to maintain good health. Vitamins are a factor in the way the body converts food into energy and living tissue. Although some of the vitamins needed can be produced by the body itself, most must be supplied by a person's diet.

Each vitamin has such specific uses that one cannot replace another. The continued absence of just one vitamin can cause a vitamin deficiency disease. For example, before the connections between diet and health were completely understood, sailors often suffered from scurvy. Although plenty of salted meat was stocked on board and some vegetables were even included in a sailor's diet, the difficulties in carrying fresh foods for long journeys presented many dietary problems. In 1753, however, James Lind, a Scottish doctor, discovered which foods would prevent scurvy. The British navy followed his advice and adjusted the daily rations of sailors. Because the foods Lind recommended contained the vitamin necessary to prevent scurvy, it has become a rare disease in modern times.

Vitamin Sources and Functions

Vitamin	Source	Function	Deficiency Disease
A	green and yellow vegetables	promotes bone growth and vision	night blindness
B_1	grains, liver, legumes	metabolizes carbohydrates	beriberi
C	citrus fruits, potatoes, tomatoes	aids immunity, helps connective tissue growth	scurvy
D	milk, yeast	regulates bone formation	rickets, bowlegs

1 What foods, in addition to citrus fruits, would Lind have recommended that sailors take on board for long voyages?
A apples
B bananas
C beans
D potatoes

2 Of what other vitamin might sailors have had a deficiency?
F Vitamin A
G Vitamin B
H Vitamin C
J Vitamin D

3 Which foods help a person metabolize carbohydrates?
A breads
B milk
C water
D lemons

Chapter
30 Vocabulary and Spelling

You encounter new words in many ways. You see new words in textbooks or in the reading you do for pleasure. In addition, you hear new words in conversations, in the classroom, and on radio and television.

Learning different ways to expand your vocabulary and improve your spelling are some of the most useful skills you can acquire. No matter how large your vocabulary is, you can always increase your knowledge of word meanings and spellings. The best way to build these skills is to work on remembering and using new words. This task requires some patience, but it is not as difficult as you may think—and the rewards of being able to read, write, and speak more successfully are well worth the effort.

▲ **Critical Viewing**
Is working in a group such as this one helpful in building vocabulary? Why or why not? **[Infer]**

Developing Your Vocabulary

In today's era of communication, words are a fundamental tool. The more words you have to choose from, the more ideas and feelings you can express. Trying to write or speak with a limited vocabulary is like trying to paint a picture with a limited number of colors.

To increase your vocabulary, you must first have a desire to expand your knowledge of word meanings, as well as a commitment to studying new words. Following are a number of helpful techniques that you can use:

Reading, Listening, and Discussing

Most of the words that we use every day we learned when we were children, just by keeping our eyes and ears open.

▷ **KEY CONCEPT** The most common ways to increase your vocabulary are listening, reading, and taking part in conversations. ■

Hearing and Using New Words There was a time when you did not know even the simplest words. You had to learn the meaning of *mother* and *father*, *run* and *walk*, *hot* and *cold*, *in* and *out*. First, you heard the words spoken. Then, you learned to repeat them. Eventually, you were able to put the new words together and use them in conversation.

Listening and discussing are still excellent ways to expand your vocabulary. When you talk to other people, follow discussions in class, watch television, hear literature on audiocassettes, or listen to the radio, be alert to unfamiliar words. Find out the meaning by using a dictionary or by asking. (Never be embarrassed to ask what a word means; it shows that you are listening and that you want to learn.) Whenever possible, try to use the new words in conversation.

Reading Extensively In general, people use a wider variety of words when they write than when they speak. Therefore, you can expand your vocabulary by reading even more than you can by listening.

The more you read, the more you will be introduced to new words. You will also encounter familiar words used in new, unfamiliar ways. To expand your vocabulary, try to read as extensively as possible: A wide variety of sources and subjects means a wide variety of words. Textbooks, newspapers, magazines, novels, and articles on the Internet can all be rich sources of vocabulary.

Recognizing Context Clues

When you come across an unfamiliar word, you may be able to guess its meaning by examining its context. The context of a word is determined by the other words in the sentence or the passage surrounding it.

A knowledge of the different types of context clues can help you use them effectively.

▶ **KEY CONCEPT** Use context clues to determine the meaning of unfamiliar words. ■

Research Tip

Find a current news-magazine, and select five unfamiliar words. Guess their meanings according to their context, and check your answers in a dictionary.

TYPES OF CONTEXT CLUES	
Clue	**Example**
Key words in the sentence that give the word's meaning	*Mountains* and *tall* buildings scare me because I have <u>acrophobia</u>. (Italicized words suggest height. <u>Acrophobia</u> must mean "fear of high places.")
Comparisons; contrasts; synonyms; antonyms	One cat is *courageous* and *loves* adventure; the other is <u>timorous</u> and hides under the sofa. (<u>Timorous</u> must mean "fearful.")
Words or phrases that follow a word closely and rename or define it	<u>Bonsai</u>, *the art of growing trees in small pots*, is well known in Japan. (The italicized phrase provides the correct meaning.)

▶ **Exercise 1** Recognizing Context Clues Use context clues to determine the meaning of each underlined word. Check your answers in a dictionary.

1. Gloria's <u>animosity</u> could be seen in her unfriendly expression and hostile tone of voice.
2. After his eight-mile run, Mel was <u>voracious</u> and ate everything in the refrigerator.
3. The newcomer appeared to be <u>morose</u>, but later her spirits lifted.
4. Sitting for a long time watching a lot of television can reduce your energy, resulting in a feeling of <u>lethargy</u>.
5. Moving not a muscle, the actor playing the victim was able to remain <u>inert</u>.

▶ **More Practice**

Academic and Workplace Skills Activity Book
• pp. 13–14

Denotation and Connotation

Context can help you determine a word's exact meaning. Knowing the denotations and connotations of a word can help you discriminate between different shades of meaning.

> **KEY CONCEPTS** The **denotation** of a word is its literal definition. Its **connotations** include the ideas, images, and feelings that are associated with the word. ■

A definition of *dictator* is "a ruler with absolute power and authority." That is the denotation of the word. However, what comes into your mind when you hear the word *dictator*? You may think of ideas such as injustice and cruelty. You may picture specific images, such as an iron fist or a specific historic figure, such as Joseph Stalin. You may even feel emotions, such as fear and anger. All of these are connotations associated with the word *dictator*. As you strengthen your vocabulary, be aware of both positive and negative connotations of the words you use.

> **Exercise 2** Discriminating Between Denotation and Connotation Read each pair of sentences below. For each pair, write a sentence explaining the different connotations of the underlined words. Use a dictionary to help you.

1. John was <u>unaware</u> of the recent events in Asia.
   John was <u>ignorant</u> of the recent events in Asia.
2. The <u>slim</u> model walked gracefully down the ramp.
   The <u>skinny</u> model walked gracefully down the ramp.
3. The <u>uninvited</u> guests arrived at three o'clock.
   The <u>unexpected</u> guests arrived at three o'clock.
4. That store carries a lot of <u>cheap</u> clothing.
   That store carries a lot of <u>inexpensive</u> clothing.
5. The fans <u>crowded</u> around their favorite movie star.
   The fans <u>swarmed</u> around their favorite movie star.

▼ Critical Viewing
Write two sentences describing this picture. In one, use words with a positive connotation; in the other, try to be neutral. **[Interpret]**

Recognizing Related Words

Discovering how words relate to other words is a good way to increase your vocabulary.

⊗ Technology Tip

Do an on-line search, and find five new pairs of homophones. Add any unfamiliar words to your notebook.

> **KEY CONCEPTS** **Synonyms** are words that are similar in meaning. **Antonyms** are words that are opposite in meaning. **Homophones** are words that sound alike but have different meanings and spellings. ■

Synonyms It is often easier to remember a one-word synonym for a word than to remember a long dictionary definition. For example, you may be able to remember the word *attain* by remembering its synonym, *achieve*.

Antonyms Remembering antonyms in pairs may help you to recall each word's meaning. For example, *happy* is the antonym of *sad*.

Homophones Knowing that certain words sound alike but have different meanings and spellings can help you use their correct forms in writing. For example, make sure that you know the difference between the homophones *stationery* (writing material) and *stationary* (not moving).

> **Exercise 3** **Recognizing Related Words** Using a dictionary, identify each pair as either *synonyms*, *antonyms*, or *homophones*.
> 1. lead/led
> 2. rustic/refined
> 3. raze/raise
> 4. whether/weather
> 5. irk/annoy
> 6. insurrection/revolt
> 7. defer/delay
> 8. random/deliberate
> 9. ample/plentiful
> 10. vertical/horizontal

▶ **Critical Viewing** What subject do you think this student is studying? How will writing vocabulary words in a notebook help him expand his vocabulary? **[Infer]**

Using Related Words in Analogies

Working with analogies strengthens your vocabulary by increasing your understanding of connections between word meanings. Analogies are often found on standardized tests.

> **KEY CONCEPT** An **analogy** is some similarity between things that are otherwise unlike. Analogy problems present pairs of words that have some relationship to each other. ■

Look at the following analogy, and see whether you can find the pair of words whose relationship is the most similar to the capitalized pair:

EXAMPLE: HINGES : DOOR ::
a. roof : chimney
b. rock : atom
c. keyboard : organ
The answer is *c*.

The key to solving analogies is to understand what the relationship is between the capitalized words. In this example, the relationship between the capitalized words is *part to whole*— *hinges* are part of a *door*. A *roof* is not a part of a *chimney*. A *rock* is not a part of an *atom*. (Although an *atom* is part of a *rock*, the words appear in a different order from the capitalized pair.) A *keyboard*, however, is a part of an *organ*.

There are other common analogy relationships. They include *type* (crocodile : reptile), *defining characteristic* (white : snow), *instrument* (knife : cut), *degree* (afraid : terrified), *sequence* (summer : autumn), and *proximity* (sidewalk : street).

> **Exercise 4** **Working With Analogies** First, identify the analogy relationship expressed in the capitalized pair. Then, choose the lettered pair that best expresses this relationship.
>
> 1. INTRODUCTION : SPEECH ::
>   a. preface : book b. speaker : audience c. scene : act
> 2. HUMOR : COMEDIAN ::
>   a. finish line : runner b. intelligence : genius c. lecture : teacher
> 3. PAINTER : STUDIO ::
>   a. sculpture : painting   b. judge : court c. writer : essay
> 4. GEOMETRY : MATHEMATICS ::
>   a. botany : science b. shape : number c. theorem : equation
> 5. NEARBY : ADJOINING ::
>   a. ocean : shore b. perpendicular : parallel   c. noisy : stentorious

> **More Practice**
>
> Academic and Workplace Skills Activity Book
> • pp. 15–16

Studying Words Systematically

Using Resource Materials

Two of the most valuable resource tools are a dictionary and a thesaurus. A dictionary is most helpful when you are reading; a thesaurus is most useful when you are writing.

KEY CONCEPTS Use a dictionary to find the meaning, spelling, pronunciation, and origin of words. Use a thesaurus to expand the meaning of words. ■

Using a Dictionary It is a good idea to keep an unabridged (complete) dictionary nearby.

• Study the pronunciation given in parentheses after the word.

• Become aware of the part of speech (*n.*, *v.*, *adj.*). The meaning of a word can change depending upon its usage.

Using a Thesaurus A thesaurus gives a list of words similar in meaning to the one you know. (For example, if you look up *give* in a thesaurus, you might find *grant*, *contribute*, *tip*, *remit*, *fork over*, and *donate*.) Be sure to check a dictionary to see whether your substitute has the correct connotation.

Learning About Etymologies Understanding word origins can help you understand words even if you have never seen them before. The English language adopts words from a variety of sources.

• English borrows or adopts words from other languages, especially Latin and Greek. (Examples: *Drama* is a Greek word. *Tycoon* is borrowed from China and Japan.)

• Words can change meaning over time and through usage. (Example: The word *dear* used to mean "expensive.")

• Words can be invented, or coined, to serve new purposes. (Example: The words *paperbacks* and *quiz* are coined.)

• Words can be shortened. (Example: The word *flu* is short for *influenza.*)

Exercise 5 Using Vocabulary Reference Aids Look up each of the following words in the references indicated. Compare and contrast the information found in each source.
1. streak (dictionary, science textbook glossary)
2. annex (social studies textbook glossary, dictionary)
3. durability (dictionary, thesaurus)
4. grow (science textbook glossary, on-line thesaurus)

Research Tip

Find five unfamiliar words. Look them up in a thesaurus. Then, look them up in a dictionary to determine differences in their meanings. Add the new words to your notebook.

More Practice

Academic and Workplace Skills Activity Book
• pp. 17–18

Remembering Vocabulary Words

To make a word part of your vocabulary, study its definition, use it in your writing and speaking, and review it to make sure that you really understand its meaning.

▶ **KEY CONCEPT** Use one or more review techniques to remember the meanings of new words. ■

Using a Vocabulary Notebook Keep a notebook for vocabulary words. Divide your page into three columns: the *words* you want to learn; hints or *bridge words* that help you remember their meanings; and their *definitions*. Test yourself by covering either the second or third column.

VOCABULARY NOTEBOOK

Word	Bridge	Definition
ornithology	oriole	study of birds
oscillate	pendulum	swing back and forth
effervescent	soda	bubbly

Making Flashcards On the front of an index card, write a *word* you want to remember and the *bridge word*. On the back, write the *definition*. Test yourself by flipping through the cards. Enter any difficult words in your vocabulary notebook. As you master the meanings, remove these cards and add new ones.

Using a Tape Recorder Record your vocabulary words. Leave a ten-second space after each word, followed by the definition and a short sentence using the word. Replay the tape. Fill in the blank space with the definition and a sentence. Replay the tape until you can give the information easily.

▶ **Exercise 6** Adding New Words to Your Vocabulary
Identify five difficult words from one of your textbooks. Enter the words and their definitions in your vocabulary notebook. Study the words using one of the above methods. Then, test yourself by using each word in a sentence. Check your answers and correct them.

Studying Word Parts and Origins

In addition to learning new words, you can improve your vocabulary by learning about *word structure*, or the parts that make up a word.

The three word parts that can combine to form a word are a root (such as *-duc-* in pro*duc*tion), a prefix (such as *pro-* in *pro*duction), and a suffix (such as *-tion* in produc*tion*). Many of these word parts come to us from Latin, Greek, and Anglo-Saxon languages.

Recognizing Word Roots

The **root** of a word contains its basic meaning. Learning to recognize the most common word roots in English is the foundation of developing your vocabulary.

KEY CONCEPT The **root** of a word carries the basic meaning of the word. ■

In some words, especially shorter words, the root may stand alone. In either case, knowing roots can help you figure out the meanings of unfamiliar words.

Roots have come into the English language from many sources, especially from Latin and Greek. (In the chart below, Latin and Greek roots are identified by the letters *L* and *G*). In the first column below, additional spellings of the roots are indicated in parentheses.

TEN COMMON ROOTS		
Root and Origin	**Meaning**	**Examples**
-cap- (-capt-, -cept-, -ceipt-) [L.]	to take, seize	*cap*able, *capt*ivate, ac*cept*, re*ceipt*
-chor- (-cho-) [Gr.]	to dance, sing	*chor*eography, *cho*ir
-duc- (-duce-, -duct-) [L.]	to lead	pro*duc*e, re*duc*e, con*duct*
-fer- [L.]	to bring, carry	trans*fer*, in*fer*ence
-graph- [Gr.]	to write	auto*graph*
-path- [Gr.]	to feel, suffer	sym*path*y, anti*path*y
-phil- [Gr.]	to love	*phil*osophy
-puls- (-pel-) [L.]	to drive	*puls*ate, pro*pel*
-tend- (-tens-, -tent-) [L.]	to stretch	dis*tend*, ex*tens*ion, ex*tent*
-vid- (-vis-) L.	to see	e*vid*ent, *vis*ion

Exercise 7 Using Roots to Define Words Using the chart on the previous page, select the definition that matches the word. Consult a dictionary if necessary.

1. pathos
2. reception
3. telegraph
4. impulse
5. tendency

   a. a system for sending messages
   b. a driving force
   c. an inclination to act in a particular way
   d. arousing pity or sorrow
   e. a social function for receiving guests

More Practice

Academic and
Workplace Skills
Activity Book
• pp.19–20

Exercise 8 Finding Common Roots Look up each pair of words below in a dictionary, paying close attention to the word's root, shown in italics. Then, write the basic meaning of the root shared by each pair of words.

1. *spec*imen, in*spec*t
2. con*vene*, in*vent*or
3. *tenure*, de*tain*
4. pro*ceed*, suc*cess*
5. con*vert*, di*version*

Using Prefixes

A **prefix** is one or more syllables at the beginning of a word.

KEY CONCEPT The *prefix* appears before the word root and adds to its meaning. ∎

Learning Prefixes Learn the meanings and origins of the prefixes below. Additional spellings are given in parentheses. The abbreviations *L, Gr,* and *AS* mean Latin, Greek, and Anglo-Saxon, the origins from which the prefixes have come. Notice that some prefixes take more than one form—as shown in parentheses—but still have the same meaning.

Spelling Tip

Don't confuse the prefix *ante-,* meaning "before," with the prefix *anti-,* meaning "against."

TEN COMMON PREFIXES		
Prefix and Origin	**Meaning**	**Examples**
ad- (ac-, af-, al-, ap-, as-, at-) [L.]	to, toward	*ad*join, *af*fix, *ac*knowledge
com- (co-, col-, con-, cor-) [L.]	with, together	*col*laborate, *cor*respond
dis- (di-, dif-) [L.]	away, apart	*dis*connect, *dif*fuse
epi- [Gr.]	on, outside, among	*epi*taph, *epi*center
ex- (e-, ec-, ef-) [L.]	forth, from, out	*ec*centric, *ef*fluent
in- (il-, im-, ir-) [L.]	in, into, on, toward	*in*dent, *ir*rigate
mis- [AS]	wrongly	*mis*calculate
mono- [Gr.]	one, alone	*mono*tonous
non- [L.]	not	*non*essential
syn- [Gr.]	together with	*syn*chronize

▶ **Exercise 9** Defining Words With Prefixes Using your knowledge of prefixes, figure out the meaning of each word below. Then, check your answers in a dictionary.

1. *ap*point
2. *con*tribute
3. *epi*dermis
4. *di*vert
5. *e*migrate

6. *mis*place
7. *il*luminate
8. *mono*cle
9. *syn*thesize
10. *non*sense

▶ **Exercise 10** Defining Prefixes and Prefix Origins Using a dictionary, write the definition of each prefix and its origin. Then, provide an example of a word using each prefix.

1. ab- (a-, abs-)
2. in- (il-, im-, ir-)
3. inter-

4. non-
5. un-

Understanding Suffixes

A **suffix** is a syllable or group of syllables added to the end of a word root to form a new word. Note that a suffix often alters the part of speech.

▶ **KEY CONCEPT** The *suffix* is added to the end of the root and can change its meaning or part of speech. ■

Learning Suffixes Suffixes are unique in that they can change both word forms and parts of speech. In the first column, additional spellings are in parentheses. Note: *L*, *Gr*, and *AS* mean Latin, Greek, and Anglo-Saxon.

TEN COMMON SUFFIXES		
Suffix and Origin	**Meaning and Examples**	**Part of Speech**
-able (-ible) [L.]	capable of being: *reliable*	*adjective*
-ate [L.]	to make: *activate*	*verb*
-fy [L.]	to cause, become: *clarify*	*verb*
-ist [Gr.]	a skilled person: *violinist*	*noun*
-ize (-ise) [Gr.]	to make: *improvise*	*verb*
-less [AS.]	without: *ageless*	*adjective*
-ly [AS.]	in a certain way: *hourly, harshly*	*adjective or adverb*
-ness [AS.]	state of: *laziness*	*noun*
-or [L.]	quality of: *error*	*noun*
-tion (-ion,-sion, -ation) [L.]	the action of; state of being: *action*	*noun*

◉ Technology Tip

Search for an on-line Web site that provides more information on Latin, Greek, and Anglo-Saxon suffixes. Find five new words, and add them and their definitions to your vocabulary notebook.

▶ **Exercise 11** Defining Suffixes For each suffix, write its definition and origin. Use a dictionary to assist you.

1. -esque
2. -ism
3. -ous (-ious)
4. -ity
5. -or

6. -ant (-ent)
7. -ful
8. -ment
9. -ance (-ence)
10. -ade

▶ **Exercise 12** Using Suffixes to Form Words Add the correct suffix to each underlined word to form a new word that will complete each sentence below. In your notebook, write each new word and its part of speech.

1. A person who conforms is usually called a ___?___ .
2. People who are unable to help themselves are considered to be ___?___ .
3. When you cause something to become active, you ___?___ it.
4. To cause an activity to become legal is to ___?___ it.
5. When someone gives the glory to someone else, they ___?___ that person.
6. One who mediates a controversy between people or groups is called a ___?___ .
7. The quality of loving one's country like a patriot is called ___?___ .
8. If you give a lot of thought to other people's feelings, you are said to be ___?___ .
9. An action intended to punish someone is called a ___?___ .
10. If it is possible to break something, that item should be considered ___?___ .

▶ **More Practice**
Academic and Workplace Skills Activity Book
• p. 21

◀ Critical Viewing Think of some words with suffixes that this photograph calls to mind. [Interpret]

Improving Your Spelling

When it comes to spelling, English is one of the most difficult languages in the world. In some languages, such as Italian or French, spelling tends to follow a few basic rules. In English, however, there are many exceptions to almost every spelling rule. As a result, the same sound might be spelled in different ways. For example, the words *so, hoe, dough, flow, sew,* and *beau* all rhyme. In addition, the same combination of letters might be pronounced different ways, as in the words *dough, rough, through,* and *bough.*

Despite this difficulty, it is important to learn to spell correctly. Careless spelling tends to indicate either that you do not know how to spell or that your writing is careless. Someone reading your writing may be less than favorably impressed, and the value of your efforts to communicate is diminished. By using a strategy that includes practice and some simple rules, you can improve your spelling and thereby have a positive effect on all of your writing.

Keeping a Spelling Notebook

You can reduce spelling errors if you keep track of and study words that are especially difficult for you. The best place to do this is in a special section of your notebook.

▶ **KEY CONCEPT** Make a personal spelling list of difficult words; enter it in your notebook; and keep it up to date. ■

Setting Up Your Spelling Notebook Prepare a page with four columns. In the first column, record the incorrectly spelled words as you wrote them. In the second column, record the correct spelling. In the third column, enter the dates when you practiced the word. In the fourth column, write hints that help you remember the correct spelling.

PERSONAL SPELLING LIST

Misspelled Words	Correct Spelling	Practice Dates	Memory Aids
artic	arctic	4/11	no art in arctic
seperate	separate	4/11, 4/18	separate means apart and both have two A's.

> **Exercise 13** Selecting Words for a Personal Spelling List
Look over all of the writing you have done in the last month.
Record any of your misspelled words on your list.

Studying Problem Words

Some words may be difficult for you to spell because you
seldom use them. Others you may repeatedly misspell. A systematic study can help you correct both kinds of mistakes.

> **KEY CONCEPT** To study problem words, use several
steps: Look, say, listen, write, and repeat.■

STEPS FOR REVIEWING PROBLEM WORDS
1. *Look* at each word carefully to notice the arrangement or pattern of the letters. Try to see the word in your mind.
2. *Pronounce* each syllable of the word to yourself.
3. *Write* the word, and check its spelling in a dictionary.
4. *Review* your list until you can write each word correctly.

> **Exercise 14** Working With Problem Words In each of
the following sentences, select the word in parentheses that
is spelled correctly. After you complete the exercise, add to
your spelling notebook the correct spellings of any words you
spelled incorrectly.
> 1. The (pronunciation, pronuncia-
>   tion) of some words is
>   difficult.
> 2. The thunder and (lightening,
>   lightning) terrified us.
> 3. The (personnel, personal) office
>   has job information.
> 4. I hate to fill out (questionnaires,
>   questionaires).
> 5. Who is (responsible, respons-
>   able) for this messy room?
> 6. The (defendant, defendent)
>   might be innocent or guilty.
> 7. Can you draw (parallel, paralel)
>   lines without a ruler?
> 8. What kind of (mileage, milage)
>   does your car get?
> 9. Your (appearance, appearence)
>   will affect your job search.
> 10. The hotel can (accommodate,
>   accomodate) 250 guests.

> **More Practice**
> Academic and
> Workplace Skills
> Activity Book
> • pp. 22–23

▼ Critical Viewing
Identify two words
associated with this
picture that might
cause spelling difficul-
ties. Explain why.
[Connect]

Developing Memory Aids

You may find the correct spelling of some words especially difficult to learn. This is often true of words that do not follow any set rules. However, many of these words can be mastered by using memory aids.

> **KEY CONCEPT** Creating and using memory aids can help you remember the correct spelling of words that you find especially difficult to learn. ■

Using Words Within Words as a Memory Aid One useful memory aid is to look for a shorter, more familiar word within the harder one. Then, use both words to compose a sentence that you will be able to remember:

EXAMPLES:

bulletin	Watch for the *bullet* in the *bullet*in.
vegetables	Did you *get* the ve*get*ables from the market?
friend	You will be my fri*end* to the *end*.

Using Association as a Memory Aid Associate the trickiest part of the problem word with a related word that you already know how to spell.

EXAMPLES:

cellar	A cell*ar* is often d*ar*k. (Both words contain *ar*.)
medicine	This medic*ine* will help you feel f*ine* (both words end in *ine*.)
clientele	Clien*tele* means a group of customers. Customers often order what they want on the *tele*phone. (Both words contain *tele*.)

> **Exercise 15** Developing Memory Aids Create memory aids for the ten words listed below. Then, choose five difficult words from your own spelling notebook, and find a memory aid for each one. Write the hints in your notebook to help you remember the correct spelling.
>
> 1. restaurant
> 2. raspberry
> 3. cushion
> 4. sophomore
> 5. cinnamon
> 6. tortoise
> 7. rehearse
> 8. comedy
> 9. environment
> 10. oyster

Research Tip

Choose five words from a dictionary that would be difficult words for you to spell. Add them to your notebook, and develop a memory aid for each one.

More Practice

Academic and Workplace Skills Activity Book
• pp. 24–25

Applying Spelling Rules

The spellings of some words must be learned by memorization. However, the correct spelling of other words can be learned without too much difficulty by using spelling rules. For example, some words follow certain rules about how to form plurals, how to add prefixes and suffixes, or when to use *ie* or *ei.*

Plural Forms

The plural form of a noun is the form that indicates "more than one." Plural forms can be either *regular* or *irregular.*

Regular Plurals As a general rule, you can just add *-s* to the end of a word to form a regular plural. With certain regular plurals, however, you may have to choose whether to add *-s* or *-es.* Occasionally, you may also have to change a letter or two in the singular form of the word.

1. Form the plurals of words ending in *s, ss, x, z, sh,* or *ch* by adding *-es* to the base word:

   circus + *-es* = circuses   mass + *-es* = masses
   fox + *-es* = foxes   fizz + *-es* = fizzes
   dish + *-es* = dishes   finch + *-es* = finches

2. Form the plurals of words ending in *y* or *o* preceded by a vowel by adding *-s* to the base word:

   donkey + *-s* = donkeys   toy + *-s* = toys
   trolley + *-s* = trolleys   birthday + *-s* = birthdays
   stereo + *-s* = stereos   studio + *-s* = studios

3. To form the plurals of words ending in *y* preceded by a consonant, change the *y* to *i* and add *-es.* For most words ending in *o* preceded by a consonant, add *-es.* (Exceptions to this rule are musical terms ending in *o*; form these plurals by simply adding *-s.*):

   baby + *-es* = babies   fly + *-es* = flies
   veto + *-es* = vetoes   hero + *-es* = heroes
   cello + *-s* = cellos   alto + *-s* = altos

4. To form the plurals of some words ending in *f* or *fe,* change the *f* or *fe* to *v* and add *-es.* For words ending in *ff,* always add *-s*:

   knife + *-es* = knives   shelf + *-es* = shelves
   half + *-es* = halves   elf + *-es* = elves
   gulf + *-s* = gulfs   proof + *-s* = proofs
   chef + *-s* = chefs   tariff + *-s* = tariffs

▲ Critical Viewing
Think of some ways that you can study spelling rules with other students.
[Support]

Irregular Plurals Irregular plurals are not formed according to the rules on the previous page. If you are unsure of how to form a plural, check a dictionary. You will usually find the spelling of an irregular plural listed right after the pronunciation of the word. If no plural form is given in the dictionary, add -*s* or -*es* to the singular form. Below is a list of common irregular plurals:

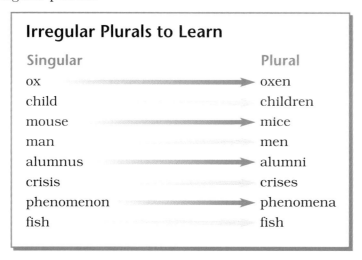

Irregular Plurals to Learn	
Singular	**Plural**
ox	oxen
child	children
mouse	mice
man	men
alumnus	alumni
crisis	crises
phenomenon	phenomena
fish	fish

Forming the Plurals of Compound Words: To form the plural of a compound word that is written as two or more separate or hyphenated words, make the word that is being modified plural by adding -*s* or -*es* to the singular form. For example, *rule of order* becomes *rules of order*, and *mother-in-law* becomes *mothers-in-law*.

Exercise 16 Forming Plurals Write the plural for each of the nouns listed below. Consult a dictionary if you need to confirm your answers.

1. ox
2. loaf
3. tax
4. chief
5. cry
6. deer
7. alley
8. stew
9. class
10. jelly
11. sheaf
12. goose
13. crisis
14. block
15. hunch
16. belief
17. brush
18. potato
19. volcano
20. heart

Prefixes and Suffixes

A prefix is one or more syllables added at the beginning of a word to form a new word. A suffix is one or more syllables added to the end of a word.

KEY CONCEPTS Adding a prefix to a word does not affect the spelling of the original word. Adding a suffix often involves a spelling change in the word. ■

Adding Prefixes When a prefix is added to a word, the spelling of the word root remains the same.

- This rule also pertains to words with double letters (*dis-* + satisfy = dissatisfy).

- A prefix may change to aid pronunciation when it is added, but the root stays the same (*ad-* becomes *al-* before *locate* to form *allocate*; *in-* becomes *ir-* before *reverent* to form *irreverent*).

Exercise 17 Spelling Words With Prefixes Form words by combining roots with prefixes. You may have to change the form of the prefix. Check a dictionary.

1. *ad-* + portion
2. *de-* + activate
3. *com-* + respond
4. *in-* + migrate
5. *ex-* + fervescent
6. *pre-* + eminent
7. *co-* + operate
8. *mis-* + speak
9. *ad-* + fluent
10. *un-* + necessary

More Practice

Academic and
Workplace Skills
Activity Book
• pp. 24–25

Adding Suffixes Some words require spelling changes when adding suffixes. The following three lists summarize the major kinds of spelling changes that can take place when a suffix is added.

Spelling Changes in Words Ending in *y:* Use the following rules for spelling changes of words ending in *y*, paying careful attention to the rules' exceptions:

1. When adding a suffix to words that end in *y* and are preceded by a consonant, change *y* to *i*. Most suffixes beginning with *i* are the exception to the rule.

   rely + *-able* = reliable   friendly + *-ness* = friendliness
   rely + *-ing* = relying   fly + *-ing* = flying

2. For words that end in *y* and are preceded by a vowel, make no change when adding most suffixes. A few short words are the exceptions.

   joy + *-ous* = joyous   employ + *-ment* = employment
   day + *-ly* = daily   pay + *-ed* = paid

30.4

Spelling Changes in Words Ending in *e:* Use the following rules for spelling changes of words ending in *e*, paying careful attention to the rules' exceptions:

1. For words ending in *e*, drop the *e* when adding a suffix beginning with a vowel. The major exceptions to this rule are (1) words ending in *ce* or *ge* with suffixes beginning with *a* or *o*, (2) words ending in *ee*, and (3) a few special words.

    love + -*able* = lovable   thrive + -*ing* = thriving
    manage + -*able* = manageable   sane + -*ity* = sanity
    agree + -*able* = agreeable   see + -*ing* = seeing
    dye + -*ing* = dyeing   be + -*ing* = being

2. For words ending in *e*, make no change when adding a suffix beginning with a consonant. A few special words are the exceptions.

    peace + -*ful* = peaceful   brave + -*ly* = bravely
    argue + -*ment* = argument   true + -*ly* = truly

Doubling the Final Consonant Before Suffixes: Use the following rules for cases in which a final consonant may or may not change, paying careful attention to the rules' exceptions:

1. For words ending consonant + vowel + consonant in a stressed syllable, double the final consonant when adding a suffix beginning with a vowel. The major exceptions to this rule are (1) words ending in *x* or *w* and (2) words in which the stress changes after the suffix is added.

    mud + -*y* = mud´dy   submit + -*ed* = submit´ted
    mix + -*ing* = mixing   row + -*ing* = rowing
    refer´ + -*ence* = ref´erence confer´ + -*ence* = con´ference

2. For words ending consonant + vowel + consonant in an unstressed syllable, make no change when adding a suffix beginning with a vowel. There are no major exceptions to this rule.

    angel + -*ic* = angelic   final + -*ize* = finalize
    hammer + -*ed* = hammered   person + -*al* = personal

▲ **Critical Viewing** Identify three adverbs that describe how these crew members are rowing. Which rules, if any, apply to the suffixes at the ends of the adverbs? [Apply]

▶ **Exercise 18** Spelling Words With Suffixes Using the rules given above, write the correct spelling for the words below. Check your answers in a dictionary.

1. fascinate + -*ion*   6. control + -*able*
2. lucky + -*ly*   7. confer + -*ence*
3. lobby + -*ist*   8. courage + -*ous*
4. swim + -*er*   9. alphabet + -*ic*
5. cease + -*less*   10. apply + -*ance*

Spelling *ie* and *ei* Words and Words Ending in *-cede*, *-ceed*, and *-sede*

Words containing *ie* and *ei*, and words with the endings *-cede*, *-ceed*, and *-sede* often prove troublesome to spell.

For most words containing *ie* or *ei*, you can use the traditional rule: "Place *i* before *e* except after *c* or when sounded like *a*, as in *neighbor* or *weigh*." For words that are exceptions to this rule as well as for words ending in *-cede*, *-ceed*, and *-sede*, it is often best to memorize the correct spellings.

ie and ei Words The *ie* and *ei* rule applies to many words, but like most rules, it has exceptions.

Exceptions for *ie* words: *counterfeit, either, foreign, forfeit, heifer, height, heir, leisure, neither, seismology, seize, seizure, sheik, sleight, sovereign, their, weird*

Exceptions for *ei* words: *ancient, conscience, efficient, financier, sufficient*

▶ **Exercise 19** Spelling *ie* and *ei* Words Fill in the blanks by inserting the missing letters. Check your work in a dictionary.
1. ach ___?___ ve
2. bel ___?___ f
3. dec ___?___ ve
4. sl ___?___ gh
5. s ___?___ zure
6. rec ___?___ pt
7. effic ___?___ nt
8. h ___?___ ress
9. r ___?___ gn
10. rel ___?___ ve

Words Ending in *-cede*, *-ceed*, and *-sede* The best way to handle words that end with these suffixes is to memorize the correct spelling. The words ending in *-cede* are *accede, concede, intercede, precede, recede, secede*. The three words endings in *-ceed* are *exceed, proceed, succeed*, and the only word ending in *-sede* is *supersede*.

▶ **Exercise 20** Working With Words Ending in *-cede*, *-ceed*, or *-sede* Complete the word for each sentence below by filling in the blanks with *-cede*, *-ceed*, or *-sede*.
1. No repairs can be done until the waters re ___?___.
2. To reach the drive-in, pro ___?___ down Elm Avenue.
3. The senator refuses to con ___?___ defeat.
4. We would like to ac ___?___ to your proposal if we can.
5. The new regulations super ___?___ the old ones.

More Practice

Academic and Workplace Skills Activity Book
• pp. 26–27

Other Confusing Endings

In certain instances, suffixes may sound alike.

> **KEY CONCEPT** Learn to distinguish between similar word endings that can cause errors. ■

COMMON WORDS ENDING IN *-able* and *-ible*

acceptable	memorable	accessible	eligible
believable	peaceable	digestible	incredible

COMMON WORDS ENDING IN *-ance* and *-ence*

acquaintance	radiance	convenience	patience
appearance	resonance	correspondence	presence

COMMON WORDS ENDING IN *-sy*

autopsy	curtsy	epilepsy	hypocrisy
biopsy	ecstasy	fantasy	idiosyncrasy

COMMON WORDS ENDING IN *-efy*

liquefy	putrefy	rarefy	stupefy

COMMON WORDS ENDING IN *-uous*, *-eous*, and *-ious*

ambiguous	gorgeous	conscious
continuous	courteous	contagious

> **Exercise 21** **Writing Words With Confusing Endings** Fill in the blanks below. Consult a dictionary if necessary.

1. court __?__ s
2. caut __?__ s
3. convert __?__ ble
4. unforgett __?__
5. liqu __?__ fy
6. irresist __?__ ble
7. hypocr __?__ y
8. correspond __?__ ce
9. stren __?__ s
10. gorg __?__ s

Proofreading Carefully

Often, spelling errors are merely the result of writing quickly to try to get your thoughts down on paper. Get into the habit of proofreading everything you write, to eliminate careless errors.

> **KEY CONCEPT** Review everything you write, and proofread for spelling errors. ■

There are a number of different proofreading skills. To discover the proofreading methods that work best for you, use a variety or combination of strategies.

PROOFREADING STRATEGIES

- Proofread your work by slowly reading it aloud or silently to yourself.

- Proofread only one line at a time. Use a ruler or other device to focus on the line you are proofreading and to cover up the lines you are not proofreading.

- Read backward, from the last word to the first. This forces you to focus only on the words themselves.

- Consult a dictionary when you come across a word that you suspect is spelled incorrectly.

- Check the spelling of proper nouns.

▶ **Exercise 22** **Proofreading Carefully** Find the misspelled word, and correct it. Use a dictionary if necessary.
1. He is quite cheerfull about the unpleasant task.
2. We need your assistence for several moments.
3. Although there were several qualified contestants, they were all farely certain of the outcome.
4. She has the abilety to do several things equally well.
5. After all that work, a peice of pie would taste delicious.
6. The exhausted speaker aksed for a glass of water.
7. The monkys ran around the cage, begging for bananas.
8. Our friends incisted that we spend a few more hours and stay for dinner.
9. The package arrived on Wensday; we found that strange because we expected it on Friday.
10. Although many people don't realize it, penguins exhist only in the Southern Hemisphere.

▶ **More Practice**
Academic and
Workplace Skills
Activity Book
• p. 28

Reflecting on Your Vocabulary, Spelling, and Proofreading Skills

Ask yourself the following questions to think about the way you learn vocabulary and spelling words:

- Do I have more trouble with pronunciations or meanings?

- Which types of spelling words are hardest for me?

- What kinds of errors do I usually make?

Standardized Test Preparation Workshop

Using Context to Determine Meaning

Many standardized tests have questions that are designed to evaluate your ability to determine the meaning of a word. You will be given a written passage. Several words will be underlined. You will need to use the context of the passage to select the correct meaning of the word.

The following sample items will provide practice answering these types of questions.

Test Tip

Look for synonyms or examples to help identify the correct answer.

Sample Test Items	Answers and Explanations
Directions: Read the passage. Then, read each question that follows the passage. Decide which is the best answer to each question. To begin a cross-stitch project, <u>thread</u> an embroidery needle with the proper color thread. Then, referring to your <u>pattern</u>, create your picture with a series of stitched *x*'s.	

1 In this passage, the word *thread* means—
 	
  A fine cotton string
 	
  B main point
 	
  C pass through
 	
  D line
	The correct answer for item 1 is C. Although the other choices offer correct definitions for *thread*, in this context, *thread* is a verb. The only choice that describes the act of putting thread through the eye of a needle is *pass through*.

2 The word *pattern* in this passage means—
 	
  F blueprint
 	
  G design
 	
  H model
 	
  J precedent
	The correct answer for item 2 is G. The word *pattern* refers to a set of written directions accompanied by a diagram of an artistic project. The correct choice, *design*, implies something artistic. Although choice F, *blueprint*, is a synonym, it is not the best choice because this word usually refers to detailed plans for building projects.

▶ **Practice 1** **Directions:** Read the passage. Then, read each question that follows the passage. Decide which is the best answer to each question.

The latest systems sold at HOTSHOT Computers are virtually virus proof. Three high school students started the company in a basement with castoff equipment they salvaged from schools, businesses, or anyone who was upgrading and getting rid of old equipment. Since the company issued its IPO on Wall Street just three months ago, stock prices have tripled!

1 In this passage, the word *systems* means—
  A living organisms
  B approaches to problem solving
  C set of computer equipment
  D orderliness

2 The word *virus* in this passage means—
  F a germ that causes illness in humans
  G a program that invades and causes damage to another computer program
  H an insect
  J a computer program that solves medical dilemmas

3 Here, the expression *castoff* means—
  A untied, as a boat from its dock
  B thrown away
  C removed, as a cast from a healed limb
  D used

4 Here, the word *upgrading* means—
  F improving
  G earning a higher grade in a computer course
  H climbing a steep rock
  J advancing

▶ **Practice 2** **Directions:** Read the passage. Then, read each question that follows the passage. Decide which is the best answer to each question.

Imagine the tedious task of cartography in the days before satellites, or even aerial photography! Humans have long recognized the need for maps, for navigation as well as for defining boundaries and borders, and have spent hours measuring and drawing out lakes, rivers, and mountains. Although most early maps were primitive, we must admire the elbow grease it took to complete the painstaking work of mapmaking.

1 In this passage, the word *tedious* means—
  A highly technical
  B wearisome
  C fascinating
  D fun-filled

2 The word *cartography* in this passage means—
  F carefully drawn primitive cartoons
  G the task of creating graphs
  H calligraphy
  J the science of making maps

3 In this passage, the word *navigation* means—
  A steering
  B a close relative to the crocodile
  C direction-finding
  D charting a course on the sea

4 In this passage, the expression *elbow grease* means—
  F an early chemical used to preserve maps
  G an ointment used to soothe the aching muscles of early cartographers
  H the ink used to draw maps on parchment
  J very hard work

Reading Skills

There are no other skills that are more essential to your success in life than reading skills. Throughout your years in school and throughout your life, you will read a wide variety of materials—from textbooks to newspapers to pamphlets to novels to road signs. It is important for you to be able to read all of these materials with a high level of comprehension and retention. In this chapter, you will learn skills and strategies that will help you increase your level of comprehension and become a more effective and efficient reader.

▲ Critical Viewing
What type of reading do you think this girl is doing? On what do you base your answer? **[Speculate]**

Reading Methods and Tools

The way in which you approach reading can vary widely, depending on the nature of the piece of writing. However, there are certain skills and strategies that you can apply to virtually anything you read.

Reading Textbooks

At least 80 percent of the reading you do for school involves textbooks. If you are able to get the most out of the textbooks you read, you will almost certainly improve your performance in school.

▶ **KEY CONCEPT** Use study aids when reading textbooks to help you understand what you are reading and to remember it better later. ■

Textbook Sections The material in a textbook is structured so that you can read it and learn it easily. Unlike most other books, textbooks include reading aids to help you make the best use of the books. Following are descriptions of these special sections:

Table of Contents This section shows how the book is organized by listing units and chapters with their page numbers. It offers a quick overview of the book.

Front of the Book

Preface or Introduction Located before or after the table of contents, these features state the author's purpose in writing the book and may give suggestions for using the book.

Front of the Book

Index This section alphabetically lists all topics covered in the book and the pages on which they can be found, making it possible to locate information quickly.

Back of the Book

Glossary The glossary lists in alphabetical order all the specialized words and terms used in the book and defines them clearly.

Appendix This feature can include such things as charts, lists, documents, or other material related to the subject of the book. An appendix can serve as an immediate reference source.

Back of the Book

Bibliography A bibliography lists books and articles that the author has used or referred to in writing the book. Many of the entries may be useful for follow-up study or for research projects.

Back of the Book

Textbook Features

Textbooks also have a number of other features designed to help you find and review material:

Titles, Headings, and Subheadings These divide the material into manageable segments. They are printed in large, boldfaced type, often in different colors. Main topics have larger headings, and subtopics have smaller ones. By scanning the headings, you can get a quick idea of the topics being covered. You can then focus on topics with which you are having difficulty or on those that your teacher has identified as being important.

Overviews The chapters in textbooks often begin with an overview, objectives, outline, or a summary of what will be covered. These features help you to preview and review what is being covered.

Questions and Exercises Most textbooks include questions or exercises at the ends of sections or chapters. Previewing the questions and exercises before you read will help you focus your reading on the most important concepts and details. After reading, answer the questions to check your understanding.

Pictures, Captions, and Graphics Pictures can add to your understanding of the ideas in the text. Look for captions that explain the content of the pictures and connect them to the reading. Use graphics, such as maps and charts, to help you understand complex concepts.

KEY CONCEPT Use titles, headings, and subheadings; overviews; questions and exercises; pictures, captions, and graphics to help you thoroughly comprehend the material. ■

Exercise 1 Examining a Textbook Choose one of your textbooks, and use it to answer the following questions:
1. Use the table of contents to identify the organization.
2. If there is a preface, does it explain the author's purpose in writing the book? If so, what is the purpose?
3. What are two specific terms found in the index?
4. Use the glossary to find the definitions of the two terms you found in the index.
5. If there is an appendix, what information does it contain?
6. Explain the format of any questions and exercises.
7. Find a chart, and explain the concept it conveys.
8. Identify at least three pictures you find useful, and explain why you think the publisher chose them.
9. What features appear at the beginning of each chapter?
10. Identify at least three different levels of headings.

Using Reading Strategies

Strong readers use various reading strategies to help them comprehend and critically examine what they're reading. In addition, they vary their reading style according to the content.

Vary Your Reading Style

> **KEY CONCEPT** Adjust your reading style to suit your purpose in reading. ■

Skimming Skimming a text means to look it over quickly to get a sense, or a general idea, of its contents. Look for highlighted or bold type, headings, and topic sentences. Use skimming to preview, review, and locate information.

Scanning Scanning involves looking through a text to find specific information. Look for words related to your topic or purpose for reading. Use scanning to research, review, and find information.

Close Reading Close reading refers to reading carefully to take in all of the main ideas and to understand the relationships among those ideas. Use this technique whenever you are reading material in your textbooks for the first time.

▲ Critical Viewing
Based on her posture, what type of reading style do you think this girl is using? Why? **[Analyze]**

> **Exercise 2** **Varying Your Reading Style** Choose a nonfiction book. Skim it in its entirety. Write down what you have learned. Then, scan it until you come across an interesting section. Read that section closely, and take detailed notes.

Use Question-Answer Relationships (QARs)

Understanding how questions are written can help you to answer them. There are four general types of questions. Learning to identify these types will help you to answer questions more easily. You can also improve your reading skills by asking and answering these types of questions as you read:

1. **Right There** This type of question deals with answers that are right there in the text, usually in one or two paragraphs or sentences.
2. **Think and Search** The answer to this type of question is in the text, but you need to think about the question's answer and then search for evidence to support it.
3. **Author and You** These questions call on you to consider what the author says and connect it to what you know.
4. **On Your Own** The answers to these questions are not in the text. They require you to draw on your experiences.

Use the SQ4R Method

To get the most out of your textbook, use the SQ4R method, a guided reading approach that involves these six skills:

1. **Survey** Preview the material you are going to read, focusing on chapter titles, headings, overviews, summaries, objectives, and questions or exercises.
2. **Question** Write down a question about each heading.
3. **Read** As you read, search for the answers to the questions that you have posed.
4. **Recite** Orally or mentally, recite the questions and their answers.
5. **Record** Take notes to further reinforce information in your mind. Include a list of main ideas and major details.
6. **Review** Review the material on a regular basis.

KEY CONCEPT Use the SQ4R method to guide your reading and to help you recall information later. ∎

THE SQ4R METHOD

Exercise 3 Using the SQ4R Method Use the SQ4R method to study a chapter in one of your textbooks. Then, write a brief review of the ways in which using SQ4R helped. Note information that you might have missed if you had not been using SQ4R, and explain how the overall use of SQ4R affected your understanding of the material.

Technology Tip

Use the SQ4R method when you visit new Web pages for research purposes. The notes that you record will guide you and save you time when you return to the Web page for more information.

Outlining What You Read

An **outline** is a structured list of information. The information is arranged according to main ideas, major details, and supporting details. Outlines are an excellent study tool that can help you prepare for tests and quizzes on information in your textbooks.

> **KEY CONCEPT** Make an outline as you read to keep track of important information and ideas. ■

Follow these steps to make an outline:

- Use Roman numerals for main ideas. Use capital letters for major details. Use Arabic numerals for supporting details.

- Use indentation to indicate importance. Main ideas begin at the left. Items begin farther to the right as they become less important.

- Never place a single item under any main idea. Always place two or more items or none at all.

The example below illustrates a formal outline on the magician Jean-Eugène Robert-Houdin:

SAMPLE OUTLINE

I. The magician Robert-Houdin ——————— Main idea
    A. Robert-Houdin in 1880's ——————— Major detail
        1. Developed rules for performing tricks
                    └─ Supporting details
        2. Created many new tricks
    B. Tools of the magician ——————— Major detail
        1. Skill with hands
        2. Secret devices
                    └─ Supporting details
        3. Misdirects people's attention
        4. Encourages false conclusions

> **Exercise 4** **Making an Outline** Using an assigned chapter of a textbook, make an outline of one section. Give your outline at least two main ideas. Then, test the effectiveness of your outline by sharing it with a schoolmate who has not read the chapter. See whether the schoolmate can answer the chapter review questions using the outline alone. If not, you may have left some key concepts out of your outline.

Using Graphic Organizers

Graphic organizers are an effective reading aid. They can help you sort out main topics and key details as well as identify relationships among the details. When choosing what organizer to use, consider the type of organization the author uses.

Analyze Chronological Order

When the events in a piece you are reading are presented in chronological order, or the order in which the events occur, you will probably find a **timeline** most effective. Use the top of the timeline to name the event, and use the bottom to indicate the elapsed time. Look at the sample below.

TIMELINE

Event 1 Event 2   Event 3   Event 4 Event 5

Time intervals (years, months, days, minutes)

Chart Main Points and Subtopics

When a piece of writing is divided clearly into main points and subtopics, you will probably want to use a **cluster diagram,** also known as a **web.** Begin by writing your topic in the center of a sheet of paper. Circle that topic. Then, write down any subtopics, and draw circles around them, making the circles large enough to add supporting details. Link the related ideas to the main topic with lines, and list the supporting details.

CLUSTER DIAGRAM

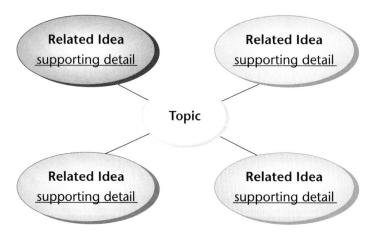

Analyze Comparison-and-Contrast Structure

Writers often make comparisons between two or more subjects. A **Venn diagram** is probably the most effective graphic organizer to help you sort out the details of such comparisons. In addition, a Venn diagram can help you make comparisons between two or more pieces of writing—a task that you will often be asked to do in school or on standardized tests.

To make a Venn diagram, draw overlapping circles. In the overlapping sections of the circles, write the subjects' shared characteristics. In the other sections of the circles, write their differences. Note that the Venn diagram below would be used for three subjects.

VENN DIAGRAM (3 Subjects)

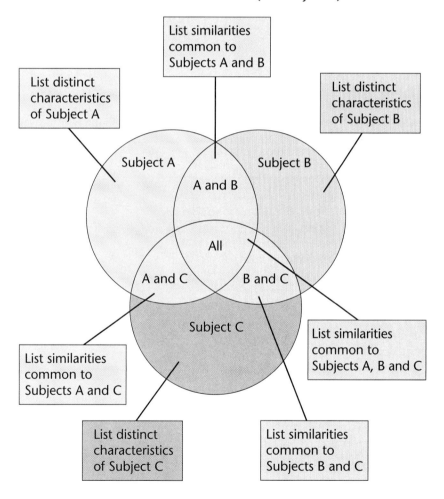

🖱 Research Tip

Discover more types of graphic organizers and variations on cluster diagrams and Venn diagrams by reviewing your textbooks. Note how information is organized and relationships are shown on the graphic organizers that you find. Use them to guide you as you create your own.

▷ **Exercise 5** **Using Graphic Organizers** Read a chapter from one of your textbooks or a work of literature. Then, use a Venn diagram, a timeline, or a cluster diagram to organize information from the text.

Reading Nonfiction Critically

Over the course of your life, you'll probably read more non-fiction than any other type of writing. Nonfiction refers to writing that has a basis in fact. Newspaper reports, reference books, and history texts are all examples of nonfiction.

Analyzing and Evaluating Nonfiction

When you read nonfiction, it is important not only to grasp the writer's main ideas and key points, but to evaluate critically the accuracy and reliability of what you read. Use a variety of reading strategies to examine, evaluate, and form judgments about what you read.

Make Inferences Nonfiction writers are generally more direct than fiction writers in making their key points. However, that doesn't mean that some information isn't left out of a typical nonfiction work. To grasp ideas that are either only hinted at or left out, you need to make inferences, or draw conclusions, based on the information the author *does* provide.

Make Generalizations When a writer provides a related set of facts and details on one topic, you can often make generalizations about that topic. For example, if an author tells numerous stories about people who experienced hardships settling in a new land, you might make the generalization that many people who came to the land faced similar hardships.

Recognize the Author's Purpose or Bias A writer's purpose, or reason for writing, can influence the choice of details and presentation of material. In addition, writers often present an issue with their own bias—their outlook on an issue or topic. Try to identify a writer's purpose, and be on the lookout for details that suggest bias.

Evaluate the Strength of the Evidence and the Writer's Credibility Check to see that a writer thoroughly supports the points with facts, examples, and details. Also, check to see that a writer has expertise or has done thorough research on the topic.

Recognize Persuasive Techniques Be on the lookout for appeals to your emotions. Make sure a writer offers sound evidence before accepting his or her position.

Judge the Writer's Work When you read many works by the same writer, try to draw some overall conclusions about the quality of his or her work.

 **Internet Tip**

Treat the information you find on the Internet the same way you would treat any nonfiction book: Critically analyze and evaluate the material using the strategies presented on this page.

Distinguishing Fact From Opinion

Don't just assume that every piece of nonfiction you read is reliable. Often, information that is presented as being the truth is simply the writer's opinion.

▶ **KEY CONCEPT** To help you evaluate the reliability of what you read, be careful to distinguish facts from opinions. ■

A statement of fact can be verified, or proved true, by experimentation, records, or personal observation. A statement of opinion cannot be proved true; before it can be accepted, it must be validated, or supported, with satisfactory sources or facts. An opinion may be based on facts, but an opinion is *not* a fact.

FACT:	To put a satellite in space, a rocket must travel fast enough to escape the Earth's gravity.
OPINION (feeling):	Space travel is too dangerous.
OPINION (judgment):	A mechanical flaw in a spacecraft could threaten an astronaut's life.
OPINION (prediction):	In the next decade, humans will colonize the moon.

Verify facts and validate opinions to determine whether the material you are reading is reliable.

▶ **Exercise 6** Analyzing Fact and Opinion Statements First, identify each of the following statements as *fact* or *opinion.* Then, analyze whether each fact statement is *true* or *false,* and analyze whether each opinion statement is *valid* or *invalid.*

1. Abraham Lincoln was the greatest president the United States has ever had.
2. Our team is sure to win the baseball game next week.
3. The blue whale is the largest animal ever to inhabit Earth.
4. The Supreme Court has eleven justices.
5. We will have snow tomorrow because a cold front is approaching.

▶ **Exercise 7** Analyzing Facts and Opinions in a Magazine Look through a newsmagazine. Write down five examples of facts. Then, find at least two examples of opinions. Tell whether the opinions are backed by facts.

▼ Critical Viewing
Based on her expression, do you think this girl agrees or disagrees with what she is reading? [Infer]

Applying Modes of Reasoning

When you read critically, you draw conclusions about what you read. These conclusions need to be sound and logical.

> **KEY CONCEPT** Think logically to draw valid conclusions. ■

Inductive and Deductive Reasoning

When you think logically, you use *reasoning* to lead to or support a conclusion. Two main forms of reasoning are *inductive* and *deductive*.

Inductive Reasoning Inductive reasoning involves drawing an overall conclusion, or making a generalization, from a set of specific facts. A valid generalization is a statement supported by evidence that holds true in a large number of cases. The more evidence you have, the more reliable your generalization will be.

Deductive Reasoning When you use deductive reasoning, you move from the general to the specific. For example, if you learn that everyone who works at a certain company has excellent health benefits, then you can deduce that someone you know who works there has excellent health benefits.

Logical Fallacies

A logical fallacy occurs when the rules of logic are not followed. Two types of logical fallacies are hasty generalizations and circular reasoning.

Hasty Generalization A hasty generalization is a statement that is made about a large number of cases or a whole group on the basis of a few examples, without taking into account exceptions or qualifying factors. Look at this example:

VALID: Every homeroom in our school has more girls than boys, so there are more girls than boys in our school.

HASTY: There are fifteen girls and ten boys in my homeroom, so there must be more girls than boys in our school.

Circular Reasoning Circular reasoning, also called *begging the question*, occurs when a person restates a general statement as if it were a fact without supplying supporting evidence.

> **◯ Research Tip**
>
> To understand the use of generalizations, research the published results of polls and surveys. Note the conclusions drawn from the results, and determine whether the generalizations are hasty or valid.

Other Forms of Reasoning

Analogies An analogy is a comparison between two unlike things that are in some way similar. A *complete analogy* is one that names the specific ways in which two things are similar. An *incomplete analogy* is one that simply states one thing is like another without offering the specifics.

COMPLETE: The cell is like a factory—it processes raw materials, produces energy, and discharges wastes.

INCOMPLETE: The human body is like a machine.

The first analogy is complete because it compares particular functions that actually are similar. The second is incomplete because it fails to acknowledge ways in which the body is *not* like a machine.

RECOGNIZE COMPLETE/INCOMPLETE ANALOGIES

1. How are the two things being compared essentially different?
2. How are the two things alike? Is the comparison logical?
3. What is the truth that the comparison tries to show?

Cause and Effect A cause-and-effect sequence is one in which something is caused by one or more events that occurred before it. When one event happens immediately after another, people sometimes conclude that the first event caused the second event. An unrelated sequence is one in which the first event did not cause the second event. In many cases, events can occur one after the other *without* signifying a cause-and-effect relationship.

> **Exercise 8** Analyzing Forms of Reasoning First, identify the form of reasoning (inference, generalization, analogy, or cause and effect) used in each of the following statements. Then, tell whether each conclusion is valid or invalid.
> 1. If you leave the lights of a car turned on, the battery will run down.
> 2. The atom is like a miniature solar system.
> 3. The two meals I got on the plane were not good, so all airline food must be terrible.
> 4. Luis has been elected class president for the past three years, so he must be a real leader.
> 5. When the available supply of a product increases, the price usually goes down.

Identifying an Author's Purpose and Evaluating Language Use

Identify an Author's Purpose

To read critically, you must also determine why the material was written. Is the author trying to inform you, persuade you, or simply entertain you?

IDENTIFYING AN AUTHOR'S PURPOSE IN WRITING	
Purpose	**Informational Clues**
To inform:	Series of factual statements that are verified by records or personal observation
To instruct:	Sequential development of an idea or a process
To offer an opinion:	Presentation of an issue with a predominant point of view backed up by valid authority
To sell:	Persuasion designed to sell an idea or a product
To entertain:	Narration of an event in a humorous way; often used to lighten a serious topic

Evaluate the Use of Language

Learning to understand and evaluate the various ways in which words are used is an important part of becoming a critical reader.

Connotation and Denotation   As you read critically, you must be sensitive to the author's tone, or attitude toward the topic. Tone can be expressed using words with *connotative*, or implied, meanings that differ from the *denotative*, or literal, meanings. Connotations can affect a person emotionally and cause a particular response to the material. The following three statements are similar, yet each gives a different impression of the event described.

DENOTATION: The speaker walked quickly up to the lectern.

CONNOTATION: The speaker strode confidently up to the lectern.

CONNOTATION: The speaker stumbled clumsily up to the lectern.

Irony Irony refers to a contrast between perception and reality; between what is said and what is actually meant.

Understatement When an idea is played down or treated casually, it is considered to be an understatement.

Inflated Language and Jargon Inflated language refers to writing that sounds very scholarly or is filled with scientific or technical terms or overly long phrases. One type of inflated language is called jargon. Jargon is the specialized vocabulary used by people in a particular field. In its place, it is useful, but jargon is often misused to impress the reader or to conceal meaning.

Euphemism A euphemism is a word or phrase used to replace words that may be considered offensive.

Slanting Slanting is the writing of a passage so that it leans toward one point of view. Choosing words with either positive or negative connotations is one type of slanting. Another type of slanting is presenting only one side of an issue by leaving out important facts that would support another point of view.

SLANTED STATEMENT:	Management offered the union a salary increase of only 7 percent.
MORE BALANCED STATEMENT:	Management offered a 7-percent salary increase plus an expanded benefits package, including profit sharing.

> ▶ **Exercise 9** **Applying Critical Reading Skills** Analyze this passage for statements of fact and opinion, forms of reasoning, author's purpose, and use of language.

Nowadays, it is impossible to drive down any street for more than a few minutes without passing at least one jogger, clad in colorful shorts and expensive running shoes, and usually panting or even gasping for air. The death from a heart attack of Jim Fixx, a fellow slave to the exercise mania, seems not to have deterred these fanatical amateur athletes. Millions of dollars are spent each year in fashionable exercise salons run by sharp entrepreneurs. If you could manage to stop one of the victims long enough to ask why he is putting himself through such torture, he would probably mumble something about the heart being a muscle that needs exercise. There is no medical evidence for this. It is true that exercise is a good thing, but overexercising is too much of a good thing. In fact, victims of the physical fitness craze may actually be harming themselves. Doctors report seeing many more injuries to joints, muscles, and tendons. And, of course, there is always the risk of a heart attack during violent exercise.

> ◀ **Speaking and Listening Tip**
> A speaker's tone of voice or facial expression is often a clue that he or she is using irony or understatement.

▼ Critical Viewing
What types of connotations might the words have in a description of this runner? **[Speculate]**

Reading Literary Writing

Although you will most often read literature for pleasure, you will get more out of what you read if you apply the strategies that follow. The reading strategies on this page can be applied to any type of literature. On the pages that follow, you'll find specific strategies for reading short stories and novels, drama, poetry, and epics and legends.

Analyzing and Evaluating Fiction

Establish a Purpose for Reading Before you begin, establish a purpose for reading to focus your thoughts. For example, you might read simply for enjoyment, or you might read to learn something about the exotic setting of a novel, or you might read to learn lessons you can apply to your life.

Ask Questions As you read, ask questions: *Why* did the character do this? *When* are the events taking place? *What* are the consequences of these events? Look for answers to these questions as you work your way through the piece.

Reread or Read Ahead When you are unsure what is happening or if the meaning of a sentence or a paragraph is unclear, reread it. At times, you may also find it helpful to read ahead to find more information and to make connections.

Make Personal Connections You will increase your understanding and enjoyment if you connect the characters and events to your own experiences. Consider what you would do and how you would feel if you were taking part in the action.

Read Aloud Read aloud to hear the sounds of the words. This technique is especially effective for poetry, in which sound is just as important as meaning.

Analyze When you analyze, you try to determine the meaning behind events and the characters' actions. Works of literature usually convey a theme, or a central message about life. Most themes are conveyed indirectly, so you may need to do some analyzing to grasp the message.

Respond As you read, think about how the characters and events make you feel, and explore the associations that they bring to mind. When you have finished reading, take some time to reflect and to consider what the work means to you. This may help you decide whether to read other works by that author.

Research Tip

Published literary criticisms reflect one writer's or a group of writers' critical readings of a work of literature. Review several books that contain literary criticisms to see how professional writers apply the critical thinking skills you are learning to use.

Reading Fiction

Following are some strategies for reading fiction:

Predict As you read, ask yourself what might happen next. Base your predictions on what you know about the characters and setting as well as on clues the author provides.

Connect to Your Own Experiences To help you understand how the characters feel, compare their experiences to those you've had in your own life.

Envision the Setting and the Action Use details from the story to create a picture in your mind, as if you were watching the story unfold on the big screen. You might even use a chart like this one to list important details of a scene and to identify the importance of the scene to the story.

Research Tip

You can view film versions of stories, novels, epics, and legends for an understanding of historical context. Be aware, however, that the historical information you see may not be completely accurate and may reflect the filmmakers' interpretations.

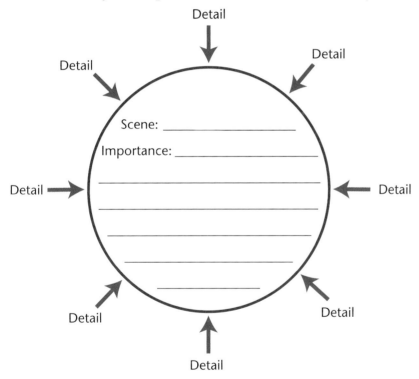

Draw Inferences and Conclusions Writers don't always tell you everything directly. Sometimes, you have to make inferences, or draw conclusions, by considering the underlying meaning of details that the writer includes or doesn't include.

> **Exercise 10** **Reading Short Stories** Read a short story. Apply all of the strategies above. When you have finished, write a brief explanation of how you used each strategy.

Reading Drama

The key difference between dramas and other forms of literature is that dramas are meant to be performed. As a result, the story unfolds and the characters are revealed through dialogue and action—there are no long passages of description and no direct revelations about how characters feel. Stage directions indicate when and how the actors move and sometimes suggest lighting and sound effects.

Envision the Action Remember that dramas are meant to be performed rather than read. As you read, try to envision how the play would look if it were being performed on stage. Use the stage directions to help you see in your mind the action taking place and to visualize the costumes.

Connect the Play to Its Historical Context Sometimes, the time in which a play is set can have a dramatic impact on how the characters act and can shape the message the play conveys. Look in the stage directions for information about the time in which the play is set.

Summarize Most dramas are broken into acts or scenes. Pause between acts or scenes to review in your mind the action that has taken place. Make a chart like the one below. List the act, and identify the scenes, characters, and conflict. Then, briefly summarize the events.

Act I: _____

   Scene I: _____

      Characters: _____

      Conflict: _____

> **Exercise 11** **Reading Drama** Read the first act of a play in your textbook or in another collection. Explain the play's setting, including its historical context. Tell how the stage directions and characters' comments and actions enabled you to envision the scene. Then, summarize the conflict and the events that occurred in the act.

Reading Poetry

Reading poetry is unlike reading other types of literature because it is a very distinctive kind of writing—it differs in its appearance, its use of language, and its sound. Poets' imaginative use of language can sometimes make a poem seem complex or hard to understand. Using specific strategies can help you to understand and appreciate poetry.

Identify the Speaker When you read a poem, you are hearing the voice of the poem's speaker. The speaker is not necessarily the poet, although it can be. The speaker may be a character created by the poet. Determine who you think is "telling" the poem, and try to determine his or her perspective on the situation in the poem.

Envision Images Use your senses to experience the pleasures of a poem. For instance, *see* the image of a storm scattering red autumn leaves and *hear* the sound of the wind howling.

Read According to Punctuation Keep in mind that even if a poem is shaped to fit a particular rhythm and rhyme, a poem's words are usually put together and punctuated as sentences. When you read a poem, don't stop at the end of each line unless a punctuation mark stops you.

Listen to the Poem One of the things that distinguishes poetry from prose is its sound. Poetry is meant to be read aloud; by doing so, you will hear the music of the poet's words.

▷ **Exercise 12** Reading Poetry Select a poem from your textbook. Read the poem aloud, according to its punctuation, and listen to its sound. Then, write a brief description of the poem in which you identify the speaker, describe three images or figures of speech, and describe the poem's sound.

Speaking and Listening Tip

To appreciate how listening to poetry differs from reading it, attend a local poetry reading. If this isn't possible, find recordings of poetry. Compare and contrast the effect of listening to a poem with the effect of reading one.

Reading From Varied Sources

Today, there are more sources of reading material than ever before. Not only can you read books, magazines, newspapers, and other forms of printed material, but you can also read an almost unlimited amount of material on the Internet. The following are just a few of the sources from which you can choose. When selecting a source, consider your purpose for reading, along with any time constraints with which you're faced.

Read Diaries, Letters, and Journals Diaries, letters, and journals are a great source for firsthand accounts of historical events. Use them to discover how it felt to be part of an event in which you are interested or as primary source material in a research paper. As you read, remember that diaries and journals present a single perspective—the writer's—of the events. To find a balanced point of view, look at several diaries and journals.

Read Newspapers Newspapers are probably the best source for up-to-date information on issues and events. When you are writing a research paper on a historical event, you may want to use newspapers to capture the way information about the event was presented to people at that time. You will also want to use newspapers when you are writing about current events. Beyond school, you'll probably continue to use newspapers as a means of keeping up with current events. Although newspapers are one of the most objective sources, be on the lookout for any words or choices of details that suggest a bias.

Read Speeches Transcripts of speeches can be another excellent source for learning about historical or current events. Keep in mind that a speech that you are reading was originally written to be presented orally to an audience. Also, consider that a speech presents a single point of view—that of the speaker. Many speeches, such as political speeches, have a persuasive purpose. As a result, speakers often carefully choose words and details to achieve a specific effect. Try to avoid being swayed by appeals to emotion or charged language. Instead, see how effectively the speaker has backed up his or her key points with facts, statistics, and other types of support.

▼ **Critical Viewing**
This painting shows Patrick Henry delivering his famous "Give Me Liberty or Give Me Death" speech. What can you tell about his delivery based on the painting? **[Analyze]**

"GIVE ME LIBERTY, OR GIVE ME DEATH !"
PATRICK HENRY delivering his great speech on the Rights of the Colonies, before the Virginia Assembly convened at Richmond, March 23rd 1775. Concluding with the words "Give me liberty or give me death" which became the war cry of the Revolution.

Read Electronic Texts The main type of electronic texts that you will encounter are Web pages. There is an incredible amount of information on the Web, and the amount is growing every day. Some of the information is reliable and objective; some is biased or targeted toward a specific audience. When you read material on the Internet, do so with a critical eye. Determine the purpose behind the material. Often, you will discover that the material has a persuasive purpose. Check whether any points made in a text on the Web are thoroughly supported by facts and details. Also, evaluate the credibility of the source.

▶ **Exercise 13** Reading Varied Sources Find at least one example of each of the sources mentioned on these pages. Read the material carefully. Then, write a brief summary of each piece. Follow your summary with an evaluation of the reliability of the material. How well has the author supported his or her main points? Is the author credible? Why or why not? Would you recommend the material to others? Explain.

Reflecting on Your Reading

After a week of applying reading skills and strategies for both nonfiction and fiction works, think about the experience of using them. Use these questions to direct your reflection:

- Which sections of the books that I read did I find most useful?

- How has varying my reading style affected my reading time?

- Which graphic organizers have I used to process and understand information from my reading?

- How do the steps of the SQ4R method help me obtain more complete information and understanding?

- How have critical reading skills helped me to analyze and evaluate the material I read?

- Which strategies for reading fiction did I find most useful? Which strategies did I find most difficult to use?

Jot down your responses and ideas in a journal or notebook. If you like, compare your thoughts and ideas with those of a partner.

Standardized Test Preparation Workshop

Make Inferences and Predictions

The reading sections of standardized tests often measure your ability to make inferences. For these types of questions, a reading passage will be supplied. The answer to the question will not be directly stated in the material you use. You will need to put together clues from the text to arrive at the correct answer. Some questions will require you to make inferences or predictions about characters' actions or probable plot events. Other questions will ask you to make inferences about the author's purpose or point of view. You may be asked to respond by choosing from among several choices or by responding in writing.

Look at the following sample items:

Test Tips

- If you are given a specific amount of space in which to write an answer, plan your points carefully before you begin writing.
- Approach multiple-choice reading questions the same way you'd approach short-answer items.

Sample Test Items

Answers and Explanations

Directions Read the passage. Then, answer the questions that follow the passage.

From "A Celebration of Grandfathers," Rudolfo Anaya

"Buenos dias le de Dios, abuelo." God give you a good day, grandfather. This is how I was taught as a child to greet my grandfather, or any grown person. It was a greeting of respect, a cultural value to be passed on from generation to generation, this respect for the old ones.

The old people I remember from my childhood were strong in their beliefs, and as we lived daily with them we learned a wise path of life to follow. They had something important to share with the young, and when they spoke, the young listened.

1. The author opens the story with a Spanish quotation to
   A impress readers with his knowledge of Spanish.
   B establish a cultural context for the work.
   C explain the essay's title.
   D teach readers a Spanish quotation.

The answer for item 1 is *B*. By opening with a quotation in the language of his childhood, the author gives readers a taste of the culture in which he was raised.

2. Answer the following question. Base your answer on "A Celebration of Grandfathers."

In what ways has the author's attitude toward the elderly changed or remained the same since he was a child? Support your answer with details from the passage

Your answer should consist of a paragraph that includes a topic sentence and details from the passage that support it.

> **Practice 1** **Directions:** Read the passage. Then, answer the questions that follow the passage.

From "Sonata for Harp and Bicycle," Joan Aiken

. . . ."No one is allowed to remain in the building after five o'clock," Mr. Manaby told his new assistant, showing him into the little room that was like the inside of a parcel.

"Why not?"

"Directorial policy," said Mr. Manaby. But that was not the real reason.

Gaunt and sooty, Grimes Buildings lurched up the side of a hill toward Clerkenwell. Every little office within its dim and crumbling exterior owned one tiny crumb of light—such was the proud boast of the architect—but toward evening the crumbs were collected as by an immense vacuum cleaner, absorbed and demolished, yielding to an uncontrollable mass of dark that came tumbling through windows to take their place. Darkness infested the building like a flight of bats returning willingly to roost.

"Wash hands, please. Wash hands, please," the intercom began to bawl in the passages at a quarter to five. Without much need of prompting, the staff hustled like lemmings along the corridors to green- and blue-tiled washrooms that mocked with an illustration of cheerfulness the encroaching dusk.

❶ Mr. Manaby could best be described as
  A a man who is friendly and outgoing.
  B a man who does not like his job.
  C a man who expects rules to be followed.
  D a clean and tidy man.

❷ Which sentence BEST describes the author's attitude toward the employees of Grimes Buildings?

  F She admires their dedication.
  G She is amused by their unquestioning obedience.
  H She is impressed by their superior intelligence.
  I She is saddened by their cruelty.

❸ The reaction of the employees to the intercom announcement indicates that
  A they are used to the announcement.
  B they resent the announcement.
  C they are surprised by the announcement.
  D they don't understand the announcement.

❹ What can you predict based on the opening dialogue?
  F The new assistant will fit in well.
  G The new assistant will have a fight with Mr. Manaby.
  H The new assistant will break the intercom.
  I The new assistant will stay in the building after five o'clock.

❺ When the author says the little room is like the inside of a parcel, she means that
  A the room is square.
  B the room is filled with paper.
  C the room is small.
  D the room is closed.

❻ Which word BEST describe the assistant's reaction to Mr. Manaby's statement that everyone must leave by five o'clock?
  F curious
  G timid
  H amused
  I sad

> **Practice 2** **Directions:** Answer the following question. Base your answer on "A Sonata for Harp and Bicycle."

READ THINK EXPLAIN What is the main impression the author gives of Grimes Buildings? Use details from the excerpt to explain your answer.

Chapter 32

Study, Reference,
and Test-Taking Skills

◀ Critical Viewing
What type of school-
work would and
would not be appro-
priate to do in the
setting shown here?
Why? [Analyze]

   Learning how to improve your study, reference, and test-
taking skills will make your schoolwork easier and prove to be
a valuable asset throughout your education. The first two sections of this chapter will show you how to improve your general
study habits and how to research specific information in printed and electronic forms. The final section will discuss strategies that you can use to improve your performance on tests.

Basic Study Skills

As with most other things, the more you think out and plan how you study, the more effective your studying will be. Develop a systematic approach to studying that includes how and where you study and how you record what you learn.

Developing a Study Plan

Good study habits begin with a strong study plan. The purpose of a study plan is to help you make the best use of the time available to you for doing your assignments. Your study plan should include setting up a study area, establishing a study schedule, and keeping a study notebook.

▶ **KEY CONCEPT** Use a *three point study plan* to manage your time and keep track of your assignments. ■

USING A STUDY PLAN

STUDY AREA
1. Set up a well-lit study area free from distractions.
2. Equip the area with work materials: pens, paper, ruler, dictionary.

STUDY NOTEBOOK
1. List assignments and include their due dates.
2. List long-term assignments in steps.
3. Check off assignments as you complete them.

STUDY SCHEDULE
1. Block out periods of time in which you have fixed activities.
2. Plan to study 2–3 hours a day, in 30–45 minute periods.
3. Study your hardest subject first.

⚙ Technology Tip

You can use a software time-management program to help you set up and keep track of your study schedule.

▶ **Exercise 1** **Evaluating Your Study Plan** Identify which area of your study plan you need to improve most: setting up a study area, making a study schedule, or keeping a study notebook. Work to improve that skill for one week, and then evaluate your progress.

Taking Notes

Notes are an important study tool. Not only will you need them to study, but the very act of writing information down helps you retain it. Divide your notebook by subject, and take notes on what you learn in class and read in your textbooks.

KEY CONCEPT Keep an organized notebook in which you take notes while listening or reading. ■

Modified Outline Because there is not enough time to write everything down, you should take notes on only the most important information. One of the fastest ways to take notes is by using a *modified outline form*, in which you list main ideas at the margin, indent to show major details, and indent further for supporting details, if necessary.

PASSAGE:

Silicon Chips are engraved with hundreds of electronic circuits. These chips are small enough to pass through the eye of a needle, yet they can store 64,000 pieces of information. They are already at work in the digital watch, the pocket calculator, and the microwave oven.

SAMPLE MODIFIED OUTLINE

Silicon Chips) ———————— Main idea
1. Engraved with hundreds of) —— Major details
      electronic circuits)
2. Extremely small,
      yet store 64,000 pieces of information
3. Used in digital watches,
      calculators, microwave ovens

Summaries A summary is an excellent tool to help you review material. It is a restatement of key ideas in your own words. Written summaries are usually arranged in paragraphs. You can use a summary to capture main ideas from a piece you've just read or a lecture you've just heard. You can also summarize a modified outline you've developed.

Exercise 2 Developing a Modified Outline and a Summary Develop a modified outline and a summary of a chapter from one of your textbooks.

Technology Tip

If you have steady access to a computer and are a strong keyboardist, you may want to record and store some of your notes on computer. Make sure that you back up your notes on a separate disk and that you keep a hard copy.

Reference Skills

The recent revolution in electronic media has made more kinds of information available than ever before. Virtually every kind of printed reference now has an electronic equivalent, either on CD-ROM or on-line or both. At public or school libraries, you can often find all these sources: fiction and non-fiction books, audiocassettes, videocassettes, periodicals (newspapers, magazines, and scholarly journals), reference works in printed and electronic form, information on micro-film, and computer access to the Internet.

Finding Library Resources

Some library resources *circulate*—that is, you can borrow them for a fixed period of time. Others are for *reference* only and must be used at the library. Some materials are displayed on *open stacks*, or shelves, where you get them yourself; oth-ers are stored on *closed stacks* open only to library staff, who will bring you the material when you request it.

Using the Library Catalog The catalog shows whether the library owns a work. Use the catalog to help you find works by specific authors or on particular subjects. The cata-log also clarifies whether a book is fiction or nonfiction and gives call numbers of nonfiction works so that you can locate them on the shelves.

▶ **KEY CONCEPT** Use the library catalog— in *card, printed*, or *electronic* form—to find important information about the materials that a library stocks. ■

Card Catalog Each work in a library has an *author card* and *title card*; each nonfiction book also has at least one *subject card*. Cards are filed alphabetically in small drawers, with au-thor cards alphabetized by last names and title cards alpha-betized by the first words of the titles, excluding *A, An*, or *The*.

CARD CATALOG (AUTHOR CARD)	
306.209C Collins, Gail	call number / <u>author</u>
Scorpion Tongues	title
New York:	city of publication
William Morrow, 1998	publisher, / <u>publication date</u>
322 p; index	number of pages / <u>index</u>
United States—Politics	subject

Electronic Catalog Most libraries now keep an electronic catalog, an on-line database or a CD-ROM that you access from special library computer terminals. Usually, you can find a book's catalog entry by typing in its title, key words in the title, its author's name, or (for nonfiction) an appropriate subject. Electronic catalogs usually indicate whether the book is available or has been checked out. Often, the catalog will also indicate whether the book is available from other local libraries through an inter-library loan system.

Printed Catalog A printed catalog is a booklet that lists each work alphabetically by author, by title, and (for nonfiction) by subject.

Technology Tip

Some electronic catalogs can be accessed remotely through the Internet. Ask your librarian if this option is available.

> **Exercise 3** Using the Library Catalog Visit your school or local library, and use the catalog to answer these questions.
> 1. What kind of catalog does the library use?
> 2. Who wrote *The Red Badge of Courage*? Is this book fiction or nonfiction?
> 3. What are the titles, subjects, and call numbers of three nonfiction books by Annie Dillard?
> 4. What are the titles, authors, and call numbers of three books about nutrition published since 1998?
> 5. What are the titles, authors, and call numbers of two nonfiction books about space exploration?

▼ Critical Viewing
How do the stacks at this library compare with those at your own library? [Compare]

Finding Books on Library Shelves Libraries generally separate fiction (made-up stories) from nonfiction (factual material). Nonfiction includes two smaller groups often shelved separately: biographies (real-life people's stories) and reference works (works to which you refer for information and which must be used at the library).

▶**KEY CONCEPT** Find fiction arranged alphabetically by authors' last names and nonfiction arranged by call number. ■

Fiction Books of fiction are shelved in a special section alphabetized by authors' last names. In the library catalog and on its spine, the book may be labeled *F* or *FIC*, followed by one or more letters of the author's last name; for example, *FIC Cis* may appear on a novel by Sandra Cisneros.

▶**KEY CONCEPT** Find nonfiction on the shelves by using the call numbers. ■

Nonfiction Works of nonfiction are assigned number-letter codes, called *call numbers*, based on their content. The call numbers are placed on the spine of each book, and the books are arranged in number-letter order on the shelves—for example, 216.1, 216.2, 216.41A, 216.41G, 216.42B, 217.1. To find a nonfiction book, look it up in the library catalog to learn its call number and then follow number-letter order to locate the book on the shelf.

Most public libraries assign call numbers according to the **Dewey Decimal System,** which divides all knowledge into ten main groups numbered from 000 to 999. The following chart shows the number spans for these ten content areas.

| MAIN CLASSES OF THE DEWEY DECIMAL SYSTEM ||
Number	Subject
000–099	General Works (encyclopedias, periodicals, etc.)
100–199	Philosophy
200–299	Religion
300–399	Social Sciences
400–499	Languages
500–599	Science
600–699	Technology (applied science)
700–799	Arts and Leisure
800–899	Literature
900–999	History

Special Sections In the Dewey Decimal System, *biographies* are often not assigned call numbers but instead are shelved in a special section alphabetized by the last names of their subjects (the people they are about). In the library catalog and on the book's spine, a biography may be labeled *B* or *BIO*, followed by one or more letters of the subject's last name; for example, *BIO Ein* may appear on a biography of Albert Einstein.

Reference works usually have their own special section—and an *R* or *REF* before their call numbers. Many libraries also have special sections for young-adult books (often labeled *YA*) and children's books (usually labeled *J* or *JUV* for *juvenile*).

The **Library of Congress System,** unlike the Dewey Decimal System, is organized letter-number. In the Library of Congress System, the call numbers begin with letters. The main classes are designated by a single letter; combinations of two letters designate the subclasses. The letter designations are followed by a numerical notation, from 1 to 9999, which can be further subdivided:

▲ Critical Viewing
What type of assistance do you imagine that the librarian is providing for the girl in this photograph? **[Speculate]**

MAIN CLASS:	H	Social Sciences
SUBCLASS:	HF	Commerce, Marketing, Advertising
DIVISION:	5717	Business Communication

▶ **Exercise 4** **Finding Fiction and Nonfiction** In your notebook, answer the following questions.

1. To find fiction by Ralph Ellison on a library shelf, would you look before or after fiction by George Eliot?
2. For a nonfiction work with call number 310.3R, would you look before or after of a work with call number 310.2J?
3. For a book with call number R032.1B, would you look in the reference, biography, or fiction section?
4. Arrange this fiction in the order that you would find them on library shelves: *Moby-Dick* by Herman Melville, *The Bluest Eye* by Toni Morrison, *Ethan Frome* by Edith Wharton, and *The Joy Luck Club* by Amy Tan.
5. Arrange these call numbers in the order that you would find them on library shelves: 519.3B, 518.1P, 518.6C, 518.1K, 519.6A. What is the general subject or content area of books with these call numbers?

Using Periodicals and Periodical Indexes

A *periodical* is a newspaper, magazine, or similar publication issued at regular intervals. Such publications are good sources of up-to-date information. To find out which periodicals a library carries, look up the title in the card catalog.

Periodical Indexes To find which periodicals contain articles on a particular subject, consult a periodical index. Issued regularly in printed or electronic form, these indexes contain *citations* that tell you where and when an article was published. They also may contain *abstracts*, or brief summaries, of the articles. In addition, many electronic indexes provide the *full text*, or complete article, for some articles cited.

▶ **KEY CONCEPT** Use articles from periodicals for up-to-date information and periodical indexes to locate the articles. ■

Some indexes—such as the *Readers' Guide to Periodical Literature*—cover articles from many periodicals; others, such as *The New York Times Index*, cover articles from only one publication. Look at this sample *Readers' Guide* entry.

SAMPLE READERS' GUIDE ENTRY

subject heading ———————[**HORSEMANSHIP**
              See also
cross-references ——————[Polo
              [Rodeos
subheading ⌐ **Competition** article topic clarified in brackets
title of article ⌐ A show of hooves [pony club rally].
             illustrated
author ⌐ J.B. Banks *National Geographic World* v288 no 4
name of periodical ⌐   volume and number ⌐
pages ——————[p. 12–15   date   ⌐ Ag 1999

▶ **Exercise 5** **Using Periodicals** Visit a school or local library to answer these questions.
1. What daily newspapers does the library carry?
2. Find an article in a current magazine that provides information you could use in an essay.
3. Use a periodical index to find four citations for articles on women in sports. Also, list the subjects you looked under.
4. Use a periodical index to find an article on a subject you are studying. Read the article, and share your findings.
5. Using a periodical index, find an article about someone you admire. Read the article, and then write a summary.

◆Technology Tip

Many newspapers and magazines now have free Internet Web sites where you can read current editions at no cost.

🔎 Research Tip

Find citations in an electronic index by typing in the subject, the author's name, or a key word in the title of the article. Find citations in printed indexes by looking up the subject or author.

Using Dictionaries

A *dictionary* is a collection of words and their meanings, along with other information about words, such as their parts of speech and pronunciations.

▶ **KEY CONCEPT** Use a dictionary to find information about words, such as spelling, pronunciation, and parts of speech. ■

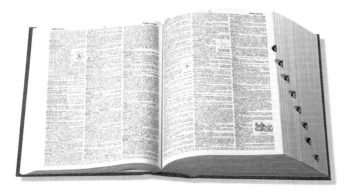

Technology Tip

Abridged electronic dictionaries are now available in a computerized form resembling pocket calculators. Foreign-language dictionaries in this form can be quite convenient for travelers.

English-Language Dictionaries An *unabridged* dictionary of the English language attempts to cover all the words in the language, including those no longer in use, and gives detailed information on each word's history. An *abridged* English-language dictionary, which is shortened for everyday use, is the kind of dictionary that most people have in their homes and offices.

Specialized Dictionaries These dictionaries are limited to words of a particular type (for example, slang) or words in a particular field (for example, legal or literary terms). They also include *foreign-language dictionaries*, which are two-part dictionaries that give English equivalents of words in a particular foreign language and vice versa.

Dictionary Organization Dictionaries are available in both printed and electronic form. In printed dictionaries, entry words are arranged in *alphabetical order*. To speed your search for a word, use the **thumb index,** a series of right-hand notches that makes it easier to thumb alphabetically through a dictionary. Each notch, labeled *A, B, C,* and so on, shows the section of entries for words that start with that particular letter.

Also use the **guide words,** two large words at the top of each dictionary page that show the first and last entry words on the page. All other entry words on the page fall alphabetically between these two guide words. For instance, if the guide words are *rider* and *rift,* the words *ridge* and *rife* will also be on that page; however, the word *right* will not be there.

In **electronic dictionaries,** you usually find a word simply by typing the word and having the dictionary search the dictionary database.

Dictionary Entries Dictionary entries contain a wealth of information about words and their use. Here is an example:

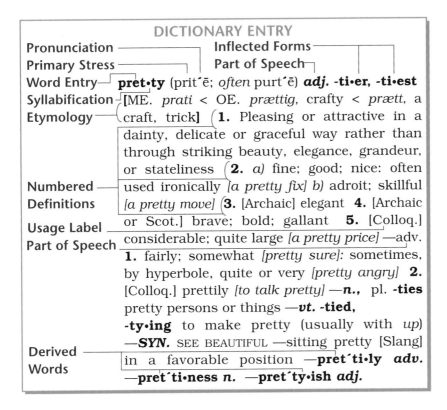

Entry Word With Syllabification The word being defined appears in dark print at the start of the entry. From it you can confirm the word's spelling and usually learn how to break it into syllables (if the word has more than one syllable). Dashes, dots, or spaces usually show the syllables.

Pronunciation Usually appearing in parentheses or brackets immediately following the entry word, the pronunciation shows how to say the word and uses accent marks (´) to show which syllable or syllables to stress. To understand the symbols in the pronunciation, you need to consult the dictionary's *pronunciation key.* When you consult the key that follows the pronunciation of *pretty,* you see that the *e* sounds like the *i* in *is* and the *y* sounds like the first *e* in *even.*

Part-of-Speech Label The dictionary uses abbreviations to show how a word functions in a sentence—as a noun (*n*), a transitive verb (*vt*), an intransitive verb (*vi*), an adjective (*adj*), an adverb (*adv*), or another part of speech.

Plurals and Inflected Forms The dictionary shows irregularly formed plurals and verb tenses and will show inflected forms, such as comparative and superlative modifiers, if there is anything unusual about their spellings.

Etymology Information about the word's origin and history also appears in brackets, parentheses, or slashes near the start or end of the entry. It often uses abbreviations for languages, all explained in the dictionary's key to abbreviations and symbols (at the front of most printed dictionaries).

Definition and Example The meanings of the entry word are numbered if there is more than one, and sometimes examples are included to illustrate their uses in phrases or sentences.

Usage and Field Labels Some definitions have labels showing how or where they are used. For instance, definitions labeled *Archaic (Arch)*, *Obsolete (Obs)*, or *Rare* are not widely used today. Those labeled *Colloquial (Colloq)* or *Slang* are not considered standard English. Those labeled *British (Brit)* or *Scottish (Scot)* are not much used in America. Those labeled with particular field names—*Electronics (Elec)*, for example, or *Music*—are not much used outside their field. American dictionaries also use a symbol (such as a star) to show whether a particular word or definition is mainly used in America.

Idioms and Derived Words The end of an entry may list and define *idioms*, or expressions, in which the entry word appears. It may also list *derived words*—words formed from the entry word—along with their part of speech.

▶ **Exercise 6** Understanding Dictionary Entries Use a dictionary to answer these questions.
1. Which of these words is NOT spelled correctly?
    a. accommodate **b.** definite **c.** hypocrasy **d.** rendezvous
2. In the word *phlegmatic*, which syllable is stressed?
3. What is the origin of the word *algebra*?
4. Identify two meanings of the word *parade*.
5. Is there an adverb derived from *nasty*? If so, what is it?

Using a Thesaurus

A *thesaurus* is a specialized dictionary providing extensive lists of *synonyms*, or words with similar meanings, and often some *antonyms*, or words with opposite meanings.

▶ **KEY CONCEPT** A thesaurus is one of the most useful writing tools, because it can help you to avoid the repetition of words and to make your language as precise as possible. ■

In a thesaurus, words may be arranged alphabetically or they may be grouped by theme. When the arrangement is thematic, you first have to look up the word in the index to find out in which thematic grouping its synonyms will appear. When the thesaurus is arranged alphabetically by word, you simply look up the word as you would in any dictionary.

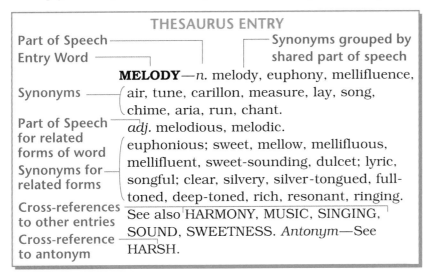

THESAURUS ENTRY

Part of Speech
Entry Word
Synonyms grouped by shared part of speech

MELODY—*n.* melody, euphony, mellifluence, air, tune, carillon, measure, lay, song, chime, aria, run, chant.

Synonyms

Part of Speech for related forms of word
adj. melodious, melodic. euphonious; sweet, mellow, mellifluous, mellifluent, sweet-sounding, dulcet; lyric, songful; clear, silvery, silver-tongued, full-toned, deep-toned, rich, resonant, ringing.

Synonyms for related forms

Cross-references to other entries
See also HARMONY, MUSIC, SINGING, SOUND, SWEETNESS. *Antonym*—See HARSH.

Cross-reference to antonym

Technology Tip

Many of the word-processing programs provide an on-line thesaurus. To use this feature, simply enter a word and you will be given a list of synonyms.

▶ **Exercise 7** **Using a Thesaurus** Use a thesaurus to find appropriate synonyms for the words in italics. For each sentence, explain whether the synonym you have identified is more effective than the original word.
1. After two workers left, the shop advertised for new *workers*.
2. The manager *managed* the search.
3. He *ran* several interviews over a two-week period.
4. The last applicant seemed very *brainy*.
5. The manager was also pleased by her *pleasant* manner.

Using Other Reference Works

Most libraries have all kinds of useful *reference works*, or resources to which you refer for information instead of reading them in their entirety. Such works are usually found in the reference section of the library. Most libraries will not allow you to check out reference works, so you must look at them while on site.

> **KEY CONCEPT** Reference works are a good source for learning general information about a topic or as a starting point for a research project. ■

SOME GENERAL ENCYCLOPEDIAS	SOME SPECIALIZED ENCYCLOPEDIAS
Encyclopædia Britannica *The World Book Encyclopedia* *Grolier's Multimedia Encyclopedia* *Compton's Pictured Encyclopedia*	*Van Nostrand's Scientific Encyclopedia* *Health Reference Center* *Encyclopedia of the Arts* *Grove's Dictionary of Music & Musicians* *The Baseball Encyclopedia*

Encyclopedias An *encyclopedia* is a collection of articles on different subjects. Encyclopedias list articles alphabetically by subject and usually span several volumes, with letters on the spine showing which subjects each volume contains; for example, a volume labeled *Ma to Mi* may contain an article on Maine but not Montana. Not all topics have their own article, but an alphabetical index, usually in a separate volume, tells you in which articles particular topics are covered.

A *general encyclopedia* collects articles offering basic information on a great many subjects. A *specialized encyclopedia* collects more complex or detailed articles in a particular field.

Almanacs These annual publications (updated more frequently in some electronic versions) offer factual information on a wide range of subjects, including history, geography, government, weather, science, industry, sports, and entertainment. In printed almanacs, the index may be in the back or the front.

Research Tip

Encyclopedias can help you gather background information to get started on a research project. However, they should not be one of your main sources of information. Instead, you should rely on nonfiction books, interviews, and reliable Internet resources.

Biographical References These works provide brief life histories of famous people, usually listed alphabetically by last name. Some biographical references, such as *Current Biography* or *Webster's Biographical Dictionary*, cover people from many walks of life; others, such as *Contemporary Authors* or *The International Who's Who of Women*, cover people in specific fields or areas.

Literary Indexes The library catalog lists books and other full-length publications, but to find a shorter work, you need to consult a literary index. A *literary index* tells you in which *anthologies*, or collections, shorter works of literature are found. Examples include *Granger's Guide to Poetry, Poem Finder*, the *Short Story Index*, the *Play Index*, and the *Essay Index*.

Books of Quotations Looking for a snappy quotation to use in a report? Trying to learn who first said an oft-quoted remark? You can perform either task with a *book of quotations*, which lists famous remarks and tells you who said them and where. Examples include *Bartlett's Book of Quotations, The Oxford Dictionary of Quotations*, and *Gale's Quotations*.

Atlases and Electronic Map Collections *Atlases* or *electronic map collections* contain maps and geographical information based on them. They also may include statistics about population, climate, agriculture, industry, natural resources, and so forth. In printed atlases, maps often have a numbered and lettered grid; to find a particular place on a map, you look it up in an alphabetical list called a *gazetteer*, which refers you to the area on the grid that the place appears.

▼ Critical Viewing What type of reference book would you use to find out what type of flowers these are and to gather information about them? [Connect]

> **Exercise 8** Using Other Reference Works Use printed or electronic reference works to find answers to these questions. Indicate the type of reference you used.
> 1. In what year was the city of Wichita, Kansas, founded?
> 2. What is Elizabeth Blackwell's claim to fame?
> 3. What is the highest dam in the United States?
> 4. Which countries border Mexico?
> 5. Find a quotation about nature from any work by Ralph Waldo Emerson. Include the name of the work.

Using the Internet and Other Media Resources

Find and Evaluate Information on the Internet

Through the Internet, you can access a virtually unlimited amount of information without ever leaving your desk. Because so much information is available, however, it is easy to get lost on the Web. For this reason, it is essential to know how to find information quickly on the Web and to critically evaluate the information you do find.

KEY CONCEPT The Internet provides a wealth of information on just about any topic. However, the information must be critically evaluated. ■

Locating Appropriate Web Sites The information on the Web is offered through thousands of individual Web sites, each of which has its own address, or URL (Universal Resource Locator). These sites usually consist of several Web pages of text, graphics, and sometimes audio or video displays. Use these tips to help you find appropriate sites:

- If you know a reliable Web site and its address (URL), simply type the address into your Web browser.

- If you don't know a particular Web site, use an Internet search engine to find the information. Use general search engines to search for a key term. Use other search engines to search in specific fields or categories.

- Also, consult reference librarians familiar with the Internet or Internet coverage in established library journals (such as *Booklist* and *The Library Journal*) for information on useful, reliable reference Web sites.

Evaluating Web Sites Since almost anyone can create a Web site, not every Web site provides useful or reliable information. Once you find a Web site, evaluate its reliability by considering the following:

- Identify who set up the site. Is the organization or individual who set it up an authority on the topics covered?

- Be on the lookout for **bias,** the presentation of a single point of view on a topic. If a site does represent a single position on a topic, it is essential that all of the arguments that are presented are backed up by facts and examples.

- Check to see that the information is up to date. What clues can you find that suggest when the site was last updated?

- Compare the information presented on the topic to information presented on other related sites.

Technology Tip

You often can print a Web page or download it onto a disk. On a home computer, you can also highlight and copy text and paste it into a file in your word-processing program.

> **Exercise 9** **Using the Internet** On a library, school, or home computer, use the Internet to do this research:
> 1. Go to the U.S. Postal Service Web site, **www.usps.gov**, to learn the ZIP Code for 146 K St., Washington, D.C.
> 2. Find the official Web site for the Metropolitan Museum of Art in New York City and from it find the museum hours.
> 3. Choose a topic for a science paper. List names and URLs of four Web sites that you think can help you.
> 4. Find the text of the poem "To Helen" by Edgar Allan Poe. Be sure to record the name and URL.
> 5. From a reliable source, find out about Lyme disease and how to prevent it. Record source information.

Use Other Media Resources

In addition to the Internet, there are a wide range of other media resources that you can use for research. These include videos, CD-ROMs, and electronic databases. You can probably find many of these resources at your local or school library.

Video Resources Videos, such as the ones below, can be an excellent reference tool and a key part of a multimedia report.

- **News Programs** provide up-to-date information on key events and issues and can offer insights into how people responded to major events at the time they happened.

- **Documentaries** can offer in-depth information on a wide range of specific topics.

CD-ROM References Most of the print references mentioned earlier in this chapter are also available on CD-ROM. For example, there are a wide range of CD-ROM encyclopedias that provide text information, photographs, video, and audio. In addition, there are CD-ROM atlases and map programs that you can use to find information about geographical regions. To use a CD-ROM reference, you simply need to type in key words and the program will take you to your topic.

Electronic Databases Electronic databases provide large collections of data on specific topics. The databases allow you to sort and examine the information in a variety of ways. You can usually find the sort feature of a database in the menu bar. To conduct a search, type in one or more key words.

> **Exercise 10** **Using Media Resources** Choose a topic that interests you. Conduct research on that topic, using two different media resources. Present your findings to the class.

Technology Tip

Electronic maps often have "zoom in" and other features in which you simply click the mouse to enlarge or change the area shown.

Technology Tip

Remember that in electronic database searches, one wrong letter can result in failure. Be sure to type carefully and spell everything correctly. If you aren't sure of a spelling, try several variations.

Test-Taking Skills

In this section, you will learn some strategies to improve your performance on tests and to deal with the different kinds of questions they often contain.

Taking Tests

Objective tests are those in which each question has a single correct answer. To prepare for such tests, carefully study the material that the test will cover. Be sure to arrive at the test on time, well rested, and with all the equipment you were told to bring—pencils, pens, and so on.

▶ KEY CONCEPT When taking a test, divide your time into three steps—previewing, answering, and proofreading. ■

PREVIEW THE TEST

1. Put your name on each sheet of paper you will hand in.
2. Look over the entire test to get an overview of the types of questions and how they are arranged.
3. Find out whether you lose points for incorrect answers. If you do, do not guess at answers.
4. Decide how much time you must spend on each section of the test.
5. Plan to devote the most time to questions that are hardest or worth the most points.

ANSWER THE QUESTIONS

1. Answer the easy questions first. Put a check next to harder questions, and come back to them later.
2. If permitted, use scratch paper to jot down your ideas.
3. Read each question at least *twice* before answering.
4. Supply the single best answer, giving only one answer to a question unless the instructions say otherwise.
5. Answer all questions on the test unless you are told not to guess or there is a penalty for wrong guesses.
6. Do not change your first answer without a good reason.

PROOFREAD YOUR ANSWERS

1. Check that you have followed directions completely.
2. Reread test questions and answers. Make sure that you have answered all of the questions.

Answering Different Kinds of Questions

Although the content of tests varies greatly, the types of questions that appear on these tests are fairly similar. This section will inform you about different types of test questions and specific strategies for answering them.

> **KEY CONCEPT** Improve your test scores by learning about different kinds of questions and the strategies for answering them. ■

True-or-False Questions True-or-false questions ask you to identify whether or not a statement is accurate.

- If a statement seems true, be sure that it is all true.
- Pay special attention to the word *not*, which often changes the whole meaning of a statement.
- Take note of the generalizing words *all, always, never, no, none,* and *only.* They often make a statement false.
- Take note of the qualifying words *generally, much, many, most, often, sometimes,* and *usually.* They often make a state-ment true.

Multiple-Choice Questions This kind of question asks you to choose from four or five possible responses.

- Try to answer the question before reading the choices. If your answer is one of the choices, select that choice.
- Eliminate obviously incorrect answers, crossing them out if you are allowed to write on the test paper.

Matching Questions Matching questions require that you match items in one group with items in another.

- Count each group to see whether any items will be left over.
- Read all the items before you start matching.
- Match the items you know first, and then match the others. If you can write on the paper, cross out items as you use them.

Fill-in Questions A fill-in question asks you to supply an answer in your own words. The answer may complete a state-ment or it may simply answer a question.

- Read the question or incomplete statement carefully.
- If you are completing a statement, look for context clues that may signal the answer. Pay special attention if the word *an* appears right before the missing word, which indicates that the missing word begins with a vowel sound.

Analogies An *analogy* is a special type of multiple-choice question that often appears on vocabulary and reading tests. Analogy items usually provide a pair of words and ask you to choose another pair that expresses a similar relationship.

EXAMPLE: FURNITURE : CHAIR ::

a. food : meat   **c.** daisy : flower
b. wall : window   **d.** olive : green

In the preceding example, the answer is *a*. The relationship between the pairs of words is *kind*. A chair is a *kind* of furniture, and meat is a *kind* of food. Notice that the sequence of the words matters. The following chart lists common analogy relationships:

COMMON ANALOGY RELATIONSHIPS	
Relationship	**Example**
Shared quality (synonyms)	impetuous : rash
Lack of a quality (antonyms)	enthusiasm : boredom
Degree (greater to lesser / lesser to greater)	guffaw : giggle / whisper : scream
Part to whole / Whole to part	drawer : desk / house : room
Kind (specific to general / general to specific)	salamander : lizard / dog : poodle
Sequence	arrest : trial
Location or proximity	knee : calf
Device	wrench : plumber

Learn More

Having a strong vocabulary will help you answer analogy questions. For more on developing your vocabulary skills, see Chapter 30.

Short-Answer Questions Short-answer questions call on you to write one or more sentences in which you provide certain information. Before you respond to a short-answer question, look carefully at the question. Identify key words, such as *explain, compare*, and *identify*. When you answer the question, provide only the information called for through the key words. Be as direct and concise as possible.

Essay Questions On many standardized tests and tests you take in school, you will be called on to write one or more essays. Sometimes, you are given a choice of prompts to which you can respond. In other instances, you are given only a single prompt. Look for key words in the prompt or prompts to determine exactly what information you are being asked to provide. Take a few minutes to gather facts, examples, and other types of details you can include in your essay. Devote most of your time to drafting your essay. However, try to allow a little time to make revisions in your work.

> **Exercise 11** Completing Analogies For each item, choose the letter of the pair of words that expresses the relationship most like the relationship of the words in capital letters. Also, indicate the type of relationship.

1. MANGO : FRUIT ::
   a. vegetable : corn **b.** peas : beans **c.** zucchini : vegetable
2. JOY : ECSTASY ::
   a. admiration : love **b.** life : hope **c.** happiness : sorrow
3. FOREWORD : EPILOGUE ::
   a. appetizer : dessert **b.** team : spirit **c.** introduction : book
4. THERMOSTAT : HEAT ::
   a. watt : light **b.** scale : weight **c.** temperature : thermometer
5. CONCEIT : MODESTY ::
   a. anger : fury **b.** vitality : sloth **c.** kindness : virtue

> **Exercise 12** Understanding the Various Types of Test Questions Using a subject you are studying in one of your classes, prepare an objective test on the material. Write five true-or-false questions, five multiple-choice questions, five matching questions, and five fill-in questions. Exchange papers with another student, and take that student's test, writing your answers on a separate sheet of paper. Exchange again, and grade the test.

Reflecting on Your Study, Reference, and Test-Taking Skills

Consider the methods you have learned for improving study skills, the reference works available for improving your research skills, and the strategies for improving your test-taking skills. Answer the following questions in a journal entry:

- What changes should I make in my study area or schedule?
- What changes should I make to take notes effectively?
- Which reference materials seem the most useful to me?
- Which reference materials do I feel I need to learn more about?
- How can I budget my time more effectively when taking tests?
- What new strategies should I adopt for different kinds of test questions?

Standardized Test Preparation Workshop

Constructing Meaning From Informational Texts

Most standardized tests will have questions designed to evaluate your reading skills. You will be given a passage to read. Following will be several questions that test your ability to construct meaning from the information provided in the passage. When answering these types of questions, you will be required to do the following:

- Distinguish between facts and nonfacts, or opinions.
- Identify the stated or implied main idea of a section of the passage.
- Choose the best summary—a brief, clear restatement of the subject and main ideas.

The following sample item will give you practice answering these types of questions.

Test Tip

The main idea of short passages is frequently, but not always, found in the first sentence.

Sample Test Item

Directions: Read the passage. Then, read each question that follows the passage. Decide which is the best answer to each question.

In 1928, T. S. Eliot became a devout member of the Church of England, after becoming a British citizen the previous year. These changes preceded radical changes in the focus of Eliot's writing, as evidenced by his exploration of religious themes in "Ash Wednesday" and "Four Quartets."

1 Which of the following is an OPINION expressed in the passage?

   A T. S. Eliot wrote "Ash Wednesday."

   B T. S. Eliot was a British citizen.

   C The Church of England existed in 1928.

   D T. S. Eliot disliked Americans.

Answer and Explanation

The correct answer is *D*. All the other choices are documented facts about Eliot's life and works. Although the reader might infer that Eliot disliked Americans based on his change in citizenship, the reader cannot enter Eliot's mind to know how he felt about Americans.

▶ **Practice 1** **Directions:** Read the passage. Then, read each question that follows the passage. Decide which is the best answer to each question.

Frederic Remington is considered the best, and certainly the most popular, painter and sculptor of the Old West. Born in New York State, he first traveled west—to Montana in 1881—not as an artist but to seek his fortune, possibly in gold mining. In 1883, he traveled west again to try his hand at sheep ranching in Kansas. Later, he tried to make his fortune as part owner of a Kansas City saloon. All these ventures met with failure. It was in the latter part of the 1880's and early 1890's that Remington became a successful artist.

1 Which of the following is an OPINION expressed in the passage?

  A Frederic Remington is the best sculptor of the Old West.

  B Remington was born in New York.

  C Remington failed as a saloon owner.

  D Remington spent time as a sheep rancher.

2 What is the main idea of the passage?

  F Remington loved the West.

  G Remington was a huge failure.

  H Remington tried many careers but found success as an artist.

  J Remington loved gold mining.

▶ **Practice 2** **Directions:** Read the passage. Then, read each question that follows the passage. Decide which is the best answer to each question.

Two basic forms of music dominated the Harlem Renaissance: blues and jazz. The roots of blues and jazz are in the work songs, spirituals, and shouts of southern slaves. These slave songs, in turn, had their roots in the music of Africa. The pattern of theme and variation and the rhythmic counterpoint common in blues and jazz are elements in west African music. The blues, specifically, evolved after the Civil War, expressing the hardships and struggles of African Americans during Reconstruction. As Langston Hughes described the blues: "The music is slow, often mournful, yet syncopated, with a kind of marching bass behind it that seems to say, 'In spite of fate, bad luck, these blues themselves, I'm going to get on! I'm going to get on!'"

1 Which of the following is an OPINION stated in the passage?

  A The roots of blues and jazz are found in the music of the Reconstruction period.

  B The pattern of theme and variation common in blues and jazz are elements in west African music.

  C The blues evolved after the Civil War.

  D Blues and jazz music were Langston Hughes's favorite form of music.

2 What is the main idea of the passage?

  F Langston Hughes loved the blues and jazz.

  G The music of the Harlem Renaissance reflects the style of west African music and the sorrowful, yet hopeful music of African Americans both before and after the Civil War.

  H Hughes wrote jazz and blues music for the Harlem Renaissance.

  J West African music was a highly specialized type of music adopted by the musicians of the Harlem Renaissance.

Workplace Skills and Competencies

Many skills that make you a successful student also help to make you a valuable employee when you begin a career. In addition to writing and speaking effectively, listening attentively, and reading carefully, you will benefit from knowing how to communicate well with others and how to accomplish tasks efficiently and creatively.

This chapter will help you improve skills you already have and develop new ones in several important areas. You will learn strategies for effective interaction, goal setting, and problem solving. In addition, you will learn how to manage your time and money wisely and how to apply math and computer skills to the workplace.

▲ **Critical Viewing**
Identify a career that requires the computer and interpersonal skills these students are demonstrating.
[Connect]

Working With People

Whether you pursue a career as a salesperson, researcher, contractor, or train conductor, you will be expected to interact effectively with people. The way you speak and interact with supervisors, co-workers, clients, or the general public will influence their impression of you and the company you represent. This section will help you to further develop skills needed for communicating in one-on-one and group situations.

Learn to Communicate One on One

In the workplace, you may need to interact in one-on-one situations involving people you know only on a professional level or people you don't know at all. The first of these one-on-one situations is the job or college interview: Performing effectively during an interview can help you get into the college of your choice, land a job, or advance in the workplace.

Interviewing Interviews are the most formal type of one-on-one communication. In addition to sharing information about training, strengths, weaknesses, and interests, interview candidates must also present a positive first impression.

> ◤ **KEY CONCEPT** A job or college interview requires preparation, professional conduct, and follow-up work. ■

Keys to a Successful Interview

Before the Interview
- Bring copies of your résumé and names of references with you.
- Review the key points of your background and experience so you will be prepared to answer questions.
- Research the employer or college, and prepare questions that demonstrate your knowledge and interest.
- Dress neatly.

During the Interview
- Be respectful and polite at all times.
- Listen carefully, and respond directly to each question.
- Smile, and maintain eye contact.
- Thank the interviewer for his or her time, and ask when a decision will be made.

After the Interview
- Send a follow-up letter, restating your interest and thanking the interviewer for his or her time.
- When the deadline for a decision arrives, call to check your status.

▶ Speaking and Listening Tip

Use your experiences outside of school to practice professionalism. Request information from store clerks and telephone operators as if you were in a work environment. Discuss with a partner how communicating in this way affects the way people respond to you.

Interacting Successfully In school or in the workplace, you will have conferences with others to discuss your performance and your plans for the future. In addition, you may have meetings with colleagues to get a job done. Whether you need to organize a project, solve an unexpected problem, or deal with customers, your ability to interact respectfully may mean the difference between success and failure.

More Practice

Academic and Workplace Skills Activity Book
• p. 54

> **KEY CONCEPT** To interact effectively in school and work situations, treat others with respect, listen carefully, and do not hesitate to communicate your thoughts and concerns. ■

Guidelines for Successful Interaction

- **Be sensitive to verbal or nonverbal messages** you receive from other people. Know when you need to be serious and when you can be casual or humorous.
- **Listen carefully,** and ask questions if necessary.
- **Find common ground**—similar interests or experiences that connect you to the other person.
- **Respect differences,** and accept that others may have different backgrounds, abilities, and opinions.
- **Use language that is appropriate** in tone, style, and complexity for your audience. For example, you may use slang with friends but not with an employer.
- **Avoid finger pointing;** instead, look for a positive resolution to problems rather than a person to blame.

> **Exercise 1** Interviewing for a Position With another student, choose a job you would like to pursue. Then, for a group, role-play a job interview for that position. The interviewer should ask questions to prompt the interviewee to describe his or her qualifications. After the role-play is over, ask the group to point out the strengths and weaknesses you demonstrated as a candidate.

> **Exercise 2** Interacting With Others in Various Situations With other students, role-play the following situations. In each case, discuss what you learned from the experience.
> 1. Two students: a new student asks a coach about joining a team in midseason.
> 2. Four students: a salesperson is helping a customer who cannot make a decision; others are growing impatient as they wait for assistance.
> 3. Two students: an employee asks a supervisor for a raise.

▼ Critical Viewing Are these students having a positive or a negative interaction? On what do you base your answer? **[Deduce]**

Learning Teamwork

Team efforts are critical to success in many arenas outside of sports. For example, you may use teamwork to develop a group project with fellow students, participate in a town committee, or work on a job-based project team. Group interaction requires basic communication skills and the ability to anticipate or avoid conflicts among the many personalities involved. To work successfully as a team, members must be willing to listen and be respectful of one another's opinions and roles.

Conducting Meetings and Group Discussions Effective meetings or group discussions will help a team work well together. Participants can take specific roles to keep the group focused. Ideally, these roles should be rotated each meeting:

- A **facilitator** guides the discussion and encourages the interaction of all group members.

- A **note-taker** records key points and distributes meeting minutes or notes after the meeting.

- A **timekeeper** keeps track of the time allotted to a topic.

> **KEY CONCEPT** For a group to work effectively, all members must be organized, focused on the task at hand, and aware of their responsibilities. ■

The following chart shows some of the other ground rules for an effective meeting:

GROUND RULES FOR A MEETING OR DISCUSSION

- ☑ Establish a time limit, and begin and end on time.
- ☑ Assign roles, including facilitator, timekeeper, and note-taker.
- ☑ Use a flip chart to record key points.
- ☑ When trying to make plans or find solutions, allow time for brainstorming—the free exchange of ideas.
- ☑ Make sure everyone participates.

>  **Exercise 3** Using Group Roles Working with five classmates, choose a group facilitator, a timekeeper, and a note-taker. Then, begin a fifteen-minute discussion about the impact on students of one of the following areas: volunteering, the Internet, after-school jobs, or sports. Have the rest of the class evaluate your teamwork.

♆ Challenge

Often, the group establishes an *agenda* that lists the order of the topics being discussed. If new issues or questions are raised during the discussion that cannot be solved during the allotted time, all of the people involved should plan to meet again.

Participating Effectively Assuming roles and setting ground rules are good first steps toward running an effective meeting or discussion. However, the success of a meeting or discussion ultimately rests on the effective participation of each group member. To participate effectively in these situations, be prepared to make suggestions, be open to the ideas of others, and give and accept constructive criticism.

KEY CONCEPT A good participant contributes ideas and constructive criticism and allows others to do the same. ■

Critical Viewing
What details of this photograph suggest that the students shown are meeting informally? **[Interpret]**

TIPS FOR EFFECTIVE PARTICIPATION

Listen respectfully to all viewpoints.

Share your perspective, and encourage others to do so.

Focus on the topic, and help others to focus on it as well.

Give and receive criticism gracefully.

Exercise 4 **Conducting a Meeting** Form a committee with a group of classmates. Assign roles, and set an agenda for a meeting in which you will identify a goal you would all like to see accomplished, such as building a new park in your community. Then, work together at your meeting to lay out plans for how this goal might be accomplished. When your meeting is complete, list contributions each group member made to the plan.

Exercise 5 **Analyzing a Group Discussion** Using the tips outlined above, evaluate a televised round-table discussion. In your notebook, describe what you have witnessed. Refer to the strategies for effective participation to explain how the group did or did not work well together.

Moving Toward Goals

Thoughtful planning is a key to success in school, the workplace, and other areas of life. When you plan and set goals, you give yourself a better chance of achieving them.

> **KEY CONCEPT** Goals should be specific and include a clear timeline for completion. ■

Personal and Professional Goals

Some goals are *personal*—for example, making a sports team or improving your reading speed. Other goals are *professional*, because they focus on accomplishments in school or your work life. Getting into college, finishing a project on time, and earning a promotion are professional goals.

Because goals can conflict with each other, it is useful to identify all the goals you are working to achieve. You can then decide which are most important. You'll find that your priorities can shift over time. For example, when schoolwork includes final exams, you may let your academic goals override some of the other goals you are working to achieve.

Setting and Achieving Goals A vague goal like "exercising more" is hard to track. Set a specific goal, such as "exercising twice a week," and then make an action plan to outline the steps for achieving it. Assign a time for completion, and be ready to adjust your goals if necessary. A chart such as the one below can help you track your progress.

GOALS CHART

GOAL	STEPS NEEDED TO ACHIEVE IT	PROGRESS
A. _____	1. _____	_____
	2. _____	_____
	3. _____	_____
B. _____	1. _____	_____
	2. _____	_____
	3. _____	

> **Exercise 6** **Developing a Goals Chart** Develop a goals chart. Include at least one personal and one professional goal, and chart your progress as you work toward achieving them.

> **Exercise 7** **Devising an Action Plan** Devise an action plan for earning money to buy a new stereo system. Include the steps needed to achieve the goal, the time frame for completing each step, and the resources required for each step.

🖱 Research Tip

To help plan your career goals, investigate fields of interest at the career center of a local college.

> **More Practice**

Academic and Workplace Skills Activity Book
• p. 55

Solving Problems and Thinking Creatively

Learn More

For more instruction about problem-and-solution writing, see Chapter 11.

As you work to achieve your personal and professional goals, you are bound to meet unexpected problems. Knowing how to face these problems calmly and devise workable solutions can help you stay on track to meet the goals you have set. To master this skill, you need a strategy for outlining problems and analyzing their solutions. For particularly difficult problems, you must also learn to think creatively to generate a number of possible solutions with which to work.

Learning to Solve Problems Most problems can be solved by using a systematic strategy that will allow you to analyze the problem and define a solution more clearly.

▶ **KEY CONCEPT** Solving a problem requires a thorough understanding of what's wrong, a number of possible solutions, and a careful review of each one. ■

Use the following steps to solve problems more efficiently, minimize setbacks, and move forward.

STEPS IN PROBLEM SOLVING

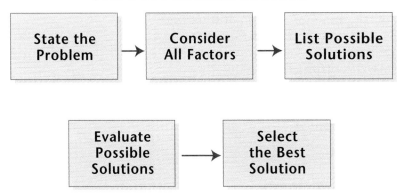

State the Problem → Consider All Factors → List Possible Solutions

Evaluate Possible Solutions → Select the Best Solution

▶ **Exercise 8** Solving Problems Using the steps outlined above, identify at least two possible solutions for one of the following problems. Then, choose the best solution.
1. A student can't master a concept in math class.
2. A store manager realizes she may be losing business because cashier lines are too long on weekends.
3. A baby can choke on the small pieces of some of his older brother's games, but the older boy enjoys playing with these games.

Thinking Creatively You can use creative thinking to come up with possible solutions for a difficult problem. All you have to do is open your mind to ideas that are new, different, and sometimes unconventional.

> **KEY CONCEPT** Creative thinking requires openness to unusual approaches from which to draw new ideas. ■

If a star pitcher was slated to appear in the championship game but also wanted to go to a friend's birthday celebration scheduled for the same time, creative thinking might help. While standard problem solving might encourage the athlete to split time between both events, creative thinking might generate a more appealing idea: The athlete could videotape a message and ask his friend to wait until the party to play the tape.

CREATIVE THINKING SUGGESTIONS

Pose the problem to others and listen to their advice.

Imagine how someone with particular talents might solve the problem, such as an inventor or artist.

Increase the number of possible solutions by listing all ideas, however fanciful or impractical.

USING CREATIVE THINKING

Interact with people from different cultures and backgrounds to widen your frame of reference.

> **Exercise 9** **Using Creative Thinking** Use creative thinking to offer two more suggestions to the problems identified in Exercise 8.

Managing Time

Although different careers require different abilities, most work situations present workers with tasks that need to be completed according to tight deadlines. In addition to the major projects you are assigned to complete, you often have to address unexpected problems and emergencies. In that case, your ability to manage your time effectively will play a critical role in determining your success.

Managing Your Time Proper time management takes planning and the ability to decide which of your goals and activities are most important. Budgeting your time well helps ensure that important projects are accomplished, time is free for other activities, and hasty decisions are prevented.

> **KEY CONCEPT** Manage your time effectively by keeping a calendar marked with appointments and key events, preparing daily or weekly "to-do" lists, prioritizing your tasks, and breaking up large tasks into manageable portions. ■

SAMPLE CALENDAR AND TO-DO LIST

To-Do List

1. Practice reading lines from play
2. Buy birthday present
3. Renew membership at gym
4. Write e-mail to my pen pal

Mon 9:30 Meeting with teacher

Tues

Wed 3:00–5:00 Drama auditions

Thur 7:00–10:00 Baby-sit

Fri

Sat 7:30 Katie's birthday party

Sun

> **Exercise 10** **Managing Your Time** Record your schedule for a week. Include a daily to-do list, with activities and appointments ranked according to importance. At the end of the week, evaluate how effectively this system worked for you.

Managing Money

The strategies of money management are simple: Spend less than you make to allow for the unexpected; treat your savings account like a bill to be paid rather than a place to put "extra" money; and plan your expenditures. Setting and sticking to a budget ensures that you will have money for what you need and want.

▶ **KEY CONCEPT** To manage money wisely, track your spending, set financial goals, and make a plan to meet these goals. ■

Developing a Budget A budget helps you manage money efficiently by tracking *credit*, or incoming money (in black), and noting *debits*, or expenses (in red). When a budget is balanced, credit and debit are equal. If debit exceeds credit, the budgeter must make choices about cutting spending or increasing income. When credit exceeds debit, the budget reveals a savings or a profit. Look at this example:

SAMPLE BUDGET

STUDENT GOVERNMENT MONTHLY BUDGET			
	INCOME	REGULAR EXPENSES	PROJECTED EXPENSES
Snack sale	200.00		
Alumni donations	50.00		
Savings for class gift		20.00	
Purchase of snacks for sale		75.00	25.00
Security deposit on tickets and chairs for dance			100.00
Total	250.00	95.00	125.00

▶ **Exercise 11** **Managing a Budget** Develop a budget for someone who earns $200 a month, spends $10–20 per week on entertainment, $5 per week on snack foods, $20 per month on gifts, and puts $50 per month in a savings account.
  1. How long will it take this person to save $400 without using money from the savings account?
  2. Make a recommendation for cutting expenses.

Research Tip

You can find easy-to-understand guides to managing your time and money at your local library.

More Practice

Academic and Workplace Skills Activity Book
• pp. 57–58

Applying Math Skills

Although there are many ways to apply your math skills to everyday life, this section addresses three of the most common ways: those used in the workplace, in shopping, and in the analysis of statistics.

> **KEY CONCEPT** Math skills are necessary to manage money properly, to make wise purchases, and to evaluate certain types of information. ∎

Following are three areas in which math will prove useful:
1. **Succeeding in the Workplace** You may need to use your math skills while at work. For example, contractors often set rates based on the materials they need plus a fee for the hours they will work. Office managers often need to balance a budget, buy supplies, and calculate payroll. Whatever job you do, a knowledge of your own pay rate will help you determine your ability to afford items you may want to purchase.
2. **Making Wise Purchases** When you are faced with multiple choices in a competitive market, use unit prices to calculate the most economical buys. For example, when you do the math, you may see that a "buy one, get one free" sale doesn't offer the bargain you had originally imagined.
3. **Analyzing Statistics** Business reports, daily newspapers, and other sources of information often use statistics to support certain points of view. Knowing how to weigh the value of those numbers helps you to make informed judgments.

▼ Critical Viewing
How can a knowledge of math skills help you as you consider purchasing CDs? **[Connect]**

> **Exercise 12** Using Math Skills to Decide Whether or Not to Accept a Job
A neighbor has offered you and a friend $350 to paint her house. From your past painting experience, you realize that it will take five eight-hour days to complete the job, six gallons of paint at $25 per gallon, and the purchase of $50 in painting materials.
1. What is the total cost of supplies?
2. What is your hourly wage on this job?
3. Identify one other factor that might influence your decision.
4. Would you accept this job? Explain your answer.

Applying Computer Skills

With computers common in many workplaces, employers in a variety of fields expect new workers to have computer skills. Consider improving your skills to increase your opportunities in the workplace.

KEY CONCEPT A knowledge of your computer means the ability to enter information accurately, format text, use a variety of software, and access Internet information. ■

Following are a few ways to make the most of a computer:

1. **Practice your keyboarding skills.** Being an accurate and quick keyboarder gives you more time to focus on other tasks. A good typing speed is 45 words per minute, but remember that accuracy is more important than speed.
2. **Learn how to format.** You can use fonts, bullets, and other features to organize and emphasize information. Consider learning a variety of programs to help you apply your skills in any working environment.
3. **Use the thesaurus and spell-check tools.** To make your work professional and accurate, get in the habit of using a word processor's language functions. For example, with a click of a mouse, you can find just the right word or catch errors you may have missed while proofreading.
4. **Learn to use the Internet.** With a teacher's guidance, discover the wealth of information available at your fingertips.

Exercise 13 Working With Computers Complete these activities:

1. Find an application that creates charts or graphs, and use the computers Help menu to create one.
2. Conduct interviews to find out how computers enhance the workplace of several people you know.

> **More Practice**
>
> Academic and Workplace Skills Activity Book
> • pp. 59–60

> ⏩ **Learn More**
>
> The Media and Technology Skills activities in Chapters 1–3 offer instruction to help you improve your computer skills.

Reflecting on Your Workplace Skills and Competencies

To reflect on your workplace skills and competencies, consider the job you most want to pursue. Then, jot down your responses to these questions:

• What skills are most important in the job or career you want to pursue?

• What skills should you improve? Why?

Standardized Test Preparation Workshop

Reading Informational Texts

Some standardized tests assess your ability to read real-world texts, such as flyers, brochures, and advertisements. Often, this involves carefully following a sequence of steps or directions. The following sample test item will give you practice in answering these types of questions.

Sample Test Item

Directions: Read the passage, and answer the question that follows.

> ## Do you know the ins and outs of exploring the Web?
>
> Come share your knowledge as a volunteer for Tech Literacy. As a volunteer, you will teach basic computer skills as well as every aspect of Internet use—from turning on the computer to setting up bookmarks.
>
> If you are interested, sign up at your local library. If you know anyone who might be interested in taking the class, have them call
>
> ### 1-800-555-TECH

1 Based on this advertisement, which of the following would you teach first?

    A using search engines

    B how to use a computer mouse

    C using the Help key

    D creating Internet bookmarks

Answer and Explanation

The correct answer is *B, how to use a computer mouse*. Because the class will first teach basic instruction, one of the first things taught would be using a computer mouse.

▶ **Practice 1** **Directions:** Read the passage, and answer the questions that follow.

Jonah has to write a report on the life and times of Anton Chekhov. After beginning with an encyclopedia and then reading a few brief biographies, Jonah asked the librarian to help him find a source that would provide him with biographical, historical, and literary information. She suggested that he use a program called *AuthorWorks* CD-ROM. After finding a computer, he began to read the following pages from the user manual.

The Author Directory
The main menu, in the form of an author directory, offers you the following choices:

- Click on Guided Tour to see a demonstration of the features and contents of *AuthorWorks*.
- Click on Contents to see a listing of topics about each author. Click on any topic to take you into the program.
- Click on Index to see a list of the articles available. Then, click on any article title to take you to the article.
- Click on Projects for a directory of sample projects for each author.
- Click on an author to explore his or her life and work. A video provides an author overview. Spoken excerpts from the author's works follow. You can play each excerpt by clicking on the highlighted arrows on the Menu Bar.

To return to the Author Directory at any time, select Author Directory from the GO menu.

Whenever you want to exit from the program, select EXIT from the FILE menu.

---

1 If Jonah wants to find out more about the personal life of an author, he should click on—
A Works
B Times
C arrow keys
D the author

2 Where did Jonah first look for information?
F concise biographies
G encyclopedias
H history books
J CD-ROMs

3 If Jonah wanted to find specific articles on the author, he would choose—
A Works
B Projects
C Index
D Contents

4 If Jonah wanted to know more about what is contained in *AuthorWorks*, he should click on —
F an author
G Guided Tour
H Contents
J Index page

5 If Jonah wanted to go back to the Author Directory at any time, he would—
A click anywhere on the screen
B click on the Back button
C use the GO menu
D click on the arrows

6 To exit the program—
F click on the Stop icon
G choose control & Q
H choose EXIT from FILE menu
J click arrow in left corner

Citing Sources *and* Preparing Manuscript

The presentation of your written work is important. Your work should be neat, clean, and easy to read. Follow your teacher's directions for placing your name and class, along with the title and date of your work, on the paper.

For handwritten work:

- Use cursive handwriting or manuscript printing, according to the style your teacher prefers. The penmanship reference below shows the accepted formation of letters in cursive writing.
- Write or print neatly.
- Write on one side of lined $8\,^1/_2$" x 11" paper with a clean edge. (Do not use pages torn from a spiral notebook.)
- Indent the first line of each paragraph.

- Leave a margin, as indicated by the guidelines on the lined paper. Write in a size appropriate for the lines provided. Do not write so large that the letters from one line bump into the ones above and below. Do not write so small that the writing is difficult to read.
- Write in blue or black ink.
- Number the pages in the upper right corner.
- You should not cross out words on your final draft. Recopy instead. If your paper is long, your teacher may allow you to make one or two small changes by neatly crossing out the text to be deleted and using a caret [^] to indicate replacement text. Alternatively, you might make one or two corrections neatly with correction fluid. If you find yourself making more than three corrections, consider recopying the work.

PENMANSHIP REFERENCE

Aa Bb Cc Dd Ee Ff
Gg Hh Ii Jj Kk Ll
Mm Nn Oo Pp Qq
Rr Ss Tt Uu Vv Ww
Xx Yy Zz 1 2 3 4 5 6 7 8 9 0

For word-processed or typed documents:

- Choose a standard, easy-to-read font.
- Type or print on one side of unlined $8\frac{1}{2}$" x 11" paper.
- Set the margins for the side, top, and bottom of your paper at approximately one inch. Most word-processing programs have a default setting that is appropriate.
- Double-space the document.
- Indent the first line of each paragraph.
- Number the pages in the upper right corner. Many word-processing programs have a header feature that will do this for you automatically.

- If you discover one or two errors after you have typed or printed, use correction fluid if your teacher allows such corrections. If you have more than three errors in an electronic file, consider making the corrections to the file and reprinting the document. If you have typed a long document, your teacher may allow you to make a few corrections by hand. If you have several errors, however, consider retyping the document.

For research papers:

Follow your teacher's directions for formatting formal research papers. Most papers will have the following features:

- Title page
- Table of Contents or Outline
- Works-Cited List

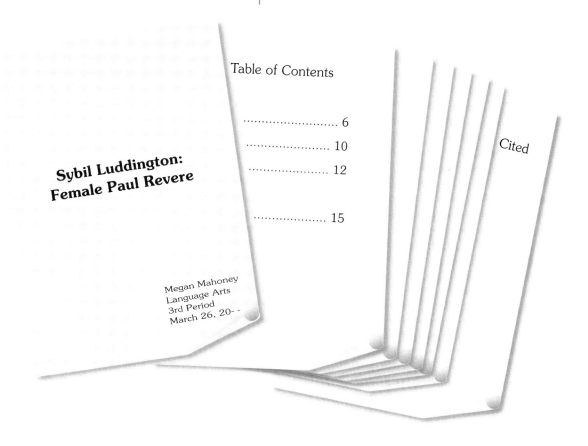

Table of Contents

.... 6

.... 10

.... 12

.... 15

Cited

Sybil Luddington:
Female Paul Revere

Megan Mahoney
Language Arts
3rd Period
March 26, 20- -

Incorporating Ideas From Research

Below are three common methods of incorporating the ideas of other writers into your work. Choose the most appropriate style by analyzing your needs in each case. In all cases, you must credit your source.

- **Direct Quotation:** Use quotation marks to indicate the exact words.
- **Paraphrase:** To share ideas without a direct quotation, state the ideas in your own words. While you haven't copied word-for-word, you still need to credit your source.
- **Summary:** To provide information about a large body of work—such as a speech, an editorial, or a chapter of a book—identify the writer's main idea.

Avoiding Plagiarism

Whether you are presenting a formal research paper or an opinion paper on a current event, you must be careful to give credit for any ideas or opinions that are not your own. Presenting someone else's ideas, research, or opinion as your own—even if you have rephrased it in different words—is *plagiarism*, the equivalent of academic stealing, or fraud.

You can avoid plagiarism by synthesizing what you learn: Read from several sources and let the ideas of experts help you draw your own conclusions and form your own opinions. Ultimately, however, note your own reactions to the ideas presented.

When you choose to use someone else's ideas or work to support your view, credit the source of the material. Give bibliographic information to cite your sources of the following information:

- Statistics
- Direct quotations
- Indirectly quoted statements of opinions
- Conclusions presented by an expert
- Facts available in only one or two sources

Crediting Sources

When you credit a source, you acknowledge where you found your information and you give your readers the details necessary for locating the source themselves. Within the body of the paper, you provide a short citation, a footnote number linked to a footnote, or an endnote number linked to an endnote reference. These brief references show the page numbers on which you found the information. To make your paper more formal, prepare a reference list at the end of the paper to provide full bibliographic information on your sources. These are two common types of reference lists:

- A **bibliography** provides a listing of all the resources you consulted during your research.
- A **works-cited list** indicates the works you have referenced in your paper.

Choosing a Format for Documentation

The type of information you provide and the format in which you provide it depend on what your teacher prefers. These are the most commonly used styles:

- **Modern Language Association (MLA) Style** This is the style used for most papers at the middle-school and high-school level and for most language arts papers.
- **American Psychological Association (APA) Style** This is used for most papers in the social sciences and for most college-level papers.
- ***Chicago Manual of Style* (CMS) Style** This is preferred by some teachers.

On the following pages, you'll find sample citation formats for the most commonly cited materials. Each format calls for standard bibliographic information. The difference is in the order of the material presented in each entry and the punctuation required.

MLA Style for Listing Sources

Book with one author	Pyles, Thomas. *The Origins and Development of the English Language.* 2nd ed. New York: Harcourt Brace Jovanovich, Inc., 1971.
Book with two or three authors	McCrum, Robert, William Cran, and Robert MacNeil. *The Story of English.* New York: Penguin Books, 1987.
Book with an editor	Truth, Sojourner. *Narrative of Sojourner Truth.* Ed. Margaret Washington. New York: Vintage Books, 1993.
Book with more than three authors or editors	Donald, Robert B., et al. *Writing Clear Essays.* Upper Saddle River, NJ: Prentice-Hall, Inc., 1996.
A single work from an anthology	Hawthorne, Nathaniel. "Young Goodman Brown." *Literature: An Introduction to Reading and Writing.* Ed. Edgar V. Roberts and Henry E. Jacobs. Upper Saddle River, NJ: Prentice-Hall, Inc., 1998. 376–385. [Indicate pages for the entire selection.]
Introduction in a published edition	Washington, Margaret. Introduction. *Narrative of Sojourner Truth.* By Sojourner Truth. Ed. Washington. New York: Vintage Books, 1993. v–xi.
Signed article in a weekly magazine	Wallace, Charles. "A Vodacious Deal." *Time* 14 Feb. 2000: 63.
Signed article in a monthly magazine	Gustaitis, Joseph. "The Sticky History of Chewing Gum." *American History* Oct. 1998: 30–38.
Unsigned editorial or story	"Selective Silence." Editorial. *Wall Street Journal* 11 Feb. 2000: A14. [If the editorial or story is signed, begin with the author's name.]
Signed pamphlet	[Treat the pamphlet as though it were a book.]
Pamphlet with no author, publisher, or date	*Are You at Risk of Heart Attack?* n.p. n.d. [n.p. n.d. indicates that there is no known publisher or date]
Filmstrips, slide programs, videocassettes, DVDs, and other audiovisual media	*The Diary of Anne Frank.* Dir. George Stevens. Perf. Millie Perkins, Shelley Winters, Joseph Schildkraut, Lou Jacobi, and Richard Beymer. 1959. DVD. Twentieth Century Fox, 2004.
Radio or television program transcript	"Washington's Crossing of the Delaware." Host Liane Hansen. Guest David Hackett Fischer. *Weekend Edition Sunday.* Natl. Public Radio. WNYC, New York City. 23 Dec. 2003. Transcript.
Internet	"Fun Facts About Gum." NACGM site. National Association of Chewing Gum Manufacturers. 19 Dec. 1999. <http://www.nacgm.org/consumer/funfacts.html>. [Indicate the date of last update if known and the date you accessed the information. Content and addresses at Web sites change frequently.]
Newspaper	Thurow, Roger. "South Africans Who Fought for Sanctions Now Scrap for Investors." *Wall Street Journal* 11 Feb. 2000: A1+ [For a multipage article that does not appear on consecutive pages, write only the first page number on which it appears, followed by a plus sign.]
Personal interview	Smith, Jane. Personal interview. 10 Feb. 2000.
CD (with multiple publishers)	Simms, James, ed. *Romeo and Juliet.* By William Shakespeare. CD-ROM. Oxford: Attica Cybernetics Ltd.; London: BBC Education; London: HarperCollins Publishers, 1995.
Article from an encyclopedia	Askeland, Donald R. "Welding." *World Book Encyclopedia.* 1991 ed.

APA Style for Listing Sources

The list of citations for APA is referred to as a Reference List and not a bibliography.

Book with one author	Pyles, T. (1971). *The Origins and Development of the English Language* (2nd ed.). New York: Harcourt Brace Jovanovich, Inc.
Book with two or three authors	McCrum, R., Cran, W., & MacNeil, R. (1987). *The Story of English.* New York: Penguin Books.
Book with an editor	Truth, S. (1993). *Narrative of Sojourner Truth* (M. Washington, Ed.). New York: Vintage Books.
Book with more than three authors or editors	Donald, R. B., Morrow, B. R., Wargetz, L. G., & Werner, K. (1996). *Writing Clear Essays.* Upper Saddle River, New Jersey: Prentice-Hall, Inc. [With six or more authors, abbreviate second and following authors as "et al."]
A single work from an anthology	Hawthorne, N. (1998) Young Goodman Brown. In E. V. Roberts, & H. E. Jacobs (Eds.), *Literature: An Introduction to Reading and Writing* (pp. 376–385). Upper Saddle River, New Jersey: Prentice-Hall, Inc.
Introduction to a work included in a published edition	[No style is offered under this heading.]
Signed article in a weekly magazine	Wallace, C. (2000, February 14). A vodacious deal. *Time, 155,* 63. [The volume number appears in italics before the page number.]
Signed article in a monthly magazine	Gustaitis, J. (1998, October). The sticky history of chewing gum. *American History, 33,* 30–38.
Unsigned editorial or story	Selective Silence. (2000, February 11). *Wall Street Journal,* p. A14.
Signed pamphlet	Pearson Education. (2000). *LifeCare* (2nd ed.) [Pamphlet]. Smith, John: Author.
Pamphlet with no author, publisher, or date	[No style is offered under this heading.]
Filmstrips, slide programs, and videotape	Stevens, G. (Producer & Director). (1959). *The Diary of Anne Frank.* [Videotape]. (Available from Twentieth Century Fox) [If the producer and the director are two different people, list the producer first and then the director, with an ampersand (&) between them.]
Radio or television program transcript	Broderick, D. (1999, May 23). The First Immortal Generation. (R. Williams, Radio Host). *Ockham's Razor.* New York: National Public Radio.
Internet	National Association of Chewing Gum Manufacturers. Available: http://www.nacgm.org/consumer/funfacts.html [References to Websites should begin with the author's last name, if available. Indicate the site name and the available path or URL address.]
Newspaper	Thurow, R. (2000, February 11). South Africans who fought for sanctions now scrap for investors. *Wall Street Journal,* pp. A1, A4.
Personal interview	[APA states that, since interviews (and other personal communications) do not provide "recoverable data," they should only be cited in text.]
CD (with multiple publishers)	[No style is offered under this heading.]
Article from an encyclopedia	Askeland, D. R. (1991). Welding. In *World Book Encyclopedia.* (Vol. 21 pp. 190–191). Chicago: World Book, Inc.

CMS Style for Listing Sources

The following chart shows the CMS author-date method of documentation.

Book with one author	Pyles, Thomas. *The Origins and Development of the English Language,* 2nd ed. New York: Harcourt Brace Jovanovich, Inc., 1971.
Book with two or three authors	McCrum, Robert, William Cran, and Robert MacNeil. *The Story of English.* New York: Penguin Books, 1987.
Book with an editor	Truth, Sojourner. *Narrative of Sojourner Truth.* Edited by Margaret Washington. New York: Vintage Books, 1993.
Book with more than three authors or editors	Donald, Robert B., et al. *Writing Clear Essays.* Upper Saddle River, New Jersey: Prentice-Hall, Inc., 1996.
A single work from an anthology	Hawthorne, Nathaniel. "Young Goodman Brown." In *Literature: An Introduction to Reading and Writing.* Ed. Edgar V. Roberts and Henry E. Jacobs. 376–385. Upper Saddle River, New Jersey: Prentice-Hall, Inc., 1998.
Introduction to a work included in a published edition	Washington, Margaret. Introduction to *Narrative of Sojourner Truth,* by Sojourner Truth. New York: Vintage Books, 1993. [According to CMS style, you should avoid this type of entry unless the introduction is of special importance to the work.]
Signed article in a weekly magazine	Wallace, Charles. "A Vodacious Deal." *Time,* 14 February 2000, 63.
Signed article in a monthly magazine	Gustaitis, Joseph. "The Sticky History of Chewing Gum." *American History,* October 1998, 30–38.
Unsigned editorial or story	*Wall Street Journal,* 11 February 2000. [CMS states that items from newspapers are seldom listed in a bibliography. Instead, the name of the paper and the relevant dates are listed.]
Signed pamphlet	[No style is offered under this heading.]
Pamphlet with no author, publisher, or date	[No style is offered under this heading.]
Filmstrips, slide programs, and videotape	Stevens, George. (director). *The Diary of Anne Frank.* 170 min. Beverly Hills, California: Twentieth Century Fox, 1994.
Radio or television program transcript	[No style is offered under this heading.]
Internet	[No style is offered under this heading.]
Newspaper	*Wall Street Journal,* 11 February 2000. [CMS states that items from newspapers are seldom listed in a bibliography. Instead, the name of the paper and the relevant dates are listed.]
Personal interview	[CMS states that, since personal conversations are not available to the public, there is no reason to place them in the bibliography. However, the following format should be followed if they are listed.] Jane Smith. Conversation with author. Wooster, Ohio, 10 February 2000.
CD (with multiple publishers)	Shakespeare, William. *Romeo and Juliet.* Oxford: Attica Cybernetics Ltd.; London: BBC Education; London: HarperCollins Publishers, 1995. CD-ROM.
Article from an encyclopedia	[According to CMS style, encyclopedias are not listed in bibliographies.]

Sample Works-Cited List (MLA)

Carwardine, Mark, Erich Hoyt, R. Ewan Fordyce, and
Peter Gill. *The Nature Company Guides: Whales,
Dolphins, and Porpoises*. New York: Time-Life
Books, 1998.

Ellis, Richard. *Men and Whales*. New York: Knopf,
1991.

Whales in Danger. "Discovering Whales." 18 Oct. 1999.
<http://whales.magna.com.au/DISCOVER>

Sample Internal Citations (MLA)

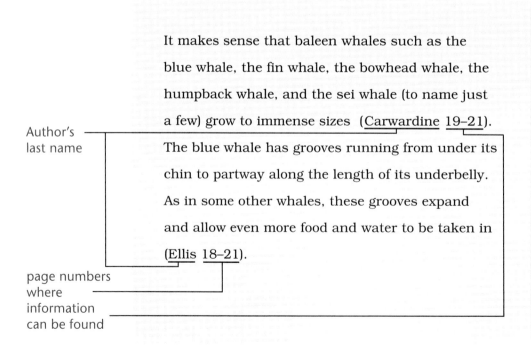

It makes sense that baleen whales such as the
blue whale, the fin whale, the bowhead whale, the
humpback whale, and the sei whale (to name just
a few) grow to immense sizes (Carwardine 19–21).

Author's
last name

The blue whale has grooves running from under its
chin to partway along the length of its underbelly.
As in some other whales, these grooves expand
and allow even more food and water to be taken in
(Ellis 18–21).

page numbers
where
information
can be found

Internet Research Handbook

Introduction to the Internet

The Internet is a series of networks that are interconnected all over the world. The Internet allows users to have almost unlimited access to information stored on the networks. Dr. Berners-Lee, a physicist, created the Internet in the 1980's by writing a small computer program that allowed pages to be linked together using key words. The Internet was mostly text-based until 1992, when a computer program called the NCSA Mosaic (National Center for Supercomputing Applications at the University of Illinois) was created. This program was the first Web browser. The development of Web browsers greatly eased the ability of the user to navigate through all the pages stored on the Web. Very soon, the appearance of the Web was altered as well. More appealing visuals were added, and sound was also implemented. This change made the Web more user-friendly and more appealing to the general public.

Using the Internet for Research

Key Word Search

Before you begin a search, you should identify your specific topic. To make searching easier, narrow your subject to a key word or a group of key words. These are your search terms, and they should be as specific as possible. For example, if you are looking for the latest concert dates for your favorite musical group, you might use the band's name as a key word. However, if you were to enter the name of the group in the query box of the search engine, you might be presented with thousands of links to information about the group that is unrelated to your needs. You might locate such information as band member biographies, the group's history, fan reviews of concerts, and hundreds of sites with related names containing information that is irrelevant to your search. Because you used such a broad key word, you might need to navigate through all that information before you find a link or subheading for concert dates. In contrast, if you were to type in "Duplex Arena and [band name]" you would have a better chance of locating pages that contain this information.

How to Narrow Your Search

If you have a large group of key words and still don't know which ones to use, write out a list of all the words you are considering. Once you have completed the list, scrutinize it. Then, delete the words that are least important to your search, and highlight those that are most important.

These **key search connectors** can help you fine-tune your search:

AND: narrows a search by retrieving documents that include both terms. For example: *baseball AND playoffs*

OR: broadens a search by retrieving documents including any of the terms. For example: *playoffs OR championships*

NOT: narrows a search by excluding documents containing certain words. For example: *baseball NOT history of*

Tips for an Effective Search

1. Keep in mind that search engines can be case-sensitive. If your first attempt at searching fails, check your search terms for misspellings and try again.

2. If you are entering a group of key words, present them in order, from the most important to the least important key word.

3. Avoid opening the link to every single page in your results list. Search engines present pages in descending order of relevancy. The most useful pages will be located at the top of the list. However, read the description of each link before you open the page.

4. When you use some search engines, you can find helpful tips for specializing your search. Take the opportunity to learn more about effective searching.

Other Ways to Search

Using On-line Reference Sites

How you search should be tailored to *what* you are hoping to find. If you are looking for data and facts, use reference sites before you jump onto a simple search engine. For example, you can find reference sites to provide definitions of words, statistics about almost any subject, biographies, maps, and concise information on many topics. Some useful on-line reference sites:

- On-line libraries
- On-line periodicals
- Almanacs
- Encyclopedias

You can find these sources using subject searches.

Conducting Subject Searches

As you prepare to go on-line, consider your subject and the best way to find information to suit your needs. If you are looking for general information on a topic and you want your search results to be extensive, consider the subject search indexes on most search engines. These indexes, in the form of category and subject lists, often appear on the first page of a search engine. When you click on a specific highlighted word, you will be presented with a new screen containing subcategories of the topic you chose. In the screen shots below, the category *Sports & Recreation* provided a second index for users to focus a search even further.

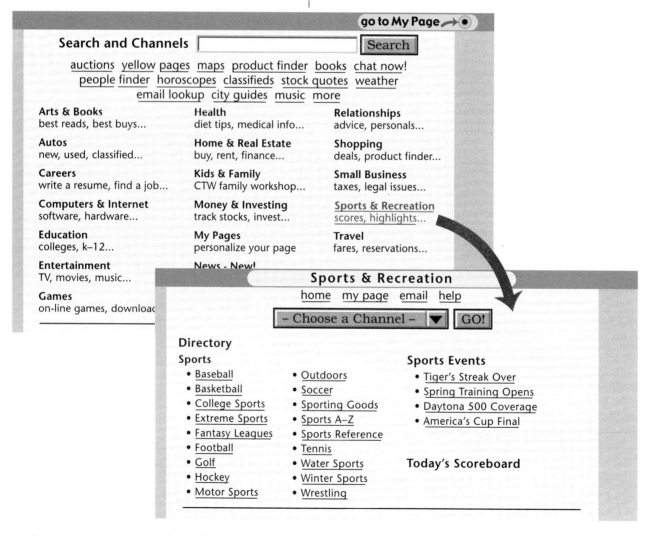

Evaluating the Reliability of Internet Resources

Just as you would evaluate the quality, bias, and validity of any other research material you locate, check the source of information you find on-line. Compare these two sites containing information on the poet and writer Langston Hughes:

Site A is a personal Web site constructed by a college student. It contains no bibliographic information or links to sites that he used. Included on the site are several poems by Langston Hughes and a student essay about the poet's use of symbolism. It has not been updated in more than six months.

Site B is a Web site constructed and maintained by the English Department of a major university. Information on Hughes is presented in a scholarly format, with a bibliography and credits for the writer. The site includes links to other sites and indicates new features that are added weekly.

For your own research, consider the information you find on Site B to be more reliable and accurate than that on Site A. Because it is maintained by experts in their field who are held accountable for their work, the university site will be a better research tool than the student-generated one.

Tips for Evaluating Internet Sources

1. Consider who constructed and who now maintains the Web page. Determine whether this author is a reputable source. Often, the URL endings indicate a source.

   - Sites ending in *.edu* are maintained by educational institutions.
   - Sites ending in *.gov* are maintained by government agencies (federal, state, or local).
   - Sites ending in *.org* are normally maintained by nonprofit organizations and agencies.
   - Sites with a *.com* ending are commercially or personally maintained.

2. Skim the official and trademarked Web pages first. It is safe to assume that the information you draw from Web pages of reputable institutions, on-line encyclopedias, on-line versions of major daily newspapers, or government-owned sites produce information as reliable as the material you would find in print. In contrast, unbranded sites or those generated by individuals tend to borrow information from other sources without providing documentation. As information travels from one source to another, the information has likely been muddled, misinterpreted, edited, or revised.

3. You can still find valuable information in the less "official" sites. Check for the writer's credentials and then consider these factors:

   - Don't let official-looking graphics or presentations fool you.
   - Make sure the information is updated enough to suit your needs. Many Web pages will indicate how recently they have been updated.
   - If the information is borrowed, see whether you can trace it back to its original source.

Respecting Copyrighted Material

Because the Internet is a relatively new and quickly growing medium, issues of copyright and ownership arise almost daily. As laws begin to govern the use and reuse of material posted on-line, they may change the way that people can access or reprint material.

Text, photographs, music, and fine art printed on-line may not be reproduced without acknowledged permission of the copyright owner.

Glossary of Internet Terms

attached file: a file containing information, such as a text document or GIF image, that is attached to an e-mail message; reports, pictures, spreadsheets, and so on transmitted to others by attaching these to messages as files

bandwidth: the amount of information, mainly compressed in bits per second (bps), that can be sent through a connection within a specific amount of time; depending on how fast your modem is, 15,000 bits (roughly one page of text) can be transferred per second

bit: a binary digit of computerized data, represented by a single digit that is either a 1 or a 0; a group of bits constitutes a byte

bookmark: a feature of your Web browser that allows you to place a "bookmark" on a Web page to which you wish to return at a later time

browser: software designed to present material accessed on the Web

bulletin-board system: a computer system that members access in order to join on-line discussion groups or to post announcements

case-sensitivity: the quality of a search engine that causes it to respond to upper- or lowercase letters in different ways

chat room: informal on-line gathering sites where people share conversations, experiences, or information on a specific topic; many chat rooms do not require users to provide their identity, so the reliability or safety of these sites is uncertain

cookie: a digitized piece of information that is sent to a Web browser by a Web server, intended to be saved on a computer; cookies gather information about the user, such as user preferences, or recent on-line purchases; a Web browser can be set to either accept or reject cookies

cyberspace: a term referring to the electronic environment connecting all computer network information with the people who use it

database: a large collection of data that have been formatted to fit a certain user-defined standard

digerati: a slang term to describe Internet experts; an offshoot of the term *literati*

download: to copy files from the Internet onto your computer

e-mail: electronic mail, or the exchange of messages via the Internet; because it is speedier than traditional mail and offers easier global access, e-mail has grown in popularity; e-mail messages can be sent to a single person or in bulk to a group of people

error message: a displayed communication or printout that reports a problem with a program or Web page

FTP site (file transfer protocol): a password-protected server on the Internet that allows the transfer of information from one computer to another

GIF (Graphic Interchange Format): a form of graphics used on the Web

graphics: information displayed as pictures or images instead of text

hits: items retrieved by a key word search; the number tracking the volume of visits to a Web site

home page: the main Web page for an individual or an organization, containing links to subpages within

HTML (HyperText Markup Language): the coding text that is the foundation for creating Web pages

interactivity: a quality of some Web pages that encourages the frequent exchange of information between user and computer

Internet: a worldwide computer network that supports services such as the World Wide Web, e-mail, and file transfer

JPEG (Joint Photo Experts Group, the developers): a file format for graphics especially suited to photographs

K: a measurement of file size or memory; short for "Kilobyte," 1,000 bytes of information (see *bit*)

key word: search term entered into the query box of a search engine to direct the results of the search

link: an icon or word on a Web page that, when clicked, transfers the user to another Web page or to a different document within the same page

login: the procedure by which users gain access to a server or a secure Web site; usually the user must enter a specific user name and password

modem: a device that transfers data to a computer through a phone line. A computer's modem connects to a server, which then sends information in the form of digital signals. The modem converts these signals into waves, for the purpose of information reception. The speed of a modem affects how quickly a computer can receive and download information

newbie: jargon used to describe Internet novices

newsgroup: an on-line discussion group, where users can post and respond to messages; the most prevalent collection of newsgroups is found on USENET

query box: the blank box in a search engine where your search terms are input

relevance ranking: the act of displaying the results of a search in the order of their relevance to the search terms

search engines: tools that help you navigate databases to locate information; search engines respond to a key word search by providing the user with a directory of multiple Web pages about the key word or containing the key word

server: a principal computer that provides services, such as storing files and providing access to the Internet, to another computer

signature: a preprogrammed section of text that is automatically added to an e-mail message

surfing: the process of reading Web pages and of moving from one Web site to another

URL (Uniform Resource Locator): a Web page's address; a URL can look like this:

http://www.phwg.phschool.com or
http://www.senate.gov/~appropriations/
 labor/testimony

usenet: a worldwide system of discussion groups, or newsgroups

vanity pages: Web sites placed on-line by people to tell about themselves or their interests; vanity pages do not have any commercial or informational value

virus: a set of instructions, hidden in a computer system or transferred via e-mail or electronic files, that can cause problems with a computer's ability to perform normally

Web page: a set of information, including graphics, text, sound, and video, presented in a browser window; a Web page can be found by its URL once it is posted on the World Wide Web

Web site: a collection of Web pages that are linked together for posting on the World Wide Web

W3: a group of Internet experts, including networking professionals, academics, scientists, and corporate interests, who maintain and develop technologies and standards for the Internet

WWW (World Wide Web): a term referring to the multitude of information systems found on the Internet; this includes FTP, Gopher, telnet, and http sites

zip: a format for compressed files (files reduced in size); used to make their transmission and storage more efficient

Commonly Overused Words

When you write, use the most precise word for your meaning, not the word that comes to mind first. Consult this thesaurus to find alternatives for some commonly overused words. Consult a full-length thesaurus to find alternatives to words that do not appear here. Keep in mind that the choices offered in a thesaurus do not all mean exactly the same thing. Review all the options, and choose the one that best expresses your meaning.

about approximately, nearly, almost, approaching, close to

absolutely unconditionally, perfectly, completely, ideally, purely

activity action, movement, operation, labor, exertion, enterprise, project, pursuit, endeavor, job, assignment, pastime, scheme, task

add attach, affix, join, unite, append, increase, amplify

affect adjust, influence, transform, moderate, incline, motivate, prompt

amazing overwhelming, astonishing, startling, unexpected, stunning, dazzling, remarkable

awesome impressive, stupendous, fabulous, astonishing, outstanding

bad defective, inadequate, poor, unsatisfactory, disagreeable, offensive, repulsive, corrupt, wicked, naughty, harmful, injurious, unfavorable

basic essential, necessary, indispensable, vital, fundamental, elementary

beautiful attractive, appealing, alluring, exqui-
site, gorgeous, handsome, stunning

begin commence, found, initiate, introduce, launch, originate

better preferable, superior, worthier

big enormous, extensive, huge, immense, massive

boring commonplace, monotonous, tedious, tiresome

bring accompany, cause, convey, create, conduct, deliver, produce

cause origin, stimulus, inspiration, motive

certain unquestionable, incontrovertible, unmistakable, indubitable, assured, confident

change alter, transform, vary, replace, diversify

choose select, elect, nominate, prefer, identify

decent respectable, adequate, fair, suitable

definitely unquestionably, clearly, precisely, positively, inescapably

easy effortless, natural, comfortable, undemanding, pleasant, relaxed

effective powerful, successful

emphasize underscore, feature, accentuate

end limit, boundary, finish, conclusion, finale, resolution

energy vitality, vigor, force, dynamism

enjoy savor, relish, revel, benefit

entire complete, inclusive, unbroken, integral

excellent superior, remarkable, splendid, unsurpassed, superb, magnificent

exciting thrilling, stirring, rousing, dramatic

far distant, remote

fast swift, quick, fleet, hasty, instant, accelerated

fill occupy, suffuse, pervade, saturate, inflate, stock

finish complete, conclude, cease, achieve, exhaust, deplete, consume

funny comical, ludicrous, amusing, droll, entertaining, bizarre, unusual, uncommon

get obtain, receive, acquire, procure, achieve

give bestow, donate, supply, deliver, distribute, impart

go proceed, progress, advance, move

good satisfactory, serviceable, functional, competent, virtuous, striking

great tremendous, superior, remarkable, eminent, proficient, expert

happy pleased, joyous, elated, jubilant, cheerful, delighted

hard arduous, formidable, complex, complicated, rigorous, harsh

help assist, aid, support, sustain, serve

hurt injure, harm, damage, wound, impair

important significant, substantial, weighty, meaningful, critical, vital, notable

interesting absorbing, appealing, entertaining, fascinating, thought-provoking

job task, work, business, undertaking, occupation, vocation, chore, duty, assignment

keep retain, control, possess

kind type, variety, sort, form

know comprehend, understand, realize, perceive, discern

like (adj) similar, equivalent, parallel

like (verb) enjoy, relish, appreciate

main primary, foremost, dominant

make build, construct, produce, assemble, fashion, manufacture

mean plan, intend, suggest, propose, indicate

more supplementary, additional, replenishment

new recent, modern, current, novel

next subsequently, thereafter, successively

nice pleasant, satisfying, gracious, charming

old aged, mature, experienced, used, worn, former, previous

open unobstructed, accessible

part section, portion, segment, detail, element, component

perfect flawless, faultless, ideal, consummate

plan scheme, design, system, plot

pleasant agreeable, gratifying, refreshing, welcome

prove demonstrate, confirm, validate, verify, corroborate

quick brisk, prompt, responsive, rapid, nimble, hasty

really truly, genuinely, extremely, undeniably

regular standard, routine, customary, habitual

see regard, behold, witness, gaze, realize, notice

small diminutive, miniature, minor, insignificant, slight, trivial

sometimes occasionally, intermittently, sporadically, periodically

take grasp, capture, choose, select, tolerate, endure

terrific extraordinary, magnificent, marvelous

think conceive, imagine, ponder, reflect, contemplate

try attempt, endeavor, venture, test

use employ, operate, utilize

very unusually, extremely, deeply, exceedingly, profoundly

want desire, crave, yearn, long

Commonly Misspelled Words

The list on these pages presents words that cause problems for many people. Some of these words are spelled according to set rules, but others follow no specific rules. As you review this list, check to see how many of the words give you trouble in your own writing. Then, read the instruction in the "Vocabulary and Spelling" chapter in the book for strategies and suggestions for improving your own spelling habits.

abbreviate	athletic	catastrophe	curious
absence	attendance	category	cylinder
absolutely	auxiliary	ceiling	deceive
abundance	awkward	cemetery	decision
accelerate	bandage	census	deductible
accidentally	banquet	certain	defendant
accumulate	bargain	changeable	deficient
accurate	barrel	characteristic	definitely
ache	battery	chauffeur	delinquent
achievement	beautiful	chief	dependent
acquaintance	beggar	clothes	descendant
adequate	beginning	coincidence	description
admittance	behavior	colonel	desert
advertisement	believe	column	desirable
aerial	benefit	commercial	dessert
affect	bicycle	commission	detcriorate
aggravate	biscuit	commitment	dining
aggressive	bookkeeper	committee	disappointed
agreeable	bought	competitor	disastrous
aisle	boulevard	concede	discipline
all right	brief	condemn	dissatisfied
allowance	brilliant	congratulate	distinguish
aluminum	bruise	connoisseur	effect
amateur	bulletin	conscience	eighth
analysis	buoyant	conscientious	eligible
analyze	bureau	conscious	embarrass
ancient	bury	contemporary	enthusiastic
anecdote	buses	continuous	entrepreneur
anniversary	business	controversy	envelope
anonymous	cafeteria	convenience	environment
answer	calendar	coolly	equipped
anticipate	campaign	cooperate	equivalent
anxiety	canceled	cordially	especially
apologize	candidate	correspondence	exaggerate
appall	capacity	counterfeit	exceed
appearance	capital	courageous	excellent
appreciate	capitol	courteous	exercise
appropriate	captain	courtesy	exhibition
architecture	career	criticism	existence
argument	carriage	criticize	experience
associate	cashier	curiosity	explanation

extension
extraordinary
familiar
fascinating
February
fiery
financial
fluorescent
foreign
forfeit
fourth
fragile
gauge
generally
genius
genuine
government
grammar
grievance
guarantee
guard
guidance
handkerchief
harass
height
humorous
hygiene
ignorant
illegible
immediately
immigrant
independence
independent
indispensable
individual
inflammable
intelligence
interfere
irrelevant
irritable
jewelry
judgment
knowledge
laboratory
lawyer
legible
legislature
leisure
liable

library
license
lieutenant
lightning
likable
liquefy
literature
loneliness
magnificent
maintenance
marriage
mathematics
maximum
meanness
mediocre
mileage
millionaire
minimum
minuscule
miscellaneous
mischievous
misspell
mortgage
naturally
necessary
negotiate
neighbor
neutral
nickel
niece
ninety
noticeable
nuclear
nuisance
obstacle
occasion
occasionally
occur
occurred
occurrence
omitted
opinion
opportunity
optimistic
outrageous
pamphlet
parallel
paralyze
parentheses

particularly
patience
permanent
permissible
perseverance
persistent
personally
perspiration
persuade
phenomenal
phenomenon
physician
pleasant
pneumonia
possess
possession
possibility
prairie
precede
preferable
prejudice
preparation
prerogative
previous
primitive
privilege
probably
procedure
proceed
prominent
pronunciation
psychology
publicly
pursue
questionnaire
realize
really
recede
receipt
receive
recognize
recommend
reference
referred
rehearse
relevant
reminiscence
renowned
repetition

restaurant
rhythm
ridiculous
sandwich
satellite
schedule
scissors
secretary
siege
solely
sponsor
subtle
subtlety
superintendent
supersede
surveillance
susceptible
tariff
temperamental
theater
threshold
truly
unmanageable
unwieldy
usage
usually
valuable
various
vegetable
voluntary
weight
weird
whale
wield
yield

Abbreviations Guide

Abbreviations, shortened versions of words or phrases, can be valuable tools in writing if you know when and how to use them. They can be very helpful in informal writing situations, such as taking notes or writing lists. However, only a few abbreviations can be used in formal writing. They are: *Mr., Mrs., Miss, Ms., Dr., A.M., P.M., A.D., B.C., M.A, B.A., Ph.D.,* and *M.D.*

The following pages provide the conventional abbreviations for a variety of words.

Abbreviations of Common Titles

Ambassador	Amb.	Lieutenant	Lt.
Attorney	Atty.	Major	Maj.
Brigadier-General	Brig. Gen.	President	Pres.
Brother	Br.	Professor	Prof.
Captain	Capt.	Representative	Rep.
Colonel	Col.	Reverend	Rev.
Commander	Cmdr.	Secretary	Sec.
Commissioner	Com.	Senator	Sen.
Corporal	Cpl.	Sergeant	Sgt.
Doctor	Dr.	Sister	Sr.
Father	Fr.	Superintendent	Supt.
Governor	Gov.	Treasurer	Treas.
Honorable	Hon.	Vice Admiral	Vice Adm.

Abbreviations of Academic Degrees

Bachelor of Arts	B.A. (or A.B.)	Esquire (lawyer)	Esq.
Bachelor of Science	B.S. (or S.B.)	Master of Arts	M.A. (or A.M.)
Doctor of Dental Surgery	D.D.S.	Master of Business Administration	M.B.A.
Doctor of Divinity	D.D.		
Doctor of Education	Ed.D.	Master of Fine Arts	M.F.A.
Doctor of Laws	LL.D.	Master of Science	M.S. (or S.M.)
Doctor of Medicine	M.D.	Registered Nurse	R.N.
Doctor of Philosophy	Ph.D.		

Abbreviations of States

State	Traditional	Postal Service	State	Traditional	Postal Service
Alabama	Ala.	AL	Montana	Mont.	MT
Alaska	Alaska	AK	Nebraska	Nebr.	NE
Arizona	Ariz.	AZ	Nevada	Nev.	NV
Arkansas	Ark.	AR	New Hampshire	N.H.	NH
California	Calif.	CA	New Jersey	N.J.	NJ
Colorado	Colo.	CO	New Mexico	N.M.	NM
Connecticut	Conn.	CT	New York	N.Y.	NY
Delaware	Del.	DE	North Carolina	N.C.	NC
Florida	Fla.	FL	North Dakota	N.Dak.	ND
Georgia	Ga.	GA	Ohio	O.	OH
Hawaii	Hawaii	HI	Oklahoma	Okla.	OK
Idaho	Ida.	ID	Oregon	Ore.	OR
Illinois	Ill.	IL	Pennsylvania	Pa.	PA
Indiana	Ind.	IN	Rhode Island	R.I.	RI
Iowa	Iowa	IA	South Carolina	S.C.	SC
Kansas	Kans.	KS	South Dakota	S.Dak.	SD
Kentucky	Ky.	KY	Tennessee	Tenn.	TN
Louisiana	La.	LA	Texas	Tex.	TX
Maine	Me.	ME	Utah	Utah	UT
Maryland	Md.	MD	Vermont	Vt.	VT
Massachusetts	Mass.	MA	Virginia	Va.	VA
Michigan	Mich.	MI	Washington	Wash.	WA
Minnesota	Minn.	MN	West Virginia	W. Va	WV
Mississippi	Miss.	MS	Wisconsin	Wis.	WI
Missouri	Mo.	MO	Wyoming	Wyo.	WY

Common Geographical Abbreviations

Apartment	Apt.	National	Natl.
Avenue	Ave.	Park, Peak	Pk.
Block	Blk.	Peninsula	Pen.
Boulevard	Blvd.	Point	Pt.
Building	Bldg.	Province	Prov.
County	Co.	Road	Rd.
District	Dist.	Route	Rte.
Drive	Dr.	Square	Sq.
Fort	Ft.	Street	St.
Island	Is.	Territory	Terr.
Mountain	Mt.		

Abbreviations of Traditional Measurements

inch(es)	in.	ounce(s)	oz.
foot, feet	ft.	pound(s)	lb.
yard(s)	yd.	pint(s)	pt.
mile(s)	mi.	quart(s)	qt.
teaspoon(s)	tsp.	gallon(s)	gal.
tablespoon(s)	tbsp.	Fahrenheit	F.

Abbreviations of Metric Measurements

millimeter(s)	mm	liter(s)	L
centimeter(s)	cm	kiloliter(s)	kL
meter(s)	m	milligram(s)	mg
kilometer(s)	km	centigram(s)	cg
milliliter(s)	mL	gram(s)	g
centiliter(s)	cL	Celsius	C

Other Commonly Used Abbreviations

about (used with dates)	c., ca., circ.	manager	mgr.
and others	et al.	manufacturing	mfg.
anonymous	anon.	market	mkt.
approximately	approx.	measure	meas.
associate, association	assoc., assn.	merchandise	mdse.
auxiliary	aux., auxil.	miles per hour	mph
bibliography	bibliog.	miscellaneous	misc.
boxes	bx(s).	money order	M.O.
bucket	bkt.	note well; take notice	N.B.
bulletin	bull.	number	no.
bushel	bu.	package	pkg.
capital letter	cap.	page	p., pg.
cash on delivery	C.O.D.	pages	pp.
department	dept.	pair(s)	pr(s).
discount	disc.	parenthesis	paren.
dozen(s)	doz.	Patent Office	pat. off.
each	ea.	piece(s)	pc(s).
edition, editor	ed.	poetical, poetry	poet.
equivalent	equiv.	private	pvt.
established	est.	proprietor	prop.
fiction	fict.	pseudonym	pseud.
for example	e.g.	published, publisher	pub.
free of charge	grat., gratis	received	recd.
General Post Office	G.P.O.	reference, referee	ref.
government	gov., govt.	revolutions per minute	rpm
graduate, graduated	grad.	rhetorical, rhetoric	rhet.
Greek, Grecian	Gr.	right	R.
headquarters	hdqrs.	scene	sc.
height	ht.	special, specific	spec.
hospital	hosp.	spelling, species	sp.
illustrated	ill., illus.	that is	i.e.
including, inclusive	incl.	treasury, treasurer	treas.
introduction, introductory	intro.	volume	vol.
italics	ital.	weekly	wkly
karat, carat	k., kt.	weight	wt.
left	L.		

Proofreading Symbols Reference

Proofreading symbols make it easier to show where changes are needed in a paper. When proofreading your own or a classmate's work, use these standard proofreading symbols.

insert	I proofred. *a*^
delete	I p̶ proofread.
close up space	I proof read.
delete and close up space	I proofreade̸.
begin new paragraph	¶ I proofread.
spell out	I proofread ⑩ papers. (sp)
lowercase	I P̸roofread. (lc)
capitalize	i̲̲ proofread. (cap)
transpose letters	I proofraed. (tr)
transpose words	I only proofread her paper. (tr)
period	I will proofread⊙
comma	I will proofread‸and she will help.
colon	We will proofread for the following errors⋮
semicolon	I will proofread‸she will help. ‸;
single quotation marks	She said, "I enjoyed the story‸The Invalid." ˅ ˅
double quotation marks	She said,‸I enjoyed the story. ‸˅ ˅
apostrophe	Did you borrow Sylvias book? ˅
question mark	Did you borrow Sylvia's book‸ ?/
exclamation point	You're kidding‸ !/
hyphen	on‸line /=/
parentheses	William Shakespeare‸1564–1616‸ ⦉ ⦊

Student Publications

To share your writing with a wider audience, consider submitting it to a local, state, or national publication for student writing. Following are several magazines and Web sites that accept and publish student work.

Periodicals

Merlyn's Pen merlynspen.org

Skipping Stones P.O. Box 3939, Eugene, OR 97403
http://www.skippingstones.org

Teen Ink Box 30, Newton, MA 02461 teenink.com

On-line Publications

Kid Pub http://www.kidpub.org

MidLink Magazine http://www.ncsu.edu/midlink

Contests

Annual Poetry Contest National Federation of State Poetry Societies, Contest Chair, Kathleen Pederzani, 121 Grande Boulevard, Reading, PA 19608-9680

http://www.nfsps.com

Paul A. Witty Outstanding Literature Award International Reading Association, Special Interest Group for Reading for Gifted and Creative Students, c/o Texas Christian University, P.O. Box 297900, Fort Worth, TX 76129

Seventeen Magazine Fiction Contest *Seventeen* Magazine, 1440 Broadway 13th Floor, New York, NY 10018

The Young Playwrights Festival National Playwriting Competition Young Playwrights Inc., Dept WEB, 306 West 38th Street #300, New York, NY 10018

webmaster@youngplaywrights.org

Glossary

accent: the emphasis on a syllable, usually in poetry

action verb: a word that tells what action someone or something is performing (*See* linking verb.)

active voice: the voice of a verb whose subject performs an action (*See* passive voice.)

adjective: a word that modifies a noun or pronoun by telling *what kind* or *which one*

adjective clause: a subordinate clause that modifies a noun or pronoun

adjective phrase: a prepositional phrase that modifies a noun or pronoun

adverb: a word that modifies a verb, an adjective, or another adverb

adverb clause: a subordinate clause that modifies a verb, an adjective, an adverb, or a verbal by telling *where, when, in what way, to what extent, under what condition,* or *why*

adverb phrase: a prepositional phrase that modifies a verb, an adjective, or an adverb

allegory: a literary work with two or more levels of meaning—a literal level and one or more symbolic levels

alliteration: the repetition of initial consonant sounds in accented syllables

allusion: an indirect reference to a well-known person, place, event, literary work, or work of art

annotated bibliography: a research writing product that provides a list of materials on a given topic, along with publication information, summaries, or evaluations

apostrophe: a punctuation mark used to form possessive nouns and contractions

appositive: a noun or pronoun placed after another noun or pronoun to identify, rename, or explain the preceding word

appositive phrase: a noun or pronoun with its modifiers, placed next to a noun or pronoun to identify, rename, or explain the preceding word

article: one of three commonly used adjectives: *a, an,* and *the*

assonance: the repetition of vowel sounds in stressed syllables containing dissimilar consonant sounds

audience: the reader(s) a writer intends to reach

autobiographical writing: narrative writing that tells a true story about an important period, experience, or relationship in the writer's life

ballad: a song that tells a story (often dealing with adventure or romance) or a poem imitating such a song

bias: the attitudes or beliefs that affect a writer's ability to present a subject objectively

bibliography: a list of the sources of a research paper, including full bibliographic references for each source the writer consulted while conducting research (*See* works-cited list.)

biography: narrative writing that tells the story of an important period, experience, or relationship in a person's life, as reported by another

blueprinting: a prewriting technique in which a writer sketches a map of a home, school, neighborhood, or other meaningful place in order to spark memories or associations for further development

body paragraph: a paragraph in an essay that develops, explains, or supports the key ideas of the writing

brainstorming: a prewriting technique in which a group jots down as many ideas as possible about a given topic

case: the form of a noun or pronoun that indicates how it functions in a sentence

cause-and-effect writing: expository writing that examines the relationship between events, explaining how one event or situation causes another

character: a person (though not necessarily a human being) who takes part in the action of a literary work

characterization: the act of creating and developing a character through narration, description, and dialogue

citation: in formal research papers, the acknowledgment of ideas found in outside sources

classical invention: a prewriting technique in which writers gather details about a topic by analyzing the category and subcategories to which the topic belongs

clause: a group of words that has a subject and a verb

climax: the high point of interest or suspense in a literary work

coherence: a quality of written work in which all the parts flow logically from one idea to the next

colon: a punctuation mark used before an extended quotation, explanation, example, or series and after the salutation in a formal letter

comma: a punctuation mark used to separate words or groups of words

comparison-and-contrast writing: expository writing that describes the similarities and differences between two or more subjects in order to achieve a specific purpose

complement: a word or group of words that completes the meaning of a verb

compound sentence: a sentence that contains two or more independent clauses with no subordinate clauses

conclusion: the final paragraph(s) of a work of writing in which the writer may restate a main idea, summarize the points of the writing, or provide a closing remark to end the work effectively (*See* introduction, body paragraph, topical paragraph, functional paragraph.)

conflict: a struggle between opposing forces

conjugation: a list of the singular and plural forms of a verb in a particular tense

conjunction: a word used to connect other words or groups of words

connotation: the emotional associations that a word calls to mind (*See* denotation.)

consonance: the repetition of final consonant sounds in stressed syllables containing dissimilar vowel sounds

contraction: a shortened form of a word or phrase that includes an apostrophe to indicate the position of the missing letter(s)

coordinating conjunctions: words such as *and, but, nor,* and *yet* that connect similar words or groups of words

correlative conjunctions: word pairs such as *neither . . . nor, both . . . and,* and *whether . . . or* used to connect similar words or groups of words

couplet: a pair of rhyming lines written in the same meter

cubing: a prewriting technique in which a writer analyzes a subject from six specified angles: description; association; application; analysis; comparison and contrast; and evaluation

 D

declarative sentence: a statement punctuated with a period

demonstrative pronouns: words such as *this, that, these,* and *those* used to single out specific people, places, or things

denotation: the objective meaning of a word; its definition independent of other associations the word calls to mind (*See* connotation.)

depth-charging: a drafting technique in which a writer elaborates on a sentence by developing a key word or idea

description: language or writing that uses sensory details to capture a subject

dialect: the form of a language spoken by people in a particular region or group

dialogue: a direct conversation between characters or people

diary: a personal record of daily events, usually written in prose

diction: a writer's word choice

direct object: a noun or a pronoun that receives the action of a transitive verb

direct quotation: a drafting technique in which writers indicate the exact words of another by enclosing them in quotation marks

documentary: nonfiction film that analyzes news events or another focused subject by combining interviews, film footage, narration, and other audio/visual components

documented essay: research writing that includes a limited number of research sources, providing full documentation parenthetically within the text

drafting: a stage of the writing process that follows prewriting and precedes revising in which a writer gets ideas on paper in a rough format

drama: a story written to be performed by actors and actresses

E

elaboration: a drafting technique in which a writer extends his or her ideas through the use of facts, examples, descriptions, details, or quotations

epic: a long narrative poem about the adventures of a god or a hero

essay: a short nonfiction work about a particular subject

etymology: the history of a word, showing where it came from and how it has evolved into its present spelling and meaning

exclamation mark: a punctuation mark used to indicate strong emotion

exclamatory sentence: a statement that conveys strong emotion and ends with an exclamation mark

exposition: writing to inform, addressing analytic purposes such as problem and solution, comparison and contrast, how-to, and cause and effect

extensive writing: writing products generated for others and from others, meant to be shared with an audience and often done for school assignments (*See* reflexive writing.)

fact: a statement that can be proved true (*See* opinion.)

fiction: prose writing about imaginary characters and events

figurative language: writing or speech not meant to be interpreted literally

firsthand biography: narrative writing that tells the story of an important period, experience, or relationship in a person's life, reported by a writer who knows the subject personally

five W's: a prewriting technique in which writers gather details about a topic by generating answers to the following questions: *Who? What? Where? When?* and *Why?*

fragment: an incomplete idea punctuated as a complete sentence

freewriting: a prewriting technique in which a writer quickly jots down as many ideas on a topic as possible

functional paragraph: a paragraph that performs a specific role in composition, such as to arouse or sustain interest, to indicate dialogue, to make a transition (*See* topical paragraph.)

G

generalization: a statement that presents a rule or idea based on particular facts

gerund: a noun formed from the present participle of a verb (ending in -*ing*)

gerund phrase: a group of words containing a gerund and its modifiers or complements that function as a noun

grammar: the study of the forms of words and the way they are arranged in phrases, clauses, and sentences

helping verb: a verb added to another verb to make a single verb phrase that indicates the time at which an action takes place or whether it actually happens, could happen, or should happen

hexagonal writing: a technique in which a

writer analyzes a subject from six angles: literal level, personal allusions, theme, literary devices, literary allusions, and evaluation

homophones: pairs of words that sound the same as each other yet have different meanings and different spellings, such as *hear/here*

how-to writing: expository writing that explains a process by providing step-by-step directions

humanities: forms of artistic expression including, but not limited to, fine art, photography, theater, film, music, and dance

hyperbole: a deliberate exaggeration or overstatement

hyphen: a punctuation mark used to combine numbers and word parts, to join certain compound words, and to show that a word has been broken between syllables at the end of a line

I-Search report: a research paper in which the writer addresses the research experience in addition to presenting the information gathered

image: a word or phrase that appeals to one or more of the senses—sight, hearing, touch, taste, or smell

imagery: the descriptive language used to recreate sensory experiences, set a tone, suggest emotions, and guide readers' reactions

imperative sentence: a statement that gives an order or a direction and ends with either a period or an exclamation mark

indefinite pronoun: a word such as *anyone, each,* or *many* that refers to a person, place, or thing, without specifying which one

independent clause: a group of words that contains both a subject and a verb and that can stand by itself as a complete sentence

indirect quotation: reporting only the general meaning of what a person said or thought; quotation marks are not needed

infinitive: the form of a verb that comes after the word *to* and acts as a noun, adjective, or adverb

infinitive phrase: a phrase introduced by an infinitive that may be used as a noun, an adjective, or an adverb

interjection: a word or phrase that expresses feeling or emotion and functions independently of a sentence

interrogative pronoun: a word such as *which* and *who* that introduces a question

interrogative sentence: a question that is punctuated with a question mark

interview: an information-gathering technique in which one or more people pose questions to one or more other people who provide opinions or facts on a topic

intransitive verb: an action verb that does not take a direct object (*See* transitive verb.)

introduction: the opening paragraphs of a work of writing in which the writer may capture the readers' attention and present a thesis statement to be developed in the writing (*See* body paragraph, topical paragraph, functional paragraph, conclusion.)

invisible writing: a prewriting technique in which a writer freewrites without looking at the product until the exercise is complete; this can be accomplished at a word processor with the monitor turned off or with carbon paper and an empty ballpoint pen

irony: the general name given to literary techniques that involve surprising, interesting, or amusing contradictions

itemizing: a prewriting technique in which a writer creates a second, more focused, set of ideas based on an original listing activity. (*See* listing.)

jargon: the specialized words and phrases unique to a specific field

journal: a notebook or other organized writing system in which daily events and personal impressions are recorded

K

key word: the word or phrase that directs an Internet or database search

L

layering: a drafting technique in which a writer elaborates on a statement by identifying and then expanding upon a central idea or word

lead: the opening sentences of a work of writing meant to grab the reader's interest, accomplished through a variety of methods, including providing an intriguing quotation, a surprising or provocative question or fact, an anecdote, or a description

learning log: a record-keeping system in which a student notes information about new ideas

legend: a widely told story about the past that may or may not be based in fact

legibility: the neatness and readability of words

linking verb: a word that expresses its subject's state of being or condition (*See* action verb.)

listing: a prewriting technique in which a writer prepares a list of ideas related to a specific topic. (*See* itemizing.)

looping: a prewriting activity in which a writer generates follow-up freewriting based on the identification of a key word or central idea in an original freewriting exercise

lyric poem: a poem expressing the observations and feelings of a single speaker

M

main clause: a group of words that has a subject and a verb and can stand alone as a complete sentence

memoir: autobiographical writing that provides an account of a writer's relationship with a person, event, or place

metaphor: a figure of speech in which one thing is spoken of as though it were something else

meter: the rhythmic pattern of a poem

monologue: a speech or performance given entirely by one person or by one character

mood: the feeling created in the reader by a literary work or passage

multimedia presentation: a technique for sharing information with an audience by enhancing narration and explanation with media, including video images, slides, audiotape recordings, music, and fine art

N

narration: writing that tells a story

narrative poem: a poem that tells a story in verse

nominative case: the form of a noun or pronoun used as the subject of a verb, as a predicate nominative, or as the pronoun in a nominative absolute (*See* objective case, possessive case.)

noun: a word that names a person, place, or thing

noun clause: a subordinate clause that acts as a noun

novel: an extended work of fiction that often has a complicated plot, many major and minor characters, a unifying theme, and several settings

O

objective case: the form of a noun or pronoun used as the object of any verb, verbal, or preposition, or as the subject of an infinitive (*See* nominative case, possessive case.)

observation: a prewriting technique involving close visual study of an object; a writing product that reports such a study

ode: a long formal lyric poem with a serious theme

onomatopoeia: words such as *buzz* and *plop* that suggest the sounds they name

open-book test: a form of assessment in which students are permitted to use books and class notes to respond to test questions

opinion: beliefs that can be supported but not proved to be true (*See* fact.)

oral tradition: the body of songs, stories, and poems preserved by being passed from generation to generation by word of mouth

outline: a prewriting or study technique that allows writers or readers to organize the presentation and order of information

oxymoron: a figure of speech that fuses two contradictory or opposing ideas, such as "freezing fire" or "happy grief"

P

parable: a short, simple story from which a moral or religious lesson can be drawn

paradox: a statement that seems to be contradictory but that actually presents a truth

paragraph: a group of sentences that share a common topic or purpose and that focus on a single main idea or thought

parallelism: the placement of equal ideas in words, phrases, or clauses of similar types

paraphrase: restating an author's idea in different words, often to share information by making the meaning clear to readers

parentheses: punctuation marks used to set off asides and explanations when the material is not essential

participial phrase: a group of words made up of a participle and its modifiers and complements that acts as an adjective

participle: a form of a verb that can act as an adjective

passive voice: the voice of a verb whose subject receives an action (*See* active voice.)

peer review: a revising technique in which writers meet with other writers to share focused feedback on a draft

pentad: a prewriting technique in which a writer analyzes a subject from five specified points: actors, acts, scenes, agencies, and purposes

period: a punctuation mark used to end a declarative sentence, an indirect question, and most abbreviations

personal pronoun: a word such as *I, me, you, we, us, he, him, she, her, they,* and *them* that refers to the person speaking; the person spoken to; or the person, place, or thing spoken about

personification a figure of speech in which a nonhuman subject is given human characteristics

persuasion: writing or speaking that attempts to convince others to accept a position on an issue of concern to the writer

phrase: a group of words without a subject and verb that functions as one part of speech

plot: the sequence of events in narrative writing

plural: the form of a word that indicates more than one item is being mentioned

poetry: a category of writing in which the final product may make deliberate use of rhythm, rhyme, and figurative language in order to express deeper feelings than those conveyed in ordinary speech (*See* prose, drama.)

point of view: the perspective, or vantage point, from which a story is told

portfolio: an organized collection of writing projects, including writing ideas, works in progress, final drafts, and the writer's reflections on the work

possessive case: the form of a noun or pronoun used to show ownership (*See* objective case, nominative case.)

prefix: one or more syllables added to the beginning of a word root (*See* root, suffix.)

preposition: a word that relates a noun or pronoun that appears with it to another word in the sentence to indicate relations of time, place, causality, responsibility, and motivation

prepositional phrase: a group of words that includes a preposition and a noun or pronoun

presenting: a stage of the writing process in which a writer shares a final draft with an audience through speaking, listening, or representing activities

prewriting: a stage of the writing process in which writers explore, choose, and narrow a topic and then gather necessary details for drafting

problem-and-solution writing: expository writing that examines a problem and provides a realistic solution

pronoun: a word that stands for a noun or for another word that takes the place of a noun

prose: a category of written language in which the end product is developed through sentences and paragraphs (*See* poetry, drama.)

publishing: a stage of the writing process in which a writer shares the written version of a final draft with an audience

punctuation: the set of symbols used to convey specific directions to the reader

purpose: the specific goal or reason a writer chooses for a writing task

Q

question mark: a punctuation mark used to end an interrogative sentence or an incomplete question

quicklist: a prewriting technique in which a writer creates an impromptu, unresearched list of ideas related to a specific topic

quotation mark: a punctuation mark used to indicate the beginning and end of a person's exact speech or thoughts

R

ratiocination: a systematic approach to the revision process that involves color-coding elements of writing for evaluation

reflective essay: autobiographical writing in which a writer shares a personal experience and then provides insight about the event

reflexive pronoun: a word that ends in *-self* or *-selves* and names the person or thing receiving an action when that person or thing is the same as the one performing the action

reflexive writing: writing generated for oneself and from oneself, not necessarily meant to be shared, in which the writer makes all decisions regarding form and purpose (*See* extensive writing.)

refrain: a regularly repeated line or group of lines in a poem or song

relative pronoun: a pronoun such as *that, which, who, whom,* or *whose* that begins a

subordinate clause and connects it to another idea in the sentence

reporter's formula: a prewriting technique in which writers gather details about a topic by generating answers to the following questions: *Who? What? Where? When?* and *Why?*

research: a prewriting technique in which writers gather information from outside sources such as library reference materials, interviews, and the Internet

research writing: expository writing that presents and interprets information gathered through an extensive study of a subject

response to literature writing: persuasive, expository, or narrative writing that presents a writer's analysis of or reactions to a published work

revising: a stage of the writing process in which a writer reworks a rough draft to improve both form and content

rhyme: the repetition of sounds at the ends of words

rhyme scheme: the regular pattern of rhyming words in a poem or stanza

rhythm: the form or pattern of words or music in which accents or beats come at certain fixed intervals

root: the base of a word (*See* prefix, suffix.)

rubric: an assessment tool, generally organized in a grid, to indicate the range of success or failure according to specific criteria

run-on sentence: two or more complete sentences punctuated incorrectly as one

S

salutation: the greeting in a formal letter

satire: writing that ridicules or holds up to contempt the faults of individuals or of groups

SEE method: an elaboration technique in which a writer presents a statement, an extension, and an elaboration to develop an idea

semicolon: a punctuation mark used to join independent clauses that are not already joined by a conjunction

sentence: a group of words with a subject and a predicate that expresses a complete thought

setting: the time and place of the action of a piece of narrative writing

short story: a brief fictional narrative told in prose

simile: a figure of speech in which *like* or *as* is used to make a comparison between two basically unrelated ideas

sonnet: a fourteen-line lyric poem with a single theme

speaker: the imaginary voice assumed by the writer of a poem

stanza: a group of lines in a poem, seen as a unit

statistics: facts presented in numerical form, such as ratios, percentages, or summaries

subject: the word or group of words in a sentence that tells whom or what the sentence is about

subordinate clause: a group of words containing both a subject and a verb that cannot stand by itself as a complete sentence

subordinating conjunction: a word used to join two complete ideas by making one of the ideas dependent on the other

suffix: one or more syllables added to the end of a word root (*See* prefix, root.)

summary: a brief statement of the main ideas and supporting details presented in a piece of writing

symbol: something that is itself and also stands for something else

T

theme: the central idea, concern, or purpose in a piece of narrative writing, poetry, or drama

thesis statement: a statement of an essay's main idea; all information in the essay supports or elaborates this idea

tone: a writer's attitude toward the readers and toward the subject

topic sentence: a sentence that states the main idea of a paragraph

topic web: a prewriting technique in which a writer generates a graphic organizer to identify categories and subcategories of a topic

topical paragraph: a paragraph that develops, explains, and supports the topic sentence related to an essay's thesis statement

transition: words, phrases, or sentences that smooth writing by indicating the relationship among ideas

transitive verb: an action verb that takes a direct object (*See* intransitive verb.)

U

unity: a quality of written work in which all the parts fit together in a complete, self-contained whole

V

verb: a word or group of words that expresses an action, a condition, or the fact that something exists while indicating the time of the action, condition, or fact

verbal: a word derived from the verb but used as a noun, adjective, or adverb (*See* gerund, infinitive, participle.)

vignette: a brief narrative characterized by precise detail

voice: the distinctive qualities of a writer's style, including diction, attitude, sentence style, and ideas

W

works-cited list: a list of the sources of a research paper, including full bibliographic references for each source named in the body of the paper (*See* bibliography.)

Note: **Bold numbers** show pages on which basic definitions or rules appear.

Viruses, Electronic, **859**
Visual Aids, **758**–759, 760
Vocabulary, 766–777
  development of, 767–771
  improving spelling of, 778–787
  notebooks for, 773
  systematic study for, 772–773
  test items for, 788–789
  word parts and origins in, 774–777
Voice
  active *vs.* passive, 87, **88**, **534**–537, **877**
  in good writing, 7
  See also Audiences; Purpose for Writing

W

Web Pages, 301, **859**
  See also Internet
Web Sites, **859**
  advertising on, 152
  art museums on, 757
  finding and evaluating, 855–857
  finding information at, 525
  finding new words at, 776
  government, 556
  locating and evaluating, 826
  for periodicals, 819
  student, 294
  using company, 179
  See also Internet; Search Engines
well, good, 592
went, gone, **616**
when, 398
when, where, **621**
where, 398
which, **620**
which, that, 235
who, **620**
who, whoever, **552**–553
who, whom, 552–555
whom, whomever, **552**, **554**
who's, whose, 163, 349, 552, **717**
will, 719
Word Choice, 7
  See also Revising Word Choice, Strategies for
Word Division, **708**–710
Word-Processing Programs
  common features of, 9
  creating flyers with, 167
  Find feature in, 187

finding words with, 210, 211
formatting with, 760
organizing writing with, 58
spell-checking with, 22, 549, 613, 845
thesaurus in, 823
using Find feature of, 90
See also Computers
Wordiness, 263
Words
  in analogies, 771
  commonly confused, 211
  commonly misspelled, 862–863
  hearing and using new, 767
  origins of, 774–777
  problem, 779
  recognizing related, 770
  systematic study of, 772–773
  within words, 780
Working With Others, 6, 835–836
Workplace Skills and Competencies, 834–847
  applying computer skills, 845
  applying math skills, 844
  managing money, 843
  managing time, 842
  moving toward goals, 839
  solving problems, 840
  teamwork, 837–838
  test items for, 846–847
  thinking creatively, 841
  working with people, 835–836
Workplace Writing, 322–335
  business letters in, 324–325
  defined, **323**
  forms and applications in, 328–329
  meeting minutes in, 326–327
  types of, **323**
Works-Cited Lists, **850**, **877**
  creating and checking, 264–265
  examples of, 249, 269
  sample of, 854
  See also Citations; Sources
Work Sheets, Peer Review, 65
World Wide Web (WWW), **859**
would, 719
Writers. *See* Authors
Writing
  types of, **12**
  using writing technologies, 9, 25, 169, 241, 301, 319, 845
  See also Autobiographical Writing; Cause-and Effect Essays; Comparison-and-

Contrast Essays; Narration; Persuasive Essays; Problem-and-Solution Essays; Research Writing; Response to Literature; Short Stories; Writing for Assessment
Writing Activities, Ideas for
  See Cooperative Writing Opportunities; Media and Technology Skills; Spotlight on the Humanities; Topic Bank Ideas
Writing for Assessment
  drafting, 308–309
  editing and proofreading, 312
  prewriting, 306–307
  publishing and presenting, 313
  revising, 310–311
  rubric for self-assessment, 313
  types of, **305**
Writing Materials, 4
Writing Process, 14–31
  developing approach to, 3–4
  overview of, 2–11
  planning for, 5
  stages in, **13**
  test prompts for, 10–11, 26–27
  types and modes in, **12**
Writing Prompts, 10–11
Writing-Reading Connections. *See* Reading-Writing Connections
Writing, Types of, 12
W's, Five, 872
W3, Internet, **859**
WWW. *See* World Wide Web

Y

yet, 397, 654, 671
you, **418**, **581**
your, you're, 163

Z

Zip, Electronic, **859**
Zooming Technique, 762

Acknowledgments

Staff Credits

The people who made up the *Prentice Hall Writing and Grammar: Communication in Action* team—representing design services, editorial, editorial services, electronic publishing technology, manufacturing & inventory planning, marketing, marketing services, market research, online services & multimedia development, product planning, production services, project office, and publishing processes—are listed below. Bold type denotes the core team members.

Ellen Backstrom, Betsy Bostwick, Evonne Burgess, **Louise B. Capuano**, **Sarah Carroll**, **Megan Chill**, Katherine Clarke, Rhett Conklin, Martha Conway, Harold Crudup, **Harold Delmonte**, Libby Forsyth, Maggie Fritz, Ellen Goldblatt, Elaine Goldman, Jonathan Goldson, **Rebecca Graziano**, **Diana Hahn**, Rick Hickox, Kristan Hoskins, Raegan Keida, Carol Lavis, **George Lychock**, **Gregory Lynch**, William McAllister, Loretta Moser, Margaret Plotkin, Maureen Raymond, Gerry Schrenk, **Melissa Shustyk**, Annette Simmons, Robin Sullivan, Julie Tomasella, **Elizabeth Torjussen**, **Doug Utigard**

Additional Credits

Ernie Albanese, Diane Alimena, Susan Andariese, Michele Angelucci, Penny Baker, Susan Barnes, John Carle, Angelo Focaccia, Kathy Gavilanes, Beth Geschwind, Michael Goodman, Jennifer Harper, Evan Holstrom, Leanne Korszoloski, Sue Langan, Rebecca Lauth, Dave Liston, Maria Keogh, Vicki Menanteaux, Gail Meyer, Artur Mkrtchyan, LaShonda Morris, Karyl Murray, Omni-Photo Communications, Kim Ortell, Carolyn Sapontzis, Mildred Schulte, Slip Jig Image Research Services, Sunnyside, NY, Debi Taffet

Grateful acknowledgment is made to the following for copyrighted material:

Barnes & Noble, Inc.
Introduction to *The Hunchback of Notre Dame* by Paul Montazzoli. Copyright © 1996 by Barnes & Noble, Inc.

The Boston Globe
"But What of Parents Whose Son Seeks Political Asylum?" by Ellen Goodman from *The Boston Globe,* August 7, 1980. Reprinted by permission of Globe Newspaper Company.

The Estate of Gwendolyn Brooks
"Maud Martha Spares the Mouse" from *Maud Martha.* Reprinted by permission of The Estate of Gwendolyn Brooks.

Channel One Network
"Growing Pains in China" by Cindy Lin. Reprinted by permission of Channel One Network.

Bernard Edelman
From *Dear America; Letters Home From Vietnam,* edited by Bernard Edelman for the New York Vietnam Veterans Memorial Commission.

Lee & Low Books, Inc.
"Mexican Magician" by Pat Mora. Text copyright © 1996 from the collection *Confetti: Poems for Children.* Permission arranged with Lee & Low Books, Inc., New York, NY.

Pat Mora
From "Uncoiling" by Pat Mora. Reprinted by permission of the author.

New Directions Publishing
From "The Street" by Octavio Paz, translated by Muriel Rukeyser, from *Early Poems of Octavio Paz,* copyright © 1973 by Octavio Paz and Muriel Rukeyser. Reprinted by permission of New Directions Publishing Corp.

The New York Times
"The Long Tale of Madonna the Iguana" by Linda Greenhouse. Copyright © 2000 by the New York Times Co. Reprinted by permission.

Random House, Inc.
"The Sun's Way" by Bashō. From *An Introduction to Haiku* by Harold G. Henderson, copyright © 1958 by Harold G. Henderson. Used by permission of Doubleday, a division of Random House, Inc.

Paul Simon Music
From "Old Friends" by Paul Simon. Copyright © 1968 by Paul Simon. Used by permission of the publisher, Paul Simon Music.

The University of Arizona Press
From "The Figurative Tradition" from *The Pueblo Storyteller: Development of the Figurative Ceramic Tradition* by Barbara Babcock, Guy Monthan, and Doris Monthan. Copyright © 1986 by The Arizona Board of Regents. Reprinted by permission of the University of Arizona Press.

The Washington Post Writers Group
"The Littlest Defector Deserves Asylum" by George Will, *Newsday,* September 4, 1980. Copyright © 1980 by The Washington Post Writers Group. Reprinted with permission.

Weldon Owen Publishing
Text from *Nature Company Guides Whales, Dolphins, and Porpoises.* © Weldon Owen Pty Ltd.

William K. Zinsser
Excerpt from *On Writing Well* by William K. Zinsser. Copyright © 1976, 1980, 1985, 1988, 1990, 1994, 1998, 2001 by William K. Zinsser.

Note: Every effort has been made to locate the copyright owner of material reprinted in this book. Omissions brought to our attention will be corrected in subsequent editions.

Photo Credits

Cover: Stamp design ©United States Postal Service, All Rights Reserved; Erika Craddock/Tony Stone Images; **iii:** PhotoEdit **ix:** Tony Stone Images **vi:** (top) LEA/Omni-Photo Communications, Inc. (bottom) Corel Professional Photos CD-ROM™ **vii:** (top) Corel Professional Photos CD-ROM™ (middle) Corel Professional Photos CD-ROM™ (bottom) David Young-Wolff PhotoEdit **x:** ©1997, G. & M. Kohler/FPG International Corp.; **xi:** PhotoDisc/Getty Images, Inc.; **xii:** Will Hart/PhotoEdit; **xiii:** PhotoDisc/Getty Images, Inc.; **xiv:** PhotoDisc/Getty Images, Inc.; **xv:** F. Hoffmann/The Image Works; **xvi:** ©1996, Walter Bibikow/FPG International Corp.; **xvii:** *Federal Brigade Commanded by General Winfield Scott,* Julian Scott, Smithsonian Institution; **xviii:** Kunsthistorisches Museum, Antikensammlung, Vienna, Austria, ©Photograph by Erich Lessing/Art Resource, NY; **xix:** *Ballet Class,* Edgar Degas, Corel Professional Photos CD-ROM™; **xx:** (top) David Young-Wolff/PhotoEdit; (bottom) Bruce Ayres/Tony Stone Images; **xxi:** (top) Corel Professional Photos CD-ROM™; (bottom) Corel Professional Photos CD-ROM™; **xxii:** (top) Corel Professional Photos CD-ROM™; (bottom) Courtesy of the Italian Government Tourist Board; **xxiii:** (top) Corel Professional Photos CD-ROM™; (bottom) Courtesy of the Library of Congress; **xxiv:** (top) Corel Professional Photos CD-ROM™; (bottom) Corel Professional Photos CD-ROM™; **xxv:** (top), (middle) & (bottom) Corel Professional Photos CD-ROM™; **xxvi:** (top) Corel Professional Photos CD-ROM™; (bottom) ©The Stock Market/Jose L. Pelaez; **xxvii:** (top) Corel Professional Photos CD-ROM™; (bottom) ©The Stock Market/Tom Stewart; **1:** *Femme Cousant,* Henri Lebasque, Christie's Images/SuperStock, ©2001 Artists Rights Society (ARS), New York, ADAGP, Paris; **2:** ©Sven Martson/The Image Works; **5:** Don Smetzer/Tony Stone Images; **6:** David De Lossy/The Image Bank; **8:** Shelley Rotner/Omni-Photo Communications, Inc.; **12:** Bob Daemmrich/Stock, Boston Inc./PictureQuest; **24:** Photofest; **28:** Tony Page/Tony Stone Images; **29:** Kindra Clineff/Index Stock Photography, Inc.; **35:** Don Spiro/Medichrome/The Stock Shop, Inc.; **37:** AP/Wide World Photos; **41:** Corel Professional Photos CD-ROM™; **43:** ©StockFood America/EISING; **44:** Tony Freeman/PhotoEdit; **48:** North Carolina Museum of Art/CORBIS; **51:** Silver Burdett Ginn; **52:** Tony Stone Images; **55:** *Backgammon,* 1976, Jane Freilicher, oil on canvas, 38 x 44 in., From the permanent collection of the Utah Museum of Fine Arts, Acc. 1979.008; **61:** LEA/Omni-Photo Communications, Inc.; **68:** Tony Stone Images; **70:** Karen Huntt Mason/CORBIS; **71:** Robert Ullmann/Monkmeyer; **72:** Photofest; **76:** Richard Hutchings/PhotoEdit; **78:** ©1997, G. & M. Kohler/FPG International Corp.; **79:** (left) © StockFood America/Mastri; (right) ©1997, G. & M. Kohler/FPG International Corp.; **81:** *Students of Modelling and Painting,* Anonymous, Private Collection/Bridgeman Art Library, NYC; **85:** Tony Freeman/PhotoEdit; **92:** PhotoDisc/Getty Images, Inc.; **94:** Richard T. Nowitz/CORBIS; **96:** *He Laid Down His Hammer and Cried,* 1944–47, Palmer C. Hayden, Museum of African American Art, Los Angeles, CA; **100:** Gottlieb/Monkmeyer; **102:** Tim Page/CORBIS; **105:** Studio Interior, 1982, Jane Freilicher, Tibor De Nagy; **108:** Kevin R. Morris/CORBIS; **113:** Michelle Bridwell/PhotoEdit; **116:** PhotoDisc/Getty Images, Inc.; **117:** David Young-Wolff/PhotoEdit; **118:** ©The Stock Market/Craig Tuttle; **120:** Portrait of Dolores Olmedo, Diego Rivera, Schalkwijk/Art Resource, NY; **121:** Mark Richards/PhotoEdit; **124:** AP Photo/Jan Bauer; **126:** Richard Derk/Chicago Sun-Times; **129:** AP/Wide World Photos; **131:** *Arrivals and Departures,* 1999, Chester Arnold, The Seven Bridges Foundation, Greenwich, CT. Photo courtesy of George Adams Gallery, New York; **136:** Bill Bachman/The Image Works; **137:** Tom Stack/Tom Stack & Associates; **141:** Will Hart/PhotoEdit; **144:** Myrleen Ferguson/PhotoEdit; **148:** *Snap the Whip,* Winslow Homer, Corel Professional Photos CD-ROM™; **152:** PhotoDisc/Getty Images, Inc.; **154:** Costa Rica Tourist Board; **166:** Amy Etra/PhotoEdit; **168:** Mitchell Gerber/CORBIS; **172:** Tony Arruza/CORBIS; **174:** ©The Stock Market/Jon Feingersh; **177:** *Minor League,* Clyde Singer, The Butler Institute of American Art; **181:** PhotoDisc/Getty Images, Inc.; **189:** (left) David Young-Wolff/PhotoEdit; (right) Amy C. Etra/PhotoEdit; **191:** Ken Karp/PH photo; **193:** Photofest; **196:** *The Landing of Columbus at San Salvador (Guanahani) in Bahamas,* 12 October 1492, The Granger Collection, New York; **198:** ©The Stock Market/Andrew Holbrooke; **199:** Bill Bachmann/PhotoEdit; **201:** *Rolling Power,* 1939, Charles Sheeler, Smith College Museum of Art, Northampton, Massachusetts. Purchased, Drayton Hillyer Fund, 1940; **204:** Ralph White/CORBIS; **213:** F. Hoffmann/The Image Works; **214:** Stephen Wilkes/The Image Bank; **215:** David Young-Wolff/PhotoEdit; **216:** City of Edinburgh Museums and Art Galleries/The Bridgeman Art Library, London/New York; **220:** Mary Kate Denny/PhotoEdit; **222:** David A. Northcott/CORBIS; **225:** *Unloading the Cargo,* 1942, Ralston Crawford; **230:** Corel Professional Photos CD-ROM™; **234:** Will Hart; **237:** Michael Newman/PhotoEdit; **238:** ©1996, Walter Bibikow/FPG International Corp.; **239:** PhotoEdit; **244:** Corel Professional Photos CD-ROM™; **246:** Jerry Jacka Photography;

249: *Storyteller,* ca. 1970, Helen Cordero, Adobe Gallery; **251:** *Federal Brigade Commanded by General Winfield Scott,* Julian Scott, Smithsonian Institution; **252:** Scribner's Publishing; **255:** PhotoEdit; **267:** Magnum Photos, Inc. ©1944 Robert Capa; **269:** Courtesy National Archives; **270:** NASA; **272:** Courtesy of Teatro all Scala; **276:** ©The Stock Market/ Tom Stewart; **278:** Corel Professional Photos CD-ROM™; **279–280:** Photofest; **283:** *Children Dancing,* Robert Gwathmey, Butler Institute of American Art. ©Estate of Robert Gwathmey/Licensed by VAGA, New York, NY; **292:** Will Faller; **295:** *Penelope at the loom and Telemachus,* Museo Nazionale, Chiusi, Italy, ©Photograph by Erich Lessing/Art Resource, NY; **296:** Kunsthistorisches Museum, Antikensammlung, Vienna, Austria, ©Photograph by Erich Lessing/Art Resource, NY; **298:** George Kleiman/CORBIS; **300:** Courtesy of the Library of Congress; **306:** ©The Stock Market/Charles Gupton; **307:** (top & bottom) The Granger Collection, New York; **310:** Tony Stone Images; **315:** The Mariner's Museum/ CORBIS; **316:** Bob Daemmrich/ The Image Works; **318:** *The Emperor Ch'ien-lung as a Young Man:* The Metropolitan Museum of Art, Rogers Fund, 1942. (42.141.8) Photograph ©1980 The Metropolitan Museum of Art; **322:** Bruce Ayers/Tony Stone Images; **330:** David Young-Wolff/ PhotoEdit; **332:** *Ballet Class,* Edgar Degas, Corel Professional Photos CD-ROM™; **336:** *Delta,* 1990, 40 x 40 inches, acrylic on canvas by Paul Giovanopoulos, Photograph Courtesy Louis K. Meisel Gallery, New York; **338:** Courtesy of the Library of Congress; **341:** Corel Professional Photos CD-ROM™; **342:** Courtesy National Archives, photo no. 111-sc-7740; **345:** Corel Professional Photos CD-ROM™; **347:** Greater Houston Convention and Visitors Bureau; **352:** NASA; **354–393:** Corel Professional Photos CD-ROM™; **398:** Silver Burdett Ginn; **399:** Modern Curriculum Press; **410–451:** Corel Professional Photos CD-ROM™; **453:** Courtesy of the Library of Congress; **454–471:** Corel Professional Photos CD-ROM™; **476:** Courtesy of the Italian Government Tourist Board; **484:** Silver Burdett Ginn; **486:** Pearson Education/Prentice Hall School; **489–497:** Corel Professional Photos CD-ROM™; **500:** Pearson Education/PH College; **503:** Silver Burdett Ginn; **505–508:** Corel Professional Photos CD-ROM™; **510:** Silver Burdett Ginn; **518–521:** Corel Professional Photos CD-ROM™; **522:** Courtesy, Museum of Fine Arts, Boston; **527:** Corel Professional Photos CD-ROM™; **530:** ©Archivo Iconografico, S.A./ CORBIS; **535:** Corel Professional Photos CD-ROM™; **542:** Courtesy of the Library of Congress; **545:** Corel Professional Photos CD-ROM™; **547–548:** Courtesy of the Library of Congress; **553–555:** NASA; **564:** Corel Professional Photos CD-ROM™; **568:** NOAA; **570–599:** Corel Professional Photos CD-ROM™; **606–609:** Courtesy of the Library of Congress; **614–639:** Corel Professional Photos CD-ROM™; **640:** EMG-Education Management Group; **648:** Pearson Education/Prentice Hall College; **650:** NASA; **655:** Pearson Education/Prentice Hall School; **660:** Corel Professional Photos CD-ROM™; **665:** Pearson Education/Prentice Hall College; **667:** Silver Burdett Ginn; **673:** *Snap the Whip,* Winslow Homer, Corel Professional Photos CD-ROM™; **675–676:** Corel Professional Photos CD-ROM™; **679:** New York Convention & Visitors Bureau; **683–686:** Corel Professional Photos CD-ROM™; **688:** Pearson Education/Prentice Hall College; **692:** Courtesy of the Library of Congress; **695:** Corel Professional Photos CD-ROM™; **701:** Pearson Education/Prentice Hall College; **703–707:** Corel Professional Photos CD-ROM™; **708:** PhotoDisc/Getty Images, Inc.; **713–721:** Corel Professional Photos CD-ROM™; **742:** *The Library,* 1960, Jacob Lawrence, National Museum of American Art, Washington, D.C./Art Resource, NY; **744:** Paul Conklin/ PhotoEdit; **746:** Morry Gash/AP/ Wide World Photos; **757:** *Dancers in Pink and Green,* Edgar Degas, oil on canvas, H. 32-3/8 in. W. 29-3/4 in. (82.2 x 75.6 cm) Signed (lower right): Degas. The Metropolitan Musem of Art, Bequest of Mrs. H. O. Havemeyer, 1929. The H. O. Havemeyer Collection. (29.100.42). Photograph Copyright © 1980 By The Metropolitan Museum of Art; **766:** Dennis MacDonald/ PhotoEdit; **769:** Corel Professional Photos CD-ROM™; **770:** David Young-Wolff/PhotoEdit; **777–779:** Corel Professional Photos CD-ROM™; **781:** ©The Stock Market/ Jose L. Pelaez; **784:** Corel Professional Photos CD-ROM™; **790:** Myrleen Ferguson/ PhotoEdit; **793:** ©The Stock Market/Gabe Palmer/Mug Shots; **799:** Tony Stone Images; **803:** Duomo/CORBIS; **808:** The Granger Collection, New York,; **812:** David Young-Wolff/ PhotoEdit; **816:** Tony Freeman/ PhotoEdit; **818:** Michelle Bridwell/ PhotoEdit; **820:** CORBIS; **825:** Corel Professional Photos CD-ROM™; **834:** ©The Stock Market/ Tom Stewart; **836:** Ken Karp/PH Photo; **838:** Michael Newman/ PhotoEdit; **844:** Kindra Clineff/ Index Stock Photography, Inc.